Readings to accompany
Experience Humanities

VOLUME II

THE RENAISSANCE
TO THE PRESENT

EDITED BY

Roy T. Matthews & F. DeWitt Platt
Michigan State University

Mc Graw Hill — Connect Learn Succeed™

READINGS TO ACCOMPANY EXPERIENCE HUMANITIES:
VOLUME II: THE RENAISSANCE TO THE PRESENT

Published by McGraw-Hill, a business unit of The McGraw-Hill Companies, Inc., 1221 Avenue of the Americas, New York, NY, 10020.

Some ancillaries, including electronic and print components, may not be available to customers outside the United States.

This book is printed on acid-free paper.

1 2 3 4 5 6 7 8 9 0 QDB/QDB 1 0 9 8 7 6 5 4 3

ISBN   978-0-07-749473-5
MHID   0-07-749473-3

Senior Vice President, Products & Markets: *Kurt L. Strand*
Vice President, General Manager, Products & Markets: *Michael J. Ryan*
Vice President, Content Production & Technology Services: *Kimberly Meriwether David*
Director: *Christopher Freitag*
Brand Manager: *Laura Wilk*
Managing Development Editor: *Nancy Crochiere*
Development Editor: *Arthur Pomponio*
Editorial Coordinator: *Jessica Holmes*
Digital Development Editor: *Betty Chen*

Marketing Manager: *Kelly Odom*
Lead Project Manager: *Susan Trentacosti*
Content Project Manager: *Emily Kline*
Senior Buyer: *Carol A. Bielski*
Designer: *Debra Kubiak*
Cover/Interior Designer: *Pam Verros*
Cover Image: *The Arch St. Louis Missouri Gateway Monument: © Phil Degginger/Alamy*
Typeface: *9/11 Palatino*
Compositor: *Thompson Type*
Printer: *Quad/Graphics*

Library of Congress Control Number: 2012955772

The Internet addresses listed in the text were accurate at the time of publication. The inclusion of a website does not indicate an endorsement by the authors or McGraw-Hill, and McGraw-Hill does not guarantee the accuracy of the information presented at these sites.

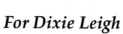

For Dixie Leigh

"Many women have done excellently, but you surpassed them all."

—Book of Proverbs 31:29

FDP

———— ∞ ————

For Randy and Elizabeth

We taught them the past, and they have brought us happiness.
Now, they show us the future by making the world a better place.

RTM

CONTENTS

Chapter 19 THE TRIUMPH OF THE BOURGEOISIE, 1830–1871 213

Chapter 20 THE AGE OF EARLY MODERNISM, 1871–1914 254

Chapter 21 THE AGE OF THE MASSES AND THE ZENITH OF MODERNISM, 1914–1945 269

Chapter 22 THE AGE OF ANXIETY AND LATE MODERNISM, 1945–1970 303

PREFACE

In this age of e-books, smartphones, social media, and whatever new technology the next news cycle brings—and the printed word seems to be in decline—we are delighted to present this edition of *Readings to accompany Experience Humanities*, called by us affectionately, "the Reader." Since the first edition (1990), both the Reader and our other textbook, *Experience Humanities*, have been widely adopted at universities and colleges across the country. This anthology offers selections from the West's literary and philosophical heritage which, if studied with care, will help students establish vital intellectual linkages to the literary and philosophical achievements of our continually evolving Western tradition.

The Western tradition, originating in about 3000 BCE and developed over five thousand years, consists of a vast, diverse, and complex tapestry of literary and philosophical writings. To keep this anthology to a manageable length, we have followed two principles as we made our selections: (1) include works that have significantly impacted Western culture, and (2) offer as many diverse and representative voices as possible without sacrificing quality. The readings, placed in chronological order, are arranged in twenty-three chapters, echoing the format of *Experience Humanities*, and comprise two volumes. Volume I covers ancient Mesopotamia through the Renaissance; Volume II, the Renaissance through postmodernism.

In Volume II, we renumbered the existing chapter layout to bring the chapters into harmony with revisions made in *Experience Humanities*,. Specifically, old Chapters 11–22 are now renumbered as Chapters 12–23. We also added or replaced two selections in response to our surveys and advice from instructors and students. These changes comprise: in Chapter 15, adding two new poems by Sister Juana Inés de la Cruz, which reflect her critique of colonial Mexico's courtly culture—the world in which she lived; and in Chapter 21, including a selection from Thomas Mann's *The Magic Mountain*, a master work by one of Germany's greatest writers, who is often ranked with Goethe .

* * *

For this edition, we express once again our appreciation to the McGraw-Hill editorial and production teams. Things get better with each edition! First, we want to thank Chris Freitag, Director, for his unfaltering support of this project. We also give a shout-out to Nancy Crochiere, Managing Development Editor, for her calm and steady hand during the year and one half required to bring this edition into print. To Art Pomponio, Development Editor, we are grateful for his many helpful suggestions and nudges, when we were falling behind schedule. We especially single out Susan Trentacosti, Lead Project Manager, for her strength and agility in bringing the production to a successful close and on time; and to Jenna Caputo, Permissions

Researcher, for her zeal in obtaining permission rights, even of the most difficult sort. We thank the library staffs of Michigan State University, American University, and Georgetown University for their helpful cooperation. To our former humanities students at Michigan State University who served as readers and critics for most of the anthology's selections, we express our thanks; their informed responses helped hone the way we interpret literature and philosophy. If our headnotes and footnotes are clear and apposite, then part of the praise must be shared with those students. And finally, we want to thank LeeAnn and Dixie, our friends and families, especially our grandchildren Clayton, Evan, and Max Matthews, and Victoria Holland Adams; and Martha Burke for their patience, forbearance, and love during this twenty-two-year-long journey—we are eternally in your debt.

12

THE EARLY RENAISSANCE
Return to Classical Roots
1400–1494

GIOVANNI PICO DELLA MIRANDOLA
Selections from *On the Dignity of Man*

The Latin oration *On the Dignity of Man* is a tour de force by Pico (1463–1494), a son of the noble house of Mirandola (Italy). Written when Pico was twenty-four, the oration is a mixture of Aristotelian, Hebraic, Arabic, Persian, and Aramaic notions held together by Neoplatonism— a blend of Plato's ideas and Christian beliefs. Its central Neoplatonic motif is that love is the divine glue unifying the universe. Christian in structure, this synthesis of ideas breaks free of its frame to become a nonsectarian philosophy.

Pico's oration embodies the Renaissance spirit. In its appeal to wide-ranging sources, it expresses Renaissance zeal for the classic texts of Greece and Rome as well as hitherto ignored ancient sources. Its theme is the Renaissance belief that the findings of reason and the truths of the Bible share a basic unity that is reflected in the history of thought. Most of all, its view that human nature has no limits is the prototype of the Renaissance idea of unlimited possibility. Today this idea, with its corollary of free expression, is a defining trait of Western culture.

The oration was composed to introduce a debate Pico scheduled for Rome in 1487. In this debate, Pico proposed to defend nine hundred theses gleaned from his vast readings; he even offered to pay his potential opponents' travel expenses. The debate, however, did not take place because Pope Innocent VIII (pope 1484–1492) forbade it. The pope also appointed a commission to examine the debate topics, with the result that seven theses were condemned as heretical and six more were suspect. Threatened by church officials, Pico subsequently settled in Florence, where he was caught up in the anti-Renaissance crusade of the monk Savonarola. Pico's plan to wander as an evangelist was cut short in 1494, when he died suddenly at age thirty-one.

Reading the Selections

The first selection from the oration *On the Dignity of Man* begins with a greeting—"Most venerable fathers"—thus establishing that the work was meant to be recited orally, ostensibly before a group of clergy. The major insights to be gained from this selection are Pico's concept of human nature and his style of reasoning.

Pico's concept of human nature is his major contribution to Western thought. For him, human nature is not fixed, and the will is perfectly free. In a burst of lyricism, he claimed that human beings are shape-shifting creatures who may be vegetative, bestial, rational, divine,

1

or even co-equal with God: When humanity's quest ends, "We shall . . . not be ourselves, but He himself who made us." Brushing aside medieval ideas, Pico expresses the radiant faith of Renaissance humanism, that human beings are not flawed by original sin but are capable of becoming godlike.

Pico's style of reasoning reflects the Renaissance trend of treating old problems in new ways. To deal with the question of human nature, he takes the Platonic concept of the Great Chain of Being, which maintains that creation is a linked cord reaching step by step from the simplest life to God, and gives it a modern twist. Ancient thinkers had used the Great Chain of Being to argue that human potential is limited, since the place of human beings in the chain is fixed, and that change would destroy the whole creation. In contrast, Pico claimed that human beings may make of themselves anything they please, because as hybrids of the whole creation, they exist both outside and above the Great Chain of Being.

∞

Most venerable fathers, I have read in the records of the Arabians that Abdul the Saracen, on being asked what thing on, so to speak, the world's stage, he viewed as most greatly worthy of wonder, answered that he viewed nothing more wonderful than man. And Mercury's, "a great wonder, Asclepius, is man!" agrees with that opinion. On thinking over the reason for these sayings, I was not satisfied by the many assertions made by many men concerning the outstandingness of human nature: that man is the messenger between creatures, familiar with the upper and king of the lower; by the sharpsightedness of the senses, by the hunting-power of reason, and by the light of intelligence, the interpreter of nature; the part in between the standstill of eternity and the flow of time, and, as the Persians say, the bond tying the world together, nay, the nuptial bond; and, according to David,[1] "a little lower than the angels." These reasons are great but not the chief ones, that is, they are not reasons for a lawful claim to the highest wonder as to a prerogative. Why should we not wonder more at the angels themselves and at the very blessed heavenly choirs?

Finally, it seemed to me that I understood why man is the animal that is most happy, and is therefore worthy of all wonder; and lastly, what the state is that is allotted to man in the succession of things, and that is capable of arousing envy not only in the brutes but also in the stars and even in minds beyond the world. It is wonderful and beyond belief. For this is the reason why man is rightly said and thought to be a great marvel and the animal really worthy of wonder. Now hear what it is, fathers; and with kindly ears and for the sake of your humanity, give me your close attention:

Now the highest Father, God the master-builder, had, by the laws of his secret wisdom, fabricated this house, this world which we see, a very superb temple of divinity. He had adorned the super-celestial region with minds. He had animated the celestial globes with eternal souls; he had filled with a diverse throng of animals the cast-off and residual parts of the lower world. But, with the work finished, the Artisan desired that there be someone to reckon up the reason of such a big work, to love its beauty, and to wonder at its greatness. Accordingly, now that all things had been completed, as Moses and Timaeus[2] testify, He lastly considered creating man. But there was nothing in the archetypes from which He could mold a new sprout, nor anything in His storehouses which He could bestow as a heritage upon a new son, nor was there an empty judiciary seat where this contemplator of the universe could sit. Everything was filled up; all things had been laid out in the highest, the lowest, and the middle orders. But it did not belong to the paternal power to have failed in the final parturition, as though exhausted by child-bearing; it did not belong to wisdom, in a case of necessity, to have been tossed back and forth through want of a plan; it did not belong to the loving-kindness which was going to praise divine liberality in others to be forced to condemn itself. Finally, the best of workmen decided that that to which nothing of its very own could be given should be, in composite fashion, whatsoever had belonged individually to each and every thing. Therefore He took up man, a work of indeterminate form; and, placing him at the midpoint of the world, He spoke to him as follows:

---

[1] **Abdul the Saracen, Mercury, Asclepius, David** Pico is including various sources to show that man is a wonder in himself and worthy of study and praise. Abdul the Saracen is probably the famous Arabian physician, Abul Kassim, who wrote a medical textbook used for more than five hundred years in Europe. Mercury is the Roman god of merchants and traders who, by the Renaissance, was seen as a symbol of the human intellect and the mediator between the human mind and divine wisdom. Asclepius was the Greek god of healing; he became a Roman god in the third century BCE after a plague. King David of the Old Testament was often referenced by writers and scholars for his wisdom as recorded in the Bible.

---

[2] **Moses and Timaeus** Moses, from the Old Testament, to whom God gave the Ten Commandments, and who led his people to the Promised Land, was considered a strong and wise leader. Timaeus was a Greek philosopher who was the major voice in Plato's work *Timaeus*. The dialogue refers to the creation of the world that Christians later associated with God as the creator. The Neoplatonists used Timaeus in their works against the Aristotelians and Scholasticism.

"We have given to thee, Adam, no fixed seat, no form of thy very own, no gift peculiarly thine, that thou mayest feel as thine own, have as thine own, possess as thine own the seat, the form, the gifts which thou thyself shalt desire. A limited nature in other creatures is confined within the laws written down by Us. In conformity with thy free judgment, in whose hand We have placed thee, thou art confined by no bounds; and thou wilt fix limits of nature for thyself. I have placed thee at the center of the world, that from there thou mayest more conveniently look around and see whatsoever is in the world. Neither heavenly nor earthly, neither mortal nor immortal have We made thee. Thou, like a judge appointed for being honorable, art the molder and maker of thyself; thou mayest sculpt thyself into whatever shape thou dost prefer. Thou canst grow downward into the lower natures which are brutes. Thou canst again grow upward from thy soul's reason into the higher natures which are divine."

O great liberality of God the Father! O great and won- 5 derful happiness of man. It is given him to have that which he chooses and to be that which he wills. As soon as brutes are born, they bring with them, "from their dam's bag," as Lucilius[3] says, what they are going to possess. Highest spirits have been, either from the beginning or soon after, that which they are going to be throughout everlasting eternity. At man's birth the Father placed in him every sort of seed and sprouts of every kind of life. The seeds that each man cultivates will grow and bear their fruit in him. If he cultivates vegetable seeds, he will become a plant. If the seeds of sensation, he will grow into brute. If rational, he will come out a heavenly animal. If intellectual, he will be an angel, and a son of God. And if he is not contented with the lot of any creature but takes himself up into the center of his own unity, then, made one spirit with God and settled in the solitary darkness of the Father, who is above all things, he will stand ahead of all things. Who does not wonder at this chameleon which we are? Or who at all feels more wonder at anything else whatsoever? It was not unfittingly that Asclepius the Athenian said that man was symbolized by Prometheus in the secret rites, by reason of our nature sloughing its skin and transforming itself; hence metamorphoses were popular among the Jews and the Pythagoreans.[4] For the more secret Hebrew theology at one time reshapes holy Enoch[5] into an angel of divinity, whom they call *malach hashechina,* and at other times reshapes other men into other divinities. According to the Pythagoreans, wicked men are deformed into brutes and, if you believe Empedocles,[6] into plants too. And copying them, Maumeth [Mohammed] often had it on his lips

that he who draws back from divine law becomes a brute. And his saying so was reasonable: for it is not the rind which makes the plant, but a dull and non-sentient nature; not the hide which makes a beast of burden, but a brutal and sensual soul; not the spherical body which makes the heavens, but right reason; and not a separateness from the body but a spiritual intelligence which makes an angel. For example, if you see a man given over to his belly and crawling upon the ground, it is a bush not a man that you see. If you see anyone blinded by the illusions of his empty and Calypso-like[7] imagination, seized by the desire of scratching, and delivered over to the senses, it is a brute not a man that you see. If you come upon a philosopher winnowing out all things by right reason, he is a heavenly not an earthly animal. If you come upon a pure contemplator, ignorant of the body, banished to the innermost places of the mind, he is not an earthly, not a heavenly animal; he more superbly is a divinity clothed with human flesh.

Who is there that does not wonder at man? And it is not unreasonable that in the mosaic and Christian holy writ man is sometimes denoted by the name "all flesh" and at other times by that of "every creature"; and man fashions, fabricates, transforms himself into the shape of all flesh, into the character of every creature. Accordingly, where Evantes the Persian tells of the Chaldaean theology, he writes that man is not any inborn image of himself, but many images coming in from the outside: hence that saying of the Chaldaeans: *enosh hu shinuy vekamah tevaoth baal chayim,* that is, man is an animal of diverse, multiform, and destructible nature.

But why all this? In order for us to understand that, after having been born in this state so that we may be what we will to be, then, since we are held in honor, we ought to take particular care that no one may say against us that we do not know that we are made similar to brutes and mindless beasts of burden. But rather, as Asaph[8] the prophet says: "Ye are all gods, and sons of the most high," unless by abusing the very indulgent liberality of the Father, we make the free choice, which he gave to us, harmful to ourselves instead of helpful toward salvation. Let a certain holy ambition invade the mind, so that we may not be content with mean things but may aspire to the highest things and strive with all our forces to attain them: for if we will to, we can. Let us spurn earthly things; let us struggle toward the heavenly. Let us put in last place whatever is of the world; and let us fly beyond the chambers of the world to the chamber nearest the most lofty divinity. There, as the sacred mysteries reveal, the seraphim, cherubim, and thrones occupy the first places. Ignorant of how to yield to them and unable to endure the second places, let us compete with the angels in dignity and glory. When we have willed it, we shall be not at all below them. . . .

---

[3] **Lucilius** Roman poet, third and second century BCE, who supposedly originated the satirical form used by later Roman poets. Only fragments of his works remain.
[4] **Pythagoreans** Followers of the sixth-century BCE Greek philosopher and mathematician Pythagoras. The Pythagoreans contributed to the study of mathematics and astronomy.
[5] **Enoch** Biblical figure who, according to the book of Genesis, did not die as a mortal because "God took him."
[6] **Empedocles** Fifth-century BCE Greek philosopher who explained the physical world as composed of four elements controlled by Strife and Love.

---

[7] **Calypso-like** Calypso, the nymph who kept Odysseus on the island for seven years, was also associated with the "hidden"; thus, an illusion or one who creates illusions.
[8] **Asaph** Several Asaphs in the Old Testament. One was the Choirmaster during David's time; his name is connected to a small collection of psalms, and he is probably the one Pico is referencing in this passage.

. . .

Not only the Mosaic or Christian mysteries but also the theology of the ancients show the advantages for us and the dignity of these liberal arts about which I have come here to dispute. For what else is meant by the degrees of initiation that are customary in the secret rites of the Greeks? First, to those who had been purified by moral and dialectic arts, which we have called, as it were, purgative, befell the reception of the mysteries. And what else can this reception be but the interpretation of more hidden nature by means of philosophy? Then lastly, to those who had been thus prepared, came that ἐποπτεία, that is, a vision of divine things by means of the light of theology. Who does not seek to be initiated into such rites? Who does not set all human things at a lower value and, contemning the goods of fortune and neglecting the body, does not desire, while still continuing on earth, to become the drinking-companion of the gods; and, drunken with the nectar of eternity, to bestow the gift of immortality upon the mortal animal? Who does not wish to have breathed into him the Socratic frenzies sung by Plato in the *Phaedrus,* that by the oarlike movement of wings and feet he may quickly escape from here, that is, from this world where he is laid down as in an evil place, and be carried in speediest flight to the heavenly Jerusalem. We shall be possessed, fathers, we shall be possessed by these Socratic frenzies, which will so place us outside of our minds that they will place our mind and ourselves in God. We shall be possessed by them if we have first done what is in us to

do. For if through morality the forces of the passions will have been so stretched to the [proper] measure, through due proportions, that they sound together in fixed concord, and if through dialectic, reason will have moved, keeping time in her forward march, then, aroused by the frenzy of the muses, we shall drink in the heavenly harmony of our ears. Then Bacchus the leader of the muses, in his own mysteries, that is, in the visible signs of nature, will show the invisible things of God to us as we philosophize, and will make us drunk with the abundance of the house of God. In this house, if we are faithful like Moses, holiest theology will approach, and will inspire us with a twofold frenzy. We, raised up into the loftiest watchtower of theology, from which, measuring with indivisible eternity the things that are, will be, and shall have been, and looking at their primeval beauty, shall be prophets of Phoebus,[9] his winged lovers, and finally, aroused with ineffable charity as with fire, placed outside of ourselves like burning Seraphim,[10] filled with divinity, we shall now not be ourselves, but He himself who made us.

---

[9] **Phoebus** Another name for Apollo, the Greek god of prophecy, the patron of music and poetry; also connected with the sun and, thus, the "shining one," as Phoebus is likewise called.
[10] **Seraphim** In the Hebrew tradition and Bible, they are supernatural beings associated with the presence of God. Pico is using both Phoebus and the Seraphim as images of light to lift the reader to new heights of knowledge and wisdom.

Questions for Critical Thinking

1. According to Pico, what are the ways man can exercise his free will and what can be the results of his using his free will?

2. Discuss and give examples of how Pico blends Christian and non-Christian sources to support his argument about the nature of man.

LEON BATTISTA ALBERTI
Selections from *On Painting* and *Dinner Pieces*

Leon Battista Alberti (1404–1472) was the "universal man," the beau ideal of the age, and his achievements rivaled those of the later Leonardo da Vinci. Besides painting, Alberti mastered music, mathematics, engineering, architecture, sculpture, poetry, drama, and civil and canon law and wrote books on most of these fields. A friend of Cosimo de' Medici (1389–1464), the merchant-banker who dominated Florence, Alberti was active in Cosimo's Platonic Academy, the club of artists and thinkers who studied Plato (see *Phaedo* and *The Republic* in Chapter 3,

Volume I). Alberti's spirit had such force that his friends called him the complete genius, hence the authority attributed to his works.

Alberti's *On Painting* helped ensure the triumph of the new Renaissance style over older medieval art. Published in Latin (1435) and Italian (1436), this was the first modern treatise on the theory of painting. It became the era's authoritative guide for painters, both within and outside Florence, including Fra Angelico (ca. 1400–1455), Piero della Francesca (1420–1492), and perhaps Leonardo da Vinci (1452–1519). From 1600 until 1800, Alberti's treatise was invoked as an authority for painting practices approved by Europe's art academies. Today's historians still find this work invaluable, for it prepared the way for the art, the artist, and the patron of the Renaissance.

On Painting is divided into three "books," or parts. Book I presents a mathematical method for creating perspective—the illusion of depth on a flat surface. Book II deals with painterly matters, such as color, drawing, and grace and beauty in poses and movements. Book III sets forth a type of humanist painting that uses Greco-Roman themes and depicts the soul's condition through bodily gestures and facial expressions.

Alberti's *Dinner Pieces*, written between 1430 and 1440, consists of dialogues, stories, and fables. Never published during Alberti's lifetime, they remained scattered and in manuscript form until the late nineteenth century, and were finally edited and translated into English in the 1980s.

According to Alberti, his brief essays or "short books," as he labeled them, were "to be read over dinner and drinks." While many of these pieces were written to entertain readers, they also allowed the author to satirize popular subjects, ridicule his contemporaries, and initiate serious discussions.

In setting up conversations on particular topics, Alberti often spoke through two characters: Philoponius (from Greek, "lover of toil") and Lepidus (from Latin, "witty"). Lepidus is the voice out of the past, derived from Cynicism, the fourth-century BCE Hellenistic philosophy, which emphasized self-control and self-sufficiency and was later made popular during the Roman Empire by the Greek satirical writer, Lucian (ca. 120–after 180 CE). Alberti also borrowed from writers and thinkers, including Aesop, Petrarch (see "Letter to Posterity" in Chapter 11, Volume I), Horace (see *Odes* in Chapter 5, Volume I), Juvenal (see *Satire III* in Chapter 5, Volume I), and Cicero (see *On the Republic* in Chapter 5, Volume I). However, he did not mix Christian sources with classical references as did most Renaissance humanists.

Reading the Selections

The selection from Book II of *On Painting* shows Alberti as a Renaissance humanist, making the case for a radical new role for the age's painters. These painters are characterized by intellect, with the ascendancy of mind over hand visible in their art. This argument echoes the familiar rationale of humanists that studying and practicing grammar, rhetoric, logic, arithmetic, geometry, music, and astronomy—the seven liberal arts—are good exercises for the soul. What is radical in Alberti's claim is the ranking of painting with the liberal arts. During the Middle Ages, painting had ranked low, on a par with crafts (shoemaking, weaving, and such). The favorable reception of this treatise encouraged the rise of independent artists, as evidenced around 1500 in the careers of Michelangelo, Leonardo da Vinci, and Raphael.

Alberti also argued that painting should be part of the core curriculum of the schools. To prove his case, he used examples from antiquity showing that the best families required that painting be taught to their sons and daughters. By 1513, Alberti's hope was realized in the well-rounded backgrounds of the idealized lady and gentleman of Castiglione's highly influential *The Book of the Courtier*.

Finally, Alberti was a pioneer in his claim for the sovereign power of painting: "Who can doubt that painting is the master art?" A generation later Leonardo gave voice to the identical claim.

The four selections from *Dinner Pieces*—Religion, Wealth, Preface to Poggio Bracciolini, and The Clouds—summarize some of Alberti's philosophical interests, record his observations on contemporary Italian life, and showcase his satirical skills. In Religion (from Book One),

Alberti has Libripeta (from Latin, "seeker of books") and Lepidus engage in a conversation about the usefulness of worshiping in temples, the nature of the gods, and their relationships to humans. In Wealth (from Book Two), Alberti, speaking through his grandfather, defines what is of real value in life and what is worthwhile that should be left to one's heirs. This selection is also autobiographical as the Alberti family was exiled from Florence in the late fourteenth century, a few years before Leon Battista's birth. In Preface to Poggio Bracciolini (from Book Four), Alberti offers an Aesopian fable to compare himself to others as a way to explain why he is writing *Dinner Pieces*. The last selection—The Clouds (from Book Ten)—opens by raising the issue of the Italian city-states employing mercenary troops, which was one of the most contentious issues at that time. Alberti then spins another Aesopian fable—about the Clouds' petitioning the gods to be given their own king—which meanders over various topics, but eventually returns to the opening question about a state hiring foreign troops.

∽

On Painting, Book II

Because this [process of] learning may perhaps appear a fatiguing thing to young people, I ought to prove here that painting is not unworthy of consuming all our time and study.

Painting contains a divine force which not only makes absent men present, as friendship is said to do, but moreover makes the dead seem almost alive. Even after many centuries they are recognized with great pleasure and with great admiration for the painter. Plutarch[11] says that Cassander, one of the captains of Alexander, trembled through all his body because he saw a portrait of his King. Agesilaos, the Lacedaemonian, never permitted anyone to paint him or to represent him in sculpture; his own form so displeased him that he avoided being known by those who would come after him. Thus the face of a man who is already dead certainly lives a long life through painting. Some think that painting shaped the gods who were adored by the nations. It certainly was their greatest gift to mortals, for painting is most useful to that piety which joins us to the gods, and keeps our souls full of religion. They say that Phidias[12] made in Aulis a god Jove[13] so beautiful that it considerably strengthened the religion then current.

The extent to which painting contributes to the most honourable delights of the soul and to the dignified beauty of things can be clearly seen not only from other things but especially from this: you can conceive of almost nothing so precious which is not made far richer and much more beautiful by association with painting. Ivory, gems and similar expensive things become more precious when worked by the hand of the painter. Gold worked by the art of painting outweighs an equal amount of unworked gold. If figures were made by the hand of Phidias or Praxiteles[14] from lead itself—the lowest of metals—they would be valued more highly than silver. The painter, Zeuxis,[15] began to give away his things because, as he said, they could not be bought. He did not think it possible to come to a just price which would be satisfactory to the painter, for in painting animals he set himself up almost as a god.

Therefore, painting contains within itself this virtue that any master painter who sees his works adored will feel himself considered another god. Who can doubt that painting is the master art or at least not a small ornament of things? The architect, if I am not mistaken, takes from the painter architraves, bases, capitals, columns, façades and other similar things. All the smiths, sculptors, shops and guilds are governed by the rules and art of the painter. It is scarcely possible to find any superior art which is not concerned with painting, so that whatever beauty is found can be said to be born of painting. *But also this, a dignified painting is held in high honour by many so that among all artists some smiths are named, only this is not the rule among smiths.* For this reason, I say among my friends that Narcissus who was changed into a flower, according to the poets, was the inventor of painting. Since painting is already the flower of every art, the story of Narcissus[16] is most to the point. What else can you call painting but a similar embracing with art of what is presented on the surface of the water in the fountain?

Quintilian[17] said that the ancient painters used to circumscribe shadows cast by the sun, and from this our art

---

[11] **Plutarch** Greek biographer who wrote *Parallel Lives,* which were character studies comparing famous Greeks and Romans who lived from antiquity to Plutarch's time in the first century CE.
[12] **Phidias** Regarded as the most famous of all Greek sculptors. Lived in fifth-century BCE Athens and produced many works, including sculptures for the Parthenon.
[13] **Jove** Another Latin name for Jupiter, who was the chief deity of the Roman system of gods and goddesses.

[14] **Praxiteles** Greek sculptor of the fourth century BCE; many of his works are extant.
[15] **Zeuxis** Fifth-century BCE Greek painter whose paintings were very realistic. None of his works exist today.
[16] **Narcissus** A handsome youth who fell in love with his own image reflected in a fountain pool and died of frustration from being unable to fulfill his love.
[17] **Quintilian** First-century CE Roman lawyer, orator, and author of a book on Roman education.

has grown. There are those who say that a certain Philocles, an Egyptian, and a Cleantes were among the first inventors of this art. The Egyptians affirm that painting was in use among them a good 6000 years before it was carried into Greece. They say that painting was brought to us from Greece after the victory of Marcellus[18] over Sicily. But we are not interested in knowing who was the inventor of the art or the first painter, since we are not telling stories like Pliny.[19] We are, however, building anew an art of painting about which nothing, as I see it, has been written in this age. They say that Euphranor of Isthmus wrote something about measure and about colours, that Antigonos and Xenocrates exchanged something in their letters about painting, and that Apelles wrote to Pelleus about painting. Diogenes Laertius recounts that Demetrius made commentaries on painting.[20] Since all the other arts were recommended in letters by our great men, and since painting was not neglected by our Latin writers, I believe that our ancient Tuscan [ancestors] were already most expert masters in painting.

Trismegistus,[21] an ancient writer, judged that painting and sculpture were born at the same time as religion, *for thus he answered Aesclepius: mankind portrays the gods in his own image from his memories of nature and his own origins.* Who can here deny that in all things public and private, profane and religious, painting has taken all the most honourable parts to itself so that nothing has ever been so esteemed by mortals?

The incredible prices of painted pictures have been recorded. Aristides the Theban sold a single picture for one hundred talents. They say that Rhodes was not burned by King Demetrius for fear that a painting of Protogenes' should perish. It could be said that the city of Rhodes was ransomed from the enemy by a single painting. Pliny collected many other such things in which you can see that good painters have always been greatly honoured by all. The most noble citizens, philosophers and quite a few kings not only enjoyed painted things but also painted with their own hands. Lucius Manilius, Roman citizen, and Fabius, a most noble man, were painters. Turpilius, a Roman knight, painted at Verona. Sitedius, praetor and proconsul, acquired renown as a painter. Pacuvius, tragic poet and nephew of the poet Ennius, painted Hercules in the Roman forum. Socrates, Plato, Metrodorus, Pyrrho were connoisseurs of painting. The emperors Nero, Val-

entinian, and Alexander Severus were most devoted to painting. It would be too long, however, to recount here how many princes and kings were pleased by painting. Nor does it seem necessary to me to recount all the throng of ancient painters. Their number is seen in the fact that 360 statues, part on horseback and part in chariots, were completed in four hundred days for Demetrius Phalerius,[22] son of Phanostratus. In a land in which there was such a great number of sculptors, can you believe that painters were lacking? I am certain that both these arts are related and nurtured by the same genius, painting with sculpture. But I always give higher rank to the genius of the painter because he works with more difficult things.

However, let us return to our work. Certainly the number of sculptors and painters was great in those times when princes and plebeians, learned and unlearned enjoyed painting, and when painted panels and portraits, considered the choicest booty from the provinces, were set up in the theatres. Finally L. Paulus Aemilius and not a few other Roman citizens taught their sons painting along with the fine arts and the art of living piously and well. This excellent custom was frequently observed among the Greeks who, because they wished their sons to be well educated, taught them painting along with geometry and music. It was also an honour among women to know how to paint. Martia, daughter of Varro,[23] is praised by the writers because she knew how to paint. Painting had such reputation and honour among the Greeks that laws and edicts were passed forbidding slaves to learn painting. It was certainly well that they did this, for the art of painting has always been most worthy of liberal minds and noble souls.

As for me, I certainly consider a great appreciation of painting to be the best indication of a most perfect mind, even though it happens that this art is pleasing to the uneducated as well as to the educated. It occurs rarely in any other art that what delights the experienced also moves the inexperienced. In the same way you will find that many greatly desire to be well versed in painting. Nature herself seems to delight in painting, for in the cut faces of marble she often paints centaurs and faces of bearded and curly headed kings. It is said, moreover, that in a gem from Pyrrhus all nine Muses, each with her symbol, are to be found clearly painted by nature. Add to this that in no other art does it happen that both the experienced and the inexperienced of every age apply themselves so voluntarily to the learning and exercising of it. Allow me to speak of myself here. Whenever I turn to painting for my recreation, which I frequently do when I am tired of more pressing affairs, I apply myself to it with so much pleasure that I am surprised that three or four hours have passed. Thus this art gives pleasure and praise to whoever is skilled in it; riches and perpetual fame to one who is master of it. Since these things are so, since painting is

---

[18] **Marcellus** Roman general who conquered Sicily in the third century BCE.
[19] **Pliny** Probably Pliny the Elder, not his son, the Younger. The Elder, who lived in the first century CE, wrote extensively on many topics, including an extant encyclopedia of natural science.
[20] **Euphranor of Isthmus, Antigonos, Xenocrates, Apelles, Pelleus, Diogenes Laertius, Demetrius** All these men were ancient Greek sculptors, painters, or philosophers who lived in the fourth and third centuries BCE. Many of their works are lost; most are known only by name or secondary references.
[21] **Trismegistus** Alberti is probably referring to the author of a set of ancient books who was supposed to be Thoth, the Egyptian god of wisdom, and whom the Greeks called Hermes Trismegistus. The books were reputed to include information on every possible topic.

[22] **Demetrius Phalerius** Fourth- and third-century BCE Athenian orator and statesman.
[23] **Varro** Probably Marcus Terentius Varro, second- and first-century BCE Roman scholar and author of many books on law, customs, religion, and philosophy.

the best and most ancient ornament of things, worthy of free men, pleasing to learned and unlearned, I greatly encourage our studious youth to exert themselves as much as possible in painting.

Therefore, I recommend that he who is devoted to painting should learn this art. The first great care of one who seeks to obtain eminence in painting is to acquire the fame and renown of the ancients. It is useful to remember that avarice is always the enemy of virtue. Rarely can anyone given to acquisition of wealth acquire renown. I have seen many in the first flower of learning suddenly sink to money-making. As a result they acquire neither riches nor praise. However, if they had increased their talent with study, they would have easily soared into great renown. Then they would have acquired much riches and pleasure. . . .

Questions for Critical Thinking

1. Discuss some of the sources and references from the past that Alberti offers in proving the value of painting.

2. What advice does Alberti give to a person who wishes to become a painter? Do you think this advice would apply to someone who wants to be an artist today? Why or why not?

Dinner Pieces, Book One
Religion

LIBRIPETA:[24] This fig tree seems to me quite pious and compassionate, for from it, as from Timon's famous tree,[25] many have hanged themselves to end life's afflictions. But here comes Lepidus,[26] whom I have expected for some time now.

LEPIDUS: Greetings, Libripeta. Did the sacrifice detain me in the temple longer than you would have wished?

LIBR.: Much longer. But tell me, what business did you have with the gods that occasioned your lengthy discussions?

LEP.: What, is it shameful to worship the gods devoutly and to pray that they favor our wishes?

LIBR.: Doubtless under that roof, with its mob of lurking priests, the gods hear you quite well!

LEP.: Don't you know that everything is filled with gods?

LIBR.: Then you could properly have done beneath this fig tree exactly what, following the superstitious custom of the ignorant, you accomplished in the temple. But tell me, please, did you pray only for yourself before those painted gods, or did you act as an agent for others?

LEP.: Why do you ask?

LIBR.: Because I would find you arrogant, if you thought that the gods hold you so dear that they are more moved by your words than by those of people who truly need assistance. Besides, in my view, whoever prays to the gods asks them above all to grant and keep his goods, present and future, and to remove and avert his ills. What do you say to this?

LEP.: I'm of the same opinion.

LIBR.: O foolish ones, do you want the gods to act as your hirelings and thieves? For no goods can come to you but those snatched from others who own them. Can you show me a servant so base that you could honorably order him to commit such a crime? Is anyone so unrestrained as to order corrupt assassins to make him rich with booty taken from others?

LEP.: I see your point. Yet I did not ask that they act as thieves, but as laborers, for I asked them to see that golden cabbages grow in my garden.

LIBR.: If they are wise, the gods will detest your impudence.

LEP.: Will you deny, Libripeta, that the gods often aid mankind in adversity?

---

[24] **Libripeta** Alberti's name for the character who acts as a foil in this dialogue. May be a reference to Niccolò Niccoli (c. 1364– 1437), the Florentine humanist, who, like Alberti, was a student of classical times and culture.

[25] **Timon's famous tree** Plutarch, in his essay on Marc Antony in *The Lives of the Noble Grecians and Romans*, includes a passage on Timon, an Athenian citizen. Timon, who disliked most people, announced before the assembled Athenians that he had a fig tree on his property on which many persons had hanged themselves, and if anyone wanted to hang himself, he should do it now before the tree was cut down. Thus, the reference is to a misanthrope—one who does not like other humans.

[26] **Lepidus** From the Latin word for "witty." Hence, the voice of Alberti in this dialogue.

LIBR.: Will you deny, Lepidus, that men are themselves the cause of all the ills that vex them? Just climb this fig tree and hang yourself from this branch; then ask the gods to rescue you. If you didn't ruin your health by reading in continual vigils, Lepidus, you would hardly be so pale or so dyspeptic. Men willingly submit to the ills they suffer. Believe me, no sailors would know of gods to calm the storm, if they didn't trust themselves to the surging sea. But such is their custom: when their own senseless folly subjects them to the gravest dangers, they turn at once to the gods. Thus, by wishing the gods to stop what they themselves have undertaken, they seem not to pray, but to engage in conflict and controversy. And you too, if you avoid whatever causes your ills, will never have need of any gods to remove them. Or if you judge that it is men who harm other men, there is no need to invoke protecting gods, but rather to reconcile men. But if the gods themselves are the cause of our ills, please consider that they will scarcely depart from their former custom because of your prayers. For ages, men have been plagued by adversity; and if something else—fate, or chance, or time—causes our afflictions, without a doubt it exercises its office freely and with the gods' assent, and will spurn your paltry supplications, O men of religion. Besides, do you think the gods resemble us small human beings? Do they make decisions on the spur of the moment, like imprudent and reckless people, and then abruptly change their former resolves? Indeed, men of learning tell me that the gods are incomparably industrious in their great task of administration, and that they rule the world according to a practically eternal order. Consequently, you rave like madmen if you think your words or arguments will sway the gods' intent and actions from their age-old course toward new undertakings. Besides, the gods would be groveling slaves if they abandoned their own resolves for your hopes and desires. In fine, you must remember that the gods are quite busy moving the sun, the moon, and the other heavenly bodies through the vast heavens. Even your men of religion assert publicly that the gods toss mountainous waves on the sea, send down winds and lightning bolts, and control countless such terrifying phenomena. Engaged in such great matters, the gods have little time to listen to the interminable, futile, and utterly ridiculous prayers of men. And if the gods paid attention to trivial matters, they would more gladly listen to the pure voices of cicadas and crickets than to the foolish entreaties of impure men. Know then that the gods are deafened only by the prayers of the wicked. For good men are clearly content with the goods they have, and they yield to adversity. But the wicked never show reason or restraint in demanding goods or bearing ills.

LEP.: I regard your remarks, Libripeta, as made for the sake of disputation, but shall always maintain my own view of the gods and believe that they welcome the prayers and vows of good men. And I remained convinced that many of the misfortunes we deserve are averted by the mercy of the gods, who are most generous to meritorious men. Goodbye.

❧

Dinner Pieces, Book Two
Wealth

My grandfather, Benedetto Alberti, a Florentine knight noted for his fine character and virtue, had been driven into exile by seditious citizens, and lay on his death bed on the island of Rhodes.[27] Urged by his friends to draw up a will, he asked them what things they wished him to include in it. His friends replied: "Your own, Benedetto, for no one doubts that you are the richest man in Tuscany."[28]

He said: "I assure you that there is nothing of which I am more ignorant and unaware. As for those things which I suppose you mean, I scarcely know now what is mine. But in my youth, I labored many years under such an error, and imprudently deemed mine those things which are popularly thought to belong to a person. I followed the common usage of my fellow-citizens, and called them *my* estates, *my* property, and *my* wealth, as people do."

"But weren't they yours?" his friends asked.

"No," my grandfather replied. "Even more surprisingly, I have long realized that even this body which confines me was never really mine. For I recall how against my will these members were always subject to cold, to heat, or to various pains, and how they hindered and opposed my nobler intentions and desires. I recall how this body continually suffered hunger, thirst, and other such harsh and savage masters. And I perceive how in a single day fortune, mistress of our affairs, has snatched from me all my wealth and goods and even my homeland, and has driven me into exile. What, then, dare I call mine, either past or present?

---

[27] **Rhodes** An island in the Aegean Sea, off the coast of Turkey. Settled by Greeks around 1000 BCE and became a prosperous island until its alliance with Rome in the second century BCE. In Alberti's times, Rhodes was under the control of Knights of St. John of Jerusalem, and then fell to the Turks in 1522. Thus, it could have been where his grandfather took refuge after being exiled from Florence.

[28] **Tuscany** The region in central Italy where Florence is located, which was the center of the early Italian Renaissance.

"Now, wealth in human life is like a game with a ball. 5 For it is not holding the ball in your hands a long time, but throwing it with skill and returning it accurately, that helps you win the victory. Just so, I judge that it is not the possession but the use of wealth that contributes to happiness. And as for myself, I admit that I have virtually nothing left that I may especially call mine, except the knowledge of my deeds and the recollection of what

I suffered in life. I wish, therefore, to leave my heirs this sole inheritance. They may claim that, above all others in our city, I was the most devoted to my country, and the most desirous of peace, tranquillity, and freedom; that I was by no means ignorant of liberal studies, letters, and arts; and that I defended the public weal with great vigilance and faith, and was always content with my private estate. Let these deeds of mine pass to my heirs."

∞

Dinner Pieces, Book Four
Preface to Poggio Bracciolini[29]

While wallowing in the lowly swamp-grass of a muddy 1 river bank, some heifers, they say, saw a she-goat seated on the ruins of an ancient temple which had collapsed atop a rocky crag, and admonished her in these words. "You there, wanton one, what temerity possesses you, that you spurn this verdant bank and attempt that arduous and virtually inaccessible height? Don't you see that it is better to fill yourself with sweet and juicy grass than always to graze thirstily amid jagged ruins, nourished on bitter wild figs? Take care that you don't come to regret your dangerous rambles on such precipices."

The she-goat, they say, replied to the heifers in these words: "Ha! grave, ill-humored, tender-footed beasts! Don't you know that the mouth carefully serves the stomach, and the feet the mouth? I have a goat's stomach, not a cow's. If you disdain what I graze on because you can't reach it, I spurn your swamp-grass because it is available everywhere to even the idlest cattle. And if others' peril bothers you in your sloth, you should have reproved the vultures, who

search for carcasses from the highest reaches of heaven. Their fall is far more dangerous than mine."

Now, the very same thing, dear Poggio, I find happening to me as I engage in writing these *Dinner Pieces*. For many of us today seek food and sustenance in the more plentiful and pleasant fields of eloquence. And the same people censure me for delighting in difficult pursuits, rather than in those filled with the juice of commonplace eloquence and material reward. But if these critics heed the goat in the fable, I think they will find no cause to reproach me. If they blame me for choosing to spurn other lucrative arts and for following my natural abilities, then they must also blame the mathematicians and all others who devote themselves to understanding the stars and profoundly recondite subjects. Can't everyone see how ruinously they fail when they fall short of the hope that led them to contemplate the farthest realms of the heavens? Yet no one denies that they pursue a liberal goal.

For myself, I take pleasure in rare subjects which, like piquant herbs in an appetizer, should not be excluded from the lavish dinners of writers who I confess are richer than myself. Besides, if I wish to prove my diligence in this field—in which zeal furthers talent, and application zeal—whose envy can distract me from bringing forth diverse and rare inventions like these?

---

[29] **Poggio Bracciolini** Famous Renaissance humanist (1380–1459) who discovered many classical writings in monasteries. He and Alberti were at the Vatican as secretaries to the Pope. Later, in the mid-1450s, Poggio served in the Florentine government.

∞

Dinner Pieces, Book Ten
The Clouds

In the recent age of our fathers, Italians employed hired 1 troops and foreign armies rather than conscripted citizens, as had been our ancestors' custom. They did this by prudent choice, I believe, since exposing the lives of ignoble mercenaries to the perils of battle seemed more practical than risking the lives of citizens in the fortunes in war. They may also have wished to prevent Italian troops from taking up arms only to abuse them later to

the ruin of their homeland, as in fact happened. For continual invaders, led by their hope of victory and their desire of booty, ravaged the peaceful and wealthy peoples of Italy; and the youths of Italy, being of fierce and aggressive stock, gradually began to rouse themselves to martial pursuits. Soon nearly countless military commanders sprang up throughout Italy. Endowed with great courage and emboldened by the glory of their exploits, they looked beyond mere victories and triumphs, and aspired to kingdoms, disdaining any conquest which did not subject the vanquished to their personal dictates and decrees.

Since the ambition of these men was to rule, they did their utmost to seize power. But the ambition of the free cities was to serve no master, and they did their utmost to defend their freedom. As a result, such great civil wars arose that not only men, but even the gods were astonished. Hence, almighty Jupiter,[30] who has always cherished mankind's peace and tranquillity, sent the gods' envoy Mercury[31] to learn the meaning of such great and widespread preparations for war. Donning his winged sandals, the god descended to a mountain in the Alps, from which he could view both the Po Valley and Tuscany.[32] There he removed his sandals and shed his divine appearance so that he could more gracefully blend into the company of mortals. Suddenly, he was joined by the Clouds, who formed a circle around him and greeted him as an old friend, for Mercury had often used their aid in his missions.

"Your arrival is indeed timely," said Mercury. "Unless I am mistaken, you may relieve me of the task which brings me here in such incertitude. Since you float above men's cities night and day and may easily know the reason, tell me why mortals have taken up arms on all sides?"

"So that you know, Mercury," the Clouds replied, "Pluto's[33] daughter is a girl named Ambition, who is perhaps not unknown to the gods themselves. Because of her singular beauty, she is greatly desired by many young noblemen and by not a few patrician youths. Being a wanton and forward young woman, she is extremely delighted by the large number of her suitors, and promises all of them that she will try to satisfy their wishes. Inflamed with love for her, they devote all their efforts and energies to courting her, and employ any means they can to thwart and hinder their rivals. Hence arise rivalries, enmities, and altercations, and in the zeal for their factions, they have resolved to fight for her, and have deployed their troops in battle formation."

Hearing this, Mercury exclaimed: "What a plague on mortals this woman is! She is the perpetual source of quarrels, discords, dissensions, and the ruin of all things public and private." Then, making ready to return to Jupiter, he asked whether the Clouds wished to request anything of him.

The Clouds replied: "We welcome your question, Mercury. For we hope that, as you bear us affection, you will not refuse to take up our cause, which is just, righteous, and hardly troublesome, and we pray and entreat you to do so. The issue is this. You know, Mercury, that we are not ignoble. We think no one is unaware that, whether our mother was Earth or Juno,[34] we were certainly begotten by our father Phoebus.[35] As for our peaceable and modest way of life, we scarcely need to describe here something so familiar to you.

"What then? The Fires have Etna[36] as their seat, and Vulcan[37] as their king. The waters fill immense and multitudinous gulfs, and are rolled far and wide by their king Neptune.[38] And the Winds, not content with their caves or their king [Neptune], sport through all the skies, seas, mountains, and the whole earth. Isn't it unjust, then, that we, who are harmless and constant in our duty, are neither honored with a king nor protected by laws? Nay, it is our harsh lot to be driven constantly as exiles and outcasts, never allowed to abide in one place or to repose in tranquillity. Shall we forever nurture the dark earth with our tears?[39] We collect dew and sustenance which make the seeds and fruits bloom and ripen, and these feed both animals sacrificed to the gods and mortal men, who are the darlings of the gods. By contrast, the Winds strike down the flowers, the Waters flood and lay low the burgeoning fields, and the Fires devastate the full-grown crops.

"You are wise, and we know that you are in haste to return to Jupiter. So we need not detain you with prolix entreaties. But there is one thing we ask again. Plead the cause of our well-being and dignity before Jupiter—but only if you judge it honorable and consonant with your affection for us. We wish you to know, Mercury, that we could hope for nothing more than to obtain this just and easily granted favor with you as our spokesman. We wish to be honored with a king and, as if after a long exile, to be granted a homeland in which, at last in peace, we may some day worship the gods devoutly and piously. We refuse no homeland or king, as long as it is honorable. If, as we hope, Mercury, you help us to attain this, you will truly find that those you have aided are grateful and mindful of your kindness."

Mercury replied: "I desire to have your honor and interests at heart. But you must decide whether it is better for Mercury to appear before the gods as the Clouds' ambassador, or as Jupiter's counselor. In my view, you should send your own emissaries to Jupiter. I shall see that the senate of the gods convenes to receive them with honor."

The Clouds thus decided to send emissaries to accompany Mercury on his return to Jupiter. They say that, when he had heard their speech and its petitions, Jupiter

---

[30] **Jupiter** Chief god of the Romans, equivalent to Zeus among the Greek deities.

[31] **Mercury** Roman god of messages or herald for the deities. Hermes in the Greek system.

[32] **Po Valley and Tuscany** Two well-known regions in Italy. Florence, the home of Alberti, is located in Tuscany. On top of the mountain in the Alps, Mercury could look south—first to the Po Valley—and beyond that, to Tuscany.

[33] **Pluto** Ruling god of the underworld. Alberti asserts that Ambition is his daughter, but there is no evidence in Roman or Greek myths that she was his daughter.

---

[34] **Earth or Juno** Earth, or Gaia, came out of primeval Chaos. Earth gave birth to the generation of Titans, who were then followed by the Olympian deities. Juno is Roman queen of the gods and goddesses and associated with Hera, the Greek goddess.

[35] **Phoebus** Another name for Apollo, who is associated with the sun and often identified as "the shining one."

[36] **Etna** An active volcano in Sicily.

[37] **Vulcan** Roman god of fire and craftsmanship; the Greek god is Hephaestos.

[38] **Neptune** Roman god of the sea, equated with Poseidon of the Greek Olympians.

[39] **our tears** Rain.

frowned slightly. Then, after briefly relecting in silence, he dismissed them with the following reply. The gods had decided to grant the Clouds whatever king and kingdom would give them joy. Yet, in order to satisfy the Clouds' desires without creating rancor, the gods delegated to the various orders of the Clouds the task of electing a king fitting and worthy of the heavenly powers. He therefore bade them hold an election, and to rest assured that the gods would not hesitate to give their appointed king both a dwelling-place and all due honors.

Soon, little Clouds were flying across the land as bailiffs[40] to summon the bearded patrician clouds to the royal elections. The latter appeared one by one, each dressed in white and sunk in deep meditation, with brows raised haughtily, as if already engaged in administering a tyrannical regime and in drafting new laws. The Clouds were so puffed with pride that they disdained their usual steeds, and arrived mounted on strange and horrible beasts like the hydra, centaur, the Lernaean beast, and such monsters.[41] They say that the Clouds' haughty arrogance disgusted their father Phoebus, who turned away, unable to bear the sight of them. As the Clouds gathered to meet, they greeted one another with an intolerable show of dignity and majesty, lowering their deep and rumbling voices to subdued and muted tones. Yet the centuriate[42] assembly had scarcely been admitted, much less all the other orders, when the Clouds bustled throughout their ranks, canvassing for votes with a zeal which can hardly be described. You could have heard their deep and husky

---

[40] **bailiffs** Used in this context as one who is a messenger. In the U.S. judiciary system, a bailiff occupies a similar role.

[41] **the hydra, centaur, the Lernaean beast, and such monsters** A hydra is a many-headed mythological beast; the centaur was a half-man, half-horse creature; the Lernaean beast refers to the second labor of Hercules, when he killed the Lernaean hydra, or snakelike beast of nine heads that lived in Lake Lerna.

[42] **centuriate** That is, the assembly was divided into sections of hundreds. Alberti thus paints a scene of many "clouds."

voices swell until they burst into thunderous roars. Then, the fierce contention between factions erupted into violence. The furious candidates wrapped their arms in their cloaks, and they used stones and firebrands as weapons against the others' stones. The din of the battle and the rumbling of the combatants inspired incredible terror in the hearts of men and gods alike. Rivers overflowed with the blood of the Clouds, and the mountains and temples of the gods shook with fright and terror. No doubt, the gods themselves were in suspense, as if the foundations of heaven were collapsing.

Only Jupiter, they say, maintained a very placid and serene countenance, and after sighing, he smiled at the great turbulence of the Clouds. When asked why, he replied that he had not rashly decided to bid the Clouds elect their own king. For he knew well the preposterous and perverse nature of the Clouds, who were puffed up with their own superiority, and whose excessive squeamishness always led them to approve a shifting and unstable way of life. He added that he was not unfamiliar with their arrogant insolence, which was clear, among other things, from their desire for a king and a kingdom. Had they acquired these, and had they learned to direct their strength, wisdom, and energies toward their common glory, their savage and reckless nature would have carried their insolence so far that they would have attempted to seize the stars, the moon, and even the sun.

Therefore, Jupiter said, he could have found no better way to restrain and repress their aggressiveness. For those who share a common vice or virtue readily associate with each other. Hence, we see that drunkards, gluttons, paramours, dicers, thieves, brigands, assassins, and other such reprobates and criminals, induced by the urging and pleasure of their common nature, all live together sociably and intimately. Only one who is proud disdains and detests his brothers in pride, and no one is harsher to his peers than proud men. It is in the nature of the proud to vex and antagonize each other incessantly.

∞

Questions for Critical Thinking

1. What are the main arguments put forward in *Religion* regarding the nature of the gods and their relationships with humans? Who do you think has the better argument, Libripeta or Lepidus?

2. Summarize the series of events regarding the Clouds' efforts to choose a king. What are the lessons Alberti is offering his reader in this *Dinner Piece*?

13

THE HIGH RENAISSANCE AND EARLY MANNERISM
1494–1564

BALDASSARE CASTIGLIONE
Selections from *The Book of the Courtier*

The Book of the Courtier (*courtier* being a "gentleman") belongs to the genre of etiquette books that flourished in Renaissance Europe as a religious-based culture gave way to a more humanistic world. Books of this type were much in evidence, in response to this period's ideal that secular life in the upper levels of society should be marked by reserved grace, especially between the sexes. Court life, whether in the royal or aristocratic domain, already had well-established rules of behavior derived from the medieval chivalric code; however, courts were still dominated by a male ethos, manifested in rough speech, crude manners, and general lack of refinement between men and women. Whereas most Renaissance etiquette books were meant to correct crude behavior and speech, *The Courtier* took a broader view by offering an idealized vision of court life in which courteous ladies became the arbiters of society. Published in 1528 and translated into most Western languages by 1600, this work became the bible of politeness for Europe's upper classes, and its rules were formalized into strict expectations. This Renaissance book is the source from which modern notions of "lady" and "gentleman" descend.

The Courtier's author, Baldassare Castiglione (1478–1529), was himself a polished courtier, growing up among the Italian nobility and studying the classics at the University of Milan. Later, he was attached to various northern Italian ducal courts (Milan, Urbino, and Mantua), for whose rulers he performed military and diplomatic missions. While serving as the Duke of Mantua's ambassador to Rome, he was brought by his duties into the cultivated court of the Medici pope, Leo X (pope 1513–1521). A later pope, Clement VII (pope 1523–1534), made Castiglione the papal representative to Spain, a post he held until he died.

The Courtier, Castiglione's only publication, was his life's work. He was moved to write it during his eleven years at the ducal court of Urbino, which was the center of an accomplished circle of artists, writers, and intellectuals presided over by the old duke and his young wife, Elisabetta. This Urbino circle, with its witty talk, integrity, and grace, came to embody Castiglione's social ideal. When he wrote *The Courtier*, Castiglione tried to capture the conversational tone of this circle by making the work a dialogue, divided into four books, set during an evening in the ducal palace. In his book, as in life, Duchess Elisabetta is the playful leader of the group.

Reading the Selections

These selections from *The Book of the Courtier* are excerpts from Books I and III, dealing respectively with the qualities that define a courtier and a lady. Not based on real life, these attributes are ideals meant as a guide for correct deportment and had been gleaned from Castiglione's readings in medieval and classical literature. Of the ideal courtier, the participants agree that he should be both a soldier trained in the bearing of arms and a scholar skilled in the liberal arts and social graces; however, they are of two minds as to which role should dominate.

No such dispute divides Castiglione's participants over the ideal lady: all concur that she should be the consummate hostess—charming, witty, graceful, physically attractive, and utterly feminine. An innovative aspect of this idealized model is the insistence that a lady be educated in the liberal arts in the same way as a gentleman. This idea swept away the barrier that, since the Middle Ages, had excluded women from higher learning. However, women remained barred from universities until the nineteenth century.

∞

Book I

. . .

"But to come to specific details, I[1] judge that the first and true profession of the courtier must be that of arms; and this above everything else I wish him to pursue vigorously. Let him also stand out from the rest as enterprising, bold, and loyal to whomever he serves. And he will win a good reputation by demonstrating these qualities whenever and wherever possible, since failure to do so always incurs the gravest censure. Just as once a woman's reputation for purity has been sullied it can never be restored, so once the reputation of a gentleman-at-arms has been stained through cowardice or some other reproachful behaviour, even if only once, it always remains defiled in the eyes of the world and covered with ignominy. The more our courtier excels in this art, therefore, the more praise he will deserve, although I do not think he needs to have the professional knowledge of such things and the other qualities appropriate to a military commander. However, since the subject of what constitutes a great captain takes us into very deep waters, we shall be content, as we said, for the courtier to show complete loyalty and an undaunted spirit, and for these to be always in evidence. For men demonstrate their courage far more often in little things than in great. Very often in the face of appalling danger but where there are numerous witnesses one will find those who, though ready to drop dead with fear, driven on by shame or the presence of others, will press forward, with their eyes closed, and do their duty; and only God knows how. But in things of trifling importance,

when they believe they can avoid danger without its being noticed, they are only too willing to play for safety. As for those who, even when they are sure they are not being observed or seen or recognized by anyone, are full of ardour and avoid doing anything, no matter how trivial, for which they would incur reproach, they possess the temper and quality we are looking for in our courtier. All the same, we do not wish the courtier to make a show of being so fierce that he is always blustering and bragging, declaring that he is married to his cuirass,[2] and glowering with the haughty looks that we know only too well in Berto.[3] To these may very fairly be said what a worthy lady once remarked jokingly, in polite company, to a certain man (I don't want just now to mention him by name) whom she had honoured by asking him to dance and who not only refused but would not listen to music or take part in the many other entertainments offered, protesting all the while that such frivolities were not his business. And when at length the lady asked what his business was, he answered with a scowl: "Fighting . . ."

"'Well then,' the lady retorted, 'I should think that since you aren't at war at the moment and you are not engaged in fighting, it would be a good thing if you were to have yourself well greased and stowed away in a cupboard with all your fighting equipment, so that you avoid getting rustier than you are already.'

"And of course everyone burst out laughing at the way she showed her contempt for his stupid presumption.

"Therefore," Count Lodovico went on, "the man we are seeking should be fierce, rough and always to the fore, in the presence of the enemy; but anywhere else he should

---

[1] **I** Count Lodovico da Canossa (1476–1532) is speaking. A noble from Verona, he was appointed papal ambassador to England and France by Pope Leo X (pope 1513–1521); made Bishop of Bayeux (in France) in 1520; appointed emissary to Venice by King Francis I of France; resident at Urbino at intervals after 1496. A relative of Castiglione.

[2] **cuirass** Breastplate armor covering the body from neck to waist.
[3] **Berto** Perhaps a papal buffoon, or fool, during the time of Pope Julius II (pope 1503–1513) or Leo X.

be kind, modest, reticent and anxious above all to avoid ostentation or the kind of outrageous self-glorification by which a man always arouses loathing and disgust among those who have to listen to him. . . .

"I should like our courtier to be a more than average 5 scholar, at least in those studies which we call the humanities; and he should have a knowledge of Greek as well as Latin, because of the many different things that are so beautifully written in that language. He should be very well acquainted with the poets, and no less with the orators and historians, and also skilled at writing both verse and prose, especially in our own language; for in addition to the satisfaction this will give him personally, it will enable him to provide constant entertainment for the ladies, who are usually very fond of such things. But if because of his other activities or through lack of study he fails to achieve a commendable standard in his writing, then he should take pains to suppress his work, to avoid ridicule, and he should show it only to a friend he can trust. And the exercise of writing will be profitable for him at least to the extent that it will teach him how to judge the work of others. For it is very unusual for someone who is not a practised writer, however erudite he may be, to understand completely the demanding work done by writers, or appreciate their stylistic accomplishments and triumphs and those subtle details characteristic of the writers of the ancient world. Moreover, these studies will make our courtier well informed and eloquent and (as Aristippus[4] said to the tyrant) self-confident and assured no matter whom he is talking to. However, I should like our courtier to keep one precept firmly in mind: namely, that in what I have just discussed and in everything else he should always be diffident and reserved rather than forward, and he should be on his guard against assuming that he knows what he does not know. For we are instinctively all too greedy for praise, and there is no sound or song that comes sweeter to our ears; praise, like Sirens'[5] voices, is the kind of music that causes shipwreck to the man who does not stop his ears to its deceptive harmony. Recognizing this danger, some of the philosophers of the ancient world wrote books giving advice on how a man can tell the difference between a true friend and a flatterer. Even so, we may well ask what use is this, seeing that there are so many who realize perfectly well that they are listening to flattery, and yet love the flatterer and detest the one who tells them the truth. Indeed, very often, deciding that the one who praises them is not being fulsome enough, they lend him a hand themselves and say such things that even the most outrageous flatterer feels ashamed. Let us leave these blind fools to their errors and decide that our courtier should possess such good judgement that he will not be told that black is white or presume anything of himself unless he is certain that it is true, and especially in regard to those flaws which, if you remember, when he was

suggesting his game for the evening Cesare[6] recalled we had often used to demonstrate the particular folly of this person or another. To make no mistake at all, the courtier should, on the contrary, when he knows the praises he receives are deserved, not assent to them too openly nor let them pass without some protest. Rather he should tend to disclaim them modestly, always giving the impression that arms are, as indeed they should be, his chief profession, and that all his other fine accomplishments serve merely as adornments; and this should especially be his attitude when he is in the company of soldiers, lest he behave like those who in the world of scholarship want to be taken for warriors and among warriors want to seem men of letters. In this way, as we have said, he will avoid affectation, and even his modest achievements will appear great."

At this point, Pietro Bembo[7] interrupted: "I cannot see, my dear Count, why you wish this courtier, who is so literate and so well endowed with other worthy qualities, to regard everything as serving to adorn the profession of arms, and not arms and the rest as serving to adorn the profession of letters, which, taken by themselves, are as superior in dignity to arms as is the soul to the body, since letters are a function of the soul, just as arms are of the body."

Then the Count answered: "On the contrary, the profession of arms pertains both to the soul and to the body. But I should not want you to be the judge of this, Pietro, because by one of the parties concerned it would be assumed that you were prejudiced. And as this is a controversy that the wisest men have already thrashed out, there is no call to re-open it. As it is, I consider that it has been settled in favour of arms; and since I may form our courtier as I wish, I want him to be of the same opinion. If you think the contrary, wait until you hear of a contest in which the man who defends the cause of arms is allowed to use them, just as those who defend the cause of letters make use of letters in their defence; for if each one uses his own weapons, you will see that the men of letters will lose."

"Ah," said Pietro Bembo, "you were only too ready earlier on to damn the French for their scant appreciation of letters, and you mentioned the glory that they bring to men and the way they make a man immortal. And now you seem to have changed your mind. Do you not remember that:

> *Giunto Alessandro alla famosa tomba*
> *del fero Achille, sospirando disse:*
> *O fortunato, che sì chiara tromba*
> *trovasti, e chi di te sì alto scrisse!*[8]

---

[6] **Cesare** Cesare Gonzaga (1475–1512), a famous warrior, from the illustrious Gonzaga family in Mantua; a cousin and friend of Castiglione.
[7] **Pietro Bembo** (1470–1547), a Venetian noble and Renaissance man; regarded as an authority on language, style, and Platonic love. Appointed papal secretary by Pope Leo X; made cardinal in 1539; resident at Urbino, 1506–1512.
[8] *. . . alto scrisse!* The first quatrain of a sonnet by Petrarch, literally: "When Alexander reached the famous tomb of fierce Achilles, he sighed and said: 'O happy man, who found so illustrious a trumpet, and one to write of you so nobly!'"

---

[4] **Aristippus** (ca. 435–366 BCE) Greek philosopher who founded a hedonistic school of philosophy in Cyrene, North Africa.
[5] **Sirens** In Homer's *Odyssey*, monstrous creatures, half-woman, half-bird, whose singing lured sailors onto destructive rocks at sea.

And if Alexander[9] was envious of Achilles[10] not because of what he had done himself but because of the way he was blessed by fortune in having his deeds celebrated by Homer, we must conclude that he put a higher value on the writings of Homer than on the arms of Achilles. What other judge do you want, or what other verdict on the relative worth of arms and letters than the one delivered by one of the greatest commanders that has ever lived?"

The Count replied: "I blame the French for believing that letters are harmful to the profession of arms, and I maintain myself that it is more fitting for a warrior to be educated than for anyone else; and I would have these two accomplishments, the one helping the other, as is most fitting, joined together in our courtier. I do not think that this means I have changed my opinion. But, as I said, I do not wish to argue which of them is more praiseworthy. Let it be enough that men of letters hardly ever choose to praise other than great men and glorious deeds, which deserve praise both on their own account and because, in addition, they provide writers with a truly noble theme. And this subject-matter embellishes what is written and, no doubt, is the reason why such writings endure, for otherwise, if they dealt not with noble deeds but with vain and trivial subjects, they would surely be read and appreciated less. And if Alexander was envious of Achilles because he was praised by Homer, it still does not necessary follow that he thought more of letters than of arms;

and if he had thought that he was as inferior to Achilles as a soldier as he believed that all those who would write about him were inferior to Homer as writers, he would, I[11] am sure, have far preferred brave exploits on his own part to brave talk from others. Therefore I believe that when he said what he did, Alexander was tacitly praising himself, and expressing a desire for what he thought he lacked, namely supreme ability as a writer, rather than for what he took for granted he already had, namely prowess as a warrior, in which he was far from acknowledging Achilles as his superior. So when he called Achilles fortunate he meant that if so far his own fame did not rival that of Achilles (which had been made bright and illustrious through so inspired a poem) this was not because his valour and merits were less notable or less deserving of the highest praise but because of the way fortune had granted Achilles a born genius to be his herald and to trumpet his deeds to the world. Moreover, perhaps Alexander wanted to encourage some gifted person to write about him, showing that his pleasure in this would be as great as his love and respect for the sacred monuments of literature. And now we have said enough about this subject."

"Indeed, far too much," remarked signor Lodovico, "for I don't think that one could discover anywhere in the world a vessel big enough to hold all the things you want to put into our courtier" . . .

---

[9] **Alexander** Alexander III, called Alexander the Great (r. 336–323 BCE). Macedonian general and founder of a great empire, stretching from his homeland to the Indus River.
[10] **Achilles** Ancient Greek hero (see Homer's *Iliad* in Chapter 2, Volume I).

[11] **I** Giuliano de' Medici (1479–1516), of Florence; son of Lorenzo de' Medici and brother of Pope Leo X; during the exile of the Medici from Florence, 1494–1512, Giuliano lived in Urbino, where he was called the "Magnifico Giuliano."

∞

Book III

. . .

"Thus just as it is very fitting that a man should display a certain robust and sturdy manliness, so it is well for a woman to have a certain soft and delicate tenderness, with an air of feminine sweetness in her every movement, which, in her going and staying and whatsoever she does, always makes her appear a woman, without any resemblance to a man. If this precept be added to the rules that these gentlemen have taught the courtier, then I think that she ought to be able to make use of many of them, and adorn herself with the finest accomplishments, as signor Gaspare[12] says. For I consider that many virtues of the mind are as necessary to a woman as to a man; as it is to be of good family; to shun affectation; to be naturally graceful; to be well mannered, clever and prudent; to be

neither proud, envious or evil-tongued, nor vain, contentious or clumsy; to know how to gain and keep the favour of her mistress and of everyone else; to perform well and gracefully the sports suitable for women. It also seems to me that good looks are more important to her than to the courtier, for much is lacking to a woman who lacks beauty. She must also be more circumspect and at greater pains to avoid giving an excuse for someone to speak ill of her; she should not only be beyond reproach but also beyond even suspicion, for a woman lacks a man's resources when it comes to defending herself. And now, seeing that Count Lodovico has explained in great detail what should be the principal occupation of a courtier, namely, to his mind, the profession of arms, it seems right for me to say what I consider ought to be that of the lady at Court. And when I have done this, then I shall believe that most of my task has been carried out.

"Leaving aside, therefore, those virtues of the mind which she must have in common with the courtier, such as

---

[12] **signor Gaspare** (1486–1511), of a distinguished Lombard family; friend of Castiglione.

prudence, magnanimity, continence[13] and many others besides, and also the qualities that are common to all kinds of women, such as goodness and discretion, the ability to take good care, if she is married, of her husband's belongings and house and children, and the virtues belonging to a good mother, I say that the lady who is at Court should properly have, before all else, a certain pleasing affability whereby she will know how to entertain graciously every kind of man with charming and honest conversation, suited to the time and the place and the rank of the person with whom she is talking. And her serene and modest behaviour, and the candour that ought to inform all her actions, should be accompanied by a quick and vivacious spirit by which she shows her freedom from boorishness; but with such a virtuous manner that she makes herself thought no less chaste, prudent and benign than she is pleasing, witty and discreet. Thus she must observe a certain difficult mean,[14] composed as it were of contrasting qualities, and take care not to stray beyond certain fixed limits. . . .

"Now since signor Gaspare also asks what are the many things a lady at Court should know about, how she ought to converse, and whether her virtues should be such as to contribute to her conversation, I declare that I want her to understand what these gentlemen have said the courtier himself ought to know; and as for the activities we have said are unbecoming to her, I want her at least to have the understanding that people can have of things they do not practise themselves; and this so that she may know how to value and praise the gentlemen concerned in all fairness, according to their merits. And, to repeat in just a few words something of what has already been said, I want this lady to be knowledgeable about literature and painting, to know how to dance and play games, adding a discreet modesty and the ability to give a good impression of herself to the other principles that have been

taught the courtier. And so when she is talking or laughing, playing or jesting, no matter what, she will always be most graceful, and she will converse in a suitable manner with whomever she happens to meet, making use of agreeable witticisms and jokes. And although continence, magnanimity, temperance, fortitude of spirit, prudence and the other virtues may not appear to be relevant in her social encounters with others, I want her to be adorned with these as well, not so much for the sake of good company, though they play a part in this too, as to make her truly virtuous, and so that her virtues, shining through everything she does, make her worthy of honour."

"I am quite surprised," said signor Gaspare with a laugh, "that since you endow women with letters, continence, magnanimity and temperance, you do not want them to govern cities as well, and to make laws and lead armies, while the men stay at home to cook and spin."

The Magnifico replied, also laughing: "Perhaps that would not be so bad, either."

Then he added: "Do you not know that Plato, who was certainly no great friend of women, put them in charge of the city and gave all the military duties to the men[15]? Don't you think that we might find many women just as capable of governing cities and armies as men? But I have not imposed these duties on them, since I am fashioning a Court lady and not a queen. I'm fully aware that you would like by implication to repeat the slander that signor Ottaviano[16] made against women yesterday, namely, that they are most imperfect creatures, incapable of any virtuous act, worth very little and quite without dignity compared with men. But truly both you and he would be very much in error if you really thought this.". . .

---

[13] **continence** Self-restraint in matters of the flesh.
[14] **mean** An idea rooted in Aristotle's ethics.

[15] **Plato . . . to the men** Plato reasoned that in the ideal state both men and women philosophers should rule (see Plato, *The Republic*, in Chapter 3, Volume I).
[16] **signor Ottaviano** Ottaviano Fregosa (d. 1524), a noble from Genoa; elected *doge,* or chief magistrate, of Genoa, in 1513; appointed governor of Genoa by King Francis I, of France.

∾

Questions for Critical Thinking

1. Discuss the influence of classical culture on Castiglione's ideal courtier and lady.

2. Are there any lingering influences of Castiglione's portrait of the ideal courtier and lady in the contemporary world today? Discuss.

NICCOLÒ MACHIAVELLI
Selections from *The Prince*

The Prince is a short and strikingly honest handbook on how to win power and keep it. Based on Niccolò Machiavelli's (1469–1527) personal experiences as diplomat and government employee (in the service of his beloved Florence), the book has become the foundation of modern political theory. In his other works, in particular his histories of Italy and Florence, Machiavelli drew upon his classical education and personal experiences to develop this message: Learn from the past what works and what does not. But nowhere else does Machiavelli express his thesis so boldly and succinctly as in *The Prince:* "The end justifies any means."

The Prince's harsh and amoral attitude toward politics sparked controversies when first published. Many of Machiavelli's contemporaries, who were witnessing the end of the medieval Age of Faith and experiencing the dawn of a secular time, were sharply divided over the meaning of his writings. Especially damaging to the book's reputation was its persistent low opinion of human nature. Succeeding generations have debated his analysis of human behavior and his consequent rationale for a strong government. In modern secular society, many readers have come to accept Machiavelli's view that political power, driven by personal or group interests, must be understood in utilitarian and practical terms.

The Prince, a treatise on the art of successful governing, is composed of three parts. The first part, comprising eleven chapters, categorizes and describes the various types of existing governments. The second part, which consists of fourteen chapters, offers advice and examples on winning and maintaining political power. In these fourteen chapters, Machiavelli instructs the ruler on how to raise and organize armies, how to keep subjects loyal, and how to avoid the pitfalls of overconfidence and flattery. Throughout *The Prince*, the author compares and contrasts key traits that make a ruler a success or a failure. He also addresses the issue of fortune—what is now called opportunity—and emphasizes how often it affects a ruler. In the third part—the concluding chapter—Machiavelli calls upon "the prince" to unite the Italians against foreign oppressors and drive them from Italy.

Reading the Selections

Chapters XV, XVI, and XVII appear in the second part of *The Prince*, in which Machiavelli discusses the most effective way for a ruler to govern his subjects. He points out that his discussion is rooted in practical politics, rather than based on imaginary regimes created by writers—a reference to the idealized commonwealths of Plato and medieval Christian authors. In Chapter XV, Machiavelli lists traits for which rulers are praised or blamed—such as being called stubborn or flexible, religious or skeptical—and notes that no ruler could continuously practice the best of these without damaging his ability to govern. Thus, in a crisis the ruler should not shrink from being blamed for vices if they are needed to safeguard the state, though most of the time, the prince should pretend to be what he is not in order to keep his subjects' loyalty.

In Chapter XVI, Machiavelli focuses on the traits of generosity and miserliness and shows, through ancient and current examples, the consequences for rulers who practiced one or the other of them. He concludes, given his dark view of human nature, that it is better for a ruler to be miserly than generous. In Chapter XVII, Machiavelli raises perhaps the most controversial question in the treatise: Is it better for the ruler to be loved or feared? Ideally, the ruler should be both loved and feared, but as this is nearly impossible, then the ruler should be feared. Machiavelli, realizing that fear has its limits, ends on a cautionary note: The "wise prince" must avoid being hated by his subjects, for hatred is the soil out of which rebellions grow.

❧

Chapter XV

The Things for Which Men, and Especially Princes, Are Praised or Blamed

It now remains for us to see how a prince should govern his conduct towards his subjects or his friends. I know that this has often been written about before, and so I hope it will not be thought presumptuous for me to do so, as, especially in discussing this subject, I draw up an original set of rules. But since my intention is to say something that will prove of practical use to the inquirer, I have thought it proper to represent things as they are in real truth, rather than as they are imagined. Many have dreamed up republics and principalities which have never in truth been known to exist; the gulf between how one should live and how one does live is so wide that a man who neglects what is actually done for what should be done learns the way to self-destruction rather than self-preservation. The fact is that a man who wants to act virtuously in every way necessarily comes to grief among so many who are not virtuous. Therefore if a prince wants to maintain his rule he must learn how not to be virtuous, and to make use of this or not according to need.

So leaving aside imaginary things, and referring only to those which truly exist, I say that whenever men are discussed (and especially princes, who are more exposed to view), they are noted for various qualities which earn them either praise or condemnation. Some, for example, are held to be generous, and others miserly (I use the Tuscan[17]

word rather than the word avaricious: we call a man who is mean with what he possesses, miserly, and a man who wants to plunder others, avaricious). Some are held to be benefactors, others are called grasping; some cruel, some compassionate; one man faithless, another faithful; one man effeminate and cowardly, another fierce and courageous; one man courteous, another proud; one man lascivious, another pure; one guileless, another crafty; one stubborn, another flexible; one grave, another frivolous; one religious, another sceptical; and so forth. I know everyone will agree that it would be most laudable if a prince possessed all the qualities deemed to be good among those I have enumerated. But, human nature being what it is, princes cannot possess those qualities, or rather they cannot always exhibit them. So a prince should be so prudent that he knows how to escape the evil reputation attached to those vices which could lose him his state, and how to avoid those vices which are not so dangerous, if he possibly can; but, if he cannot, he need not worry so much about the latter. And then, he must not flinch from being blamed for vices which are necessary for safeguarding the state. This is because, taking everything into account, he will find that some of the things that appear to be virtues will, if he practises them, ruin him, and some of the things that appear to be wicked will bring him security and prosperity.

---

[17] **Tuscan** Having to do with Tuscany, the Italian region, whose capital is Florence, Machiavelli's home.

❧

Chapter XVI

Generosity and Parsimony

So, starting with the first of the qualities I enumerated above, I say it would be splendid if one had a reputation for generosity; nonetheless if your actions are influenced by the desire for such a reputation you will come to grief. This is because if your generosity is good and sincere it may pass unnoticed and it will not save you from being reproached for its opposite. If you want to acquire a reputation for generosity, therefore, you have to be ostentatiously lavish; and a prince acting in that fashion will soon squander all his resources, only to be forced in the end, if he wants to maintain his reputation, to lay excessive burdens on the people, to impose extortionate taxes, and to do everything else he can to raise money. This will start to make his subjects hate him, and, since he will have impoverished himself, he will be generally despised. As a result, because of this generosity of his, having injured

many and rewarded few, he will be vulnerable to the first minor setback, and the first real danger he encounters will bring him to grief. When he realizes this and tries to retrace his path he will immediately be reputed a miser.

So as a prince cannot practise the virtue of generosity in such a way that he is noted for it, except to his cost, he should if he is prudent not mind being called a miser. In time he will be recognized as being essentially a generous man, seeing that because of his parsimony his existing revenues are enough for him, he can defend himself against an aggressor, and he can embark on enterprises without burdening the people. So he proves himself generous to all those from whom he takes nothing, and they are innumerable, and miserly towards all those to whom he gives nothing, and they are few. In our own times great things have been accomplished only by those who have been held miserly, and the others have met disaster. Pope Julius II[18] made use of a reputation for generosity to win the papacy, but subsequently he made no effort to maintain this reputation, because he wanted to be able to finance his wars. The present king of France[19] has been able to wage so many wars without taxing his subjects excessively only because his long-standing parsimony enabled him to meet the additional expenses involved. Were the present king of Spain[20] renowned for his generosity he would not have started and successfully concluded so many enterprises.

So if a prince does not have to rob his subjects, if he can defend himself, if he is not plunged into poverty and shame, if he is not forced to become rapacious, he ought not to worry about being called a miser. Miserliness is one of those vices which sustain his rule. Someone may object: Caesar[21] came to power by virtue of his generosity, and many others, because they practised and were known for their generosity, have risen to the very highest positions. My answer to this is as follows. Either you are already a prince, or you are on the way to becoming one. In the first case, your generosity will be to your cost; in the second, it is certainly necessary to have a reputation for generosity. Caesar was one of those who wanted to establish his

own rule over Rome; but if, after he had established it, he had remained alive and not moderated his expenditure he would have fallen from power.

Again, someone may retort: there have been many princes who have won great successes with their armies, and who have had the reputation of being extremely generous. My reply to this is: the prince gives away what is his own or his subjects', or else what belongs to others. In the first case he should be frugal; in the second, he should indulge his generosity to the full. The prince who campaigns with his armies, who lives by pillaging, sacking, and extortion, disposes of what belongs to aliens; and he must be open-handed, otherwise the soldiers would refuse to follow him. And you can be more liberal with what does not belong to you or your subjects, as Caesar, Cyrus,[22] and Alexander were. Giving away what belongs to strangers in no way affects your standing at home; rather it increases it. You hurt yourself only when you give away what is your own. There is nothing so self-defeating as generosity: in the act of practising it, you lose the ability to do so, and you become either poor and despised or, seeking to escape poverty, rapacious and hated. A prince should try to avoid, above all else, being despised and hated; and generosity results in your being both. Therefore it is wiser to incur the reputation of being a miser, which invites ignominy but not hatred, than to be forced by seeking a name for generosity to incur a reputation for rapacity, which brings you hatred as well as ignominy.

---

[18]**Pope Julius II** (pope 1503–1513).
[19]**king of France** Louis XII (r. 1498–1515).
[20]**king of Spain** Ferdinand V (r. 1474–1504), joint ruler, with Isabella, of Castile; their marriage created the modern state of Spain; served as regent of Castile for his daughter, Joanna the Mad, 1506–1516. As Ferdinand II, he ruled Aragon, 1479–1516.
[21]**Caesar** Julius Caesar (100–44 BCE). Roman general and statesman.

---

[22]**Cyrus** Cyrus II, known as the Great (ca. 585–ca. 529 BCE). King of Persia and founder of the Achaemenian dynasty and empire.

∞

Chapter XVII

Cruelty and Compassion; and Whether It Is Better to Be Loved than Feared, or the Reverse

Taking others of the qualities I enumerated above, I say that a prince should want to have a reputation for compassion rather than for cruelty: nonetheless, he should be careful that he does not make bad use of compassion. Cesare Borgia[23] was accounted cruel; nevertheless, this cruelty of his reformed the Romagna, brought it unity, and restored order and obedience. On reflection, it will be seen

that there was more compassion in Cesare than in the Florentine people, who, to escape being called cruel, allowed Pistoia to be devastated.[24] So a prince should not worry if he incurs reproach for his cruelty so long as he keeps his subjects united and loyal. By making an example or two he will prove more compassionate than those who, being too compassionate, allow disorders which lead to murder and rapine. These nearly always harm the whole community, whereas executions ordered by a prince only affect individuals. A new prince, of all rulers, finds it impossible to avoid a reputation for cruelty, because of the abundant

---

[23]**Cesare Borgia** (1475/1476–1507) Member of an illustrious Italian family of Spanish origin. Son of Pope Alexander VI (d. 1503) by the Roman woman Vannozza Cattanei; appointed bishop of Pamplona in 1491, archbishop of Valencia in 1492, and cardinal in 1493; served as papal legate in 1497 and 1498; gave up cardinal's hat in 1498. Captain general of papal army in 1499; conquered, with French aid, Romagna and the Marches, 1499–1501; made duke by his father, 1501; seized Urbino in 1501; opposed by enemies, including Pope Julius II (elected 1503); imprisoned, 1504–1506; escaped and killed.

---

[24]**Pistoia . . . devastated** Pistoia was a subject-city of Florence, which forcibly restored order there when conflict broke out between two rival factions in 1501–1502. Machiavelli was concerned with this business at first hand.

dangers inherent in a newly won state. Vergil,[25] through the mouth of Dido,[26] says:

Res dura, et regni novitas me talia cogunt
Moliri, et late fines custode tueri.[27]

Nonetheless, a prince should be slow to take action, and should watch that he does not come to be afraid of his own shadow; his behaviour should be tempered by humanity and prudence so that over-confidence does not make him rash or excessive distrust make him unbearable.

From this arises the following question: whether it is better to be loved than feared, or the reverse. The answer is that one would like to be both the one and the other; but because it is difficult to combine them, it is far better to be feared than loved if you cannot be both. One can make this generalization about men: they are ungrateful, fickle, liars, and deceivers, they shun danger and are greedy for profit; while you treat them well, they are yours. They would shed their blood for you, risk their property, their lives, their children, so long, as I said above, as danger is remote; but when you are in danger they turn against you. Any prince who has come to depend entirely on promises and has taken no other precautions ensures his own ruin; friendship which is bought with money and not with greatness and nobility of mind is paid for, but it does not last and it yields nothing. Men worry less about doing an injury to one who makes himself loved than to one who makes himself feared. The bond of love is one which men, wretched creatures that they are, break when it is to their advantage to do so; but fear is strengthened by a dread of punishment which is always effective.

The prince should nonetheless make himself feared in such a way that, if he is not loved, at least he escapes being hated. For fear is quite compatible with an absence of hatred; and the prince can always avoid hatred if he abstains from the property of his subjects and citizens and from their women. If, even so, it proves necessary to execute someone, this should be done only when there is proper justification and manifest reason for it. But above all a prince should abstain from the property of others; because men sooner forget the death of their father than the loss of their patrimony.[28] It is always possible to find pretexts for confiscating someone's property; and a prince who starts to live by rapine always finds pretexts for seizing what belongs to others. On the other hand, pretexts for executing someone are harder to find and they are less easily sustained.

However, when a prince is campaigning with his soldiers and is in command of a large army then he need 5

not worry about having a reputation for cruelty; because, without such a reputation, he can never keep his army united and disciplined. Among the admirable achievements of Hannibal[29] is included this: that although he led a huge army, made up of countless different races, on foreign campaigns, there was never any dissension, either among the troops themselves or against their leader, whether things were going well or badly. For this, his inhuman cruelty was wholly responsible. It was this, along with his countless other qualities, which made him feared and respected by his soldiers. If it had not been for his cruelty, his other qualities would not have been enough. The historians, having given little thought to this, on the one hand admire what Hannibal achieved, and on the other condemn what made his achievements possible.

That his other qualities would not have been enough by themselves can be proved by looking at Scipio,[30] a man unique in his own time and through all recorded history. His armies mutinied against him in Spain, and the only reason for this was his excessive leniency, which allowed his soldiers more licence than was good for military discipline. Fabius Maximus[31] reproached him for this in the Senate and called him a corrupter of the Roman legions.[32] Again, when the Locri[33] were plundered by one of Scipio's officers, he neither gave them satisfaction nor punished his officer's insubordination; and this was all because of his having too lenient a nature. By way of excuse for him some senators argued that many men were better at not making mistakes themselves than at correcting them in others. But in time Scipio's lenient nature would have spoilt his fame and glory had he continued to indulge it during his command; when he lived under orders from the Senate, however, this fatal characteristic of his was not only concealed but even brought him glory.

So, on this question of being loved or feared, I conclude that since some men love as they please but fear when the prince pleases, a wise prince should rely on what he controls, not on what he cannot control. He should only endeavour, as I said, to escape being hated.

---

[25] **Vergil** Also spelled Virgil (70–19 BCE); Roman poet (see *The Aeneid* in Chapter 5, Volume I).

[26] **Dido** Legendary Queen of Carthage. Originally a Phoenician princess from Tyre, she fled to Africa and founded Carthage. Vergil made her tragic love affair with Aeneas, the founder of ancient Rome, the unifying theme for the first four books of the *Aeneid*.

[27] *Res . . . custode tueri.* "Harsh necessity, and the newness of my kingdom, force me to do such things and to guard my frontiers everywhere" (*Aeneid* I, 563).

[28] **patrimony** An estate inherited from one's father.

[29] **Hannibal** (247–183 BCE) Carthaginian general. In the Second Punic War, led his troops from Spain, across the Alps, and into Italy, where he fought various battles and eventually marched on Rome, 218–211 BCE; Romans held on and waited him out; recalled to Carthage in 203, and defeated at battle of Zama in 202 BCE; headed Carthaginian government, 202–195 BCE; fled to Asia Minor; committed suicide.

[30] **Scipio** Scipio Africanus (236–184/183 BCE) Roman general. In the Second Punic War, led army in Spain, 210–206 BCE; led Roman invasion of Carthage; defeated **Hannibal** at battle of Zama in 202 BCE.

[31] **Fabius Maximus** (d. 203 BCE) Called *Cunctator,* the "Delayer." Roman general, famous for his delaying strategy against Hannibal in the Second Punic War. Fabius successfully made quick incursions against Hannibal's forces, while avoiding set battles. A group of English socialists in the late 1800s adopted the name Fabian in honor of this strategy.

[32] **legions** Roman army units, each composed of three thousand to six thousand foot soldiers with cavalry.

[33] **Locri** Ancient city founded by the Greeks, located on the eastern side of the "toe" of Italy; Locri changed sides between Rome and its enemies until it was captured by **Scipio Africanus** and made Roman, in the Second Punic War.

Questions for Critical Thinking

1. According to Machiavelli, which is more important for a prince: to be feared or to be loved? Explain.

2. *The Prince* has been charged with creating the mind-set called "Machiavellian," meaning that "the end justifies any means." Is this a valid judgment of Machiavelli's ideas? Explain.

MICHELANGELO
Poems

Michelangelo Buonarroti (1475–1564) and Leonardo da Vinci (1452–1519) are recognized today as the most influential and famous artists of the High Renaissance. Michelangelo, like Leonardo da Vinci, was a Universal Man, a person blessed and cursed with many talents. With his conflicted sense of his successes and failures, a bigger-than-life ego, a commanding physical presence, and a driving ambition, he found himself constantly at odds with his patrons and always seeking approval from his friends. Nonetheless, he was honored and admired in his own times for his contributions to the arts. Painters and sculptors have looked to him for inspiration and as their ideal ever since his death, and posterity considers him to be the personification of the Italian Renaissance.

He spent most of his career serving the powerful Medici family in Florence and the popes in Rome—a situation which, over his lifetime, intensified his troubled relationships with supporters, complicated his personal life, and channeled his creativity into nearly every art form. Despite his fluctuating moods and being overburdened with too many commissions and commitments, Michelangelo left the world some of the most lasting works in the history of art.

While his reputation and legacy rest principally on his paintings, sculpture, architecture, and urban planning, Michelangelo is also known for his literary contributions, especially his poems. He wrote over three hundred, including sonnets and madrigals, philosophical poems, and love poems. The three central themes running through his poems were love, both physical and Platonic, or spiritual; the passing of time, or the phases of life and death; and religious faith, especially the yearning for the love of God, and salvation. They also record his lifelong conflict between his admiration for classical or pagan values, which he acquired as a young artist while living in Florence, and his Christian beliefs and faith, which deepened in his later years.

Michelangelo, though considering himself to be an amateur poet, wanted his poems to be published during his lifetime. He was not a polished stylist, and literary critics do not judge his works to be "high" poetry. However, what he said in his poems—the outpouring of his inner thoughts—has endeared them to readers. His literary efforts reveal his creative talents and processes as a visual artist because, in his poems, Michelangelo broods over his works and what they mean to him and others. His sense of success and failure weaves in and out of the poems, and they leave a self-portrait of a person who was constantly in doubt about himself and life.

Reading the Selections

Poems 166 and 248 touch upon some of Michelangelo's most personal concerns and pay tribute to two individuals who had inspired and influenced him—one a female friend and the other a historical figure. Poem 166, a madrigal, was written to Vittoria Colonna (1490–1547), a woman whom he knew in Rome. She was the subject of many of his poems, in which he expressed his love and respect for her, his thoughts on religion, and the prospect of death. She seemed to be the only woman to whom he was ever closely attached, even though their relationship was clearly intellectual and spiritual. They communicated with one another for over a decade, and she became his inspiration and ideal. She was, in his life, what Beatrice was to Dante (see *The Divine Comedy* in Chapter 10, Volume I) and Laura was to Petrarch (see the *Canzoniere* and "Letter to Posterity" in Chapter 11, Volume I). Poem 248 is a paean, or tribute, to Dante in which Michelangelo compares his life to Dante's life and legacy.

Poem 285, one of his best-known sonnets, was written around 1552–1554 in the later years of his life, and focuses on old age. Michelangelo laments what he considers to be what was once an idol—art—and how he, now, faces his demise. In his later years, confronting his own mortality and worried about the future of the Catholic Church in its struggle with the newly unleashed Protestant Reformation movement, Michelangelo wrote several poems expressing these themes.

Poems

166

My eyes can easily see your beautiful face[34]
wherever it appears, near or far away;
but my feet, lady, are prevented from bearing
my arms or either hand to that same place.[35]

The soul, the intellect complete and sound,
more free and unfettered, can rise through the eyes
up to your lofty beauty; but great ardor
gives no such privilege to the human body,
which, weighed down and mortal, and still lacking
        wings,
can hardly follow the flight of a little angel;
so sight alone can take pride and pleasure in doing so.[36]

If you have as much power in heaven as here among us,
make my whole body nothing but an eye:
let there be no part of me that can't enjoy you.

---

[34] **My eyes can easily see your beautiful face** The opening refers to the Neoplatonic argument that the human eyes see human or bodily beauty, but there is a higher or spiritual beauty that can be "seen" at a higher level. Thus, Michelangelo sees Vittoria Colonna's physical beauty (actually, she was rather homely), but her beauty is only a step to a higher level of beautiful, which is on a metaphysical plane.

[35] **my arms or either hand to that same place** That is, so I, Michelangelo, might be able to embrace you, Vittoria.

[36] **so sight alone can take pride and pleasure in doing so** This means that only the eyes can follow her.

248

He came down from heaven, and once he had seen
the just hell and the merciful one, he went
back up, with his body alive, to contemplate God,
in order to give us the true light of it all.[37]
For such a shining star, who with his rays
undeservedly brightened the nest where I was born,[38]

the whole wicked world would not be enough reward;
only you,[39] who created him, could ever be that.
I speak of Dante, for his deeds were poorly
appreciated by that ungrateful people
who fail to welcome only righteous men.[40]
If only I were he! To be born to such good fortune,
to have his harsh exile along with his virtue,
I would give up the happiest state in the world.

---

[37] **He came down from heaven . . . as the true light of it all.** These four lines refer to Dante, who, born as a human, made a journey through Hell, Purgatory, and Heaven in *The Divine Comedy*.

[38] **undeservedly brightened the nest where I was born** The city of Florence, home to Dante and Michelangelo.

[39] **only you** God.

[40] **who fail to welcome only righteous men** Both Dante and Michelangelo were exiled from Florence.

285

The voyage of my life at last has reached,   1
across a stormy sea, in a fragile boat,[41]
the common port[42] all must pass through, to give
an accounting for every evil and pious deed.
   So now I recognize how laden with error
was the affectionate fantasy
that made art an idol and sovereign to me,
like all things men want in spite of their best interests.[43]

What will become of all my thoughts of love,
once gay and foolish, now that I'm nearing two deaths?[44]   10
I'm certain of one and the other looms over me.
   Neither painting nor sculpture will be able any longer
to calm my soul, now turned toward that divine love
that opened his arms on the cross to take us in.[45]

---

[41] **across a stormy sea, in a fragile boat** Life is like being in a stormy sea in a small, light boat.
[42] **the common port** Death.
[43] **So now I recognize . . . of their best interests.** This four-line verse is a confession from Michelangelo that he, like most men, pursued worldly goals and ambition—in this case, art—which is sinful and distracts from the true meaning of life.

---

[44] **two deaths** The death of the body, which is certain, and the fear of the death of the soul, which would be even worse.
[45] **that opened his arms on the cross to take us in** The image of Christ opening his arms to embrace sinners. Michelangelo drew such a scene and also used this image in other poems.

✺

Questions for Critical Thinking

1. How does Michelangelo compare his respect and admiration for Vittoria Colonna and Dante? Which do you think is more persuasive?

2. Discuss the major themes in all three poems, and note how they are manifested in images and references.

14

NORTHERN HUMANISM, NORTHERN RENAISSANCE, RELIGIOUS REFORMATIONS, AND LATE MANNERISM

1500–1603

FRANÇOIS RABELAIS
Selection from *The Histories of Gargantua and Pantagruel*

Rabelais' *The Histories of Gargantua and Pantagruel* marks a fresh departure in Western letters. These robust satires, the first literary works to treat bodily functions and copulation graphically and without apology, gave the world the adjective *Rabelaisian*, meaning "earthiness of speech." Because of their crudeness, the works became an underground classic—enjoyed in private but very little imitated. Only today, with the rise of freer public discourse, has Rabelais' legacy come into its own.

Another reason these works represent a milestone in Western letters is that they signal the coming of the Renaissance to France. Lasting from 1515 until 1604, the French Renaissance was inspired by writers' and artists' "discovery" of Italy; literature and art clearly were altered by closer contact with ancient culture and classical forms. The classic ideal—the dominance of order over diversity, reason over passion—became a guiding force in French culture. François Rabelais (ca. 1494–1553) was a leader of this rebirth, though his sprawling books did not chime with classicism's orderly ideal. More to the point, his works reflected this period's transitional nature. On one side he mocked the dying Middle Ages, with its tedious theological study; on the other side he praised the dawning Renaissance, with its love of classical lore. In his works he was also friendly to Protestantism, stressing simple piety just as its reformers did.

The Histories of Gargantua and Pantagruel is actually five books dealing with a legendary family of giants. *Gargantua* (1534), the second written, is now known as Book I, opening the series with the bawdy tale of Gargantua, focusing on his childhood and training for kingship. *Pantagruel* (1532), the first written, tells of Gargantua's giant son, Pantagruel, and is known as Book II. Basically a satire on scholastic education (see Aquinas's *Summa theologica* in Chapter 10, Volume I), it also ridicules many timely topics—courtroom delays, lying lawyers, and pseudointellectuals. The other three books (the last published posthumously) contain further adventures of Pantagruel.

Rabelais' career mirrored this stormy age. Entered in a monastery as a youth, he abandoned the cloister and theology to study medicine. He later served as physician in a number of posts, mainly in France. To the disgust of critics, he spent his last years as a parish priest, delegating the duties but keeping the income. Because of his books, he was hounded by the authorities, but friends in church and state always came to his rescue.

Reading the Selection

This selection contains probably the most famous passage from Book I on *Gargantua*. It features Gargantua's friend, the rascally Friar John ("the monk") and his "ideal" Abbey of Thélème, where "monks" and "nuns" were to live in accordance with the abbey's unchristian rule: "Do what you will." This abbey, with its pleasure-driven inmates, satirizes the faults that the Protestant reformers claimed against sixteenth-century monks. Beneath the broad satire, the story seems to reinforce humanist morals: the best way to regulate one's life is "by the promptings of reason and good sense," and free people have a "natural spur and instinct" to seek virtue and avoid vice.

This passage also shows Rabelais' passion for words. For example, in the inscription over the Great Gate of Thélème, the words tumble down like a waterfall, offering an exaggerated list of those to be denied entry as well as those to be welcomed to the abbey.

⟨∞⟩

Book I

How Gargantua Had the Abbey of Thélème[1] Built for the Monk

There only remained the monk[2] to be provided for, and Gargantua wanted to make him abbot of Seuilly,[3] but he refused the post. He next proposed to give him the abbey of Bourgueil[4] or of Saint-Florant,[5] whichever would suit him better, or both, if he fancied them. But the monk answered categorically that he wanted neither charge nor government of monks.

"For how should I be able to govern others," he said, "when I don't know how to govern myself? If it seems to you that I have done you, and may in the future do you welcome service, give me leave to found an abbey after my own devices."

This request pleased Gargantua, and he offered him all his land of Thélème, beside the River Loire, to within six miles of the great forest of Port-Huault.[6] The monk then requested Gargantua to institute his religious order in an exactly contrary way to all others.

"First of all, then," said Gargantua, "you mustn't build walls round it. For all other abbeys have lofty walls (*murs*[7])."

"Yes," said the monk, "and not without reason. Where there's a *mur* before and a *mur* behind, there are plenty of murmurs, envy, and mutual conspiracy."

Moreover, seeing that in certain monasteries in this world it is the custom that if any woman enters—I speak of chaste and honest women—they wash the place where she trod, it was ordained that if any monk or nun happened to enter here, the spot where he or she had stood should be scrupulously washed likewise. And because in the religious foundations of this world everything is encompassed, limited, and regulated by hours, it was decreed that there should be no clock or dial at all, but that affairs should be conducted according to chance and opportunity. For Gargantua said that the greatest waste of time he knew was the counting of hours—what good does it do?—and the greatest nonsense in the world was to regulate one's life by the sound of a bell, instead of by the promptings of reason and good sense. Item, because at that time they put no women into religious houses unless they were one-eyed, lame, hunchbacked, ugly, malformed, lunatic, half-witted, bewitched, and blemished, or men that were not sickly, low-born, stupid, or a burden on their family. . . .

"By the way," said the monk, "if a woman is neither fair nor good, what can you do with her?"

"Make her a nun," said Gargantua.

"Yes," said the monk, "and a sempstress[8] of shirts."

It was decreed that here no women should be admitted unless they were beautiful, well-built, and sweet-natured, nor any men who were not handsome, well-built, and of pleasant nature also.

Item, because men never entered nunneries except secretly and by stealth, it was decreed that here there should

---

[1] **Thélème** Latin, *theleme,* "the will of God." The Abbey of Thélème functions as an anti-abbey in Rabelais' satire.
[2] **the monk** Friar John, a companion of Gargantua. Modeled perhaps on an actual person, who served as a legal agent for the monks of Seuilly.
[3] **Seuilly** Monastery in the Loire River valley (see footnote 1).
[4] **Bourgueil** Abbey in the Loire River valley, famous for its wine since about 1000.
[5] **Saint-Florant** Also spelled Saint-Florent; abbey in Loire River valley, near Saumur; famous for its wine.
[6] **Port-Huault** Near Chinon in the Loire River valley, the birthplace of Rabelais.
[7] **mur** French, "wall."

---

[8] **sempstress** Variation of seamstress.

be no women when there were no men, and no men when there were no women.

Item, because both men and women once accepted into a monastic order, after their novitiate[9] year, were compelled and bound to remain for ever, so long as they lived, it was decreed that both men and women, once accepted, could depart from there whenever they pleased, without let or hindrance.

Item, because ordinarily monks and nuns made three vows, that is of chastity, poverty, and obedience, it was decreed that there anyone could be regularly married, could become rich, and could live at liberty.

With regard to the lawful age of entry, women were to be received at from ten to fifteen, and men at from twelve to eighteen.

. . .

THE INSCRIPTION SET ABOVE THE GREAT GATE OF THÉLÈME

Enter not here, vile hypocrites and bigots,   1
Pious old apes, and puffed-up snivellers,
Wry-necked creatures sawnier than the Goths,[10]
Or Ostrogoths,[11] precursors of Gog and Magog,[12]
Woe-begone scoundrels, mock-godly sandal-wearers,
Beggars in blankets, flagellating[13] canters,
Hooted at, pot-bellied, stirrers up of troubles,
Get along elsewhere to sell your dirty swindles.
    Your hideous deceits
    Would fill my fields and streets   10
    With villainy
    And with their falsity
    Would untune my song's notes,
    Your hideous deceits.
Enter not here, lawyers insatiable,
Ushers, lawyers' clerks, devourers of the people,
Holders of office, scribes, and pharisees,[14]
Ancient judges who tie up good citizens
Like stray dogs with cord on their necks,
Your reward is earned now, and it is the gibbet.[15]   20
So go and bray there. Here is done no violence,
Such as in your courts sets men fighting lawsuits.

Lawsuits and wrangling
Set us not jangling;
We come here for pleasure.
But may your leisure
Be filled up with tangling
Lawsuits and wrangling.
Enter not here, miserly usurers,[16]
Gluttons and lechers, everlasting gatherers,   30
Tricksters and swindlers, mean pettifoggers,
Hunchbacked and snub-nosed, who in your lockers
Never have enough of gold coin and silver.
However much you pocket you're never satisfied.
You pile up still more, you mean-featured dastards,[17]
May cruel death for this spoil your faces.
    Most hideous of faces,
    Take them and their grimaces,
    Shave them elsewhere, for here
    They're out of place, I fear.   40
    Shift them to other places,
    Most hideous of faces.
Enter not here, you rambling mastiff curs,
Morning nor evening, jealous, old and spiteful,
Nor you either, seditious mutineers,
Spirits, goblins, and fond husbands' familiars,[18]
Greeks or Latins, more to be feared than wolves,
Nor you with your sores, gnawed to the bone by pox,
Take your ulcers elsewhere and show them to others,
Scabby from head to toe and brimful of dishonour,   50
    Grace, honour, praise, and light
    Are here our sole delight;
    Of them we make our song,
    Our limbs are sound and strong.
    This blessing fills us quite,
    Grace, honour, praise, and light.
Enter in here, and you shall be most welcome,
And having come, stay noble gentlemen!
Here is the place where income comes in well,
And having come affords good entertainment   60
For great and small, though thousands of them come.
Be then my cronies, my especial favourites,
Merry and nimble, jolly, gay, and sprightly,
And, in a word, the best of good companions.
    All worthy gentlemen,
    Keen witted and serene,
    From every coarseness free,
    Here find civility,
    Among your hosts will reign,
    All worthy gentlemen.   70
Enter in here, you who preach with vigour
Christ's Holy Gospel, never mind who scoffs,

---

[9] **novitiate** Probationary period. From "novice," a person admitted to probationary membership in a monastery.

[10] **the Goths** Germanic invaders, made up of the East Goths, or Ostrogoths, and the West Goths, or Visigoths; overran the Roman Empire in the early Christian period.

[11] **Ostrogoths** East Goths (see footnote 10); founded a short-lived kingdom in Italy, 493–ca. 550.

[12] **Gog and Magog** In Jewish and Christian scriptures, two hostile powers, in the service of Satan, that will appear immediately before the end of the world.

[13] **flagellating** From *flagellate*, to whip oneself, as part of a religious ritual.

[14] **pharisee** Member of a Jewish sect, dating from the time of Jesus, that was noted for its strict adherence to the letter of the Jewish law.

[15] **gibbet** Gallows.

[16] **usurers** Those who loan money at interest. Historically, the Christian Church considered usury, the loaning of money at interest, a sin.

[17] **dastard** Coward.

[18] **familiar** A spirit that serves or guards a person.

Here you will find a refuge and a tower
Against the foeman's[19] error, the picked arguments,
Which falsely seek to spread about their poison.
Enter, here let us found a faith profound,
And then let us confound by speech and writing,
All that are the foemen of the Holy Writ.

> *Our Holy Writ and Word*
> *For ever shall be heard*   80
> *In this most holy spot.*
> *Each wears it on his heart,*
> *Each wears it as a sword,*
> *Our Holy Writ and Word.*

Enter in here, you ladies of high lineage,
Here be frank and fearless, enter gaily in,
Flowers of all beauty, with heaven in your faces,
Upright in bearing, modest in behaviour,
Here you will find the dwelling-place of honour.
That noble gentleman who of this place was donor,   90
And gives rewards, has destined it for you.
He has provided gold sufficient for its upkeep.

> *Gold freely given,*
> *A man's freely shriven,*
> *In exchange for awards.*
> *For it brings rewards*
> *To all mortal men,*
> *Gold freely given.*

· · ·

The Rules according to Which the Thélèmites Lived

All their life was regulated not by laws, statutes, or rules,   1
but according to their free will and pleasure. They rose
from bed when they pleased, and drank, ate, worked, and
slept when the fancy seized them. Nobody woke them;
nobody compelled them either to eat or to drink, or to do
anything else whatever. So it was that Gargantua had established it. In their rules there was only one clause:

Do what you will

---

[19]**foeman** Enemy.

because people who are free, well-born, well-bred, and
easy in honest company have a natural spur and instinct
which drives them to virtuous deeds and deflects them
from vice; and this they called honour. When these same
men are depressed and enslaved by vile constraint and
subjection, they use this noble quality which once impelled them freely towards virtue, to throw off and break
this yoke of slavery. For we always strive after things forbidden and covet what is denied us.

Making use of this liberty, they most laudably rivalled
one another in all of them doing what they saw pleased
one. If some man or woman said, "Let us drink," they all
drank; if he or she said, "Let us play," they all played; if
it was "Let us go and amuse ourselves in the fields," everyone went there. If it were for hawking or hunting, the
ladies, mounted on fine mares, with their grand palfreys[20]
following, each carried on their daintily gloved wrists a
sparrow-hawk, a lanneret,[21] or a merlin,[22] the men carrying the other birds.

So nobly were they instructed that there was not a
man or woman among them who could not read, write,
sing, play musical instruments, speak five or six languages, and compose in them both verse and prose.
Never were seen such worthy knights, so valiant, so nimble both on foot and horse; knights more vigorous, more
agile, handier with all weapons than they were. Never
were seen ladies so good-looking, so dainty, less tiresome,
more skilled with the fingers and the needle, and in every
free and honest womanly pursuit than they were.

For that reason, when the time came that anyone in
that abbey, either at his parents' request or for any other
reason, wished to leave it, he took with him one of the ladies, the one who had accepted him as her admirer, and
they were married to one another; and if at Thélème they
had lived in devotion and friendship, they lived in still
greater devotion and friendship when they were married.
Indeed, they loved one another to the end of their days as
much as they had done on their wedding day.

---

[20]**palfrey** Saddle horse.
[21]**lanneret** Male falcon, used in the sport of falconry.
[22]**merlin** A type of falcon used in the sport of falconry.

∞

Questions for Critical Thinking

1. Show how Rabelais' description of the Abbey of Thélème was a criticism of the medieval monastic ideal.

2. In the long inscription set above the Great Gate of Thélème, Rabelais identifies many annoying social types
in Renaissance France. What sort of society would Rabelais seem to prefer?

DESIDERIUS ERASMUS
Selection from *The Praise of Folly*

Between 1470 and the onset of the Protestant Reformation in the 1520s, the Renaissance spread from Italy north across the Alps, where it fused with existing Christian thought to create northern humanism. As in Italy, humanists in the north looked to the Greco-Roman past for inspiration, thereby reviving widespread interest in classicism. Unlike in Italy, however, scholars in northern Europe were Christians first and humanists second; they used classical learning to shed light on perceived religious problems, namely, corruption in the clergy, the church's emphasis on ritual to the neglect of moral order, and the general breakdown in spiritual life. In this way, the northern humanists pointed the way to the Protestant Reformation and helped shape mannerism, the dominant cultural style between 1520 and 1600.

The most influential voice of northern humanism was the Dutch scholar Desiderius Erasmus (ca. 1466–1536), who was called by his colleagues the Prince of Humanists. Though educated in traditional classical studies, he planned a career in the church, joining a monastery and also becoming a priest. But his love of learning and his distaste for monastic life combined to lead him to literature. His writings, beginning with the *Adagia* (1500), a collection of his commentaries on quotations from classical authors, quickly made him a well-known scholar. He traveled across Europe as the guest of princes, kings, and church leaders, and his gentle manner brought a calm to the period's religious debates. But as the Protestant revolt divided Europe, Erasmus's plea for tolerance was swept away by both sides. Still, Erasmus's treatises, letters, and especially his Greek edition of the New Testament (based on the latest sources at that time) ensured his position as the leader of northern humanism.

Reading the Selection

Erasmus is best remembered for *The Praise of Folly* (1516), a biting satire on human vanity that still rings true today. Written during one of his visits to England and dedicated to his friend and fellow humanist Sir Thomas More (see *Utopia*), it held up to ridicule his period's leaders (such as scholars, lawyers, monks, and cardinals) and exposed their hypocrisy and worldly appetites. Though Erasmus thought his book had little lasting merit, deeming it an intellectual joke tossed off to amuse his friends, *The Praise of Folly* nonetheless echoed the thoughts of many contemporaries, and subsequent generations have enjoyed its wicked satire. Today, it is the one work by Erasmus most likely to be known to educated readers.

Erasmus, in *The Praise of Folly*, uses the literary device of personification, employed earlier by Boethius (see *The Consolation of Philosophy* in Chapter 8, Volume I) and Christine de Pizan (see *The Book of the City of Ladies* in Chapter 11, Volume I). He speaks through Dame Folly, a "goddess" who delights in her foolish followers. As this section opens, Dame Folly speaks, identifying herself, her parents, and her attendants: self-love, flattery, forgetfulness, pleasure, and sensuality. Ironically, she says human life would be unbearable without her (folly), for if people were always sensible, then everyone would be miserable.

Dame Folly then surveys the human comedy, laying out the foolish things in which each profession excels. Beneath the satire against the church, Erasmus's Christian humanism shines forth; for example, the work claims that points of theology and monkish pride have become more important than "mending a poor man's shoes"—a metaphor for the church's neglect of the needy.

❧

[Folly is speaking.] In the same realm are those who are authors of books. All of them are highly indebted to me, especially those who blacken their pages with sheer triviality. For those who write learnedly to be criticized by a few scholars, not even ruling out a Persius[23] or a Laelius[24] as a judge, seem to be more pitiable than happy to me, simply because they are continuously torturing themselves. They add, they alter, they cross something out, they reinsert it, they recopy their work, they rearrange it, they show it to friends, and they keep it for nine years; yet they still are not satisfied with it. At such a price, they buy an empty reward, namely praise—and the praise of only a handful, at that. They buy this at the great expense of long hours, no sleep, so much sweat, and so many vexations. Add also the loss of health, the deterioration of their physical appearance, the possibility of blindness or partial loss of their sight, poverty, malice, premature old age, an early death, and if you can think of more, add them to this list. The scholar feels that he has been compensated for such ills when he wins the sanction of one or two other weakeyed scholars. But my author is crazy in a far happier way for he, without any hesitation, rapidly writes down anything that comes to mind, his pen, or even his dreams. There is little or no waste of paper, since he knows that if the trifles are trivial enough the majority of the readers, that is, the fools and ignoramuses, will approve of them. What is the difference if one should ignore two or three scholars, even though he may have read them? Or what weight will the censure of a few scholars carry, so long as the multitudes give it acclaim?

Actually, the wiser writers are those who put out the work of someone else as their own. By a few alterations they transfer someone else's glory to themselves, disregarding the other person's long labor and comforting themselves with the thought that even though they might be publicly convicted of plagiarism, meanwhile they shall have enjoyed the fruits and glory of authorship. It is worth one's while to observe how pleased authors are with their own works when they are popular and pointed out in a crowd—as celebrities! Their work is on display in bookstores, with three cryptic words in large type on the title page, something like a magician's spell. Ye gods! After all, what are they but words? Few people will ever hear of them, compared to the total world population, and far fewer will admire them, since people's tastes vary so, even among the common people. And why is it that the very names of the authors are often false, or stolen from the

books of the ancients? One calls himself Telemachus,[25] another Stelenus[26] or Laertes,[27] still another Polycrates,[28] and another Thrasymachus.[29] As a result, nowadays it does not matter whether you dedicate your book to a chameleon or a gourd, or simply to alpha or beta, as the philosophers do.

The most touching event is when they compliment each other and turn around in an exchange of letters, verses, and superfluities.[30] They are fools praising fools and dunces praising dunces. The first, in the opinion of the second, is an Alcaeus,[31] and the second, in the opinion of the first, is a Callimachus.[32] One holds another in higher esteem than Cicero,[33] the other finds the one more learned than Plato.[34] Or sometimes they will choose a competitor and increase their reputation by rivaling themselves with him. As a result the public is split with opposing viewpoints, until finally, when the dispute is over, each reigns as victor and has a triumphal parade. Wise men deride this as being absolute nonsense, which is just what it is. Who will deny it? Meanwhile, our authors are leading a luxurious life because of my excellence, and they would not exchange their accomplishments for even those of Scipius.[35] And while the scholars most certainly derive a great deal of pleasure from laughing at them, relishing to the utmost the madnesses of others, they themselves owe me a great deal, which they cannot deny without being most ungrateful men.

Among men of the learned professions, a most self-satisfied group of men, the lawyers may hold themselves in the highest esteem. For while they laboriously roll up the stone of Sisyphus[36] by the force of weaving six hundred laws together at the same time, by the stacking of commentary upon commentary and opinion upon opinion regardless of how far removed from the purpose, they contrive to make their profession seem to be most difficult

---

[23] **Persius** Uncertain; either a character in **Cicero's** *On Oratory* who represents a learned person, or Aulus Persius Flaccus (34–62 CE), Roman author of satires with a high moral tone.
[24] **Laelius** Uncertain; either a character in **Cicero's** *On Oratory* who represents a not-so-learned person, or a Roman official (fl.150–140 BCE) and friend of the Roman general Scipio the Younger (185/184–124 BCE). **Cicero** admired the latter Laelius and used his name for the title of a book, namely, *Laelius, or, on Friendship*.

[25] **Telemachus** Son of the legendary Greek hero Odysseus (see Homer, *Odyssey,* in Chapter 2, Volume I).
[26] **Stelenus** Folly apparently makes a mistake; this is not a classical name. Perhaps she meant to say Sthelenus, a fifth-century BCE tragic poet.
[27] **Laertes** Father of the legendary hero Odysseus (see Homer, *Odyssey*).
[28] **Polycrates** (440–370 BCE), Athenian orator and **sophist,** who wrote a (now lost) work denouncing Socrates in 394/393 BCE.
[29] **Thrasymachus** (fl. late fourth century BCE), Greek **sophist** from Chalcedon (in modern Turkey), who quarreled with Socrates in Plato's *Republic.*
[30] **superfluities** Unnecessary things.
[31] **Alcaeus** (ca. 620–ca. 580 BCE), Greek lyric poet.
[32] **Callimachus** (ca. 305–ca. 240 BCE), Greek scholar at the Library in Alexandria.
[33] **Cicero** (106–43 BCE), Roman orator, statesman, and philosopher (see Cicero, "The Dream of Scipio," in Chapter 5, Volume I).
[34] **Plato** (ca. 428–348/347 BCE), Greek philsopher (see Plato, *The Republic,* in Chapter 3, Volume I).
[35] **Scipius** Another form of Scipio; either Publius Cornelius, called Scipio the Elder (236–184/183 BCE), or Scipio Aemilianus, called the Younger (185/184–129 BCE).
[36] **Sisyphus** Greek mortal condemned by the gods to roll a rock endlessly up a mountain, only to have it fall down again.

of all. What is actually tedious they consider brilliant. Let us include with them the logicians and sophists,[37] a breed of men more loquacious than the famed brass kettles of Dodona.[38] Any one of them can outtalk any twenty women. They would be happier, though, if they were just talkative and not quarrelsome as well. In fact, they are so quarrelsome that they will argue and fight over a lock of a goat's wool, absurdly losing sight of the truth in the furor of their dispute. Their egotistical love keeps them happy, and manned with but three syllogisms, they will unflinchingly argue on any subject with any man. Their mere obstinacy affords them victory, even though you place Stentor[39] against them.

Next in line are the scientists, revered for their beards and the fur on their gowns. They feel that they are the only men with any wisdom, and all other men float about as shadows. How senilely they daydream, while they construct their countless worlds and shoot the distance to the sun, the moon, the stars, and spheres,[40] as with a thumb and line. They postulate causes for lightning, winds, eclipses, and other inexplicable things, never hesitating for a moment, as if they had exclusive knowledge about the secrets of nature, designer of elements, or as if they visited us directly from the council of the gods. Yet all this time nature is heartily laughing at them and their conjectures. It is a sufficient argument just proving that they have good intelligence for nothing. They can never explain why they always disagree with each other on every subject. In summation, knowing nothing in general they profess to know everything in particular. They are ignorant even to themselves, and at times they do not see the ditch or stone lying across their path, because many of them are day-dreamers and are absent-minded. Yet they proclaim that they perceive ideas, universals, forms without matter, primary substances, quiddities,[41] entities, and things so tenuous that I'm afraid that Lynceus[42] could not see them himself. The common people are especially disdained when they bring out their triangles, quadrangles, circles, and mathematical figures of the like. They place one on top of the other and arrange them into a maze. Then they deploy some letters precisely, as if in a battle formation, and finally they reverse them. And all of this is done only to confuse those who are ignorant of the field. These scientists do not like those who predict the future from the stars, and promise even more fantastic miracles. And these fortunate men find people who believe them.

Perhaps it would be better to pass silently over the theologians. Dealing with them, since they are hot-tempered, is like crossing Lake Camarina[43] or eating poisonous beans. They may attack me with six hundred arguments and force me to retract what I hold; for if I refuse, they will immediately declare me a heretic. By this blitz action they show a desire to terrify anyone to whom they are ill-disposed. No other people are so adverse to acknowledge my favors to them, yet the divines are bound to me by extraordinary obligations. These theologians are happy in their self-love, and as if they were presently inhabiting a third heaven, they look down on all men as though they were animals that crawled along the ground, coming near to pity them. They are protected by a wall of scholastic definitions, arguments, corollaries, and implicit and explicit propositions.[44] They have so many hideouts that not even the net of Vulcan[45] would be able to catch them; for they back down from their distinctions, by which they also cut through the knots of an argument, as if with a double-blade ax from Tenedos[46]; and they come forth with newly invented terms and monstrous-sounding words. Furthermore, they explain the most mysterious matters to suit themselves, for instance, the method by which the world was set in order and began, through what channels original sin has come down to us through generations, by what means, in what measure, and how long the Omnipotent Christ was in the Virgin's womb, and how accidents subsist in the Eucharist without their substance.[47]

But those have been beaten to death down through the ages. Here are some questions that are worthy of great (and some call them) illuminated theologians, questions that will really make them think, if they should ever encounter them. Did divine generation take place at a particular time? Are there several sonships in Christ? Whether this is a possible proposition: Does God the Father hate the Son? Could God the Father have taken upon Himself the likeness of a woman, a devil, an ass, a gourd, or a piece of flint? Then how would that gourd have preached, performed miracles, or been crucified? Also, what would Peter[48] have consecrated, if he had administered the Eucharist, while Christ's

---

[37] **sophists** School of rhetoric, philosophy, and successful living, in fifth-century BCE Athens. Because they seemingly would teach any point of view, so long as they were paid, the word *sophist* became synonymous with "faulty reasoner."
[38] **Dodona** Site of oracle of Zeus, the oldest oracle in Greece, located in the north, near the border with modern Albania; the oracle interpreted the rustling of oak leaves, the sounds of bronze vessels clanking in the trees, and the cooing of doves and other birds.
[39] **Stentor** In Homer's *Iliad*, the Greek warrior whose voice was as loud as that of fifty men.
[40] **spheres** Folly holds the medieval worldview that nine crystalline spheres, each set within the other and carrying the sun, the moon, the planets, and the stars, encircle the earth and produce harmonious sounds as they move—the music of the spheres.
[41] **quiddities** Essences.
[42] **Lynceus** In Greek mythology, one of the Argonauts; he had supernatural sight, which even enabled him to see things belowground.

---

[43] **Camarina** Lake in Sicily, fabled for its pestilential stench during drought periods.
[44] **scholastic . . . propositions** Folly catalogs the varied types of reasoning used by scholastic thinkers, who are generally portrayed as disinterested in truth.
[45] **Vulcan** Roman god of metalworking, comparable to the Greek Hephaestus.
[46] **Tenedos** Island in the Aegean, today called Bozcaada (in modern Turkey).
[47] **accidents . . . substance** *Accidents* and *substance* were terms from Aristotle, used by medieval philosophers to explain the miracle of the Eucharist; the "accidents" of the wine and bread were transformed into the "substance" of Christ's blood and flesh.
[48] **Peter** (d. ca. 64 CE), one of the twelve original apostles of Jesus. Traditionally, the church regarded Peter as the first pope, the successor to Jesus Christ on earth.

body hung on the cross? Another thought: could Christ have been said to be a man at that very moment? Will we be forbidden to eat and drink after the resurrection? (Now, while there is time, they are providing against hunger and thirst!) These intricate subtleties are infinite, and there are others that are even more subtle, concerning instances of time, notions, relations, accidents, quiddities, and entities, which no one can perceive unless, like Lynceus, he can see in the blackest darkness things that aren't there.

We must insert those maxims, rather contradictions, that, compared to the Stoic paradoxes,[49] appear to be the most common simplicity. For instance: it is a lesser crime to cut the throats of a thousand men than to sew a stitch on a poor man's shoe on the sabbath; it is better to want the earth to perish, body, boots, and breeches (as the saying goes), than to tell a single lie, however inconsequential. The methods that our scholastics follow only render more subtle the subtlest of subtleties; for you will more easily escape from a labyrinth than from the snares of the Realists,[50] Nominalists,[51] Thomists,[52] Albertists,[53] Occamists,[54] and Scotists.[55] I have not named them all, only a few of the major ones. But there is so much learning and difficulty in all of these sects that I should think the apostles themselves must have the need of some help from some other's spirit if they were to try to argue these topics with our new generation of theologians. . . .

Those who are the closest to these in happiness are generally called "the religious" or "monks," both of which are deceiving names, since for the most part they stay as far away from religion as possible and frequent every sort of place. I cannot, however, see how any life could be more gloomy than the life of these monks if I did not assist them in many ways. Though most people detest these men so much that accidentally meeting one is considered to be bad luck,[56] the monks themselves believe that they are magnificent creatures. One of the chief beliefs is that to be illiterate is to be of a high state of sanctity, and so they make sure that they are not able to read. Another is that when braying out their gospels in church they are making themselves very pleasing and satisfying to God, when in fact they are uttering these psalms as a matter of repetition rather than from their hearts. Indeed, some of these men make a good living through their uncleanliness and beggary by bellowing their petitions for food from door to door; there is not an inn, an announcement board, or a ship into which they are not accessible, here having a great advantage over other common beggars. According to them, though, they are setting an apostolic example for us by their filthiness, their ignorance, their bawdiness, and their insolence. . . .

---

[49] **Stoic paradoxes** A feature of ancient Stoic thought that recognized the complex way that seemingly good and bad are woven into human existence. Examples are "The wise man is happy on the rack," and "Only the wise man is king, and all fools are slaves."
[50] **Realists** Those who believed that universal concepts exist independently of physical objects and the human mind.
[51] **Nominalists** Those who claimed that only particular objects and events are real.
[52] **Thomists** Followers of St. Thomas Aquinas (1225–1274).
[53] **Albertists** Followers of Albertus Magnus (ca. 1200–1280).
[54] **Occamists** Followers of William of Occam or Ockham (ca. 1285–ca. 1349).
[55] **Scotists** Followers of Duns Scotus (ca. 1266–1308).

---

[56] **bad luck** Personal reference to Erasmus, who took monastic vows and lived in a monastery from 1485 until he was ordained a priest in 1492.

∽

Questions for Critical Thinking

1. In this passage, Erasmus criticizes three groups: the writing establishment, the learned professions, and religious orders. Summarize, using specific examples, his criticisms of these three groups.

2. *The Praise of Folly* is a work of *satire*. What means does Erasmus use to make his satirical points? Compare and contrast Erasmus's satirical methods with those used by social critics today.

SIR THOMAS MORE
Selection from *Utopia*

Sir Thomas More's *Utopia* (1516) is the first work of utopian literature in modern times. It is also the source of this genre's name, *utopia* (from Greek, "not-place") being a pun on *eutopia* (from Greek, "well-place," or "place [where all is] well"). Written in Latin, *Utopia* was printed both abroad and in England and soon became the talk of Europe. Since Thomas More (1478–1535) wrote it, more than one hundred books have appeared on this idea.

The idea of a perfect place grew as Western history unfolded. It was first glimpsed by the immortal Utnapishtim, the Babylonian Noah, in *The Epic of Gilgamesh* (see Chapter 1, Volume I; ca. 2500 BCE). In the *Odyssey* (see Chapter 2, Volume I), Homer named it the Elysian Fields. Another version was the Isles of the Blessed, as described by Horace. In Christianity it became paradise, called by St. Augustine (see *Confessions* in Chapter 7, Volume I) the Heavenly City. For the next thousand years, the celestial paradise (in contrast to the Earthly City) held sway in Europe. The Renaissance and the rise of secularism opened the way for More's earthly utopia.

More's *Utopia*, inspired by Plato's *The Republic* (see Chapter 3, Volume I), was in tune with Christian humanism (1500–1550), the literary movement (see Erasmus's *The Praise of Folly*) that used both classical texts and the Bible as guides. To effect his goal—a critique of Europe—More presented an ideal society in the New World. This disguise was necessary, for rash opinions could and did lead to prison or death in this age. More, a Catholic, was eventually beheaded for his beliefs, at the command of Henry VIII, the founder of the Protestant sect called Anglicanism.

The inhabitants of More's Utopia are portrayed as having solved the problems plaguing Europe at the time. Utopia was a welfare state run on communistic lines, with no private property and no money. There was universal free education, six hours' labor daily, uniforms for citizens, free medical treatment, and communal meals (with musical and reading accompaniment) in civic restaurants. Tolerance was granted to all religions. The penal code was simple, and parties to legal suits were expected to plead their own cases, as no lawyers were allowed. The law was harsh in sexual matters; adultery could result in slavery, repeated offenses in death. Divorce, however, was allowed by mutual consent. Gold was not to be used as currency but for useful objects such as chamber pots. Common storehouses of grains were maintained as reserves against famine. Completing More's dreamworld was a Utopian alphabet and language.

When first published, this work was so convincing that some readers, unable to decode More's intellectual puzzles (such as his made-up Greek names), downgraded its literary value, thinking it merely a translation of a travel book to the New World.

Scholars now disagree over the meaning of More's playful work. One group labels it a Catholic allegory whose purpose was to shame Christians into behaving better than the Utopians. Another group claims More as a Marxist before Marx, and the book as a political tract whose goal was to make Utopia's communism a model for Europe.

Reading the Selection

In this selection from Book II, Raphael Hythlodaeus (from Greek, "speaker of nonsense") describes Utopia's perfect society. In its communist system, all citizens worked to eat, except for thinkers and elected officials. The economy was run by syphogrants, controllers in charge of thirty households. In terms of war, the Utopians were peaceable, choosing violence only when all other methods failed.

Book II

Their Economy and Occupations

All the Utopians, men and women alike, work at agriculture, and no one is inexperienced in it. They are trained in it from childhood, partly by school instruction and partly by practice. School children are often taken into the nearby fields as though for play, where they not only see men and women working, but get exercise by working themselves.

Besides sharing in the farm work, every person has some particular trade of his own, such as the manufacture of wool or linen, masonry, metal work, or carpentry. There is no other craft which is practiced by any considerable number of them. People wear the same sort of clothes throughout the island, except for the distinctions which mark the difference between the married and the unmarried. The fashion of clothing never changes. Their clothing looks well, does not hinder their movements, and is suitable both for summer and winter. Every household makes its own clothing, but each man and woman also learns one of the other trades I have mentioned. The women, being the weaker, practice the lighter crafts, such as working with wool or linen. The heavier crafts are left to the men. Generally the same trade passes down from father to son, often by natural inclination. But if anyone's interests lie elsewhere, he is adopted into a family practicing the trade he prefers. When anyone makes such a change, both his father and the magistrates see to it that he is transferred to a responsible and upright house-holder. After a man has learned one trade, if he desires to acquire another, it is managed in the same manner. When he has learned both, he follows whichever he likes better, unless the public has special need for the other.

The chief and almost the only business of the syphogrants is to see that no one sits around in idleness, and that everyone works hard at his trade. But no one has to wear himself out with endless toil from morning till night, as if he were a beast of burden. Such a life, though it is the common life of workmen in all other countries, is no better than a slave's. The Utopians work six hours out of the twenty-four. They work three hours before dinner. After dinner they rest two hours, and then go to work for another three hours. Then they have supper and at eight o'clock, counting from noon, they go to bed and sleep eight hours.

The other hours of the day, those that are not used for work, sleep, and meals, are left to their individual choice, on the understanding that they shall not waste them idly and wantonly. They use their free time busily on any pursuit that pleases them. Many of them fill these intervals with reading. They have the custom of giving public lectures daily before daybreak, which none are obliged to attend except such as are selected for pursuit of learning. Yet a great many from all ranks, both men and women, go to hear lectures of one sort or another, according to their

interests. If anyone whose mind does not delight in intellectual pursuits prefers to spend his free time at his trade, as many do, this is not forbidden, but commended as beneficial to the commonwealth. After supper they spend an hour in some recreation, in summer gardening, in winter diverting themselves in their dining halls with music or talk. They know nothing about gambling with dice or other such foolish and ruinous games. They play two games not unlike our chess. One is a battle of numbers, in which one number plunders another. The other is a game in which the vices battle against the virtues. In this game the co-operation of the vices against the virtues and their opposition to each other is shown up very cleverly, as well as the special oppositions between particular virtues and vices, and the methods by which the vices openly assault or secretly undermine the virtues, and how the virtues break the strength of the vices and by what means finally one side or the other wins the victory.

To understand their way of life fully we must look at one point more carefully. They allot only six hours to labor, and you might think that a scarcity of essential goods would result. Actually their working hours are sufficient to provide not only an abundance, but even a superabundance of all the necessities and conveniences of life. You will easily understand this if you consider how large a part of the population in other countries is idle. In the first place, the women (and they are half the whole population) usually do no work, or if they do, their husbands lie snoring. Secondly, there is the multitude of priests and so-called religious men, as numerous as they are idle. Add to these all the rich men, especially great landlords, who are commonly called wellborn and noble. Add their henchmen, the whole flock of swaggering bullies. Reckon in with these the strong and lusty beggars, who go about feigning some disease to excuse their laziness. You will find that the actual number of workers who supply the needs of mankind is much smaller than you would think. And now consider how few of these workers are employed in really necessary work. Because we measure values by money, we have to carry on many superfluous trades to support luxury and wantonness. If the multitude of our workers produced only what men need for good living, there would be such an abundance of goods that prices would go down and workmen could not subsist. You can easily imagine how little time would be enough to produce the goods that man's needs and convenience demand (and his pleasure too if it were true and natural pleasure), if only the workers in useless trades were placed in worthwhile occupations and all the idlers who languish in sloth but eat twice as much as laborers were put to work on useful tasks.

The truth of this supposition is very apparent in Utopia. Out of all the men and women whose age or health permit them to work, scarcely five hundred are exempted in each city and its surrounding area. Among these are the syphogrants, who are excused from labor by law. Yet they do not excuse themselves from it, because they incite others to work more easily by setting them an example. The Utopians grant the same exemption to some who apply themselves exclusively to learning, but only at the recommendation of the priests and in accordance with a secret vote of the syphogrants. If one of these persons disappoints their hopes, he is made a workman again. On the other hand it sometimes happens that a worker devotes his free time so zealously to learning and progresses so far through his diligence, that he is excused from his trade and is transferred to the class of the learned men. From this class are chosen ambassadors, priests, tranibors,[57] and the prince himself (of old called the Barzanes,[58] but later the Ademus[59]). Since the rest of the entire population is neither idle nor engaged in useless occupations, it is easy to understand how they produce so much in so short a work day. . . .

Their Warfare

They hate and detest war as a thing manifestly brutal, and yet practiced by man more constantly than by any kind of beast. Contrary to almost all other peoples they consider nothing so inglorious as the glory won in war. Nevertheless both the men and the women of Utopia regularly practice military exercises on certain days, so that they will be prepared when the need arises. They go to war cautiously and reluctantly, only to protect their own territory or that of their friends if an enemy has invaded it, or to free some wretched people from tyrannous oppression and servitude. They help their friends not only in defense, but also to avenge injuries. They do this only if they are consulted in the whole affair, if the facts are proved, and if the stolen plunder is not returned. Then they think they should wage war against the aggressor. They decide on this policy when booty is taken from their friends by force or when the merchants of one country are oppressed in another country by unjust laws or by twisting good laws. This they think is a greater evil than direct attack.

This was the sole cause of the war which the Utopians waged against the Alaopolitans[60] for the sake of the Nephelogetes[61] some time before our arrival, when a wrong seemed to have been done under pretext of right to Nephelogete merchants resident among the Alaopolitans. Whether or not an injustice was done, it was avenged by a terrible war, the strength of each side being augmented by the resources and the hatred of their neighbors. Some prosperous nations were ruined and others were greatly shaken. In the end after a series of misfortunes, the Alaopolitans, who had been a very thriving people compared

---

[57] **tranibor** High-ranking official who supervises ten syphogrants.
[58] **Barzanes** Persian title, derived perhaps from Mithrobarzanes, the learned guide to the underworld, in the Greek writer Lucian's *Menippus,* which More translated into Latin.
[59] **Ademus** From Greek, "without a people."
[60] **Alaopolitans** From Greek, "citizens blind to their own country."
[61] **Nephelogetes** From Greek, "people born in the clouds."

to the Nephelogetes, were conquered and reduced to bondage by the Nephelogetes. Vigorously as the Utopians stood by their friends in the matter of reparations, they sought none for themselves.

If the Utopians themselves are cheated in this way, they carry their anger only to the point of cutting off trade with that country, provided no bodily injury is done. Not that they care less for their own citizens than for their neighbors, but they think it worse for their neighbors' property to be seized than their own. Their neighbors' merchants suffer a great injury because they lose their own property, but the Utopians think little of their loss, for only common goods have been lost. Besides whatever is exported must be in superfluous abundance at home, or it would not be shipped out. So they think it cruel to avenge a relatively unimportant loss by killing many men, whose death would only affect the lives and livelihood of others. But if any Utopian citizens are unjustly hurt or killed, whether by private or public policy, they send envoys demanding that the guilty persons be handed over to them. If that is refused, they declare war. If the guilty men are given up, their punishment is death or bondage.

The Utopians are troubled and ashamed when they gain a bloody victory, like merchants who have paid too high a price for what they have bought. If they overwhelm the enemy by skill and cunning, they exult and celebrate a public triumph, and erect a memorial for a victory efficiently won. When they win a victory by the strength of understanding (as only men can), they pride themselves on acting bravely and manfully. Bears, lions, boars, wolves, dogs, and other wild beasts fight with their bodies, and many of them surpass us in strength and ferocity as much as we surpass them in understanding and reason. 10

The Utopians have this one aim in war, to accomplish what they would gladly have achieved without war if just terms had been granted in time. Or if that cannot be done, they aim to exact so severe a revenge from those that have injured them that they will be afraid to do it again. Their policies are directed to these ends, which they strive toward in such a way as to avoid danger rather than to attain glory and fame.

As soon as war is declared, they at once arrange to have many small notices, which are marked with their official seal, set up by stealth in the most conspicuous places in the enemy's country. In these proclamations they promise great rewards to any one who will kill the enemy's king, and smaller rewards (but still very great) for killing those whom they regard as most responsible after the king for plotting aggression against them. They double the reward for anyone who brings in the proscribed man alive. Also they offer like rewards, as well as exemption from punishment, to any of the proscribed men who turn against their countrymen. As a result the proscribed men soon suspect everyone, distrust each other, and become distracted by their danger. It has often turned out that many of them, and even princes, have been betrayed by those whom they most trusted. The Utopians realize that rewards will spur men on to any sort of crime, and consequently they promise incredible gifts. Mindful of the danger which the assassins run, they see to it that the compensation is proportionate to the risk, and promise an immense amount of gold and also rich estates safely placed in neighboring countries. They keep these promises most faithfully. Though this manner of waging war by bidding for and buying enemies may seem like the cruel villainy of an ignoble mind, it is considered by the Utopians as a wise and praiseworthy policy, since it enables them to wage great wars without any battle at all. They even think themselves humane and merciful, because by the death of a few bad men they spare the lives of many innocent men who would otherwise die in battle, some fighting on their own side, some on the enemy's. Indeed they pity the mass of enemy soldiers no less than their own, for they know that they do not fight willingly, but are driven to it by the madness of their rulers.

If this method does not succeed, they sow the seeds of discord among the enemy by inciting the king's brother or some member of the nobility to plot for the crown. If these internal factions languish, then they arouse the neighboring people against the enemy and induce them to revive some old claims, such as kings never lack.

When they promise their resources to help in a war, they furnish money abundantly, but citizens very sparingly. They hold their own men most dear and of such account that they will not willingly exchange one of the citizens for an enemy's king. Since they keep their gold and silver for this single purpose, they spend it without reluctance, the more so as they will live no less well if they spend it all. Besides the wealth which they have at home, they have also boundless treasure abroad, many neighboring nations being in their debt, as I have said. So they hire mercenary soldiers from all sides, especially from the Zapoletes.[62]

These people live five hundred miles from Utopia toward the east. They are a rude, fierce, wild people, who delight in the forests and mountains among which they

are brought up. They are sturdy, well able to endure heat, cold, and hard work. They are unacquainted with luxuries or with agriculture, and are indifferent about housing and clothing. Their only productive occupation is taking care of cattle. For the most part they live by hunting and theft. It is as if they were born for war, and they watch carefully for any chance to engage in it. When they find such a chance they eagerly embrace it, great numbers of them going out and offering themselves at a low price to any one seeking soldiers. They know only one art for earning a living, the art of taking away life. They fight for their employers fiercely and with incorruptible fidelity. But they will not bind themselves to serve for any set time. They stipulate that they may fight next day for the enemy, if higher pay is offered, and come back on the day after that for still higher pay. There is seldom a war in which a considerable number of them are not fighting on both sides. So it commonly happens that men who are related to one another by blood and have served together in intimacy in the same campaigns are enlisted on opposite sides. Forgetful of their relationship and their friendship, they kill one another for no other reason than that they have been hired for a paltry wage by different kings. They think so much of money that they will change sides readily for an increase of only a penny a day. Thus they grow greedier and greedier for money, but money is of no use to them, for what they acquire with their blood, they soon waste profligately on contemptible pleasures.

This nation serves the Utopians against all people whatsoever, for they give higher pay than any others. Just as the Utopians seek out the best possible men to use at home, by the same principle they seek the worst men to misuse in war. When need requires, they induce the Zapoletes with promises of rich rewards to face hazards from which most of them never return. The Utopians pay the rewards in good faith to those who escape death, to incite them to similar deeds of daring later. And the Utopians have no concern over how many are killed, thinking they would deserve the thanks of the human race if they could purge the world of the whole of that disgusting and vicious people. . . .

---

[62] **Zapoletes** From Greek, "people who are open to corrupt influences." The reference may be to the Swiss, whose men often served as mercenary soldiers during the Renaissance.

Questions for Critical Thinking

1. Summarize *Utopia*'s economic and warfare policies. Compare and contrast them with the prevailing systems of Renaissance Europe, when this book was written.

2. Does More's *Utopia* have anything to teach us today? Explain.

MICHEL DE MONTAIGNE
Selection from *Essays*

The essay is ancient in form but the name is modern, coined by the French writer Montaigne in his *Essays* (from the French, *essai,* "attempt"), the first series published in 1580. Montaigne's personal essays were "attempts" at self-definition, to discover a sane and kindly way of living. With quiet authority, yet treating all truths as opinions, these essays impress his readers, then and now. His works made the essay the West's most versatile literary form.

In form, Montaigne's essays are rambling and long (most run to several thousand words) and cover diverse topics (Smells, The Affection of Fathers for Their Children, and The Length of Life). They are learned, yet jargon free; serious, yet marked by dry wit; and based on personal experience, while making points applicable to all. Widely read, Montaigne packed his pages with ideas from Plato (see *Phaedo* and *The Republic* in Chapter 3, Volume I), Plutarch, Cicero (see "The Dream of Cicero" in Chapter 5, Volume I), St. Augustine (see *Confessions* in Chapter 7, Volume I), and his own contemporaries, without always giving them credit. The result was a style linking pagan and Christian antiquity with the modern era.

Montaigne's constant subject is himself. Michel Eyquem de Montaigne (1533–1592) lived a divided life. He was a highly public figure (as counselor to the *Parlement* [law court] of Bordeaux, 1561–1570, and mayor of Bordeaux, 1581–1585), and he was a quiet philosopher, devoting himself to reading and writing. He worked on the *Essays* from 1572 until his death. With few references to career and family, the essays paint a "self-portrait" of his body, mind, and character. Driven by self-awareness—unique in this period but common today—he offers a running commentary on his kidney stones, eating habits, and vanity. He claimed he was "various and wavering," and the essays demonstrate these qualities in frequent digressions and shifting points of view.

What ultimately gives unity to the *Essays* is Montaigne's growing skepticism. He was repulsed by the fanatical wars between Protestants and Catholics that engulfed France and Europe at this time. In private siding with Catholic tradition, he nevertheless, in his essays, attached little weight to Christian ethics. Nor did he find in the ancient philosophies a moral code able to control humanity. He concluded that humans were vain and doomed to doubt— a view often voiced in the Age of Mannerism (1520–1600), a period marked by anti-Renaissance norms and the belief in human depravity.

Reading the Selection

"Of Cannibals" is part of Chapter XXXI of Book I of the *Essays*. It reflected Montaigne's knowledge of the New World, which was gleaned from the works of historians, including those who detailed the horrors of the conquest, or heard from American Indians themselves in France. Montaigne learned of the "cannibals" from Antarctic France (modern Brazil) in a work (1557) by Durand de Villegaignon, a French noble.

As horizons opened in the New World, old certainties gave way to doubts about European values. Montaigne, brought face to face with New World "cannibals," reacted with unusual (for his time) insight: "Each man calls barbarism whatever is not his own practice"—one of the West's first instances of cultural relativism.

Montaigne's cultural relativism has been termed "primitivism," meaning respect for barbarous peoples and admiration for much of their culture based on an understanding of their motives. It resembles the "noble savage" belief of Rousseau (see *Confessions* in Chapter 17), except that Montaigne accepted that savages can be as cruel as Europeans.

Book I

Chapter XXXI. Of Cannibals

When King Pyrrhus[63] passed over into Italy, after he had reconnoitered the formation of the army that the Romans were sending to meet him, he said: "I do not know what barbarians these are" (for so the Greeks called all foreign nations), "but the formation of this army that I see is not at all barbarous." The Greeks said as much of the army that Flaminius[64] brought into the country, and so did Philip,[65] seeing from a knoll the order and distribution of the Roman camp, in his kingdom, under Publius Sulpicius Galba.[66] Thus we should beware of clinging to vulgar opinions, and judge things by reason's way, not by popular say.

I had with me for a long time a man who had lived for ten or twelve years in that other world which has been discovered in our century, in the place where Villegaignon[67] landed, and which he called Antarctic France.[68] This discovery of a boundless country seems worthy of consideration. I don't know if I can guarantee that some other such discovery will not be made in the future, so many personages greater than ourselves having been mistaken about this one. I am afraid we have eyes bigger than our stomachs, and more curiosity than capacity. We embrace everything, but we clasp only wind.

Plato brings in Solon,[69] telling how he had learned from the priests of the city of Saïs in Egypt[70] that in days of old, before the Flood, there was a great island named Atlantis,[71] right at the mouth of the Strait of Gibraltar, which contained more land than Africa and Asia put together, and that the kings of that country, who not only possessed that island but had stretched out so far on the mainland that they held the breadth of Africa as far as Egypt, and the length of Europe as far as Tuscany, undertook to step over into Asia and subjugate all the nations that border

on the Mediterranean, as far as the Black Sea; and for this purpose crossed the Spains, Gaul, Italy, as far as Greece, where the Athenians checked them; but that some time after, both the Athenians and themselves and their island were swallowed up by the Flood.

It is quite likely that that extreme devastation of waters made amazing changes in the habitations of the earth, as people maintain that the sea cut off Sicily from Italy—

> 'Tis said an earthquake once asunder tore
> These lands with dreadful havoc, which before
> Formed but one land, one coast
> —VIRGIL[72]

—Cyprus from Syria, the island of Euboea[73] from the mainland of Boeotia[74]; and elsewhere joined lands that were divided, filling the channels between them with sand and mud:

> A sterile marsh, long fit for rowing, now
> Feeds neighbor towns, and feels the heavy plow.
> —HORACE[75]

But there is no great likelihood that that island was the new world which we have just discovered; for it almost touched Spain, and it would be an incredible result of a flood to have forced it away as far as it is, more than twelve hundred leagues; besides, the travels of the moderns have already almost revealed that it is not an island, but a mainland connected with the East Indies on one side, and elsewhere with the lands under the two poles; or, if it is separated from them, it is by so narrow a strait and interval that it does not deserve to be called an island[76] on that account.

It seems that there are movements, some natural, others feverish, in these great bodies, just as in our own. When I consider the inroads that my river, the Dordogne,[77] is making in my lifetime into the right bank in its descent, and that in twenty years it has gained so much ground and stolen away the foundations of several buildings, I clearly see that this is an extraordinary disturbance; for if it had always gone at this rate, or was to do so in the future, the face of the world would be turned topsy-turvy.

---

[63] **Pyrrhus** King of Epirus in northern Greece (r. 306–302 BCE, 297–272 BCE). Invaded Italy and defeated the Romans at Heraclea in 280 BCE and at Asculum in 279 BCE, but heavy troop losses gave rise to the phrase "Pyrrhic victory."

[64] **Flaminius** (ca. 230–175 BCE), Roman general and statesman. Defeated **Philip V** of Macedon at Cynoscephalae in 197 BCE.

[65] **Philip** Philip V, king of Macedon (r. 221–179 BCE), decisively defeated in 197 BCE and forced to give up control of Greece (see footnote 64).

[66] **Publius Sulpicius Galba** (fl. 211–200 BCE), Roman general and consul, defeated Philip V of Macedon in 200 BCE.

[67] **Villegaignon** Nicolas Durand de Villegaignon (1510–1571), French explorer and writer, founded a colony on the site of modern Rio de Janeiro in 1555; the Portuguese forced the abandonment of the colony in 1560.

[68] **Antarctic France** Modern Brazil.

[69] **Solon** (ca. 630–ca. 560 BCE), Athenian statesman. Reformed Athenian constitution, after which he traveled for ten years in Egypt, Cyprus, and Lydia.

[70] **Saïs in Egypt** Ancient capital of Lower Egypt, located in the Nile River delta.

[71] **Atlantis** A digression: Montaigne considers whether the New World may be the legendary Atlantis.

---

[72] **Virgil** Also spelled Vergil (70–19 BCE); Roman poet, author of The *Aeneid* (q.v.).

[73] **Euboea** A large island off the east coast of Greece, in the Aegean Sea.

[74] **Boeotia** A district in Greece, stretching from central Greece to the coast.

[75] **Horace** (65–8 BCE), Roman poet (see the *Odes* in Chapter 5, Volume I).

[76] **mainland . . . island** Montaigne thinks that the New World is the East Indies.

[77] **Dordogne** River in southwest France, which merges with the Garonne River north of Bordeaux to form the Gironde Estuary.

But rivers are subject to changes: now they overflow in one direction, now in another, now they keep to their course. I am not speaking of the sudden inundations whose causes are manifest. In Médoc,[78] along the seashore, my brother, the sieur[79] d'Arsac, can see an estate of his buried under the sands that the sea spews forth; the tops of some buildings are still visible; his farms and domains have changed into very thin pasturage. The inhabitants say that for some time the sea has been pushing toward them so hard that they have lost four leagues of land. These sands are its harbingers; and we see great dunes of moving sand that march half a league ahead of it and keep conquering land.

The other testimony of antiquity with which some would connect this discovery is in Aristotle, at least if that little book *Of Unheard-of Wonders*[80] is by him. He there relates that certain Carthaginians,[81] after setting out upon the Atlantic Ocean from the Strait of Gibraltar and sailing a long time, at last discovered a great fertile island, all clothed in woods and watered by great deep rivers, far remote from any mainland; and that they, and others since, attracted by the goodness and fertility of the soil, went there with their wives and children, and began to settle there. The lords of Carthage, seeing that their country was gradually becoming depopulated, expressly forbade anyone to go there any more, on pain of death, and drove out these new inhabitants, fearing, it is said, that in course of time they might come to multiply so greatly as to supplant their former masters and ruin their state. This story of Aristotle does not fit our new lands any better than the other.

This man I had was a simple, crude fellow—a character fit to bear true witness; for clever people observe more things and more curiously, but they interpret them; and to lend weight and conviction to their interpretation, they cannot help altering history a little. They never show you things as they are, but bend and disguise them according to the way they have seen them; and to give credence to their judgment and attract you to it, they are prone to add something to their matter, to stretch it out and amplify it. We need a man either very honest, or so simple that he has not the stuff to build up false inventions and give them plausibility; and wedded to no theory. Such was my man; and besides this, he at various times brought sailors and merchants, whom he had known on that trip, to see me. So I content myself with his information, without inquiring what the cosmographers[82] say about it.

We ought to have topographers[83] who would give us an exact account of the places where they have been. But

because they have over us the advantage of having seen Palestine, they want to enjoy the privilege of telling us news about all the rest of the world. I would like everyone to write what he knows, and as much as he knows, not only in this, but in all other subjects; for a man may have some special knowledge and experience of the nature of a river or a fountain, who in other matters knows only what everybody knows. However, to circulate this little scrap of knowledge, he will undertake to write the whole of physics. From this vice spring many great abuses.

Now, to return to my subject, I think there is nothing barbarous and savage in that nation,[84] from what I have been told, except that each man calls barbarism whatever is not his own practice; for indeed it seems we have no other test of truth and reason than the example and pattern of the opinions and customs of the country we live in. *There* is always the perfect religion, the perfect government, the perfect and accomplished manners in all things. Those people are wild, just as we call wild the fruits that Nature has produced by herself and in her normal course; whereas really it is those that we have changed artificially and led astray from the common order, that we should rather call wild. The former retain alive and vigorous their genuine, their most useful and natural, virtues and properties, which we have debased in the latter in adapting them to gratify our corrupted taste. And yet for all that, the savor and delicacy of some uncultivated fruits of those countries is quite as excellent, even to our taste, as that of our own. It is not reasonable that art should win the place of honor over our great and powerful mother Nature. We have so overloaded the beauty and richness of her works by our inventions that we have quite smothered her. Yet wherever her purity shines forth, she wonderfully puts to shame our vain and frivolous attempts:

> *Ivy comes readier without our care;*
> *In lonely caves the arbutus grows more fair;*
> *No art with artless bird song can compare.*
> —PROPERTIUS[85]

All our efforts cannot even succeed in reproducing the nest of the tiniest little bird, its contexture, its beauty and convenience; or even the web of the puny spider. All things, says Plato, are produced by nature, by fortune, or by art; the greatest and most beautiful by one or the other of the first two, the least and most imperfect by the last.

These nations, then, seem to me barbarous in this sense, that they have been fashioned very little by the human mind, and are still very close to their original naturalness. The laws of nature still rule them, very little corrupted by ours; and they are in such a state of purity that I am sometimes vexed that they were unknown earlier, in the days when there were men able to judge them better than we. I am sorry that Lycurgus[86] and Plato did

---

[78] **Médoc** District in southwest France, north of Bordeaux; famous for its wine.
[79] **sieur** Lord of the realm; Montaigne's family belongs to the French aristocracy.
[80] **Of Unheard-of Wonders** [by Aristotle] Scholars today believe *On Marvelous Things Heard* (ca. 300 BCE), about an island paradise, was not written by Aristotle.
[81] **Carthaginians** People of Carthage, a Phoenician city-state in North Africa, utterly destroyed by Rome in 146 BCE.
[82] **cosmographer** Scholar who studies the constitution of the whole order of nature.
[83] **topographer** Scholar who designs a map or chart of the natural features of the land.

[84] **that nation** Indigenous people in what is now Brazil, the subject of this essay.
[85] **Propertius** (ca. 50–ca. 15 BCE), Roman poet.
[86] **Lycurgus** Legendary lawgiver of ancient Sparta; perhaps ninth century BCE.

not know of them; for it seems to me that what we actually see in these nations surpasses not only all the pictures in which poets have idealized the golden age and all their inventions in imagining a happy state of man, but also the conceptions and the very desire of philosophy. They could not imagine a naturalness so pure and simple as we see by experience; nor could they believe that our society could be maintained with so little artifice and human solder. This is a nation, I should say to Plato, in which there is no sort of traffic, no knowledge of letters, no science of numbers, no name for magistrate or for political superiority, no custom of servitude, no riches or poverty, no contracts, no successions, no partitions, no occupations but leisure ones, no care for any but common kinship, no clothes, no agriculture, no metal, no use of wine or wheat. The very words that signify lying, treachery, dissimulation, avarice, envy, belittling, pardon—unheard of. How far from this perfection would he find the republic that he imagined: *Men fresh sprung from the gods* [Seneca].[87]

> *These manners nature first ordained.*
> —VIRGIL

For the rest, they live in a country with a very pleasant and temperate climate, so that according to my witnesses it is rare to see a sick man there; and they have assured me that they never saw one palsied, bleary-eyed, toothless, or bent with age. They are settled along the sea and shut in on the land side by great high mountains, with a stretch about a hundred leagues wide in between. They have a great abundance of fish and flesh which bear no resemblance to ours, and they eat them with no other artifice than cooking. The first man who rode a horse there, though he had had dealings with them on several other trips, so horrified them in this posture that they shot him dead with arrows before they could recognize him.

Their buildings are very long, with a capacity of two or three hundred souls; they are covered with the bark of great trees, the strips reaching to the ground at one end and supporting and leaning on one another at the top, in the manner of some of our barns, whose covering hangs down to the ground and acts as a side. They have wood so hard that they cut with it and make of it their swords and grills to cook their food. Their beds are of a cotton weave, hung from the roof like those in our ships, each man having his own; for the wives sleep apart from their husbands.

They get up with the sun, and eat immediately upon rising, to last them through the day; for they take no other meal than that one. Like some other Eastern[88] peoples, of whom Suidas[89] tells us, who drank apart from meals, they do not drink then; but they drink several times a day, and to capacity. Their drink is made of some root, and is of the color of our claret[90] wines. They drink it only lukewarm. This beverage keeps only two or three days; it has a slightly sharp taste, is not at all heady, is good for the stomach, and has a laxative effect upon those who are not used to it; it is a very pleasant drink for anyone who is accustomed to it. In place of bread they use a certain white substance like preserved coriander. I have tried it; it tastes sweet and a little flat.

The whole day is spent in dancing. The younger men go to hunt animals with bows. Some of the women busy themselves meanwhile with warming their drink, which is their chief duty. Some one of the old men, in the morning before they begin to eat, preaches to the whole barnful in common, walking from one end to the other, and repeating one single sentence several times until he has completed the circuit (for the buildings are fully a hundred paces long). He recommends to them only two things: valor against the enemy and love for their wives. And they never fail to point out this obligation, as their refrain, that it is their wives who keep their drink warm and seasoned.

There may be seen in several places, including my own house, specimens of their beds, of their ropes, of their wooden swords and the bracelets with which they cover their wrists in combats, and of the big canes, open at one end, by whose sound they keep time in their dances. They are close shaven all over, and shave themselves much more cleanly than we, with nothing but a wooden or stone razor. They believe that souls are immortal, and that those who have deserved well of the gods are lodged in that part of heaven where the sun rises, and the damned in the west.

They have some sort of priests and prophets, but they rarely appear before the people, having their home in the mountains. On their arrival there is a great feast and solemn assembly of several villages—each barn, as I have described it, makes up a village, and they are about one French league from each other. The prophet speaks to them in public, exhorting them to virtue and their duty; but their whole ethical science contains only these two articles: resoluteness in war and affection for their wives. He prophesies to them things to come and the results they are to expect from their undertakings, and urges them to war or holds them back from it; but this is on the condition that when he fails to prophesy correctly, and if things turn out otherwise than he has predicted, he is cut into a thousand pieces if they catch him, and condemned as a false prophet. For this reason, the prophet who has once been mistaken is never seen again.

Divination[91] is a gift of God; that is why its abuse should be punished as imposture. Among the Scythians,[92] when the soothsayers failed to hit the mark, they were laid, chained hand and foot, on carts full of heather and drawn by oxen, on which they were burned. Those who

15

---

[87] **Seneca** (ca. 4 BCE–65 CE), Roman statesman, playwright, and philosopher.
[88] **Eastern** Montaigne thinks Brazil is part of the Eastern Hemisphere.
[89] **Suidas** Montaigne makes up this name, based on *The Suda,* a tenth-century encyclopedia on Greek history and literature.

[90] **claret** Red Bordeaux wine.
[91] **Divination** The art of foretelling the future.
[92] **Scythians** Ancient nomads, ranging from central Asia to southern Russia; founded a kingdom centered on the Crimea, seventh century BCE to about 200 CE.

handle matters subject to the control of human capacity are excusable if they do the best they can. But these others, who come and trick us with assurances of an extraordinary faculty that is beyond our ken, should they not be punished for not making good their promise, and for the temerity of their imposture?

They have their wars with the nations beyond the mountains, further inland, to which they go quite naked, with no other arms than bows or wooden swords ending in a sharp point, in the manner of the tongues of our boar spears. It is astonishing what firmness they show in their combats, which never end but in slaughter and bloodshed; for as to routs and terror, they know nothing of either.

Each man brings back as his trophy the head of the enemy he has killed, and sets it up at the entrance to his dwelling. After they have treated their prisoners well for a long time with all the hospitality they can think of, each man who has a prisoner calls a great assembly of his acquaintances. He ties a rope to one of the prisoner's arms, by the end of which he holds him, a few steps away, for fear of being hurt, and gives his dearest friend the other arm to hold in the same way; and these two, in the presence of the whole assembly, kill him with their swords. This done, they roast him and eat him in common and send some pieces to their absent friends. This is not, as people think, for nourishment, as of old the Scythians used to do; it is to betoken an extreme revenge. And the proof of this came when they saw the Portuguese, who had joined forces with their adversaries, inflict a different kind of death on them when they took them prisoner, which was to bury them up to the waist, shoot the rest of their body full of arrows, and afterward hang them. They thought that these people from the other world, being men who had sown the knowledge of many vices among their neighbors and were much greater masters than themselves in every sort of wickedness, did not adopt this sort of vengeance without some reason, and that it must be more painful than their own; so they began to give up their old method and to follow this one.

I am not sorry that we notice the barbarous horror of such acts, but I am heartily sorry that, judging their faults rightly, we should be so blind to our own. I think there is more barbarity in eating a man alive than in eating him dead; and in tearing by tortures and the rack a body still full of feeling, in roasting a man bit by bit in having him bitten and mangled by dogs and swine[93] (as we have not only read but seen within fresh memory, not among ancient enemies, but among neighbors and fellow citizens, and what is worse, on the pretext of piety and religion), than in roasting and eating him after he is dead.

Indeed, Chrysippus[94] and Zeno,[95] heads of the Stoic sect, thought there was nothing wrong in using our carcasses for any purpose in case of need, and getting nour-

ishment from them; just as our ancestors, when besieged by Caesar[96] in the city of Alésia,[97] resolved to relieve their famine by eating old men, women, and other people useless for fighting.

> The Gascons[98] once, 'tis said, their life renewed
> By eating of such food.
> —JUVENAL[99]

And physicians do not fear to use human flesh[100] in all sorts of ways for our health, applying it either inwardly or outwardly. But there never was any opinion so disordered as to excuse treachery, disloyalty, tyranny, and cruelty, which are our ordinary vices.

So we may well call these people barbarians, in respect to the rules of reason, but not in respect to ourselves, who surpass them in every kind of barbarity.

Their warfare is wholly noble and generous, and as excusable and beautiful as this human disease can be; its only basis among them is their rivalry in valor. They are not fighting for the conquest of new lands, for they still enjoy that natural abundance that provides them without toil and trouble with all necessary things in such profusion that they have no wish to enlarge their boundaries. They are still in that happy state of desiring only as much as their natural needs demand; anything beyond that is superfluous to them.

They generally call those of the same age, brothers; those who are younger, children; and the old men are fathers to all the others. These leave to their heirs in common the full possession of their property, without division or any other title at all than just the one that Nature gives to her creatures in bringing them into the world.

If their neighbors cross the mountains to attack them and win a victory, the gain of the victor is glory, and the advantage of having proved the master in valor and virtue; for apart from this they have no use for the goods of the vanquished, and they return to their own country, where they lack neither anything necessary nor that great thing, the knowledge of how to enjoy their condition happily and be content with it. These men of ours do the same in their turn. They demand of their prisoners no other ransom than that they confess and acknowledge their defeat. But there is not one in a whole century who does not choose to die rather than to relax a single bit, by word or look, from the grandeur of an invincible courage; not one who would not rather be killed and eaten than so much as ask not to be. They treat them very freely, so that life may be all the dearer to them, and usually entertain them with threats of their coming death, of the torments they will

---

[93] **dogs and swine** Religious wars between Catholics and Protestants, accompanied by various atrocities, raged in France during Montaigne's lifetime.
[94] **Chrysippus** (ca. 280–ca. 206 BCE), Greek philosopher, who, with Zeno, founded the Stoa Academy in Athens.
[95] **Zeno** (ca. 335–263 BCE), Greek philosopher (see footnote 94).

[96] **Caesar** Julius Caesar (100–44 BCE), Roman general, statesman, and historian.
[97] **Alésia** Town in east central Gaul (modern France).
[98] **Gascons** People of Gascony, a region in southwestern France, on the Atlantic Ocean, with mainly a Basque population. Montaigne was a Gascon.
[99] **Juvenal** (ca. 55/60–ca. 127 CE), Roman satirist.
[100] **human flesh** Mummified flesh, obtained from Egyptian tombs, was used in certain medications.

have to suffer, the preparations that are being made for that purpose, the cutting up of their limbs, and the feast that will be made at their expense. All this is done for the sole purpose of extorting from their lips some weak or base word, or making them want to flee, so as to gain the advantage of having terrified them and broken down their firmness. For indeed, if you take it the right way, it is in this point alone that true victory lies:

It is no victory
Unless the vanquished foe admits your mastery.
                                    —CLAUDIAN[101]

The Hungarians, very bellicose fighters, did not in olden times pursue their advantage beyond putting the enemy at their mercy. For having wrung a confession from him to this effect, they let him go unharmed and un-ransomed, except, at most, for exacting his promise never again to take up arms against them.

We win enough advantages over our enemies that are borrowed advantages, not really our own. It is the quality of a porter,[102] not of valor, to have sturdier arms and legs; agility is a dead and corporeal quality; it is a stroke of luck to make our enemy stumble, or dazzle his eyes by the sunlight; it is a trick of art and technique, which may be found in a worthless coward, to be an able fencer. The worth and value of a man is in his heart and his will; there lies his real honor. Valor is the strength, not of legs and arms, but of heart and soul; it consists not in the worth of our horse or our weapons, but in our own. He who falls obstinate in his courage, *if he has fallen, he fights on his knees* [Seneca]. He who relaxes none of his assurance, no matter how great the danger of imminent death; who, giving up his soul, still looks firmly and scornfully at his enemy—he is beaten not by us, but by fortune; he is killed, not conquered.

The most valiant are sometimes the most unfortunate. Thus there are triumphant defeats that rival victories. Nor did those four sister victories, the fairest that the sun ever set eyes on—Salamis,[103] Plataea,[104] Mycale,[105] and Sicily[106]—ever dare match all their combined glory against the glory of the annihilation of King Leonidas[107] and his men at the pass of Thermopylae.[108]

Who ever hastened with more glorious and ambitious desire to win a battle than Captain Ischolas[109] to lose one? Who ever secured his safety more ingeniously and pains-takingly than he did his destruction? He was charged to defend a certain pass in the Peloponnesus[110] against the Arcadians.[111] Finding himself wholly incapable of doing this, in view of the nature of the place and the inequality of the forces, he made up his mind that all who confronted the enemy would necessarily have to remain on the field. On the other hand, deeming it unworthy both of his own virtue and magnanimity and of the Lacedaemonian[112] name to fail in his charge, he took a middle course between these two extremes, in this way. The youngest and fittest of his band he preserved for the defense and service of their country, and sent them home; and with those whose loss was less important, he determined to hold this pass, and by their death to make the enemy buy their entry as dearly as he could. And so it turned out. For he was presently sur-rounded on all sides by the Arcadians, and after slaugh-tering a large number of them, he and his men were all put to the sword. Is there a trophy dedicated to victors that would not be more due to these vanquished? The role of true victory is in fighting, not in coming off safely; and the honor of valor consists in combating, not in beating.

To return to our story. These prisoners are so far from giving in, in spite of all that is done to them, that on the contrary, during the two or three months that they are kept, they wear a gay expression; they urge their captors to hurry and put them to the test; they defy them, insult them, reproach them with their cowardice and the num-ber of battles they have lost to the prisoners' own people.

I have a song composed by a prisoner which con-tains this challenge, that they should all come boldly and gather to dine off him, for they will be eating at the same time their own fathers and grandfathers, who have served to feed and nourish his body. "These muscles," he says, "this flesh and these veins are your own, poor fools that you are. You do not recognize that the substance of your ancestors' limbs is still contained in them. Savor them well; you will find in them the taste of your own flesh." An idea that certainly does not smack of barbarity. Those that paint these people dying, and who show the execu-tion, portray the prisoner spitting in the face of his slayers and scowling at them. Indeed, to the last gasp they never stop braving and defying their enemies by word and look. Truly here are real savages by our standards; for either they must be thoroughly so, or we must be; there is an amazing distance between their character and ours.

The men there have several wives, and the higher their reputation for valor the more wives they have. It is a remarkably beautiful thing about their marriages that the

[101] **Claudian** (ca. 370–ca. 404 CE), Roman poet.
[102] **porter** Person who carries heavy things.
[103] **Salamis** Island in Saronic Gulf, off Athens; site of major battle in 480 BCE, in which the Greeks defeated the Persians.
[104] **Plataea** Ancient city in Boeotia; site of battle in 479 BCE, in which the Greeks decisively defeated the Persians and ensured the independence of Greece.
[105] **Mycale** Ancient promontory in Ionia on the coast of Asia Minor; off this site, in the Aegean Sea, the Greeks defeated the Persians in a major battle in 479 BCE.
[106] **Sicily** Island off the "toe" of Italy, settled by Greek colonists in ancient times; site of major battle in 480 BCE, won by the Greek settlers against Carthaginian invaders.
[107] **King Leonidas** Ruler of ancient Sparta (ca. 490–ca. 480 BCE).
[108] **Thermopylae** Greek, "Hot Gates." Narrow pass in northern Greece that, in ancient times, controlled the only road between Thessaly and central Greece.

[109] **Captain Ischolas** Spartan soldier; this anecdote is taken from a universal history by the ancient Greek historian Diodorus Siculus.
[110] **Peloponnesus** Large peninsula forming the southern part of mainland Greece.
[111] **Arcadians** People of Arcady, an ancient country in the Greek Peloponnesus; dominated by Sparta for years; liberated after Thebes defeated Sparta in 371 BCE.
[112] **Lacedaemonian** Another name for ancient Sparta.

same jealousy our wives have to keep us from the affection and kindness of other women, theirs have to win this for them. Being more concerned for their husbands' honor than for anything else, they strive and scheme to have as many companions as they can, since that is a sign of their husbands' valor.

Our wives will cry "Miracle!" but it is no miracle. It is a properly matrimonial virtue but one of the highest order. In the Bible, Leah,[113] Rachel,[114] Sarah,[115] and Jacob's wives[116] gave their beautiful handmaids to their husbands; and Livia[117] seconded the appetites of Augustus,[118] to her own disadvantage; and Stratonice, the wife of King Deiotarus,[119] not only lent her husband for his use a very beautiful young chambermaid in her service, but carefully brought up her children, and backed them up to succeed to their father's estates.

And lest it be thought that all this is done through a simple and servile bondage to usage and through the pressure of the authority of their ancient customs, without reasoning or judgment, and because their minds are so stupid that they cannot take any other course, I must cite some examples of their capacity. Besides the warlike song I have just quoted, I have another, a love song, which begins in this vein: "Adder,[120] stay; stay, adder, that from the pattern of your coloring my sister may draw the fashion and the workmanship of a rich girdle that I may give to my love; so may your beauty and your pattern be forever preferred to all other serpents." This first couplet is the refrain of the song. Now I am familiar enough with poetry to be a judge of this: not only is there nothing barbarous in this fancy, but it is altogether Anacreontic.[121] Their language, moreover, is a soft language, with an agreeable sound, somewhat like Greek in its endings.

Three of these men, ignorant of the price they will ₃₅ pay some day, in loss of repose and happiness, for gaining

knowledge of the corruptions of this side of the ocean; ignorant also of the fact that of this intercourse will come their ruin (which I suppose is already well advanced: poor wretches, to let themselves be tricked by the desire for new things, and to have left the serenity of their own sky to come and see ours!)—three of these men were at Rouen,[122] at the time the late King Charles IX[123] was there. The king talked to them for a long time; they were shown our ways, our splendor, the aspect of a fine city. After that, someone asked their opinion, and wanted to know what they had found most amazing. They mentioned three things, of which I have forgotten the third, and I am very sorry for it; but I still remember two of them. They said that in the first place they thought it very strange that so many grown men, bearded, strong, and armed, who were around the king (it is likely that they were talking about the Swiss[124] of his guard) should submit to obey a child, and that one of them was not chosen to command instead. Second (they have a way in their language of speaking of men as halves of one another), they had noticed that there were among us men full and gorged with all sorts of good things, and that their other halves were beggars at their doors, emaciated with hunger and poverty; and they thought it strange that these needy halves could endure such an injustice, and did not take the others by the throat, or set fire to their houses.

I had a very long talk with one of them; but I had an interpreter who followed my meaning so badly, and who was so hindered by his stupidity in taking in my ideas, that I could get hardly any satisfaction from the man. When I asked him what profit he gained from his superior position among his people (for he was a captain, and our sailors called him king), he told me that it was to march foremost in war. How many men followed him? He pointed to a piece of ground, to signify as many as such a space could hold; it might have been four or five thousand men. Did all his authority expire with the war? He said that this much remained, that when he visited the villages dependent on him, they made paths for him through the underbrush by which he might pass quite comfortably.

All this is not too bad—but what's the use? They don't wear breeches.

---

[113] **Leah** Wife of Jacob, whom God later named as Israel (Genesis 29:15–30).
[114] **Rachel** Younger sister of **Leah** and preferred wife of **Jacob** (see footnote 113).
[115] **Sarah** Wife of Moses (Genesis 17:15–16).
[116] **Jacob's wives** **Leah** and **Rachel.**
[117] **Livia** Livia Drusilla (58 BCE–29 CE), Roman empress, wife of Augustus.
[118] **Augustus** Original name, Gaius Octavius. Roman emperor (r. 27 BCE–14 CE), founder of the Roman Empire (see footnote 117).
[119] **Stratonice, the wife of King Deiotarus** Uncertain, based perhaps in an account in *Moral Essays* by the Greek writer Plutarch.
[120] **Adder** A type of venomous snake.
[121] **Anacreontic** In the style of Anacreon (ca. 582–ca. 485 BCE), Greek poet, famous for verses on love and wine.

---

[122] **Rouen** Port city on the Seine River, in western France.
[123] **Charles IX** (r. 1560–1574), ruler of France. He was ten years old when he became king. In early years, his mother, Catherine de' Medici (1519–1589), served as regent.
[124] **Swiss** Mercenary troops from Switzerland.

❧

Questions for Critical Thinking

1. According to Montaigne, which set of morals is superior: those of the Old [European] World or those of New World peoples?

2. What evidence of Eurocentrism do you see in Montaigne's essay? In what way was Montaigne farsighted in his outlook?

WILLIAM SHAKESPEARE
Hamlet

Excepting the Bible, Shakespeare's *Hamlet* is perhaps the West's most famous literary work. Hardly a day passes without this play being acted, either on a commercial stage or in a school or college; and many versions of the play, on film and on tape, ensure its universal visibility. Hamlet's role is usually defined as the most difficult in the theater, and many actors, and a few actresses, often choose to play Hamlet as a crown to their careers. It is so well known that the world uses the term *Hamletlike* to describe people unable to make up their minds.

The hectic world in which *Hamlet* appeared gave no forecast of the play's future greatness. First staged in 1600, the play was one of a series that William Shakespeare (1564–1616) was turning out for the nearly insatiable demands of the commercial stage. He was fresh to London in 1590 from a middle-class youth in Stratford-upon-Avon. When Shakespeare retired to gentlemanly leisure in Stratford in 1610, he had written thirty-seven dramas—almost two plays a year.

The London audiences did not want masterpieces; instead, they craved violence, ghosts, and murders galore. They wanted revenge tragedies, the most popular dramatic form in the Age of Elizabeth (1558–1603), England's golden age. This taste for blood is not surprising, for Elizabethan England made national heroes of pirate patriots like Francis Drake and accepted as normal that Protestants and Catholics should burn heretics alive. It was for this violence-filled age that Shakespeare wrote *Hamlet*, based on a bloody revenge tale that had already inspired one play during the 1580s.

Reading the Selection

Shakespeare's *Hamlet* is set at the royal Danish court. Its revenge theme is activated by the murder of old King Hamlet. Prince Hamlet, depressed by his father's death, is plunged into a court seething with intrigue, carousing, ghosts, and spies. There are also wandering actors, an oath sworn on swords, a secret letter, a deadly duel, and a hasty funeral. Lest these devices be insufficiently entertaining, Hamlet himself veers from madman to scholar to prince to swordsman before he gets his revenge. At the end, the stage is littered with corpses, and the major characters are all dead.

What rescues *Hamlet* from mere melodrama and pushes it into the stratosphere of great art are Shakespeare's majestic language and complete mastery of psychology. The theater, reborn in medieval productions like *Everyman*, with its simple morals and even simpler psychology, now came to maturity in Shakespeare's hands.

Dramatis Personae

CLAUDIUS *King of Denmark*
HAMLET *Son to the late, and nephew to the present king*
POLONIUS *Lord Chamberlain*
HORATIO *Friend to Hamlet*
LAERTES *Son to Polonius*
VOLTIMAND
CORNELIUS
ROSENCRANTZ
GUILDENSTERN } *Courtiers*
OSRIC
A GENTLEMAN
A PRIEST
MARCELLUS } *Officers*
BERNARDO

FRANCISCO *A soldier*
REYNALDO *Servant to Polonius*
PLAYERS
TWO CLOWNS *Grave-diggers*
FORTINBRAS *Prince of Norway*
A CAPTAIN
ENGLISH AMBASSADORS
GERTRUDE *Queen of Denmark, and mother to Hamlet*
OPHELIA *Daughter to Polonius*
LORDS, LADIES, OFFICERS, SOLDIERS, SAILORS, MESSENGERS,
    and OTHER ATTENDANTS
GHOST *of Hamlet's father*

SCENE—DENMARK

Act I

Scene I—Elsinore. A Platform[125] Before the Castle

The two opening scenes put the spectator in full possession of the situation of affairs in Denmark. The death and character of the late king, his reappearance to denote some unknown evil, the threats of war, and the consequent need for strong men are emphasized in the first; the second adds the personal relations of HAMLET *with the royal house, and depicts his state of mind at the beginning of the action.*

HORATIO is carefully differentiated from MARCELLUS, BERNARDO, *and* FRANCISCO: *they are unlettered soldiers; he is a scholar, and, as such, has his touches both of imagination and scepticism.*

The scene opens amid nervous suspense; there is a tradition that it was written in a charnel-house. "'Tis bitter cold," and silent, and the watcher is "sick at heart." On two previous nights the ghost has appeared to BERNARDO *and* MARCELLUS. BERNARDO's *agitation shows itself in the way he challenges the guard, instead of waiting to be challenged.*

FRANCISCO at his post. Enter to him BERNARDO

BERNARDO: Who's there?

FRANCISCO: Nay, answer me:[126] stand, and unfold yourself.   1

BER.: Long live the king![127]

FRAN.: Bernardo?

BER.: He.

FRAN.: You come most carefully upon your hour.

BER.: 'Tis now struck twelve; get thee to bed, Francisco.

FRAN.: For this relief much thanks: 'tis bitter cold,
    And I am sick at heart.

BER.: Have you had quiet guard?   10

FRAN.:   Not a mouse stirring.

BER.: Well, good night.
    If you do meet Horatio and Marcellus,
    The rivals[128] of my watch, bid them make haste.

FRAN.: I think I hear them. Stand, ho! Who's there?

Enter HORATIO *and* MARCELLUS

HORATIO: Friends to this ground.

MARCELLUS: And liegemen to the Dane.

FRAN.: Give you[129] good night.

MAR.:   O, farewell, honest soldier:
    Who hath relieved you?   20

FRAN.:   Bernardo has my place.
    Give you good night.   [*Exit.*

MAR.: Holla! Bernardo!

BER.:   Say,
    What, is Horatio there?

HOR.:   A piece of him.

BER.: Welcome, Horatio: welcome, good Marcellus.

HOR.: What, has this thing appear'd again tonight?

BER.: I have seen nothing.

MAR.: Horatio says 'tis but our fantasy,   30
    And will not let belief take hold of him
    Touching this dreaded sight, twice seen of us:
    Therefore I have entreated him along
    With us to watch the minutes of this night;
    That if again this apparition come,
    He may approve[130] our eyes and speak to it.

HOR.: Tush, tush, 't will not appear.

BER.:   Sit down awhile;
    And let us once again assail your ears,
    That are so fortified against our story   40
    What we have two nights seen.

HOR.:   Well, sit we down,
    And let us hear Bernardo speak of this.

BER.: Last night of all,
    When yond same star that's westward from the pole[131]
    Had made his course to illume that part of heaven
    Where now it burns, Marcellus and myself,
    The bell then beating one—

Enter GHOST

MAR.: Peace, break thee off; look, where it comes again!

BER.: In the same figure, like the king that's dead.   50

MAR.: Thou art a scholar[132]; speak to it, Horatio.

BER.: Looks it not like the king? mark it, Horatio.

HOR.: Most like: it harrows[133] me with fear and wonder.

BER.: It would be spoke to.[134]

MAR.:   Question it, Horatio.

HOR.: What art thou that usurp'st this time of night,
    Together with that fair and warlike form
    In which the majesty of buried Denmark[135]
    Did sometimes march? by heaven I charge thee,
        speak!

MAR.: It is offended.   60

BER.:   See, it stalks away!

HOR.: Stay! speak, speak! I charge thee, speak!

                    [*Exit Ghost.*

MAR.: 'Tis gone, and will not answer.

BER.: How now, Horatio! you tremble and look pale:
    Is not this something more than fantasy?
    What think you on 't?

HOR.: Before my God, I might not this believe
    Without the sensible and true avouch
    Of mine own eyes.

MAR.:   Is it not like the king?   70

I.i. [125] **platform** A level space on the battlements of the royal castle at Elsinore, a Danish seaport; now Helsingör.

[126] **me** This is emphatic, since Francisco is the sentry.

[127] **Long live the king!** Either a password or greeting; Horatio and Marcellus use a different one in line 15.

[128] **rivals** Partners.

[129] **Give you** God give you.

[130] **approve** Corroborate.

[131] **pole** Polestar.

[132] **scholar** Exorcisms were performed in Latin, which Horatio as an educated man would be able to speak.

[133] **harrows** Lacerates the feelings.

[134] **It . . . to.** A ghost could not speak until spoken to.

[135] **buried Denmark** The buried king of Denmark.

HOR.: As thou art to thyself:
    Such was the very armour he had on
    When he the ambitious Norway combated;
    So frown'd he once, when, in an angry parle,
    He smote[136] the sledded pole-axe[137] on the ice.
    'Tis strange.
MAR.: Thus twice before, and jump at this dead hour,
    With martial stalk hath he gone by our watch.
HOR.: In what particular thought to work I know not;
    But in the gross and scope[138] of my opinion,   80
    This bodes some strange eruption to our state.
MAR.: Good now,[139] sit down, and tell me, he that knows,
    Why this same strict and most observant watch
    So nightly toils[140] the subject[141] of the land,
    And why such daily cast[142] of brazen cannon,
    And foreign mart[143] for implements of war;
    Why such impress[144] of shipwrights, whose sore task
    Does not divide the Sunday from the week;
    What might be toward, that this sweaty haste
    Doth make the night joint-labourer with the day: 90
    Who is 't that can inform me?
HOR.:   That can I;
    At least, the whisper goes so. Our last king,
    Whose image even but now appear'd to us,
    Was, as you know, by Fortinbras of Norway,
    Thereto prick'd on[145] by a most emulate[146] pride,
    Dared to the combat; in which our valiant Hamlet—
    For so this side of our known world esteem'd him—
    Did slay this Fortinbras; who, by a seal'd compact,
    Well ratified by law and heraldry,[147]   100
    Did forfeit, with his life, all those his lands
    Which he stood seized[148] of, to the conqueror:
    Against the which, a moiety competent[149]
    Was gaged by our king; which had return'd
    To the inheritance of Fortinbras,
    Had he been vanquisher; as, by the same covenant,[150]
    And carriage[151] of the article design'd,
    His fell to Hamlet. Now, sir, young Fortinbras,
    Of unapproved[152] mettle hot and full,[153]
    Hath in the skirts of Norway here and there   110
    Shark'd up[154] a list of lawless resolutes,[155]

For food and diet,[156] to some enterprise
    That hath a stomach in 't; which is no other—
    As it doth well appear unto our state—
    But to recover of us, by strong hand
    And terms compulsatory, those foresaid lands
    So by his father lost: and this, I take it,
    Is the main motive of our preparations,
    The source of this our watch and the chief head
    Of this post-haste and romage[157] in the land.   120
BER.: I think it be no other but e'en so:
    Well may it sort[158] that this portentous figure
    Comes armed through our watch; so like the king
    That was and is the question of these wars.
HOR.: A mote[159] it is to trouble the mind's eye.
    In the most high and palmy state[160] of Rome,
    A little ere the mightiest Julius fell,
    The graves stood tenantless and the sheeted dead
    Did squeak and gibber in the Roman streets:
    As stars with trains of fire[161] and dews of blood,   130
    Disasters[162] in the sun; and the moist star[163]
    Upon whose influence Neptune's empire[164] stands
    Was sick almost to doomsday with eclipse:
    And even the like precurse[165] of fierce events,
    As harbingers preceding still the fates
    And prologue to the omen coming on,
    Have heaven and earth together demonstrated
    Unto our climatures and countrymen.—
    But soft, behold! lo, where it comes again!

Re-enter GHOST

    I'll cross[166] it, though it blast me. Stay, illusion!   140
    If thou hast any sound, or use of voice

                       [*It*[167] *spreads its arms.*

    Speak to me:
    If there be any good thing to be done,
    That may to thee do ease and grace to me,
    Speak to me:
    If[168] thou art privy to thy country's fate,
    Which, happily, foreknowing may avoid,
    O, speak!
    Or if thou hast uphoarded in thy life
    Extorted treasure in the womb of earth,
    For which, they say, you spirits oft walk in death,   150

                       [*The cock crows.*

    Speak of it: stay, and speak! Stop it, Marcellus.

---

[136] **smote** Defeated.
[137] **sledded pole-axe** Sometimes written as *Polacks*, meaning Polish warriors.
[138] **gross and scope** General drift.
[139] **Good now** An expression denoting entreaty or expostulation.
[140] **toils** Causes or makes to toil.
[141] **subject** People, subjects.
[142] **cast** Casting, founding.
[143] **mart** Buying and selling, traffic.
[144] **impress** Impressment.
[145] **prick'd on** Incited.
[146] **emulate** Rivaling.
[147] **law and heraldry** Heraldic law, governing combat.
[148] **seized** Possessed.
[149] **moiety competent** Adequate or sufficient portion.
[150] **covenant** Joint bargain.
[151] **carriage** Import, bearing.
[152] **unapproved** Not turned to account.
[153] **hot and full** Full of fight.
[154] **Shark'd up** Got together in haphazard fashion.
[155] **resolutes** Desperadoes.

---

[156] **food and diet** No pay but their keep.
[157] **romage** Bustle, commotion.
[158] **sort** Suit.
[159] **mote** Speck of dust.
[160] **palmy state** Triumphant sovereignty.
[161] **stars . . . fire** i.e., Comets.
[162] **Disasters** Unfavorable aspects.
[163] **moist star** The moon, governing tides.
[164] **Neptune's empire** The sea.
[165] **precurse** Heralding.
[166] **cross** Meet, face, thus bringing down the evil influence on the person who crosses it.
[167] **It** The Ghost, or perhaps Horatio.
[168] **If . . .** In the following seven lines, Horatio recites the traditional reasons ghosts might walk.

MAR.: Shall I strike at it with my partisan[169]?
HOR.: Do, if it will not stand.
BER.:   'Tis here!
HOR.:   'Tis here!
MAR.: 'Tis gone!   [*Exit Ghost.*
    We do it wrong, being so majestical,
    To offer it the show of violence;
    For it is, as the air, invulnerable,   160
    And our vain blows malicious mockery.
BER.: It was about to speak, when the cock crew.[170]
HOR.: And then it started like a guilty thing
    Upon a fearful summons. I have heard,
    The cock, that is the trumpet to the morn,
    Doth with his lofty and shrill-sounding throat
    Awake the god of day; and, at his warning,
    Whether in sea or fire, in earth or air,
    The extravagant[171] and erring spirit hies
    To his confine:[172] and of the truth herein   170
    This present object made probation.[173]
MAR.: It faded on the crowing of the cock.
    Some say that ever 'gainst[174] that season comes
    Wherein our Saviour's birth is celebrated,
    The bird of dawning singeth all night long:
    And then, they say, no spirit dare stir abroad;
    The nights are wholesome; then no planets strike,[175]
    No fairy takes, nor witch hath power to charm,
    So hallow'd and so gracious[176] is the time.
HOR.: So have I heard and do in part believe it.   180
    But, look, the morn, in russet mantle clad,
    Walks o'er the dew of yon high eastward hill:
    Break we our watch up; and by my advice,
    Let us impart what we have seen to-night
    Unto young Hamlet; for, upon my life,
    This spirit, dumb to us, will speak to him.
    Do you consent we shall acquaint him with it,
    As needful in our loves, fitting our duty?
MAR.: Let's do 't, I pray; and I this morning know
    Where we shall find him most conveniently. [*Exeunt.* 190

Scene II—A Room of State in the Castle

HAMLET's brief dialogue with the KING *and* QUEEN *and his subsequent soliloquy sufficiently acquaint us with his mood. He has no idea of his uncle's crime, though he detests his character; but his moral sense has received a severe shock from his mother's marriage. The whole world appears to him, in consequence, under the dominion of evil; he would gladly be quit of it. But that cannot be, and, moreover, he cannot do anything, nor even utter his feelings.*

He must take refuge in irony and sarcasm, or, when possible, in silence.

CLAUDIUS *is a hypocrite, but his hypocrisy is that of a statesman; he plays his part with a dignity and a keen insight into what is needful for the welfare of the state, which explains how the council came to choose him king.*

The scene opens with a bridal procession. It is the custom of the stage for HAMLET *to come on last, slowly and reluctantly, and clad in black, among the glittering draperies of the court.*

Enter CLAUDIUS, *King of Denmark,* GERTRUDE *the Queen,* HAMLET, POLONIUS, LAERTES *and his sister* OPHELIA, LORDS ATTENDANT

KING: Though yet of Hamlet our dear brother's death   1
    The memory be green, and that it us befitted
    To bear our hearts in grief and our whole kingdom
    To be contracted in one brow of woe,
    Yet so far hath discretion fought with nature
    That we with wisest sorrow think on him,
    Together with remembrance of ourselves.
    Therefore our sometime sister, now our queen,
    The imperial jointress[177] to this warlike state,
    Have we, as 't were with a defeated joy,—   10
    With an auspicious and a dropping eye,
    With mirth in funeral and with dirge in marriage,
    In equal scale weighing delight and dole,—
    Taken to wife: nor have we herein barr'd
    Your better wisdoms, which have freely gone
    With this affair along. For all, our thanks.
    Now follows, that[178] you know, young Fortinbras,
    Holding a weak[179] supposal of our worth,
    Or thinking by our late dear brother's death
    Our state to be disjoint[180] and out of frame,[181]   20
    Colleagued[182] with the dream of his advantage,[183]
    He hath not fail'd to pester us with message,
    Importing[184] the surrender of those lands
    Lost by his father, with all bonds of law,
    To our most valiant brother. So much for him.
    Now for ourself and for this time of meeting:
    Thus much the business is: we have here writ
    To Norway, uncle of young Fortinbras,—
    Who, impotent and bed-rid, scarcely hears
    Of this his nephew's purpose,—to suppress   30
    His further gait[185] herein; in that the levies,
    The lists and full proportions, are all made
    Out of his subject:[186] and we here dispatch
    You, good Cornelius, and you, Voltimand,
    For bearers of this greeting to old Norway;
    Giving to you no further personal power

---

[169] **partisan** Long-handled spear with a blade having lateral projections.
[170] **cock crew** According to traditional ghost lore, spirits returned to their confines at cockcrow.
[171] **extravagant and erring** Wandering. Both words mean the same thing.
[172] **confine** Place of confinement.
[173] **probation** Proof, trial.
[174] **'gainst** Just before.
[175] **planets strike** It was thought that planets were malignant and might strike travelers by night.
[176] **gracious** Full of goodness.

I.ii. [177] **jointress** Woman possessed of a jointure, or, joint tenancy of an estate.
[178] **that** That which.
[179] **weak supposal** Low estimate.
[180] **disjoint** Distracted, out of joint.
[181] **frame** Order.
[182] **Colleagued** Added to.
[183] **dream . . . advantage** Visionary hope of success.
[184] **Importing** Purporting, pertaining to.
[185] **gait** Proceeding.
[186] **Out of his subject** At the expense of Norway's subjects (collectively).

To business with the king, more than the scope
Of these delated[187] articles allow.
Farewell, and let your haste commend your duty.

CORNELIUS: ⎫
VOLTIMAND: ⎭ In that and all things will we show our duty.   40
KING: We doubt it nothing: heartily farewell.

[*Exeunt Voltimand and Cornelius.*

And now, Laertes, what's the news with you?
You told us of some suit; what is 't, Laertes?
You cannot speak of reason to the Dane,[188]
And lose your voice:[189] what wouldst thou beg,
    Laertes,
That shall not be my offer, not thy asking?
The head is not more native[190] to the heart,
The hand more instrumental[191] to the mouth,
Than is the throne of Denmark to thy father.
What wouldst thou have, Laertes?   50
LAERTES: My dread lord,
Your leave and favour to return to France;
From whence though willingly I came to Denmark,
To show my duty in your coronation,
Yet now, I must confess, that duty done,
My thoughts and wishes bend again toward France
And bow them to your gracious leave and pardon.[192]
KING: Have you your father's leave? What says Polonius?
POLONIUS: He hath, my lord, wrung from me my slow   60
    leave
By laboursome petition, and at last
Upon his will I seal'd my hard consent:
I do beseech you, give him leave to go.
KING: Take thy fair hour, Laertes; time be thine,
And thy best graces spend it at thy will!
But now, my cousin[193] Hamlet, and my son,—
HAMLET: [*Aside*] A little more than kin, and less than
    kind.[194]
KING: How is it that the clouds still hang on you?
HAM.: Not so, my lord; I am too much i' the sun.[195]   70
QUEEN: Good Hamlet, cast thy nighted colour off,
And let thine eye look like a friend on Denmark.
Do not for ever with thy vailed lids
Seek for thy noble father in the dust:
Thou know'st 'tis common; all that lives must die,
Passing through nature to eternity.
HAM.: Ay, madam, it is common.[196]

---

[187] **delated** Expressly stated.
[188] **the Dane** Danish king.
[189] **lose your voice** Speak in vain.
[190] **native** Closely connected, related.
[191] **instrumental** Serviceable.
[192] **leave and pardon** Permission to depart.
[193] **cousin** Any kin not of the immediate family.
[194] **A little . . . kind.** i.e., My relation to you has become more than kinship warrants; it has also become unnatural.
[195] **I am . . . sun** The senses seem to be: I am too much out of doors, I am too much in the sun of your grace (ironical), I am too much of a son to you. Possibly an allusion to the proverb "Out of heaven's blessing into the warm sun"; i.e., Hamlet is out of house and home in being deprived of the kingship.
[196] **Ay . . . common.** i.e., It is common, but it hurts nevertheless; possibly a reference to the commonplace quality of the queen's remark.

QUEEN: If it be,
Why seems it so particular with thee?
HAM.: Seems, madam! nay, it is; I know not "seems."
'Tis not alone my inky cloak, good mother,   80
Nor customary suits[197] of solemn black,
Nor windy suspiration[198] of forced breath,
No, nor the fruitful river in the eye,
Nor the dejected 'haviour of the visage,
Together with all forms, moods, shows of grief,
That can denote me truly: these indeed seem,
For they are actions that a man might play:
But I have that within which passeth show;
These but the trappings and the suits of woe.
KING: 'Tis sweet and commendable in your nature,   90
    Hamlet,
To give these mourning duties to your father:
But, you must know, your father lost a father;
That father lost, lost his, and the survivor bound
In filial obligation for some term
To do obsequious[199] sorrow: but to persever
In obstinate condolement[200] is a course
Of impious stubbornness; 'tis unmanly grief;
It shows a will most incorrect[201] to heaven,
A heart unfortified, a mind impatient,   100
An understanding simple and unschool'd:
For what we know must be and is as common
As any the most vulgar thing[202] to sense,
Why should we in our peevish opposition
Take it to heart? Fie! 'tis a fault to heaven,
A fault against the dead, a fault to nature,
To reason most absurd; whose common theme
Is death of fathers, and who still hath cried,
From the first corse till he that died to-day,
"This must be so." We pray you, throw to earth   110
This unprevailing[203] woe, and think of us
As of a father: for let the world take note,
You are the most immediate[204] to our throne;
And with no less nobility[205] of love
Than that which dearest father bears his son,
Do I impart[206] toward you. For your intent
In going back to school in Wittenberg,[207]
It is most retrograde[208] to our desire:
And we beseech you, bend you[209] to remain
Here, in the cheer and comfort of our eye,   120
Our chiefest courtier, cousin, and our son.
QUEEN: Let not thy mother lose her prayers, Hamlet:
I pray thee, stay with us; go not to Wittenberg.
HAM.: I shall in all my best obey you, madam.

---

[197] **customary suits** Suits prescribed by custom for mourning.
[198] **windy suspiration** Heavy sighing.
[199] **obsequious** Dutiful.
[200] **condolement** Sorrowing.
[201] **incorrect** Untrained, uncorrected.
[202] **vulgar thing** Common experience.
[203] **unprevailing** Unavailing.
[204] **most immediate** Next in succession.
[205] **nobility** High degree.
[206] **impart** The object is apparently love (1.110).
[207] **Wittenberg** Famous German university founded in 1502.
[208] **retrograde** Contrary.
[209] **bend you** Incline yourself; imperative.

KING: Why, 'tis a loving and a fair reply:
 Be as ourself in Denmark. Madam, come;
 This gentle and unforced accord of Hamlet
 Sits smiling to my heart: in grace whereof,
 No jocund health that Denmark drinks to-day,
 But the great cannon to the clouds shall tell,   130
 And the king's rouse[210] the heavens shall bruit[211]
  again,
 Re-speaking earthly thunder. Come away.

  [*Exeunt all but Hamlet.*

HAM.: O, that this too too solid flesh would melt,
 Thaw and resolve itself into a dew!
 Or that the Everlasting had not fix'd
 His canon 'gainst self-slaughter! O God! God!
 How weary, stale, flat and unprofitable,
 Seem to me all the uses of this world!
 Fie on 't! ah fie! 'tis an unweeded garden,
 That grows to seed; things rank and gross in nature   140
 Possess it merely.[212] That it should come to this!
 But two months dead: nay, not so much, not two:
 So excellent a king; that was, to this,
 Hyperion[213] to a satyr; so loving to my mother
 That he might not beteem[214] the winds of heaven
 Visit her face too roughly. Heaven and earth!
 Must I remember? why, she would hang on him,
 As if increase of appetite had grown
 By what it fed on: and yet, within a month—
 Let me not think on 't—Frailty, thy name is   150
  woman!—
 A little month, or ere those shoes were old
 With which she follow'd my poor father's body,
 Like Niobe,[215] all tears:—why she, even she—
 O God! a beast, that wants discourse of reason,[216]
 Would have mourn'd longer—married with my
  uncle,
 My father's brother, but no more like my father
 Than I to Hercules: within a month:
 Ere yet the salt of most unrighteous tears
 Had left the flushing in her galled[217] eyes,
 She married. O, most wicked speed, to post   160
 With such dexterity[218] to incestuous sheets!
 It is not nor it cannot come to good:
 But break, my heart; for I must hold my tongue.

Enter HORATIO, MARCELLUS, *and* BERNARDO

HOR.: Hail to your lordship!
HAM.:   I am glad to see you well:
 Horatio,—or I do forget myself.

HOR.: The same, my lord, and your poor servant ever.
HAM.: Sir, my good friend; I'll change that name with
  you:[219]
 And what make you from Wittenberg, Horatio?
 Marcellus?   170
MAR.: My good lord—
HAM.: I am very glad to see you. Good even, sir.
 But what, in faith, make you from Wittenberg?
HOR.: A truant disposition, good my lord.
HAM.: I would not hear your enemy say so,
 Nor shall you do mine ear that violence,
 To make it truster of your own report
 Against yourself: I know you are no truant.
 But what is your affair in Elsinore?
 We'll teach you to drink deep ere you depart.   180
HOR.: My lord, I came to see your father's funeral.
HAM.: I pray thee, do not mock me, fellow-student;
 I think it was to see my mother's wedding.
HOR.: Indeed, my lord, it follow'd hard[220] upon.
HAM.: Thrift, thrift, Horatio! the funeral baked meats[221]
 Did coldly furnish forth the marriage tables.
 Would I had met my dearest[222] foe in heaven
 Or ever I had seen that day, Horatio!
 My father—me thinks I see my father.
HOR.: Where, my lord?   190
HAM.:   In my mind's eye, Horatio.
HOR.: I saw him—once; he was a goodly king.
HAM.: He was a man, take him for all in all,
 I shall not look upon his like again.
HOR.: My lord, I think I saw him yesternight.
HAM.: Saw? who?
HOR.: My lord, the king your father.
HAM.:   The king my father!
HOR.: Season your admiration[223] for a while
 With an attent ear, till I may deliver,   200
 Upon the witness of these gentlemen,
 This marvel to you.
HAM.:   For God's love, let me hear.
HOR.: Two nights together had these gentlemen,
 Marcellus and Bernardo, on their watch,
 In the dead waste and middle of the night,
 Been thus encounter'd. A figure like your father,
 Armed at point exactly, cap-a-pe,[224]
 Appears before them, and with solemn march
 Goes slow and stately by them: thrice he walk'd   210
 By their oppress'd[225] and fear-surprised eyes,
 Within his truncheon's[226] length; whilst they,
  distill'd[227]

---

[210] **rouse** Draft of liquor.
[211] **bruit again** Echo.
[212] **merely** Completely, entirely.
[213] **Hyperion** God of the sun in the older regime of ancient gods.
[214] **beteem** Allow.
[215] **Niobe** Tantalus's daughter, who boasted that she had more sons and daughters than Leto; for this, Apollo and Artemis slew her children. She was turned into stone by Zeus on Mount Sipylus.
[216] **discourse of reason** Process or faculty of reason.
[217] **galled** Irritated.
[218] **dexterity** Facility.

[219] **I'll . . . you** I'll be your servant, you shall be my friend; also explained as "I'll exchange the name of friend with you."
[220] **hard** Close.
[221] **baked meats** Meat pies.
[222] **dearest** Direst; the adjective *dear* in Shakespeare has two different origins; O.E. *deore,* "beloved," and O.E. *deore,* "fierce." *Dearest* is the superlative of the second.
[223] **Season your admiration** Restrain your astonishment.
[224] **cap-a-pe** From head to foot.
[225] **oppress'd** Distressed.
[226] **truncheon** Officer's staff.
[227] **distill'd** Softened, weakened.

Almost to jelly with the act[228] of fear,
Stand dumb and speak not to him. This to me
In dreadful secrecy impart they did;
And I with them the third night kept the watch:
Where, as they had deliver'd, both in time,
Form of the thing, each word made true and good,
The apparition comes: I knew your father;
These hands are not more like.   220

HAM.:   But where was this?
MAR.: My lord, upon the platform where we watch'd.
HAM.: Did you not speak to it?
HOR.:   My lord, I did;
But answer made it none: yet once methought
It lifted up its head and did address
Itself to motion, like as it would speak;
But even then the morning cock crew loud,
And at the sound it shrunk in haste away,
And vanish'd from our sight.   230
HAM.:   'Tis very strange.
HOR.: As I do live, my honour'd lord, 'tis true;
And we did think it writ down in our duty
To let you know of it.
HAM.: Indeed, indeed, sirs, but this troubles me.
Hold you the watch to-night?

MAR.: }
BER.: }   We do, my lord.

HAM.: Arm'd, say you?

MAR.: }
BER.: } Arm'd, my lord.

HAM.: From top to toe?   240

MAR.: }
BER.: }   My lord, from head to foot.

HAM.: Then saw you not his face?
HOR.: Oh, yes, my lord; he wore his beaver[229] up.
HAM.: What, look'd he frowningly?
HOR.: A countenance more in sorrow than in anger.
HAM.: Pale or red?
HOR.: Nay, very pale.
HAM.:   And fix'd his eyes upon you?
HOR.: Most constantly.
HAM.:   I would I had been there.   250
HOR.: It would have much amazed you.
HAM.: Very like, very like. Stay'd it long?
HOR.: While one with moderate haste might tell a
hundred.

MAR.: }
BER.: } Longer, longer.

HOR.: Not when I saw 't.
HAM.:   His beard was grizzled,—no?
HOR.: It was, as I have seen it in his life,
A sable[230] silver'd.
HAM.:   I will watch to-night;   260
Perchance 't will walk again.
HOR.:   I warrant it will.
HAM.: If it assume my noble father's person,
I'll speak to it, though hell itself should gape

And bid me hold my peace. I pray you all,
If you have hitherto conceal'd this sight,
Let it be tenable in your silence still;
And whatsoever else shall hap to-night,
Give it an understanding, but no tongue:
I will requite your loves. So, fare you well: 270
Upon the platform, 'twixt eleven and twelve,
I'll visit you.
ALL: Our duty to your honour.
HAM.: Your loves, as mine to you: farewell.

                              [*Exeunt all but Hamlet.*

My father's spirit in arms! all is not well;
I doubt[231] some foul play: would the night were
come!
Till then sit still, my soul: foul deeds will rise,
Though all the earth o'erwhelm them, to men's eyes.

                                              [*Exit.*

Scene III—A Room in Polonius' House

The principal elements in the situation of things at Elsinore have been put before us in the first two scenes: the need for a man of action and the supernatural suggestion of some hidden evil in Scene I, and the position and nature of HAMLET *in Scene II. The present scene completes the picture by showing the contrast to* HAMLET *afforded by the family of* POLONIUS, *who may be taken as typical of the court at Elsinore. All are carefully drawn on a lower scale than his, shallow where he is subtle, commonplace where he is original. Nonetheless, the portrait of the gentle maiden,* OPHELIA, *is touched so as to win our sympathies. She is no mate for* HAMLET; *yet in her own sphere she is a beautiful and lovable character.* POLONIUS *is a politician without being a statesman,* LAERTES *an apt representative of gilded youth as it existed at the court of Elizabeth. Both have low ideals: the father is consumed with the conceit of his own intellect and experience, which have shown him only the lower side of humanity; the son is "Italianate," degraded in tone by his life in a foreign city. Both are incredulous, not only of the purity and honor of* HAMLET *but of that of* OPHELIA *herself.*

Enter LAERTES *and* OPHELIA

LAER.: My necessaries are embark'd: farewell: 1
And, sister, as the winds give benefit
And convoy is assistant,[232] do not sleep,
But let me hear from you.
OPHELIA: Do you doubt that?
LAER.: For Hamlet and the trifling of his favour,
Hold it a fashion[233] and a toy in blood,[234]
A violet in the youth of primy[235] nature,
Forward,[236] not permanent, sweet, not lasting,
The perfume and suppliance of a minute[237];   10
No more.
OPH.: No more but so?

---

[228] **act** Action.
[229] **beaver** Visor on the helmet.
[230] **sable** Black color.

---

[231] **doubt** Fear.
I.iii. [232] **convoy is assistant** Means of conveyance are available.
[233] **fashion** Custom, prevailing usage.
[234] **toy in blood** Passing amorous fancy.
[235] **primy** In its prime.
[236] **Forward** Precocious.
[237] **suppliance of a minute** Diversion to fill up a minute.

LAER.:   Think it no more:
For nature, crescent,[238] does not grow alone
In thews[239] and bulk, but, as this temple[240] waxes,
The inward service of the mind and soul
Grows wide withal. Perhaps he loves you now,
And now no soil[241] nor cautel[242] doth besmirch
The virtue of his will: but you must fear,
His greatness weigh'd,[243] his will is not his own;   20
For he himself is subject to his birth:
He may not, as unvalued persons do,
Carve for himself; for on his choice depends
The safety and health of this whole state;
And therefore must his choice be circumscribed
Unto the voice and yielding[244] of that body
Whereof he is the head. Then if he says he loves you,
It fits your wisdom so far to believe it
As he in his particular act and place
May give his saying deed[245]; which is no further   30
Than the main voice of Denmark goes withal.
Then weigh what loss your honour may sustain,
If with too credent[246] ear you list his songs,
Or lose your heart, or your chaste treasure open
To his unmaster'd[247] importunity.
Fear it, Ophelia, fear it, my dear sister,
And keep you in the rear of your affection,
Out of the shot and danger of desire.
The chariest[248] maid is prodigal enough,
If she unmask her beauty to the moon: 40
Virtue itself 'scapes not calumnious strokes:
The canker galls the infants of the spring,[249]
Too oft before their buttons[250] be disclosed,
And in the morn and liquid dew[251] of youth
Contagious blastments[252] are most imminent.
Be wary then; best safety lies in fear:
Youth to itself rebels, though none else near.
OPH.:   I shall the effect of this good lesson keep,
As watchman to my heart. But, good my brother,
Do not, as some ungracious[253] pastors do,   50
Show me the steep and thorny way to heaven;
Whiles, like a puff'd[254] and reckless libertine,
Himself the primrose path of dalliance treads,
And recks[255] not his own rede.[256]

LAER.:   O, fear me not.
I stay too long: but here my father comes.

Enter POLONIUS

A double[257] blessing is a double grace;
Occasion[258] smiles upon a second leave.
POL.:   Yet here, Laertes! aboard, aboard, for shame!
The wind sits in the shoulder of your sail,   60
And you are stay'd for. There; my blessing with thee!
And these few precepts[259] in thy memory
See thou character.[260] Give thy thoughts no tongue,
Nor any unproportion'd[261] thought his act.
Be thou familiar, but by no means vulgar.[262]
Those friends thou hast, and their adoption tried,
Grapple them to thy soul with hoops of steel;
But do not dull thy palm with entertainment
Of each new-hatch'd, unfledged[263] comrade. Beware
Of entrance to a quarrel, but being in,   70
Bear 't that the opposed may beware of thee.
Give every man thy ear, but few thy voice;
Take each man's censure, but reserve thy judgement.
Costly thy habit as thy purse can buy,
But not express'd in fancy[264]; rich, not gaudy;
For the apparel oft proclaims the man,
And they in France of the best rank and station
Are of a most select and generous choice in that.[265]
Neither a borrower nor a lender be;
For loan oft loses both itself and friend,   80
And borrowing dulls the edge of husbandry.[266]
This above ALL: to thine own self be true,
And it must follow, as the night the day,
Thou canst not then be false to any man.
Farewell: my blessing season[267] this in thee!
LAER.:   Most humbly do I take my leave, my lord.
POL.:   The time invites you; go; your servants tend.
LAER.:   Farewell, Ophelia; and remember well
What I have said to you.
OPH.:   'Tis in my memory lock'd,   90
And you yourself shall keep the key of it.
LAER.:   Farewell.   [*Exit.*
POL.:   What is 't, Ophelia, he hath said to you?
OPH.:   So please you, something touching the Lord
Hamlet.
POL.:   Marry, well bethought:
'Tis told me, he hath very oft of late
Given private time to you; and you yourself

---

[238] **crescent** Growing, waxing.
[239] **thews** Bodily strength.
[240] **temple** Body.
[241] **soil** Blemish.
[242] **cautel** Crafty device.
[243] **greatness weigh'd** High position considered.
[244] **voice and yielding** Assent, approval.
[245] **deed** Effect.
[246] **credent** Credulous.
[247] **unmaster'd** Unrestrained.
[248] **chariest** Most scrupulously modest.
[249] **The canker . . . spring** The cankerworm destroys the young plants of spring.
[250] **buttons** Buds.
[251] **liquid dew** i.e., Time when dew is fresh.
[252] **blastments** Blights.
[253] **ungracious** Graceless.
[254] **puff'd** Bloated.
[255] **recks** Heeds.
[256] **rede** Counsel.

---

[257] **double** i.e., Laertes has already bade his father good-bye.
[258] **Occasion** Opportunity.
[259] **precepts** Many parallels have been found to the series of maxims that follows, one of the closer being that in Lyly's *Euphues: The Anatomy of Wit.*
[260] **character** Inscribe.
[261] **unproportion'd** Inordinate.
[262] **vulgar** Common.
[263] **unfledged** Immature.
[264] **express'd in fancy** Fantastical in design.
[265] **Are . . . that.** Choice is usually taken as a substantive meaning "head," "eminence."
[266] **husbandry** Thrift.
[267] **season** Mature.

Have of your audience been most free and
   bounteous:
If it be so, as so 'tis put on[268] me,   100
And that in way of caution, I must tell you,
You do not understand yourself so clearly
As it behoves my daughter and your honour.
What is between you? give me up the truth.

OPH.: He hath, my lord, of late made many tenders[269]
   Of his affection to me.

POL.: Affection! pooh! you speak like a green girl,
   Unsifted[270] in such perilous circumstance.
   Do you believe his tenders, as you call them?

OPH.: I do not know, my lord, what I should think.   110

POL.: Marry, I'll teach you: think yourself a baby;
   That you have ta'en these tenders[271] for true pay,
   Which are not sterling.[272] Tender[273] yourself more
     dearly;
   Or—not to crack the wind[274] of the poor phrase,
   Running it thus—you'll tender me a fool.[275]

OPH.: My lord, he hath importuned me with love
   In honourable fashion.[276]

POL.: Ay, fashion you may call it; go to, go to.

OPH.: And hath given countenance[277] to his speech, my
   lord,
   With almost all the holy vows of heaven.   120

POL.: Ay, springes[278] to catch woodcocks.[279] I do know,
   When the blood burns, how prodigal the soul
   Lends the tongue vows: these blazes, daughter,
   Giving more light than heat, extinct in both,
   Even in their promise, as it is a-making,
   You must not take for fire. From this time
   Be somewhat scanter of your maiden presence;
   Set your entreatments[280] at a higher rate
   Than a command to parley.[281] For Lord Hamlet,
   Believe so much in him,[282] that he is young,   130
   And with a larger tether may he walk
   Than may be given you: in few,[283] Ophelia,
   Do not believe his vows; for they are brokers,[284]
   Not of that dye[285] which their investments[286] show,
   But mere implorators of[287] unholy suits,
   Breathing[288] like sanctified and pious bonds,

The better to beguile. This is for all:
I would not, in plain terms, from this time forth,
Have you so slander[289] any moment leisure,
As to give words or talk with the Lord Hamlet.   140
Look to 't, I charge you: come your ways.

OPH.: I shall obey my lord.   [*Exeunt.*

Scene IV—The Platform

*The elements of the tragedy are now before the mind of the specta-
tor; the revelation of the* GHOST *is the spark that sets them in
motion. With this the first act, or prologue to the main action,
naturally ends.* HAMLET's *problem is presented to him; the question is, "What will he make of it?" This must be decided in the
course of the play by the laws of his character and circumstances.
His first impulse is to believe and to revenge; yet, even so early
as this, the hastily conceived design of simulating madness is a
foretaste of what is to follow.*

   *Scenes IV and V are dramatically continuous; they are only
separated scenically by the need for a slight change of locality.*

Enter HAMLET, HORATIO, *and* MARCELLUS

HAM.: The air bites shrewdly; it is very cold.   1

HOR.: It is a nipping and an eager air.

HAM.: What hour now?

HOR.:   I think it lacks of twelve.

MAR.: No, it is struck.

HOR.: Indeed? I heard it not: then it draws near the
   season
   Wherein the spirit held his wont to walk.

    [*A flourish of trumpets, and ordnance shot off, within.*

   What does this mean, my lord?

HAM.: The king doth wake[290] to-night and takes his rouse,[291]
   Keeps wassail,[292] and the swaggering up-spring[293]   10
     reels[294];
   And, as he drains his draughts of Rhenish[295] down,
   The kettle-drum and trumpet thus bray out
   The triumph of his pledge.[296]

HOR.:   Is it a custom?

HAM.: Ay, marry, is 't:
   But to my mind, though I am native here
   And to the manner born,[297] it is a custom
   More honour'd in the breach than the observance.
   This heavy-headed revel east and west
   Makes us traduced and tax'd of other nations: 20
   They clepe[298] us drunkards, and with swinish phrase[299]
   Soil our addition[300]; and indeed it takes

---

[268] **put on** Impressed on.
[269] **tenders** Offers.
[270] **Unsifted** Untried.
[271] **tenders** Promises to pay.
[272] **sterling** Legal currency.
[273] **Tender** Hold.
[274] **crack the wind** i.e., Run it until it is broken-winded.
[275] **tender . . . fool** Show me a fool (for a daughter).
[276] **fashion** Mere form, pretense.
[277] **countenance** Credit, support.
[278] **springes** Snares.
[279] **woodcocks** Birds easily caught, type of stupidity.
[280] **entreatments** Conversations, interviews.
[281] **command to parley** Mere invitation to talk.
[282] **so . . . him** This much concerning him.
[283] **in few** Briefly.
[284] **brokers** Go-betweens, procurers.
[285] **dye** Color or sort.
[286] **investments** Clothes.
[287] **implorators of** Solicitors of.
[288] **Breathing** Speaking.

---

[289] **slander** Bring disgrace or reproach upon.
I.iv. [290] **wake** Stay awake, hold revel.
[291] **rouse** Carouse, drinking bout.
[292] **wassail** Carousal.
[293] **up-spring** Last and wildest dance at German merrymakings.
[294] **reels** Reels through.
[295] **Rhenish** Rhine wine.
[296] **Triumph . . . pledge.** His glorious achievement as a drinker.
[297] **to . . . born** Destined by birth to be subject to the custom in
question.
[298] **clepe** Call.
[299] **with swinish phrase** By calling us swine.
[300] **addition** Reputation.

From our achievements, though perform'd at height
The pith and marrow of our attribute.[301]
So, oft it chances in particular men,
That for some vicious mole of nature[302] in them,
As, in their birth—wherein they are not guilty,
Since nature cannot choose his origin—
By the o'ergrowth of some complexion,
Oft breaking down the pales[303] and forts of reason,   30
Or by some habit that too much o'er-leavens[304]
The form of plausive[305] manners, that these men,
Carrying, I say, the stamp of one defect,
Being nature's livery,[306] or fortune's star,[307]—
Their virtues else—be they as pure as grace,
As infinite as man may undergo—
Shall in the general censure take corruption
From that particular fault: the dram of eale[308]
Doth all the noble substance of a doubt
To his own scandal.[309]   40

HOR.:   Look, my lord, it comes!

Enter GHOST

HAM.: Angels and ministers of grace[310] defend us!
Be thou a spirit of health or goblin damn'd,
Bring with thee airs from heaven or blasts from hell,
Be thy intents wicked or charitable,
Thou comest in such a questionable[311] shape
That I will speak to thee: I'll call thee Hamlet,
King, father, royal Dane: O, answer me!
Let me not burst in ignorance; but tell
Why thy canonized[312] bones, hearsed[313] in death,   50
Have burst their cerements[314]; why the sepulchre,
Wherein we saw thee quietly inurn'd,
Hath oped his ponderous and marble jaws,
To cast thee up again. What may this mean,
That thou, dead corse, again in complete steel
Revisit'st thus the glimpses of the moon,[315]
Making night hideous; and we fools of nature[316]
So horridly to shake our disposition
With thoughts beyond the reaches of our souls?
Say, why is this? wherefore? what should we do?   60

[*Ghost beckons Hamlet.*

HOR.: It beckons you to go away with it,
       As if it some impartment[317] did desire
       To you alone.
MAR.:   Look, with what courteous action
       It waves you to a more removed[318] ground:
       But do not go with it.
HOR.:   No, by no means.
HAM.: It will not speak; then I will follow it.
HOR.: Do not, my lord.
HAM.:   Why, what should be the fear?   70
       I do not set my life at a pin's fee;
       And for my soul, what can it do to that,
       Being a thing immortal as itself?
       It waves me forth again: I'll follow it.
HOR.: What if it tempt you toward the flood, my lord,
       Or to the dreadful summit of the cliff
       That beetles o'er[319] his base into the sea,
       And there assume some other horrible form,
       Which might deprive your sovereignty of reason[320]
       And draw you into madness? think of it: 80
       The very place puts toys of desperation,[321]
       Without more motive, into every brain
       That looks so many fathoms to the sea
       And hears it roar beneath.
HAM.:   It waves me still.
       Go on; I'll follow thee.
MAR.: You shall not go, my lord.
HAM.:   Hold off your hands.
HOR.: Be ruled; you shall not go.
HAM.:   My fate cries out,   90
       And makes each petty artery in this body
       As hardy as the Nemean lion's[322] nerve.[323]
       Still am I call'd. Unhand me, gentlemen.
       By heaven, I'll make a ghost of him that lets[324] me!
       I say, away! Go on; I'll follow thee.

[*Exeunt Ghost and Hamlet.*

HOR.: He waxes desperate with imagination.
MAR.: Let's follow; 'tis not fit thus to obey him.
HOR.: Have after. To what issue[325] will this come?
MAR.: Something is rotten in the state of Denmark.
HOR.: Heaven will direct it.[326]   100
MAR.:   Nay, let's follow him. [*Exeunt.*

---

[301] **attribute** Reputation.
[302] **mole of nature** Natural blemish in one's constitution.
[303] **pales** Palings (as of a fortification).
[304] **o'er-leavens** Induces a change throughout (as yeast works in bread).
[305] **plausive** Pleasing.
[306] **nature's livery** Endowment from nature.
[307] **fortune's star** The position in which one is placed by fortune, a reference to astrology. The two phrases are aspects of the same thing.
[308] **dram of eale** Has had various interpretations, the preferred one being probably, "a dram of evil."
[309] **the dram . . . scandal** A famous crux.
[310] **ministers of grace** Messengers of God.
[311] **questionable** Inviting question or conversation.
[312] **canonized** Buried according to the canons of the church.
[313] **hearsed** Coffined.
[314] **cerements** Grave-clothes.
[315] **glimpses of the moon** The earth by night.
[316] **fools of nature** Mere men, limited to natural knowledge.

---

[317] **impartment** Communication.
[318] **removed** Remote.
[319] **beetles o'er** Overhangs threateningly.
[320] **deprive . . . reason** Take away the sovereignty of your reason. It was thought that evil spirits would sometimes assume the form of departed spirits in order to work madness in a human creature.
[321] **toys of desperation** Freakish notions of suicide.
[322] **Nemean lion's** One of the monsters slain by Hercules.
[323] **nerve** Sinew, tendon. The point is that the arteries that were carrying the spirits out into the body were functioning and were as stiff and hard as the sinews of the lion.
[324] **lets** Hinders.
[325] **issue** Outcome.
[326] **it** i.e., The outcome.

Scene V—Another Part of the Platform

(See synopsis for Act I, Scene IV.)

Enter GHOST *and* HAMLET

HAM.: Where wilt thou lead me? speak; I'll go no further. 1
GHOST: Mark me.
HAM.: I will.
GHOST: My hour is almost come,
 When I to sulphurous and tormenting flames
 Must render up myself.
HAM.: Alas, poor ghost!
GHOST: Pity me not, but lend thy serious hearing
 To what I shall unfold.
HAM.: Speak; I am bound to hear. 10
GHOST: So art thou to revenge, when thou shalt hear.
HAM.: What?
GHOST: I am thy father's spirit,
 Doom'd for a certain term to walk the night,
 And for the day confined to fast[327] in fires
 Till the foul crimes done in my days of nature
 Are burnt and purged away. But that I am forbid
 To tell the secrets of my prison-house,
 I could a tale unfold whose lightest word
 Would harrow up thy soul, freeze thy young blood, 20
 Make thy two eyes, like stars, start from their
 spheres,[328]
 Thy knotted[329] and combined[330] locks to part
 And each particular hair to stand an end,
 Like quills upon the fretful porpentine:[331]
 But this eternal blazon[332] must not be
 To ears of flesh and blood. List, list, O, list!
 If thou didst ever thy dear father love—
HAM.: O God!
GHOST: Revenge his foul and most unnatural[333] murder.
HAM.: Murder! 30
GHOST: Murder most foul, as in the best it is;
 But this most foul, strange and unnatural.
HAM.: Haste me to know 't, that I, with wings as swift
 As meditation or the thoughts of love,
 May sweep to my revenge.
GHOST: I find thee apt;
 And duller shouldst thou be than the fat weed[334]
 That roots itself in ease on Lethe wharf,[335]
 Wouldst thou not stir in this. Now, Hamlet, hear:
 'Tis given out that, sleeping in my orchard, 40
 A serpent stung me; so the whole ear of Denmark
 Is by a forged process of my death

Rankly abused: but know, thou noble youth,
 The serpent that did sting thy father's life
 Now wears his crown.
HAM.: O my prophetic soul!
 My uncle!
GHOST: Ay, that incestuous, that adulterate[336] beast,
 With witchcraft of his wit, with traitorous gifts,—
 O wicked wits and gifts, that have the power 50
 So to seduce—won to his shameful lust
 The will of my most seeming-virtuous queen:
 O Hamlet, what a falling-off was there!
 From me, whose love was of that dignity
 That it went hand in hand even with the vow
 I made to her in marriage, and to decline
 Upon a wretch whose natural gifts were poor
 To those of mine!
 But virtue, as it never will be moved,
 Though lewdness court it in a shape of heaven, 60
 So lust, though to a radiant angel link'd,
 Will sate itself in a celestial bed,
 And prey on garbage.
 But, soft! methinks I scent the morning air;
 Brief let me be. Sleeping within my orchard,
 My custom always of the afternoon,
 Upon my secure[337] hour thy uncle stole,
 With juice of cursed Hebona[338] in a vial,
 And in the porches of my ears did pour
 The leperous[339] distilment; whose effect 70
 Holds such an enmity with blood of man
 That swift as quicksilver it courses through
 The natural gates and alleys of the body,
 And with a sudden vigour it doth posset[340]
 And curd, like eager[341] droppings into milk,
 The thin and wholesome blood: so did it mine;
 And a most instant tetter bark'd about,
 Most lazar-like,[342] with vile and loathsome crust,
 All my smooth body.
 Thus was I, sleeping, by a brother's hand 80
 Of life, of crown, of queen, at once dispatch'd:[343]
 Cut off even in the blossoms of my sin,
 Unhousel'd,[344] disappointed,[345] unaneled,[346]
 No reckoning made, but sent to my account
 With all my imperfections on my head:
 O, horrible! O, horrible! most horrible![347]
 If thou hast nature in these, bear it not;
 Let not the royal bed of Denmark be

I.v. [327] **fast** Probably, do without food. It has been sometimes taken in the sense of doing general penance.
[328] **spheres** Orbits.
[329] **knotted** Perhaps intricately arranged.
[330] **combined** Tied, bound.
[331] **porpentine** Porcupine.
[332] **eternal blazon** Promulgation or proclamation of eternity, revelation of the hereafter.
[333] **unnatural** i.e., Pertaining to fratricide.
[334] **fat weed** Many suggestions have been offered as to the particular plant intended, including asphodel; probably a general reference for plants growing along rotting wharves and piles.
[335] **Lethe wharf** Bank of the river of forgetfulness in Hades.

---

[336] **adulterate** Adulterous.
[337] **secure** Confident, unsuspicious.
[338] **Hebona** Generally supposed to mean henbane, conjectured hemlock; ebenus, meaning "yew."
[339] **leperous** Causing leprosy.
[340] **posset** Coagulate, curdle.
[341] **eager** Sour, acid.
[342] **lazar-like** Leperlike.
[343] **dispatch'd** Suddenly bereft.
[344] **Unhousel'd** Without having received the sacrament.
[345] **disappointed** Unready, without equipment for the last journey.
[346] **unaneled** Without having received extreme unction.
[347] **O . . . horrible!** Many editors give this line to Hamlet; Garrick and Sir Henry Irving spoke it in that part.

A couch for luxury[348] and damned incest.
But, howsoever thou pursuest this act,   90
Taint not thy mind,[349] nor let thy soul contrive
Against thy mother aught: leave her to heaven
And to those thorns that in her bosom lodge,
To prick and sting her. Fare thee well at once!
The glow-worm shows the matin[350] to be near,
And 'gins to pale his uneffectual fire:[351]
Adieu, adieu! Hamlet, remember me.   [*Exit.*

HAM.: O all you host of heaven! O earth! what else?
And shall I couple[352] hell? O, fie! Hold, hold, my heart;
And you, my sinews, grow not instant old,   100
But bear me stiffly up. Remember thee!
Ay, thou poor ghost, while memory holds a seat
In this distracted globe.[353] Remember thee!
Yea, from the table of my memory
I'll wipe away all trivial fond records,
All saws[354] of books, all forms, all pressures[355] past,
That youth and observation copied there;
And thy commandment all alone shall live
Within the book and volume of my brain,
Unmix'd with baser matter: yes, by heaven!   110
O most pernicious woman!
O villain, villain, smiling, damned villain!
My tables,[356]—meet it is I set it down,
That one may smile, and smile, and be a villain;
At least I'm sure it may be so in Denmark: [*Writing.*
So, uncle, there you are. Now to my word[357];
It is "Adieu, adieu! remember me."
I have sworn 't.

HOR.: ⎫
MAR.: ⎭ [*Within*] My lord, my lord—

MAR.:   [*Within*] Lord Hamlet,—   120

HOR.:   [*Within*] Heaven secure him!

HAM.: So be it!

HOR.: [*Within*] Hillo, ho, ho,[358] my lord!

HAM.: Hillo, ho, ho, boy! come, bird, come.

Enter HORATIO *and* MARCELLUS

MAR.: How is 't, my noble lord?

HOR.:   What news, my lord?

HAM.: O, wonderful!

HOR.:   Good my lord, tell it.

HAM.: No; you'll reveal it.

HOR.: Not I, my lord, by heaven.   130

MAR.:   Nor I, my lord.

HAM.: How say you, then; would heart of man once
    think it?
But you'll be secret?

HOR.: ⎫
MAR.: ⎭   Ay, by heaven, my lord.

HAM.: There's ne'er a villain dwelling in all Denmark
    But he's an arrant[359] knave.

HOR.: There needs no ghost, my lord, come from the grave
    To tell us this.

HAM.:   Why, right; you are i' the right;
And so, without more circumstance at all,   140
I hold it fit that we shake hands and part:
You, as your business and desire shall point you;
For every man has business and desire,
Such as it is; and for mine own poor part,
Look you, I'll go pray.

HOR.: These are but wild and whirling words, my lord.

HAM.: I'm sorry they offend you, heartily;
Yes, 'faith, heartily.

HOR.:   There's no offence, my lord.

HAM.: Yes, by Saint Patrick,[360] but there is, Horatio,   150
And much offence too. Touching this vision here,
It is an honest[361] ghost, that let me tell you:
For your desire to know what is between us,
O'ermaster 't as you may. And now, good friends,
As you are friends, scholars and soldiers,
Give me one poor request.

HOR.: What is 't, my lord? we will.

HAM.: Never make known what you have seen to-night.

HOR.: ⎫
MAR.: ⎭ My lord, we will not.

HAM.:   Nay, but swear 't.   160

HOR.: In faith,
    My lord, not I.

MAR.:   Nor I, my lord, in faith.

HAM.: Upon my sword.

MAR.:   We have sworn, my lord, already.

HAM.: Indeed, upon my sword,[362] indeed.

GHOST: [*Beneath*] Swear.

HAM.: Ah, ha, boy! say'st thou so? art thou there,
    true-penny[363]?
Come on—you hear this fellow in the cellarage—   170
Consent to swear.

HOR.:   Propose the oath, my lord.

HAM.: Never to speak of this that you have seen,
Swear by my sword.

GHOST: [*Beneath*] Swear.

HAM.: Hic et ubique?[364] then we'll shift our ground.
Come hither, gentlemen,
And lay your hands again upon my sword:
Never to speak of this that you have heard,
Swear by my sword.

---

[348] **luxury** Lechery.
[349] **Taint . . . mind** Probably, deprave not thy character, do nothing except in the pursuit of a natural revenge.
[350] **matin** Morning.
[351] **uneffectual fire** Cold light.
[352] **couple** Add.
[353] **distracted globe** Confused head.
[354] **saws** Wise sayings.
[355] **pressures** Impressions stamped.
[356] **tables** Probably a small portable writing tablet carried at the belt.
[357] **word** Watchword.
[358] **Hillo, ho, ho** A falconer's call to a hawk in air.

---

[359] **arrant** Thoroughgoing.
[360] **Saint Patrick** St. Patrick was the keeper of purgatory and patron saint of all blunders and confusion.
[361] **honest** i.e., A real ghost, not an evil spirit.
[362] **sword** i.e., The hilt in the form of a cross.
[363] **true-penny** Good old boy, or the like.
[364] **Hic et ubique?** Here and everywhere?

GHOST: [*Beneath*] Swear.   180
HAM.: Well said, old mole! canst work i' the earth so fast?
       A worthy pioneer[365]! Once more remove, good
            friends.
HOR.: O day and night, but this is wondrous strange!
HAM.: And therefore as a stranger give it welcome.
       There are more things in heaven and earth, Horatio,
       Than are dreamt of in our philosophy.
       But come;
       Here, as before, never, so help you mercy,
       How strange or odd soe'er I bear myself,
       As I perchance hereafter shall think meet   190
       To put an antic[366] disposition on,
       That you, at such times seeing me, never shall,
       With arms encumber'd[367] thus, or this head-shake,
       Or by pronouncing of some doubtful phrase,
       As "Well, well, we know," or "We could, an if we
            would,"

_____
[365] **Pioneer** Digger, miner.
[366] **antic** Fantastic.
[367] **encumber'd** Folded or entwined.

       Or "If we list to speak," or "There be, and if they
            might,"
       Or such ambiguous giving out,[368] to note[369]
       That you know aught of me: this not to do,
       So grace and mercy at your most need help you,
       Swear.   200
GHOST: [*Beneath*] Swear.
HAM.: Rest, rest, perturbed spirit! [*They swear.*]
       So, gentlemen,
       With all my love I do commend me to you:
       And what so poor a man as Hamlet is
       May do, to express his love and friending[370] to you,
       God willing, shall not lack. Let us go in together;
       And still your fingers on your lips, I pray.
       The time is out of joint: O cursed spite,
       That ever I was born to set it right!
       Nay, come, let's go together.   [*Exeunt.* 210

_____
[368] **giving out** Profession of knowledge.
[369] **to note** To give a sign.
[370] **friending** Friendliness.

∞

Act II

Scene I—A Room in Polonius' House

*Act I has been a sort of prologue; it contains the possibilities of
which the remaining acts show the tragic development. As usual
with Shakespeare, there is a crisis or turning-point at about the
middle of the play, in the scene where* HAMLET *has a definite
opportunity of killing the* KING *and misses it (Act III, Scene III).
Up to that point we are concerned with the cause of the tragedy,
the action and reaction of the* GHOST's *injunction and* HAMLET's
*character upon each other, the puttings off, the assumed madness.
After that follows the effect; the successive fatal consequences due
to that one cause are unrolled before us.*

*   The first part of Scene I is important chiefly as showing us
at once that a considerable interval has elapsed.* LAERTES *has had
time to reach Paris and make friends there. It leads up to the more
important questions, What has become of* HAMLET *during the
interval? Is* CLAUDIUS *dead yet?*

Enter POLONIUS *and* REYNALDO

POL.: Give him this money and these notes, Reynaldo.   1
REY.: I will, my lord.
POL.: You shall do marvellous wisely, good Reynaldo,
       Before you visit him, to make inquire
       Of his behaviour.
REY.:   My lord, I did intend it.
POL.: Marry, well said; very well said. Look you, sir,
       Inquire me first what Danskers[371] are in Paris;

_____
II.i. [371] **Danskers** Danke was a common variant for "Denmark";
hence "Dane."

       And how, and who, what means, and where they
            keep,[372]
       What company, at what expense; and finding   10
       By this encompassment[373] and drift[374] of question
       That they do know my son, come you more nearer
       Than your particular demands will touch it.[375]
       Take[376] you, as 't were, some distant knowledge of
            him;
       As thus, "I know his father and his friends,
       And in part him": do you mark this, Reynaldo?
REY.: Ay, very well, my lord.
POL.: "And in part him; but" you may say "not well:
       But, if 't be he I mean, he's very wild;
       Addicted so and so": and there put on[377] him   20
       What forgeries[378] you please: marry, none so rank
       As may dishonour him; take heed of that;
       But, sir, such wanton,[379] wild and usual slips
       As are companions noted and most known
       To youth and liberty.
REY.:   As gaming, my lord.

_____
[372] **keep** Dwell.
[373] **encompassment** Roundabout talking.
[374] **drift** Gradual approach or course.
[375] **come . . . it** i.e., You will find out more this way than by asking pointed questions.
[376] **Take** Assume, pretend.
[377] **put on** Impute to.
[378] **forgeries** Invented tales.
[379] **wanton** Sportive, unrestrained.

POL.: Ay, or drinking, fencing,[380] swearing, quarrelling,
    Drabbing:[381] you may go so far.
REY.: My lord, that would dishonour him.
POL.: 'Faith, no; as you may season it in the charge.   30
    You must not put another scandal on him,
    That he is open to incontinency[382];
    That's not my meaning: but breathe his faults so
      quaintly[383]
    That they may seem the taints of liberty,[384]
    The flash and outbreak of a fiery mind,
    A savageness in unreclaimed[385] blood,
    Of general assault.[386]
REY.:   But, my good lord,—
POL.: Wherefore should you do this?
REY.:   Ay, my lord,   40
    I would know that.
POL.:   Marry, sir, here's my drift;
    And, I believe, it is a fetch of warrant:[387]
    You laying these slight sullies on my son,
    As 't were a thing a little soil'd i' the working,
    Mark you,
    Your party in converse, him you would sound,
    Having ever[388] seen in the prenominate[389] crimes
    The youth you breathe of guilty, be assured
    He closes with you in this consequence[390];   50
    "Good sir," or so, or "friend," or "gentleman,"
    According to the phrase or the addition
    Of man and country.
REY.:   Very good, my lord.
POL.: And then, sir, does he this—he does—
    What was I about to say? By the mass, I was about to
      say something: where did I leave?
REY.: At "closes in the consequence," at "friend or so,"
    and "gentleman."
POL.: At "closes in the consequence," ay, marry;
    He closes thus: "I know the gentleman;
    I saw him yesterday, or t' other day,   60
    Or then, or then; with such, or such; and, as you say,
    There was a' gaming; there o'ertook in 's rouse[391];
    There falling out at tennis": or perchance,
    "I saw him enter such a house of sale,"
    Videlicet,[392] a brothel, or so forth.
    See you now;
    Your bait of falsehood takes this carp of truth:
    And thus do we of wisdom and of reach,[393]

With windlasses[394] and with assays of bias,[395]
By indirections[396] find directions[397] out: 70
So by my former lecture[398] and advice,
Shall you my son. You have me, have you not?
REY.: My lord, I have.
POL.:   God be wi' you; fare you well.
REY.: Good my lord!
POL.: Observe his inclination in yourself.[399]
REY.: I shall, my lord.
POL.: And let him ply his music.[400]
REY.:   Well, my lord.
POL.: Farewell!   [*Exit Reynaldo.*   80

Enter OPHELIA

    How now, Ophelia! what's the matter?
OPH.: O, my lord, my lord, I have been so affrighted!
POL.: With what, i' the name of God?
OPH.: My lord, as I was sewing in my closet,[401]
    Lord Hamlet, with his doublet[402] all unbraced[403];
    No hat upon his head; his stockings foul'd,
    Ungarter'd, and down-gyved[404] to his ancle;
    Pale as his shirt; his knees knocking each other;
    And with a look so piteous in purport
    As if he had been loosed out of hell   90
    To speak of horrors,—he comes before me.
POL.: Mad for thy love?
OPH.:   My lord, I do not know;
    But truly, I do fear it.
POL.:   What said he?
OPH.: He took me by the wrist and held me hard;
    Then goes he to the length of all his arm;
    And, with his other hand thus o'er his brow,
    He falls to such perusal of my face
    As he would draw it. Long stay'd he so;   100
    At last, a little shaking of mine arm
    And thrice his head thus waving up and down,
    He raised a sigh so piteous and profound
    As it did seem to shatter all his bulk[405]
    And end his being: that done, he lets me go:
    And, with his head over his shoulder turn'd,
    He seem'd to find his way without his eyes;
    For out o' doors he went without their helps,
    And, to the last, bended their light on me.
POL.: Come, go with me: I will go seek the king.   110
    This is the very ecstasy of love,

---

[380] **fencing** Indicative of the ill repute of professional fencers and fencing schools in Elizabethan times.
[381] **Drabbing** Associated with immoral women.
[382] **incontinency** Habitual loose behavior.
[383] **quaintly** Delicately, ingeniously.
[384] **taints of liberty** Blemishes due to freedom.
[385] **unreclaimed** Untamed.
[386] **general assault** Tendency that assails all untrained youth.
[387] **fetch of warrant** Clever trick.
[388] **ever** At any time.
[389] **prenominate** Before-mentioned.
[390] **closes . . . consequence** Agrees with you in this conclusion.
[391] **o'ertook in's rouse** Overcome by drink.
[392] **Videlicet** Namely.
[393] **reach** Capacity, ability.

[394] **windlasses** i.e., Circuitous paths.
[395] **assays of bias** Attempts that resemble the course of the bowl, which, being weighted on one side, has a curving motion.
[396] **indirections** Devious courses.
[397] **directions** Straight courses, i.e., the truth.
[398] **lecture** Admonition.
[399] **Observe . . . yourself.** In your own person, not by spies; or conform your own conduct to his inclination; or test him by studying yourself.
[400] **ply his music** Probably to be taken literally.
[401] **closet** Private chamber.
[402] **doublet** Close-fitting coat.
[403] **unbraced** Unfastened.
[404] **down-gyved** Fallen to the ankles (like gyves, or fetters).
[405] **bulk** Body.

Whose violent property[406] fordoes[407] itself
And leads the will to desperate undertakings
As oft as any passion under heaven
That does afflict our natures. I am sorry.
What, have you given him any hard words of late?

OPH.: No, my good lord, but, as you did command,
I did repel his letters and denied
His access to me.

POL.:   That hath made him mad.   120
I am sorry that with better heed and judgement
I had not quoted[408] him: I fear'd he did but trifle.
And meant to wreck thee; but, beshrew[409] my
    jealousy!
By heaven, it is as proper to our age
To cast beyond[410] ourselves in our opinions
As it is common for the younger sort
To lack discretion. Come, go we to the king:
This must be known; which, being kept close, might
    move
More grief to hide than hate to utter love.[411]   [*Exeunt.*

Scene II—A Room in the Castle

This long scene contains two main dramatic motives. In the latter part of it, from the entry of the PLAYERS, *we get the gradual approach to that crisis of the action that is brought about by the play scene. The rest gives us, so to speak, a summary of the mental condition of* HAMLET *and of his attitude to the court during the months of delay. The points to notice are (1) the assumption of madness, which deceives* GERTRUDE, OPHELIA, POLONIUS, ROSENCRANTZ, *and* GUILDENSTERN, *though the* KING, *who has a better key to* HAMLET's *behavior than any of these, is not without his suspicions; (2) the delight that* HAMLET *takes in the opportunity thus afforded him of venting irony upon his enemies, and especially upon* POLONIUS; (3) *his invariable tendency to pass from the consideration of his own position into general satire and invective upon society. It is to be observed that* HAMLET *is not always acting the madman; he does so, for instance, with* ROSENCRANTZ *and* GUILDENSTERN *only when he begins to suspect their good faith. And further, the pretense is easy for him. It requires only a slight exaggeration of his natural self. His thoughts and feelings, especially under conditions of nervous excitement, are always on a plane hardly intelligible to ordinary mortals. To appear mad he has only to relax the control that he normally exerts.*

Enter KING, QUEEN, ROSENCRANTZ, GUILDENSTERN, *and*
ATTENDANTS

KING: Welcome, dear Rosencrantz and Guildenstern!   1
Moreover that[412] we much did long to see you,
The need we have to use you did provoke
Our hasty sending. Something have you heard
Of Hamlet's transformation; so call it,

Since nor the exterior nor the inward man
Resembles that it was. What it should be,
More than his father's death, that thus hath put him
So much from the understanding of himself,
I cannot dream of: I entreat you both,   10
That, being of so young days[413] brought up with him,
And since so neighbour'd to his youth and humour,
That you vouchsafe your rest[414] here in our court
Some little time: so by your companies
To draw him on to pleasures, and to gather,
So much as from occasion you may glean,
Whether aught, to us unknown, afflicts him thus,
That, open'd, lies within our remedy.

QUEEN: Good gentlemen, he hath much talk'd of you;
And sure I am two men there are not living   20
To whom he more adheres. If it will please you
To show us so much gentry[415] and good will
As to expend your time with us awhile,
For the supply and profit[416] of our hope,
Your visitation shall receive such thanks
As fits a king's remembrance.

ROS.:   Both your majesties
Might, by the sovereign power you have of us,
Put your dread pleasures more into command
Than to entreaty.   30

GUIL.:   But we both obey,
And here give up ourselves, in the full bent[417]
To lay our service freely at your feet,
To be commanded.

KING: Thanks, Rosencrantz and gentle Guildenstern.

QUEEN: Thanks, Guildenstern and gentle Rosencrantz:
And I beseech you instantly to visit
My too much changed son. Go, some of you,
And bring these gentlemen where Hamlet is.

GUIL.: Heavens make our presence and our practices   40
Pleasant and helpful to him!

QUEEN: Ay, amen!

[*Exeunt Rosencrantz, Guildenstern, and some Attendants.*

Enter POLONIUS

POL.: The ambassadors from Norway, my good lord,
Are joyfully return'd.

KING: Thou still hast been the father of good news.

POL.: Have I, my lord? I assure my good liege,
I hold my duty, as I hold my soul,
Both to my God and to my gracious king:
And I do think, or else this brain of mine
Hunts not the trail of policy so sure   50
As it hath used to do, that I have found
The very cause of Hamlet's lunacy.

KING: O, speak of that; that do I long to hear.

POL.: Give first admittance to the ambassadors;
My news shall be the fruit to that great feast.

---

[406] **property** Nature.
[407] **fordoes** Destroys.
[408] **quoted** Observed.
[409] **beshrew my jealousy** Curse my suspicions.
[410] **cast beyond** Overshoot, miscalculate.
[411] **might . . . love** i.e., I might cause more grief to others by hiding the knowledge of Hamlet's love to Ophelia than hatred to me and mine by telling of it.
II.ii. [412] **Moreover that** Besides the fact that.

---

[413] **of so young days** From such early youth.
[414] **vouchsafe your rest** Please to stay.
[415] **gentry** Courtesy.
[416] **supply and profit** Aid and successful outcome.
[417] **in . . . bent** To the utmost degree of our mental capacity.

KING: Thyself do grace to them, and bring them in.

                          [*Exit Polonius.*

He tells me, my dear Gertrude, he hath found
The head and source of all your son's distemper.
QUEEN: I doubt[418] it is no other but the main[419];
    His father's death, and our o'erhasty marriage.   60
KING: Well, we shall sift him.

Re-enter POLONIUS, *with* VOLTIMAND *and* CORNELIUS

                   Welcome, my good friends!
Say, Voltimand, what from our brother Norway?
VOLT.: Most fair return of greetings and desires.
    Upon our first, he sent out to suppress
    His nephew's levies; which to him appear'd
    To be a preparation 'gainst the Polack;
    But, better look'd into, he truly found
    It was against your highness: whereat grieved,
    That so his sickness, age and impotence   70
    Was falsely borne in hand,[420] sends out arrests
    On Fortinbras; which he, in brief, obeys;
    Receives rebuke from Norway, and in fine[421]
    Makes vow before his uncle never more
    To give the assay[422] of arms against your majesty.
    Whereon old Norway, overcome with joy,
    Gives him three thousand crowns in annual fee,
    And his commission to employ those soldiers,
    So levied as before, against the Polack:
    With an entreaty, herein further shown,   80

                          [*Giving a paper.*

    That it might please you to give quiet pass
    Through your dominions for this enterprise,
    On such regards of safety and allowance[423]
    As therein are set down.
KING: It likes[424] us well;
    And at our more consider'd[425] time we'll read,
    Answer, and think upon this business.
    Meantime we thank you for your well-took labour:
    Go to your rest; at night we'll feast together: 90
    Most welcome home!

                [*Exeunt Voltimand and Cornelius.*

POL.:   This business is well ended.
    My liege, and madam, to expostulate
    What majesty should be, what duty is,
    Why day is day, night night, and time is time,
    Were nothing but to waste night, day and time.
    Therefore, since brevity is the soul of wit,[426]
    And tediousness the limbs and outward flourishes,[427]

I will be brief: your noble son is mad:
    Mad call I it; for, to define true madness,
    What is 't but to be nothing else but mad?   100
    But let that go.
QUEEN: More matter, with less art.
POL.: Madam, I swear I use no art at all.
    That he is mad, 'tis true: 'tis true 'tis pity;
    And pity 'tis 'tis true: a foolish figure[428];
    But farewell it, for I will use no art.
    Mad let us grant him, then: and now remains
    That we find out the cause of this effect,
    Or rather say, the cause of this defect,
    For this effect defective comes by cause: 110
    Thus it remains, and the remainder thus.
    Perpend.[429]
    I have a daughter—have while she is mine—
    Who, in her duty and obedience, mark,
    Hath given me this: now gather, and surmise. [*Reads.*
    "To the celestial and my soul's idol, the most
        beautified Ophelia,"—
    That's an ill phrase, a vile phrase; "beautified" is a
        vile phrase: but you shall hear. Thus: [*Reads.*
    "In her excellent white bosom, these, &c."
QUEEN: Came this from Hamlet to her?
POL.: Good madam, stay awhile; I will be faithful.   [*Reads.* 120
    "Doubt thou the stars are fire;
      Doubt that the sun doth move;
     Doubt truth to be a liar;
      But never doubt I love.
    "O dear Ophelia, I am ill at these numbers[430]; I have
      not art to reckon[431] my groans: but that I love
      thee best,
    O most best, believe it. Adieu.
        "Thine evermore, most dear lady, whilst
              this machine[432] is to him, HAMLET."
    This, in obedience, hath my daughter shown me,
    And more above,[433] hath his solicitings,   130
    As they fell out[434] by time, by means[435] and place,
    All given to mine ear.
KING: But how hath she
    Received his love?
POL.:   What do you think of me?
KING: As of a man faithful and honourable.
POL.: I would fain prove so. But what might you think,
    When I had seen this hot love on the wing—
    As I perceived it, I must tell you that,
    Before my daughter told me—what might you,   140
    Or my dear majesty your queen here, think,
    If I had play'd the desk or table-book,[436]

---

[418] **doubt** Fear.
[419] **main** Chief point, principal concern.
[420] **borne in hand** Deluded.
[421] **in fine** In the end.
[422] **assay** Assault, trial (of arms).
[423] **safety and allowance** Pledges of safety to the country and terms of permission for the troops to pass.
[424] **likes** Pleases.
[425] **consider'd** Suitable for deliberation.
[426] **wit** Sound sense or judgment.
[427] **flourishes** Ostentation, embellishments.

---

[428] **figure** Figure of speech.
[429] **Perpend** Consider.
[430] **ill . . . numbers** Unskilled at writing verses.
[431] **reckon** Number metrically, scan.
[432] **machine** Bodily frame.
[433] **more above** Moreover.
[434] **fell out** Occurred.
[435] **means** Opportunities (of access).
[436] **play'd . . . table-book** i.e., Remained shut up, concealed this information.

Or given my heart a winking,[437] mute and dumb,
Or look'd upon this love with idle sight;
What might you think? No, I went round to work,
And my young mistress thus I did bespeak:[438]
"Lord Hamlet is a prince, out of thy star[439];
This must not be": and then I prescripts gave her,
That she should lock herself from his resort,
Admit no messengers, receive no tokens.   150
Which done, she took the fruits of my advice;
And he, repulsed—a short tale to make—
Fell into a sadness, then into a fast,
Thence to a watch,[440] thence into a weakness,
Thence to a lightness,[441] and, by this declension,[442]
Into the madness wherein now he raves,
And all we mourn for.

KING: Do you think 'tis this?
QUEEN: It may be, very likely.
POL.: Hath there been such a time—I'd fain know that—   160
       That I have positively said " 'Tis so,"
       When it proved otherwise?
KING: Not that I know.
POL.: [*Pointing to his head and shoulder*] Take this from this,
       if this be otherwise:
       If circumstances lead me, I will find
       Where truth is hid, though it were hid indeed
       Within the centre.[443]
KING: How may we try it further?
POL.: You know, sometimes he walks four hours together
       Here in the lobby.   170
QUEEN: So he does indeed.
POL.: At such a time I'll loose my daughter to him:
       Be you and I behind an arras[444] then;
       Mark the encounter: if he love her not
       And be not from his reason fall'n thereon,[445]
       Let me be no assistant for a state,
       But keep a farm and carters.
KING: We will try it.
QUEEN: But, look, where sadly the poor wretch comes
       reading.
POL.: Away, I do beseech you, both away: 180
       I'll board[446] him presently.

                   [*Exeunt King, Queen, and Attendants.*

Enter HAMLET, *reading*

             O, give me leave:
       How does my good Lord Hamlet?
HAM.: Well, God-a-mercy.
POL.: Do you know me, my lord?

HAM.: Excellent well; you are a fishmonger.[447]
POL.: Not I, my lord.
HAM.: Then I would you were so honest a man.
POL.: Honest, my lord!
HAM.: Ay, sir; to be honest, as this world goes, is to be one   190
       man picked out of ten thousand.
POL.: That's very true, my lord.
HAM.: For if the sun breed maggots in a dead dog, being
       a god kissing carrion,[448]—Have you a daughter?
POL.: I have, my lord.
HAM.: Let her not walk i' the sun:[449] conception[450] is a
       blessing: but not as your daughter may conceive.
       Friend, look to 't.
POL.: [*Aside*] How say you by[451] that? Still harping on my
       daughter: yet he knew me not at first; he said I was a   200
       fishmonger: he is far gone, far gone: and truly in my
       youth I suffered much extremity for love; very near
       this. I'll speak to him again. What do you read, my
       lord?
HAM.: Words, words, words.
POL.: What is the matter,[452] my lord?
HAM.: Between who?[453]
POL.: I mean, the matter that you read, my lord.
HAM.: Slanders, sir: for the satirical rogue says here
       that old men have grey beards, that their faces are   210
       wrinkled, their eyes purging[454] thick amber and
       plum-tree gum and that they have a plentiful lack
       of wit, together with most weak hams: all which, sir,
       though I most powerfully and potently believe, yet
       I hold it not honesty[455] to have it thus set down, for
       yourself, sir, should be old as I am, if like a crab you
       could go backward.
POL.: [*Aside*] Though this be madness, yet there is method
       in 't. Will you walk out of the air, my lord?
HAM.: Into my grave.   220
POL.: Indeed, that is out o' the air. [*Aside*] How pregnant
       sometimes his replies are! a happiness[456] that often
       madness hits on, which reason and sanity could
       not so prosperously[457] be delivered of. I will leave
       him, and suddenly contrive the means of meeting
       between him and my daughter.—My honourable
       lord, I will most humbly take my leave of you.
HAM.: You cannot, sir, take from me any thing that I will
       more willingly part withal: except my life, except
       my life, except my life.   230

---

[437] **given . . . winking** Given my heart a signal to keep silent.
[438] **bespeak** Address.
[439] **out . . . star** Above thee in position.
[440] **watch** State of sleeplessness.
[441] **lightness** Lightheartedness.
[442] **declension** Decline, deterioration.
[443] **centre** Middle point of the earth.
[444] **arras** Hanging, tapestry.
[445] **thereon** On that account.
[446] **board** Accost.

---

[447] **fishmonger** An opprobrious expression meaning "bawd,"
"procurer."
[448] **god kissing carrion** In mythology, the sun was thought to be
a god. Hamlet's coarse imagery shows that a disgusting thing
can arise from a seemingly beneficial source—a veiled attack on
Polonius and his hypocrisy.
[449] **i' the sun** In the sunshine of princely favors.
[450] **conception** Quibble on "understanding" and "pregnancy."
[451] **by** Concerning.
[452] **matter** Substance.
[453] **Between who?** Hamlet deliberately takes matter as meaning
"basis of dispute."
[454] **purging** Discharging.
[455] **honesty** Decency.
[456] **happiness** Felicity of expression.
[457] **prosperously** Successfully.

POL.: Fare you well, my lord.

HAM.: These tedious old fools!

Enter ROSENCRANTZ *and* GUILDENSTERN

POL.: You go to seek the Lord Hamlet; there he is.

ROS.: [*To* POLONIUS] God save you, sir!   [*Exit Polonius.*

GUIL.: My honoured lord!

ROS.: My most dear lord!

HAM.: My excellent good friends! How dost thou, Guildenstern? Ah, Rosencrantz! Good lads, how do ye both?

ROS.: As the indifferent[458] children of the earth.   240

GUIL.: Happy, in that we are not over-happy;
On fortune's cap we are not the very button.

HAM.: Nor the soles of her shoe?

ROS.: Neither, my lord.

HAM.: Then you live about her waist, or in the middle of her favours? What's the news?

ROS.: None, my lord, but that the world's grown honest.

HAM.: Then is doomsday near: but your news is not true. Let me question more in particular: what have you, my good friends, deserved at the hands of fortune, that she sends you to prison hither?   250

GUIL.: Prison, my lord!

HAM.: Denmark's a prison.

ROS.: Then is the world one.

HAM.: A goodly one; in which there are many confines,[459] wards and dungeons, Denmark being one o' the worst.

ROS.: We think not so, my lord.

HAM.: Why, then, 'tis none to you; for there is nothing either good or bad, but thinking makes it so: to me it is a prison.   260

ROS.: Why then, your ambition makes it one; 'tis too narrow for your mind.

HAM.: O God, I could be bounded in a nutshell and count myself a king of infinite space, were it not that I have bad dreams.

GUIL.: Which dreams indeed are ambition, for the very substance of the ambitious[460] is merely the shadow of a dream.

HAM.: A dream itself is but a shadow.

ROS.: Truly, and I hold ambition of so airy and light a quality that it is but a shadow's shadow.   270

HAM.: Then are our beggars bodies, and our monarchs and outstretched heroes the beggars' shadows. Shall we to the court? for, by my fay,[461] I cannot reason.[462]

ROS.:
GUIL.: } We'll wait upon you.

HAM.: No such matter: I will not sort you with the rest of my servants, for, to speak to you like an honest man, I am most dreadfully attended. But, in the beaten way of friendship,[463] what make you at Elsinore?   280

ROS.: To visit you, my lord; no other occasion.

HAM.: Beggar that I am, I am even poor in thanks; but I thank you: and sure, dear friends, my thanks are too dear a[464] halfpenny. Were you not sent for? Is it your own inclining? Is it a free visitation? Come, deal justly with me: come, come; nay, speak.

GUIL.: What should we say, my lord?

HAM.: Why, any thing, but to the purpose. You were sent for; and there is a kind of confession in your looks which your modesties have not craft enough to colour: I know the good king and queen have sent for you.   290

ROS.: To what end, my lord?

HAM.: That you must teach me. But let me conjure[465] you, by the rights of our fellowship, by the consonancy of our youth,[466] by the obligation of our ever-preserved love, and by what more dear a better proposer[467] could charge you withal, be even and direct with me, whether you were sent for, or no?

ROS.: [*Aside to* GUIL.] What say you?   300

HAM.: [*Aside*] Nay, then, I have an eye of you.—If you love me, hold not off.

GUIL.: My lord, we were sent for.

HAM.: I will tell you why; so shall my anticipation prevent your discovery,[468] and your secrecy to the king and queen moult no feather. I have of late—but wherefore I know not—lost all my mirth, forgone all custom of exercises; and indeed it goes so heavily with my disposition that this goodly frame, the earth, seems to me a sterile promontory, this   310 most excellent canopy, the air, look you, this brave o'erhanging firmament, this majestical roof fretted[469] with golden fire, why, it appears no other thing to me than a foul and pestilent congregation of vapours. What a piece of work is a man! how noble in reason! how infinite in faculty[470]! In form and moving how express[471] and admirable! in action how like an angel! in apprehension[472] how like a god! the beauty of the world! the paragon of animals! And yet, to me, what is this quintessence[473] of dust? man delights not me: 320 no, nor woman neither, though by your smiling you seem to say so.

ROS.: My lord, there was no such stuff in my thoughts.

HAM.: Why did you laugh then, when I said "man delights not me"?

ROS.: To think, my lord, if you delight not in man, what lenten[474] entertainment the players shall receive from

---

[458] **indifferent** Ordinary.
[459] **confines** Places of confinement.
[460] **very . . . ambitious** That seemingly most substantial thing that the ambitious pursue.
[461] **fay** Faith.
[462] **reason** Argue.
[463] **in the . . . friendship** As a matter of course among friends.

[464] **a** i.e., At a.
[465] **conjure** Adjure, entreat.
[466] **consonancy of our youth** The fact that we are of the same age.
[467] **better proposer** One more skillful in finding proposals.
[468] **prevent your discovery** Forestall your disclosure.
[469] **fretted** Adorned.
[470] **faculty** Capacity.
[471] **express** Well-framed (?), exact (?).
[472] **apprehension** Understanding.
[473] **quintessence** The fifth essence of ancient philosophy, supposed to be the substance of the heavenly bodies and to be latent in all things.
[474] **lenten** Meager.

you: we coted[475] them on the way; and hither are they coming, to offer you service.

HAM.: He that plays the king shall be welcome; His majesty shall have tribute of me; the adventurous knight shall use his foil and target[476]; the lover shall not sigh gratis; the humorous man[477] shall end his part in peace; the clown shall make those laugh whose lungs are tickle o' the sere[478]; and the lady shall say her mind freely, or the blank verse shall halt for 't.[479] What players are they? 330

ROS.: Even those you were wont to take delight in, the tragedians of the city.

HAM.: How chances it they travel? their residence,[480] both in reputation and profit, was better both ways. 340

ROS.: I think their inhibition[481] comes by the means of the late innovation.[482]

HAM.: Do they hold the same estimation they did when I was in the city? are they so followed?

ROS.: No, indeed, are they not.

HAM.: How[483] comes it? do they grow rusty?

ROS.: Nay, their endeavour keeps in the wonted pace: but there is, sir, an aery[484] of children, little eyases,[485] that cry out on the top of question,[486] and are most tyrannically[487] clapped for 't: these are now the fashion, and so berattle[488] the common stages[489]—so they call them—that many wearing rapiers[490] are afraid of goose-quills[491] and dare scarce come thither. 350

HAM.: What, are they children? who maintains 'em? how are they escoted[492]? Will they pursue the quality[493] no longer than they can sing[494]? will they not say afterwards, if they should grow themselves to common[495] players—as it is most like, if their means

are no better—their writers do them wrong, to make them exclaim against their own succession[496]? 360

ROS.: 'Faith, there has been much to do on both sides; and the nation holds it no sin to tarre[497] them to controversy: there was, for a while, no money bid for argument,[498] unless the poet and the player went to cuffs[499] in the question.[500]

HAM.: Is 't possible?

GUIL.: O, there has been much throwing about of brains.

HAM.: Do the boys carry it away[501]?

ROS.: Ay, that they do, my lord; Hercules and his load[502] too. 370

HAM.: It is not very strange; for mine uncle is king of Denmark, and those that would make mows[503] at him while my father lived, give twenty, forty, fifty an hundred ducats[504] a-piece for his picture in little.[505] 'Sblood, there is something in this more than natural, if philosophy could find it out. [*Flourish of trumpets within.*]

GUIL.: There are the players.

HAM.: Gentlemen, you are welcome to Elsinore. Your hands, come then: the appurtenance of welcome is fashion and ceremony: let me comply[506] with you in this garb,[507] lest my extent[508] to the players, which, I tell you, must show fairly outward, should more appear like entertainment than yours. You are welcome: but my uncle-father and aunt-mother are deceived. 380

GUIL.: In what, my dear lord?

HAM.: I am but mad north-north-west:[509] when the wind is southerly I know a hawk from a handsaw.[510]

Re-enter POLONIUS

POL.: Well be with you, gentlemen! 390

HAM.: Hark you, Guildenstern; and you too: at each ear a hearer: that great baby you see there is not yet out of his swaddling-clouts.[511]

ROS.: Happily he's the second time come to them; for they say an old man is twice a child.

---

[475] **coted** Overtook and passed beyond.
[476] **foil and target** Sword and shield.
[477] **humorous man** Actor who takes the part of the humor characters.
[478] **tickle o' the sere** Easy on the trigger.
[479] **the lady . . . for 't** The lady (fond of talking) shall have opportunity to talk, blank verse or no blank verse.
[480] **residence** Remaining in one place.
[481] **inhibition** Formal prohibition (from acting plays in the city or, possibly, at court).
[482] **innovation** The new fashion in satirical plays performed by boy actors in the "private" theaters.
[483] **How . . .** Here begins the famous passage dealing with the War of the Theatres (1599–1602)—namely, the rivalry between the children's companies and the adult actors.
[484] **aery** Nest.
[485] **eyases** Young hawks.
[486] **cry . . . question** Speak in a high key dominating conversation; clamor forth the height of controversy; probably "excel"; perhaps intended to decry leaders of the dramatic profession.
[487] **tyrannically** Outrageously.
[488] **berattle** Berate.
[489] **common stages** Public theaters.
[490] **many wearing rapiers** Many men of fashion, who were afraid to patronize the common players for fear of being satirized by the poets who wrote for the children.
[491] **goose-quills** i.e., Pens of satirists.
[492] **escoted** Maintained.
[493] **quality** Acting profession.
[494] **no longer . . . sing** i.e., Until their voices change.
[495] **common** Regular, adult.

---

[496] **succession** Future careers.
[497] **tarre** Set on (as dogs).
[498] **argument** Probably, plot for a play.
[499] **went to cuffs** Came to blows.
[500] **question** Controversy.
[501] **carry it away** Win the day.
[502] **Hercules . . . load** Regarded as an allusion to the sign of the Globe Theatre, which was Hercules bearing the world on his shoulder.
[503] **mows** Grimaces.
[504] **ducats** Gold coins worth 9s. 4d.
[505] **in little** In miniature.
[506] **comply** Observe the formalities of courtesy.
[507] **garb** Manner.
[508] **extent** Showing of kindness.
[509] **I am . . . north-north-west** I am only partly mad, i.e., in only one point of the compass.
[510] **handsaw** A proposed reading of hernshaw would mean "heron"; handsaw may be an early corruption of hernshaw. Another view regards hawk as the variant of hack, a tool of the pickax type, and handsaw as a saw operated by hand.
[511] **swaddling-clouts** Clothes in which to wrap a newborn baby.

HAM.: I will prophesy he comes to tell me of the players; mark it. You say right, sir: o' Monday morning[512]; 'twas so indeed.

POL.: My lord, I have news to tell you.

HAM.: My lord, I have news to tell you. When Roscius[513] was an actor in Rome, 400

POL.: The actors are come hither, my lord.

HAM.: Buz, buz![514]

POL.: Upon mine honour,—

HAM.: Then came each actor on his ass,—

POL.: The best actors in the world, either for tragedy, comedy, history, pastoral, pastoral-comical, historical-pastoral, tragical-historical, tragical-comical-historical-pastoral, scene individable,[515] or poem unlimited:[516] Seneca[517] cannot be too heavy, 410 nor Plautus[518] too light. For the law of writ and the liberty,[519] these are the only men.

HAM.: O Jephthah, judge of Israel,[520] what a treasure hadst thou!

POL.: What a treasure had he, my lord?

HAM.: Why,
> "One fair daughter, and no more,
> The which he loved passing[521] well."

POL.: [*Aside*] Still on my daughter.

HAM.: Am I not i' the right, old Jephthah? 420

POL.: If you call me Jephthah, my lord, I have a daughter that I love passing well.

HAM.: Nay, that follows not.

POL.: What follows, then, my lord?

HAM.: Why,
> "As by lot, God wot,"

and then, you know,
> "It came to pass, as most like[522] it was,"—

the first row[523] of the pious chanson[524] will show you
more; for look, where my abridgement[525] comes. 430

Enter four or five PLAYERS

You are welcome, masters; welcome, all. I am glad to see thee well. Welcome, good friends. O, my old friend! thy face is valanced[526] since I saw thee last: comest thou to beard me in Denmark? What, my young lady and mistress! By 'r lady, your ladyship is nearer to heaven than when I saw you last, by the altitude of a chopine.[527] Pray God, your voice, like a piece of uncurrent[528] gold, be not cracked within the ring.[529] Masters, you are all welcome. We'll e'en to 't like French falconers, fly at any thing we see: we'll 440 have a speech straight: come, give us a taste of your quality; come, a passionate speech.

FIRST PLAYER: What speech, my lord?

HAM.: I heard thee speak me a speech once, but it was never acted; or, if it was, not above once; for the play, I remember, pleased not the million; 'twas caviare to the general:[530] but it was—as I received it, and others, whose judgements in such matters cried in the top of[531] mine—an excellent play, well digested in the scenes, set down with as much modesty as 450 cunning.[532] I remember, one said there were no sallets[533] in the lines to make the matter savoury, nor no matter in the phrase that might indict[534] the author of affectation; but called it an honest method, as wholesome as sweet, and by very much more handsome than fine.[535] One speech in it I chiefly loved: 'twas Aeneas' tale to Dido[536]; and thereabout of it especially, where he speaks of Priam's slaughter: if it live in your memory, begin at this line: let me see, let me see— 460
> "The rugged Pyrrhus,[537] like the Hyrcanian beast,"[538]

—it is not so:—it begins with Pyrrhus:—
> "The rugged Pyrrhus, he whose sable arms,
> Black as his purpose, did the night resemble
> When he lay couched in the ominous horse,[539]
> Hath now this dread and black complexion smear'd
> With heraldry more dismal; head to foot
> Now is he total gules[540]; horridly trick'd[541]
> With blood of fathers mothers, daughters, sons,
> Baked and impasted[542] with the parching streets, 470
> That lend a tyrannous and damned light
> To their lord's murder: roasted in wrath and fire,

---

[512] **o' Monday morning** Said to mislead Polonius.
[513] **Roscius** A famous Roman actor.
[514] **Buz, buz!** An interjection used at Oxford to denote stale news.
[515] **scene individable** A play observing the unity of place.
[516] **poem unlimited** A play disregarding the unities of time and place.
[517] **Seneca** Writer of Latin tragedies, model of early Elizabethan writers of tragedy.
[518] **Plautus** Writer of Latin comedy.
[519] **law . . . liberty** Pieces written according to rules and without rules, i.e., "classical" and "romantic" dramas.
[520] **Jephthah . . . Israel** Jephthah had to sacrifice his daughter (see Judges 11).
[521] **passing** Surpassingly.
[522] **like** Probable.
[523] **row** Stanza.
[524] **chanson** Ballad.
[525] **abridgement comes** Opportunity comes for cutting short the conversation.
[526] **valanced** Fringed (with a beard).

[527] **chopine** Kind of shoe raised by the thickness of the heel; worn in Italy, particularly in Venice.
[528] **uncurrent** Not passable as lawful coinage.
[529] **cracked within the ring** In the center of coins were rings enclosing the sovereign's head; if the coin was cracked within this ring, it was unfit for currency.
[530] **caviare to the general** Not relished by the multitude.
[531] **cried in the top of** Spoke with greater authority than.
[532] **cunning** Skill.
[533] **sallets** Salads: here, spicy improprieties.
[534] **indict** Convict.
[535] **as wholesome . . . fine** Its beauty was not that of elaborate ornament, but that of order and proportion.
[536] **Aeneas' tale to Dido** The lines recited by the player are imitated from Marlowe and Nashe's *Dido, Queen of Carthage*. They are written in such a way that the conventionality of the play within a play is raised above that of ordinary drama.
[537] **Pyrrhus** A Greek hero in the Trojan War.
[538] **Hyrcanian beast** The tiger (see *Aeneid* in Chapter 5, Volume I).
[539] **ominous horse** Trojan horse.
[540] **gules** Red, a heraldic term.
[541] **trick'd** Spotted, smeared.
[542] **impasted** Made into a paste.

And thus o'er-sized[543] with coagulate gore,
With eyes like carbuncles, the hellish Pyrrhus
Old grandsire Priam seeks."
So, proceed you.

POL.: 'Fore God, my lord, well spoken, with good accent and good discretion.

FIRST PLAYER: "Anon he finds him
Striking too short at Greeks; his antique sword,   480
Rebellious to his arm, lies where it falls,
Repugnant[544] to command: unequal match'd,
Pyrrhus at Priam drives; in rage strikes wide;
But with the whiff and wind of his fell sword
The unnerved father falls. Then senseless Ilium,[545]
Seeming to feel this blow, with flaming top
Stoops to his base, and with a hideous crash
Takes prisoner Pyrrhus' ear: for, lo! his sword
Which was declining on the milky head
Of reverend Priam, seem'd i' the air to stick: 490
So, as a painted tyrant,[546] Pyrrhus stood,
And like a neutral to his will and matter,[547]
Did nothing.
But, as we often see, against[548] some storm,
A silence in the heavens, the rack[549] stand still,
The bold winds speechless and the orb below
As hush as death, anon the dreadful thunder
Doth rend the region,[550] so, after Pyrrhus' pause,
Aroused vengeance sets him new a-work:
And never did the Cyclops' hammers fall   500
On Mars's armour forged for proof eterne[551]
With less remorse than Pyrrhus' bleeding sword
Now falls on Priam.
Out, out, thou strumpet, Fortune! All you gods,
In general synod,[552] take away her power:
Break all the spokes and fellies[553] from her wheel,
And bowl the round nave[554] down the hill of heaven,
As low as to the fiends!"

POL.: This is too long.

HAM.: It shall to the barber's, with your beard. Prithee,   510
say on: he's for a jig[555] or a tale of bawdry,[556] or he
sleeps: say on: come to Hecuba.[557]

FIRST PLAYER: "But who, O, who had seen the
mobled[558] queen—"

HAM.: "The mobled queen?"

POL.: That's good; "mobled queen" is good.

---

[543] **o'er-sized** Covered as with size or glue.
[544] **Repugnant** Disobedient.
[545] **Then senseless Ilium** Insensate Troy.
[546] **painted tyrant** Tyrant in a picture.
[547] **matter** Task.
[548] **against** Before.
[549] **rack** Mass of clouds.
[550] **region** Assembly.
[551] **proof eterne** External resistance to assault.
[552] **synod** Assembly.
[553] **fellies** Pieces of wood forming the rim of a wheel.
[554] **nave** Hub.
[555] **jig** Comic performance given at the end or in an interval of a play.
[556] **bawdry** Indecency.
[557] **Hecuba** Wife of Priam, king of Troy.
[558] **mobled** Muffled.

FIRST PLAYER: "Run barefoot up and down, threatening the flames
With bisson rheum[559]; a clout[560] upon that head
Where late the diadem stood, and for a robe,   520
About her lank and all o'er-teemed[561] loins,
A blanket, in the alarm of fear caught up;
Who this had seen, with tongue in venom steep'd,
'Gainst Fortune's state would treason have
     pronounced:[562]
But if the gods themselves did see her then
When she saw Pyrrhus make malicious sport
In mincing with his sword her husband's limbs,
The instant burst of clamour that she made,
Unless things mortal move them not at all,
Would have made milch[563] the burning eyes of   530
     heaven,
And passion in the gods."

POL.: Look, whether he has not turned[564] his colour and has tears in 's eyes. Pray you, no more.

HAM.: 'Tis well; I'll have thee speak out the rest soon. Good my lord, will you see the players well bestowed? Do you hear, let them be well used; for they are the abstract[565] and brief chronicles of the time: after your death you were better have a bad epitaph than their ill report while you live.

POL.: My lord, I will use them according to their desert.

HAM.: God's bodykins,[566] man, much better: use every   540
man after his desert, and who should 'scape whipping? Use them after your own honour and dignity: the less they deserve, the more merit is in your bounty. Take them in.

POL.: Come, sirs.

HAM.: Follow him, friends; we'll hear a play to-morrow. [*Exit Polonius with all the Players but the First.*] Dost thou hear me, old friend; can you play the Murder of Gonzago?

FIRST PLAYER: Ay, my lord.   550

HAM.: We'll ha 't to-morrow night. You could, for a need, study a speech of some dozen or sixteen lines,[567] which I would set down and insert in 't, could you not?

FIRST PLAYER: Ay, my lord.

HAM.: Very well. Follow that lord; and look you mock him not. [*Exit First Player.*] My good friends, I'll leave you till night: you are welcome to Elsinore.

ROS.: Good my lord!

HAM.: Ay, so, God be wi' ye; [*Exeunt Rosencrantz and   560
Guildenstern.*] Now I am alone.
O, what a rogue and peasant[568] slave am I!

---

[559] **bisson rheum** Blinding tears.
[560] **clout** Piece of cloth.
[561] **o'er-teemed** Worn out with bearing children.
[562] **pronounced** Proclaimed.
[563] **milch** Moist with tears.
[564] **turned** Changed.
[565] **abstract** Summary account.
[566] **bodykins** Diminutive form of the oath "by God's body."
[567] **dozen or sixteen lines** Critics have amused themselves by trying to locate Hamlet's lines.
[568] **peasant** Base.

Is it not monstrous that this player here,
But in a fiction, in a dream of passion,
Could force his soul so to his own conceit
That from her working all his visage wann'd,[569]
Tears in his eyes, distraction in 's aspect,
A broken voice, and his whole function suiting
With forms to his conceit[570]? and all for nothing!
For Hecuba!   570
What's Hecuba to him, or he to Hecuba,
That he should weep for her? What would he do,
Had he the motive and the cue for passion
That I have? He would drown the stage with tears
And cleave the general ear with horrid speech,
Make mad the guilty and appal the free,
Confound the ignorant, and amaze indeed
The very faculties of eyes and ears.
Yet I,
A dull and muddy-mettled[571] rascal, peak,[572]   580
Like John-a-dreams,[573] unpregnant of[574] my cause,
And can say nothing; no, not for a king,
Upon whose property[575] and most dear life
A damn'd defeat was made. Am I a coward?
Who calls me villain? breaks my pate across?
Plucks off my beard, and blows it in my face?
Tweaks me by the nose? gives me the lie i' the throat,
As deep as to the lungs? who does me this?
Ha!
'Swounds, I should take it; for it cannot be   590
But I am pigeon-liver'd[576] and lack gall
To make oppression bitter, or ere this

I should have fatted all the region kites[577]
With this slave's offal: bloody, bawdy villain!
Remorseless, treacherous, lecherous, kindless[578]
    villain!
O, vengeance!
Why, what an ass am I! This is most brave,
That I, the son of a dear father murder'd,
Prompted to my revenge by heaven and hell,
Must, like a whore, unpack my heart with words,   600
And fall a-cursing, like a very drab,[579]
A scullion[580]!
Fie upon 't! foh! About,[581] my brain! I have heard
That guilty creatures sitting at a play
Have by the very cunning of the scene
Been struck so to the soul that presently
They have proclaim'd their malefactions;
For murder, though it have no tongue, will speak
With most miraculous organ. I'll have these players
Play something like the murder of my father   610
Before mine uncle: I'll observe his looks;
I'll tent[582] him to the quick: if he but blench,[583]
I know my course. The spirit that I have seen
May be the devil:[584] and the devil hath power
To assume a pleasing shape; yea, and perhaps
Out of my weakness and my melancholy,
As he is very potent with such spirits,[585]
Abuses me to damn me: I'll have grounds
More relative[586] than this:[587] the play's the thing
Wherein I'll catch the conscience of the king.   [*Exit.* 620

---

[569] **wann'd** Grew pale.
[570] **his whole . . . conceit** His whole being responded with forms to suit his thought.
[571] **muddy-mettled** Dull-spirited.
[572] **peak** Mope, pine.
[573] **John-a-dreams** An expression occurring elsewhere in Elizabethan literature to indicate a dreamer.
[574] **unpregnant of** Not quickened by.
[575] **property** Proprietorship (of crown and life).
[576] **pigeon-liver'd** The pigeon was supposed to secrete no gall; if Hamlet, so he says, had had gall, he would have felt the bitterness of oppression and avenged it.

[577] **region kites** Kites of the air.
[578] **kindless** Unnatural.
[579] **drab** Prostitute.
[580] **scullion** Prostitute.
[581] **About** About it, or turn thou right about.
[582] **tent** Probe.
[583] **blench** Quail, flinch.
[584] **May be the devil** Hamlet's suspicion is properly grounded in the belief of the time.
[585] **spirits** Humors.
[586] **relative** Closely related, definite.
[587] **this** i.e., The ghost's story.

Act III

Scene I—A Room in the Castle

This short scene sums up the precise situation of affairs at the moment when the crisis is coming on. There are three points to be noticed:

HAMLET *has resolved to make the play the solution of all his doubts; if that test shows the* KING *guilty, he shall die. Even as he forms this determination, his heart fails him. He turns to an alternative that has dimly presented itself before (Act I, Scene II, Line 133), and deliberately considers the desirability of suicide. But such a way out of the difficulty is too simple, too easy for his over-speculative nature. He sees the future filled with countless*

possibilities, which puzzle his will, and this enterprise also loses the name of action.

HAMLET *has long known that no help is to be had from* OPHELIA. *Yet when she appears before him, his old tenderness revives. He speaks gently to her, and then—discovers that she is deceiving him, acting as a decoy for* POLONIUS. *This obliges him to play the madman again, and his paradoxes express a feeling of revulsion from the poor foolish girl. His mother's sin has already made him lose faith in womanhood, and now he sees* OPHELIA, *too, spotted with all the vileness of her sex. He assails her with reproaches so inappropriate to herself that she can only take them as the sign of a shattered mind.*

With POLONIUS *and the like* HAMLET's *acting is successful; but the* KING *is shrewder. His suspicions are awakened, and he at once plots to get his nephew out of the way.* HAMLET *has, therefore, gone too far on the path of delay, and though he does not know it, the opportunities of revenge are fast slipping away from him.*

Enter KING, QUEEN, POLONIUS, OPHELIA, ROSENCRANTZ, *and* GUILDENSTERN

KING: And can you, by no drift of circumstance,[588]   1
    Get from him why he puts on this confusion,
    Grating so harshly all his days of quiet
    With turbulent and dangerous lunacy?
ROS.: He does confess he feels himself distracted;
    But from what cause he will by no means speak.
GUIL.: Nor do we find him forward[589] to be sounded,
    But, with a crafty madness, keeps aloof,
    When we would bring him on to some confession
    Of his true state.   10
QUEEN: Did he receive you well?
ROS.: Most like a gentleman.
GUIL.:   But with much forcing of his disposition.[590]
ROS.: Niggard of question,[591] but, of our demands,
    Most free in his reply.
QUEEN: Did you assay[592] him
    To any pastime?
ROS.: Madam, it so fell out, that certain players
    We o'er-raught[593] on the way: of these we told him;
    And there did seem in him a kind of joy   20
    To hear of it: they are about the court,
    And, as I think, they have already order
    This night to play before him.
POL.:   'Tis most true:
    And he beseech'd me to entreat your majesties
    To hear and see the matter.
KING: With all my heart; and it doth much content me
    To hear him so inclined.
    Good gentlemen, give him a further edge,[594]
    And drive his purpose on to these delights.   30
ROS.: We shall, my lord.

          [*Exeunt Rosencrantz and Guildenstern.*

        Sweet Gertrude, leave us too;
    For we have closely[595] sent for Hamlet hither,
    That he, as 't were by accident, may here
    Affront[596] Ophelia:
    Her father and myself, lawful espials,[597]
    Will so bestow ourselves that, seeing, unseen,
    We may of their encounter frankly judge,
    And gather by him, as he is behaved,

    If 't be the affliction of his love or no   40
    That thus he suffers for.
QUEEN: I shall obey you;
    And for your part, Ophelia, I do wish
    That your good beauties be the happy cause
    Of Hamlet's wildness:[598] so shall I hope your virtues
    Will bring him to his wonted way again,
    To both your honours.
OPH.:   Madam, I wish it may. [*Exit Queen.*
POL.: Ophelia, walk you here. Gracious,[599] so please you,
    We will bestow ourselves. [*To* OPHELIA] Read on this   50
      book;
    That show of such an exercise[600] may colour[601]
    Your loneliness. We are oft to blame in this,—
    'Tis too much proved—that with devotion's visage
    And pious action we do sugar o'er
    The devil himself.
KING: [*Aside*] O, 'tis too true!
    How smart a lash that speech doth give my
      conscience!
    The harlot's cheek, beautied with plastering art,
    Is not more ugly to[602] the thing[603] that helps it
    Than is my deed to my most painted word:
    O heavy burthen!   60
POL.: I hear him coming: let's withdraw, my lord.

           [*Exeunt King and Polonius.*

Enter HAMLET

HAM.: To be, or not to be: that is the question:
    Whether 'tis nobler in the mind to suffer
    The slings and arrows of outrageous fortune,
    Or to take arms against a sea[604] of troubles,
    And by opposing end them? To die: to sleep;
    No more; and by a sleep to say we end
    The heart-ache and the thousand natural shocks
    That flesh is heir to, 'tis a consummation
    Devoutly to be wish'd. To die, to sleep;
    To sleep: perchance to dream: ay, there's the rub;   70
    For in that sleep of death what dreams may come
    When we have shuffled[605] off this mortal coil,[606]
    Must give us pause: there's the respect[607]
    That makes calamity of so long life[608];
    For who would bear the whips and scorns of time,[609]

III.i. [588] **drift of circumstance** Vice of conversation.
[589] **forward** Willing.
[590] **forcing of his disposition** i.e., Against his will.
[591] **Niggard of question** Sparing of conversation.
[592] **assay** Try to win.
[593] **o'er-raught** Overtook.
[594] **edge** Incitement.
[595] **closely** Secretly.
[596] **Affront** Confront.
[597] **lawful espials** Legitimate spies.

[598] **wildness** Madness.
[599] **Gracious** Your grace (addressed to the king).
[600] **exercise** Act of devotion (the book she reads is one of devotion).
[601] **colour** Give a plausible appearance to.
[602] **to** Compared to.
[603] **thing** i.e., The cosmetic.
[604] **sea** The mixed metaphor of this speech has often been commented on; a later emendation, *siege*, has sometimes been spoken on the stage.
[605] **shuffled** Sloughed, cast.
[606] **coil** Usually means "turmoil"; here, possibly "body" (conceived of as wound about the soul like rope); *clay, soil, veil* have been suggested as emendations.
[607] **respect** Consideration.
[608] **of . . . life** So long-lived.
[609] **time** The world.

The oppressor's wrong, the proud man's
    contumely,
The pangs of despised[610] love, the law's delay,
The insolence of office[611] and the spurns[612]   80
That patient merit of the unworthy takes,
When he himself might his quietus[613] make
With a bare bodkin[614]? who would fardels[615] bear,
To grunt and sweat under a weary life,
But that the dread of something after death,
The undiscover'd country from whose bourn[616]
No traveller returns, puzzles the will
And makes us rather bear those ills we have
Than fly to others that we know not of?
Thus conscience[617] does make cowards of us all;   90
And thus the native hue[618] of resolution
Is sicklied o'er[619] with the pale cast[620] of thought,
And enterprises of great pitch[621] and moment[622]
With this regard[623] their currents[624] turn awry,
And lose the name of action.—Soft you now!
The fair Ophelia! Nymph, in thy orisons[625]
Be all my sins remember'd.
OPH.:   Good my lord,
How does your honour for this many a day?
HAM.: I humbly thank you; well, well, well.   100
OPH.: My lord, I have remembrances of yours,
That I have longed long to re-deliver;
I pray you, now receive them.
HAM.:   No, not I;
I never gave you aught.
OPH.: My honour'd lord, you know right well you did;
And, with them, words of so sweet breath composed
As made the things more rich: their perfume lost,
Take these again; for to the noble mind
Rich gifts wax poor when givers prove unkind.   110
There, my lord.
HAM.: Ha, ha! are you honest?[626]
OPH.: My lord?
HAM.: Are you fair[627]?
OPH.: What means your lordship?

HAM.: That if you be honest and fair, your honesty[628] should admit no discourse to[629] your beauty.
OPH.: Could beauty, my lord, have better commerce[630] than with honesty?
HAM.: Ay, truly; for the power of beauty will sooner 120 transform honesty from what it is to a bawd than the force of honesty can translate beauty into his likeness: this was sometime a paradox, but now the time[631] gives it proof. I did love you once.
OPH.: Indeed, my lord, you made me believe so.
HAM.: You should not have believed me; for virtue cannot so inoculate[632] our old stock but we shall relish of it:[633] I loved you not.
OPH.: I was the more deceived.
HAM.: Get thee to a nunnery: why wouldst thou be a 130 breeder of sinners? I am myself indifferent honest[634]; but yet I could accuse me of such things that it were better my mother had not borne me: I am very proud, revengeful, ambitious, with more offences at my beck[635] than I have thoughts to put them in, imagination to give them shape, or time to act them in. What should such fellows as I do crawling between earth and heaven? We are arrant knaves, all; believe none of us. Go thy ways to a nunnery. Where's your father? 140
OPH.: At home, my lord.
HAM.: Let the doors be shut upon him, that he may play the fool no where but in 's own house. Farewell.
OPH.: O, help him, you sweet heavens!
HAM.: If thou dost marry, I'll give thee this plague for thy dowry: be thou as chaste as ice, as pure as snow, thou shalt not escape calumny. Get thee to a nunnery, go: farewell. Or, if thou wilt needs marry, marry a fool; for wise men know well enough what monsters[636] you make of them. To a nunnery, go, and 150 quickly too. Farewell.
OPH.: O heavenly powers, restore him!
HAM.: I have heard of your[637] paintings too, well enough; God has given you one face, and you make yourselves another: you jig,[638] you amble, and you lisp, and nick-name God's creatures, and make your wantonness your ignorance.[639] Go to, I'll no more on 't; it hath made me mad. I say, we will have no more marriages: those that are married already, all but

---

[610] **despised** Rejected.
[611] **office** Office-holders.
[612] **spurns** Insults.
[613] **quietus** Acquittance; here, death.
[614] **bare bodkin** Mere dagger; bare is sometimes understood as "unsheathed."
[615] **fardels** Burdens.
[616] **bourn** Boundary.
[617] **conscience** Probably, inhibition by the faculty of reason restraining the will from doing wrong.
[618] **native hue** Natural color; metaphor derived from the color of the face.
[619] **sicklied o'er** Given a sickly tinge.
[620] **cast** Shade of color.
[621] **pitch** Height (as of falcon's flight).
[622] **moment** Importance.
[623] **regard** Respect, consideration.
[624] **currents** Courses.
[625] **orisons** Prayers.
[626] **are you honest?** Honest meaning "truthful" and "chaste."
[627] **fair** Meaning "just, honorable, and beautiful." The speech has the irony of a double entendre.

[628] **your honesty** Your chastity.
[629] **discourse to** Familiar intercourse with.
[630] **commerce** Intercourse.
[631] **the time** The present age.
[632] **inoculate** Graft (metaphorical).
[633] **but . . . it** i.e., That we do not still have about us a taste of the old stock, i.e., retain our sinfulness.
[634] **indifferent honest** Moderately virtuous.
[635] **beck** Command.
[636] **monsters** An allusion to the horns of a cuckold.
[637] **your** Indefinite use.
[638] **jig** Move with jerky motion; probably allusion to the jig, or song and dance, of the current stage.
[639] **make . . . ignorance** i.e., Excuse your wantonness on the ground of your ignorance.

one,[640] shall live; the rest shall keep as they are. To a   160
nunnery, go.   [*Exit.*

OPH.: O, what a noble mind is here o'erthrown!
    The courtier's, soldier's, scholar's, eye, tongue, sword;
    The expectancy and rose[641] of the fair state,
    The glass of fashion and the mould of form,[642]
    The observed of all observers,[643] quite, quite down!
    And I, of ladies most deject and wretched,
    That suck'd the honey of his music vows,
    Now see that noble and most sovereign reason.
    Like sweet bells jangled, out of tune and harsh;   170
    That unmatch'd form and feature of blown[644] youth
    Blasted with ecstasy:[645] O, woe is me,
    To have seen what I have seen, see what I see!

Re-enter KING *and* POLONIUS

KING: Love! his affections do not that way tend;
    Nor what he spake, though it lack'd form a little,
    Was not like madness. There's something in his soul,
    O'er which his melancholy sits on brood;
    And I do doubt[646] the hatch and the disclose[647]
    Will be some danger: which for to prevent,
    I have in quick determination   180
    Thus set it down: he shall with speed to England,
    For the demand of our neglected tribute:
    Haply the seas and countries different
    With variable[648] objects shall expel
    This something-settled[649] matter in his heart,
    Whereon his brains still beating puts him thus
    From fashion of himself.[650] What think you on 't?
POL.: It shall do well: but yet do I believe
    The origin and commencement of his grief
    Sprung from neglected love. How now, Ophelia!   190
    You need not tell us what Lord Hamlet said;
    We heard it all. My lord, do as you please;
    But, if you hold it fit, after the play
    Let his queen mother all alone entreat him
    To show his grief: let her be round[651] with him;
    And I'll be placed, so please you, in the ear
    Of all their conference. If she find him not,
    To England send him, or confine him where
    Your wisdom best shall think.
KING: It shall be so: 200
    Madness in great ones must not unwatch'd go.

[*Exeunt.*

---

[640] **one** i.e., The king.
[641] **expectancy and rose** Source of hope.
[642] **The glass . . . form** The mirror of fashion and the pattern of courtly behavior.
[643] **observed . . . observers** i.e., The center of attention in the court.
[644] **blown** Blooming.
[645] **ecstasy** Madness.
[646] **doubt** Fear.
[647] **disclose** Disclosure or revelation (by chipping of the shell).
[648] **variable** Various.
[649] **something-settled** Somewhat settled.
[650] **From . . . himself** Out of his natural manner.
[651] **round** Blunt.

Scene II—A Hall in the Castle

This important scene finally convinces HAMLET *of the* KING'S *guilt; it closes with a resolution to "do bitter business." * HAMLET *is throughout in a state of extreme nervous tension; at the success of his plot he breaks into the wildest excitement. Hence the nonsense he talks to* OPHELIA *and his riotous fooling with the* COURTIERS. *The episodes with the* PLAYERS *and* HORATIO *serve partly as a quiet opening to the turbulent emotions of the play scene, partly to show that* HAMLET'S *action is fundamentally sane and rational. It is characteristic of him to be able to interest himself at such a critical moment in the niceties of the actor's art.*

Enter HAMLET *and* PLAYERS

HAM.: Speak the speech, I pray you, as I pronounced it   1
    to you, trippingly on the tongue: but if you mouth
    it, as many of your[652] players do, I had as lief the
    town-crier spoke my lines. Nor do not saw the air
    too much with your hand, thus, but use all gently;
    for in the very torrent, tempest, and, as I may say,
    the whirlwind of passion, you must acquire and
    beget a temperance that may give it smoothness.
    O, it offends me to the soul to hear a robustious[653]
    periwigpated[654] fellow tear a passion to tatters, to very   10
    rags, to split the ears of the groundlings,[655] who for the
    most part are capable of[656] nothing but inexplicable[657]
    dumb-shows and noise: I would have such a fellow
    whipped for o'erdoing Termagant;[658] it out-herods
    Herod:[659] pray you, avoid it.
FIRST PLAYER: I warrant your honour.
HAM.: Be not too tame neither, but let your own discretion
    be your tutor: suit the action to the word, the word to
    the action; with this special observance, that you o'er-
    step not the modesty of nature: for any thing so over-   20
    done is from the purpose of playing, whose end, both
    at the first and now, was and is, to hold, as 't were,
    the mirror up to nature; to show virtue her own fea-
    ture, scorn her own image, and the very age and body
    of the time his form and pressure.[660] Now this
    overdone, or come tardy off,[661] though it make the
    unskilful laugh, cannot but make the judicious
    grieve; the censure of the which one[662] must in your
    allowance o'erweigh a whole theatre of others. O,
    there be players that I have seen play, and heard oth-   30
    ers praise, and that highly, not to speak it profanely,

III.ii. [652] **your** Indefinite use.
[653] **robustious** Violent, boisterous.
[654] **periwigpated** Wearing a wig.
[655] **groundlings** Those who stood in the yard of the theater.
[656] **capable of** Susceptible of being influenced by.
[657] **inexplicable** Of no significance worth explaining.
[658] **Termagant** A god of the Saracens; a character in the St. Nicholas play, where one of his worshipers, leaving him in charge of goods, returns to find them stolen; whereupon he beats the god (or idol), which howls vociferously.
[659] **Herod** Herod of Jewry; a character in *The Slaughter of the Innocents* and other cycle plays. The part was played with great noise and fury.
[660] **pressure** Stamp, impressed character.
[661] **come tardy off** Inadequately done.
[662] **the censure . . . one** The judgment of even one of whom.

that, neither having the accent of Christians nor the gait of Christian, pagan, nor man, have so strutted and bellowed that I have thought some of nature's journeymen[663] had made men and not made them well, they imitated humanity so abominably.

FIRST PLAYER: I hope we have reformed that indifferently[664] with us, sir.

HAM.: O, reform it altogether. And let those that play your clowns speak no more than is set down for 40 them; for there be of[665] them that will themselves laugh, to set on some quantity of barren[666] spectators to laugh too; though, in the mean time, some necessary question of the play be then to be considered: that's villainous, and shows a most pitiful ambition in the fool that uses it. Go, make you ready.

[*Exeunt Players.*

Enter POLONIUS, ROSENCRANTZ, *and* GUILDENSTERN

How now, my lord: will the king hear this piece of work?

POL.: And the queen too, and that presently.

HAM.: Bid the players make haste. [*Exit Polonius.*] Will you two help to hasten them?

ROS.: ⎫
GUIL.: ⎭ We will, my lord.

[*Exeunt Rosencrantz and Guildenstern.*

HAM.: What ho! Horatio!

Enter HORATIO

HOR.: Here, sweet lord, at your service.

HAM.: Horatio, thou art e'en as just[667] a man
As e'er my conversation coped withal.

HOR.: O, my dear lord,—

HAM.: 　　　　　　　　　Nay, do not think I flatter;
For what advancement may I hope from thee
That no revenue hast but thy good spirits,
To feed and clothe thee? Why should the poor be 60
　　flatter'd?
No, let the candied tongue lick absurd pomp,
And crook the pregnant[668] hinges of the knee
Where thrift[669] may follow fawning. Dost thou
　　hear?
Since my dear soul was mistress of her choice
And could of men distinguish, her election
Hath seal'd thee for herself; for thou hast been
As one, in suffering all, that suffers nothing,
A man that fortune's buffets and rewards
Hast ta'en with equal thanks: and blest are those
Whose blood and judgement are so well 70
　　commingled,
That they are not a pipe for fortune's finger

To sound what stop[670] she please. Give me that man
That is not passion's slave, and I will wear him
In my heart's core, ay, in my heart of heart,
As I do thee.—Something too much of this.—
There is a play to-night before the king;
One scene of it comes near the circumstance
Which I have told thee of my father's death:
I prithee, when thou seest that act afoot,
Even with the very comment of thy soul[671] 80
Observe mine uncle: if his occulted[672] guilt
Do not itself unkennel in one speech,
It is a damned[673] ghost that we have seen,
And my imaginations are as foul
As Vulcan's stithy.[674] Give him heedful note;
For I mine eyes will rivet to his face,
And after we will both our judgements join
In censure of his seeming.[675]

HOR.: 　　　　　　　　　Well, my lord:
If he steal aught the whilst this play is playing, 90
And 'scape detecting, I will pay the theft.

HAM.: They are coming to the play; I must be idle:[676]
Get you a place.

Danish march. A flourish. Enter KING, QUEEN, POLONIUS, OPHELIA, ROSENCRANTZ, GUILDENSTERN *and others*

KING: How fares our cousin Hamlet?

HAM.: Excellent, i' faith; of the chameleon's dish:[677]
I eat the air, promise-crammed: you cannot feed capons so.

KING: I have nothing with[678] this answer, Hamlet; these words are not mine.[679]

HAM.: No, nor mine now. [*To* POLONIUS] My lord, you 100 played once i' the university, you say?

POL.: That I did, my lord; and was accounted a good actor.

HAM.: What did you enact?

POL.: I did enact Julius Caesar: I was killed i' the Capitol; Brutus killed me.

HAM.: It was a brute part of him to kill so capital a calf there. Be the players ready?

ROS.: Ay, my lord; they stay upon your patience.

QUEEN: Come hither, my dear Hamlet, sit by me. 110

HAM.: No, good mother, here's metal more attractive.

[*Lying down at Ophelia's feet.*

POL.: [*To the* KING] O, ho! do you mark that?

OPH.: You are merry, my lord.

HAM.: Who, I?

---

[663] **journeymen** Laborers not yet masters in their trade.
[664] **indifferently** Fairly, tolerably.
[665] **of** i.e., Some among them.
[666] **barren** i.e., Of wit.
[667] **just** Honest, honorable.
[668] **pregnant** Pliant.
[669] **thrift** Profit.

[670] **stop** Hole in a wind instrument for controlling the sound.
[671] **very . . . soul** Inward and sagacious criticism.
[672] **occulted** Hidden.
[673] **damned** In league with Satan.
[674] **stithy** Smithy, place of stiths (anvils).
[675] **censure . . . seeming** Judgment of his appearance or behavior.
[676] **idle** Crazy, or not attending to anything serious.
[677] **chameleon's dish** Chameleons were supposed to feed on air. (Hamlet deliberately misinterprets the king's "fares" as "feeds.")
[678] **have . . . with** Make nothing of.
[679] **are not mine** Do not respond to what I ask.

OPH.: Ay, my lord.

HAM.: O God, your only[680] jig-maker.[681] What should a man do but be merry? for, look you, how cheerfully my mother looks, and my father died within these two hours.

OPH.: Nay, 'tis twice two months, my lord.   120

HAM.: So long? Nay then, let the devil wear black, for I'll have a suit of sables.[682] O heavens! die two months ago, and not forgotten yet? Then there's hope a great man's memory may outlive his life half a year: but, by 'r, lady, he must build churches, then; or else shall he suffer not thinking on,[683] with the hobby-horse, whose epitaph is "For, O, for, O, the hobby-horse is forgot."[684]

Hautboys play. The dumb-show enters.

Enter a KING *and a* QUEEN *very lovingly; the* QUEEN *embracing him, and he her. She kneels, and makes show of protestation unto him. He takes her up, and declines his head upon her neck. He lies him down upon a bank of flowers; she, seeing him asleep, leaves him. Anon comes in a fellow, takes off his crown, kisses it, pours poison in the* KING's *ears, and exits. The* QUEEN *returns, finds the* KING *dead, and makes passionate action. The* POISONER, *with some two or three* MUTES, *comes in again, seeming to lament with her. The dead body is carried away. The* POISONER *wooes the* QUEEN *with gifts; she seems loath and unwilling awhile, but in the end accepts his love.*   [*Exeunt.*

OPH.: What means this, my lord?

HAM.: Marry, this is miching mallecho[685]; it means   130
mischief.

OPH.: Belike this show imports the argument of the play.

Enter PROLOGUE

HAM.: We shall know by this fellow: the players cannot keep counsel; they'll tell all.

PRO.: For us, and for our tragedy,
Here, stooping[686] to your clemency,
We beg your hearing patiently.   [*Exit.*

HAM.: Is this a prologue, or the posy[687] of a ring?

OPH.: 'Tis brief, my lord.

HAM.: As woman's love.

Enter two PLAYERS, KING *and* QUEEN

P. KING: Full thirty times hath Phoebus' cart gone round   140
Neptune's salt-wash[688] and Tellus'[689] orbed ground,
And thirty dozen moons with borrow'd[690] sheen

---

[680] **your only** Only your.
[681] **jig-maker** Composer of jigs (song and dance).
[682] **suit of sables** Garments trimmed with the fur of the sable, with a quibble on sable meaning "black."
[683] **suffer . . . on** Undergo oblivion.
[684] **"For . . . forgot."** Verse of a song occurring also in *Love's Labour's Lost,* III.i.; the hobby horse was a character in the Morris Dance.
[685] **miching mallecho** Sneaking mischief.
[686] **stooping** Bowing.
[687] **posy** Motto.
[688] **salt-wash** The sea.
[689] **Tellus** Goddess of the earth (*orbed ground*).
[690] **borrow'd** i.e., Reflected.

About the world have times twelve thirties been
Since love our hearts and Hymen[691] did our hands
Unite commutual[692] in most sacred bands.

P. QUEEN: So many journeys may the sun and moon
Make us again count o'er ere love be done!
But, woe is me, you are so sick of late,
So far from cheer and from your former state,
That I distrust[693] you. Yet, though I distrust,   150
Discomfort you, my lord, it nothing must:
For women's fear and love holds quantity;[694]
In neither aught, or in extremity.
Now, what my love is, proof hath made you know;
And as my love is sized, my fear is so:
Where love is great, the littlest doubts are fear;
Where little fears grow great, great love grows there.

P. KING: 'Faith, I must leave thee, love, and shortly too;
My operant[695] powers their functions leave[696] to do:
And thou shalt live in this fair world behind,   160
Honour'd, beloved; and haply one as kind
For husband shalt thou—

P. QUEEN: O, confound the rest!
Such love must needs be treason in my breast:
In second husband let me be accurst!
None wed the second but who kill'd the first.

HAM.: [*Aside*] Wormwood, wormwood.

P. QUEEN: The instances that second marriage move
Are base respects of thrift, but none of love:
A second time I kill my husband dead,   170
When second husband kisses me in bed.

P. KING: I do believe you think what now you speak;
But what we do determine oft we break.
Purpose is but the slave to memory,
Of violent birth, but poor validity:
Which now, like fruit unripe, sticks on the tree;
But fall, unshaken, when they mellow be.
Most necessary 'tis that we forget
To pay ourselves what to ourselves is debt:
What to ourselves in passion we propose,   180
The passion ending, both the purpose lose.
The violence of either grief or joy
Their own enactures[697] with themselves destroy:
Where joy most revels, grief doth most lament;
Grief joys, joy grieves, on slender accident.
This world is not for aye,[698] nor 'tis not strange
That even our loves should with our fortunes
change;
For 'tis a question left us yet to prove,
Whether love lead fortune, or else fortune love.
The great man down, you mark his favourite flies;   190
The poor advanced makes friends of enemies.
And hitherto doth love on fortune tend;

---

[691] **Hymen** God of matrimony.
[692] **commutual** Mutually.
[693] **distrust** Am anxious about.
[694] **holds quantity** Keeps proportion between.
[695] **operant** Active.
[696] **leave** Cease.
[697] **enactures** Fulfillments.
[698] **aye** Ever.

For who[699] not needs shall never lack a friend,
And who in want a hollow friend doth try,
Directly seasons[700] him his enemy.
But, orderly to end where I begun,
Our wills and fates do so contrary run
That our devices still are overthrown;
Our thoughts are ours, their ends[701] none of our own:
So think thou wilt no second husband wed;   200
But die thy thoughts when thy first lord is dead.

P. QUEEN: Nor earth to me give food, nor heaven light!
Sport and repose lock from me day and night!
To desperation turn my trust and hope!
An anchor's[702] cheer[703] in prison be my scope!
Each opposite[704] that blanks[705] the face of joy
Meet what I would have well and it destroy!
Both here and hence pursue me lasting strife,
If, once a widow, ever I be wife!

HAM.: If she should break it now!   210

P. KING: 'Tis deeply sworn. Sweet, leave me here awhile;
My spirits grow dull, and fain I would beguile
The tedious day with sleep.   [*Sleeps.*

P. QUEEN: Sleep rock thy brain;
And never come mischance between us twain! [*Exit.*

HAM.: Madam, how like you this play?

QUEEN: The lady doth protest too much, methinks.

HAM.: O, but she'll keep her word.

KING: Have you heard the argument? Is there no offence
in 't?   220

HAM.: No, no, they do but jest, poison in jest; no offence i'
the world.

KING: What do you call the play?

HAM.: The Mouse-trap. Marry, how? Tropically.[706] This
play is the image of a murder done in Vienna:
Gonzago[707] is the duke's name; his wife, Baptista: you
shall see anon; 'tis a knavish piece of work: but what
o' that? your majesty and we that have free souls, it
touches us not: let the galled jade[708] wince, our
withers[709] are unwrung.[710]   230

Enter LUCIANUS

This is one Lucianus, nephew to the king.

OPH.: You are as good as a chorus,[711] my lord.

HAM.: I could interpret between you and your love, if I
could see the puppets dallying.[712]

OPH.: You are keen, my lord, you are keen.

HAM.: It would cost you a groaning to take off my edge.

OPH.: Still better, and worse.[713]

HAM.: So you mistake[714] your husbands. Begin, murderer;
pox,[715] leave thy damnable faces, and begin. Come:
"the croaking raven doth bellow for revenge."   240

LUC.: Thoughts black, hands apt, drugs fit, and time
agreeing;
Confederate[716] season, else no creature seeing;
Thou mixture rank, of midnight weeds collected,
With Hecate's[717] ban[718] thrice blasted, thrice infected,
Thy natural magic and dire property,
On wholesome life usurp immediately.

[*Pours poison into the sleeper's ears.*

HAM.: He poisons him i' the garden for 's estate. His
name's Gonzago: the story is extant, and writ in
choice Italian: you shall see anon how the murderer
gets the love of Gonzago's wife.   250

OPH.: The king rises.

HAM.: What, frighted with false fire[719]!

QUEEN: How fares my lord?

POL.: Give o'er the play.

KING: Give me some light: away!

ALL: Lights, lights, lights!

[*Exeunt all but Hamlet and Horatio.*

HAM.: Why, let the stricken deer go weep,
The hart ungalled play;
For some must watch, while some must sleep:
So runs the world away.[720]   260
Would not this,[721] sir, and a forest of feathers[722]—if the
rest of my fortunes turn Turk with[723] me—with two
Provincial roses[724] on my razed[725] shoes, get me a
fellowship in a cry[726] of players,[727] sir?

HOR.: Half a share.[728]

---

[699] **who** Whoever.
[700] **seasons** Matures, ripens.
[701] **ends** Results.
[702] **anchor** An anchorite, a religious hermit.
[703] **cheer** Fare; sometimes printed as *chair.*
[704] **opposite** Adverse thing.
[705] **blanks** Causes to blanch or grow pale.
[706] **Tropically** Figuratively, *tropically* suggests a pun on *trap* in Mouse-trap.
[707] **Gonzago** In 1538 Luigi Gonzago murdered the Duke of Urbano by pouring poisoned lotion in his ears.
[708] **galled jade** Horse whose hide is rubbed by saddle or harness.
[709] **withers** The part between the horse's shoulder blades.
[710] **unwrung** Not wrung or twisted.
[711] **chorus** In many Elizabethan plays, the action was explained by an actor known as the "chorus"; at a puppet show, the actor who explained the action was known as an "interpreter," as indicated by the lines following.

[712] **dallying** With sexual suggestion, continued in **keen** (sexually aroused), **groaning** (i.e., in pregnancy), and **edge** (i.e., sexual desire or impetuosity).
[713] **Still . . . worse.** More keen, less decorous.
[714] **mistake** Err in taking.
[715] **pox** An imprecation.
[716] **Confederate** Conspiring (to assist the murderer).
[717] **Hecate** The goddess of witchcraft.
[718] **ban** Curse.
[719] **false fire** Fireworks, or a blank discharge.
[720] **Why . . . away** Probably from an old ballad, with allusion to the popular belief that a wounded deer retires to weep and die.
[721] **this** i.e., The play.
[722] **feathers** Allusion to the plumes that Elizabethan actors were fond of wearing.
[723] **turn Turk with** Go back on.
[724] **two Provincial roses** Rosettes of ribbon like the roses of Provins near Paris, or else the roses of Provence.
[725] **razed** Cut, slashed (by way of ornament).
[726] **cry** Pack (as of hounds).
[727] **fellowship . . . players** Partnership in a theatrical company.
[728] **Half a share.** Allusion to the custom in dramatic companies of dividing the ownership into a number of shares among the householders.

HAM.: A whole one, I.
     For thou dost know, O Damon dear,
       This realm dismantled[729] was
     Of Jove himself; and now reigns here
       A very, very[730]—pajock.[731]   270

HOR.: You might have rhymed.

HAM.: O good Horatio, I'll take the ghost's word for a
     thousand pound. Didst perceive?

HOR.: Very well, my lord.

HAM.: Upon the talk of the poisoning?

HOR.: I did very well note him.

HAM.: Ah, ha! Come, some music! come, the recorders[732]!
     For if the king like not the comedy,
     Why then, belike, he likes it not, perdy.[733]
     Come, some music!   280

Re-enter ROSENCRANTZ *and* GUILDENSTERN

GUIL.: Good my lord, vouchsafe me a word with you.

HAM.: Sir, a whole history.

GUIL.: The king, sir,—

HAM.: Ay, sir, what of him?

GUIL.: Is in his retirement marvellous distempered.

HAM.: With drink, sir?

GUIL.: No, my lord, rather with choler.[734]

HAM.: Your wisdom should show itself more richer to
     signify this to his doctor; for, for me to put him to his
     purgation would perhaps plunge him into far more   290
     choler.

GUIL.: Good my lord, put your discourse into some
     frame,[735] and start not so wildly from my affair.

HAM.: I am tame, sir: pronounce.

GUIL.: The queen, your mother, in most great affliction of
     spirit, hath sent me to you.

HAM.: You are welcome.

GUIL.: Nay, good my lord, this courtesy is not of the
     right breed. If it shall please you to make me a
     wholesome[736] answer, I will do your mother's   300
     commandment: if not, your pardon and my return
     shall be the end of my business.

HAM.: Sir, I cannot.

GUIL.: What, my lord?

HAM.: Make you a wholesome answer; my wit's diseased:
     but, sir, such answer as I can make, you shall command;
     or, rather, as you say, my mother: therefore no more,
     but to the matter:[737] my mother, you say,—

ROS.: Then thus she says; your behaviour hath struck her
     into amazement and admiration.   310

HAM.: O wonderful son, that can so astonish a mother!
     But is there no sequel at the heels of this mother's
     admiration? Impart.

ROS.: She desires to speak with you in her closet, ere you
     go to bed.

HAM.: We shall obey, were she ten times our mother.
     Have you any further trade with us?

ROS.: My lord, you once did love me.

HAM.: So I do still, by these pickers and stealers.[738]

ROS.: Good my lord, what is your cause of distemper?   320
     you do, surely, bar the door upon your own liberty,
     if you deny your griefs to your friend.

HAM.: Sir, I lack advancement.

ROS.: How can that be, when you have the voice[739] of the
     king himself for your succession in Denmark?

HAM.: Ay, sir, but "While the grass grows,"[740]—the
     proverb is something musty.

Re-enter PLAYERS *with recorders*

     O, the recorders! let me see one. To withdraw[741] with
     you:—why do you go about to recover the wind[742]
     of me, as if you would drive me into a toil[743]?   330

GUIL.: O, my lord, if my duty be too bold, my love is too
     unmannerly.[744]

HAM.: I do not well understand that. Will you play upon
     this pipe?

GUIL.: My lord, I cannot.

HAM.: I pray you.

GUIL.: Believe me, I cannot.

HAM.: I do beseech you.

GUIL.: I know no touch of it, my lord.

HAM.: 'Tis as easy ay lying: govern these ventages[745] with   340
     your fingers and thumb, give it breath with your
     mouth, and it will discourse most eloquent music.
     Look you, these are the stops.

GUIL.: But these cannot I command to any utterance of
     harmony; I have not the skill.

HAM.: Why, look you now, how unworthy a thing you
     make of me! You would play upon me; you would
     seem to know my stops; you would pluck out the
     heart of my mystery; you would sound me from my
     lowest note to the top of my compass:[746] and there is   350
     much music, excellent voice, in this little organ[747]; yet
     cannot you make it speak. 'Sblood, do you think I
     am easier to be played on than a pipe? Call me what
     instrument you will, though you can fret[748] me, yet
     you cannot play upon me.

---

[729] **dismantled** Stripped, divested.

[730] **For . . . very** Probably from an old ballad having to do with
Damon and Pythias.

[731] **pajock** Peacock (a bird with a bad reputation). Possibly the
word was *patchock*, diminutive of patch clown.

[732] **recorders** Wind instruments of the flute kind.

[733] **perdy** Corruption of *par dieu*.

[734] **choler** Bilious disorder, with quibble on the sense "anger."

[735] **frame** Order.

[736] **wholesome** Sensible.

[737] **matter** Matter in hand.

[738] **pickers and stealers** Hands, so called from the catechism "to
keep my hands from picking and stealing."

[739] **voice** Support.

[740] **"While . . . grows"** The rest of the proverb is "the silly horse
starves." Hamlet may be destroyed while he is waiting for the
succession to the kingdom.

[741] **withdraw** Speak in private.

[742] **recover the wind** Get to the windward side.

[743] **toil** Snare.

[744] **if . . . unmannerly** If I am using an unmannerly boldness, it
is my love that occasions it.

[745] **ventages** Stops of the recorder.

[746] **compass** Range of voice.

[747] **organ** Musical instrument, i.e., the pipe.

[748] **fret** Quibble on meaning "irritate" and the piece of wood,
gut, or metal that regulates the fingering.

Enter POLONIUS

God bless you, sir!

POL.: My lord, the queen would speak with you, and presently.

HAM.: Do you see yonder cloud that's almost in shape of a camel? 360

POL.: By the mass, and 'tis like a camel, indeed.

HAM.: Methinks it is like a weasel.

POL.: It is backed like a weasel.

HAM.: Or like a whale?

POL.: Very like a whale.

HAM.: Then I will come to my mother by and by. They fool me to the top of my bent.[749] I will come by and by.

POL.: I will say so.

HAM.: By and by[750] is easily said.   [*Exit Polonius.*
Leave me, friends.   [*Exeunt all but Hamlet.* 370
'Tis now the very witching time[751] of night,
When churchyards yawn and hell itself breathes out
Contagion to this world: now could I drink hot
        blood,
And do such bitter business as the day
Would quake to look on. Soft! now to my mother.
O heart, lose not thy nature; let not ever
The soul of Nero[752] enter this firm bosom:
Let me be cruel, not unnatural:
I will speak daggers to her, but use none;
My tongue and soul in this be hypocrites; 380
How in my words soever she be shent,[753]
To give them seals[754] never, my soul, consent!   [*Exit.*

Scene III—A Room in the Castle

HAMLET *has his opportunity to translate resolution into action and misses it. Critics have objected to what they regard as the cold-blooded cruelty of his reasons for not killing the* KING *while he is praying. But they do not observe that these are not reasons, only excuses.* HAMLET *would like the* KING *if he could, but he has delayed so long that he cannot now commit himself to the definite immediate act. But the hour is slipping from him.* CLAUDIUS, *in spite of his momentary weakness of contrition, is determined to get rid, in one way or another, of this dangerous prince.*

Enter KING, ROSENCRANTZ, *and* GUILDENSTERN

KING: I like him not, nor stands it safe with us 1
To let his madness range. Therefore prepare you;
I your commission will forthwith dispatch,[755]
And he to England shall along with you:
The terms[756] of our estate[757] may not endure
Hazard so near us as doth hourly grow
Out of his lunacies.

GUIL.: We will ourselves provide:
Most holy and religious fear it is
To keep those many many bodies safe 10
That live and feed upon your majesty.

ROS.: The single and peculiar[758] life is bound,
With all the strength and armour of the mind,
To keep itself from noyance;[759] but much more
That spirit upon whose weal depend and rest
The lives of many. The cease[760] of majesty
Dies not alone; but, like a gulf,[761] doth draw
What's near it with it: it is a massy wheel,
Fix'd on the summit of the highest mount,
To whose huge spokes ten thousand lesser things 20
Are mortised and adjoin'd; which, when it falls,
Each small annexment, petty consequence,
Attends[762] the boisterous ruin. Never alone
Did the king sigh, but with a general groan.

KING: Arm[763] you, I pray you, to this speedy voyage;
For we will fetters put upon this fear,
Which now goes too free-footed.

ROS.:
GUIL.: } We will haste us.

            [*Exeunt Rosencrantz and Guildenstern.*

Enter POLONIUS

POL.: My lord, he's going to his mother's closet:
Behind the arras[764] I'll convey[765] myself, 30
To hear the process;[766] I'll warrant she'll tax him
        home:[767]
And, as you said, and wisely was it said,
'Tis meet that some more audience than a mother,
Since nature makes them partial, should o'erhear
The speech, of vantage:[768] Fare you well, my liege:
I'll call upon you ere you go to bed,
And tell you what I know.

KING: Thanks, dear my lord.

            [*Exit Polonius.*

O, my offence is rank, it smells to heaven;
It hath the primal eldest curse[769] upon 't, 40
A brother's murder. Pray can I not,
Though inclination be as sharp as will:[770]
My stronger guilt defeats my strong intent;
And, like a man to double business bound,
I stand in pause where I shall first begin,

---

[749] **top of my bent** Limit of endurance, i.e., extent to which a bow may be bent.
[750] **By and by** Immediately.
[751] **witching time** i.e., Time when spells are cast.
[752] **Nero** Murderer of his mother, Agrippina.
[753] **shent** Rebuked.
[754] **give them seals** Confirm with deeds.
III.iii. [755] **dispatch** Prepare.
[756] **terms** Conditions, circumstances.
[757] **estate** State.

---

[758] **single and peculiar** Individual and private.
[759] **noyance** Harm.
[760] **cease** Decease.
[761] **gulf** Whirlpool.
[762] **Attends** Participates in.
[763] **Arm** Prepare.
[764] **arras** Screen of tapestry placed around the walls of household apartments.
[765] **convey** Implication of secrecy; convey was often used to mean "steal."
[766] **process** Proceedings.
[767] **tax him home** Reprove him severely.
[768] **of vantage** From an advantageous place.
[769] **primal eldest curse** The curse of Cain, the first to kill his brother.
[770] **sharp as will** i.e., His desire is as strong as his determination.

And both neglect. What if this cursed hand
Were thicker than itself with brother's blood,
Is there not rain enough in the sweet heavens
To wash it white as snow? Whereto serves mercy
But to confront[771] the visage of offence?   50
And what's in prayer but this two-fold force,
To be forestalled[772] ere we come to fall,
Or pardon'd being down? Then I'll look up;
My fault is past. But, O, what form of prayer
Can serve my turn? "Forgive me my foul murder"?
That cannot be; since I am still possess'd
Of those effects for which I did the murder,
My crown, mine own ambition[773] and my queen.
May one be pardon'd and retain the offence[774]?
In the corrupted currents[775] of this world   60
Offence's gilded hand[776] may shove by justice,
And oft 'tis seen the wicked prize[777] itself
Buys out the law: but 'tis not so above;
There is no shuffling,[778] there the action lies[779]
In his true nature; and we ourselves compell'd,
Even to the teeth and forehead[780] of our faults,
To give in evidence. What then? what rests[781]?
Try what repentance can: what can it not?
Yet what can it when one can not repent?
O wretched state! O bosom black as death!   70
O limed[782] soul, that, struggling to be free,
Art more engaged[783]! Help, angels! Make assay[784]!
Bow, stubborn knees; and, heart with strings of steel,
Be soft as sinews of the new-born babe!
All may be well.   [Retires and kneels.

Enter HAMLET

HAM.: Now might I do it pat,[785] now he is praying;
            And now I'll do 't. And so he goes to heaven:
            And so am I revenged. That would be scann'd:[786]
            A villain kills my father; and for that,
            I, his sole son, do this same villain send   80
            To heaven.
            O, this is hire and salary, not revenge.
            He took my father grossly, full of bread[787];
            With all his crimes broad blown,[788] as flush[789] as May;
            And how his audit stands who knows save heaven?

But in our circumstance and course[790] of thought,
'Tis heavy with him: and am I then revenged,
To take him in the purging of his soul,
When he is fit and season'd for his passage[791]?
No!   90
Up, sword; and know thou a more horrid hent:[792]
When he is drunk asleep,[793] or in his rage,
Or in the incestuous pleasure of his bed;
At gaming, swearing, or about some act
That has no relish of salvation in 't;
Then trip him, that his heels may kick at heaven,
And that his soul may be as damn'd and black
As hell, where to it goes. My mother stays:
This physic[794] but prolongs thy sickly days.   [Exit.

KING: [Rising] My words fly up, my thoughts remain   100
            below:
            Words without thoughts never to heaven go.   [Exit.

Scene IV—The Queen's Closet

There has been much critical controversy on the question of GERTRUDE's *guilt or innocence in the matter of her husband's murder. The natural inference from this scene (especially Line 46), and from the* GHOST's *story in Act I, Scene V, is that she knew nothing of it. She was guilty of a sinful love for* CLAUDIUS *but was not an accomplice in his greater crime.* HAMLET, *indeed, assumes throughout that the stain of murder as well as of adultery is upon her, but he is naturally inclined to take the blackest view.*

In any case, it is his mother's faithlessness in love that HAMLET *resents most bitterly, and with this chiefly he upbraids her. At first he is successful: the stings of remorse begin to make themselves felt. Then comes the* GHOST, *and she is convinced that* HAMLET *is mad. From that moment she is overcome with fear, and his words pass over her unheeded. For the rest of the play her heart is cleft in twain; she vacillates to the end between good and evil, between her son and her lover.*

Enter QUEEN *and* POLONIUS

POL.: He will come straight. Look you lay[795] home to him: 1
            Tell him his pranks have been too broad[796] to bear
                with,
            And that your grace hath screen'd and stood
                between
            Much heat[797] and him. I'll silence[798] me even here.
            Pray you, be round[799] with him.
HAM.: [Within] Mother, mother, mother!
QUEEN: I'll warrant you,
            Fear me not: withdraw, I hear him coming.

                        [Polonius hides behind the arras.

---

[771] **confront** Oppose directly.
[772] **forestalled** Prevented.
[773] **ambition** i.e., Realization of ambition.
[774] **offence** Benefit accruing from offense.
[775] **currents** Courses.
[776] **gilded hand** Hand offering gold as a bribe.
[777] **wicked prize** Prize won by wickedness.
[778] **shuffling** Escape by trickery.
[779] **lies** Is sustainable.
[780] **teeth and forehead** Very face.
[781] **rests** Remains.
[782] **limed** Caught as with birdlime.
[783] **engaged** Embedded.
[784] **assay** Trial.
[785] **pat** Opportunely.
[786] **would be scann'd** Needs to be looked into.
[787] **full of bread** Enjoying his worldly pleasures (see Ezekiel 16:49).
[788] **broad blown** In full bloom.
[789] **flush** Lusty.

---

[790] **in . . . course** As we see it in our mortal situation.
[791] **fit . . . passage** i.e., Reconciled to heaven by forgiveness of his sins.
[792] **hent** Seizing; or more likely, occasion of seizure.
[793] **drunk asleep** In a drunken sleep.
[794] **physic** Purging (by prayer).
III.iv. [795] **lay** Thrust.
[796] **broad** Unrestrained.
[797] **Much heat** i.e., The king's anger.
[798] **silence** Hide.
[799] **round** Blunt.

Enter HAMLET

HAM.: Now, mother, what's the matter?

QUEEN: Hamlet, thou hast thy father much offended. 10

HAM.: Mother, you have my father[800] much offended.

QUEEN: Come, come, you answer with an idle tongue.

HAM.: Go, go, you question with a wicked tongue.

QUEEN: Why, how now, Hamlet!

HAM.: What's the matter now?

QUEEN: Have you forgot me?

HAM.: No, by the rood,[801] not so:
You are the queen, your husband's brother's wife;
And—would it were not so!—you are my mother.

QUEEN: Nay, then, I'll set those to you that can speak. 20

HAM.: Come, come, and sit you down; you shall not budge;
You go not till I set you up a glass
Where you may see the inmost part of you.

QUEEN: What wilt thou do? thou wilt not murder me?
Help, help, ho!

POL.: [*Behind*] What, ho! help, help, help!

HAM.: [*Drawing*] How now! a rat? Dead, for a ducat, dead!   [*Makes a pass through the arras.*

POL.: [*Behind*] O, I am slain!   [*Falls and dies.*

QUEEN: O me, what hast thou done? 30

HAM.: Nay, I know not:
Is it the king?

QUEEN: O, what a rash and bloody deed is this:

HAM.: A bloody deed! almost as bad, good mother,
As kill a king, and marry with his brother.

QUEEN: As kill a king!

HAM.: Ay, lady, 't was my word.

[*Lifts up the arras and discovers Polonius.*

Thou wretched, rash, intruding fool, farewell!
I took thee for thy better: take thy fortune;
Thou find'st to be too busy is some danger. 40
Leave wringing of your hands: peace! sit you down,
And let me wring your heart; for so I shall,
If it be made of penetrable stuff,
If damned custom have not brass'd[802] it so
That it be proof and bulwark against sense.

QUEEN: What have I done, that thou darest wag thy tongue
In noise so rude against me?

HAM.: Such an act
That blurs the grace and blush of modesty,
Calls virtue hypocrite, takes off the rose 50
From the fair forehead of an innocent love
And sets a blister[803] there, makes marriage-vows
As false as dicers' oaths: O, such a deed
As from the body of contraction[804] plucks
The very soul, and sweet religion[805] makes
A rhapsody[806] of words: heaven's face doth glow;

Yea, this solidity and compound mass,
With tristful visage, as against the doom,
Is thought-sick at the act.[807]

QUEEN: Ay me, what act, 60
That roars so loud, and thunders in the index[808]?

HAM.: Look here, upon this picture, and on this,
The counterfeit presentment[809] of two brothers.
See, what a grace was seated on this brow;
Hyperion's[810] curls; the front[811] of Jove himself;
An eye like Mars, to threaten and command;
A station[812] like the herald Mercury
New-lighted on a heaven-kissing hill;
A combination and a form indeed,
Where every god did seem to set his seal, 70
To give the world assurance[813] of a man:
This was your husband. Look you now, what follows:
Here is your husband; like a mildew'd ear,[814]
Blasting his wholesome brother. Have you eyes?
Could you on this fair mountain leave to feed,
And batten[815] on this moor[816]? Ha! have you eyes?
You cannot call it love; for at your age
The hey-day[817] in the blood is tame, it's humble,
And waits upon the judgement: and what judgement
Would step from this to this? Sense, sure, you have, 80
Else could you not have motion[818]; but sure, that sense
Is apoplex'd[819]; for madness would not err,
Nor sense to ecstasy was ne'er so thrall'd[820]
But it reserved some quantity of choice,[821]
To serve in such a difference. What devil was 't
That thus hath cozen'd[822] you at hoodman blind[823]?
Eyes without feeling, feeling without sight,
Ears without hands or eyes, smelling sans[824] all,
Or but a sickly part of one true sense
Could not so mope.[825] 90
O shame! where is thy blush? Rebellious hell,
If thou canst mutine[826] in a matron's bones,

---

[807] **heaven's . . . act** Heaven's face blushes to look down upon this world, compounded of the four elements, with hot face as though the day of doom were near, and thought-sick at the deed (i.e., Gertrude's marriage).

[808] **index** Prelude or preface.

[809] **counterfeit presentment** Portrayed representation.

[810] **Hyperion's** The sun god's.

[811] **front** Brow.

[812] **station** Manner of standing.

[813] **assurance** Pledge, guarantee.

[814] **mildew'd ear** Blighted ear of grain (Genesis 41:6).

[815] **batten** Grow fat.

[816] **moor** Barren upland.

[817] **hey-day** State of excitement

[818] **Sense . . . motion** Sense and motion are functions of the middle or sensible soul, the possession of sense being the basis of motion.

[819] **apoplex'd** Paralyzed; mental derangement was thus of three sorts: apoplexy, ecstasy, and diabolic possession.

[820] **thrall'd** Enslaved.

[821] **quantity of choice** Fragment of the power to choose.

[822] **cozen'd** Tricked, cheated.

[823] **hoodman blind** Blindman's bluff.

[824] **sans** Without.

[825] **mope** Be in a depressed, spiritless state, act aimlessly.

[826] **mutine** Mutiny, rebel.

---

[800] **thy father . . . my father** i.e., Claudius, the elder Hamlet.

[801] **rood** Cross.

[802] **brass'd** Brassed, hardened.

[803] **sets a blister** Brands as a harlot.

[804] **contraction** The marriage contract.

[805] **religion** Religious vows.

[806] **rhapsody** Senseless string.

To flaming youth let virtue be as wax,
And melt in her own fire: proclaim no shame
When the compulsive ardour gives the charge,[827]
Since frost itself as actively doth burn
And reason panders will.[828]

QUEEN: O Hamlet, speak no more:
Thou turn'st mine eyes into my very soul;
And there I see such black and grained[829] spots   100
As will not leave their tinct. O, speak to me no more;
These words, like daggers, enter in mine ears;
No more, sweet Hamlet!

HAM.:   A murderer and a villain;
A slave that is not twentieth part the tithe
Of your precedent lord[830]; a vice of kings,[831]
A cutpurse of the empire and the rule,
That from a shelf the precious diadem stole,
And put it in his pocket!

QUEEN: No more!   110

HAM.: A king of shreds and patches,[832]—

Enter GHOST

Save me, and hover o'er me with your wings,
You heavenly guards! What would your gracious
          figure?

QUEEN: Alas, he's mad!

HAM.: Do you not come your tardy son to chide,
That, lapsed in time and passion,[833] lets go by
The important[834] acting of your dread command?
O, say!

GHOST: Do not forget: this visitation
Is but to whet thy almost blunted purpose.   120
But, look, amazement[835] on thy mother sits:
O, step between her and her fighting soul.
Conceit in weakest bodies strongest works:
Speak to her, Hamlet.

HAM.:   How is it with you, lady?

QUEEN: Alas, how is 't with you,
That you do bend your eye on vacancy
And with the incorporal[836] air do hold discourse?
Forth at your eyes your spirits wildly peep;
And, as the sleeping soldiers in the alarm,   130
Your bedded[837] hair, like life in excrements,[838]

Start up, and stand an[839] end. O gentle son,
Upon the heat and flame of thy distemper
Sprinkle cool patience. Whereon do you look?

HAM.: On him, on him! Look you, how pale he glares!
His form and cause conjoin'd,[840] preaching to stones,
Would make them capable. Do not look upon me;
Lest with this piteous action you convert
My stern effects:[841] then what I have to do
Will want true colour[842]; tears perchance for blood.   140

QUEEN: To whom do you speak this?

HAM.:   Do you see nothing there?

QUEEN: Nothing at all; yet all that is I see.

HAM.: Nor did you nothing hear?

QUEEN: No, nothing but ourselves.

HAM.: Why, look you there! look, how it steals away!
My father, in his habit as he lived!
Look, where he goes, even now, out at the portal!

[*Exit Ghost.*

QUEEN: This is the very coinage of your brain:
This bodiless creation ecstasy   150
Is very cunning in.

HAM.:   Ecstasy!
My pulse, as yours, doth temperately keep time,
And makes as healthful music: it is not madness
That I have utter'd: bring me to the test,
And I the matter will re-word[843]; which madness
Would gambol[844] from. Mother, for love of grace,
Lay not that flattering unction[845] to your soul,
That not your trespass, but my madness speaks:
It will but skin and film the ulcerous place,   160
Whiles rank corruption, mining[846] all within,
Infects unseen. Confess yourself to heaven;
Repent what's past; avoid what is to come[847];
And do not spread the compost[848] on the weeds,
To make them ranker. Forgive me this my virtue[849];
For in the fatness[850] of these pursy[851] times
Virtue itself of vice must pardon beg,
Yea, curb[852] and woo for leave to do him good.

QUEEN: O Hamlet, thou hast cleft my heart in twain.

HAM.: O, throw away the worser part of it,   170
And live the purer with the other half.
Good night: but go not to mine uncle's bed;
Assume a virtue, if you have it not.

---

[827] **gives the charge** Delivers the attack.
[828] **reason panders will** The normal and proper situation was one in which reason guided the will in the direction of good; here, reason is perverted and leads in the direction of evil.
[829] **grained** Dyed in grain.
[830] **precedent lord** i.e., The elder Hamlet.
[831] **vice of kings** Buffoon of kings; a reference to the Vice, or clown, of the morality plays and interludes.
[832] **shreds and patches** i.e., Motley, the traditional costume of the Vice.
[833] **lapsed . . . passion** Having suffered time to slip and passion to cool; also explained as "engrossed in casual events and lapsed into mere fruitless passion, so that he no longer entertains a rational purpose."
[834] **important** Urgent.
[835] **amazement** Frenzy, distraction.
[836] **incorporal** Immaterial.
[837] **bedded** Laid in smooth layers.
[838] **excrements** The hair was considered an excrement or voided part of the body.

---

[839] **an** On.
[840] **conjoin'd** United.
[841] **convert . . . effects** Divert me from my stern duty. For effects, possibly affects (affections of the mind).
[842] **want true color** Lack good reason so that (with a play on the normal sense of color) I shall shed tears instead of blood.
[843] **re-word** Repeat in words.
[844] **gambol** Skip away.
[845] **unction** Ointment used medicinally or as a rite; suggestion that forgiveness for sin may not be so easily achieved.
[846] **mining** Working under the surface.
[847] **what is to come** i.e., The sins of the future.
[848] **compost** Manure.
[849] **this my virtue** My virtuous talk in reproving you.
[850] **fatness** Grossness.
[851] **pursy** Short-winded, corpulent.
[852] **curb** Bow, bend the knee.

That monster, custom, who all sense doth eat,
Of habits devil, is angel yet in this,
That to the use of actions fair and good
He likewise gives a frock or livery,
That aptly is put on. Refrain to-night,
And that shall lend a kind of easiness
To the next abstinence: the next more easy;   180
For use almost can change the stamp of nature,
And either . . . the devil, or throw him out[853]
With wondrous potency. Once more, good night:
And when you are desirous to be bless'd,[854]
I'll blessing beg of you. For this same lord,

                        [Pointing to Polonius.

I do repent: but heaven hath pleased it so,
To punish me with this and this with me,
That I must be their scourge and minister.
I will bestow him, and will answer well
The death I gave him. So, again, good night.   190
I must be cruel, only to be kind:
Thus bad begins and worse remains behind.
One word more, good lady.
QUEEN: What shall I do?
HAM.: Not this, by no means, that I bid you do:
Let the bloat[855] king tempt you again to bed;
Pinch wanton on your cheek; call you his mouse;
And let him, for a pair of reechy[856] kisses,
Or paddling in your neck with his damn'd fingers,
Make you to ravel all this matter out,   200
That I essentially[857] am not in madness,
But mad in craft. 'T were good you let him know;
For who, that's but a queen, fair, sober, wise,
Would from a paddock,[858] from a bat, a gib,[859]
Such dear concernings[860] hide? who would do so?

---

[853] **And . . . out** Defective line. Line usually emended by inserting *master* after *either*.
[854] **be bless'd** Become blessed, i.e., repentant.
[855] **bloat** Bloated.
[856] **reechy** Dirty, filthy.
[857] **essentially** In my essential nature.
[858] **paddock** Toad.
[859] **gib** Tomcat.
[860] **dear concernings** Important affairs.

No, in despite of sense and secrecy,
Unpeg the basket on the house's top,
Let the birds fly, and, like the famous ape,[861]
To try conclusions,[862] in the basket creep,
And break your own neck down.   210
QUEEN: Be thou assured, if words be made of breath,
And breath of life, I have no life to breathe
What thou hast said to me.
HAM.: I must to England; you know that?
QUEEN: Alack,
I had forgot: 'tis so concluded on.
HAM.: There's letters seal'd: and my two schoolfellows,
Whom I will trust as I will adders fang'd,
They bear the mandate; they must sweep my way,[863]
And marshal me to knavery. Let it work;   220
For 'tis the sport to have the enginer[864]
Hoist[865] with his own petar:[866] and 't shall go hard
But I will delve one yard below their mines,
And blow them at the moon: O, 'tis most sweet,
When in one line two crafts[867] directly meet.
This man shall set me packing:[868]
I'll lug the guts into the neighbour room.
Mother, good night. Indeed this counsellor
Is now most still, most secret and most grave,
Who was in life a foolish prating knave.   230
Come, sir, to draw[869] toward an end with you.
Good night, mother.

    [Exeunt severally; Hamlet dragging in Polonius.

---

[861] **the famous ape** A letter from Sir John Suckling seems to supply other details of the story, otherwise not identified: "It is the story of the jackanapes and the partridges; thou starest after a beauty till it be lost to thee, then let'st out another, and starest after that till it is gone too."
[862] **conclusions** Experiments.
[863] **sweep my way** Clear my path.
[864] **enginer** Constructor of military works, or possibly, artilleryman.
[865] **Hoist** Blown up.
[866] **petar** Defined as a small engine of war used to blow in a door or make a breach, and as a case filled with explosive materials.
[867] **two crafts** Two acts of guile, with quibble on the sense of "two ships."
[868] **set me packing** Set me to making schemes, and set me to lugging (him), and, also, send me off in a hurry.
[869] **draw** Come, with quibble on literal sense.

Act IV

Scene I—A Room in the Castle

This scene is practically continuous with Act III, Scene IV. As soon as HAMLET *has left his mother's closet,* CLAUDIUS *enters to learn the result of the interview. He finds the* QUEEN *over- whelmed and hardly able to speak—the combined effect of her son's reproaches and of her grief at his insanity.*

Enter KING, QUEEN, ROSENCRANTZ, *and* GUILDENSTERN

KING: There's matter in these sighs, these profound heaves: 1
You must translate: 'tis fit we understand them.
Where is your son?
QUEEN: Bestow this place on us a little while.

    [Exeunt Rosencrantz and Guildenstern.

Ah, mine own lord, what have I seen to-night!
KING: What, Gertrude? How does Hamlet?

QUEEN: Mad as the sea and wind, when both contend
　　Which is the mightier: in his lawless fit,
　　Behind the arras hearing something stir,
　　Whips out his rapier, cries, "A rat, a rat!"　　　　10
　　And, in this brainish[870] apprehension,[871] kills
　　The unseen good old man.
KING:　　　　　　　　　　　　O heavy deed!
　　It had been so with us, had we been there:
　　His liberty is full of threats to all;
　　To you yourself, to us, to every one.
　　Alas, how shall this bloody deed be answer'd?
　　It will be laid to us, whose providence[872]
　　Should have kept short,[873] restrain'd and out of haunt,[874]
　　This mad young man: but so much was our love,　　20
　　We would not understand what was most fit;
　　But, like the owner of a foul disease,
　　To keep it from divulging,[875] let it feed
　　Even on the pith of life. Where is he gone?
QUEEN: To draw apart the body he hath kill'd:
　　O'er whom his very madness, like some ore
　　Among a mineral[876] of metals base,
　　Shows itself pure; he weeps for what is done.
KING: O Gertrude, come away!
　　The sun no sooner shall the mountains touch,　　30
　　But we will ship him hence: and this vile deed
　　We must, with all our majesty and skill,
　　Both countenance and excuse. Ho, Guildenstern!

Re-enter ROSENCRANTZ *and* GUILDENSTERN

　　Friends both, go join you with some further aid:
　　Hamlet in madness hath Polonius slain,
　　And from his mother's closet hath he dragg'd him:
　　Go seek him out; speak fair, and bring the body
　　Into the chapel. I pray you, haste in this.

　　　　　　　[*Exeunt Rosencrantz and Guildenstern.*

　　Come, Gertrude, we'll call up our wisest friends;
　　And let them know, both what we mean to do,　　40
　　And what's untimely done . . .[877]
　　Whose whisper o'er the world's diameter,[878]
　　As level[879] as the cannon to his blank,[880]
　　Transports his poison'd shot, may miss our name,
　　And hit the woundless[881] air. O, come away!
　　My soul is full of discord and dismay.　　[*Exeunt.*

IV.i. [870] **brainish** Headstrong, passionate.
[871] **apprehension** Conception, imagination.
[872] **providence** Foresight.
[873] **short** i.e., On a short tether.
[874] **out of haunt** Secluded.
[875] **divulging** Becoming evident.
[876] **mineral** Mine.
[877] **done . . .** Defective line; some editors add: *so haply, slander;* others add: *for, haply, slander;* other conjectures.
[878] **diameter** Extent from side to side.
[879] **level** Straight.
[880] **blank** White spot in the center of a target.
[881] **woundless** Invulnerable.

Scene II—Another Room in the Castle

In this scene and the following, HAMLET *continues his assumption of madness. He is not at all unwilling to be sent to England; it will compel him to further delay; and he promises himself an intellectual treat in checkmating any design that his companions may have against him.*

Enter HAMLET

HAM.: Safely stowed.　　　　　　　　　　　　　1
ROS.:
GUIL.: } [*Within*] Hamlet! Lord Hamlet!
HAM.: But soft, what noise? who calls on Hamlet?
　　O, here they come.

Enter ROSENCRANTZ *and* GUILDENSTERN

ROS.: What have you done, my lord, with the dead body?
HAM.: Compounded it with dust, whereto 'tis kin.
ROS.: Tell us where 'tis, that we may take it thence
　　And bear it to the chapel.
HAM.: Do not believe it.
ROS.: Believe what?　　　　　　　　　　　　　10
HAM.: That I can keep your counsel[882] and not mine own.
　　Besides, to be demanded of a sponge! what replication[883] should be made by the son of a king?
ROS.: Take you me for a sponge, my lord?
HAM.: Ay, sir, that soaks up the king's countenance, his rewards, his authorities.[884] But such officers do the king best service in the end: he keeps them, like an ape, in the corner of his jaw; first mouthed, to be last swallowed: when he needs what you have gleaned, it is but squeezing you, and, sponge, you shall be dry　　20
　　again.
ROS.: I understand you not, my lord.
HAM.: I am glad of it: a knavish speech sleeps in a foolish ear.
ROS.: My lord, you must tell us where the body is, and go with us to the king.
HAM.: The body is with the king, but the king is not with the body.[885] The king is a thing—
GUIL.: A thing, my lord!
HAM.: Of nothing: bring me to him. Hide fox, and all after.[886]　30

　　　　　　　　　　　　　　　　[*Exeunt.*

Scene III—Another Room in the Castle

(See synopsis for Act IV, Scene II.)

Enter KING, *attended*

KING: I have sent to seek him, and to find the body.　　1
　　How dangerous is it that this man goes loose!

IV.ii. [882] **keep your counsel** Hamlet is aware of their treachery but says nothing about it.
[883] **replication** Reply.
[884] **authorities** Authoritative backing.
[885] **The body . . . body.** There are many interpretations; possibly, "The body lies in death with the king, my father; but my father walks disembodied"; or "Claudius has the bodily possession of kingship, but kingliness, or justice of inheritance, is not with him."
[886] **Hide . . . after.** An old signal cry in the game of hide-and-seek.

Yet must not we put the strong law on him:
He's loved of the distracted[887] multitude,
Who like not in their judgement, but their eyes;
And where 'tis so, the offender's scourge[888] is weigh'd,[889]
But never the offence. To bear all smooth and even,
This sudden sending him away must seem
Deliberate pause:[890] diseases desperate grown
By desperate appliance are relieved,   10
Or not at all.

Enter ROSENCRANTZ

How now! what hath befall'n?
ROS.: Where the dead body is bestow'd, my lord,
    We cannot get from him.
KING: But where is he?
ROS.: Without, my lord; guarded, to know your pleasure.
KING: Bring him before us.
ROS.: Ho, Guildenstern! bring in my lord.

Enter HAMLET *and* GUILDENSTERN

KING: Now, Hamlet, where's Polonius?
HAM.: At supper.
KING: At supper! where?   20
HAM.: Not where he eats, but where he is eaten: a certain
    convocation of politic[891] worms[892] are e'en at him. Your
    worm is your only emperor for diet: we fat all crea-
    tures else to fat us, and we fat ourselves for maggots:
    your fat king and your lean beggar is but variable
    service,[893] two dishes, but to one table: that's the end.
KING: Alas, alas!
HAM.: A man may fish with the worm that hath eat of a
    king, and eat of the fish that hath fed of that worm.   30
KING: What dost thou mean by this?
HAM.: Nothing but to show you how a king may go a
    progress[894] through the guts of a beggar.
KING: Where is Polonius?
HAM.: In heaven; send thither to see: if your messenger
    find him not there, seek him i' the other place
    yourself. But indeed, if you find him not within this
    month, you shall nose him as you go up the stairs
    into the lobby.
KING: Go seek him there.   [*To some Attendants.*   40
HAM.: He will stay till you come.   [*Exeunt Attendants.*
KING: Hamlet, this deed, for thine especial safety,—
    Which we do tender,[895] as we dearly grieve
    For that which thou hast done,—must send thee
        hence
    With fiery quickness: therefore prepare thyself;
    The bark is ready, and the wind at help,

The associates tend, and every thing is bent
    For England.
HAM.:   For England!
KING: Ay, Hamlet.   50
HAM.:   Good.
KING: So is it, if thou knew'st our purposes.
HAM.: I see a cherub[896] that sees them. But, come; for
    England! Farewell, dear mother.
KING: Thy loving father, Hamlet.
HAM.: My mother: father and mother is man and wife;
    man and wife is one flesh; and so, my mother. Come,
    for England!   [*Exit.*
KING: Follow him at foot[897]; tempt him with speed
        aboard;
    Delay it not; I'll have him hence to-night: 60
    Away! for every thing is seal'd and done
    That else leans on the affair: pray you, make haste.

        [*Exeunt Rosencrantz and Guildenstern.*

And, England, if my love thou hold'st at aught—
As my great power thereof may give thee sense,
Since yet thy cicatrice[898] looks raw and red
After the Danish sword, and thy free awe[899]
Pays homage to us—thou mayst not coldly set
Our sovereign process; which imports at full,
By letters congruing to that effect,
The present death of Hamlet. Do it, England;   70
For like the hectic[900] in my blood he rages,
And thou must cure me: till I know 'tis done,
Howe'er my haps,[901] my joys were ne'er begun.   [*Exit.*

Scene IV—A Plain in Denmark

The present act works out the results of HAMLET*'s failure until
they bring about the catastrophe of Act V. There are two main
threads of incident: (1) there is the failure of the plot against*
HAMLET*'s life, which leads to his return to Denmark, and drives*
CLAUDIUS *to new devices; and (2)* HAMLET*'s unkindness to*
OPHELIA, *together with the death of* POLONIUS, *makes her insane.*
LAERTES *returns, burning for revenge, and readily becomes the*
KING*'s accomplice.*

The stress laid upon the fortunes of OPHELIA *in the latter
part of the play has its dramatic purpose. It impresses us with the
fact that* HAMLET*'s ineffectiveness has its tragic results outside his
own life; and at the same time the pathos of the situation makes us
feel pity rather than anger toward him, since his deep affection for*
OPHELIA *is manifest throughout. And it is essential to the effect
of tragedy that the sympathies of the spectator should be at the end
with the hero.*

The scene with the CAPTAIN *serves as a transition to the
new act; at the same time, it strikes the note of contrast between*
HAMLET *and* FORTINBRAS, *the strong, practical man. The*

IV.iii. [887]**distracted** i.e., Without power of forming logical
judgments.
[888]**scourge** Punishment.
[889]**weigh'd** Taken into consideration.
[890]**Deliberate pause** Considered action.
[891]**politic** Crafty.
[892]**convocation . . . worms** Allusion to the Diet of Worms
(1521).
[893]**variable service** A variety of dishes.
[894]**progress** Royal journey of state.
[895]**tender** Regard, hold dear.

---

[896]**cherub** Cherubim are angels of knowledge.
[897]**at foot** Close behind, at heel.
[898]**cicatrice** Scar.
[899]**free awe** England, awed by Danish power, "freely" pays
homage to Denmark.
[900]**hectic** Fever.
[901]**haps** Fortunes.

perception of this contrast is characteristically put in HAMLET's *own mouth.*

Enter FORTINBRAS, *a* CAPTAIN, *and* SOLDIERS, *marching*

FORTINBRAS: Go, captain, from me greet the Danish king;   1
    Tell him that, by his license,[902] Fortinbras
    Craves the conveyance[903] of a promised march
    Over his kingdom. You know the rendezvous.
    If that his majesty would aught with us,
    We shall express our duty in his eye[904];
    And let him know so.
CAPTAIN: I will do 't, my lord.
FORT.: Go softly[905] on.   [*Exeunt Fortinbras and Soldiers.*

Enter HAMLET, ROSENCRANTZ, GUILDENSTERN, *and others*

HAM.: Good sir, whose powers are these?   10
CAP.: They are of Norway, sir.
HAM.: How purposed, sir, I pray you?
CAP.: Against some part of Poland.
HAM.: Who commands them, sir?
CAP.: The nephew to old Norway, Fortinbras.
HAM.: Goes it against the main[906] of Poland, sir,
    Or for some frontier?
CAP.: Truly to speak, and with no addition,
    We go to gain a little patch of ground
    That hath in it no profit but the name.   20
    To pay five ducats, five, I would not farm it:[907]
    Nor will it yield to Norway or the Pole
    A ranker rate, should it be sold in fee.[908]
HAM.: Why, then the Polack never will defend it.
CAP.: Yes, it is already garrison'd.
HAM.: Two thousand souls and twenty thousand ducats
    Will not debate the question of this straw:[909]
    This is the imposthume[910] of much wealth and peace,
    That inward breaks, and shows no cause without
    Why the man dies. I humbly thank you, sir.   30
CAP.: God be wi' you, sir.   [*Exit.*
ROS: Will 't please you go, my lord?
HAM.: I'll be with you straight. Go a little before.

            [*Exeunt all except Hamlet.*

    How all occasions[911] do inform against[912] me,
    And spur my dull revenge! What is a man,
    If his chief good and market of his time[913]
    Be but to sleep and feed? a beast, no more.

IV.iv. [902] **license** Leave.
[903] **conveyance** Escort, convey.
[904] **in his eye** In his presence.
[905] **softly** Slowly.
[906] **main** Country itself.
[907] **farm it** Take a lease of it.
[908] **fee** Fee simple.
[909] **debate . . . straw** Settle this trifling matter.
[910] **imposthume** Purulent abscess or swelling.
[911] **occasions** Incidents, events.
[912] **inform against** Generally defined as "show," "betray" (i.e., his tardiness); more probably inform means "take shape," as in *Macbeth*, II.i.
[913] **market of his time** The best use he makes of his time, or, that for which he sells his time.

    Sure, he that made us with such large discourse,
    Looking before and after, gave us not
    That capability and god-like reason   40
    To fust[914] in us unused. Now, whether it be
    Bestial oblivion, or some craven scruple
    Of thinking too precisely on the event,
    A thought which, quarter'd, hath but one part
        wisdom
    And ever three parts coward, I do not know
    Why yet I live to say "This thing's to do";
    Sith I have cause and will and strength and means
    To do 't. Examples gross as earth exhort me:
    Witness this army of such mass and charge
    Led by a delicate and tender prince,   50
    Whose spirit with divine ambition puff'd
    Makes mouths at the invisible event,
    Exposing what is mortal and unsure
    To all that fortune, death and danger dare,
    Even for an egg-shell. Rightly to be great
    Is not to stir without great argument,
    But greatly to find quarrel in a straw
    When honour's at the stake. How stand I then,
    That have a father kill'd, a mother stain'd,
    Excitements of[915] my reason and my blood,   60
    And let all sleep? while, to my shame, I see
    The imminent death of twenty thousand men,
    That, for a fantasy and trick[916] of fame,
    Go to their graves like beds, fight for a plot[917]
    Whereon the numbers cannot try the cause,
    Which is not tomb enough and continent
    To hide the slain? O, from this time forth,
    My thoughts be bloody, or be nothing worth!   [*Exit.*

Scene V—Elsinore. A Room in the Castle

The interest of Scenes V and VII lies partly in the ingenuity with which the KING *turns* LAERTES *to his purposes, partly in the pathos of* OPHELIA's *madness and death.* LAERTES *is a youth of high spirit and true emotions, but his French training has left him without high principle, and he is weak enough to be easily led. The genuine insanity of* OPHELIA *is a pendant to that assumed by* HAMLET; *the immediate cause is her father's death, yet the loss of her lover must also have affected her deeply. The character of the songs she sings—they are not given in full in this edition—is not inconsistent with perfect purity; all who have had experience with mad patients can confirm this; and therefore it gives no support to the curious theory, held by no less a critic than Goethe, that she had been* HAMLET's *mistress.*

Enter QUEEN, HORATIO, *and a* GENTLEMAN

QUEEN: I will not speak with her.   1
GENTLEMAN: She is importunate, indeed distract:
    Her mood will needs be pitied.
QUEEN: What would she have?

---

[914] **fust** Grow moldy.
[915] **Excitements of** Incentives to.
[916] **trick** Toy, trifle.
[917] **plot** i.e., Of ground.

GENT.: She speaks much of her father; says she hears
 There's tricks[918] i' the world; and hems, and beats her
  heart[919];
 Spurns enviously at straws[920]; speaks things in doubt,
 That carry but half sense: her speech is nothing,
 Yet the unshaped[921] use of it doth move
 The hearers to collection[922]; they aim[923] at it,   10
 And botch[924] the words up fit to their own thoughts;
 Which, as her winks, and nods, and gestures yield[925]
  them,
 Indeed would make one think there might be thought,
 Though nothing sure, yet much unhappily.[926]
HOR.: 'T were good she were spoken with; for she may
  strew
 Dangerous conjectures in ill-breeding minds.[927]
QUEEN: Let her come in.   [*Exit Horatio.*
 To my sick soul, as sin's true nature is,
 Each toy seems prologue to some great amiss:[928]
 So full of artless jealousy is guilt,   20
 It spills itself in fearing to be spilt.[929]

Re-enter HORATIO, *with* OPHELIA

OPH.: Where is the beauteous majesty of Denmark?
QUEEN: How now, Ophelia!
OPH.: [*Sings*] How should I your true love know
   From another one?
  By his cockle hat[930] and staff,
   And his sandal shoon.[931]
QUEEN: Alas, sweet lady, what imports this song?
OPH.: Say you? nay, pray you, mark.
 [*Sings*] He is dead and gone, lady,   30
   He is dead and gone;
  At his head a grass-green turf,
   At his heels a stone.
QUEEN: Nay, but, Ophelia,—
OPH.: Pray you, mark.
 [*Sings*] White his shroud as the mountain snow,—

Enter KING

QUEEN: Alas, look here, my lord.
OPH.: [*Sings*] Larded[932] with sweet flowers;
  Which bewept to the grave did go
   With true-love showers.   40
KING: How do you, pretty lady?

OPH.: Well, God 'ild[933] you! They say the owl[934] was a
 baker's daughter. Lord, we know what we are, but
 know not what we may be. God be at your table!
KING: Conceit upon her father.
OPH.: Pray you, let's have no words of this; but when
 they ask you what it means, say you this:
 [*Sings*] To-morrow is Saint Valentine's day,
   All in the morning betime,
  And I a maid at your window,   50
   To be your Valentine.[935]
KING: How long hath she been thus?
OPH.: I hope all will be well. We must be patient: but I
 cannot choose but weep, to think they should lay
 him i' the cold ground. My brother shall know of it:
 and so I thank you for your good counsel. Come, my
 coach! Good night, ladies; good night, sweet ladies;
 good night, good night.   [*Exit.*
KING: Follow her close; give her good watch, I pray you.

       [*Exit Horatio.*

 O, this is the poison of deep grief; it springs 60
 All from her father's death. O Gertrude, Gertrude,
 When sorrows come, they come not single spies,
 But in battalions. First, her father slain:
 Next, your son gone; and he most violent author
 Of his own just remove: the people muddied,
 Thick and unwholesome in their thoughts and
  whispers,
 For good Polonius' death; and we have done but
  greenly,[936]
 In hugger-mugger[937] to inter him: poor Ophelia
 Divided from herself and her fair judgement,
 Without the which we are pictures, or mere beasts: 70
 Last, and as much containing as all these,
 Her brother is in secret come from France:
 Feeds on his wonder, keeps himself in clouds,[938]
 And wants not buzzers[939] to infect his ear
 With pestilent speeches of his father's death;
 Wherein necessity, of matter beggar'd,[940]
 Will nothing stick[941] our person to arraign
 In ear and ear.[942] O my dear Gertrude, this,
 Like to a murdering-piece,[943] in many places
 Gives me superfluous death. [*A noise within.* 80
QUEEN: Alack, what noise is this?
KING: Where are my Switzers[944]? Let them guard the door.

IV.v. [918] **tricks** Deceptions.
[919] **heart** i.e., Breast.
[920] **Spurns . . . straws** Kicks spitefully at small objects in her path.
[921] **unshaped** Unformed, artless.
[922] **collection** Inference, a guess at some sort of meaning.
[923] **aim** Wonder.
[924] **botch** Patch.
[925] **yield** Deliver, bring forth (her words).
[926] **much unhappily** Expressive of much unhappiness.
[927] **ill-breeding minds** Minds bent on mischief.
[928] **great amiss** Calamity, disaster.
[929] **So . . . spilt.** Guilt is so full of suspicion that it unskillfully betrays itself in fearing to be betrayed.
[930] **cockle hat** Hat with cockleshell stuck in it as a sign that the wearer has been a pilgrim to the shrine of St. James of Composte-la; the pilgrim's garb was a conventional disguise for lovers.
[931] **shoon** Shoes.
[932] **Larded** Decorated.

[933] **God 'ild** God yield or reward.
[934] **owl** Reference to a monkish legend that a baker's daughter was turned into an owl for refusing bread to the Savior.
[935] **Valentine** This song alludes to the belief that the first girl seen by a man on the morning of this day was his valentine or true love.
[936] **greenly** Foolishly.
[937] **hugger-mugger** Secret haste.
[938] **in clouds** Invisible.
[939] **buzzers** Gossipers.
[940] **of matter beggar'd** Unprovided with facts.
[941] **nothing stick** Not hesitate.
[942] **In ear and ear** In everybody's ears.
[943] **murdering-piece** Small cannon or mortar; suggestion of numerous missiles fired.
[944] **Switzers** Swiss guards, mercenaries.

Enter another GENTLEMAN

    What is the matter?

GENT.:   Save yourself, my lord:
    The ocean, overpeering[945] of his list,[946]
    Eats not the flats with more impetuous haste
    Than young Laertes, in a riotous head,
    O'erbears your officers. The rabble call him lord;
    And, as the world were now but to begin,
    Antiquity forgot, custom not known,   90
    The ratifiers and props of every word,[947]
    They cry "Choose we: Laertes shall be king":
    Caps, hands and tongues, applaud it to the clouds:
    "Laertes shall be king, Laertes king!"

QUEEN: How cheerfully on the false trail they cry!
    O, this is counter,[948] you false Danish dogs!

KING: The doors are broke.   [*Noise within.*

Enter LAERTES, *armed; Danes following*

LAER.: Where is this king? Sirs, stand you all without.

DANES: No, let's come in.

LAER.:   I pray you, give me leave.   100

DANES: We will, we will.   [*They retire without the door.*

LAER.: I thank you: keep the door. O thou vile king,
    Give me my father!

QUEEN: Calmly, good Laertes.

LAER.: That drop of blood that's calm proclaims me
        bastard,
    Cries cuckold to my father, brands the harlot
    Even here, between the chaste unsmirched brows
    Of my true mother.

KING: What is the cause, Laertes,
    That thy rebellion looks so giant-like?   110
    Let him go, Gertrude; do not fear our person:
    There's such divinity doth hedge a king,
    That treason can but peep to[949] what it would,[950]
    Acts little of his will. Tell me, Laertes,
    Why thou art thus incensed. Let him go, Gertrude.
    Speak, man.

LAER.: Where is my father?

KING: Dead.

QUEEN: But not by him.

KING: Let him demand his fill.   120

LAER.: How came he dead? I'll not be juggled with:
    To hell, allegiance! vows, to the blackest devil!
    Conscience and grace, to the profoundest pit!
    I dare damnation. To this point I stand,
    That both the worlds I give to negligence,[951]
    Let come what comes; only I'll be revenged
    Most thoroughly for my father.

KING: Who shall stay you?

LAER.: My will,[952] not all the world:
    And for my means, I'll husband them so well,   130
    They shall go far with little.

KING: Good Laertes,
    If you desire to know the certainty
    Of your dear father's death, is 't writ in your revenge,
    That, swoopstake,[953] you will draw both friend and foe,
    Winner and loser?

LAER.: None but his enemies.

KING: Will you know them then?

LAER.: To his good friends thus wide I'll ope my arms;
    And like the kind life-rendering pelican,[954]   140
    Repast[955] them with my blood.

KING: Why, now you speak
    Like a good child and a true gentleman.
    That I am guiltless of your father's death,
    And am most sensibly in grief for it,
    It shall as level to your judgement pierce
    As day does to your eye.

DANES: [*Within*] Let her come in.

LAER.: How now! what noise is that?

Re-enter OPHELIA

    O heat,[956] dry up my brains! tears seven times salt,   150
    Burn out the sense and virtue of mine eye!
    By heaven, thy madness shall be paid with weight,
    Till our scale turn the beam. O rose of May!
    Dear maid, kind sister, sweet Ophelia!
    O heavens! is 't possible, a young maid's wits
    Should be as mortal as an old man's life?
    Nature is fine in love, and where 'tis fine,
    It sends some precious instance of itself
    After the thing it loves.

OPH.: [*Sings*]
        They bore him barefaced on the bier;   160
        Hey non nonny, nonny, hey nonny;
        And in his grave rain'd many a tear:—
    Fare you well, my dove!

LAER.: Hadst thou thy wits, and didst persuade revenge,
    It could not move thus.

OPH.: [*Sings*] You must sing a-down a-down,
        An you call him a-down-a.
    O, how the wheel[957] becomes it! It is the false steward,
        that stole his master's daughter.[958]

LAER.: This nothing's more than matter.   170

OPH.: There's rosemary,[959] that's for remembrance; pray,
    love, remember: and there is pansies,[960] that's for
    thoughts.

---

[945] **overpeering** Overflowing.

[946] **list** Shore.

[947] **word** Promise.

[948] **counter** A hunting term meaning to follow the trail in a direction opposite to that which the game has taken.

[949] **peep to** i.e., Look at from afar off.

[950] **would** Wishes to do.

[951] **give to negligence** He despises both the here and the hereafter.

[952] **My will** He will not be stopped except by his own will.

[953] **swoopstake** Literally, drawing the whole stake at once, i.e., indiscriminately.

[954] **pelican** Reference to the belief that the pelican feeds its young with its own blood.

[955] **Repast** Feed.

[956] **heat** Probably the heat generated by the passion of grief.

[957] **wheel** Spinning wheel as accompaniment to the song refrain.

[958] **false steward . . . daughter** The story is unknown.

[959] **rosemary** Used as a symbol of remembrance both at weddings and at funerals.

[960] **pansies** Emblems of love and courtship. Cf. French *penseés*.

LAER.: A document[961] in madness, thoughts and
    remembrance fitted.

OPH.: There's fennel[962] for you, and columbines:[963] there's
    rue[964] for you; and here's some for me: we may call it
    herb grace o' Sundays: O, you must wear your rue
    with a difference. There's a daisy:[965] I would give you
    some violets,[966] but they withered all when my father   180
    died: they say he made a good end,—
    [*Sings*] For bonny sweet Robin is all my joy.[967]

LAER.: Thought[968] and affliction, passion, hell itself,
    She turns to favour and to prettiness.

OPH.: [*Sings*] And will he not come again?[969]

        And will he not come again?
          No, no, he is dead:
          Go to thy death-bed:
        He never will come again.

        His beard was as white as snow,   190
        All flaxen was his poll:[970]
          He is gone, he is gone,
          And we cast away[971] moan:
        God ha' mercy on his soul!
    And of all Christian souls, I pray God. God be wi' ye.

                          [*Exit.*

LAER.: Do you see this, O God?

KING: Laertes, I must commune with your grief,
    Or you deny me right[972]? Go but apart,
    Make choice of whom your wisest friends you will,
    And they shall hear and judge 'twixt you and me: 200
    If by direct or by collateral[973] hand
    They find us touch'd,[974] we will our kingdom give,
    Our crown, our life, and all that we call ours,
    To you in satisfaction; but if not,
    Be you content to lend your patience to us,
    And we shall jointly labour with your soul
    To give it due content.

LAER.:   Let this be so;
    His means of death, his obscure burial—
    No trophy, sword, nor hatchment[975] o'er his bones,   210

No noble rite nor formal ostentation—
    Cry to be heard, as 't were from heaven to earth,
    That I must call 't in question.

KING: So you shall;
    And where the offence is let the great axe fall.
    I pray you, go with me.   [*Exeunt.*

Scene VI—Another Room in the Castle

This scene serves to keep the fortunes of HAMLET *in our mind
during the period of his absence. It is simultaneous with Scenes
V and VII, the action of which is practically continuous, and in a
modern play it would probably be made to take place in a corner
of the same hall, while the* KING *and* LAERTES *whisper apart.*

Enter HORATIO *and a* SERVANT

HOR.: What are they that would speak with me?   1

SERV.: Sea-faring men, sir: they say they have letters for
    you.

HOR.: Let them come in.   [*Exit Servant.*
    I do not know from what part of the world
    I should be greeted, if not from lord Hamlet.

Enter SAILORS

FIRST SAILOR: God bless you, sir.

HOR.: Let him bless thee too.

FIRST SAILOR: He shall, sir, an 't please him. There's a
    letter for you, sir; it comes from the ambassador that   10
    was bound for England; if your name be Horatio, as I
    am let to know it is.

HOR.: [*Reads*] "Horatio, when thou shalt have overlooked
    this, give these fellows some means[976] to the king:
    they have letters for him. Ere we were two days old
    at sea, a pirate of very warlike appointment gave us
    chase. Finding ourselves too slow of sail, we put on
    a compelled valour, and in the grapple I boarded
    them: on the instant they got clear of our ship; so I
    alone became their prisoner. They have dealt with me   20
    like thieves of mercy:[977] but they knew what they did;
    I am to do a good turn for them. Let the king have
    the letters I have sent; and repair thou to me with as
    much speed as thou wouldst fly death. I have words
    to speak in thine ear will make thee dumb; yet
    are they much too light for the bore[978] of the matter.
    These good fellows will bring thee where I am.
    Rosencrantz and Guildenstern hold their course for
    England: of them I have much to tell thee. Farewell.
        "He that thou knowest thine, HAMLET."   30
    Come, I will make you way for these your letters;
    And do 't the speedier, that you may direct me
    To him from whom you brought them.   [*Exeunt.*

---

[961] **document** Piece of instruction or lesson.

[962] **fennel** Emblem of flattery.

[963] **columbines** Emblem of unchastity (?) or ingratitude (?).

[964] **rue** Emblem of repentance. It was usually mingled with holy
water and then known as herb of grace. Ophelia is probably
playing on the two meanings of rue "repentant" and "even for
Ruth (pity)"; the former signification is for the queen, the latter
for herself.

[965] **daisy** Emblem of dissembling, faithlessness.

[966] **violets** Emblems of faithfulness.

[967] **For . . . joy.** Probably a line from a Robin Hood ballad.

[968] **Thought** Melancholy thought.

[969] **And . . . again?** This song appeared in the songbooks as "The
Merry Milkmaids' Dumps."

[970] **poll** Head.

[971] **cast away** Shipwrecked.

[972] **right** My rights.

[973] **collateral** Indirect.

[974] **touch'd** Implicated.

[975] **hatchment** Tablet displaying the armorial bearings of a
deceased person.

IV.vi. [976] **means** Means of access.

[977] **thieves of mercy** Merciful thieves.

[978] **bore** Caliber, importance.

Scene VII—Another Room in the Castle

The LAERTES *motive and the* OPHELIA *motive of Scene V are continued here.* LAERTES *proves an easy tool for the* KING'S *ingenious villainy. His naturally impetuous temper, made degenerate by such a life in France as is suggested in Act III, Scene I, snatches at even an ignoble chance of revenge.*

Enter KING *and* LAERTES

KING: Now must your conscience[979] my acquittance seal, 1
And you must put me in your heart for friend,
Sith you have heard, and with a knowing ear,
That he which hath your noble father slain
Pursued my life.
LAER.:   It well appears: but tell me
Why you proceeded not against these feats,
So crimeful and so capital[980] in nature,
As by your safety, wisdom, all things else,
You mainly[981] were stirr'd up. 10
KING: O, for two special reasons;
Which may to you, perhaps, seem much unsinew'd,[982]
But yet to me they are strong. The queen his mother
Lives almost by his looks; and for myself—
My virtue or my plague, be it either which—
She's so conjunctive[983] to my life and soul,
That, as the star moves not but in his sphere,[984]
I could not but by her. The other motive,
Why to a public count[985] I might not go,
Is the great love the general gender[986] bear him; 20
Who, dipping all his faults in their affection,
Would, like the spring[987] that turneth wood to stone,
Convert his gyves[988] to graces; so that my arrows,
Too slightly timber'd[989] for so loud[990] a wind,
Would have reverted to my bow again,
And not where I had aim'd them.
LAER.: And so have I a noble father lost;
A sister driven into desperate terms,[991]
Whose worth, if praises may go back[992] again,
Stood challenger on mount[993] of all the age[994] 30
For her perfections: but my revenge will come.
KING: Break not your sleeps for that: you must not think
That we are made of stuff so flat and dull
That we can let our beard be shook with danger

And think it pastime. You shortly shall hear more:
I loved your father, and we love ourself;
And that, I hope, will teach you to imagine—

Enter a MESSENGER

How now! what news?
MESS.: Letters, my lord, from Hamlet:
This to your majesty; this to the queen.[995] 40
KING: From Hamlet! who brought them?
MESS.: Sailors, my lord, they say; I saw them not:
They were given me by Claudio[996]; he received them
Of him that brought them.
KING: Laertes, you shall hear them.
Leave us.   [*Exit Messenger.*
[*Reads*] "High and mighty, You shall know I am set
naked[997] on your kingdom. To-morrow shall I
beg leave to see your kingly eyes: when I shall,
first asking your pardon thereunto, recount the 50
occasion of my sudden and more strange return.
     "HAMLET."
What should this mean? Are all the rest come back?
Or is it some abuse, and no such thing?
LAER.: Know you the hand?
KING: 'Tis Hamlet's character. "Naked!"
And in a postcript here, he says, "alone."
Can you advise me?
LAER.: I'm lost in it, my lord. But let him come;
It warms the very sickness in my heart, 60
That I shall live and tell him to his teeth,
"Thus didest thou."
KING: If it be so, Laertes—
As how should it be so? how otherwise?[998]—
Will you be ruled by me?
LAER.:   Ay, my lord;
So you will not o'errule me to a peace.
KING: To thine own peace. If he be now return'd,
As checking at[999] his voyage, and that he means
No more to undertake it, I will work him 70
To an exploit, now ripe in my device,
Under the which he shall not choose but fall:
And for his death no wind of blame shall breathe,
But even his mother shall uncharge the practice[1000]
And call it accident.
LAER.:   My lord, I will be ruled;
The rather, if you could devise it so
That I might be the organ.[1001]
KING: It falls right.
You have been talk'd of since your travel much, 80
And that in Hamlet's hearing, for a quality

IV.vii. [979]**conscience** Knowledge that this is true.
[980]**capital** Punishable by death.
[981]**mainly** Greatly.
[982]**unsinew'd** Weak.
[983]**conjunctive** Conformable (the next line suggesting planetary conjunction).
[984]**sphere** The hollow sphere in which, according to Ptolemaic astronomy, the planets were supposed to move.
[985]**count** Account, reckoning.
[986]**general gender** Common people.
[987]**spring** i.e., One heavily charged with lime.
[988]**gyves** Fetters; here, faults, or possibly, punishments inflicted (on him).
[989]**slightly timber'd** Light.
[990]**loud** Strong.
[991]**terms** State, condition.
[992]**go back** i.e., To Ophelia's former virtues.
[993]**on mount** Set up on high, mounted (on horseback).
[994]**of all the age** Qualifies *challenger*, not *mount*.

---

[995]**to the queen** One hears no more of the letter to the queen.
[996]**Claudio** This character does not appear in the play.
[997]**naked** Unprovided (with retinue).
[998]**As . . . otherwise?** How can this (Hamlet's return) be true? (Yet) how otherwise than true (since we have the evidence of his letter)? Some editors read "How should it not be so?" etc., making the words refer to Laertes' desire to meet with Hamlet.
[999]**checking at** Falconry term for when a hawk leaves the quarry to fly at a chance bird; turn aside.
[1000]**uncharge the practice** Acquit the stratagem of being a plot.
[1001]**organ** Agent, instrument.

Wherein, they say, you shine: your sum of parts
Did not together pluck such envy from him
As did that one, and that, in my regard,
Of the unworthiest siege.[1002]

LAER.:   What part is that, my lord?
KING: A very riband in the cap of youth,
Yet needful too; for youth no less becomes
The light and careless livery that it wears
Than settled age his sables[1003] and his weeds,   90
Importing health and graveness. Two months since,
Here was a gentleman of Normandy:—
I've seen myself, and served against, the French,
And they can well[1004] on horseback: but this gallant
Had witchcraft in 't; he grew onto his seat;
And to such wondrous doing brought his horse,
As had he been incorpsed and demi-natured[1005]
With the brave beast: so far he topp'd[1006] my thought,
That I, in forgery[1007] of shapes and tricks,
Come short of what he did.   100

LAER.:   A Norman, was 't?
KING: A Norman.
LAER.: Upon my life, Lamond.[1008]
KING: The very same.
LAER.: I know him well: he is the brooch indeed
And gem of all the nation.
KING: He made confession[1009] of you,
And gave you such a masterly report
For art and exercise[1010] in your defence[1011]
And for your rapier most especial,   110
That he cried out, 't would be a sight indeed,
If one could match you: the scrimers[1012] of their nation,
He swore, had neither motion, guard, nor eye
If you opposed them. Sir, this report of his
Did Hamlet so envenom with his envy
That he could nothing do but wish and beg
Your sudden coming o'er, to play[1013] with him.
Now, out of this,—

LAER.:   What out of this, my lord?
KING: Laertes, was your father dear to you?   120
Or are you like the painting of a sorrow,
A face without a heart?

LAER.:   Why ask you this?
KING: Not that I think you did not love your father;
But that I know love is begun by time;
And that I see, in passages of proof,[1014]
Time qualifies the spark and fire of it.

There lives within the very flame of love
A kind of wick or snuff that will abate it;
And nothing is at a like goodness still;   130
For goodness, growing to a plurisy,[1015]
Dies in his own too much:[1016] that we would do,
We should do when we would; for this "would" changes
And hath abatements[1017] and delays as many
As there are tongues, are hands, are accidents[1018];
And then this "should" is like a spendthrift[1019] sigh,
That hurts by easing. But, to the quick o' the ulcer:[1020]—
Hamlet comes back: what would you undertake,
To show yourself your father's son in deed
More than in words?   140

LAER.:   To cut his throat i' the church.
KING: No place, indeed, should murder sanctuarize[1021];
Revenge should have no bounds. But, good Laertes,
Will you do this, keep close within your chamber.
Hamlet return'd shall know you are come home:
We'll put on those shall praise your excellence
And set a double varnish on the fame
The Frenchman gave you, bring you in fine together
And wager on your heads: he, being remiss,
Most generous and free from all contriving,   150
Will not peruse the foils; so that, with ease,
Or with a little shuffling, you may choose
A sword unbated,[1022] and in a pass of practice[1023]
Requite him for your father.

LAER.:   I will do 't:
And, for that purpose, I'll anoint my sword.
I bought an unction of a mountebank,[1024]
So mortal that, but dip a knife in it,
Where it draws blood no cataplasm[1025] so rare,
Collected from all simples[1026] that have virtue   160
Under the moon,[1027] can save the thing from death
That is but scratch'd withal: I'll touch my point
With this contagion, that, if I gall[1028] him slightly,
It may be death.

KING: Let's further think of this;
Weigh what convenience both of time and means
May fit us to our shape:[1029] If this should fail,

[1002] **siege** Rank.
[1003] **sables** Rich garments.
[1004] **can well** Are skilled.
[1005] **incorpsed and demi-natured** Of one body and nearly of one nature (like the centaur).
[1006] **topp'd** Surpassed.
[1007] **forgery** Invention.
[1008] **Lamond** This refers possibly to Pietro Monte, instructor to Louis XII's master of the horse.
[1009] **confession** Grudging admission of superiority.
[1010] **art and exercise** Skillful exercise.
[1011] **defence** Science of defense in sword practice.
[1012] **scrimers** Fencers.
[1013] **play** Fence.
[1014] **passages of proof** Proved instances.

[1015] **plurisy** Excess, plethora.
[1016] **in his own too much** Of its own excess.
[1017] **abatements** Diminutions.
[1018] **accidents** Occurrences, incidents.
[1019] **spendthrift** An allusion to the belief that each sigh cost the heart a drop of blood.
[1020] **quick o' the ulcer** Heart of the difficulty.
[1021] **sanctuarize** Protect from punishment; allusion to the right of sanctuary with which certain religious places were invested.
[1022] **unbated** Not blunted, having no button.
[1023] **pass of practice** Treacherous thrust.
[1024] **mountebank** Quack doctor.
[1025] **cataplasm** Plaster or poultice.
[1026] **simples** Herbs.
[1027] **Under the moon** i.e., When collected by moonlight to add to their medicinal value.
[1028] **gall** Graze, wound.
[1029] **shape** Part we propose to act.

And that our drift look through our bad
    performance,[1030]
'T were better not assay'd: therefore this project
Should have a back or second, that might hold,   170
If this should blast in proof.[1031] Soft! let me see:
We'll make a solemn wager on your cunnings:[1032]
I ha 't:
When in your motion you are hot and dry—
As make your bouts more violent to that end—
And that he calls for drink, I'll have prepared him
A chalice[1033] for the nonce, whereon but sipping,
If he by chance escape your venom'd stuck,[1034]
Our purpose may hold there.

Enter QUEEN

                        How now, sweet queen! 180
QUEEN: One woe doth tread upon another's heel,
    So fast they follow: your sister's drown'd, Laertes.
LAER.: Drown'd! O, where?
QUEEN: There is a willow[1035] grows aslant a brook,
    That shows his hoar[1036] leaves in the glassy stream;
    There with fantastic garlands did she come
    Of crow-flowers,[1037] nettles, daisies, and long purples[1038]
    That liberal[1039] shepherds give a grosser name,

————————

[1030] **drift ... performance** Intention be disclosed by our bungling.
[1031] **blast in proof** Burst in the test (like a cannon).
[1032] **cunnings** Skills.
[1033] **chalice** Cup.
[1034] **stuck** Thrust (from *stoccado*).
[1035] **willow** For its significance of forsaken love.
[1036] **hoar** White (i.e., on the underside).
[1037] **crow-flowers** Buttercups.
[1038] **long purples** Early purple orchids.
[1039] **liberal** Probably, free-spoken.

But our cold maids do dead men's fingers call them:
There, on the pendent boughs her coronet weeds 190
Clambering to hang, an envious sliver[1040] broke;
When down her weedy[1041] trophies and herself
Fell in the weeping brook. Her clothes spread wide;
And, mermaid-like, awhile they bore her up:
Which time she chanted snatches of old tunes;
As one incapable[1042] of her own distress,
Or like a creature native and indued[1043]
Unto that element: but long it could not be
Till that her garments, heavy with their drink,
Pull'd the poor wretch from her melodious lay 200
To muddy death.
LAER.:   Alas, then, she is drown'd?
QUEEN: Drown'd, drown'd.
LAER.: Too much of water hast thou, poor Ophelia,
    And therefore I forbid my tears: but yet
    It is our trick[1044]; nature her custom holds,
    Let shame say what it will: when these are gone,
    The woman will be out.[1045] Adieu, my lord:
    I have a speech of fire, that fain would blaze,
    But that this folly douts it.   [*Exit.* 210
KING: Let's follow, Gertrude!
    How much I had to do to calm his rage!
    Now fear I this will give it start again;
    Therefore let's follow.   [*Exeunt.*

————————

[1040] **sliver** Branch.
[1041] **weedy** i.e., Of plants.
[1042] **incapable** Lacking capacity to apprehend.
[1043] **indued** Endowed with qualities fitting her for living in water.
[1044] **trick** Way.
[1045] **when ... out** When my tears are all shed, the woman in me will be satisfied.

∞

Act V

Scene I—A Churchyard

This scene does not advance the action much, for HAMLET's *quarrel with* LAERTES *has very little to do with their subsequent encounter; it only serves to bring into contrast the opposing characters of the two men. But we want a moment or two of relief before the breathless rush with which the play closes, and this the grim humor of the grave-diggers and* HAMLET's *moralizing afford. The solemnity of* OPHELIA's *burial helps us to realize the pathos of her fate, and therein the tragedy of* HAMLET's *failure.*

    The dialogue between the CLOWNS *affords an example of Shakespeare's unrivaled power of insight into the mental habits and modes of reasoning of uneducated people.*

Enter two CLOWNS,[1046] *with spades, &c.*

FIRST CLOWN: Is she to be buried in Christian burial that 1
    wilfully seeks her own salvation?
SECOND CLOWN: I tell thee she is: and therefore make her
    grave straight:[1047] the crowner[1048] hath sat on her, and
    finds it Christian burial.
FIRST CLO.: How can that be, unless she drowned herself
    in her own defence?
SEC. CLO.: Why, 'tis found so.
FIRST CLO.: It must be "se offendendo"[1049]; it cannot be else.
    For here lies the point: if I drown myself wittingly,[1050] 10

————————

[1047] **straight** Straightway, immediately; some editors interpret "from east to west in a direct line, parallel with the church."
[1048] **crowner** Coroner.
[1049] **"se offendendo"** For *se defendendo,* term used in verdicts of justifiable homicide.
[1050] **wittingly** Intentionally.

————————

V.i. [1046] **clowns** The word *clown* was used to denote peasants as well as humorous characters; here, applied to the rustic type of clown.

it argues an act: and an act hath three branches[1051]; it is, to act, to do, and to perform: argal,[1052] she drowned herself wittingly.

SEC. CLO.: Nay, but hear you, goodman delver,[1053]—

FIRST CLO.: Give me leave. Here lies the water; good: here stands the man; good: if the man go to this water, and drown himself, it is, will he, nill he, he goes,—mark you that; but if the water come to him and drown him, he drowns not himself: argal, he that is not guilty of his own death shortens not his own life.   20

SEC. CLO.: But is this law?

FIRST CLO.: Ay, marry, is 't; crowner's quest[1054] law.

SEC. CLO.: Will you ha' the truth on 't? If this had not been a gentlewoman, she should have been buried out o' Christian burial.

FIRST CLO.: Why, there thou say'st:[1055] and the more pity that great folk should have countenance[1056] in this world to drown or hang themselves, more than their even[1057] Christian. Come, my spade. There is no ancient gentlemen but gardeners, ditchers, and grave-makers: they hold up[1058] Adam's profession.   30

SEC. CLO.: Was he a gentleman?

FIRST CLO.: 'A was the first that ever bore arms.

SEC. CLO.: Why, he had none.

FIRST CLO.: What, art a heathen? How dost thou understand the Scripture? The Scripture says "Adam digged": could he dig without arms? I'll put another question to thee: if thou answerest me not to the purpose, confess thyself[1059]—   40

SEC. CLO.: Go to.[1060]

FIRST CLO.: What is he that builds stronger than either the mason, the shipwright, or the carpenter?

SEC. CLO.: The gallows-maker; for that frame outlives a thousand tenants.

FIRST CLO.: I like thy wit well, in good faith: the gallows does well; but how does it well? it does well to those who do ill: now thou dost ill to say the gallows is built stronger than the church: argal, the gallows may do well to thee. To 't again, come.   50

SEC. CLO.: "Who builds stronger than a mason, a shipwright, or a carpenter?"

FIRST CLO.: Ay, tell me that, and unyoke.[1061]

SEC. CLO.: Marry, now I can tell.

FIRST CLO.: To 't.

SEC. CLO.: Mass,[1062] I cannot tell.

Enter HAMLET *and* HORATIO, *at a distance*

FIRST CLO.: Cudgel thy brains no more about it, for your dull ass will not mend his pace with beating; and when you are asked this question next, say "a grave-maker": the houses that he makes last till doomsday. Go, get thee to Yaughan: fetch me a stoup[1063] of liquor.   60

[*Exit Sec. Clown.*

[*He digs, and sings.*

> In youth, when I did love, did love,
>   Methought it was very sweet,
> To contract, O, the time, for, ah, my behove,[1064]
>   O, methought, there was nothing meet.

HAM.: Has this fellow no feeling of his business, that he sings at grave-making?

HOR.: Custom hath made it in him a property of easiness.[1065]

HAM.: 'Tis e'en so: the hand of little employment hath the daintier sense.   70

FIRST CLO.: [*Sings*]

> But age, with his stealing steps
>   Hath claw'd me in his clutch,
> And hath shipped me intil the land,
>   As if I had never been such.

[*Throws up a skull.*

HAM.: That skull had a tongue in it, and could sing once: how the knave jowls[1066] it to the ground, as if it were Cain's jawbone,[1067] that did the first murder! It might be the pate of a politician,[1068] which this ass now o'er-reaches[1069]; one that would circumvent God, might it not?   80

HOR.: It might, my lord.

HAM.: Or of a courtier: which could say "Good morrow, sweet lord! How dost thou, good lord?" This might be my lord such-a-one, that praised my lord such-a-one's horse, when he meant to beg it; might it not?

HOR.: Ay, my lord.

HAM.: Why, e'en so: and now my Lady Worm's; chapless,[1070] and knocked about the mazzard[1071] with a sexton's spade: here's fine revolution, an we had the trick to see 't. Did these bones cost no more the breeding, but to play at loggats[1072] with 'em? mine ache to think on 't.   90

[1051] **three branches** Parody of legal phraseology.
[1052] **argal** Corruption of ergo, therefore.
[1053] **delver** Digger.
[1054] **quest** Inquest.
[1055] **there thou say'st** That's right.
[1056] **countenance** Privilege.
[1057] **even** Fellow.
[1058] **hold up** Maintain, continue.
[1059] **confess thyself** "And be hanged" completes the proverb.
[1060] **Go to.** Perhaps "begin," or some other form of concession.
[1061] **unyoke** After this great effort, you may unharness the team of your wits.
[1062] **Mass** By the Mass.

[1063] **stoup** Two-quart measure.
[1064] **behove** Benefit.
[1065] **property of easiness** A peculiarity that now is easy.
[1066] **jowls** Dashes.
[1067] **Cain's jawbone** Allusion to the old tradition that Cain slew Abel with the jawbone of an ass.
[1068] **politician** Schemer, plotter.
[1069] **o'er-reaches** Quibble on the literal sense and the sense "circumvent."
[1070] **chapless** Having no lower jaw.
[1071] **mazzard** Head.
[1072] **loggats** A game in which six sticks are thrown to lie as near as possible to a stake fixed in the ground, or block of wood on a floor.

FIRST CLO.: [*Sings*]

> A pick-axe, and a spade, a spade,
> For and[1073] a shrouding sheet:
> O, a pit of clay for to be made
> For such a guest is meet.

[*Throws up another skull.*

HAM.: There's another: why may not that be the skull of a lawyer? Where be his quiddities[1074] how, his quillets,[1075] his cases, his tenures,[1076] and his tricks? why does he suffer this rude knave now to knock him about the sconce[1077] with a dirty shovel, and will not tell him of his action of battery? Hum! This fellow might be in 's time a great buyer of land, with his statutes, his recognizances,[1078] his fines, his double vouchers,[1079] his recoveries:[1080] is this the fine of his fines, and the recovery of his recoveries, to have his fine[1081] pate full of fine dirt? will his vouchers vouch him no more of his purchases, and double ones too, than the length and breadth of a pair of indentures[1082]? The very conveyances of his lands will hardly lie in this box; and must the inheritor[1083] himself have no more, ha? 110

HOR.: Not a jot more, my lord.

HAM.: Is not parchment made of sheep-skins?

HOR.: Ay, my lord, and of calf-skins[1084] too.

HAM.: They are sheep and calves which seek out assurance in that.[1085] I will speak to this fellow. Whose grave's this, sirrah?

FIRST CLO.: Mine, sir.

> [*Sings*] O, a pit of clay for to be made 120
> For such a guest is meet.

HAM.: I think it be thine, indeed; for thou liest in 't.

FIRST CLO.: You lie out on 't, sir, and therefore it is not yours: for my part, I do not lie in 't, and yet it is mine.

HAM.: Thou dost lie in 't, to be in 't and say it is thine: 'tis for the dead, not for the quick; therefore thou liest.

FIRST CLO.: 'Tis a quick lie, sir; 't will away again, from me to you.

HAM.: What man dost thou dig it for?

FIRST CLO.: For no man, sir. 130

HAM.: What woman, then?

FIRST CLO.: For none, neither.

HAM.: Who is to be buried in 't?

FIRST CLO.: One that was a woman, sir; but, rest her soul, she's dead.

HAM.: How absolute[1086] the knave is! we must speak by the card,[1087] or equivocation[1088] will undo us. By the Lord, Horatio, these three years I have taken note of it; the age is grown so picked[1089] that the toe of the peasant comes so near the heel of the courtier, 140 he galls[1090] his kibe.[1091] How long hast thou been a grave-maker?

FIRST CLO.: Of all the days i' the year, I came to 't that day that our last king Hamlet overcame Fortinbras.

HAM.: How long is that since?

FIRST CLO.: Cannot you tell that? every fool can tell that it was the very day that young Hamlet was born; he that is mad, and sent into England.

HAM.: Ay, marry, why was he sent into England?

FIRST CLO.: Why, because he was mad: he shall recover 150 his wits there; or, if he do not, it's no great matter there.

HAM.: Why?

FIRST CLO.: 'T will not be seen in him there; there the men are as mad as he.

HAM.: How came he mad?

FIRST CLO.: Very strangely, they say.

HAM.: How strangely?

FIRST CLO.: Faith, e'en with losing his wits.

HAM.: Upon what ground? 160

FIRST CLO.: Why, here in Denmark: I have been sexton here, man and boy, thirty years.[1092]

HAM.: How long will a man lie i' the earth ere he rot?

FIRST CLO.: I' faith, if he be not rotten before he die, he will last you some eight year or nine year: a tanner will last you nine year.

HAM.: Why he more than another?

FIRST CLO.: Why, sir, his hide is so tanned with his trade, that he will keep out water a great while; and your water is a sore decayer of your dead body. Here's a 170 skull now; this skull has lain in the earth three and twenty years.

HAM.: Whose was it?

FIRST CLO.: A mad fellow's it was: whose do you think it was?

HAM.: Nay, I know not.

FIRST CLO.: A pestilence on him for a mad rogue! a' poured a flagon of Rhenish on my head once. This same skull, sir, was Yorick's skull, the king's jester.

HAM.: This? 180

FIRST CLO.: E'en that.

HAM.: Let me see.   [*Takes the skull.*
Alas, poor Yorick! I knew him, Horatio: a fellow of infinite jest, of most excellent fancy: he hath borne

---

[1073] **For and** And moreover.
[1074] **quiddities** Subtleties, quibbles.
[1075] **quillets** Verbal niceties, subtle distinctions.
[1076] **tenures** The holding of a piece of property or office or the conditions or period of such holding.
[1077] **sconce** Head.
[1078] **statutes, recognizances** Legal terms connected with the transfer of land.
[1079] **vouchers** Persons called on to warrant a tenant's title.
[1080] **recoveries** Process for transfer of entailed estate.
[1081] **fine** The four uses of this word are as follows: (1) end, (2) legal process, (3) elegant, (4) small.
[1082] **indentures** Conveyances or contracts.
[1083] **inheritor** Possessor, owner.
[1084] **calf-skins** Parchments.
[1085] **assurance in that** Safety in legal parchments.

[1086] **absolute** Positive, decided.
[1087] **by the card** With precision, i.e., by the mariner's card on which the points of the compass were marked.
[1088] **equivocation** Ambiguity in the use of terms.
[1089] **picked** Refined, fastidious.
[1090] **galls** Chafes.
[1091] **kibe** Chilblain.
[1092] **thirty years** This statement shows Hamlet's age to be thirty years.

me on his back a thousand times; and now, how
abhorred in my imagination it is! my gorge rises at
it. Here hung those lips that I have kissed I know not
how oft. Where be your gibes now? your gambols?
your songs? your flashes of merriment, that were
wont to set the table on a roar? Not one now, to mock   190
your own grinning? quite chap-fallen? Now get you
to my lady's chamber, and tell her, let her paint an
inch thick, to this favour she must come; make her
laugh at that. Prithee, Horatio, tell me one thing.

HOR.: What's that, my lord?

HAM.: Dost thou think Alexander looked o' this fashion
i' the earth?

HOR.: E'en so.

HAM.: And smelt so? pah!   [*Puts down the skull.* 200

HOR.: E'en so, my lord.

HAM.: To what base uses we may return, Horatio!
Why may not imagination trace the noble dust of
Alexander, till he find it stopping a bung-hole?

HOR.: 'T were to consider too curiously,[1093] to consider so.

HAM.: No, faith, not a jot; but to follow him thither with
modesty enough, and likelihood to lead it: as thus:
Alexander died, Alexander was buried, Alexander
returneth into dust; the dust is earth; of earth we
make loam[1094]; and why of that loam, whereto he was
converted, might they not stop a beer-barrel?   210
Imperious[1095] Caesar, dead and turn'd to clay,
Might stop a hole to keep the wind away:
O, that that earth, which kept the world in awe
Should patch a wall to expel the winter's flaw[1096]!
But soft! but soft! aside: here comes the king,

Enter PRIESTS, *&c. in procession; the Corpse of* OPHELIA,
LAERTES *and* MOURNERS *following;* KING, QUEEN, *their
trains, &c.*

The queen, the courtiers: who is this they follow?
And with such maimed rites? This doth betoken
The corse they follow did with desperate hand
Fordo[1097] it[1098] own life: 't was of some estate.
Couch[1099] we awhile, and mark. [*Retiring with Horatio.* 220

LAER.: What ceremony else?

HAM.: That is Laertes,
A very noble youth: mark.

LAER.: What ceremony else?

FIRST PRIEST: Her obsequies have been as far enlarged[1100]
As we have warranty: her death was doubtful;
And, but that great command o'ersways the order,
She should in ground unsanctified have lodged
Till the last trumpet; for charitable prayers,
Shards,[1101] flints and pebbles should be thrown on her: 230

Yet here she is allow'd her virgin crants,[1102]
Her maiden strewments[1103] and the bringing home
Of bell and burial.[1104]

LAER.: Must there no more be done?

FIRST PRIEST: No more be done:
We should profane the service of the dead
To sing a requiem and such rest to her
As to peace-parted[1105] souls.

LAER.:   Lay her i' the earth:
And from her fair and unpolluted flesh   240
May violets spring! I tell thee, churlish priest,
A ministering angel shall my sister be,
When thou liest howling.[1106]

HAM.:   What, the fair Ophelia!

QUEEN: Sweets to the sweet: farewell! [*Scattering flowers.*
I hoped thou shouldst have been my Hamlet's wife;
I thought thy bride-bed to have deck'd, sweet maid,
And not have strew'd thy grave.

LAER.:   O, treble woe
Fall ten times treble on that cursed head,   250
Whose wicked deed thy most ingenious sense[1107]
Deprived thee of! Hold off the earth awhile,
Till I have caught her once more in mine arms:

                         [*Leaps into the grave.*

Now pile your dust upon the quick and dead,
Till of this flat a mountain you have made,
To o'ertop old Pelion,[1108] or the skyish head
Of blue Olympus.

HAM.: [*Advancing*] What is he whose grief
Bears such an emphasis? whose phrase of sorrow
Conjures the wandering stars,[1109] and makes them   260
stand
Like wonder-wounded heroes? This is I,
Hamlet the Dane.   [*Leaps into the grave.*

LAER.:   The devil take thy soul!

                         [*Grappling with him.*

HAM.: Thou pray'st not well.
I prithee, take thy fingers from my throat;
For, though I am not splenitive[1110] and rash,
Yet have I something in me dangerous,
Which let thy wiseness fear: hold off thy hand.

KING: Pluck them asunder.

QUEEN: Hamlet, Hamlet!   270

ALL: Gentlemen,—

HOR.:   Good my lord, be quiet.

[1093] **curiously** Minutely.
[1094] **loam** Clay paste for brickmaking.
[1095] **Imperious** Imperial.
[1096] **flaw** Gust of wind.
[1097] **Fordo** Destroy.
[1098] **it** Its.
[1099] **Couch** Hide, lurk.
[1100] **enlarged** Extended, referring to the fact that suicides are not given full burial rites.
[1101] **Shards** Broken bits of pottery.

[1102] **crants** Garlands customarily hung upon the biers of unmarried women.
[1103] **strewments** Traditional strewing of flowers.
[1104] **bringing...burial** The laying to rest of the body, to the sound of the bell.
[1105] **peace-parted** Allusion to the text "Lord, now lettest thy servant depart in peace."
[1106] **howling** i.e., In hell.
[1107] **ingenious sense** Mind endowed with finest qualities.
[1108] **Pelion** Olympus, Pelion, and Ossa are mountains in the north of Thessaly.
[1109] **wandering stars** Planets.
[1110] **splenitive** Quick-tempered.

[The attendants part them, and they come out of the grave.

HAM.: Why, I will fight with him upon this theme
    Until my eyelids will no longer wag.[1111]
QUEEN: O my son, what theme?
HAM.: I loved Ophelia: forty thousand brothers
    Could not, with all their quantity[1112] of love,
    Make up my sum. What wilt thou do for her?
KING: O, he is mad, Laertes.
QUEEN: For love of God, forbear[1113] him.   280
HAM.: 'Swounds,[1114] show me what thou 'lt do:
    Woo 't[1115] weep? woo 't fight? woo 't fast? woo 't tear
      thyself?
    Woo 't drink up eisel[1116]? eat a crocodile?
    I'll do 't. Dost thou come here to whine?
    To outface me with leaping in her grave?
    Be buried quick with her, and so will I:
    And, if thou prate of mountains, let them throw
    Millions of acres on us, till our ground,
    Singeing his pate against the burning zone,[1117]
    Make Ossa like a wart! Nay, an thou 'lt mouth,   290
    I'll rant as well as thou.
QUEEN: This is mere madness:
    And thus awhile the fit will work on him;
    Anon, as patient as the female dove,
    When that her golden couplets[1118] are disclosed,
    His silence will sit drooping.
HAM.:   Hear you, sir;
    What is the reason that you use me thus?
    I loved you ever: but it is no matter;
    Let Hercules himself do what he may,   300
    The cat will mew and dog will have his day.   *[Exit.*
KING: I pray you, good Horatio, wait upon him.

                      [Exit Horatio.

[To LAERTES] Strengthen your patience in[1119] our last
    night's speech;
    We'll put the matter to the present push.[1120]
    Good Gertrude, set some watch over your son.
    This grave shall have a living[1121] monument:
    An hour of quiet shortly shall we see;
    Till then, in patience our proceeding be.   *[Exeunt.*

[1111] **wag** Move (not used ludicrously).
[1112] **quantity** Some suggest that the word is used in a deprecatory sense (little bits, fragments).
[1113] **forbear** Leave alone.
[1114] **'Swounds** Oath, "God's wounds."
[1115] **Woo 't** Wilt thou.
[1116] **eisel** Vinegar. Some editors have taken this to be the name of a river, such as the Yssel, the Weissel, and the Nile.
[1117] **burning zone** Sun's orbit.
[1118] **golden couplets** The pigeon lays two eggs; the young when hatched are covered with golden down.
[1119] **in** By recalling.
[1120] **present push** Immediate test.
[1121] **living** Lasting; also refers (for Laertes' benefit) to the plot against Hamlet.

Scene II—A Hall in the Castle

It is necessary first that HAMLET's *reappearance should be explained. This is done by his narrative to* HORATIO. *Then follows the brief scene with* OSRIC, *which declares* HAMLET's *character to be fundamentally unchanged; and then comes the end.* HAMLET's *revenge is accomplished at last, not deliberately, but by a sudden impulse, and at what a cost!* CLAUDIUS *died justly, but—over and beyond* OPHELIA—*the blood that is shed is at* HAMLET's *door. "The rest is silence," and the entry of* FORTINBRAS *and* HAMLET's *dying submission symbolize the triumph of another order of mind.*

Enter HAMLET *and* HORATIO

HAM.: So much for this, sir: now shall you see the other: 1
    You do remember all the circumstance?
HOR.: Remember it, my lord!
HAM.: Sir, in my heart there was a kind of fighting,
    That would not let me sleep: methought I lay
    Worse than the mutines[1122] in the bilboes.[1123] Rashly,[1124]
    And praised be rashness for it, let us know,
    Our indiscretion sometimes serves us well,
    When our deep plots do pall:[1125] and that should
      teach us
    There's a divinity that shapes our ends,   10
    Rough-hew[1126] them how we will,—
HOR.: That is most certain.
HAM.: Up from my cabin,
    My sea-gown[1127] scarf'd about me, in the dark
    Groped I to find out them; had my desire,
    Finger'd[1128] their packet, and in fine[1129] withdrew
    To mine own room again; making so bold,
    My fears forgetting manners, to unseal
    Their grand commission; where I found, Horatio,—
    O royal knavery!—an exact command,   20
    Larded[1130] with many several sorts of reasons
    Importing Denmark's health and England's too,
    With, ho! such bugs[1131] and goblins in my life,[1132]
    That, on the supervise,[1133] no leisure bated,[1134]
    No, not to stay the grinding of the axe,
    My head should be struck off.
HOR.:   Is 't possible?
HAM.: Here's the commission: read it at more leisure.
    But wilt thou hear me how I did proceed?
HOR.: I beseech you.   30
HAM.: Being thus be-netted round with villanies,—
    Ere I could make a prologue to my brains,

V.ii. [1122] **mutines** Mutineers.
[1123] **bilboes** Shackles.
[1124] **Rashly** Goes with line 7.
[1125] **pall** Fail.
[1126] **Rough-hew** Shape roughly; it may mean "bungle."
[1127] **sea-gown** "A sea-gown, or a corase, high-collered, and short-sleeved gowne, reaching down to the mid-leg, and used most by seamen and saylors" (Cotgrave, quoted by Singer).
[1128] **Finger'd** Pilfered, filched.
[1129] **in fine** Finally.
[1130] **Larded** Enriched.
[1131] **bugs** Bug-bears.
[1132] **such . . . life** Such imaginary dangers if I were allowed to live.
[1133] **supervise** Perusal.
[1134] **leisure bated** Delay allowed.

They had begun the play[1135]—I sat me down,
Devised a new commission, wrote it fair:
I once did hold it, as our statists[1136] do,
A baseness to write fair[1137] and labour'd much
How to forget that learning, but, sir, now
It did me yeoman's[1138] service: wilt thou know
The effect of what I wrote?

HOR.:   Ay, good my lord.   40

HAM.: An earnest conjuration from the king,
As England was his faithful tributary,
As love between them like the palm might flourish,
As peace should still her wheaten garland[1139] wear
And stand a comma[1140] 'tween their amities,
And many such-like "As" es[1141] of great charge,[1142]
That, on the view and knowing of these contents,
Without debatement further, more or less,
He should the bearers put to sudden death,
Not shriving-time[1143] allow'd.   50

HOR.:   How was this seal'd?

HAM.: Why, even in that was heaven ordinant.[1144]
I had my father's signet in my purse,
Which was the model of that Danish seal;
Folded the writ up in form of the other,
Subscribed it, gave 't the impression, placed it safely,
The changeling never known. Now, the next day
Was our sea-fight; and what to this was sequent[1145]
Thou know'st already.

HOR.: So Guildenstern and Rosencrantz go to 't.   60

HAM.: Why, man, they did make love to this
employment;
They are not near my conscience; their defeat
Does by their own insinuation[1146] grow:
'Tis dangerous when the baser nature comes
Between the pass[1147] and fell incensed[1148] points
Of mighty opposites.

HOR.:   Why, what a king is this!

HAM.: Does it not, think'st thee, stand[1149] me now upon—
He that hath kill'd my king and whored my mother,
Popp'd in between the election[1150] and my hopes,   70
Thrown out his angle[1151] for my proper life,

And with such cozenage[1152]—is 't not perfect
conscience,
To quit[1153] him with this arm? and is 't not to be
damn'd,
To let this canker[1154] of our nature come
In further evil?

HOR.: It must be shortly known to him from England
What is the issue of the business there.

HAM.: It will be short: the interim is mine;
And a man's life's no more than to say "One."
But I am very sorry, good Horatio,   80
That to Laertes I forgot myself;
For, by the image of my cause, I see
The portraiture of his: I'll court his favours:
But, sure, the bravery[1155] of his grief did put me
Into a towering passion.

HOR.:   Peace! who comes here?

Enter OSRIC

OSRIC: Your lordship is right welcome back to Denmark.

HAM.: I humbly thank you, sir. Dost know this
water-fly[1156]?

HOR.: No, my good lord.   90

HAM.: Thy state is the more gracious; for 'tis a vice to
know him. He hath much land, and fertile: let a beast
be lord of beasts,[1157] and his crib shall stand at the
king's mess:[1158] 'tis a chough[1159]; but, as I say, spacious
in the possession of dirt.

OSR.: Sweet lord, if your lordship were at leisure, I should
impart a thing to you from his majesty.

HAM.: I will receive it, sir, with all diligence of spirit. Put
your bonnet to his right use; 'tis for the head.

OSR.: I thank your lordship, it is very hot.   100

HAM.: No, believe me, 'tis very cold; the wind is
northerly.

OSR.: It is indifferent[1160] cold, my lord, indeed.

HAM.: But yet methinks it is very sultry and hot for my
complexion.

OSR.: Exceedingly, my lord; it is very sultry,—as 't
were,—I cannot tell how. But, my lord, his majesty
bade me signify to you that he has laid a great wager
on your head: sir, this is the matter,—

HAM.: I beseech you, remember[1161]—   110

[1135] **prologue . . . play** i.e., Before I could begin to think, my mind had made its decision.
[1136] **statists** Statesmen.
[1137] **fair** In a clear hand.
[1138] **yeoman's** i.e., Faithful.
[1139] **wheaten garland** Symbol of peace.
[1140] **comma** Smallest break or separation. Here, amity begins and amity ends the period, and peace stands between like a dependent clause. The comma indicates continuity, link.
[1141] **"As" es** The "whereases" of a formal document, with play on the word *ass.*
[1142] **charge** Import; burden.
[1143] **shriving-time** Time for absolution.
[1144] **ordinant** Directing.
[1145] **sequent** Subsequent.
[1146] **insinuation** Interference.
[1147] **pass** Thrust.
[1148] **fell incensed** Fiercely angered.
[1149] **stand** Become incumbent.
[1150] **election** The Danish throne was filled by election.
[1151] **angle** Fishing line.

[1152] **cozenage** Trickery.
[1153] **quit** Repay.
[1154] **canker** Ulcer, or possibly the worm that destroys buds and leaves.
[1155] **bravery** Bravado.
[1156] **water-fly** Vain or busily idle person.
[1157] **lord of beasts** Cf. Genesis 1:28: "God said to [the first man and the first woman], 'Be fruitful and multiply, and fill the earth and subdue it; and have dominion over the fish of the sea and over the birds of the air and over every living thing that moves upon the earth.' "
[1158] **his crib . . . mess** He shall eat at the king's table, i.e., be one of the group of persons (usually four) constituting a mess at a banquet.
[1159] **chough** Probably, chattering jackdaw; also explained as chuff, provincial boor, or churl.
[1160] **indifferent** Somewhat.
[1161] **remember** i.e., Remember thy courtesy; conventional phrase for "Be covered."

[Hamlet moves him to put on his hat.

osr.: Nay, good my lord; for mine ease,[1162] in good faith. Sir, here is newly come to court Laertes; believe me, an absolute gentleman, full of most excellent differences, of very soft[1163] society and great showing:[1164] indeed, to speak feelingly[1165] of him, he is the card[1166] or calendar of gentry,[1167] for you shall find in him the continent of what part a gentleman would see.

ham.: Sir, his definement[1168] suffers no perdition[1169] in you; though, I know, to divide him inventorially[1170] would dizzy the arithmetic of memory, and yet but yaw[1171]   120 neither, in respect of his quick sail. But, in the verity of extolment, I take him to be a soul of great article[1172]; and his infusion[1173] of such dearth and rareness,[1174] as, to make true diction of him, his semblable[1175] is his mirror; and who else would trace[1176] him, his umbrage,[1177] nothing more.

osr.: Your lordship speaks most infallibly of him.

ham.: The concernancy,[1178] sir? why do we wrap the gentleman in our more rawer breath[1179]?

osr.: Sir?   130

hor.: Is 't not possible to understand in another tongue?[1180] You will do 't, sir, really.

ham.: What imports the nomination[1181] of this gentleman?

osr.: Of Laertes?

hor.: His purse is empty already; all 's golden words are spent.

ham.: Of him, sir.

osr.: I know you are not ignorant—

ham.: I would you did, sir; yet, in faith, if you did, it would not much approve[1182] me. Well, sir?   140

osr.: You are not ignorant of what excellence Laertes is—

ham.: I dare not confess that, lest I should compare with him in excellence; but, to know a man well, were to know himself.[1183]

[1162] **mine ease** Conventional reply declining the invitation of "Remember thy courtesy."
[1163] **soft** Gentle.
[1164] **showing** Distinguished appearance.
[1165] **feelingly** With just perception.
[1166] **card** Chart, map.
[1167] **gentry** Good breeding.
[1168] **definement** Definition.
[1169] **perdition** Loss, diminution.
[1170] **divide him inventorially** i.e., Enumerate his graces.
[1171] **yaw** To move unsteadily (of a ship).
[1172] **article** Moment or importance.
[1173] **infusion** Infused temperament, character imparted by nature.
[1174] **dearth and rareness** Rarity.
[1175] **semblable** True likeness.
[1176] **trace** Follow.
[1177] **umbrage** Shadow.
[1178] **concernancy** Import.
[1179] **breath** Speech.
[1180] **Is 't . . . tongue?** i.e., Can one converse with Osric only in this outlandish jargon?
[1181] **nomination** Naming.
[1182] **approve** Command.
[1183] **but . . . himself** But to know a man as excellent were to know Laertes.

osr.: I mean, sir, for his weapon; but in the imputation[1184] laid on him by them, in his meed[1185] he's unfellowed.

ham.: What's his weapon?

osr.: Rapier and dagger.

ham.: That's two of his weapons: but, well.

osr.: The king, sir, hath wagered with him six Barbary   150 horses: against the which he has imponed,[1186] as I take it, six French rapiers and poniards, with their assigns, as girdle, hangers,[1187] and so: three of the carriages, in faith, are very dear to fancy,[1188] very responsible[1189] to the hilts, most delicate[1190] carriages, and of very liberal conceit.[1191]

ham.: What call you the carriages?

hor.: I knew you must be edified by the margent[1192] ere you had done.

osr.: The carriages, sir, are the hangers.   160

ham.: The phrase would be more german[1193] to the matter, if we could carry cannon by our sides: I would it might be hangers till then. But, on: six Barbary horses against six French swords, their assigns, and three liberal-conceited carriages; that's the French bet against the Danish. Why is this "imponed," as you call it?

osr.: The king, sir, hath laid, that in a dozen passes between yourself and him, he shall not exceed you three hits: he hath laid on twelve for nine; and it   170 would come to immediate trial, if your lordship would vouchsafe the answer.

ham.: How if I answer "no"?

osr.: I mean, my lord, the opposition of your person in trial.

ham.: Sir, I will walk here in the hall: if it please his majesty, 'tis the breathing time[1194] of day with me; let the foils be brought, the gentleman willing, and the king hold his purpose, I will win for him an I can; if not, I will gain nothing but my shame and the   180 odd hits.

osr.: Shall I re-deliver you e'en so?

ham.: To this effect, sir; after what flourish your nature will.

osr.: I commend my duty to your lordship.

ham.: Yours, yours. [*Exit Osric.*] He does well to commend it himself; there are no tongues else for 's turn.

hor.: This lapwing[1195] runs away with the shell on his head.

[1184] **imputation** Reputation.
[1185] **meed** Merit.
[1186] **he has imponed** He has wagered.
[1187] **hangers** Straps on the sword belt from which the sword hung.
[1188] **dear to fancy** Fancifully made.
[1189] **responsible** Probably, well balanced, corresponding closely.
[1190] **delicate** i.e., In workmanship.
[1191] **liberal conceit** Elaborate design.
[1192] **margent** Margin of a book, place for explanatory notes.
[1193] **german** Germane, appropriate.
[1194] **breathing time** Exercise period.
[1195] **lapwing** Peewit; noted for its wiliness in drawing a visitor away from its nest and its supposed habit of running about when newly hatched with its head in the shell; possibly an allusion to Osric's hat.

HAM.: He did comply with his dug,[1196] before he sucked it. 190
Thus has he—and many more of the same breed that
I know the drossy[1197] age dotes on—only got the
tune[1198] of the time and outward habit of encounter[1199];
a kind of yesty[1200] collection, which carries them
through and through the most fond and winnowed[1201]
opinions; and do but blow them to their trial, the
bubbles are out.[1202]

Enter a LORD

LORD: My lord, his majesty commended him to you by
young Osric, who brings back to him, that you attend
him in the hall; he sends to know if your pleasure 200
hold to play with Laertes, or that you will take longer
time.
HAM.: I am constant to my purposes; they follow the
king's pleasure: if his fitness speaks, mine is ready;
now or whensoever, provided I be so able as now.
LORD: The king and queen and all are coming down.
HAM.: In happy time.[1203]
LORD: The queen desires you to use some gentle
entertainment to Laertes before you fall to play.
HAM.: She well instructs me. [*Exit Lord.* 210
HOR.: You will lose this wager, my lord.
HAM.: I do not think so; since he went into France, I have
been in continual practice; I shall win at the odds. But
thou wouldst not think how ill all 's here about my
heart: but it is no matter.
HOR.: Nay, good my lord,—
HAM.: It is but foolery; but it is such a kind of gain-
giving,[1204] as would perhaps trouble a woman.
HOR.: If your mind dislike any thing, obey it: I will
forestal their repair hither, and say you are not fit. 220
HAM.: Not a whit, we defy augury: there's a special
providence in the fall of a sparrow. If it be now, 'tis
not to come; if it be not to come, it will be now; if it be
not now, yet it will come: the readiness is all:[1205] since
no man knows aught of what he leaves, what is 't to
leave betimes?

Enter KING, QUEEN, LAERTES, LORDS, OSRIC, *and*
ATTENDANTS *with foils, &c.*

KING: Come, Hamlet, come, and take this hand from me.

[*The King puts Laertes' hand into Hamlet's.*

HAM.: Give me your pardon, sir: I've done you wrong;
But pardon 't as you are a gentleman.
This presence[1206] knows, 230

And you must needs have heard, how I am punish'd
With sore distraction. What I have done,
That might your nature, honour and exception[1207]
Roughly awake, I here proclaim was madness.
Was 't Hamlet wrong'd Laertes? Never Hamlet:
If Hamlet from himself be ta'en away,
And when he's not himself does wrong Laertes,
Then Hamlet does it not, Hamlet denies it.
Who does it, then? His madness: if 't be so,
Hamlet is of the faction that is wrong'd; 240
His madness is poor Hamlet's enemy.
Sir, in this audience,
Let my disclaiming from a purposed evil
Free me so far in your most generous thoughts,
That I have shot mine arrow o'er the house,
And hurt my brother.
LAER.:   I am satisfied in nature,[1208]
Whose motive, in this case, should stir me most
To my revenge: but in my terms of honour
I stand aloof; and will no reconcilement, 250
Till by some elder masters, of known honour,
I have a voice[1209] and precedent of peace,
To keep my name ungored. But till that time,
I do receive your offer'd love like love,
And will not wrong it.
HAM.:   I embrace it freely;
And will this brother's wager frankly play.
Give us the foils. Come on.
LAER.:   Come, one for me.
HAM.: I'll be your foil,[1210] Laertes: in mine ignorance 260
Your skill shall, like a star i' the darkest night,
Stick fiery off[1211] indeed.
LAER.:   You mock me, sir.
HAM.: No, by this hand.
KING: Give them the foils, young Osric. Cousin Hamlet,
You know the wager?
HAM.:   Very well, my lord;
Your grace hath laid the odds o' the weaker side.
KING: I do not fear it; I have seen you both:
But since he is better'd, we have therefore odds. 270
LAER.: This is too heavy, let me see another.
HAM.: This likes me well. These foils have all a length?

[*They prepare to play.*

OSR.: Ay, my good lord.
KING: Set me the stoups of wine upon that table.
If Hamlet give the first or second hit,
Or quit in answer of the third exchange,
Let all the battlements their ordnance fire;
The king shall drink to Hamlet's better breath;
And in the cup an union[1212] shall he throw,

[1196] **did comply . . . dug** Paid compliments to his mother's breast.
[1197] **drossy** Frivolous.
[1198] **tune** Temper, mood.
[1199] **habit of encounter** Demeanor of social intercourse.
[1200] **yesty** Frothy.
[1201] **fond and winnowed** Select and refined.
[1202] **blow . . . out** i.e., Put them to the test, and their ignorance is exposed.
[1203] **In happy time.** A phrase of courtesy.
[1204] **gain-giving** Misgiving.
[1205] **all** All that matters.
[1206] **presence** Royal assembly.

[1207] **exception** Disapproval.
[1208] **nature** i.e., He is personally satisfied, but his honor must be satisfied by the rules of the code of honor.
[1209] **voice** Authoritative pronouncement.
[1210] **foil** Quibble on the two senses: "background which sets something off," and "blunted rapier for fencing."
[1211] **Stick fiery off** Stand out brilliantly.
[1212] **union** Pearl.

Richer than that which four successive kings   280
In Denmark's crown have worn. Give me the cups;
And let the kettle[1213] to the trumpet speak,
The trumpet to the cannoneer without,
The cannons to the heavens, the heavens to earth,
"Now the king drinks to Hamlet." Come, begin:
And you, the judges, bear a wary eye.

HAM.: Come on, sir.

LAER.:   Come, my lord.   *[They play.*

HAM.:   One.

LAER.:   No.   290

HAM.:   Judgement.

OSR.: A hit, a very palpable hit.

LAER.:   Well; again.

KING: Stay; give me drink. Hamlet, this pearl[1214] is thine;
Here's to thy health.

    [Trumpets sound, and cannon shot off within.

Give him the cup.

HAM.: I'll play this bout first; set it by awhile.
Come. [*They play.*] Another hit; what say you?

LAER.: A touch, a touch, I do confess.

KING: Our son shall win.   300

QUEEN: He's fat,[1215] and scant of breath.
Here, Hamlet, take my napkin, rub thy brows:
The queen carouses[1216] to thy fortune, Hamlet.

HAM.: Good madam!

KING: Gertrude, do not drink.

QUEEN: I will, my lord; I pray you, pardon me.

KING: [*Aside*] It is the poison'd cup: it is too late.

HAM.: I dare not drink yet, madam; by and by.

QUEEN: Come, let me wipe thy face.

LAER.: My lord, I'll hit him now.   310

KING: I do not think 't.

LAER.: [*Aside*] And yet 'tis almost 'gainst my conscience.

HAM.: Come, for the third, Laertes: you but dally;
I pray you, pass with your best violence;
I am afeard you make a wanton[1217] of me.

LAER.: Say you so? come on.   *[They play.*

OSR.: Nothing, neither way.

LAER.: Have at you now!

    [*Laertes wounds Hamlet; then, in scuffling, they
    change rapiers,[1218] and Hamlet wounds Laertes.*

KING: Part them; they are incensed.

HAM.: Nay, come, again.   [*The Queen falls.* 320

OSR.:   Look to the queen there, ho!

HOR.: They bleed on both sides. How is it, my lord?

1213 **kettle** Kettledrum.
1214 **pearl** i.e., The poison.
1215 **fat** Not physically fit, out of training. Some earlier editors speculated that the term applied to the corpulence of Richard Burbage, who originally played the part, but the allusion now appears unlikely. "Fat" may also suggest "sweaty."
1216 **carouses** Drinks a toast.
1217 **wanton** Spoiled child.
1218 **in scuffling, they change rapiers** According to a widespread stage tradition, Hamlet receives a scratch, realizes that Laertes' sword is unbated (not blunted), and accordingly forces an exchange.

OSR.: How is 't, Laertes?

LAER.: Why, as a woodcock[1219] to mine own springe,[1220]
Osric;
I am justly kill'd with mine own treachery.

HAM.: How does the queen?

KING: She swounds[1221] to see them bleed.

QUEEN: No, no, the drink, the drink,—O my dear
Hamlet,—
The drink, the drink! I am poison'd.   [*Dies.*

HAM.: O villany! Ho! let the door be lock'd: 330
Treachery! Seek it out.

LAER.: It is here, Hamlet: Hamlet, thou art slain;
No medicine in the world can do thee good;
In thee there is not half an hour of life;
The treacherous instrument is in thy hand,
Unbated[1222] and envenom'd: the foul practice
Hath turn'd itself on me; lo, here I lie,
Never to rise again: thy mother's poison'd:
I can no more: the king, the king's to blame.

HAM.: The point envenom'd too!   340
Then, venom, to thy work.   [*Stabs the King.*

ALL: Treason! treason!

KING: O, yet defend me, friends; I am but hurt.

HAM.: Here, thou incestuous, murderous, damned Dane,
Drink off this potion. Is thy union here?
Follow my mother.   [*King dies.*

LAER.:   He is justly served;
It is a poison temper'd[1223] by himself.
Exchange forgiveness with me, noble Hamlet:
Mine and my father's death come not upon thee,   350
Nor thine on me!   [*Dies.*

HAM.: Heaven make thee free of it! I follow thee.
I am dead, Horatio. Wretched queen, adieu!
You that look pale and tremble at this chance,
That are but mutes[1224] or audience to this act,
Had I but time—as this fell sergeant,[1225] death,
Is strict in his arrest—O, I could tell you—
But let it be. Horatio, I am dead;
Thou livest; report me and my cause aright
To the unsatisfied.   360

HOR.:   Never believe it:
I am more an antique Roman[1226] than a Dane:
Here's yet some liquor left.

HAM.:   As thou 'rt a man,
Give me the cup: let go; by heaven, I'll have 't.
O good Horatio, what a wounded name,
Things standing thus unknown, shall live behind me!
If thou didst ever hold me in thy heart,
Absent thee from felicity awhile,
And in this harsh world draw thy breath in pain,   370
To tell my story.   [*March afar off, and shot within.*
    What warlike noise is this?

1219 **woodcock** As type of stupidity or as decoy.
1220 **springe** Trap, snare.
1221 **swounds** Swoons.
1222 **Unbated** Not blunted with a button.
1223 **temper'd** Mixed.
1224 **mutes** Performers in a play who speak no words.
1225 **sergeant** Sheriff's officer.
1226 **Roman** It was the Roman custom to follow masters in death.

OSR.: Young Fortinbras, with conquest come from Poland,
To the ambassadors of England gives
This warlike volley.
HAM.:   O, I die, Horatio;
The potent poison quite o'er-crows[1227] my spirit:
I cannot live to hear the news from England;
But I do prophesy the election lights
On Fortinbras: he has my dying voice;   380
So tell him, with the occurrents,[1228] more and less,
Which have solicited.[1229] The rest is silence.   [*Dies.*
HOR.: Now cracks a noble heart. Good night, sweet
     prince:
And flights of angels sing thee to thy rest!
Why does the drum come hither?   [*March within.*

Enter FORTINBRAS, *the* ENGLISH AMBASSADORS, *and others*

FORT.: Where is this sight?
HOR.:   What is it ye would see?
If aught of woe or wonder, cease your search.
FORT.: This quarry[1230] cries on havoc.[1231] O proud death,
What feast is toward in thine eternal cell,   390
That thou so many princes at a shot
So bloodily hast struck?
FIRST AMBASSADOR: The sight is dismal;
And our affairs from England come too late:
The ears are senseless that should give us hearing,
To tell him his commandment is fulfill'd,
That Rosencrantz and Guildenstern are dead:
Where should we have our thanks?
HOR.:   Not from his mouth,[1232]
Had it the ability of life to thank you: 400
He never gave commandment for their death.
But since, so jump[1233] upon this bloody question,[1234]

1227 **o'er-crows** Triumphs over.
1228 **occurrents** Events, incidents.
1229 **solicited** Moved, urged.
1230 **quarry** Heap of dead.
1231 **cries on havoc** Proclaims a general slaughter.
1232 **his mouth** i.e., The king's.
1233 **jump** Precisely.
1234 **question** Dispute.

You from the Polack wars, and you from England,
Are here arrived, give order that these bodies
High on a stage[1235] be placed to the view;
And let me speak to the yet unknowing world
How these things came about: so shall you hear
Of carnal, bloody, and unnatural acts,
Of accidental judgements, casual slaughters,
Of deaths put on by cunning and forced cause,   410
And, in this upshot, purposes mistook
Fall'n on the inventors' heads: all this can I
Truly deliver.
FORT.:   Let us haste to hear it,
And call the noblest to the audience.
For me, with sorrow I embrace my fortune:
I have some rights of memory[1236] in this kingdom,
Which now to claim my vantage doth invite me.
HOR.: Of that I shall have also cause to speak,
And from his mouth whose voice will draw on   420
     more:[1237]
But let this same be presently perform'd,
Even while men's minds are wild; lest more
     mischance
On[1238] plots and errors happen.
FORT.:   Let four captains
Bear Hamlet, like a soldier to the stage;
For he was likely, had he been put on,
To have proved most royally: and, for his passage,[1239]
The soldiers' music and the rites of war
Speak loudly for him.
Take up the bodies: such a sight as this   430
Becomes the field,[1240] but here shows much amiss.
Go, bid the soldiers shoot.

[*A dead march. Exeunt, bearing off the dead bodies; after which*
a peal of ordnance is shot off.

1235 **stage** Platform.
1236 **of memory** Traditional, remembered.
1237 **voice . . . more** Vote will influence still others.
1238 **On** On account of, or possibly, on top of, in addition to.
1239 **passage** Death.
1240 **field** i.e., Of battle.

∞

Questions for Critical Thinking

1. Is Hamlet mad? Explain.
2. The character of Hamlet has sometimes been portrayed in one of four ways: a disappointed office-seeker; a mother's boy with an Oedipal complex; a weak-willed intellectual unable to make up his mind; and an overly refined dandy living in a coarse and cruel age. Discuss, using passages from the play to support each of these interpretations.

MARTIN LUTHER
Selections from the *Ninety-Five Theses*

Martin Luther (1483–1546), founder of the Protestant Reformation, changed not only the structure and theology of Western Christianity but profoundly influenced social, economic, and political developments and thought across Europe and around the world. Luther, an unknown German monk who was upset over how the church was raising money, intended only to draw attention to some specific issues and never suspected that his criticisms would arouse much interest. Yet, soon after publication of the *Ninety-Five Theses* his followers were calling for reforms of the clergy, demanding a reorganization of the Catholic hierarchy, and introducing a radical set of religious beliefs and practices. Within a decade after Luther broke with the church, the Protestant movement had spread beyond Germany and had begun to splinter into various denominations. Along with the economic and political changes already transforming European society, these religious upheavals hastened the end of the medieval world.

Luther's early life and education reflected the social and intellectual movements sweeping across Germany. His parents, who came from peasant stock, were moving up the economic ladder. Hans Luther, his father, became a petty capitalist who had high hopes for his son's future success. Luther's education was a mixture of medieval scholasticism and Renaissance humanism. He studied Aristotle's works and, at the same time, encountered the new learning based on recently discovered classical sources. The young Luther earned two degrees and seemed destined for a career in law—a goal that pleased his father. Then, suddenly, in 1505, Luther entered a monastery to become a monk and to study for the priesthood. During the next five years, he pursued his doctoral degree and continued to perform his priestly duties. In 1510 Luther journeyed to Rome, where he observed an indifferent and sometimes corrupt clergy. While searching for the sacred shrines of Christian Rome, he could not avoid seeing Renaissance Rome, thus sharpening the contrasts between the Italian and German churches.

A year later, in 1511, he became a teacher of the Bible at the University of Wittenberg, where he also preached and served as pastor of a church. Here he found answers to questions that had troubled him since his early days as a monk. Luther had always been deeply concerned with his own sense of sin and guilt, which brought on periods of doubt and despair. Likewise, his perception of God's justice, which demanded punishment for sinners, conflicted with the image of a loving and forgiving God, thus intensifying his doubts and anxieties. Luther eventually worked out his dilemmas and fears by closely studying the books of the Bible, talking to his students, and preaching to his congregation. Basing many of his conclusions on the writings of St. Paul, Luther formulated his famous doctrine of justification by faith. His articulation of this doctrine, along with his assertion that every man is his own priest, became the cornerstones of Lutheranism and Protestantism.

Although he expanded on his new theology in lectures and sermons, he took on more administrative duties. He soon became aware of certain church policies that greatly disturbed him. One of these was the use of indulgences as a way to raise money. Indulgences were pardons issued by the church that reduced the amount of penance Christians had to perform to atone for their sins. Indulgences had been used for centuries, and over time the church had extended their efficacy. In early 1517 Pope Leo X (pope 1513–1521), who needed money to build St. Peter's in Rome, and a German prince, who desired a bishopric, launched a campaign to sell indulgences in Germany to fund their respective projects. When Luther's parishioners returned to his church with papers of pardon, he decided to issue a set of theses, or points for debate concerning indulgences. Posting theses in public was a traditional device to elicit discussions in universities, and Luther expected only a lively debate. Once his ideas became public, however, he emerged as a hero to his congregation and a suspect in the eyes of church authorities. Within three years, Martin Luther was leading an incipient movement that would soon expand into a religious revolution.

Reading the Selections

When Luther posted the *Ninety-Five Theses,* in Latin, on the door of the Castle Church in Wittenberg on October 31, 1517, he wanted to keep the issues in the hands of the church officials. In respect to his superiors, he sent a copy to the Archbishop of Mainz to explain his position and to ask him to stop the sale of indulgences. Regardless of Luther's initial intentions, someone translated the document into German and passed it on to some printers. The theses were distributed to the local population and soon were being read in many German states. In early 1518 Luther wrote the *Explanations of the Ninety-Five Theses* in Latin, which supplied additional information and commentaries to support his original arguments. Both publications focus on Luther's criticisms and objections to indulgences, on his denial of the pope's power over purgatory, and on his concern about the welfare of sinners. His logic and his command of the language are evident in the two works.

The first selection from the opening sections of the *Ninety-Five Theses* includes Luther's refutation of the church's definition of penance and denies that the pope can remit sins by himself. Luther states that only God can remit guilt. The next selection defines a truly contrite Christian and lists what Christians should be taught regarding indulgences and the meaning of charity. The third selection compares the true treasury of the church with the treasury of indulgences. The final selection criticizes church officials who abuse indulgences and lists a series of questions that the laity were then asking of their religious leaders.

∞

Out of love and zeal for truth and the desire to bring it to light, the following theses will be publicly discussed at Wittenberg under the chairmanship of the reverend father Martin Luther, Master of Arts and Sacred Theology and regularly appointed Lecturer on these subjects at that place. He requests that those who cannot be present to debate orally with us will do so by letter.

In the Name of Our Lord Jesus Christ. Amen.

1. When our Lord and Master Jesus Christ said, "Repent,"[1241] he willed the entire life of believers to be one of repentance.

2. This word cannot be understood as referring to the sacrament of penance, that is, confession and satisfaction, as administered by the clergy.

3. Yet it does not mean solely inner repentance; such inner repentance is worthless unless it produces various outward mortifications[1242] of the flesh.

4. The penalty of sin remains as long as the hatred of self, that is, true inner repentance, until our entrance into the kingdom of heaven.

5. The pope neither desires nor is able to remit[1243] any penalties except those imposed by his own authority or that of the canons.

6. The pope cannot remit any guilt, except by declaring and showing that it has been remitted by God; or, to be sure, by remitting guilt in cases reserved to his judgment. If his right to grant remission in these cases were disregarded, the guilt would certainly remain unforgiven.

7. God remits guilt to no one unless at the same time he humbles him in all things and makes him submissive to his vicar, the priest.

8. The penitential canons[1244] are imposed only on the living, and, according to the canons themselves, nothing should be imposed on the dying.

. . .

40. A Christian who is truly contrite[1245] seeks and loves to pay penalties for his sins; the bounty of indulgences, however, relaxes penalties and causes men to hate them—at least it furnishes occasion for hating them.

41. Papal indulgences must be preached with caution, lest people erroneously think that they are preferable to other good works of love.

42. Christians are to be taught that the pope does not intend that the buying of indulgences should in any way be compared with works of mercy.

43. Christians are to be taught that he who gives to the poor or lends to the needy does a better deed than he who buys indulgences.

[1241] **"Repent"** Matthew 4:17.
[1242] **mortification** The subjection and denial of human passions and appetites by abstinence or self-inflicted pain or punishment.
[1243] **remit** To release from the guilt or penalty of a sin.

[1244] **canons** The laws of the church.
[1245] **contrite** Grieving or penitent for a sin.

44. Because love grows by works of love, man thereby becomes better. Man does not, however, become better by means of indulgences but is merely freed from penalties.

45. Christians are to be taught that he who sees a needy man and passes him by, yet gives his money for indulgences, does not buy papal indulgences but God's wrath.

46. Christians are to be taught that, unless they have more than they need, they must reserve enough for their family needs and by no means squander it on indulgences.

47. Christians are to be taught that the buying of indulgences is a matter of free choice, not commanded.

48. Christians are to be taught that the pope, in granting indulgences, needs and thus desires their devout prayer more than their money.

49. Christians are to be taught that papal indulgences are useful only if they do not put their trust in them, but very harmful if they lose their fear of God because of them.

50. Christians are to be taught that if the pope knew the exactions of the indulgence preachers, he would rather that the basilica of St. Peter were burned to ashes than built up with the skin, flesh, and bones of his sheep.

51. Christians are to be taught that the pope would and should wish to give of his own money, even though he had to sell the basilica of St. Peter, to many of those from whom certain hawkers of indulgences cajole money.

. . .

62. The true treasure of the church is the most holy gospel of the glory and grace of God.

63. But this treasure is naturally most odious, for it makes the first to be last.[1246]

64. On the other hand, the treasure of indulgences[1247] is naturally most acceptable, for it makes the last to be first.

65. Therefore the treasures of the gospel are nets with which one formerly fished for men of wealth.

66. The treasures of indulgences are nets with which one now fishes for the wealth of men.

67. The indulgences which the demagogues acclaim as the greatest graces are actually understood to be such only insofar as they promote gain.

68. They are nevertheless in truth the most insignificant graces when compared with the grace of God and the piety of the cross.

69. Bishops and curates[1248] are bound to admit the commissaries[1249] of papal indulgences with all reverence.

70. But they are much more bound to strain their eyes and ears lest these men preach their own dreams instead of what the pope has commissioned.

71. Let him who speaks against the truth concerning papal indulgences be anathema[1250] and accursed;

72. But let him who guards against the lust and license of the indulgence preachers be blessed.

. . .

79. To say that the cross emblazoned with the papal coat of arms, and set up by the indulgence preachers, is equal in worth to the cross of Christ is blasphemy.[1251]

80. The bishops, curates, and theologians who permit such talk to be spread among the people will have to answer for this.

81. This unbridled preaching of indulgences makes it difficult even for learned men to rescue the reverence which is due the pope from slander or from the shrewd questions of the laity,

82. Such as: "Why does not the pope empty purgatory for the sake of holy love and the dire need of the souls that are there if he redeems an infinite number of souls for the sake of miserable money with which to build a church? The former reasons would be most just; the latter is most trivial."

83. Again, "Why are funeral and anniversary masses for the dead continued and why does he not return or permit the withdrawal of the endowments founded for them, since it is wrong to pray for the redeemed?"

84. Again, "What is this new piety of God and the pope that for a consideration of money they permit a man who is impious and their enemy to buy out of purgatory the pious soul of a friend of God and do not rather, because of the need of that pious and beloved soul, free it for pure love's sake?"

85. Again, "Why are the penitential canons, long since abrogated[1252] and dead in actual fact and through disuse, now satisfied by the granting of indulgences as though they were still alive and in force?"

86. Again, "Why does not the pope, whose wealth is today greater than the wealth of the richest Crassus,[1253] build this one basilica of St. Peter with his own money rather than with the money of poor believers?"

87. Again, "What does the pope remit or grant to those who by perfect contrition already have a right to full remission and blessings?"

88. Again, "What greater blessing could come to the church than if the pope were to bestow these remissions and blessings on every believer a hundred times a day, as he now does but once?"

1246 . . . to be last Matthew 20:16.
1247 treasure of indulgences Treasury of merit built by Jesus and Christian saints, which could be shared with penitent sinners—an idea that developed in the medieval church.
1248 curates Parish priests.
1249 commissaries Agents.

1250 anathema Cursed by ecclesiastical authority.
1251 blasphemy Showing contempt for God.
1252 abrogated Made null and void.
1253 Crassus (ca. 115–53 BCE), Roman politician and fabulously wealthy financier.

Questions for Critical Thinking

1. What are indulgences? Explain Luther's argument against the practice of indulgences, using the *Ninety-Five Theses* to buttress your case.

2. Luther's most radical idea was "All men [and women] are priests." Show how this idea is made manifest in his *Ninety-Five Theses.*

MIGUEL DE CERVANTES
Selection from *Don Quixote*

Cervantes' *Don Quixote,* arguably the greatest work in the Spanish language, has been one of the world's best-selling books since it appeared in the early seventeenth century. Over the centuries, this work has entertained millions with its satirical adventures of the dim-witted Don Quixote and his coarse sidekick, Sancho Panza. These unlikely heroes have been embraced by the world as lovable characters and have often been celebrated in other media (art, music, and films).

Don Quixote is essentially a satire on chivalry, the courtly code of the Middle Ages practiced by knights and ladies, especially in literature (see Chrètien de Troyes' *Arthurian Romances* in Chapter 10, Volume I). Chivalry was on the wane from 1400 onward, but chivalrous romances and love ballads retained their appeal in Spain throughout the 1500s. Spain's mania for the ballads and stories of chivalry led Cervantes to write this satire. More than half in love with the object of his satire, he in fact composed a book more romantically adventurous than the material he parodied.

In form, *Don Quixote* is one of the earliest novels. This should come as no surprise, since the novel form was more advanced in Spain than in the rest of Europe. This work, like early novels elsewhere, has a rambling structure, covering about one thousand pages. Its plot is rather planless, consisting of a string of episodes enlivened with flashes of wit and happy phrases.

Carried along on Cervantes' river of words are the ridiculous heroes, the knight Don Quixote and the son of the soil Sancho Panza. Don Quixote is a hopeless romantic whose exploits come to nothing. He is forever either the butt of the jokes of others (for instance, when he is tricked by the priest disguised as a damsel in distress) or the victim of his own madness (for example, when he mistakes an ugly serving girl for Dulcinea, the beautiful lady of his dreams). In contrast, Sancho Panza is the soul of common sense who doggedly tries to save his master from misadventures. Together, they stand for Spain's divided soul: Quixote symbolizes the self-absorbed aristocratic spirit consumed by honor and titles; Panza, the enduring peasant eternally exploited by the nobility.

These characters also embody the novel's theme—the tension between dreams and reality. To live in dreams is to build castles in the air, like Don Quixote. But life without dreams leads to despair, like Sancho Panza. As Panza rides with Quixote through filthy ditches and over rampaging pigs, he comes to love and admire the don's saintly nature, even though he considers him mad. Thus the moral is, Follow one's dreams, even though they come to naught.

For years Miguel de Cervantes (1547–1615) led a swashbuckling life as a soldier, being wounded, captured, enslaved, and ransomed. After 1580 he tried to support his family through writing and often wound up in prison. His fortune was made when Part I of *Don Quixote* was published in 1605; Part II followed in 1615.

Reading the Selection

This selection, Chapter VIII of Part I, contains the best-known episode in *Don Quixote:* Quixote attacks forty windmills, mistaking them for giants. Deaf to Panza's pleas, Quixote winds up utterly defeated. This episode is the source of the English saying "to tilt at windmills," meaning to fight with phantom enemies.

The second part of this selection deals with a Basque knight. It shows Cervantes resorting to an old literary device; he pretends that his "history" is actually a translation from an Arabic work.

∽

Part I

Chapter VIII. Of the Valorous Don Quixote's Success in the Dreadful and Never Before Imagined Adventure of the Windmills, with Other Events Worthy of Happy Record.

At that moment they caught sight of some thirty or forty windmills, which stand on that plain, and as soon as Don Quixote saw them he said to his squire: "Fortune is guiding our affairs better than we could have wished. Look over there, friend Sancho Panza, where more than thirty monstrous giants appear. I intend to do battle with them and take all their lives. With their spoils we will begin to get rich, for this is a fair war, and it is a great service to God to wipe such a wicked brood from the face of the earth."

"What giants?" asked Sancho Panza.

"Those you see there," replied his master, "with their long arms. Some giants have them about six miles long."

"Take care, your worship," said Sancho; "those things over there are not giants but windmills, and what seem to be their arms are the sails, which are whirled round in the wind and make the millstone turn."

"It is quite clear," replied Don Quixote, "that you are not experienced in this matter of adventures. They are giants, and if you are afraid, go away and say your prayers, whilst I advance and engage them in fierce and unequal battle."

As he spoke, he dug his spurs into his steed Rocinante,[1254] paying no attention to his squire's shouted warning that beyond all doubt they were windmills and no giants he was advancing to attack. But he went on, so positive that they were giants that he neither listened to Sancho's cries nor noticed what they were, even when he got near them. Instead he went on shouting in a loud voice: "Do not fly, cowards, vile creatures, for it is one knight alone who assails you."

At that moment a slight wind arose, and the great sails began to move. At the sight of which Don Quixote shouted: "Though you wield more arms than the giant

Briareus,[1255] you shall pay for it!" Saying this, he commended himself with all his soul to his Lady Dulcinea,[1256] beseeching her aid in his great peril. Then, covering himself with his shield and putting his lance in the rest, he urged Rocinante forward at a full gallop and attacked the nearest windmill, thrusting his lance into the sail. But the wind turned it with such violence that it shivered his weapon in pieces, dragging the horse and his rider with it, and sent the knight rolling badly injured across the plain. Sancho Panza rushed to his assistance as fast as his ass could trot, but when he came up he found that the knight could not stir. Such a shock had Rocinante given him in their fall.

"O my goodness!" cried Sancho. "Didn't I tell your worship to look what you were doing, for they were only windmills? Nobody could mistake them, unless he had windmills on the brain."

"Silence, friend Sancho," replied Don Quixote. "Matters of war are more subject than most to continual change. What is more, I think—and that is the truth—that the same sage Friston[1257] who robbed me of my room and my books has turned those giants into windmills, to cheat me of the glory of conquering them. Such is the enmity he bears me; but in the very end his black arts shall avail him little against the goodness of my sword."

"God send it as He will," replied Sancho Panza, helping the knight to get up and remount Rocinante, whose shoulders were half dislocated.

As they discussed this last adventure they followed the road to the pass of Lapice[1258] where, Don Quixote said, they could not fail to find many and various adventures, as many travellers passed that way. He was much concerned, however, at the loss of his lance, and, speaking of it to his squire, remarked: "I remember reading that a certain

---

[1254] **Rocinante** From Spanish, *rocin*, meaning "a common drudge-horse."

[1255] **Briareus** In Greek mythology, a monster with one hundred hands and fifty heads.
[1256] **Dulcinea** From Spanish, *dulce*, "sweet."
[1257] **Friston** Don Quixote imagines that Friston is a magician and his mortal enemy.
[1258] **Lapice** A mountain pass in the Spanish region of La Mancha, the setting for this novel.

Spanish knight called Diego Perez de Vargas,[1259] having broken his sword in battle, tore a great bough or limb from an oak, and performed such deeds with it that day, and pounded so many Moors,[1260] that he earned the surname of the Pounder, and thus he and his descendants from that day onwards have been called Vargas y Machuca.[1261] I mention this because I propose to tear down just such a limb from the first oak we meet, as big and as good as his; and I intend to do such deeds with it that you may consider yourself most fortunate to have won the right to see them. For you will witness things which will scarcely be credited."

"With God's help," replied Sancho, "and I believe it all as your worship says. But sit a bit more upright, sir, for you seem to be riding lop-sided. It must be from the bruises you got when you fell."

"That is the truth," replied Don Quixote. "And if I do not complain of the pain, it is because a knight errant is not allowed to complain of any wounds, even though his entrails may be dropping out through them."

"If that's so, I have nothing more to say," said Sancho, "but God knows I should be glad if your worship would complain if anything hurt. I must say, for my part, that I have to cry out at the slightest twinge, unless this business of not complaining extends to knights errants' squires as well."

Don Quixote could not help smiling at his squire's simplicity, and told him that he could certainly complain how and when he pleased, whether he had any cause or no, for up to that time he had never read anything to the contrary in the law of chivalry.

Sancho reminded him that it was time for dinner, but his master replied that he had need of none, but that his squire might eat whenever he pleased. With this permission Sancho settled himself as comfortably as he could on his ass and, taking out what he had put into the saddle-bags, jogged very leisurely along behind his master, eating all the while; and from time to time he raised the bottle with such relish that the best-fed publican in Malaga[1262] might have envied him. Now, as he went along like this, taking repeated gulps, he entirely forgot the promise his master had made him, and reckoned that going in search of adventures, however dangerous, was more like pleasure than hard work.

They passed that night under some trees, from one of which our knight tore down a dead branch to serve him as some sort of lance, and stuck into it the iron head of the one that had been broken. And all night Don Quixote did not sleep but thought about his Lady Dulcinea, to conform to what he had read in his books about knights errant spending many sleepless nights in woodland and desert dwelling on the memory of their ladies. Not so Sancho Panza; for, as his stomach was full, and not of chicory water, he slept right through till morning. And, if his master had not called him, neither the sunbeams, which struck him full on the face, nor the song of the birds, who in great number and very joyfully greeted the dawn of the new day, would have been enough to wake him. As he got up he made a trial of his bottle, and found it rather limper than the night before; whereat his heart sank, for he did not think they were taking the right road to remedy this defect very quickly. Don Quixote wanted no breakfast for, as we have said, he was determined to subsist on savoury memories. Then they turned back on to the road they had been on before, towards the pass of Lapice, which they sighted about three in the afternoon.

"Here," exclaimed Don Quixote on seeing it, "here, brother Sancho Panza, we can steep our arms to the elbows in what they call adventures. But take note that though you see me in the greatest danger in the world, you must not put your hand to your sword to defend me, unless you know that my assailants are rabble and common folk; in which case you may come to my aid. But should they be knights, on no account will it be legal or permissible, by the laws of chivalry, for you to assist me until you are yourself knighted."

"You may be sure, sir," replied Sancho, "that I shall obey your worship perfectly there. Especially as I am very peaceable by nature and all against shoving myself into brawls and quarrels. But as to defending myself, sir, I shan't take much notice of those rules, because divine law and human law allow everyone to defend himself against anyone who tries to harm him."

"I never said otherwise," replied Don Quixote, "but in the matter of aiding me against knights, you must restrain your natural impulses."

"I promise you I will," replied Sancho, "and I will observe this rule as strictly as the Sabbath."

In the middle of this conversation two monks of the order of St. Benedict[1263] appeared on the road, mounted on what looked like dromedaries[1264]; for the two mules they were riding were quite as big. They were wearing riding-masks against the dust and carrying sunshades. And behind them came a coach, with four or five horsemen escorting it, and two muleteers on foot.

In the coach, as it afterwards turned out, was a Basque[1265] lady travelling to Seville[1266] to join her husband, who was going out to take up a very important post in the Indies.[1267] The monks were not of her company, but merely journeying on the same road.

[1259] **Diego Perez de Vargas** Satiric example, used by Cervantes to ridicule the Spanish custom of dual surnames, the first half with the father's family name and the second half with the mother's family name.

[1260] **Moors** Spanish Muslims, of either Arab or Berber descent. The last Moors were driven from Spain in 1492.

[1261] **Machuca** From Spanish, "Pounder." See footnote 1259.

[1262] **Malaga** Port in southern Spain, on the Mediterranean; famous for wines.

[1263] **order of St. Benedict** Benedictine monastic order.

[1264] **dromedaries** Camels.

[1265] **Basque** Member of ethnic group in northern Spain, in the western Pyrenees Mountains; the Basque language has no known relationship to other languages.

[1266] **Seville** River port in southwestern Spain, on the Guadalquivir River.

[1267] **the Indies** Either the East Indies, the lands of Asia, or, more likely, the West Indies, the islands of the Caribbean Sea, where Spain had colonies, dating from 1492.

Now no sooner did Don Quixote see them in the distance than he said to his squire: "Either I am much mistaken, or this will prove the most famous adventure ever seen. For those dark shapes looming over there must, beyond all doubt, be enchanters bearing off in that coach some princess they have stolen; and it is my duty to redress this wrong with all my might."

"This will be a worse job than the windmills," said Sancho. "Look, sir, those are Benedictine monks, and the coach must belong to some travellers. Listen to me, sir. Be careful what you do, and don't let the Devil deceive you."

"I have told you," replied Don Quixote, "that you know very little of this subject of adventures. What I say is true, and now you will see it."

So saying, he rode forward and took up his position in the middle of the road along which the monks were coming; and when they got so near that he thought they could hear him, he called out in a loud voice: "Monstrous and diabolical crew! Release immediately the noble princesses whom you are forcibly carrying off in that coach, or prepare to receive instant death as the just punishment for your misdeeds."

The monks reined in their mules, and stopped in astonishment at Don Quixote's appearance and at his speech.

"Sir Knight," they replied, "we are neither monstrous nor diabolical, but two monks of St. Benedict travelling about our business, nor do we know whether there are any princesses being carried off in that coach or not."

"No fair speeches for me, for I know you, perfidious scoundrels!" cried Don Quixote. Then, without waiting for their reply, he spurred Rocinante and, with his lance lowered, charged at the foremost monk with such vigour and fury that, if he had not slid from his mule, he would have been thrown to the ground and badly hurt, if not killed outright. The second monk, on seeing his companion so treated, struck his heels into his stout mule's flanks and set her galloping over the plain fleeter than the wind itself. When Sancho Panza saw the monk on the ground, he got down lightly from his ass, ran up and started to strip him of his clothes. Upon this, two servants of the monks arrived and asked him why he was stripping their master. Sancho replied that the clothes fell rightly to his share as spoils of the battle which his master, Don Quixote, had won. The lads, who did not get the joke nor understand this talk of spoils and battles, saw that Don Quixote had gone off and was talking with the ladies in the coach, and so fell upon Sancho and knocked him down. And, pulling every hair from his beard, they kicked him mercilessly, and left him stretched on the ground, breathless and stunned. Then, without a moment's hesitation, the monk remounted his mule, trembling, terrified and as white as a sheet; and as soon as he was up he spurred after his comrade, who was waiting for him some distance off, watching to see the upshot of this sudden attack. But without caring to wait for the end of the adventure, they went on their way, crossing themselves more often than if they had had the Devil himself at their backs.

Don Quixote, as we have said, was talking with the lady in the coach: "Your fair ladyship may now dispose of yourself as you desire, for now the pride of your ravishers lies in the dust, overthrown by this strong arm of mine. And lest you be racked with doubt as to the name of your deliverer, know that I am Don Quixote de la Mancha, knight errant, adventurer and captive to the peerless and beautiful lady, Dulcinea del Toboso. And in requital of the benefit you have received from me, I would ask no more of you than to go to El Toboso[1268] and present yourself on my behalf before that lady, telling her what I have done for your deliverance."

All that Don Quixote said was overheard by one of the squires accompanying the coach, a Basque. And when he saw that the knight would not let them pass, but was talking of their turning back at once to El Toboso, he went up to Don Quixote and, grasping his lance, addressed him in bad Castilian[1269] and worse Basque.

"Get along, you ill-gotten knight. By God who made me, if you do not leave coach I kill you, sure as I be Basque."

Don Quixote understood him very well, and replied with great calm: "If you were a knight, as you are not, I should have punished your rash insolence by now, you slavish creature."

"I not gentleman? I swear you liar, as I am a Christian. You throw down lance and draw sword, and you will see you are carrying the water to the cat.[1270] Basque on land, gentleman at sea. A gentleman, by the devil, and you lie if you say otherwise!"

"'Now you shall see,' said Agrages,"[1271] quoted Don Quixote, and threw his lance down on the ground. Then, drawing his sword and grasping his shield, he rushed at his antagonist, determined to take his life. When the Basque saw him coming he would have liked to get down from his mule, as it was a poor sort of hired beast and not to be trusted, but there was nothing for it but to draw his sword. He was, however, lucky enough to be near the coach, from which he was able to snatch a cushion to serve as a shield; whereupon they immediately fell to, as if they had been two mortal enemies. The rest of the party tried to pacify them, but could not; for the Basque swore in his uncouth language that if they did not let him finish the battle, he would himself kill his mistress and all who hindered him.

The lady in the coach, amazed and terrified at the sight, made the coachman drive off a little way, and sat watching the deadly struggle from a distance. In the course of the fight the Basque dealt Don Quixote a mighty blow on one shoulder, thrusting above his shield, and had our knight been without defence he would have been cleft to the waist. When Don Quixote felt the weight of that tremendous stroke he cried out aloud: "O lady of my soul,

---

[1268] **El Toboso** The town of Toboso, the home of Dulcinea.
[1269] **Castilian** The language of Castile, northern and central Spain. Modern Spain was formed in 1479, following the marriage of Queen Isabella of Castile and King Ferdinand of Aragon (1469), which united their two lands.
[1270] **carrying the water to the cat** Garbled speech, spoken by the Basque squire.
[1271] **Agrages** Character in a chivalric romance—a source for Don Quixote's mad quest.

Dulcinea, flower of beauty, come to the aid of this your knight, who for the sake of your great goodness is now in this dire peril!"

To speak, to raise his sword, to cover himself with his shield and attack the Basque: all this was the work of a moment. For he had resolved to risk everything upon a single stroke. The Basque, seeing him come on, judged Don Quixote's courage by his daring, and decided to do the same as he. So he covered himself well with his cushion and waited, unable to turn his mule in either direction, for the beast was now dead weary, and not being made for such games, could not budge a step.

Don Quixote, as we have said, rushed at the wary Basque with sword aloft, determined to cleave him to the waist; and the Basque watched, with his sword also raised and well guarded by his cushion; while all the by-standers trembled in terrified suspense, hanging upon the issue of the dreadful blows with which they threatened one another. And the lady of the coach and her waiting-women offered a thousand vows and prayers to all the images and places of devotion in Spain, that God might deliver their squire and them from the great peril they were in.

But the unfortunate thing is that the author of this history[1272] left the battle in suspense at this critical point, with the excuse that he could find no more records of Don Quixote's exploits than those related here. It is true that the second author[1273] of this work would not believe that such a curious history could have been consigned to oblivion, or that the learned of La Mancha could have been so incurious as not to have in their archives or in their registries some documents relating to this famous knight. So, strong in this opinion, he did not despair of finding the conclusion of this delightful story and, by the favour of Heaven, found it, as shall be told in our second part.

40

———

[1272] **author of this history** Cervantes is deliberately deceptive about the authorship of *Don Quixote*, claiming in the Preface to be the novel's stepfather. He first says he is relying on an unnamed source, which ends with this passage. He claims then to continue the work with a translation from the Arabic by Cide Hamete Benengeli, a spurious name.

[1273] **second author** See footnote 1272.

Questions for Critical Thinking

1. *"Don Quixote* is a satire on courtly love." Explain, using the selection as the basis of your discussion.
2. Identify Don Quixote and Sancho Panza. What is their relationship with one another? Identify similar pairs of comrades-in-arms in later literature, films, and popular culture. How do you account for the persistence of this model of male companionship in Western culture?

15

THE BAROQUE AGE I
Glamour and Grandiosity
1600–1715

SISTER JUANA INÉS DE LA CRUZ
Poems and Essay

The writer Sister (Sor) Juana Inés de la Cruz (1651–1695) has long been admired and studied in the Spanish-speaking world. Only in the late twentieth century, prompted by feminist scholars, did the English-speaking world become acquainted with this remarkable woman. Her adult years began in the worldly climate of Mexico's viceregal court presided over by the Spanish governor and ended in the cloistered atmosphere of a nunnery (1669–1695). Her literary legacy reflects this divided existence: secular and religious poetry, lyric verses, court poems, secular plays, liturgical plays, and a theological treatise. These works establish her as one of the great literary figures of the colonial period in the Americas.

Sister Juana has been called the "quintessence of the baroque" and the "bridge to the Enlightenment," and both are true. Her writings, in terms of genres, subjects, and complexity, express the baroque style of contemporary Spanish authors; and in certain poems she enriches the already elaborate baroque by drawing on local dialects and native languages of Mexico. At the same time, she anticipates the Enlightenment by urging the right of women to be educated and to think for themselves. She made this claim in *Respuesta a Sor Filotea (The Reply to Sister Filotea)* (1691), an autobiographical letter addressed to the bishop of Puebla, her ecclesiastical superior. Ironically, having made this plea, she submitted to male religious authority and lapsed into silence. She died of the plague in 1695, not knowing that three centuries later scholars would hail her as "the first feminist of the New World."

That Sister Juana succeeded in religiously conformist and tradition-bound Mexico is a tribute to her genius and strong will. To even be received at court, she had to overcome obstacles such as illegitimacy, financial hardship, lack of formal education, and rural upbringing. Here, education was the key. In her life story she claimed to be self-taught in the classics, except for twenty Latin lessons. Celebrated as a child prodigy, she caught the eye of the viceroy's wife, who made her a maid-in-waiting. For five years she remained in this capacity, joining in the court's ceremonial and social life while pursuing scholarly interests. Her abrupt decision to become a nun probably reflected her lack of suitable prospects for marriage. Without family or dowry, she ultimately was dependent on her wits and charm to survive.

Reading the Selections

The first poem, Sister Juana's sonnet "She refutes the praises dedicated to her portrait," expresses the baroque sensibility, which sees death in the midst of life. Baroque-era clerics preached this message, and England's metaphysical poets made it a major theme in their verses. This sonnet is chilling, as the poet deflects an unnamed person's admiration of her portrait by pointing out that painting is "a highly colored hoax" and all humans are mortal.

The second poem, addressed to a male audience, reflects Sister Juana's exasperation with *macho* culture. In the poem she describes the sexual double bind that court ladies suffer: If they refuse men's overtures, they are called heartless; if they yield, they are whores. Either way, women can't win. Sister Juana's vision for escaping from this trap is to educate women to make them virtuous ("make them what you'd like to see")—an idea she espoused to the church hierarchy (see Essay).

The essay is from *Respuesta a Sor Filotea (The Reply to Sister Filotea)*. Written in the form of a letter, the work is addressed to Sor Filotea, the pen name adopted by the bishop of Puebla, Don Manuel Fernandez de Santa Cruz y Sahagun (bishop 1676–1699). The bishop, although a protector of Sor Juana, had apparently yielded to pressure from the male-dominated Mexican court to silence her voice. What, in particular, had caused offense was a treatise by Sor Juana in which she contradicted a leading male interpreter of the Bible. Sor Juana's *Respuesta* is a complex work of several strands, part memoir, part defense of her literary mission, and part defense of the right to free speech for women.

In the selection, Sor Juana first makes clear her desire not to stray from orthodox belief: "I wish no quarrel with the Holy Office," that is, the Inquisition, which used its considerable powers to enforce conformity on the people of colonial Mexico. Next, she makes the case for herself as a person of reason, and, as such, she claims to have a native-born inclination to search for the truth—a rationale that in some ways is prophetic of the Enlightenment. She traces her educational history, showing how she was inevitably and irresistibly drawn to the pursuit of truth. Then, she universalizes a claim for free speech for all women by assembling a roster of learned women, drawn from the Bible and ancient history. Last, she addresses the thorniest question facing anyone who would advocate free speech for women, namely the admonition from St. Paul (1 Corinthians 14:34) that "women keep silence in the church." This scriptural passage historically has been used by church authorities to relegate women to a secondary role in the life of the church.

∽

Poem 1

This that you see, a highly colored hoax   1
Which demonstrates the excellence of art,
Upon the senses plays its crafty jokes
With faulty syllogisms on its part.

This, with which flattery tries to evade
The relenting horrors of the years
And, conquering the sallies time has made,
The triumph over age and all its cares.

Is just a vain device of apprehension,
Is just a fragile flower in the wind,   10
Is just a vain defense against our lot,
Is a foolish and impossible intention,
Is labor lost, and, to the thoughtful mind,
Is but a corpse, is dust, is shade, is nought.

∞

Poem 2

In which she condemns the inconsistency of men, who   1
blame women for what they themselves have caused
Stupid men, fond of abusing
All women, without any shame,
Not seeing you're the ones to blame
For the very faults that you're accusing.

If, with a single-minded will,
You seek her well-deserved disdain,
Why do you want her to remain
Good, while inciting her to ill?

You strive to conquer her resistance,   10
Then with a solemn treachery
Attribute to her lechery
What was only done through your persistence.

Your mad position seems to fit
That of a child who draws a spook
And, when he dares to take a look,
Finds that he's afraid of it.

Showing presumptuous indiscretion,
You want to find her you're pursuing
To be Thais[1] while you are wooing   20
And Lucretia[2] when she's in possession.

What quirky humor could be more queer
Than his who, from all reason banned,
Smudges a mirror with his hand,
Then whines because it isn't clear?

If favor or disdain we tell,
You give us the same reception, madly—
Complaining when we treat you badly,
And sneering when we treat you well?

No female reputation's sure: 30
The most cautious woman in the town
Is an ingrate if she turns you down;
If she gives in to you she's a whore.

In stupidity you're all the same,
Each one an inconsistent fool;
You blame one girl for being cruel,
While the yielding one you also blame.

Your expectation is truly curious,
Of the woman who would seek your love;
The one who's ungrateful you reprove,   40
And the one who's available makes you furious.

But whatever the rage, whatever the plaints
That your capricious minds may fashion,
Lucky is one who feels no passion;
Just go somewhere else with your complaints.

Your amorous blandishments give wing
To a lady's libertine inclination,
But having seduced her in sinful fashion,
You want her to be a most virtuous thing.

In the errant passion two may loll in,   50
Whose fault would you describe as baser:
Hers who falls because you chase her,
Or his who chases because he's fallen?

Or who the greater guilt does win,
Whatever shameful pact is made:
She who sins because she's paid,
Or he who pays so he may sin.

But why do you pretend to be
Surprised at your sins, when you've displayed them?
Wish women to be what you have made them,   60
Or make them what you'd like to see.

Stop your own solicitations,
And then you may possess the right
To accuse a girl of being light
When she comes to you with unchaste persuasions.

Your arrogance fights on every level,
I note, with strong and well-aimed batteries,
For with ceaseless promises and flatteries
You unite the world, the flesh, the devil.

---

[1] **Thais** Prostitute. Thais (fl. fourth century BCE) was a Greek courtesan at the court of Alexander the Great. Later, Thais became a generic name for prostitutes in Greek and Roman comedy. The Greek Orthodox Church honors St. Thais (fl. fourth century CE), a reformed courtesan in Roman Alexandria, in Egypt.
[2] **Lucretia** Legendary figure in Roman history, fabled for her protection of her honor. According to ancient sources, Lucretia, raped by the son of Rome's last Etruscan king, committed suicide, thus inciting a rebellion that overthrew the monarchy and established the Roman Republic.

Selection from *Respuesta a Sor Filotea (The Reply to Sister Filotea)*

. . . How [have] I dared take in my unworthy hands these ₁ verses, defying gender, age, and, above all, custom? And thus I confess that many times this fear has plucked my pen from my hand and has turned my thoughts back toward the very same reason from which they had wished to be born: which obstacle did not impinge upon profane matters, for a heresy against art is not punished by the Holy Office[3] but by the judicious with derision, and by critics with censure, and censure, *just or unjust, is not to be feared,* as it does not forbid the taking of communion or hearing of mass, and offers me little or no cause for anxiety, because in the opinion of those who defame my art, I have neither the obligation to know nor the aptitude to triumph. If, then, I err, I suffer neither blame nor discredit: I suffer no blame, as I have no obligation; no discredit, as I have no possibility of triumphing—*and no one is obliged to do the impossible.* And, in truth, I have written nothing except when compelled and constrained, and then only to give pleasure to others; not alone without pleasure of my own, but with absolute repugnance, for I have never deemed myself one who has any worth in letters or the wit necessity demands of one who would write; and thus my customary response to those who press me, above all in sacred matters, is, what capacity of reason have I? what application? what resources? what rudimentary knowledge of such matters beyond that of the most superficial scholarly degrees? Leave these matters to those who understand them; I wish no quarrel with the Holy Office, for I am ignorant, and I tremble that I may express some proposition that will cause offense or twist the true meaning of some scripture. I do not study to write, even less to teach—which in one like myself were unseemly pride— but only to the end that if I study, I will be ignorant of less. This is my response, and these are my feelings.

I have never written of my own choice, but at the urging of others, to whom with reason I might say, *You have compelled me.*[4] But one truth I shall not deny (first, because it is well-known to all, and second, because although it has not worked in my favor, God has granted me the mercy of loving truth above all else), which is that from the moment I was first illuminated by the light of reason, my inclination toward letters has been so vehement, so overpowering, that not even the admonitions of others—and I have suffered many—nor my own meditations—and they have not been few—have been sufficient to cause me to forswear this natural impulse that God placed in me: the Lord God knows why, and for what purpose. And He knows that I have prayed that He dim the light of my reason, leaving only that which is needed to keep His Law, for there are those who would say that all else is unwanted in a woman,

and there are even those who would hold that such knowledge does injury. And my Holy Father[5] knows too that as I have been unable to achieve this (my prayer has not been answered), I have sought to veil the light of my reason— along with my name—and to offer it up only to Him who bestowed it upon me, and He knows that none other was the cause for my entering into Religion,[6] notwithstanding that the spiritual exercises and company of a community[7] were repugnant to the freedom and quiet I desired for my studious endeavors. And later, in that community, the Lord God knows—and, in the world, only the one who must know—how diligently I sought to obscure my name, and how this was not permitted, saying it was temptation: and so it would have been. If it were in my power, lady,[8] to repay you in some part what I owe you, it might be done by telling you this thing which has never before passed my lips, except to be spoken to the one who should hear it. It is my hope that by having opened wide to you the doors of my heart, by having made patent to you its most deeply hidden secrets, you will deem my confidence not unworthy of the debt I owe to your most august person and to your most uncommon favors.

Continuing the narration of my inclinations, of which I wish to give you a thorough account, I will tell you that I was not yet three years old when my mother determined to send one of my elder sisters to learn to read at a school for girls we call the *Amigas.*[9] Affection, and mischief, caused me to follow her, and when I observed how she was being taught her lessons I was so inflamed with the desire to know how to read, that deceiving—for so I knew it to be—the mistress, I told her that my mother had meant for me to have lessons too. She did not believe it, as it was little to be believed, but, to humor me, she acceded. I continued to go there, and she continued to teach me, but now, as experience had disabused her, with all seriousness; and I learned so quickly that before my mother knew of it I could already read, for my teacher had kept it from her in order to reveal the surprise and reap the reward at one and the same time. And I, you may be sure, kept the secret, fearing that I would be whipped for having acted without permission. The woman who taught me, may God bless and keep her, is still alive and can bear witness to all I say.

I also remember that in those days, my tastes being those common to that age, I abstained from eating cheese because I had heard that it made one slow of wits, for in me the desire for learning was stronger than the desire

---

[3] **Holy Office** Inquisition.
[4] *You have compelled me.* 2 Corinthians 12:11.

[5] **Holy Father** God.
[6] **Religion** Monastic vows; those who take monastic vows are called "religious."
[7] **community** Convent of Santa Paula in Mexico City, where Sor Juana took her vows.
[8] **lady** Sor Filotea.
[9] *Amigas* Friends.

for eating—as powerful as that is in children. When later, being six or seven, and having learned how to read and write, along with all the other skills of needlework and household arts that girls learn, it came to my attention that in Mexico City there were Schools, and a University, in which one studied the sciences. The moment I heard this, I began to plague my mother with insistent and importunate pleas: she should dress me in boy's clothing and send me to Mexico City to live with relatives, to study and be tutored at the University. She would not permit it, and she was wise, but I assuaged my disappointment by reading the many and varied books belonging to my grandfather, and there were not enough punishments, nor reprimands, to prevent me from reading: so that when I came to the city many marveled, not so much at my natural wit, as at my memory, and at the amount of learning I had mastered at an age when many have scarcely learned to speak well.

I began to study Latin grammar—in all, I believe, I had no more than twenty lessons—and so intense was my concern that though among women (especially a woman in the flower of her youth) the natural adornment of one's hair is held in such high esteem, I cut off mine to the breadth of some four to six fingers, measuring the place it had reached, and imposing upon myself the condition that if by the time it had again grown to that length I had not learned such and such a thing I had set for myself to learn while my hair was growing, I would again cut it off as punishment for being so slow-witted. And it did happen that my hair grew out and still I had not learned what I had set for myself—because my hair grew quickly and I learned slowly—and in fact I did cut it in punishment for such stupidity: for there seemed to me no cause for a head to be adorned with hair and naked of learning—which was the more desired embellishment. And so I entered the religious order, knowing that life there entailed certain conditions (I refer to superficial, and not fundamental, regards) most repugnant to my nature; but given the total antipathy I felt for marriage, I deemed convent life the least unsuitable and the most honorable I could elect if I were to insure my salvation. Working against that end, first (as, finally, the most important) was the matter of all the trivial aspects of my nature that nourished my pride, such as wishing to live alone, and wishing to have no obligatory occupation that would inhibit the freedom of my studies, nor the sounds of a community that would intrude upon the peaceful silence of my books. These desires caused me to falter some while in my decision, until certain learned persons enlightened me, explaining that they were temptation, and, with divine favor, I overcame them, and took upon myself the state which now so unworthily I hold. I believed that I was fleeing from myself, but—wretch that I am!—I brought with me my worst enemy, my inclination, which I do not know whether to consider a gift or a punishment from Heaven, for once dimmed and encumbered by the many activities common to Religion, that inclination exploded in me like gunpowder, proving how *privation is the source of appetite.*

I turned again (which is badly put, for I never ceased), I continued, then, in my studious endeavour (which for

me was respite during those moments not occupied by my duties) of reading and more reading, of study and more study, with no teachers but my books. Thus I learned how difficult it is to study those soulless letters, lacking a human voice or the explication of a teacher. But I suffered this labor happily for my love of learning. Oh, had it only been for love of God, which were proper, how worthwhile it would have been! I strove mightily to elevate these studies, to dedicate them to His service, as the goal to which I aspired was to study Theology—it seeming to me debilitating for a Catholic not to know everything in this life of the Divine Mysteries that can be learned through natural means—and, being a nun and not a layperson, it was seemly that I profess my vows to learning through ecclesiastical channels; and especially, being a daughter of a Saint Jerome[10] and a Saint Paula,[11] it was essential that such erudite parents not be shamed by a witless daughter. This is the argument I proposed to myself, and it seemed to me well-reasoned. It was, however (and this cannot be denied) merely glorification and approbation of my inclination, and enjoyment of it offered as justification.

And so I continued, as I have said, directing the course of my studies toward the peak of Sacred Theology, it seeming necessary to me, in order to scale those heights, to climb the steps of the human sciences and arts; for how could one undertake the study of the Queen of Sciences[12] if first one had not come to know her servants? How, without Logic, could I be apprised of the general and specific way in which the Holy Scripture is written? How, without Rhetoric,[13] could I understand its figures, its tropes, its locutions? How, without Physics, so many innate questions concerning the nature of animals, their sacrifices, wherein exist so many symbols, many already declared, many still to be discovered? How should I know whether Saul's[14] being refreshed by the sound of David's[15] harp was due to the virtue and natural power of Music, or to a transcendent power God wished to place in David? How, without Arithmetic, could one understand the computations of the years, days, months, hours, those mysterious weeks communicated by Gabriel[16] to Daniel,[17] and others for whose understanding one must know the nature, concordance,

---

[10] **Saint Jerome** (ca. 347–419/420), one of the Fathers of the Church. Translator of the Latin version of the Bible, called the Vulgate. Sor Juana calls him "my father."

[11] **Saint Paula** (347–404), early Christian saint and disciple of Saint Jerome. She, along with her daughter **Eustochium**, left Rome in 385, and followed him to Bethlehem in Palestine and became nuns. **Jerome's** Letter CVIII offers a biography of this early Christian saint. Sor Juana belonged to the monastic order of **Saint Paula.**

[12] **Queen of Sciences** Theology.

[13] **Rhetoric** Sor Juana studied the medieval trivium: grammar, logic, and rhetoric.

[14] **Saul** (eleventh century BCE), first king of Judah and Israel.

[15] **David** (ca. 1000–962 BCE), second king of Judah and Israel. According to 1 Samuel 8:10, when King **Saul** was plagued by a demon, David calmed him by playing on a harp.

[16] **Gabriel** Archangel; one of three mentioned in the Bible.

[17] **Daniel** Biblical prophet visited by the angel **Gabriel** (Daniel 9), who said that seventy weeks of years would elapse before the coming of the Messiah.

and properties of numbers? How, without Geometry, could one measure the Holy Arc of the Covenant[18] and the Holy City of Jerusalem, whose mysterious measures are four-square in all their dimensions, as well as the miraculous proportions of all their parts? How, without Architecture, could one know the great Temple of Solomon, of which God Himself was the Author who conceived the disposition and the design, and the Wise King but the overseer who executed it, of which temple there was no foundation without mystery no column without symbolism, no cornice without allusion, no architrave without significance; and similarly others of its parts, of which the least fillet was never intended solely for the service and complement of Art, but as symbol of greater things? How, without great knowledge of the laws and parts of which History is comprised, could one understand historical Books? Or those recapitulations in which many times what happened first is seen in the narrated account to have happened later? How, without great learning in Canon and Civil Law,[19] could one understand Legal Books? . . .

I confess, too, that . . . books . . . have been no little inspiration, in divine as in human letters. Because I find a Debbora[20] administering the law, both military and political, and governing a people among whom there were many learned men. I find a most wise Queen of Saba,[21] so learned that she dares to challenge with hard questions the wisdom of the greatest of all wise men, without being reprimanded for doing so, but, rather, as a consequence, to judge unbelievers. I see many and illustrious women; some blessed with the gift of prophecy, like Abigail[22]; others of persuasion, like Esther[23]; others with pity, like Rahab[24]; others with perseverance, like Anna,[25] the mother of Samuel[26]; and an infinite number of others, with divers gifts and virtues.

If I again turn to the Gentiles,[27] the first I encounter are the Sibyls,[28] those women chosen by God to prophesy the principal mysteries of our Faith, and with learned and elegant verses that surpass admiration. I see adored as a goddess of the sciences a woman like Minerva,[29] the daughter of the first Jupiter[30] and mistress over all the wisdom of Athens. I see a Polla Argentaria,[31] who helped Lucan,[32] her husband, write his epic *Pharsalia*. I see the daughter of the divine Tiresias,[33] more learned than her father. I see a Zenobia, Queen of the Palmyrans,[34] as wise as she was valiant. An Arete,[35] most learned daughter of Aristippus.[36] A Nicostrata,[37] framer of Latin verses and most erudite in Greek. An Aspasia of Miletus,[38] who taught philosophy and rhetoric, and who was a teacher of the philosopher Pericles.[39] An Hypatia,[40] who taught astrology, and studied many years in Alexandria. A Leontium,[41] a Greek woman, who questioned the philosopher Theophrastus,[42] and convinced him. A Jucia,[43] a Corinna,[44] a Cornelia[45]; and, finally, a great throng of women deserving to be named, some as Greeks, some as muses, some as seers; for all were nothing more than learned women, held, and celebrated—and venerated as well—as such by antiquity. Without mentioning an infinity of other women whose names fill books. For example, I find the Egyptian Catherine,[46] studying and influencing the wisdom of all the wise men of Egypt. I see a Gertrude studying, writing, and teaching. And not to overlook examples close to home, I see my most holy mother Paula,[47] learned in Hebrew, Greek, and Latin, and most

---

[18] **Holy Arc of the Covenant** Usually spelled Holy Ark. A chest containing the sacred objects of the Hebrews (Numbers 10:33).
[19] **Canon and Civil Law** Church law and law of secular society.
[20] **Debbora** Hebrew prophetess and judge (Judges 4:5).
[21] **Queen of Saba** Queen of Sheba, in modern Arabia, who visited King Solomon of ancient Judah and Israel (1 Kings 10:13).
[22] **Abigail** Wife of David (1 Samuel 25).
[23] **Esther** Jewish heroine and queen; queen of Persia and wife of King Ahasuerus. Through her influence, she saved the Persian Jews from massacre—the triumph commemorated in the Jewish festival of Purim (book of Esther).
[24] **Rahab** Canaanite prostitute, who heard and believed the story of the Jewish exodus from Egypt; repented and became a believer in God (Joshua 2 and 6).
[25] **Anna** Also, Hannah. Second wife of Elkanah, from Ephraim; unable to bear children; prayed to God and was rewarded with the birth of **Samuel** (1 Samuel 1–2).
[26] **Samuel** Hebrew judge and prophet; anointed **Saul** as king (1 Samuel 1–25).
[27] **Gentiles** Non-Jews.
[28] **Sibyls** Ancient prophetesses at varied sites, including Delphi (Greece), Cumae (Italy), and Libya (Africa).
[29] **Minerva** Roman goddess of wisdom; equivalent of the Greek god Athena.
[30] **Jupiter** Roman king of the gods; equivalent of the Greek god Zeus.
[31] **Polla Argentaria** (fl. 80s CE), wife and later widow of the poet **Lucan.**
[32] **Lucan** (39–65 CE), Roman poet, author of *Pharsalia*, a historical epic.
[33] **daughter of . . . Tiresias** Daphne, prophetess at Delphi. Tiresias was a fabled prophet from Thebes, who often appeared in Greek literature, beginning with Homer's *Odyssey*.
[34] **Zenobia, Queen of the Palmyrans** (third century CE), wife of King Odenathus, in modern Syria; after king's death, she became regent and expanded empire to include Egypt and Asia Minor; defeated and captured by the Romans.
[35] **Arete** (fl. fourth century BCE), daughter of Aristippus. Succeeded father as head of school in Cyrene (in modern Libya). Author of forty (now lost) books; hailed as "Light of Hellas," by her native city (see footnote 36).
[36] **Aristippus** (435–355 BCE), Greek philosopher, founded school of hedonism in his native city, Cyrene (in modern Libya).
[37] **Nicostrata** Ancient woman philosopher, known as Carmentis to the Italians; claimed to be part author of Greek alphabet and a writer in Latin.
[38] **Aspasia of Miletus** (ca. 470–410 BCE), Greek courtesan, famed for learning, beauty, and wit; companion to **Pericles** (see footnote 39).
[39] **Pericles** (ca. 495–429 BCE), Athenian general and statesman.
[40] **Hypatia** (ca. 370–415), pagan Greek philosopher, head of school of Neoplatonism in Alexandria; killed by rampaging Christian mob.
[41] **Leontium** (fl. third century BCE), Greek woman philosopher.
[42] **Theophrastus** (ca. 372–ca. 287 BCE), Greek philosopher and scientist; succeeded Aristotle as head of the Peripatetic school in Athens.
[43] **Jucia** Unidentified, perhaps Julia or Lucia.
[44] **Corinna** (fifth century BCE), Greek woman poet.
[45] **Cornelia** (second century BCE), Roman matron, daughter of Scipio Africanus and mother of the Gracchi Brothers; famed for her "noble nature and education" (Plutarch).
[46] **Catherine** (fourth century CE), of Alexandria; legendary Christian saint, disputed with philosophers; converted the wife of the Roman emperor; martyred on a spiked wheel.
[47] **Paula** Founder of Sor Juana's monastic order (see footnote 11).

able in interpreting the Scriptures. And what greater praise than, having as her chronicler a Jeronimus Maximus,[48] that Saint scarcely found himself competent for his task, and says, with that weighty deliberation and energetic precision with which he so well expressed himself: "If all the members of my body were tongues, they still would not be sufficient to proclaim the wisdom and virtue of Paula." Similarly praiseworthy was the widow Blesilla[49]; also, the illustrious virgin Eustochium,[50] both daughters of this same saint; especially the second, who, for her knowledge, was called the Prodigy of the World. The Roman Fabiola[51] was most well-versed in the Holy Scripture. Proba Falconia,[52] a Roman woman, wrote elegant centos,[53] containing verses from Virgil,[54] about the mysteries of Our Holy Faith. It is well-known by all that Queen Isabella,[55] wife of the tenth Alfonso,[56] wrote about astrology. Many others I do not list, out of the desire not merely to transcribe what others have said[57] (a vice I have always abominated); and many are flourishing today, as witness Christina Alexandra, Queen of Sweden,[58] as learned as she is valiant and magnanimous, and the Most Honorable Ladies, the Duquesa of Aveyro[59] and the Condesa of Villaumbrosa.[60]. . .

All this demands more investigation than some believe, who . . . attempt to interpret the Scriptures while clinging to that *Let the women keep silence in the church,*[61] not knowing how it is to be interpreted. As well as that other verse, *Let the women learn in silence.*[62] For this latter

10

scripture works more to women's favor than their disfavor, as it commands them to learn; and it is only natural that they must maintain silence while they learn. And it is also written, *Hear, oh Israel, and be silent.*[63] Which addresses the entire congregation of men and women, commanding all to silence, because if one is to hear and learn, it is with good reason that he attend and be silent. And if it is not so, I would want these interpreters and expositors of Saint Paul to explain to me how they interpret that scripture, *Let the women keep silence in the church.* For either they must understand it to refer to the material church, that is the church of pulpits and cathedras,[64] or to the spiritual, the community of the faithful, which is the Church. If they understand it to be the former, which, in my opinion, is its true interpretation, then we see that if in fact it is not permitted of women to read publicly in church, nor preach, why do they censure those who study privately? And if they understand the latter, and wish that the prohibition of the Apostle be applied transcendentally—that not even in private are women to be permitted to write or study— how are we to view the fact that the Church permitted a Gertrude,[65] a Santa Teresa,[66] a Saint Birgitta,[67] the Nun of Agreda,[68] and so many others, to write? And if they say to me that these women were saints, they speak the truth; but this poses no obstacle to my argument. First, because Saint Paul's proposition is absolute, and encompasses all women not excepting saints, as Martha and Mary,[69] Marcella,[70] Mary mother of Jacob,[71] and Salome,[72] all were in their time, and many other zealous women of the early Church. But we see, too, that the Church allows women who are not saints to write, for the Nun of Agreda and

---

[48] **Jeronimus Maximus** Term of respect for **Saint Jerome** (see footnote 10).
[49] **Blesilla** (d. 384), daughter of Saint **Paula** (see footnote 11).
[50] **Eustochium** (d. 419), daughter of Saint **Paula** (see footnote 11).
[51] **Fabiola** (d. 399/400), Roman matron and philanthropist. She converted to Christianity after 384; in Rome, built both a hospice for pilgrims and a hospital, where she served as a nurse; spent time in Bethlehem with **Saint Jerome**.
[52] **Proba Falconia** Possibly **Proba Faltonia** or simply **Proba;** (fourth century), Roman matron and poet. A Christian convert, she wrote an epic (now lost) about the wars of Emperor Constantine as well as verses on biblical history, in the style of **Virgil.**
[53] **cento** Latin, "patchwork." A patchwork poem of lines taken from several poets.
[54] **Virgil** Also spelled Vergil (70–19 BCE), Roman poet, author of the *Aeneid* (q.v.).
[55] **Queen Isabella** Confused; the wife of **Alfonso X** (see footnote 56) was Yolanda, daughter of James I of Aragon.
[56] **Alfonso** Alfonso X, the Wise, king of Castile and Leon (r. 1252–1284). Patron of the arts; established basis of Spanish law; stimulated growth of Castilian Spanish as literary language.
[57] **others have said** For comparison purposes, all of the illustrious women named by Sor Juana are also in the list compiled by the English educator, Bathsua Makin (ca. 1600–ca. 1674), titled *An Essay to Revive the Antient Education of Gentlewomen* and published in 1675, except that Makin's list doesn't mention **Jucia** (see footnote 43) and, most especially, Makin's list has many names not included in Sor Juana's work.
[58] **Christina Alexandra, Queen of Sweden** (r. 1640–1654), abdicated throne and converted to Catholicism; lived in Rome and patronized the arts.
[59] **Duquesa of Aveyro** (1630–1715), Guadelupe Alencastre, Portuguese lady, famed for piety and charity.
[60] **Condesa of Villaumbrosa** Unidentified.
[61] *Let the women keep silence in the church.* 1 Corinthians 14:34.
[62] *Let the women learn in silence.* 1 Timothy 2:11.

[63] *Hear, oh Israel, and be silent.* Statement in Christian liturgy, echoing in part, Deuteronomy 6:4: "Hear, oh Israel, the Lord is our God, the Lord alone." This scripture is also the text of the Shema (Hebrew for "hear") prayer recited in Hebrew in the Jewish liturgy.
[64] **cathedra** Latin, "chair" or "throne" of a bishop; by extension, a cathedral is a bishop's church. In this context, Sor Juana refers to the throne from which a bishop delivers his sermon or homily, while seated and facing the church congregation.
[65] **Gertrude** (1256–1301/1302), Saint Gertrude the Great, German nun, visionary, and author of various Latin works, of which three survive.
[66] **Santa Teresa** (1515–1582), of Avila, in Spain; Spanish nun; a leading mystic of the Catholic Church; author of a well-regarded spiritual autobiography in Latin.
[67] **Saint Birgitta** Also Saint Bridget (1303–1373), Swedish nun, visionary, and founder of a monastic order for women, the Brigittines.
[68] **Nun of Agreda** (1601–1665), Maria of Agreda or Maria of Jesus, her convent name; Castilian nun, visionary, author of various works in Latin.
[69] **Martha and Mary** Sisters of Lazarus, the man whom Jesus raised from the dead. Jesus blessed both women for their faith (Luke 10:38–42).
[70] **Marcella** (d. 410), Roman widow and head of a religious society; friend of **Saint Jerome;** some of **Jerome's** letters to her survive. Killed during Visigoth sack of Rome.
[71] **Mary mother of Jacob** Perhaps Mary, mother of the apostle James; she, Mary Magdalene, and a woman named **Salome** discovered Jesus's empty tomb (Mark 16:1–8).
[72] **Salome** Christian woman who discovered Jesus's empty tomb (see footnote 71).

Sor María de la Antigua[73] are not canonized, yet their writings are circulated. And when Santa Teresa and the others were writing, they were not as yet canonized. In which case, Saint Paul's prohibition was directed solely to the public office of the pulpit, for if the Apostle had forbidden women to write, the Church would not have allowed it. Now I do not make so bold as to teach—which in me would be excessively presumptuous—and as for writing, that requires a greater talent than mine, and serious reflection. As Saint Cyprian[74] says: *The things we* *write require most conscientious consideration.* I have desired to study that I might be ignorant of less; for (according to Saint Augustine[75]) some things are learned to be enacted and others only to be known: *We learn some things to know them, others, to do them.* Then, where is the offense to be found if even what is licit to women—which is to teach by writing—I do not perform, as I know that I am lacking in means following the counsel of Quintilian:[76] *Let each person learn not only from the precepts of others, but also let him reap counsel from his own nature.*

---

[73] **María de la Antigua** (fl. late seventeenth century), convent name for Sor Leonor de Ahumada, mother superior of the Convent of Our Lady of the Snows, in Córdoba.
[74] **Saint Cyprian** (third century), Christian martyr, bishop of Carthage, and writer.

[75] **Saint Augustine** (354–430), a Father of the Church and a philosopher; author of *Confessions* (q.v.) and *The City of God* (q.v.).
[76] **Quintilian** (ca. 35–ca. 100), Roman orator and educator; author of famous work on oratory.

Questions for Critical Thinking

1. Based on Sor Juana's two poems, what role does she believe women should play in society? Assess whether or not her position would carry weight in today's world.

2. Summarize Sister Juana's argument in favor of free speech for women. Which particular Bible passage did she have to address in order to make her case?

JOHN MILTON
Selection from *Paradise Lost*

Milton's *Paradise Lost* reflected the craze for the epic that swept Europe in the 1600s. It towers above this period's other epics, which are largely unread today. Often called the Protestant epic, it was intended by Milton (who belonged to the Calvinist faith) as a response to Dante's *Divine Comedy.* Although not the greatest poem in English (as some admirers claim)—its religious theme is out of tune with the pervasive secularism of the modern world—it most certainly is the most ambitious poem in the English language.

Milton's ambition is evident both in his poem's great length—more than ten thousand lines divided into twelve books, or chapters—and in its grand theme—original sin, or the belief that all humans, male and female, are born evil. This Christian belief has few supporters today, being replaced by the secular belief of socially created "evil"; but when Milton wrote, original sin was a defining feature of Western culture. Milton thus tackled one of his period's basic beliefs in an effort to "justify the ways of God to men."

Milton's three major sources are the epics of Homer (see *Iliad, Odyssey* in Chapter 2, Volume I) and Virgil (see *Aeneid* in Chapter 5, Volume I) and the book of Genesis (see *The Holy Scriptures* in Chapter 6, Volume I). From Homer and Virgil come the full epic apparatus of invocations, digressions, similes, long speeches, history, folklore, perilous journeys, battles, and scenes in the underworld. The range is colossal, the sweep majestic, and the tone lofty. From Genesis comes the plot: the creation of Adam and Eve, their first sin, and expulsion from the Garden of Eden, or paradise. Milton's artistic purpose was to transform the Genesis story, along with related theological problems, into epic poetry.

Paradise Lost reflects the era of its birth, Restoration England (1661–1688), when the Stuarts once again ruled and the Puritan experiment was over. Milton now had leisure to write, since from 1639 to 1659 he had lived for politics; first he was a propagandist for the Puritan cause and then an official in the Protectorate, Oliver Cromwell's dictatorship. Milton, though blind, composed this epic between 1660 and 1665, publishing it in 1665. The descriptions of Satan, "his horrid crew," and the construction of hell may be interpreted as political allegory—Satan has been associated with both Charles I and Cromwell. The story, the loss of paradise, may express Milton's despair over the failure of the Protectorate, which had been regarded by its leaders as biblical doctrine in political and social practice, a kind of substitute for Eden before the fall.

Reading the Selection

This selection contains about one-fourth of Book I of Paradise Lost. "The Argument" gives a general overview and a summary of Book I. The poem is in blank verse, the verse form used by Shakespeare (see Hamlet in Chapter 14), but not heretofore adopted by poets. Milton's example blazed a path for later poets, such as Wordsworth (see "Tintern Abbey" in Chapter 18).

The opening lines announce Milton's theme: "man's first disobedience, and [its] fruit . . . death . . . and all our woe." As Homer invoked Calliope, the muse of epic poetry, so Milton prays that the Holy Ghost, the third member of the Christian Trinity, will act as a "Heavenly Muse." This passage also introduces Milton's glamorous anti-hero, Satan, the Prince of Darkness and fallen angel, who takes pleasure in his evil work: "[E]ver to do ill our sole delight." Pious readers of Milton have often complained that Satan steals the show with his fascinating villainy, as shown here in verbal exchanges with his second-in-command, Beëlzebub.

Book I

The Argument

This first book proposes, first in brief, the whole subject, man's disobedience, and the loss thereupon of Paradise, wherein he was placed: then touches the prime cause of his fall, the serpent, or rather Satan in the serpent; who revolting from God, and drawing to his side many legions of angels, was, by the command of God, driven out of Heaven with all his crew, into the great deep. Which action passed over, the poem hastes into the midst of things; presenting Satan, with his angels, now fallen into Hell—described here not in the center (for heaven and earth may be supposed as yet not made, certainly not yet accursed), but in a place of utter darkness, fitliest called Chaos. Here Satan with his angels lying on the burning lake, thunder-struck and astonished, after a certain space recovers, as from confusion; calls up him who, next in order and dignity, lay by him; they confer of their miserable fall. Satan awakens all his legions, who lay till then in the same manner confounded. They rise: their numbers; array of battle; their chief leaders named, according to the idols known afterwards in Canaan and the countries adjoining. To these Satan directs his speech; comforts them with hope yet of regaining Heaven; but tells them, lastly,

of a new world and new kind of creature to be created, according to an ancient prophecy or report in Heaven; for that angels were long before this visible creation was the opinion of many ancient fathers. To find out the truth of this prophecy, and what to determine thereon, he refers to a full council. What his associates thence attempt. Pandemonium, the palace of Satan, rises, suddenly built out of the deep: the infernal peers there sit in council.

Of man's first disobedience, and the fruit
Of that forbidden tree whose mortal taste
Brought death into the world, and all our woe,
With loss of Eden, till one greater Man[77]
Restore us, and regain the blissful seat,
Sing, Heavenly Muse, that on the secret top
Of Oreb,[78] or of Sinai,[79] didst inspire
That shepherd who first taught the chosen seed
In the beginning how the heavens and earth

---

[77] **one greater Man** Jesus Christ; 1 Corinthians 15:21–22.
[78] **Oreb** Usually **Horeb.** General name for mountain district, which includes Mount **Sinai;** Exodus 3:1.
[79] **Sinai** Mountain in the **Horeb** district; **Sinai** and **Horeb** are used interchangeably.

Rose out of Chaos: or, if Sion hill[80]
Delight thee more, and Siloa's brook[81] that flowed
Fast by the oracle of God, I thence
Invoke thy aid to my adventurous song,
That with no middle flight intends to soar
Above th' Aonian mount,[82] while it pursues
Things unattempted yet in prose or rhyme.
And chiefly thou, O Spirit, that dost prefer
Before all temples th' upright heart and pure,
Instruct me, for thou know'st; thou from the first
Was present, and, with mighty wings outspread,   20
Dovelike[83] sat'st brooding on the vast abyss,
And mad'st it pregnant: what in me is dark
Illumine; what is low, raise and support;
That to the height of this great argument
I may assert Eternal Providence,
And justify the ways of God to men.
    Say first (for Heaven hides nothing from thy view,
Nor the deep tract of Hell, say first what cause
Moved our grandparents,[84] in that happy state,
Favored of Heaven so highly, to fall off   30
From their Creator, and transgress his will
For one restraint, lords of the world besides?
Who first seduced them to that foul revolt?
    Th' infernal serpent; he it was, whose guile,
Stirred up with envy and revenge, deceived
The mother of mankind,[85] what time his pride
Had cast him out from Heaven, with all his host
Of rebel angels, by whose aid aspiring
To set himself in glory above his peers,
He trusted to have equaled the Most High,   40
If he opposed; and with ambitious aim
Against the throne and monarchy of God
Raised impious war in Heaven and battle proud,
With vain attempt. Him the Almighty Power
Hurled headlong flaming from th' ethereal sky
With hideous ruin and combustion down
To bottomless perdition, there to dwell
In adamantine[86] chains and penal fire,
Who durst defy th' Omnipotent to arms.
    Nine times the space that measures day and night   50
To mortal men, he with his horrid crew
Lay vanquished, rolling in the fiery gulf
Confounded though immortal. But his doom
Reserved him to more wrath; for now the thought
Both of lost happiness and lasting pain
Torments him; round he throws his baleful eyes,

That witnessed huge affliction and dismay,
Mixed with obdurate pride and steadfast hate.
At once, as far as angels ken,[87] he views
The dismal situation waste and wild: 60
A dungeon horrible, on all sides round
As one great furnace flamed; yet from those flames
No light, but rather darkness visible
Served only to discover sights of woe,
Regions of sorrow, doleful shades, where peace
And rest can never dwell, hope never comes
That comes to all, but torture without end
Still urges, and a fiery deluge, fed
With ever-burning sulphur unconsumed:
Such place Eternal Justice had prepared   70
For those rebellious; here their prison ordained
In utter darkness and their portion set
As far removed from God and light of Heaven
As from the center thrice to th' utmost pole.
O how unlike the place from whence they fell!
There the companions of his fall, o'erwhelmed
With floods and whirlwinds of tempestuous fire,
He soon discerns; and, weltering by his side,
One next himself in power, and next in crime,
Long after known in Palestine, and named   80
Beëlzebub.[88] To whom th' arch-enemy,
And thence in Heaven called Satan, with bold words
Breaking the horrid silence thus began:
    "If thou beëst he—but O how fallen! how changed
From him who in the happy realms of light
Clothed with transcendent brightness didst outshine
Myriads, though bright! if he whom mutual league,
United thoughts and counsels, equal hope
And hazard in the glorious enterprise,
Joined with me once, now misery hath joined   90
In equal ruin; into what pit thou seest
From what height fallen, so much the stronger proved
He with his thunder: and till then who knew
The force of those dire arms? Yet not for those,
Nor what the potent Victor in his rage
Can else inflict, do I repent or change,
Though changed in outward luster, that fixed mind
And high disdain, from sense of injured merit,
That with the Mightiest raised me to contend,
And to the fierce contention brought along   100
Innumerable force of spirits armed,
That durst dislike his reign, and me preferring,
His utmost power with adverse power opposed
In dubious battle on the plains of Heaven,
And shook his throne. What though the field be lost?
All is not lost: the unconquerable will,
And study of revenge, immortal hate,
And courage never to submit or yield:
And what is else not to be overcome?
That glory never shall his wrath or might   110
Extort from me. To bow and sue for grace

---

[80] **Sion hill** Jerusalem. "Sion" or "Zion" is a poetical name for Jerusalem. Jerusalem is a mountain city, built on two mountains. See Psalm 68:15.
[81] **Siloa's brook** Also Siloah or, in Hebrew, Shelah; a pool in Jerusalem. See Nehemiah 3:15.
[82] **Aonian mount** In Greece, the site where the Muses dance. Milton means that his Muse, the Holy Spirit, is to soar above Greece and journey to the Holy Land.
[83] **Dovelike** In Christian scripture and tradition, the Holy Spirit is represented as a dove; Matthew 3:16.
[84] **grandparents** Lucifer and the rebel angels.
[85] **mother of mankind** Eve.
[86] **adamantine** Diamondlike, that is, hard as a diamond.

---

[87] **ken** Recognize.
[88] **Beëlzebub** From Hebrew, *Baal zebhubh*, a Palestinian pagan god, literally "Lord of the Flies."

With suppliant knee, and deify his power
Who from the terror of this arm so late
Doubted his empire—that were low indeed;
That were an ignominy and shame beneath
This downfall; since by fate, the strength of gods
And this empyreal[89] substance cannot fail;
Since, through experience of this great event,
In arms not worse, in foresight much advanced,
We may with more successful hope resolve   120
To wage by force or guile eternal war,
Irreconcilable to our grand Foe,
Who now triùmphs, and in th' excess of joy
Sole reigning holds the tyranny of Heaven."
    So spake th' apostate angel, though in pain,
Vaunting aloud, but racked with deep despair;
And him thus answered soon his bold compeer:
    "O prince, O chief of many thronèd powers,
That led th' embattled seraphim[90] to war
Under thy conduct, and in dreadful deeds   130
Fearless, endangered Heaven's perpetual King,
And put to proof his high supremacy,
Whether upheld by strength, or chance, or fate!
Too well I see and rue the dire event
That with sad overthrow and foul defeat
Hath lost us Heaven, and all this mighty host
In horrible destruction laid thus low,
As far as gods and heavenly essences
Can perish: for the mind and spirit remains
Invincible, and vigor soon returns,   140
Though all our glory extinct, and happy state
Here swallowed up in endless misery.
But what if he our Conqueror (whom I now
Of force believe almighty, since no less
Than such could have o'erpowered such force as ours)
Have left us this our spirit and strength entire,
Strongly to suffer and support our pains,
That we may so suffice his vengeful ire,
Or do him mightier service as his thralls
By right of war, whate'er his business be,   150

Here in the heart of Hell to work in fire,
Or do his errands in the gloomy deep?
What can it then avail though yet we feel
Strength undiminished, or eternal being
To undergo eternal punishment?"
    Whereto with speedy words th' arch-fiend replied:
"Fallen cherub,[91] to be weak is miserable,
Doing or suffering: but of this be sure,
To do aught good never will be our task,
But ever to do ill our sole delight,   160
As being the contrary to his high will
Whom we resist. If then his providence
Out of our evil seek to bring forth good,
Our labor must be to pervert that end,
And out of good still to find means of evil;
Which ofttimes may succeed, so as perhaps
Shall grieve him, if I fail not, and disturb
His inmost counsels from their destined aim.
But see! the angry Victor hath recalled
His ministers of vengeance and pursuit   170
Back to the gates of Heaven; the sulphurous hail,
Shot after us in storm, o'erblown hath laid
The fiery surge that from the precipice
Of Heaven received us falling; and the thunder,
Winged with red lightning and impetuous rage,
Perhaps hath spent his shafts, and ceases now
To bellow through the vast and boundless deep.
Let us not slip th' occasion, whether scorn
Or satiate fury yield it from our Foe.
Seest thou yon dreary plain, forlorn and wild,   180
The seat of desolation, void of light,
Save what the glimmering of these livid flames
Casts pale and dreadful? Thither let us tend
From off the tossing of these fiery waves;
There rest, if any rest can harbor there;
And reassembling our afflicted powers,
Consult how we may henceforth most offend
Our enemy, our own loss how repair,
How overcome this dire calamity,
What reinforcement we may gain from hope,   190
If not, what resolution from despair." . . .

---

[89] **empyreal** From "empyrean," the highest heaven; celestial.
[90] **seraphim** The highest order of angels, with six sets of wings;
Isaiah 6:2. The celestial hierarchy consists of nine orders, ranging from lowest to highest: angels, archangels, principalities,
powers, virtues, dominions, thrones, **cherubim, and seraphim.**

---

[91] **cherub** A member of the **cherubim** order of angels; Genesis
3:24 (see footnote [90]).

Questions for Critical Thinking

1. What connection does Milton draw between Satan and his legions, on one side, and the fall of Adam and Eve, on the other?

2. According to Milton, what is the purpose of human life? Of world history? Compare and contrast Milton's views with those of your own.

APHRA BEHN
Selection from *Oroonoko, or The Royal Slave: A True History*

Aphra Behn (1640–1689) was England's first professional woman of letters. She was not financially successful, though, for the literary world was still ruled by rich patrons. Ignored by would-be patrons, she was forced into debtors' prison for a time. Undaunted, she pressed on and left a distinguished literary legacy. She blamed her failure partly on being marginal in a male domain. In one play, for example, she railed against men who abused her for being a *woman* writer, and she claimed instead that wit has no gender. Of Behn, Virginia Woolf (see *A Room of One's Own* in Chapter 21) wrote in 1915: "All [English] women together ought to let flowers fall upon the tomb of Aphra Behn, for it was she who earned them the right to speak their minds."

Of obscure origins, Behn is thought to have spent two years in the then English colony of Surinam (modern Suriname) before settling in London. To some degree, this encounter with the world beyond Europe freed her of Eurocentrism, giving her a unique outlook for the time. She drew on this colonial world for *Oroonoko* (1688), a short story set in Surinam and focused on the doomed love of a black slave-prince and a slave woman. In this story she expressed, through the slave heroes, her fantasy of a golden age of social and sexual frankness—a type of primitivism similar to that of Montaigne (see "Of Cannibals" in Chapter 14). Works like *Oroonoko* prepared the way for the next century's long romantic novels, often with non-European settings.

Behn also won renown as a comic dramatist. In form, her plays (almost twenty in number) belong to Restoration comedy, the comedy genre that flourished after the restoration of the monarchy (the later Stuart dynasty) in 1661; it featured sexual and marital intrigue. Her works, such as *The Rover* (1677) and *The City Heiress* (1682), have been described as quite "as obscene and successful as" other plays of this period.

Behn also composed poetry and it, like her plays, chimed with the ruling artistic code in Restoration England. She wrote mainly love lyrics that catered to her audience's need to see themselves as members of an elegant and stylish society.

Reading the Selection

Behn's masterpiece, *Oroonoko, or The Royal Slave: A True History*, continues to fascinate modern readers, not only for its romantic story but, most especially, because it looks forward to the diverse, global culture emerging today. Focused on a black African prince caught in the slave trade, this story represented much that was new in seventeenth-century Europe: the growth of empire overseas, the rise of women writers, interest in non-Western cultures, and the development of a belief in natural rights. Although critics debate Behn's literary purpose—was she writing a "true history" or telling a tall tale? Did she condemn slavery or did she gloss over its cruelty?—*Oroonoko* retains its unique place in Western literature as one of the first works to challenge the Eurocentric perspective.

Three episodes are included in this selection from *Oroonoko*. In the first, Behn, speaking in the first person, introduces herself as a character in the tale. By injecting an autobiographical voice, she establishes a tension, never resolved, between the romantic elements and the realism created by her narrative presence. The second episode depicts the abduction of Prince Oroonoko and his court by a slave trader. In the third episode, Oroonoko is sold to John Trefry, plantation overseer to one of Surinam's proprietors, and is given a slave name, *Caesar*. Oroonoko is reunited with Imoinda, the black princess now enslaved as *Clemene*, whom he thought was left behind in Africa. At the end (not included here) the star-crossed lovers die heroically: Oroonoko, knowing he's going to die, kills Imoinda rather than have her live enslaved; and he, captured during a slave revolt, is hacked to death and quartered, his remains scattered around the colony.

❧

I do not pretend, in giving you the History of this *Royal Slave,* to entertain my Reader with the Adventures of a feign'd *Hero,* whose Life and Fortunes Fancy may manage at the Poet's Pleasure; nor in relating the Truth, design to adorn it with any Accidents, but such as arriv'd in earnest to him: And it shall come simply into the World, recommended by its own proper Merits, and natural Intrigues; there being enough of Reality to support it, and to render it diverting, without the Addition of Invention.

I was my self an Eye-Witness to a great part, of what you will find here set down; and what I cou'd not be Witness of, I receiv'd from the Mouth of the chief Actor in this History, the *Hero* himself, who gave us the whole Transactions of his Youth; and though I shall omit, for Brevity's sake, a thousand little Accidents of his Life, which, however pleasant to us, where History was scarce, and Adventures very rare; yet might prove tedious and heavy to my Reader, in a World where he finds Diversions for every Minute, new and strange: But we who were perfectly charm'd with the Character of this great Man, were curious to gather every Circumstance of his Life.

The Scene of the last part of his Adventures lies in a Colony in *America,* called *Surinam,*[92] in the *West-Indies.*

. . .

Oroonoko[93] was no sooner return'd from this last Conquest . . . when there arriv'd in the Port an *English* Ship.

This Person[94] had often before been in these Countries, and was very well known to *Oroonoko,* with whom he had traffick'd for Slaves, and had us'd to do the same with his Predecessors.

This Commander was a Man of a finer sort of Address, and Conversation, better bred, and more engaging, than most of that sort of Men are; so that he seem'd rather never to have been bred out of a Court, than almost all his Life at Sea. This Captain therefore was always better receiv'd at Court, than most of the Traders to those Countries were; and especially by *Oroonoko,* who was more civiliz'd, according to the *European* Mode, than any other had been, and took more Delight in the *White* Nations; and, above all, Men of Parts and Wit. To this Captain he sold abundance of his Slaves; and for the Favour and Esteem he had for him, made him many Presents, and oblig'd him to stay at Court as long as possibly he cou'd. Which the Captain seem'd to take as a very great Honour done him, entertaining the Prince every Day with Globes and Maps, and Mathematical Discourses and Instruments; eating, drinking, hunting and living with him with so much Familiarity, that it was not to be doubted, but he had gain'd very greatly upon the Heart of this gallant young Man. And the Captain, in Return of all these mighty Favours, besought the Prince to honour his Vessel with his Presence, some Day or other, to Dinner, before he shou'd set Sail; which he condescended to accept, and appointed his Day. The Captain, on his part, fail'd not to have all things in a Readiness, in the most magnificent Order he cou'd possibly: And the Day being come, the Captain, in his Boat, richly adorn'd with Carpets and Velvet-Cushions, row'd to the shore to receive the Prince; with another Long-Boat, where was plac'd all his Musick and Trumpets, with which *Oroonoko* was extreamly delighted; who met him on the shore, attended by his *French* Governor, *Jamoan, Aboan,* and about an hundred of the noblest of the Youths of the Court: And after they had first carry'd the Prince on Board, the Boats fetch'd the rest off; where they found a very splendid Treat, with all sorts of fine Wines; and were as well entertain'd, as 'twas possible in such a place to be.

The Prince having drunk hard of Punch, and several Sorts of Wine, as did all the rest (for great Care was taken, they shou'd want nothing of that part of the Entertainment) was very merry, and in great Admiration of the Ship, for he had never been in one before; so that he was curious of beholding every place, where he decently might descend. The rest, no less curious, who were not quite overcome with Drinking, rambl'd at their pleasure *Fore* and *Aft,* as their Fancies guided 'em: So that the Captain, who had well laid his Design before, gave the Word, and seiz'd on all his Guests; they clapping great Irons suddenly on the Prince, when he was leap'd down in the Hold, to view that part of the Vessel; and locking him fast down, secur'd him. The same Treachery was us'd to all the rest; and all in one Instant, in several places of the Ship, were lash'd fast in Irons, and betray'd to Slavery. That great Design over, they set all Hands to work to hoise[95] Sail; and with as treacherous and fair a Wind, they made from the Shore with this innocent and glorious Prize, who thought of nothing less than such an Entertainment.

Some have commended this Act, as brave, in the Captain; but I will spare my sense of it, and leave it to my Reader, to judge as he pleases.

. . .

I ought to tell you, that the *Christians* never buy any Slaves but they give 'em some Name of their own, their native ones being likely very barbarous, and hard to pronounce; so that Mr. *Trefry* gave *Oroonoko* that of *Caesar,*[96]

---

[92] *Surinam* An English colony within the larger district of Guiana, on the South American coast east of Venezuela; later Dutch Guiana, now Suriname. During the 1650s it was settled by experienced planters from the main colony of Barbados, where the land supply was exhausted.
[93] *Oroonoko* The hero's name evokes the 1,280-mile Orinoco River in southern Venezuela.
[94] **Person** The ship's captain.

[95] **hoise** Hoist. The abduction and enslavement of Africans who visited on board ships or traveled as pawns or passengers is recorded with disapproval in many early reports, official and unofficial, if never on this scale. Victims of high rank were sometimes ransomed or returned to avoid retaliation and the closing of trade.
[96] *Caesar* Such classical names as Pompey and Scipio, or even Cupid or Apollo, were frequently given to slaves. Julius Caesar was famed as both a military and a political leader, sometimes portrayed as a strong ruler who acted for the people but who was betrayed by members of the oligarchy. Behn regularly referred to both Charles II and James II as "Caesar" in celebratory poems.

which Name will live in that Country as long as that (scarce more) glorious one of the great *Roman;* for 'tis most evident, he wanted[97] no part of the Personal Courage of that *Caesar,* and acted things as memorable, had they been done in some part of the World replenish'd with People, and Historians, that might have given him his due. But his Misfortune was, to fall in an obscure World, that afforded only a Female Pen to celebrate his Fame; though I doubt not but it had liv'd from others Endeavours, if the *Dutch,* who, immediately after his Time, took that Country[98] had not kill'd, banish'd and dispers'd all those that were capable of giving the World this great Man's Life, much better than I have done. And Mr. *Trefry,* who design'd it, dy'd before he began it; and bemoan'd himself for not having undertook it in time.

For the future therefore, I must call *Oronooko, Caesar,* since by that Name only he was known in our Western World, and by that Name he was receiv'd on Shore at *Parham-House,* where he was destin'd a Slave. But if the King himself (God bless him) had come a-shore, there cou'd not have been greater Expectations by all the whole Plantation, and those neighbouring ones, than was on ours at that time; and he was receiv'd more like a Governor, than a Slave. Notwithstanding, as the Custom was, they assign'd him his Portion of Land, his House, and his Business, up in the Plantation. But as it was more for Form, than any Design, to put him to his Task, he endur'd no more of the Slave but the Name, and remain'd some Days in the House, receiving all Visits that were made him, without stirring towards that part of the Plantation where the *Negroes* were.

At last, he wou'd needs go view his Land, his House, and the Business assign'd him. But he no sooner came to the Houses of the Slaves, which are like a little Town by it self, the *Negroes* all having left Work, but they all came forth to behold him, and found he was that Prince who had, at several times, sold most of 'em to these Parts; and, from a Veneration they pay to great Men, especially if they know 'em, and from the Surprize and Awe they had at the sight of him, they all cast themselves at his Feet, crying out, in their Language, *Live, O King! Long Live, O King!* And kissing his Feet, paid him even Divine Homage.

Several *English* Gentlemen were with him; and what Mr. *Trefry* had told 'em, was here confirm'd; of which he himself before had no other Witness than *Caesar* himself: But he was infinitely glad to find his Grandure confirm'd by the Adoration of all the Slaves.

Caesar troubl'd with their Over-Joy, and Over-Ceremony, besought 'em to rise, and to receive him as their Fellow-Slave; assuring them, he was no better. At which they set up with one Accord a most terrible and hidious Mourning and condoling, which he and the *English* had much a-do to appease; but at last they prevail'd with 'em, and they prepar'd all their barbarous Musick, and every one kill'd and dress'd something of his own Stock (for every Family has their Land a-part, on which, at their leisure-times they

breed all eatable things); and clubbing it together,[99] made a most magnificent Supper, inviting their *Grandee*[100] *Captain,* their *Prince,* to honour it with his Presence; which he did, and several *English* with him; where they all waited on him, some playing, others dancing before him all the time, according to the Manners of their several Nations; and with unwearied Industry, endeavouring to please and delight him.

While they sat at Meat Mr. *Trefry* told *Caesar,* that most of these young *Slaves* were undone in Love, with a fine she-*Slave,* whom they had had about Six Months on their Land; the *Prince,* who never heard the Name of *Love* without a Sigh, nor any mention of it without the Curiosity of examining further into that tale, which of all Discourses was most agreeable to him, asked, how they came to be so Unhappy, as to be all undone for one fair *Slave? Trefry,* who was naturally Amorous, and lov'd to talk of Love as well as any body, proceeded to tell him, they had the most charming Black that ever was beheld on their *Plantation,* about Fifteen or Sixteen Years old, as he guess'd; that, for his part, he had done nothing but Sigh for her ever since she came; and that all the white Beautys he had seen, never charm'd him so absolutely as this fine Creature had done; and that no Man, of any Nation, ever beheld her, that did not fall in Love with her; and that she had all the *Slaves* perpetually at her Feet; and the whole Country resounded with the Fame of *Clemene,* for so, said he, we have Christ'ned her: But she denys us all with such a noble Disdain, that 'tis a Miracle to see, that she, who can give such eternal Desires, shou'd herself be all Ice, and all Unconcern. She is adorn'd with the most Graceful Modesty that ever beautifyed Youth; the softest Sigher—that, if she were capable of Love, one would swear she languish'd for some absent happy Man; and so retir'd, as if she fear'd a Rape even from the God of Day[101]; or that the Breezes would steal Kisses from her delicate Mouth. Her Task of Work some sighing Lover every day makes it his Petition to perform for her, which she accepts blushing, and with reluctancy, for fear he will ask her a Look for a Recompence, which he dares not presume to hope; so great an Awe she strikes into the Hearts of her Admirers. *I do not wonder,* replied the Prince, *that Clemene shou'd refuse Slaves, being as you say so Beautiful, but wonder how she escapes those who can entertain her as you can do; or why, being your Slave, you do not oblige her to yield. I confess,* said Trefry, *when I have, against her will, entertain'd her with Love so long, as to be transported with my Passion; even above Decency, I have been ready to make use of those advantages of Strength and Force Nature has given me. But oh! she disarms me, with that Modesty and Weeping so tender and so moving, that I retire, and thank my Stars she overcame me.* The Company laugh'd at his Civility to a *Slave,* and *Caesar* only

---

[97] **wanted** Lacked.
[98] **Country** In 1667 the Dutch attacked and conquered Surinam, and England ceded it by the Treaty of Breda in exchange for New York.

---

[99] **clubbing it together** Contributing jointly. The slaves' private plots (enabling them to feed themselves) and communal festivities with music are noted by many observers.
[100] ***Grandee*** Not simply fractured English; originally a Spanish nobleman of the highest rank, the name was applied to any man of eminence, including planters and merchants.
[101] **God of Day** The sun. Apollo, sometimes called the sun god, pursued Daphne in one famous episode (see Ovid, *Metamorphoses,* in Chapter 5, Volume I).

applauded the nobleness of his Passion and Nature; since that Slave might be Noble, or, what was better, have true Notions of Honour and Vertue in her. Thus pass'd they this Night, after having received, from the *Slaves*, all imaginable Respect and Obedience.

The next Day *Trefry* ask'd *Caesar* to walk, when the heat was allay'd, and designedly carried him by the Cottage of the *fair Slave;* and told him, she whom he spoke of last Night liv'd there retir'd. *But,* says he, *I would not wish you to approach, for, I am sure, you will be in Love as soon as you behold her.* Caesar assur'd him, he was proof against all the Charms of that Sex; and that if he imagin'd his Heart cou'd be so perfidious to Love again, after *Imoinda*, he believ'd he shou'd tear it from his Bosom: They had no sooner spoke, but a little shock Dog, that *Clemene* had presented[102] her, which she took great Delight in, ran out; and she, not knowing any body was there, ran to get it in again, and bolted out on those who were just Speaking of her: When seeing them, she wou'd have run in again; but *Trefry* caught her by the Hand, and cry'd, Clemene, *however you fly a Lover, you ought to pay some Respect to this Stranger* (pointing to *Caesar*). But she, as if she had resolv'd never to raise her Eyes to the Face of a Man again, bent 'em the more to the Earth, when he spoke, and gave the *Prince* the leisure to look the more at her. There needed no long Gazing, or Consideration, to examin who this fair Creature was; he soon saw *Imoinda* all over her; in a Minute he saw her Face, her Shape, her Air, her Modesty, and all that call'd forth his Soul with Joy at his Eyes, and left his Body destitute of almost Life; it stood without Motion, and, for a Minute, knew not that it had a Being; and, I believe, he had never come to himself, so opprest he was with Over-Joy, if he had not met with this Allay, that he perceiv'd *Imoinda* fall dead in the Hands of *Trefry*: this awaken'd him, and he ran to her aid, and caught her in his Arms, where, by degrees, she came to herself; and 'tis needless to tell with what transports, what extasies of Joy, they both a while beheld each other, without Speaking; then Snatch each other to their Arms; then Gaze again, as if they still doubted whether they possess'd the Blessing:[103] They Graspt; but when they

15

recovered their Speech, 'tis not to be imagin'd, what tender things they exprest to each other; wondering what strange Fate had brought 'em again together. They soon inform'd each other of their Fortunes, and equally bewail'd their Fate; but, at the same time, they mutually protested, that even Fetters and Slavery were Soft and Easy; and wou'd be supported with Joy and Pleasure, while they cou'd be so happy to possess each other, and to be able to make good their Vows. *Caesar* swore he disdain'd the Empire of the World, while he cou'd behold his *Imoinda*; and she despis'd Grandure and Pomp, those Vanities of her Sex, when she cou'd Gaze on *Oroonoko*. He ador'd the very Cottage where she resided, and said, That little Inch of the World wou'd give him more Happiness than all the Universe cou'd do; and she vow'd, It was a Pal-lace, while adorn'd with the Presence of *Oroonoko*.

Trefry was infinitely pleas'd with this Novel,[104] and found this *Clemene* was the Fair Mistress of whom *Caesar* had before spoke; and was not a little satisfied, that Heaven was so kind to the *Prince,* as to sweeten his Misfortunes by so lucky an Accident; and leaving the Lovers to themselves, was impatient to come down to *Parham House,* (which was on the same *Plantation*) to give me an Account of what had happened. I was as impatient to make these Lovers a Visit, having already made a Friendship with *Caesar;* and from his own Mouth learn'd what I have related, which was confirm'd by his *French*-man, who was set on Shore to seek his Fortunes; and of whom they cou'd not make a Slave, because a Christian; and he came daily to *Parham Hill* to see and pay his Respects to his Pupil *Prince:* So that concerning and intresting my self, in all that related to *Caesar,* whom I had assur'd of Liberty, as soon as the Governor arriv'd, I hasted presently to the Place where the Lovers were, and was infinitely glad to find this Beautiful young *Slave* (who had already gain'd all our Esteems, for her Modesty and her extraordinary Prettyness) to be the same I had heard *Caesar* speak so much of. One may imagine then, we paid her a treble Respect; and though from her being carv'd in fine Flowers and Birds all over her Body, we took her to be of Quality before, yet, when we knew *Clemene* was *Imoinda*, we cou'd not enough admire her.

---

[102] **had presented** Clear modern usage would add a second *had:* "had had presented." "Shock Dog," a long-haired dog or a poodle, especially associated with women of fashion.

[103] **Blessing** Modern editions often alter the syntax at this point, but the early editors did not.

---

[104] **Novel** Novel event or piece of news.

Questions for Critical Thinking

1. In this tale of star-crossed lovers, how do Oroonoko and Imoinda become separated? And how do they get back together?

2. Does Behn condemn slavery in this story? Or does she simply gloss over the cruelty of human bondage? Explain.

16

THE BAROQUE AGE II
Revolutions in Scientific and Political Thought
1600–1715

GALILEO GALILEI
Selections from *Dialogue Concerning the Two Chief World Systems—Ptolemaic and Copernican*

The contributions of Galileo Galilei (1564–1642) in astronomy, physics, cosmology, and mathematics in the seventeenth century have continued to have an impact down to the present day. His use of instruments, his establishment of precise and orderly experiments, his mathematical calculations, and his willingness to embrace new theories challenged and changed ideas that had been held for nearly two thousand years. Likewise, his methods of inquiry furthered the adoption of the scientific method as one of the most effective learning devices in modern times. In his own day, Galileo became a hero to the proponents of early modern science and a threat to the Catholic Church and to many centers of higher learning. Consequently, he ran afoul of the ecclesiastical authorities and academics. In spite of his efforts to convince them that his scientific discoveries were not a threat to Christian beliefs, he suffered at their hands and was humiliated in public for publishing his findings about the structure of the universe and the motion of the planets. For centuries he remained a martyr to the cause of scientific inquiry and a victim of the struggle between religion and science. Only in 1992 did the Catholic Church absolve Galileo of the heretical charges leveled against him in 1633.

Galileo was born into an impoverished noble family in Pisa. His father, a musician and author, taught him several instruments, which Galileo played throughout his life. The family moved to Florence, where Galileo received his early education grounded in a Renaissance curriculum. In 1581 he returned to Pisa to study medicine at the university but left before receiving his degree. Back in Florence, Galileo studied mathematics, a subject that had attracted him while a student in Pisa. His reputation as a scientist and mathematician began to grow as a result of his scientific experiments and was further enhanced by his paper on the center of gravity, or the balancing point, of solid bodies. In 1589 he was, once again, in Pisa, but this time as a lecturer in mathematics. He started his research on the theory of motion, which, through his experiments, led him to refute Aristotle's conclusion that bodies of different weights fall at different speeds.

Three years later, in 1592, Galileo went to the University of Padua, where he remained for eighteen years. Here he conducted some of his most important research in the study of motion and discovered new features of the moon and some planets. He became a convert to the

Copernican school but held his views in private. He learned about the telescope and then built his own—one powerful enough to be used for astronomical observations. His publications based on his observations of the moon, the Milky Way, Venus, the satellites of Jupiter, and sunspots (dark spots on the sun) heightened his reputation.

Galileo traveled to Rome in 1611, and church officials welcomed him and his findings. Encouraged by their reception, he decided to publish a paper on his discovery of sunspots, which reinforced the Copernican argument. Academics who supported the Aristotelian view of the universe felt threatened, and soon they and a group of Dominican preachers launched a campaign against Galileo. He made several pleas to the authorities in Rome to recognize the Copernican theory, but, in 1616, the church declared Copernicanism "false and erroneous" and admonished Galileo for holding such opinions. For the next few years Galileo worked in relative obscurity outside of Florence at his home. Then, in 1624, Galileo returned to Rome to see his friend and supporter Maffeo Barberini, who was the new pope, Urban VIII (pope 1623–1644). The pope's comments and support led to Galileo being granted permission to write a book about the Ptolemaic and Copernican "systems of the two worlds"—the geocentric and the heliocentric systems. *Dialogue Concerning the Two Chief World Systems—Ptolemaic and Copernican* was an instant success, but it created a major crisis in the Catholic Church. In 1633, Galileo, now old and sick, was summoned to Rome to stand trial. He was found guilty of teaching the Copernican theory and put under house arrest. Galileo spent his last years in his villa, where he continued to write and to carry out scientific experiments.

Reading the Selections

Galileo employed a popular literary device of his day by having three persons, representing different points of view, engage in a series of conversations ranging over numerous but related topics. Salviati, modeled on a friend, takes the Copernican position and speaks for Galileo. Simplicio is the Aristotelian who puts forth the Greek philosopher's opinions on physics and astronomy. Both set out to convince Sagredo, who personifies the educated and reasonable individual open to all arguments, willing to ask questions, and anxious to discover the truth. These two selections from *Dialogue Concerning the Two Chief World Systems—Ptolemaic and Copernican* are the preface, titled "To the Discerning Reader," and the first few pages of "The First Day," or the first chapter. In the preface, Galileo notes the recent edicts issued in Rome banning certain works, asserts that he will take the Copernican side, and explains the role of the three characters. The second selection is the opening exchange between Salviati and Simplicio. Both men engage in a discussion of the importance and meaning of numbers, which serves as a device to lay out some of the broader concepts of Aristotelian thought and reasoning. Simplicio defends Aristotle by saying that if there were something else to discover about the dimensions of an object Aristotle would have done it; so, by implication, Aristotle is the final authority. Thus, Simplicio's position shows that he is not open to new ideas.

To the Discerning Reader

Several years ago there was published in Rome a salutary edict which, in order to obviate the dangerous tendencies of our present age, imposed a seasonable silence upon the Pythagorean[1] opinion that the earth moves. There were those who impudently asserted that this decree had its origin not in judicious inquiry, but in passion none too well informed. Complaints were to be heard that advisers who were totally unskilled at astronomical observations ought not to clip the wings of reflective intellects by means of rash prohibitions.

Upon hearing such carping insolence, my zeal could not be contained. Being thoroughly informed about that prudent determination, I decided to appear openly in the

[1] **Pythagorean** The Pythagoreans were the followers of the sixth-century BCE Greek philosopher Pythagoras. He left no writings, but his disciples preserved and spread his ideas, particularly his contributions to mathematics and astronomy.

theater of the world as a witness of the sober truth. I was at that time in Rome; I was not only received by the most eminent prelates of that Court, but had their applause; indeed, this decree was not published without some previous notice of it having been given to me. Therefore I propose in the present work to show to foreign nations that as much is understood of this matter in Italy, and particularly in Rome, as transalpine diligence can ever have imagined. Collecting all the reflections that properly concern the Copernican system, I shall make it known that everything was brought before the attention of the Roman censorship, and that there proceed from this clime not only dogmas for the welfare of the soul, but ingenious discoveries for the delight of the mind as well.

To this end I have taken the Copernican side in the discourse, proceeding as with a pure mathematical hypothesis and striving by every artifice to represent it as superior to supposing the earth motionless—not, indeed, absolutely, but as against the arguments of some professed Peripatetics.[2] These men indeed deserve not even that name, for they do not walk about; they are content to adore the shadows, philosophizing not with due circumspection but merely from having memorized a few ill-understood principles.

Three principal headings are treated. First, I shall try to show that all experiments practicable upon the earth are insufficient measures for proving its mobility, since they are indifferently adaptable to an earth in motion or at rest. I hope in so doing to reveal many observations unknown to the ancients. Secondly, the celestial phenomena will be examined, strengthening the Copernican hypothesis until it might seem that this must triumph absolutely. Here new reflections are adjoined which might be used in order to simplify astronomy, though not because of any necessity imposed by nature. In the third place, I shall propose an ingenious speculation. It happens that long ago I said that the unsolved problem of the ocean tides might receive some light from assuming the motion of the earth. This assertion of mine, passing by word of mouth, found loving fathers who adopted it as a child of their own ingenuity. Now, so that no stranger may ever appear who, arming himself with our weapons, shall charge us with want of attention to such an important matter, I have thought it good to reveal those probabilities which might render this plausible, given that the earth moves.

---

[2] **Peripatetics** Another name for the Aristotelians: the followers of Aristotle, the famous fourth-century BCE Greek philosopher.

I hope that from these considerations the world will come to know that if other nations have navigated more, we have not theorized less. It is not from failing to take count of what others have thought that we have yielded to asserting that the earth is motionless, and holding the contrary to be a mere mathematical caprice, but (if for nothing else) for those reasons that are supplied by piety, religion, the knowledge of Divine Omnipotence, and a consciousness of the limitations of the human mind.

I have thought it most appropriate to explain these concepts in the form of dialogues, which, not being restricted to the rigorous observance of mathematical laws, make room also for digressions which are sometimes no less interesting than the principal argument.

Many years ago I was often to be found in the marvelous city of Venice, in discussions with Signore Giovanni Francesco Sagredo, a man of noble extraction and trenchant wit. From Florence came Signore Filippo Salviati, the least of whose glories were the eminence of his blood and the magnificence of his fortune. His was a sublime intellect which fed no more hungrily upon any pleasure than it did upon fine meditations. I often talked with these two of such matters in the presence of a certain Peripatetic philosopher whose greatest obstacle in apprehending the truth seemed to be the reputation he had acquired by his interpretations of Aristotle.

Now, since bitter death has deprived Venice and Florence of those two great luminaries in the very meridian of their years, I have resolved to make their fame live on in these pages, so far as my poor abilities will permit, by introducing them as interlocutors in the present argument. (Nor shall the good Peripatetic lack a place; because of his excessive affection toward the *Commentaries* of Simplicius, I have thought fit to leave him under the name of the author he so much revered, without mentioning his own.) May it please those two great souls, ever venerable to my heart, to accept this public monument of my undying love. And may the memory of their eloquence assist me in delivering to posterity the promised reflections.

It happened that several discussions had taken place casually at various times among these gentlemen, and had rather whetted than satisfied their thirst for learning. Hence very wisely they resolved to meet together on certain days during which, setting aside all other business, they might apply themselves more methodically to the contemplation of the wonders of God in the heavens and upon the earth. They met in the palace of the illustrious Sagredo; and, after the customary but brief exchange of compliments, Salviati commenced as follows.

∞

The First Day

Interlocutors

Salviati, Sagredo, and Simplicio

SALVIATI: Yesterday we resolved to meet today and dis- ₁
cuss as clearly and in as much detail as possible the
character and the efficacy of those laws of nature
which up to the present have been put forth by the
partisans of the Aristotelian and Ptolemaic position on the one hand, and by the followers of the
Copernican system on the other. Since Copernicus
places the earth among the movable heavenly bodies, making it a globe like a planet, we may well
begin our discussion by examining the Peripatetic 10
steps in arguing the impossibility of that hypothesis;
what they are, and how great is their force and effect. For this it is necessary to introduce into nature
two substances which differ essentially. These are
the celestial and the elemental, the former being
invariant and eternal; the latter, temporary and
destructible. This argument Aristotle treats in his
book *De Caelo*, introducing it with some discourses
dependent upon certain general assumptions, and
afterwards confirming it by experiments and specific 20
demonstrations. Following the same method, I shall
first propound, and then freely speak my opinion,
submitting myself to your criticisms—particularly
those of Simplicio, that stout champion and defender
of Aristotelian doctrines.

The first step in the Peripatetic arguments is
Aristotle's proof of the completeness and perfection of the world. For, he tells us, it is not a mere
line, nor a bare surface, but a body having length,
breadth, and depth. Since there are only these three 30
dimensions, the world, having these, has them all,
and, having the Whole, is perfect. To be sure, I much
wish that Aristotle had proved to me by rigorous
deductions that simple length constitutes the dimension which we call a line, which by the addition of
breadth becomes a surface; that by further adding
altitude or depth to this there results a body, and
that after these three dimensions there is no passing
farther—so that by these three alone, completeness,
or, so to speak, wholeness is concluded. Especially 40
since he might have done so very plainly and speedily.

SIMPLICIO: What about the elegant demonstrations in the
second, third, and fourth texts, after the definition of
"continuous"? Is it not there first proved that there
are no more than three dimensions, since Three
is everything, and everywhere? And is this not
confirmed by the doctrine and authority of the Pythagoreans, who say that all things are determined
by three—beginning, middle, and end—which is the
number of the Whole? Also, why leave out another 50
of his reasons; namely, that this number is used,
as if by a law of nature, in sacrifices to the gods?

Furthermore, is it not dictated by nature that we attribute the title of "all" to those things that are three,
and not less? For two are called "both," and one does
not say "all" unless there are three.

You have all this doctrine in the second text.
Afterwards, in the third we read, *ad pleniorem scientiam*,[3] that All, and Whole, and Perfect are formally
one and the same; and that therefore among figures 60
only the solid is complete. For it alone is determined
by three, which is All; and, being divisible in three
ways, it is divisible in every possible way. Of the
other figures, one is divisible in one way, and the
other in two, because they have their divisibility and
their continuity according to the number of dimensions allotted to them. Thus one figure is continuous
in one way, the other in two; but the third, namely
the solid, is so in every way.

Moreover, in the fourth text, after some other 70
doctrines, does he not clinch the matter with another
proof? To wit: a transition is made only according
to some defect; thus there is a transition in passing
from the line to the surface, because the line is lacking in breadth. But it is impossible for the perfect to
lack anything, being complete in every way; therefore there is no transition beyond the solid or body
to any other figure.

Do you not think that in all these places he has
sufficiently proved that there is no passing beyond 80
the three dimensions length, breadth, and thickness;
and that therefore the body, a solid, which has them
all, is perfect?

SALV.: To tell you the truth, I do not feel impelled by
all these reasons to grant any more than this: that
whatever has a beginning, middle, and end may
and ought to be called perfect. I feel no compulsion
to grant that the number three is a perfect number,
nor that it has a faculty of conferring perfection
upon its possessors. I do not even understand, let 90
alone believe, that with respect to legs, for example,
the number three is more perfect than four or two;
neither do I conceive the number four to be any
imperfection in the elements, nor that they would be
more perfect if they were three. Therefore it would
have been better for him to leave these subtleties to
the rhetoricians, and to prove his point by rigorous
demonstrations such as are suitable to make in the
demonstrative sciences.

SIMP.: It seems that you ridicule these reasons, and 100
yet all of them are doctrines to the Pythagoreans,

---

[3] *ad pleniorem scientiam* Latin, "for greater knowledge."

who attribute so much to numbers. You, who are a mathematician, and who believe many Pythagorean philosophical opinions, now seem to scorn their mysteries.

SALV.: That the Pythagoreans held the science of numbers in high esteem, and that Plato himself admired the human understanding and believed it to partake of divinity simply because it understood the nature of numbers, I know very well; nor am I far from being of the same opinion. But that these mysteries which caused Pythagoras and his sect to have such veneration for the science of numbers are the follies that abound in the sayings and writings of the vulgar, I do not believe at all. Rather I know that, in order to prevent the things they admired from being exposed to the slander and scorn of the common people, the Pythagoreans condemned as sacrilegious the publication of the most hidden properties of numbers or of the incommensurable and irrational quantities which they investigated. They taught that anyone

who had revealed them was tormented in the other world. Therefore I believe that some one of them, just to satisfy the common sort and free himself from their inquisitiveness, gave it out that the mysteries of numbers were those trifles which later spread among the vulgar. Such astuteness and prudence remind one of the wise young man who, in order to stop the importunity of his mother or his inquisitive wife—I forget which—who pressed him to impart the secrets of the Senate, made up some story which afterwards caused her and many other women to be the laughing-stock of that same Senate.

SIMP.: I do not want to join the number of those who are too curious about the Pythagorean mysteries. But as to the point in hand, I reply that the reasons produced by Aristotle to prove that there are not and cannot be more than three dimensions seem to me conclusive; and I believe that if a more cogent demonstration had existed, Aristotle would not have omitted it.

Questions for Critical Thinking

1. In Galileo's *Dialogue,* Salviati and Simplicio represent which thinkers? Summarize the philosophical position of each.

2. Describe the historical setting in which Galileo's *Dialogue* is composed. Why was a dialogue a good tactic for Galileo to use in setting forth his ideas?

FRANCIS BACON
Selection from *Essays*

Sir Francis Bacon (1561–1626), the son of a high-ranking official under England's Queen Elizabeth I, seemed destined for a career as a courtier. He did indeed spend much of his life serving Elizabeth and her successor, James I, but he also found time to write extensively about the implications of the Scientific Revolution, which during the 1600s was destroying the medieval world picture and establishing the scientific method as the basic way to understand the natural world. Inspired by the Renaissance, and in revolt against Aristotle and scholastic logic, Bacon proposed an inductive method of discovering truth; founded upon empirical observation, he proposed analysis of observed data resulting in hypotheses and verification of hypotheses through continued observation and experiment. The purpose of the Baconian method was to enable humanity to gain mastery over nature for humanity's own benefit.

Although Bacon had no laboratory and made no discoveries, he became the period's most persuasive champion of the "new learning." With his encouragement, science became a movement as he gave it a sense of direction, wrote endlessly about its usefulness, and predicted that it would improve life. Both his enthusiasm for a better tomorrow built on the scientific method and his abiding faith in the capacity of humans to advance themselves inspired later generations to believe that they could make the world better. The zenith of Bacon's influence was in the eighteenth-century Enlightenment when Voltaire (see *Candide* in Chapter 17), the age's leading thinker, called him "the Secretary of Nature."

Bacon's scientific works included *The Advancement of Learning* and the *New Organon, or New Method* (1620). He also wrote a history of King Henry VII of England, legal works, and treatises on religious matters. Probably his most lasting impact was on English letters, as he made the essay genre a standard prose form. Borrowed from Montaigne (see *Essays* in Chapter 14), the essay, in Bacon's hands, became a short composition: terse, moralistic, and aloof in style, it seldom exceeded a few hundred words.

Despite outstanding achievements as a writer, Bacon ended his political career in scandal. Made Lord Chancellor, the highest position a commoner could hold in the English government under James I, he quickly fell from power. Charged with receiving bribes, to which he confessed, he died five years later in disgrace, his political reputation ruined.

Reading the Selection

Much like Montaigne's, Bacon's essays embrace a miscellany of subjects, reflecting his restless intellect. Many appeal to the highest ideals, such as love, friendship, and truth; others are incisive, sometimes cynical, observations on greed and riches, or on ambition and the struggle for power. As a rule, he omits his own experiences and instead distills what he has witnessed into political guidelines, advice, and aphorisms (pithy sayings).

"Of Studies," taken from Bacon's first group of *Essays* (1597), offers sound advice about learning, then and now. He claims that all knowledge is useful and defines three goals of study: studying for private pleasure, for public discourse, and for practical application. He recommends three paths to learning: reading, discussing, and writing. He also thinks that studying many different subjects, such as history, mathematics, poetry, and natural philosophy (science), makes humans more versatile.

∞

Of Studies

Studies serve for delight, for ornament, and for ability. Their chief use for delight is in privateness and retiring; for ornament, is in discourse; and for ability, is in the judgment and disposition of business. For expert men can execute, and perhaps judge of particulars, one by one; but the general counsels, and the plots and marshaling of affairs, come best from those that are learned. To spend too much time in studies is sloth; to use them too much for ornament is affectation; to make judgment wholly by their rules is the humor of a scholar. They perfect nature, and are perfected by experience; for natural abilities are like natural plants, that need pruning by study; and studies themselves do give forth directions too much at large, except they be bounded in by experience. Crafty men condemn studies, simple men admire them, and wise men use them, for they teach not their own use; but that is a wisdom without them, and above them, won by observation. Read not to contradict and confute, nor to believe and take for granted, nor to find talk and discourse, but to weigh and consider. Some books are to be tasted, others to be swallowed, and some few to be chewed and digested; that is, some books are to be read only in parts; others to be read, but not curiously; and some few to be read wholly, and with diligence and attention. Some books also may be read by deputy and extracts made of them by others, but that would be only in the less important arguments and the meaner sort of books; else distilled books are like common distilled waters, flashy things. Reading maketh a full man, conference a ready man, and writing an exact man. And therefore, if a man write little, he had need have a great memory; if he confer little, he had need have a present wit; and if he read little, he had need have much cunning, to seem to know that he doth not. Histories make men wise; poets, witty; the mathematics, subtle; natural philosophy, deep; moral, grave; logic and rhetoric, able to contend. *Abeunt studia in mores.*[4] Nay,

---

[4] *Abeunt studia in mores.* Latin, "Studies pass into and influence manners." Attributed to the Roman poet Ovid (43 BCE–17 CE).

there is no stond [obstacle] or impediment in the wit but may be wrought out by fit studies, like as diseases of the body may have appropriate exercises. Bowling is good for the stone and reins [kidneys], shooting for the lungs and breast, gentle walking for the stomach, riding for the head, and the like. So if a man's wit be wandering, let him study the mathematics; for in demonstrations, if his wit be called away never so little, he must begin again. If his wit be not apt to distinguish or find differences, let him study the schoolmen, for they are *cumini sectores.*[5] If he be not apt to beat over matters and to call up one thing to prove and illustrate another, let him study the lawyer's cases. So every defect of the mind may have a special receipt.

––––––

[5] *cumini sectores* Latin, "splitters of hairs."

Questions for Critical Thinking

1. Explain Bacon's justification for study or learning.

2. Compare and contrast your reasons for obtaining an education with those offered by Bacon in this essay.

RENÉ DESCARTES
Selections from *Discourse on Method*

The French thinker and mathematician René Descartes (1596–1650) is one of the intellectual founders of the modern world. He lived during the age of the Scientific Revolution, 1550–1700, when the earth-centered model of the universe was slowly giving way to the sun-centered model, when medieval modes of reasoning were being replaced by mathematics and induction. He made important contributions to the new science, such as helping to establish the final form of the law of inertia and developing analytic geometry; however, it is for his rational (deductive) method that he is best remembered today.

Descartes' reasoning method first appeared in an introductory essay called *Discourse of the Method of Rightly Conducting the Reason and Seeking Truth in the Field of Science* (1637), which was attached to a treatise setting forth his discoveries in optics, meteorology, and geometry. The treatise is seldom read today, but the *Discourse on Method* (the essay's short title) has become a classic text of modern thought. Proposing a rational, deductive approach to all problems, Descartes' method had a double-edged effect: helping to end the reign of Aristotle and scholastic logic, while ensuring that deduction would play a major role in the new science. Cartesian deduction, with its mathematical emphasis, and Baconian (see "Of Studies") induction, with its stress on experimentation, became the twin pillars of modern science. And Cartesian skepticism, as shown in the *Discourse*, became the starting point of modern philosophy.

Ironically, Descartes, the advocate of rationalism, became a philosopher because of a mystical experience. After completing his schooling in 1612 at the Jesuit school at La Flèche, France, he spent the next nine years in travel and military service. Even though he profited from La Flèche, he was disillusioned by traditional studies, with their crumbling worldview. Especially troubling was that in the sciences no new absolute criterion of truth seemed available to replace the old. While on military duty in 1619, he had a series of dreams, which according to his later accounts, pointed the way to certainty in the sciences, using mathematics. After 1621, he devoted the remainder of his life to study and writing, in fulfillment of this mystical mission.

Reading the Selections

These two excerpts from Descartes' *Discourse on Method* contain the heart of the argument justifying his method. Part II lays out his four-step method. Step one declares that he will accept as true only those ideas that register on his reason as clear, distinct, and free from internal contradiction—his standard of certainty in philosophy, which he thought would give results equivalent to those reached in science using geometry. These are the remaining steps of his method: divide each problem into manageable parts; solve each part in an orderly fashion, moving from the simplest to the most complex; and finally, check the results.

Part IV shows Descartes doubting everything as a necessary stage to clear the slate of philosophic confusion and to define the truths that can "clearly and distinctly" be affirmed without question. At the end of this process, he is left with the undeniable idea, "I think, therefore I am," meaning that he can doubt everything, except that *he himself is doubting*. From this first principle of self-awareness, Descartes deduces the existence of the physical world and, finally, God.

∾

Part II

. . . Thus it is by custom and example that we are persuaded, much more than by any certain knowledge; at the same time, a majority of votes is worthless as a proof, in regard to truths that are even a little difficult of discovery; for it is much more likely that one man should have hit upon them for himself than that a whole nation should. Accordingly I could choose nobody whose opinions I thought preferable to other men's; and I was as it were forced to become my own guide.

But, like a man walking alone in the dark, I resolved to go so slowly, and use so much circumspection in all matters, as to be secured against falling, even if I made very little progress. In fact, I would not begin rejecting out of hand any of the opinions that might have previously crept into my belief without being introduced by reason, until I had first taken enough time to plan the work I was undertaking, and to look for the true method of attaining knowledge of everything that my mind could grasp.

The subjects I had studied a little when I was younger included, among the branches of philosophy, logic, and in mathematics, geometrical analysis and algebra. These three arts or sciences, it appeared, ought to make some contribution towards my design. But on examination I found that so far as logic is concerned, syllogisms and most of the other techniques serve for explaining to others what one knows; or even, like the art of Lully,[6] for talking without judgment about matters one is ignorant of; rather than for learning anything. And although logic comprises many correct and excellent rules, there are mixed up with

these so many others that are harmful or superfluous, that sorting them out is almost as difficult as extracting a Diana or Minerva[7] from a block of rough marble. As for the analysis of the ancients, and the algebra of our time, besides their covering only a highly abstract and apparently useless range of subjects, the former is always so restricted to the consideration of figures, that it cannot exercise the understanding without greatly wearying the imagination; and in the latter, there is such a complete slavery to certain rules and symbols that there results a confused and obscure art that embarrasses the mind, instead of a science that develops it. That was why I thought I must seek for some other method, which would comprise the advantages of these three and be exempt from their defects. And as a multitude of laws often gives occasion for vices, so that a State is much better ruled when it has only a very few laws which are very strictly observed; in the same way, instead of the great number of rules that make up logic, I thought the following four would be enough, provided that I made a firm and constant resolution not to fail even once in the observance of them.

The first was never to accept anything as true if I had not evident knowledge of its being so; that is, carefully to avoid precipitancy and prejudice, and to embrace in my judgment only what presented itself to my mind so clearly and distinctly that I had no occasion to doubt it.

The second, to divide each problem I examined into as many parts as was feasible, and as was requisite for its better solution.

---

[6] **Lully** Ramon Llull or Raymond Lully, thirteenth-century Catalan (Spain) mystic, philosopher, poet, and missionary. Devoted his life to Christian theological and Neoplatonic philosophical questions and traveled in Asia Minor, trying to convert Muslims to Christianity.

[7] **Diana or Minerva** Diana, the Roman nature goddess (closely associated with the Greek goddess Artemis), and Minerva, the Roman goddess of war and wisdom (the Roman equivalent to Athena, the Greek goddess), were known for their beauty and thus were subjects for sculptors.

The third, to direct my thoughts in an orderly way; beginning with the simplest objects, those most apt to be known, and ascending little by little, in steps as it were, to the knowledge of the most complex; and establishing an order in thought even when the objects had no natural priority one to another.

And the last, to make throughout such complete enumerations and such general surveys that I might be sure of leaving nothing out.

Those long chains of perfectly simple and easy reasonings by means of which geometers are accustomed to carry out their most difficult demonstrations had led me to fancy that everything that can fall under human knowledge form a similar sequence; and that so long as we avoid accepting as true what is not so, and always preserve the right order for deduction of one thing from another, there can be nothing too remote to be reached in the end, or too well hidden to be discovered. . . .

∞

Part IV

. . . I had noticed long before, as I said just now, that in conduct one sometimes has to follow opinions that one knows to be most uncertain just as if they were indubitable; but since my present aim was to give myself up to the pursuit of truth alone, I thought I must do the very opposite, and reject as if absolutely false anything as to which I could imagine the least doubt, in order to see if I should not be left at the end believing something that was absolutely indubitable. So, because our senses sometimes deceive us, I chose to suppose that nothing was such as they lead us to imagine. Because there are men who make mistakes in reasoning even as regards the simplest points of geometry and perpetrate fallacies, and seeing that I was as liable to error as anyone else, I rejected as false all the arguments I had so far taken for demonstrations. Finally, considering that the very same experiences *(pensées)* as we have in waking life may occur also while we sleep, without there being at that time any truth in them, I decided to feign that everything that had entered my mind hitherto was no more true than the illusions of dreams. But immediately upon this I noticed that while I was trying to think everything false, it must needs be that I, who was thinking this *(qui le pensais),* was something. And observing that this truth "I am thinking *(je pense),* therefore I exist" was so solid and secure that the most extravagant suppositions of the sceptics could not overthrow it, I judged that I need not scruple to accept it as the first principle of philosophy that I was seeking. . . .

∞

Questions for Critical Thinking

1. What does Descartes mean when he writes, "I think, therefore I am"?

2. Descartes has been called the "father of modern philosophy." Explain.

―――――――――― ∞ ――――――――――

BLAISE PASCAL
Selections from *Pensées*

Blaise Pascal [BLEHZ pas-KAHL] (1623–1662), like his contemporary and fellow countryman René Descartes (see *Discourse on Method*), made contributions to Western science and philosophy. Pascal established a new branch of geometry, founded modern probability studies, discovered laws governing air pressure, and invented several scientific instruments, including one of the first calculating machines. However, he is primarily known today for his religious and philosophical writings, the most famous being his *Pensées,* or *Thoughts,* which he wrote at the end of his life and was published posthumously.

Blaise Pascal was born near Angers, France, into a moderately wealthy family that claimed rank among the lesser nobility. His father, a mathematician and avid reader, educated his children, including his son whose intellect and talents as a mathematician were evident from an early age. The family moved to Paris in 1631 where Pascal continued his education. In 1640, at age seventeen, he published an essay on conic sections—an aspect of geometry—and his subsequent work in mathematics and geometry, especially hexagons, caught Descartes' attention. At age nineteen Pascal constructed a calculating machine to help his father, who was a tax collector for the French government, with his tax computations. Pascal hoped to patent his machine, but it was never a commercial success, although a few are still in existence. They were the first digital calculators as they operated by counting integers, and his machines are now seen as a forerunner of the modern electronic computer.

In 1646 Pascal, then in his early twenties, was converted to a mystical religious faith called Jansenism, which was identified with the Port Royal convent in Paris. Jansenism, named for Cornelius Jansen (1585–1638), a Flemish professor of theology, had its roots in the writings of St. Augustine, the fourth-century church father (see *Confessions* and *The City of God* in Chapter 7, Volume I). Jansenism, a Catholic reform movement, stressed the role of divine grace in conversion, advocated predestination, repudiated free will, and de-emphasized good works. Although the movement seemed similar to some Protestant faiths, such as Calvinism, Jansenism remained within the fold of the Roman Catholic Church until it was banned by Pope Clement XI (pope 1700–1721) and Louis XIV in 1713. At the time of his conversion to Jansenism, Pascal became ill, and, upon recovery, his doctors advised him to expand his social life. Accordingly, he immersed himself in his scientific studies, began to gamble and to enlarge his circle of friends, and read more widely—from Stoicism to Montaigne, the French essayist and skeptic (see *Essays* in Chapter 14). Then, on the night of November 23, 1654, at age thirty-one, Pascal experienced a revelation or illumination—his second conversion—an event that changed his life forever when, as he immediately recorded, he felt the presence of God.

Afterward, Pascal retired to the Port Royal convent, where he spent the rest of his life and wrote his two most famous works. The first, *Les Provinciales* (1656–1657), written as a dialogue in a series of letters, was an explanation and a defense of Jansenism, an attack on the Jesuits, who were then waging their own war on Jansenism, and a plea for a more spiritual approach to Christianity. For Pascal this meant recognizing the sacrifice of Christ, practicing charity, and living a simple life. The second work, *Pensées,* or *Thoughts* (1670), was Pascal's notes, fragments, aphorisms, and short essays that he recorded in the late 1650s, two or three years before his death. *Pensées* is considered to be a religious and philosophical classic that is still read by believers and nonbelievers today.

In *Pensées,* Pascal came to grips with his own doubts and anguish over the fate of the soul. He examined the nature of humanity and the existence of God, and he concluded that humans must, finally, put their faith in God because there is no rational answer as to God's existence. A human, as Pascal wrote, is "but a reed, the most feeble thing in nature" and a "cesspool of uncertainty and error." Human reason cannot help save us; it is inadequate to satisfy our hopes or answer our most basic questions. We must, therefore, listen to our hearts and embrace God. The heart, Pascal argued, is the best proof of the existence of God, for, as he famously wrote: "The heart has its reasons, which reason does not know."

Reading the Selections

In the first selection, Pascal observes that humankind lives in darkness, with some people performing a few religious ceremonies, which they think will save them, while others appear oblivious as to their soul's future. Taking the argument of "the reasonable man," he concludes that nothing is more important than the state of one's own soul and its prospects for eternity. The second selection, which may derive from Pascal's gambling experience and his studies of probabilities as well as his own questioning of faith, is the author's well-known "wager" regarding the existence of God. In entries 277–282, Pascal notes that the heart and reason are quite different, yet both help humans understand God. In entries 346–348, he offers some opinions of the lowly estate of "man," which reflect his Jansenist faith. In the last selections, Pascal discusses the role, nature, and "mystery" of Jesus Christ.

∞

Section III

Of the Necessity of the Wager

194

. . . Let them [unbelievers] at least learn what is the religion they attack, before attacking it. If this religion boasted of having a clear view of God, and of possessing it open and unveiled, it would be attacking it to say that we see nothing in the world which shows it with this clearness. But since, on the contrary, it says that men are in darkness and estranged from God, that He has hidden Himself from their knowledge, that this is in fact the name which He gives Himself in the Scriptures, *Deus absconditus;*[8] and finally, if it endeavours equally to establish these two things: that God has set up in the Church visible signs to make Himself known to those who should seek Him sincerely, and that He has nevertheless so disguised them that He will only be perceived by those who seek Him with all their heart; what advantage can they obtain, when, in the negligence with which they make profession of being in search of the truth, they cry out that nothing reveals it to them; and since that darkness in which they are, and with which they upbraid the Church, establishes only one of the things which she affirms, without touching the other, and, very far from destroying, proves her doctrine?

In order to attack it, they should have protested that they had made every effort to seek Him everywhere, and even in that which the Church proposes for their instruction, but without satisfaction. If they talked in this manner, they would in truth be attacking one of her pretensions. But I hope here to show that no reasonable person can speak thus, and I venture even to say that no one has ever done so. We know well enough how those who are of this mind behave. They believe they have made great efforts for their instruction, when they have spent a few hours in reading some book of Scripture, and have questioned some priest on the truths of the faith. After that, they boast of having made vain search in books and among men. But, verily, I will tell them what I have often said, that this negligence is insufferable. We are not here concerned with the trifling interests of some stranger, that we should treat it in this fashion; the matter concerns ourselves and our all.

The immortality of the soul is a matter which is of so great consequence to us, and which touches us so profoundly, that we must have lost all feeling to be indifferent as to knowing what it is. All our actions and thoughts must take such different courses, according as there are or are not eternal joys to hope for, that it is impossible to take one step with sense and judgment, unless we regulate our course by our view of this point which ought to be our ultimate end.

Thus our first interest and our first duty is to enlighten ourselves on this subject, whereon depends all our conduct. Therefore among those who do not believe, I make a vast difference between those who strive with all their power to inform themselves, and those who live without troubling or thinking about it.

I can have only compassion for those who sincerely bewail their doubt, who regard it as the greatest of misfortunes, and who, sparing no effort to escape it, make of this inquiry their principal and most serious occupations.

But as for those who pass their life without thinking of this ultimate end of life, and who, for this sole reason that they do not find within themselves the lights which convince them of it, neglect to seek them elsewhere, and to examine thoroughly whether this opinion is one of those which people receive with credulous simplicity, or one of those which, although obscure in themselves, have nevertheless a solid and immovable foundation, I look upon them in a manner quite different.

This carelessness in a matter which concerns themselves, their eternity, their all, moves me more to anger than pity; it astonishes and shocks me; it is to me monstrous. I do not say this out of the pious zeal of a spiritual devotion. I expect, on the contrary, that we ought to have this feeling from principles of human interest and self-love; for this we need only see what the least enlightened persons see.

We do not require great education of the mind to understand that here is no real and lasting satisfaction; that our pleasures are only vanity; that our evils are infinite; and, lastly, that death, which threatens us every moment, must infallibly place us within a few years under the dreadful necessity of being for ever either annihilated or unhappy.

There is nothing more real than this, nothing more terrible. Be we as heroic as we like, that is the end which awaits the noblest life in the world. Let us reflect on this,

---

[8] *Deus absconditus* Latin, "the hidden God"—unknowable to the human mind.

and then say whether it is not beyond doubt that there is no good in this life but in the hope of another; that we are happy only in proportion as we draw near it; and that, as there are no more woes for those who have complete assurance of eternity, so there is no more happiness for those who have no insight into it.

Surely then it is a great evil thus to be in doubt, but it is at least an indispensable duty to seek when we are in such doubt; and thus the doubter who does not seek is altogether completely unhappy and completely wrong. And if besides this he is easy and content, professes to be so, and indeed boasts of it; if it is this state itself which is the subject of his joy and vanity, I have no words to describe so silly a creature.

How can people hold these opinions? What joy can we find in the expectation of nothing but hopeless misery? What reason for boasting that we are in impenetrable darkness? And how can it happen that the following argument occurs to a reasonable man?

"I know not who put me into the world, nor what the world is, nor what I myself am. I am in terrible ignorance of everything. I know not what my body is, nor my senses, nor my soul, not even that part of me which thinks what I say, which reflects on all and on itself, and knows itself no more than the rest. I see those frightful spaces of the universe which surround me, and I find myself tied to one corner of this vast expanse, without knowing why I am put in this place rather than in another, nor why the short time which is given me to live is assigned to me at this point rather than at another of the whole eternity which was before me or which shall come after me. I see nothing but infinites on all sides, which surround me as an atom, and as a shadow which endures only for an instant and returns no more. All I know is that I must soon die, but what I know least is this very death which I cannot escape.

"As I know not whence I come, so I know not whither I go. I know only that, in leaving this world, I fall for ever either into annihilation or into the hands of an angry God, without knowing to which of these two states I shall be for ever assigned. Such is my state, full of weakness and uncertainty. And from all this I conclude that I ought to spend all the days of my life without caring to inquire into what must happen to me. Perhaps I might find some solution to my doubts, but I will not take the trouble, nor take a step to seek it; and after treating with scorn those who are concerned with this care, I will go without foresight and without fear to try the great event, and let myself be led carelessly to death, uncertain of the eternity of my future state."

Who would desire to have for a friend a man who talks in this fashion? Who would choose him out from others to tell him of his affairs? Who would have recourse to him in affliction? And indeed to what use in life could one put him?

In truth, it is the glory of religion to have for enemies men so unreasonable: and their opposition to it is so little dangerous that it serves on the contrary to establish its truths. For the Christian faith goes mainly to establish these two facts, the corruption of nature, and redemption by Jesus Christ. Now I contend that if these men do not serve to prove the truth of the redemption by the holiness of their behaviour, they at least serve admirably to show the corruption of nature by sentiments so unnatural.

Nothing is so important to man as his own state, nothing is so formidable to him as eternity; and thus it is not natural that there should be men indifferent to the loss of their existence, and to the perils of everlasting suffering. They are quite different with regard to all other things. They are afraid of mere trifles; they foresee them; they feel them. And this same man who spends so many days and nights in rage and despair for the loss of office, or for some imaginary insult to his honour, is the very one who knows without anxiety and without emotion that he will lose all by death. It is a monstrous thing to see in the same heart and at the same time this sensibility to trifles and this strange insensibility to the greatest objects. It is an incomprehensible enchantment, and a supernatural slumber, which indicates as its cause an all-powerful force. . . .

233

Infinite—nothing.—Our soul is cast into a body, where it finds number, time, dimension. Thereupon it reasons, and calls this nature, necessity, and can believe nothing else.

Unity joined to infinity adds nothing to it, no more than one foot to an infinite measure. The finite is annihilated in the presence of the infinite, and becomes a pure nothing. So our spirit before God, so our justice before divine justice. There is not so great a disproportion between our justice and that of God, as between unity and infinity.

The justice of God must be vast like His compassion. Now justice to the outcast is less vast, and ought less to offend our feelings than mercy towards the elect.

We know that there is an infinite, and are ignorant of its nature. As we know it to be false that numbers are finite, it is therefore true that there is an infinity in number. But we do not know what it is. It is false that it is even, it is false that it is odd; for the addition of a unit can make no change in its nature. Yet it is a number, and every number is odd or even (this is certainly true of every finite number). So we may well know that there is a God without knowing what He is. Is there not one substantial truth, seeing there are so many things which are not the truth itself?

We know then the existence and nature of the finite, because we also are finite and have extension. We know the existence of the infinite, and are ignorant of its nature, because it has extension like us, but not limits like us. But we know neither the existence nor the nature of God, because He has neither extension nor limits.

But by faith we know His existence; in glory we shall know His nature. Now, I have already shown that we may well know the existence of a thing, without knowing its nature.

Let us now speak according to natural lights.

If there is a God, He is infinitely incomprehensible, since, having neither parts nor limits, He has no affinity to us. We are then incapable of knowing either what He is or if He is. This being so, who will dare to undertake the decision of the question? Not we, who have no affinity to Him.

Who then will blame Christians for not being able to give a reason for their belief, since they profess a religion for which they cannot give a reason? They declare, in expounding it to the world, that it is a foolishness, *stultitiam*,[9] and then you complain that they do not prove it! If they proved it, they would not keep their word; it is in lacking proofs, that they are not lacking in sense. "Yes, but although this excuses those who offer it as such, and takes away from them the blame of putting it forward without reason, it does not excuse those who receive it." Let us then examine this point, and say, "God is, or He is not." But to which side shall we incline? Reason can decide nothing here. There is an infinite chaos which separated us. A game is being played at the extremity of this infinite distance where heads or tails will turn up. What will you wager? According to reason, you can do neither the one thing nor the other; according to reason, you can defend neither of the propositions.

Do not then reprove for error those who have made a choice; for you know nothing about it. "No, but I blame them for having made, not this choice, but a choice; for again both he who chooses heads and he who chooses tails are equally at fault, they are both in the wrong. The true course is not to wager at all."

Yes; but you must wager. It is not optional. You are embarked. Which will you choose then? Let us see. Since you must choose, let us see which interests you least. You have two things to lose, the true and the good; and two things to stake, your reason and your will, your knowledge and your happiness; and your nature has two things to shun, error and misery. Your reason is no more shocked in choosing one rather than the other, since you must of necessity choose. This is one point settled. But your happiness? Let us weigh the gain and the loss in wagering that God is. Let us estimate these two chances. If you gain, you gain all; if you lose, you lose nothing. Wager, then, without hesitation that He is.—"That is very fine. Yes, I must wager; but I may perhaps wager too much."—Let us see. Since there is an equal risk of gain and of loss, if you had only to gain two lives, instead of one, you might still wager. But if there were three lives to gain, you would have to play (since you are under the necessity of playing), and you would be imprudent, when you are forced to play, not to chance your life to gain three at a game where there is an equal risk of loss and gain. But there is an eternity of life and happiness. And this being so, if there were an infinity of chances, of which one only would be for you, you would still be right in wagering one to win two, and you, would act stupidly, being obliged to play, by refusing to stake one life against three at a game in which out of an infinity of chances there is one for you, if there were an infinity of an infinitely happy life to gain. But there is here an infinity of an infinitely happy life to gain, a chance of gain against a finite number of chances of loss, and what you stake is finite. If is all divided; wherever the infinite is and there is not an infinity of chances of loss against that of gain, there is no time to hesitate, you must give all. And

thus, when one is forced to play, he must renounce reason to preserve his life, rather than risk it for infinite gain, as likely to happen as the loss of nothingness.

For it is no use to say it is uncertain if we will gain, and it is certain that we risk, and that the infinite distance between the *certainty* of what is staked and the *uncertainty* of what will be gained, equals the finite good which is certainly staked against the uncertain infinite. It is not so, as every player stakes a certainty to gain an uncertainty, and yet he stakes a finite certainty to gain a finite uncertainty, without transgressing against reason. There is not an infinite distance between the certainty staked and the uncertainty of the gain; that is untrue. In truth, there is an infinity between the certainty of gain and the certainty of loss. But the uncertainty of the gain is proportioned to the certainty of the stake according to the proportion of the chances to gain and loss. Hence it comes that, if there are as many risks on one side as on the other, the course is to play even; and then the certainty of the stake is equal to the uncertainty of the gain, so far is it from fact that there is an infinite distance between them. And so our proposition is of infinite force, when there is the finite to stake in a game where there are equal risks of gain and of loss, and the infinite to gain. This is demonstrable; and if men are capable of any truths, this is one.

"I confess it, I admit it, But, still, is there no means of seeing the faces of the cards?"—Yes, Scripture and the rest, etc. "Yes, but I have my hands tied and my mouth closed; I am forced to wager, and am not free. I am not released, and am so made that I cannot believe. What, then, would you have me do?"

True. But at least learn your inability to believe, since reason brings you to this, and yet you cannot believe. Endeavour then to convince yourself, not by increase of proofs of God, but by the abatement of your passions. You would like to attain faith, and do not know the way; you would like to cure yourself of unbelief, and ask the remedy for it. Learn of those who have been bound like you, and who now stake all their possessions. These are people who know the way which you would follow, and who are cured of an ill of which you would be cured. Follow the way by which they began; by acting as if they believed, taking the holy water, having masses said, etc. Even this will naturally make you believe, and deaden your acuteness.—"But this is what I am afraid of."—And why? What have you to lose?

But to show you that this leads you there, it is this which will lessen the passions, which are your stumbling-blocks.

The end of this discourse.—Now, what harm will befall you in taking this side? You will be faithful, honest, humble, grateful, generous, a sincere friend, truthful. Certainly you will not have those poisonous pleasures, glory and luxury; but will you not have others? I will tell you that you will thereby gain in this life, and that, at each step you take on this road, you will see so great certainty of gain, so much nothingness in what you risk, that you will at last recognise that you have wagered for something certain and infinite, for which you have given nothing.

---

[9] ***stultitiam*** Latin, "foolishness"; "silliness."

"Ah! This discourse transports me, charms me," etc.

If this discourse pleases you and seems impressive, know that it is made by a man who has knelt, both before and after it, in prayer to that Being, infinite and without parts, before whom he lays all he has, for you also to lay before Him all you have for your own good and for His glory, that so strength may be given to lowliness. . . .

277

The heart has its reasons, which reason does not know. We feel it in a thousand things. I say that the heart naturally loves the Universal Being, and also itself naturally, according as it gives itself to them; and it hardens itself against one or the other at its will. You have rejected the one, and kept the other. Is it by reason that you love yourself?

278

It is the heart which experiences God, and not the reason. This, then, is faith: God felt by the heart, not by the reason.

279

Faith is a gift of God; do not believe that we said it was a gift of reasoning. Other religions do not say this of their faith. They only gave reasoning in order to arrive at it, and yet it does not bring them to it.

280

The knowledge of God is very far from the love of Him.

281

Heart, instinct, principles.

282

We know truth, not only by the reason, but also by the heart, and it is in this last way that we know first principles; and reason, which has no part in it, tries in vain to impugn them. The sceptics, who have only this for their object, labour to no purpose. We know that we do not dream, and however impossible it is for us to prove it by reason, this inability demonstrates only the weakness of our reason, but not, as they affirm, the uncertainty of all our knowledge. For the knowledge of first principles, as space, time, motion, number, is as sure as any of those which we get from reasoning. And reason must trust these intuitions of the heart, and must base them on every argument. (We have intuitive knowledge of the tri-dimensional nature of space, and of the infinity of number, and reason then shows that there are no two square numbers one of which is double of the other. Principles are intuited, propositions are inferred, all with certainty, though in different ways.) And it is as useless and absurd for reason to demand from the heart proofs of her first principles, before admitting them, as it would be for the heart to demand from reason an intuition of all demonstrated propositions before accepting them.

This inability ought, then, to serve only to humble reason, which would judge all, but not to impugn our certainty, as if only reason were capable of instructing us. Would to God, on the contrary, that we had never need of it, and that we knew everything by instinct and intuition! But nature has refused us this boon. On the contrary, she has given us but very little knowledge of this kind; and all the rest can be acquired only by reasoning. . . .

Section VI
The Philosophers

. . .

346

Thought constitutes the greatness of man.

347

Man is but a reed, the most feeble thing in nature; but he is a thinking reed. The entire universe need not arm itself to crush him. A vapour, a drop of water suffices to kill him. But, if the universe were to crush him, man would still be more noble than that which killed him, because he knows that he dies and the advantage which the universe has over him; the universe knows nothing of this.

All our dignity consists, then, in thought. By it we must elevate ourselves, and not by space and time which we cannot fill. Let us endeavour, then, to think well; this is the principle of morality.

348

A thinking reed.—It is not from space that I must seek my dignity, but from the government of my thought. I shall have no more if I possess worlds. By space the universe encompasses and swallows me up like an atom; by thought I comprehend the world.

∞

Section VII
Morality and Doctrine

· · ·

544

Jesus Christ did nothing but teach men that they loved themselves, that they were slaves, blind, sick, wretched, and sinners; that He must deliver them, enlighten, bless, and heal them; that this would be effected by hating self, and by following Him through suffering and the death on the cross.

545

Without Jesus Christ man must be in vice and misery; with Jesus Christ man is free from vice and misery; in Him is all our virtue and all our happiness. Apart from Him there is but vice, misery, darkness, death, despair.

546

We know God only by Jesus Christ. Without this mediator all communion with God is taken away; through Jesus Christ we know God. All those who have claimed to know God, and to prove Him without Jesus Christ, have had only weak proofs. But in proof of Jesus Christ we have the prophecies, which are solid and palpable proofs. And these prophecies, being accomplished and proved true by the event, mark the certainty of these truths, and therefore the divinity of Christ. In Him then, and through Him, we know God. Apart from Him, and without the Scripture, without original sin, without a necessary Mediator promised and come, we cannot absolutely prove God, nor teach right doctrine and right morality. But through Jesus Christ, and in Jesus Christ, we prove God, and teach morality and doctrine. Jesus Christ is then the true God of men.

But we know at the same time our wretchedness; for this God is none other than the Saviour of our wretchedness. So we can only know God well by knowing our iniquities. Therefore those who have known God, without knowing their wretchedness, have not glorified Him, but have glorified themselves. *Quia . . . non cognovit per sapientiam . . . placuit Deo per stultitiam prædicationis salvos facere.*[10]

547

Not only do we know God by Jesus Christ alone, but we know ourselves only by Jesus Christ. We know life and death only through Jesus Christ. Apart from Jesus Christ, we do not know what is our life, nor our death, nor God, nor ourselves.

Thus without the Scripture, which has Jesus Christ alone for its object, we know nothing, and see only darkness and confusion in the nature of God, and in our own nature.

548

It is not only impossible but useless to know God without Jesus Christ. They have not departed from Him, but approached; they have not humbled themselves, but . . .

Quo quisque optimus est, pessimus, si hoc ipsum, quod optimus est, adscribat sibi.[11]

549

I love poverty because He loved it. I love riches because they afford me the means of helping the very poor. I keep faith with everybody; I do not render evil to those who wrong me, but I wish them a lot like mine, in which I receive neither evil nor good from men. I try to be just, true, sincere, and faithful to all men; I have a tender heart for those to whom God has more closely united me; and whether I am alone, or seen of men, I do all my actions in the sight of God, who must judge of them, and to whom I have consecrated them all.

These are my sentiments; and every day of my life I bless my Redeemer, who has implanted them in me, and who, of a man full of weakness, of miseries, of lust, of pride, and of ambition, has made a man free from all these evils by the power of His grace, to which all the glory of it is due, as of myself I have only misery and error.

550

Dignior plagis quam osculis non timeo quia amo.[12]

551

The Sepulchre of Jesus Christ.—Jesus Christ was dead, but seen on the Cross. He was dead, and hidden in the Sepulchre.

---

[10] *Quia . . . non cognovit . . . salvos facere.* Latin, "Which . . . by wisdom knew not . . . it pleased God by the foolishness of preaching to save them that believe" (1 Corinthians 1:21).

[11] *Quo quisque . . . adscribat sibi.* Latin, "The better one is, the worse one becomes, if one attributes the cause of this goodness to one's self"; a quotation from *Cantica Canticorum,* LXXXIV, a collection of sermons by St. Bernard of Clairvaux (1090–1153), French saint, intellectual, and author.

[12] *Dignior plagis . . . quia amo.* Latin, "Meriting blows more than kisses, I fear not, because I love" (St. Bernard, see footnote 11).

Jesus Christ was buried by the saints alone.

Jesus Christ wrought no miracle at the Sepulchre.

Only the saints entered it.

It is there, not on the Cross, that Jesus Christ takes a new life.

It is the last mystery of the Passion and the Redemption.

Jesus Christ had nowhere to rest on earth but in the Sepulchre.

His enemies only ceased to persecute Him at the Sepulchre.

552

The Mystery of Jesus.—Jesus suffers in His passions the torments which men inflict upon Him; but in His agony He suffers the torments which He inflicts on Himself; *turbare semetipsum.*[13] This is a suffering from no human, but an almighty hand, for He must be almighty to bear it.

Jesus seeks some comfort at least in His three dearest friends, and they are asleep. He prays them to bear with Him for a little, and they leave Him with entire indifference, having so little compassion that it could not prevent their sleeping even for a moment. And thus Jesus was left alone to the wrath of God.

Jesus is alone on the earth, without any one not only to feel and share His suffering, but even to know of it; He and Heaven were alone in that knowledge.

Jesus is in a garden, not of delight as the first Adam, where he lost himself and the whole human race, but in one of agony, where He saved Himself and the whole human race.

He suffers this affliction and this desertion in the horror of night.

I believe that Jesus never complained but on this single occasion; but then He complained as if he could no longer bear His extreme suffering. "My soul is sorrowful, even unto death."

Jesus seeks companionship and comfort from men. This is the sole occasion in all His life, as it seems to me. But He receives it not, for His disciples are asleep.

Jesus will be in agony even to the end of the world. We must not sleep during that time.

Jesus, in the midst of this universal desertion, including that of His own friends chosen to watch with Him, finding them asleep, is vexed because of the danger to which they expose, not Him, but themselves; He cautions them for their own safety and their own good, with a sincere tenderness for them during their ingratitude, and warns them that the spirit is willing and the flesh weak.

Jesus, finding them still asleep, without being restrained by any consideration for themselves or for Him, has the kindness not to waken them, and leaves them in repose.

Jesus prays, uncertain of the will of His Father, and fears death; but, when He knows it, He goes forward to offer Himself to death. *Eamus. Processit* (John).[14]

_____
[13] *turbare semetipsum* Latin, "he troubled himself" or "was troubled" (John 11:33).
[14] *Eamus. Processit* Latin, "Let us be going" (Matthew 26:46); Jesus went forth (John 18:2).

Jesus asked of men and was not heard.

Jesus, while His disciples slept, wrought their salvation. He has wrought that of each of the righteous while they slept, both in their nothingness before their birth, and in their sins after their birth.

He prays only once that the cup pass away, and then with submission; and twice that it come if necessary.

Jesus is weary.

Jesus, seeing all His friends asleep and all His enemies wakeful, commits Himself entirely to His Father.

Jesus does not regard in Judas his enmity, but the order of God, which He loves and admits, since He calls him friend.

Jesus tears Himself away from His disciples to enter into His agony; we must tear ourselves away from our nearest and dearest to imitate Him.

Jesus being in agony and in the greatest affliction, let us pray longer.

We implore the mercy of God, not that He may leave us at peace in our vices, but that He may deliver us from them.

If God gave us masters by His own hand, oh! how necessary for us to obey them with a good heart! Necessity and events follow infallibly.

—"Console thyself, thou wouldst not seek Me, if thou hadst not found Me.

"I thought of thee in Mine agony, I have sweated such drops of blood for thee.

"It is tempting Me rather than proving thyself, to think if thou wouldst do such and such a thing on an occasion which has not happened; I shall act in thee if it occur.

"Let thyself be guided by My rules; see how well I have led the Virgin and the saints who have let Me act in them.

"The Father loves all that I do.

"Dost thou wish that it always cost Me the blood of My humanity, without thy shedding tears?

"Thy conversion is My affair; fear not, and pray with confidence as for Me.

"I am present with thee by My Word in Scripture, by My Spirit in the Church and by inspiration, by My power in the priests, by My prayer in the faithful.

"Physicians will not heal thee, for thou wilt die at last. But it is I who heal thee, and make the body immortal.

"Suffer bodily chains and servitude, I deliver thee at present only from spiritual servitude.

"I am more a friend to thee than such and such an one, for I have done for thee more than they, they would not have suffered what I have suffered from thee, and they would not have died for thee as I have done in the time of thine infidelities and cruelties, and as I am ready to do, and do, among my elect and at the Holy Sacrament."

"If thou knewest thy sins, thou wouldst lose heart."

—I shall lose it then, Lord, for on Thy assurance I believe their malice.

—"No, for I, by whom thou learnest, can heal thee of them and what I say to thee is a sign that I will heal thee. In proportion to thy expiation of them, thou wilt know them, and it will be said to thee: 'Behold, thy sins are forgiven thee,' Repent then, for thy hidden sins, and for the secret malice of those which thou knowest."

—Lord, I give Thee all.

—"I love thee more ardently than thou hast loved thine abominations, *ut immundus pro luto*.[15]

"To Me be the glory, not to thee, worm of the earth.

"Ask thy confessor, when My own words are to thee occasion of evil, vanity, or curiosity."

—I see in me depths of pride, curiosity, and lust. 40 There is no relation between me and God, nor Jesus Christ the Righteous. But He has been made sin for me; all Thy scourges are fallen upon Him. He is more abominable than I, and, far from abhorring me, He holds Himself honoured that I go to Him and succour Him.

But He has healed Himself, and still more so will He heal me.

I must add my wounds to His, and join myself to Him; and He will save me in saving Himself. But this must not be postponed to the future.

Eritis sicut dii scientes bonum et malum.[16] Each one creates his god, when judging, "This is good or bad"; and men mourn or rejoice too much at events.

Do little things as though they were great, because of the majesty of Jesus Christ who does them in us, and who lives our life; and do the greatest things as though they were little and easy, because of His omnipotence.

---

[15] *ut immundus pro luto* Latin, "as foul as clay."
[16] *Eritis sicut dii scientes bonum et malum.* Latin, "You will be, like God, conscious of good and evil" (Genesis 3:5).

553

It seems to me that Jesus Christ only allowed His wounds 1 to be touched after His resurrection: *Noli me tangere*.[17] We must unite ourselves only to His sufferings.

At the Last Supper He gave Himself in communion as about to die; to the disciples at Emmaus as risen from the dead; to the whole Church as ascended into heaven.

554

"Compare not thyself with others, but with Me. If thou 1 dost not find Me in those with whom thou comparest thyself, thou comparest thyself to one who is abominable. If thou findest Me in them, compare thyself to Me. But whom wilt thou compare? Thyself, or Me in thee? If it is thyself, it is one who is abominable. If it is I, thou comparest Me to Myself. Now I am God in all.

"I speak to thee, and often counsel thee, because thy director cannot speak to thee, for I do not want thee to lack a guide.

"And perhaps I do so at his prayers, and thus he leads thee without thy seeing it. Thou wouldst not seek Me, if thou didst not possess Me.

"Be not therefore troubled."

---

[17] *Noli me tangere* "Touch me not" (John 20:17)—Jesus's words to Mary Magdalene after his resurrection.

Questions for Critical Thinking

1. What is Pascal's "wager" with God? Do you find it persuasive? Explain.

2. What role does the "heart" have in Pascal's ideas?

THOMAS HOBBES
Selection from *Leviathan*

The English philosopher Thomas Hobbes (1588–1679) was probably the most radical thinker to be spawned by the Scientific Revolution of the 1600s. He was a scandalous figure to his contemporaries, for he was thought to be an atheist, and possibly was, though he denied it. Well-placed friends, including King Charles II, who forgave Hobbes's religious doubts and welcomed his defense of monarchy, intervened to save him from prison or burning at the stake. Hobbes developed a philosophy of mechanistic materialism that was characterized by lack of free will and identification of mind as a "motion in the head." It owed its method to the geometric reasoning of Descartes (see *Discourse on Method*), its empiricism to Bacon ("Of Studies"), and its atomistic structure of nature to the ancient atomists (see Epicurus's "Letter to Menoe-ceus" in Chapter 4, Volume 1) and their modern followers, such as Galileo Galilei (1564–1642). Galileo, whom Hobbes met in Italy, especially impressed him with the idea that human matter is in constant motion, guided by natural laws—the notion that Hobbes later made the guiding principle in *Leviathan,* his pioneering work in modern political theory. It is for his political writings that he is known today, his scientific works having passed into oblivion.

Hobbes's *Leviathan* (1651), in which he advocated absolute monarchy, reflected his disgust at the English Civil War, 1642–1647, which resulted in the abolition of England's kingship and the setting up of a republic. Having sat out the war in France, where he sought sanctuary, 1640–1651, he became convinced that only an absolute king could restore social order and maintain national unity. He found the word *Leviathan* in the book of Job (chapter 41), where God used it as a term for a sea monster "king" who rules "over all the children of pride"—an image of divine power. In Hobbes's book, "Leviathan" refers to an all-encompassing state, or commonwealth, that absorbs and directs all human actions.

Hobbes's method in *Leviathan* was to try to found a science of politics based on the idea that the world is a machine of matter, moving according to law. Like Descartes, he wanted to establish an undeniable truth from which to deduce the rest of his philosophy. He located his truth in his gloomy view of human nature: Left to their own devices, human beings would fight with each other all the time. This is his notion of the "war of every man against every man" that he thought existed in a "state of nature," that is, in periods when rule by law had broken down or else had never been established. It is to escape this anarchy that humanity gives up all its rights and its claims to self-government to a powerful state—Leviathan—that will protect them from themselves.

Reading the Selection

"Of Man," taken from Chapter XIII of Part I of *Leviathan,* sets forth Hobbes's theory of human nature as imagined in the state of nature. It is not that human beings are naturally evil, for there are no laws at first to prescribe what is good and bad; rather, it is that humans are by nature more selfish than social. They are created equal—"Nature hath made men . . . equal in the faculties of body and mind"—but they are driven by their passions, or desires, and all want the same things: "gain," "safety," and "reputation." Since "there is no power able to overawe them all," the result is a "time of war, where every man is enemy to every man." Thus, given free rein in the state of nature, humans create a form of life that is "solitary, poor, nasty, brutish, and short."

Part I

Chapter XIII
Of the Natural Condition of Mankind, as Concerning Their Felicity and Misery

Nature hath made men so equal in the faculties of body and mind as that though there be found one man sometimes manifestly stronger in body, or of quicker mind than another, yet when all is reckoned together, the difference between man and man is not so considerable as that one man can thereupon claim to himself any benefit to which another may not pretend as well as he. For as to the strength of body, the weakest has strength enough to kill the strongest, either by secret machination, or by confederacy with others that are in the same danger with himself.

And as to the faculties of the mind, setting aside the arts grounded upon words, and especially that skill of proceeding upon general and infallible rules, called science, which very few have, and but in few things as being not a native faculty, born with us, nor attained, as prudence, while we look after somewhat else, I find yet a greater equality amongst men than that of strength. For prudence is but experience; which equal time equally bestows on all men, in those things they equally apply themselves unto. That which may perhaps make such equality incredible is but a vain conceit of one's own wisdom, which almost all men think they have in a greater degree than the vulgar; that is, than all men but themselves and a few others, whom by fame or for concurring with themselves they approve. For such is the nature of men, that howsoever they may acknowledge many others to be more witty or more eloquent or more learned, yet they will hardly believe there be many so wise as themselves. For they see their own wit at hand, and other men's at a distance. But this proveth rather that men are in that point equal, than unequal. For there is not ordinarily a greater sign of the equal distribution of anything than that every man is contented with his share.

From this equality of ability ariseth equality of hope in the attaining of our ends. And therefore if any two men desire the same thing, which nevertheless they cannot both enjoy, they become enemies; and in the way to their end (which is principally their own conservation, and sometimes their delectation only), endeavor to destroy or subdue one another. And from hence it comes to pass, that where an invader hath no more to fear than another man's single power, if one plant, sow, build or possess a convenient seat, others may probably be expected to come prepared with forces united to dispossess and deprive him, not only of the fruit of his labor, but also of his life or liberty. And the invader again is in the like danger of another.

And from this difference of one another, there is no way for any man to secure himself so reasonable as anticipation; that is, by force or wiles to master the persons of all men he can, so long till he see no other power great enough to endanger him; and this is no more than his own conservation requireth, and is generally allowed. Also because there be some, that taking pleasure in contemplating their own power in the acts of conquest, which they pursue farther than their security requires; if others, that otherwise would be glad to be at ease within modest bounds, should not by invasion increase their power, they would not be able, long time, by standing only on their defense, to subsist. And by consequence, such augmentation of dominion over men, being necessary to a man's conservation, it ought to be allowed him.

Again, men have no pleasure, but on the contrary a great deal of grief, in keeping company, where there is no power able to overawe them all. For every man looketh that his companion should value him at the same rate he sets upon himself; and upon all signs of contempt or undervaluing, naturally endeavors, as far as he dares (which amongst them that have no common power to keep them in quiet, is far enough to make them destroy each other), to extort a greater value from his contemners, by damage; and from others, by the example.

So that in the nature of man, we find three principal causes of quarrel. First, competition; secondly, diffidence; thirdly, glory.

The first maketh men invade for gain; the second, for safety; and the third, for reputation. The first use violence, to make themselves masters of other men's persons, wives, children, and cattle; the second, to defend them; the third, for trifles, as a word, a smile, a different opinion, and any other sign of undervalue, either direct in their persons, or by reflection in their kindred, their friends, their nation, their profession, or their name.

Hereby it is manifest, that during the time men live without a common power to keep them all in awe, they are in that condition which is called war; and such a war as is of every man, against every man. For war consisteth not in battle only or the act of fighting; but in a tract of time, wherein the will to contend by battle is sufficiently known; and therefore the notion of time is to be considered in the nature of war, as it is in the nature of weather. For as the nature of foul weather lieth not in a shower or two of rain, but in an inclination thereto of many days together; so the nature of war consisteth not in actual fighting, but in the known disposition thereto during all the time there is no assurance of the contrary. All other time is peace.

Whatsoever therefore is consequent to a time of war, where every man is enemy to every man, the same is consequent to the time wherein men live without other security than what their own strength and their own invention shall furnish them withal. In such condition there is no place for industry, because the fruit thereof is uncertain; and consequently no culture of the earth; no navigation, nor use of the commodities that may be imported by sea; no commodious building; no instruments of moving and removing such things as require much force; no knowledge of the face of the earth; no account of time; no arts; no letters; no society; and, which is worst of all, continual fear, and danger of violent death; and the life of man, solitary, poor, nasty, brutish, and short.

It may seem strange to some man that has not well weighed these things, that nature should thus dissociate and render men apt to invade and destroy one another; and he may therefore, not trusting to this inference made from the passions, desire perhaps to have the same confirmed by experience. Let him therefore consider with himself; when taking a journey, he arms himself, and seeks to go well accompanied; when going to sleep, he locks his doors; when even in his house he locks his chests; and then when he knows there be laws and public officers, armed, to revenge all injuries shall be done him; what opinion he has of his fellow-subjects, when he rides armed; of his fellow-citizens, when he locks his doors; and of his children and servants, when he locks his chests. Does he not there as much accuse mankind by his actions as I do by my words? But neither of us accuse man's nature in it. The desires and other passions of man are in themselves no sin. No more are the actions that proceed from those passions, till they know a law that forbids them; which till laws be made they cannot know; nor can any law be made till they have agreed upon the person that shall make it.

It may peradventure be thought there was never such a time nor condition of war as this; and I believe it was never generally so over all the world; but there are many places where they live so now. For the savage people in many places of America, except the government of small families, the concord whereof dependeth on natural lust, have no government at all, and live at this day in that brutish manner, as I said before. Howsoever, it may be perceived what manner of life there would be, where there were no common power to fear, by the manner of life which men that have formerly lived under a peaceful government used to degenerate into in a civil war.

But though there had never been any time wherein particular men were in a condition of war one against another, yet in all times, kings and persons of sovereign authority, because of their independency, are in continual jealousies, and in the state and posture of gladiators; having their weapons pointing, and their eyes fixed on one another; that is, their forts, garrisons, and guns, upon the frontiers of their kingdoms; and continual spies upon their neighbors; which is a posture of war. But because they uphold thereby the industry of their subjects, there does not follow from it that misery which accompanies the liberty of particular men.

To this war of every man against every man, this also is consequent, that nothing can be unjust. The notions of right and wrong, justice and injustice, have there no place. Where there is no common power, there is no law; where no law, no injustice. Force and fraud are in war the two cardinal virtues. Justice and injustice are none of the faculties neither of the body nor mind. If they were, they might be in a man that were alone in the world, as well as his senses and passions. They are qualities that relate to men in society, not in solitude. It is consequent also to the same condition that there be no propriety, no dominion, no "mine" and "thine" distinct; but only that to be every man's that he can get; and for so long as he can keep it. And thus much for the ill condition which every man by mere nature is actually placed in; though with a possibility to come out of it, consisting partly in the passions, partly in his reason.

The passions that incline men to peace are fear of death, desire of such things as are necessary to commodious living, and a hope by their industry to obtain them. And reason suggesteth convenient articles of peace, upon which men may be drawn to agreement. These articles are they which otherwise are called the laws of nature. . . .

Questions for Critical Thinking

1. What is Hobbes's theory of human nature? What part does his view of human nature play in his political philosophy?

2. According to Hobbes, where do rights come from? Are these rights inalienable—that is, not able to be taken away? Explain.

JOHN LOCKE
Selections from the *Second Treatise of Civil Government*

No other modern thinker has influenced Western political thought as much as the English philosopher John Locke (1632–1704). He lived during an age of political upheaval called the Glorious (or Bloodless) Revolution (1688), in which the Tories and the Whigs, England's first two political parties, joined together to rid their country of the tyrannical James II and welcomed as their new co-rulers his daughter, Mary, and her Dutch husband, William (William III and Mary II). Locke witnessed these events from the Netherlands, where he had fled in 1683 because he foresaw the accession of the absolutist and Catholic-leaning James II. When the entourage of William sailed to England in 1689 to claim the throne, Locke was on the ship that carried the future Queen Mary.

Locke's political theory is set forth in *Two Treatises of Government* (1690), which were published in the shadow of England's change in its ruling dynasty. The *First Treatise*, directed against Sir Robert Filmer's *Patriarcha* (1680), is an attack on the theory of absolute monarchy as based on the father's role in the family. In the more famous *Second Treatise of Civil Government*, Locke explains his own views in opposition to Filmer and (indirectly) Hobbes. Advocating the right to revolution and calling for government by consent of the governed, the *Second Treatise* seems to be simply a justification for the Glorious Revolution. But Locke had been working on both treatises since the 1680s, so they represent his mature political views.

Although Hobbes is never mentioned by name in the *Second Treatise*, it is clear that *Leviathan* was very much on Locke's mind when he wrote this little work. In contrast to Hobbes's centralized government with its claim to absolute power, Locke proposed a weak centralized government, its powers limited by a set of clearly defined personal rights: life, liberty, and most especially, property. Locke also took a more optimistic view of human nature than Hobbes, seeing human beings as basically rational and capable of both controlling their passions on an individual level and ruling themselves in society. In the long run, Locke's *Second Treatise* laid the foundations for liberalism—a political theory that advocated natural rights and representative government.

The son of a lawyer, Locke graduated from Oxford, where he was disillusioned with its outdated curriculum. He practiced medicine off and on during his life, tutored the sons of the wealthy, and served as private secretary for several prominent nobles. He held high government positions under William and Mary until his death.

Reading the Selections

The selection from Chapter IX of Locke's *Second Treatise* shows Locke giving a point-by-point refutation of Hobbes's political theory. Like Hobbes, Locke sees life as violent in the state of nature, but unlike Hobbes, he attributes this violence to the lack of an "established, settled, known law," "an indifferent judge," and an independent executive (the germ of "the separation of powers" idea). These three things, while lacking in the state of nature, are acquired by humans when they enter into a social contract, thus enabling natural rights to be enjoyed in civil society.

The selection from Chapter XIX lays out Locke's argument in support of the right to revolution, pointing out that the innate conservatism of human beings will prevent its abuse.

Chapter IX

Of the Ends of Political Society and Government

If man in the state of Nature be so free as has been said, if he be absolute lord of his own person and possessions, equal to the greatest and subject to nobody, why will he part with his freedom, this empire, and subject himself to the dominion and control of any other power? To which it is obvious to answer, that though in the state of Nature he hath such a right, yet the enjoyment of it is very uncertain and constantly exposed to the invasion of others; for all being kings as much as he, every man his equal, and the greater part no strict observers of equity and justice, the enjoyment of the property he has in this state is very unsafe, very insecure. This makes him willing to quit this condition which, however free, is full of fears and continual dangers; and it is not without reason that he seeks out and is willing to join in society with others who are already united, or have a mind to unite for the mutual preservation of their lives, liberties and estates, which I call by the general name—property.

The great and chief end, therefore, of men uniting into commonwealths, and putting themselves under government, is the preservation of their property; to which in the state of Nature there are many things wanting.

Firstly, there wants an established, settled, known law, received and allowed by common consent to be the standard of right and wrong, and the common measure to decide all controversies between them. For though the law of Nature be plain and intelligible to all rational creatures, yet men, being biased by their interest, as well as ignorant for want of study of it, are not apt to allow of it as a law binding to them in the application of it to their particular cases.

Secondly, in the state of Nature there wants a known and indifferent judge, with authority to determine all differences according to the established law. For every one in that state being both judge and executioner of the law of Nature, men being partial to themselves, passion and revenge is very apt to carry them too far, and with too much heat in their own cases, as well as negligence and unconcernedness, make them too remiss in other men's.

Thirdly, in the state of Nature there often wants power to back and support the sentence when right, and to give it due execution. They who by any injustice offended will seldom fail where they are able by force to make good their injustice. Such resistance many times makes the punishment dangerous, and frequently destructive to those who attempt it.

Thus mankind, notwithstanding all the privileges of the state of Nature, being but in an ill condition while they remain in it are quickly driven into society. Hence it comes to pass, that we seldom find any number of men live any time together in this state. The inconveniences that they are therein exposed to by the irregular and uncertain exercise of the power every man has of punishing the transgressions of others, make them take sanctuary under the established laws of government, and therein seek the preservation of their property. It is this makes them so willingly give up every one his single power of punishing to be exercised by such alone as shall be appointed to it amongst them, and by such rules as the community, or those authorised by them to that purpose, shall agree on. And in this we have the original right and rise of both the legislative and executive power as well as of the governments and societies themselves.

For in the state of Nature to omit the liberty he has of innocent delights, a man has two powers. The first is to do whatsoever he thinks fit for the preservation of himself and others within the permission of the law of Nature; by which law, common to them all, he and all the rest of mankind are one community, make up one society distinct from all other creatures, and were it not for the corruption and viciousness of degenerate men, there would be no need of any other, no necessity that men should separate from this great and natural community, and associate into lesser combinations. The other power a man has in the state of Nature is the power to punish the crimes committed against that law. Both these he gives up when he joins in a private, if I may so call it, or particular political society, and incorporates into any commonwealth separate from the rest of mankind.

The first power—viz., of doing whatsoever he thought fit for the preservation of himself and the rest of mankind, he gives up to be regulated by laws made by the society, so far forth as the preservation of himself and the rest of that society shall require; which laws of the society in many things confine the liberty he had by the law of Nature.

Secondly, the power of punishing he wholly gives up, and engages his natural force, which he might before employ in the execution of the law of Nature, by his own single authority, as he thought fit, to assist the executive power of the society as the law thereof shall require. For being now in a new state, wherein he is to enjoy many conveniences from the labour, assistance, and society of others in the same community, as well as protection from its whole strength, he is to part also with as much of his natural liberty, in providing for himself, as the good, prosperity, and safety of the society shall require, which is not only necessary but just, since the other members of the society do the like.

But though men when they enter into society give up the equality, liberty, and executive power they had in the state of Nature in the hands of the society, to be so far disposed of by the legislative as the good of the society shall require, yet it being only with an intention in every one the better to preserve himself, his liberty and property (for no rational creature can be supposed to change his condition with an intention to be worse), the power of the society or legislative constituted by them can never be supposed to extend farther than the common good, but is obliged to secure every one's property by providing against those three defects above mentioned that made the state of Nature so unsafe and uneasy. And so, whoever has the legislative or supreme power of any commonwealth, is bound to govern by established standing laws, promulgated and known to the people, and not by extemporary decrees, by indifferent and upright judges, who are to decide controversies by those laws; and to employ the force of the community at home only in the execution of such laws, or abroad to prevent or redress foreign injuries and secure the community from inroads and invasion. And all this to be directed to no other end but the peace, safety, and public good of the people. . . .

∽

Chapter XIX

Of the Dissolution of Governments

. . . He that will, with any clearness, speak of the dissolution of government, ought in the first place to distinguish between the dissolution of the society and the dissolution of the government. That which makes the community, and brings men out of the loose state of Nature into one political society, is the agreement which everyone has with the rest to incorporate and act as one body, and so be one distinct commonwealth. The usual, and almost only way whereby this union is dissolved, is the inroad of foreign force making a conquest upon them. For in that case (not being able to maintain and support themselves as one entire and independent body) the union belonging to that body, which consisted therein, must necessarily cease, and so every one return to the state he was in before, with a liberty to shift for himself and provide for his own safety, as he thinks fit, in some other society. Whenever the society is dissolved, it is certain the government of that society cannot remain. Thus conquerors' swords often cut up governments by the roots, and mangle societies to pieces, separating the subdued or scattered multitude from the protection of and dependence on that society which ought to have preserved them from violence. The world is too well instructed in, and too forward to allow of this way of dissolving of governments, to need any more to be said of it; and there wants not much argument to prove that where the society is dissolved, the government cannot remain; that being as impossible as for the frame of a house to subsist when the materials of it are scattered and displaced by a whirlwind, or jumbled into a confused heap by an earthquake.

Besides this overturning from without, governments are dissolved from within:

First. When the legislative is altered, civil society being a state of peace amongst those who are of it, from whom the state of war is excluded by the umpirage which they have provided in their legislative for the ending of all differences that may arise amongst any of them; it is in their legislative that the members of a commonwealth are united and combined together into one coherent living body. This is the soul that gives form, life, and unity to the commonwealth; from hence the several members have their mutual influence, sympathy, and connection; and therefore when the legislative is broken, or dissolved, dissolution and death follows. For the essence and union of the society consisting in having one will, the legislative, when once established by the majority, has the declaring and, as it were, keeping of that will. The constitution of the legislative is the first and fundamental act of society, whereby provision is made for the continuation of their union under the direction of persons and bonds of laws, made by persons authorized thereunto, by the consent and appointment of the people, without which no one man, or number of men, amongst them can have authority of making laws that shall be binding to the rest. When any one, or more, shall take upon them to make laws whom the people have not appointed so to do, they make laws without authority, which the people are not therefore bound to obey; by which means they come again to be out of subjection, and may constitute to themselves a new legislative, as they think best, being in full liberty to resist the force of those who, without authority, would impose anything upon them. Every one is at the disposure of his own will, when those who had, by the delegation of the society, the declaring of the public will, are excluded from it, and others usurp the place, who have no such authority or delegation.

This being usually brought about by such in the commonwealth, who misuse the power they have, it is hard to consider it aright, and know at whose door to lay it, without knowing the form of government in which it happens. Let us suppose, then, the legislative placed in the concurrence of three distinct persons: First, a single hereditary person having the constant, supreme, executive power, and with it power of convoking and dissolving the other two within certain periods of time. Secondly, an assembly of hereditary nobility. Thirdly, an assembly of representatives chosen, *pro tempore,* by the people. Such a form of government supposed, it is evident—

First, that when such a single person or prince sets up his own arbitrary will in place of the laws which are the will of the society declared by the legislative, then the legislative is changed. For that being, in effect, the legislative whose rules and laws are put in execution, and required to be obeyed when other laws are set up, and other rules pretended and enforced than what the legislative, constituted by the society, have enacted, it is plain that the legislative is changed. Whoever introduces new laws, not being thereunto authorized, by the fundamental appointment of the society, or subverts the old, disowns and overturns the power by which they were made, and so sets up a new legislative.

Secondly, when the prince hinders the legislative from assembling in its due time, or from acting freely, pursuant to those ends for which it was constituted, the legislative is altered. For it is not a certain number of men—no, nor their meeting, unless they have also freedom of debating and leisure of perfecting what is for the good of the society wherein the legislative consists; when these are taken away, or altered, so as to deprive the society of the due exercise of their power, the legislative is truly altered. For it is not names that constitute governments, but the use and exercise of those powers that were intended to accompany them; so that he who takes away the freedom, or hinders the acting of the legislative in its due seasons, in effect takes away the legislative, and puts an end to the government.

Thirdly, when, by the arbitrary power of the prince, the electors or ways of election are altered without the consent and contrary to the common interest of the people, there also the legislative is altered. For if others than those whom the society hath authorized thereunto do choose, or in another way than what the society hath prescribed, those chosen are not the legislative appointed by the people.

Fourthly, the delivery also of the people into the subjection of a foreign power, either by the prince or by the legislative, is certainly a change of the legislative, and so a dissolution of the government. For the end why people entered into society being to be preserved one entire, free, independent society, to be governed by its own laws, this is lost whenever they are given up into the power of another.

Why, in such a constitution as this, the dissolution of the government in these cases is to be imputed to the prince is evident, because he, having the force, treasure, and offices of the State to employ, and often persuading himself or being flattered by others, that, as supreme magistrate, he is incapable of control; he alone is in a condition to make great advances towards such changes under pretense of lawful authority, and has it in his hands to terrify or suppress opposers as factious, seditious, and enemies to the government; whereas no other part of the legislative, or people, is capable by themselves to attempt any alteration of the legislative without open and visible rebellion, apt enough to be taken notice of, which, when it prevails, produces effects very little different from foreign conquest. Besides, the prince, in such a form of government, having the power of dissolving the other parts of the legislative, and thereby rendering them private persons, they can never, in opposition to him, or without his concurrence, alter the legislative by a law, his consent being necessary to give any of their decrees that sanction. But yet so far as the other parts of the legislative any way contribute to any attempt upon the government, and do either promote, or not, what lies in them, hinder such designs, they are guilty, and partake in this, which is certainly the greatest crime men can be guilty of one towards another.

There is one way more whereby such a government 10 may be dissolved, and that is: When he who has the supreme executive power neglects and abandons that charge, so that the laws already made can no longer be put in execution; this is demonstratively to reduce all to anarchy, and so effectually to dissolve the government. For laws not being made for themselves, but to be, by their execution, the bonds of the society to keep every part of the body politic in its due place and function. When that totally ceases, the government visibly ceases, and the people become a confused multitude without order or connection. Where there is no longer the administration of justice for the securing of men's rights, nor any remaining power within the community to direct the force, or provide for the necessities of the public, there certainly is no government left. Where the laws cannot be executed it is all one as if there were no laws, and a government without laws is, I suppose, a mystery in politics inconceivable to human capacity, and inconsistent with human society.

In these, and the like cases, when the government is dissolved, the people are at liberty to provide for themselves by erecting a new legislative differing from the other by the change of persons, or form, or both, as they shall find it most for their safety and good. For the society can never, by the fault of another, lose the native and original right it has to preserve itself, which can only be done by a settled legislative and a fair and impartial execution of the laws made by it. But the state of mankind is not so miserable that they are not capable of using this remedy till it be too late to look for any. To tell people they may provide for themselves by erecting a new legislative, when, by oppression, artifice, or being delivered over to a foreign power, their old one is gone, is only to tell them they may expect relief when it is too late, and the evil is past cure. This is, in effect, no more than to bid them first be slaves, and then to take care of their liberty, and, when their chains are on, tell them they may act like free men. This, if barely so, is rather mockery than relief, and men can never be secure from tyranny if there be no means to escape it till they are perfectly under it; and, therefore, it is that they have not only a right to get out of it, but to prevent it.

There is, therefore, secondly, another way whereby governments are dissolved, and that is, when the legislative, or the prince, either of them act contrary to their trust.

First: the legislative acts against the trust reposed in them when they endeavor to invade the property of the subject, and to make themselves, or any part of the community, masters or arbitrary disposers of the lives, liberties, or fortunes of the people.

The reasons why men enter into society is the preservation of their property; and the end while they choose and authorize a legislative is that there may be laws made, and rules set, as guards and fences to the properties of all the society, to limit the power, and moderate the dominion of every part and member of the society. For since it can never be supposed to be the will of the society that the legislative should have a power to destroy that which everyone designs to secure by entering into society, and for which the people submitted themselves to legislators of their own making; whenever the legislators endeavor to take away and destroy the property of the people, or to reduce them to slavery under arbitrary power, they put themselves into a state of war with the people, who are thereupon absolved from any further obedience, and are left to the common refuge which God hath provided for all men against force and violence. Whensoever, therefore, the legislative shall transgress this fundamental rule of society, and either by ambition, fear, folly, or corruption, endeavor to grasp themselves, or put into the hands of any other, an absolute power over the lives, liberties, and estates of the people; by this breach of trust they forfeit the power the people had put into their hands for quite contrary ends, and it devolves to the people, who have a right to resume their original liberty, and by the establishment of a new legislative (such as they shall think fit), provide for their own safety and security, which is the end for which they are in society. What I have said here concerning the legislative in general holds true also concerning the supreme executor, who having a double trust put in him, both to have a part in the legislative and the supreme execution of the law, acts against both; when he goes about to set up his own arbitrary will as the law of the society. He acts also contrary to his trust when he employs the force, treasure, and offices of the society to corrupt the representatives, and gain them to his purposes, when he openly preengages the electors, and prescribes, to their choice, such whom he has, by solicitation, threats, promises, or otherwise, won to his designs, and employs them to bring in such who have promised beforehand what to vote and what to enact. Thus to regulate candidates and electors, and new model the ways of election, what is it but to cut up the government by the roots, and poison the very fountain of public security? For the people having reserved to themselves the choice of their representatives as the fence to their properties, could do it for no other end but that they might always be freely chosen, and so chosen, freely act and advise as the necessity of the commonwealth and the public good should, upon examination and mature debate, be judged to require. This, those who give their votes before they hear the debate, and have weighed the reasons on all sides, are not capable of doing. To prepare such an assembly as this, and endeavor to set up the declared abettors of his own will, for the true representatives of the people, and the law-makers of the society, is certainly as great a breach of trust, and as perfect a declaration of a design to subvert the government, as is possible to be met with. To which, if one shall add rewards and punishments visibly employed to the same end, and all the arts of perverted law made use of to take off and destroy all that stand in the way of such a design, and will not comply and consent to betray the liberties of their country, it will be past doubt what is doing. What power they ought to have in the society who thus employ it contrary to the trust went along with it in its first institution, is easy to determine; and one cannot but see that he who has once attempted any such thing as this cannot any longer be trusted.

To this, perhaps, it will be said that the people being 15 ignorant and always discontented, to lay the foundation of government in the unsteady opinion and uncertain humor of the people is to expose it to certain ruin; and no government will be able long to subsist if the people may set up a new legislative whenever they take offense at the old one. To this I answer, quite the contrary. People are not so easily got out of their old forms as some are apt to suggest. They are hardly to be prevailed with to amend the acknowledged faults in the frame they have been accustomed to. And if there be any original defects, or adventitious ones introduced by time or corruption, it is not an easy thing to get them changed, even when all the world sees there is an opportunity for it. This slowness and aversion in the people to quit their old constitutions has in the many revolutions that have been seen in this kingdom, in this and former ages, still kept us to, or after some interval of fruitless attempts, still brought us back again to our old legislative of king, lords and commons; and whatever provocations have made the crown be taken from some of our princes' heads, they never carried the people so far as to place it in another line.

But it will be said this hypothesis lays a ferment for frequent rebellion. To which I answer:

First: no more than any other hypothesis. For when the people are made miserable, and find themselves exposed to the ill usage of arbitrary power, cry up their governors as much as you will for sons of Jupiter, let them be sacred and divine, descended or authorized from Heaven; give them out for whom or what you please, the same will happen. The people generally ill treated, and contrary to right, will be ready upon any occasion to ease themselves of a burden that sits heavy upon them. They will wish and seek for the opportunity, which in the change, weakness, and accidents of human affairs, seldom delays long to offer itself. He must have lived but a little while in the world, who has not seen examples of this in his time; and he must have read very little who cannot produce examples of it in all sorts of governments in the world.

Secondly: I answer, such revolutions happen not upon every little mismanagement in public affairs. Great mistakes in the ruling part, many wrong and inconvenient laws, and all the slips of human frailty will be borne by the people without mutiny or murmur. But if a long train of abuses, prevarications, and artifices, all tending the same way, make the design visible to the people, and they cannot but feel what they lie under, and see whither they are going, it is not to be wondered that they should then rouse themselves, and endeavor to put the rule into such hands which may secure to them the ends for which government was at first erected, and without which, ancient names and specious forms are so far from being better, that they are much worse than the state of Nature or pure anarchy; the inconveniences being all as great and as near, but the remedy farther off and more difficult.

Thirdly: I answer, that this power in the people of providing for their safety anew by a new legislative when their legislators have acted contrary to their trust by invading their property, is the best fence against rebellion, and the probablest means to hinder it. For rebellion being an opposition, not to persons, but authority, which is founded only in the constitutions and laws of the government; those, whoever they be, who, by force, break through, and, by force, justify their violation of them, are truly and properly rebels. For when men, by entering into society and civil government, have excluded force, and introduced laws for the preservation of property, peace, and unity amongst themselves, those who set up force again in opposition to the laws, do *rebellare*—that is, bring back again the state of war, and are properly rebels, which they who are in power, by the pretense they have to authority, the temptation of force they have in their hands, and the flattery of those about them being likeliest to do, the properest way to prevent the evil is to show them the danger and injustice of it who are under the greatest temptation to run into it. . . .

But if they who say it lays a foundation for rebellion 20 mean that it may occasion civil wars or intestine broils to tell the people they are absolved from obedience when illegal attempts are made upon their liberties or properties, and may oppose the unlawful violence of those who were their magistrates when they invade their properties, contrary to the trust put in them, and that, therefore, this doctrine is not to be allowed, being so destructive to the peace of the world; they may as well say, upon the same ground, that honest men may not oppose robbers or pirates, because this may occasion disorder or bloodshed. If any mischief come in such cases, it is not to be charged upon him who defends his own right, but on him that invades his neighbor's. If the innocent honest man must quietly quit all he has for peace sake to him who will lay violent hands upon it, I desire it may be considered what a kind of peace there will be in the world which consists only in violence and rapine, and which is to be maintained only for the benefit of robbers and oppressors. Who would not think it an admirable peace betwixt the mighty and the mean, when the lamb, without resistance, yielded his throat to be torn by the imperious wolf? Polyphemus's den gives us a perfect pattern of such a peace. Such a government wherein Ulysses[18] and his companions had nothing to do but quietly to suffer themselves to be devoured. And no doubt Ulysses, who was a prudent man, preached up passive obedience, and exhorted them to a quiet submission

---

[18] **Polyphemus, Ulysses** Reference to Book 9 from Homer's *Odyssey* (see Chapter 2, Volume I). Ulysses (Odysseus) and his men are in Polyphemus's cave or den, and Ulysses has to decide whether they will or will not confront the one-eyed monster.

by representing to them of what concernment peace was to mankind, and by showing the inconveniences might happen if they should offer to resist Polyphemus, who had now the power over them.

The end of government is the good of mankind; and which is best for mankind, that the people should be always exposed to the boundless will of tyranny, or that the rulers should be sometimes liable to be opposed when they grow exorbitant in the use of their power, and employ it for the destruction, and not the preservation, of the properties of their people? . . .

Here it is like the common question will be made, Who shall be judge whether the prince or legislative act contrary to their trust? This, perhaps, ill-affected and factious men may spread amongst the people, when the prince only makes use of his due prerogative. To this I reply, The people shall be judge; for who shall be judge whether his trustee or deputy acts well and according to the trust reposed in him, but he who deputes him and must, by having deputed him, have still a power to discard him when he fails in his trust? If this be reasonable in particular cases of private men, why should it be otherwise in that of the greatest moment, where the welfare of millions is concerned and also where the evil, if not prevented, is greater, and the redress very difficult, dear, and dangerous?

But, farther, this question, Who shall be judge? cannot mean that there is no judge at all. For where there is no judicature on earth to decide controversies amongst men, God in heaven is judge. He alone, it is true, is judge of the right. But every man is judge for himself, as in all other cases so in this, whether another hath put himself into a state of war with him, and whether he should appeal to the supreme Judge, as Jephtha did.

If a controversy arise betwixt a prince and some of the people in a matter where the law is silent or doubtful, and the thing be of great consequence, I should think the proper umpire in such a case should be the body of the people. For in cases where the prince hath a trust reposed in him, and is dispensed from the common, ordinary rules of the law, there, if any men find themselves aggrieved, and think the prince acts contrary to, or beyond that trust, who so proper to judge as the body of the people (who at first lodged that trust in him) how far they meant it should extend? But if the prince, or whoever they be in the administration, decline that way of determination, the appeal then lies nowhere but to Heaven. Force between either persons who have no known superior on earth, or which permits no appeal to a judge on earth, being properly a state of war, wherein the appeal lies only to Heaven; and in that state the injured party must judge for himself when he will think fit to make use of that appeal and put himself upon it.

To conclude. The power that every individual gave the society when he entered into it can never revert to the individuals again, as long as the society lasts, but will always remain in the community; because without this there can be no community—no commonwealth, which is contrary to the original agreement; so also when the society hath placed the legislative in any assembly of men, to continue in them and their successors, with direction and authority for providing such successors, the legislative can never revert to the people whilst that government lasts; because, having provided a legislative with power to continue for ever, they have given up their political power to the legislative, and cannot resume it. But if they have set limits to the duration of their legislative, and made this supreme power in any person or assembly only temporary; or else, when, by the miscarriages of those in authority, it is forfeited; upon the forfeiture of their rulers, or at the determination of the time set, it reverts to the society, and the people have a right to act as supreme, and continue the legislative in themselves or place it in a new form, or new hands, as they think good.

Questions for Critical Thinking

1. Describe the transition from a natural state to civil society in Locke's political theory. What do humans give up during this transition? What do they gain?

2. According to Locke, where do rights come from? Are these rights inalienable—that is, not able to be taken away? Explain.

17

THE AGE OF REASON
1700–1789

IMMANUEL KANT
Answer to the Question: What Is Enlightenment?

Immanuel Kant (1724–1804), the German philosopher and author who challenged many of the basic assumptions of Western thought and raised fundamental ethical, moral, and epistemological questions about the nature of knowledge, has influenced every serious thinker since his death. The early-nineteenth-century German idealists, including G. F. W. Hegel (see *Reason in History* in Chapter 18), the late-nineteenth-century Neo-Kantian schools of German thinkers, the twentieth-century American pragmatists, such as William James and John Dewey, and today's scientists, anthropologists, and historians are all indebted to Kant. Yet, he also engendered diverse and often contentious schools of thought that have set the tone and context of intellectual history for the past two hundred years.

To summarize Kant's fundamental thoughts is extremely difficult. He left a voluminous collection of books, essays, treatises, and scholarly papers that nearly overwhelm all but the most dedicated scholar. He often diverged from his central arguments that challenge the reader in following Kant's basic propositions. His ponderous prose has made it even more demanding to understand his writings.

Yet, some themes come through in his works. For example, humans possess limited reason and, therefore, can understand and comprehend only so much of their physical and metaphysical surroundings. How humans go about their methods of inquiry and what they conclude from these examinations will, in turn, become the foundations of their beliefs. However, such conclusions are always built on the reality of the limitations of human reason. Even though human reason has its limitations, human reason is superior to and must take precedent over passions, blind faith, tradition, or the supernatural. Regardless of reason's limitations, reason also points the way toward a feeling of kinship with others who share this common human trait.

Kant established two distinct categories of what humans can know. What humans can know from experience and from their limited reason is categorized as *phenomena;* what humans cannot know because it lies beyond their experience or reason is known as *noumena.* Noumena includes such metaphysical issues as God, freedom, and immortality, because they cannot be understood by human speculative thought. Therefore, they cannot be either confirmed or denied.

Whereas humans will never achieve their final goals, they must strive and learn to live with reality. Humans, at the same time, must recognize and struggle against evil.

Consequently, human achievements will be limited. Yet, some goals—such as self-worth, human dignity, and self-government—are within the realm of possibility.

Kant, who had so much influence, lived a relatively quiet and modest life. He was born in Koenigsberg (now called Kaliningrad, Russia), which was, in the early eighteenth century, an out-of-the-way small port city in East Prussia on the Baltic Sea. His father, a leather worker, had to rear a large family, and prospects for Kant receiving a formal education appeared minimal until his minister encouraged and supported the young man to attend the local university. He first studied Latin literature, but soon became a convert to the natural sciences. After graduation he served as a tutor for several wealthy families, which introduced him to a cultured and sophisticated way of life. He returned to the university a few years later, and in 1755 he received his doctor of philosophy degree. Kant then became a lecturer, which guaranteed him an academic position but no salary. He therefore had to teach the students, who paid him directly, whatever they wanted to learn. He was quickly forced to expand his interest and expertise and to do research in many fields. From his interest in the natural sciences, he moved into metaphysics and the study of the foundations of knowledge.

During the 1760s Kant began to attract attention with his essays on metaphysics and moral philosophy, and in 1770 he was named to the position of professor of logic at Koenigsberg University, where he would remain for the rest of his life. In 1781 he published his *Critique of Pure Reason,* one of the most influential philosophical works in the history of Western thought, although his book was not so recognized at that time. Nonetheless, the work launched the most productive period of his career; during the next ten years, Kant wrote influential studies in history, moral philosophy, and aesthetics.

In the midst of this flurry of writing, in 1784, he drafted his essay *Answer to the Question: What Is Enlightenment?* His essay was in response to a conservative cleric who argued that no further study of political or religious issues was needed since no one had been able to define the term *enlightenment.* Kant's reply is still considered one of the most distinct and concise explanations of the basic concepts of the Enlightenment.

As his reputation grew in the 1780s, Kant became the center of many controversies. In the early 1790s he ran afoul of the government when the new Prussian monarch, Friedrich Wilhelm II, moved to cut off debate about religion. Edicts were issued to test the religious beliefs of clergymen and professors, and Kant was threatened with warnings not to write on religious topics. The crisis passed after the death of the king in 1797, and Kant resumed his publications on religion. Before his death in 1804, Kant completed his works on ethics, published many of his lectures, and started a book on the sciences and their philosophical implications.

Reading the Selection

Compared to many of his works, *Answer to the Question: What Is Enlightenment?* is a model of clarity and exposition. Kant sets out to answer the question from the very beginning and emphatically states his response. Determination and courage to use one's intelligence, without help from others, is enlightenment. *Sapere Aude!,* "Dare to Be Wise!" or—in Kant's translation of the words of the Roman poet Horace—"Have the courage to use your own intelligence!" is, he asserts without equivocation, the "motto of enlightenment."

Kant then discusses the power of the "guardians" of society who have taken it upon themselves to make certain that the majority of the populace, including the "the entire 'fair sex,'" not become enlightened. These "guardians" contend that becoming a mature and independent individual is a difficult and dangerous step to take. Dismissing their arguments, Kant declares that enlightenment can be achieved through freedom—in particular, the exercise of freedom for a person to make "public use" of his or her reason. He then explains what he means by the public use of one's reason and provides specific examples as they relate to clergymen and monarchs. Kant returns to his opening statements to answer the question of whether his generation is living in an enlightened age. His answer is No; but, he declares, his generation is living in an "age of enlightenment," which, he believes, offers hope for a better future. He does recognize the conflict between individual thought and the power of the state, but concludes his essay on a positive note that government—that is, the Prussian monarchy—is now treating men with dignity.

Enlightenment is man's release from his self-incurred tutelage. Tutelage is man's inability to make use of his understanding without direction from another. Self-incurred is this tutelage when its cause lies not in lack of reason but in lack of resolution and courage to use it without direction from another. *Sapere aude!*[1] "Have courage to use your own reason!"—that is the motto of enlightenment.

Laziness and cowardice are the reasons why so great a portion of mankind, after nature has long since discharged them from external direction *(naturalizer maiorennes),* nevertheless remains under lifelong tutelage, and why it is so easy for others to set themselves up as their guardians. It is so easy not to be of age. If I have a book which understands for me, a pastor who has a conscience for me, a physician who decides my diet, and so forth, I need not trouble myself. I need not think, if I can only pay—others will readily undertake the irksome work for me.

That the step to competence is held to be very dangerous by the far greater portion of mankind (and by the entire fair sex)—quite apart from its being arduous—is seen to by those guardians who have so kindly assumed superintendence over them. After the guardians have first made their domestic cattle dumb and have made sure that these placid creatures will not dare take a single step without the harness of the cart to which they are confined, the guardians then show them the danger which threatens if they try to go alone. Actually, however, this danger is not so great, for by falling a few times they would finally learn to walk alone. But an example of this failure makes them timid and ordinarily frightens them away from all further trials.

For any single individual to work himself out of the life under tutelage which has become almost his nature is very difficult. He has come to be fond of this state, and he is for the present really incapable of making use of his reason, for no one has ever let him try it out. Statutes and formulas, those mechanical tools of the rational employment or rather misemployment of his natural gifts, are the fetters of an everlasting tutelage. Whoever throws them off makes only an uncertain leap over the narrowest ditch because he is not accustomed to that kind of free motion. Therefore, there are only a few who have succeeded by their own exercise of mind both in freeing themselves from incompetence and in achieving a steady pace.

But that the public should enlighten itself is more possible; indeed, if only freedom is granted, enlightenment is almost sure to follow. For there will always be some independent thinkers, even among the established guardians of the great masses, who, after throwing off the yoke of tutelage from their own shoulders, will disseminate the spirit of the rational appreciation of both their own worth and every man's vocation for thinking for himself. But be it noted that the public, which has first been brought under this yoke by their guardians, forces the guardians themselves to remain bound when it is incited to do so by some of the guardians who are themselves capable of some enlightenment—so harmful is it to implant prejudices, for they later take vengeance on their cultivators or on their descendants. Thus the public can only slowly attain enlightenment. Perhaps a fall of personal despotism or of avaricious or tyrannical oppression may be accomplished by revolution, but never a true reform in ways of thinking. Rather, new prejudices will serve as well as old ones to harness the great unthinking masses.

For this enlightenment, however, nothing is required but freedom, and indeed the most harmless freedom of all, which alone should be called by this name. It is the freedom to make public use of one's reason at every point. But I hear on all sides, "Do not argue!" The officer says: "Do not argue but drill!" The tax-collector: "Do not argue but pay!" The cleric: "Do not argue but believe!" Only one prince in the world says, "Argue as much as you will, and about what you will, but obey!" Everywhere there is restriction on freedom.

Which restriction is an obstacle to enlightenment, and which is not an obstacle but a promoter of it? I answer: The public use of one's reason must always be free, and it alone can bring about enlightenment among men. The private use of reason, on the other hand, may often be very narrowly restricted without particularly hindering the progress of enlightenment. By the public use of one's reason I understand the use which a person makes of it as a scholar before the reading public. Private use I call that which one may make of it in a particular civil post or office which is intrusted to him. Many affairs which are conducted in the interest of the community require a certain mechanism through which some members of the community must passively conduct themselves with an artificial unanimity, so that the government may direct them to public ends, or at least prevent them from destroying those ends. Here argument is certainly not allowed—one must obey. But so far as a part of the mechanism regards himself at the same time as a member of the whole community or of a society of world citizens, and thus in the role of a scholar who addresses the public (in the proper sense of the word) through his writings, he certainly can argue without hurting the affairs for which he is in part responsible as a passive member. Thus it would be ruinous for an officer in service to debate about the suitability or utility of a command given to him by his superior; he must obey. But the right to make remarks on errors in the military service and to lay them before the public for judgment cannot equitably be refused him as a scholar. The citizen cannot refuse to pay the taxes imposed on him; indeed, an impudent complaint at those levied on him can be punished as a scandal (as it could occasion general refractoriness). But the same person nevertheless does not act contrary to his duty as a citizen when, as a scholar,

---

[1] *Sapere Aude!* "Dare to Be Wise!" Kant liberally translated this quote from the first-century BCE Roman poet and satirist Horace to fit his argument, which read, "Have the courage to use your own intelligence!"

he publicly expresses his thoughts on the inappropriateness or even the injustice of these levies. Similarly, a clergyman is obligated to make his sermon to his pupils in catechism and his congregation conform to the symbol of the church which he serves, for he has been accepted on this condition. But as a scholar he has complete freedom, even the calling, to communicate to the public all his carefully tested and well-meaning thoughts on that which is erroneous in the symbol and to make suggestions for the better organization of the religious body and church. In doing this, there is nothing that could be laid as a burden on his conscience. For what he teaches as a consequence of his office as a representative of the church, this he considers something about which he has no freedom to teach according to his own lights; it is something which he is appointed to propound at the dictation of and in the name of another. He will say, "Our church teaches this or that; those are the proofs which it adduces." He thus extracts all practical uses for his congregation from statutes to which he himself would not subscribe with full conviction but to the enunciation of which he can very well pledge himself because it is not impossible that truth lies hidden in them, and, in any case, there is at least nothing in them contradictory to inner religion. For if he believed he had found such in them, he could not conscientiously discharge the duties of his office; he would have to give it up. The use, therefore, which an appointed teacher makes of his reason before his congregation is merely private, because this congregation is only a domestic one (even if it be a large gathering); with respect to it, as a priest, he is not free, nor can he be free, because he carries out the orders of another. But as a scholar, whose writings speak to his public, the world, the clergyman in the public use of his reason enjoys an unlimited freedom to use his own reason and to speak in his own person. That the guardians of the people (in spiritual things) should themselves be incompetent is an absurdity which amounts to the eternalization of absurdities.

But would not a society of clergymen, perhaps a church conference or a venerable classis (as they call themselves among the Dutch), be justified in obligating itself by oath to a certain unchangeable symbol in order to enjoy an unceasing guardianship over each of its members and thereby over the people as a whole, and even to make it eternal? I answer that this is altogether impossible. Such a contract, made to shut off all further enlightenment from the human race, is absolutely null and void even if confirmed by the supreme power, by parliaments, and by the most ceremonious of peace treaties. An age cannot bind itself and ordain to put the succeeding one into such a condition that it cannot extend its (at best very occasional) knowledge, purify itself of errors, and progress in general enlightenment. That would be a crime against human nature, the proper destination of which lies precisely in this progress; and the descendants would be fully justified in rejecting those decrees as having been made in an unwarranted and malicious manner.

The touchstone of everything that can be concluded as a law for a people lies in the question whether the people could have imposed such a law on itself. Now such a religious compact might be possible for a short and definitely limited time, as it were, in expectation of a better. One might let every citizen, and especially the clergyman, in the role of the scholar, make his comments freely and publicly, i.e., through writing, on the erroneous aspects of the present institution. The newly introduced order might last until insight into the nature of these things had become so general and widely approved that through uniting their voices (even if not unanimously) they could bring a proposal to the throne to take those congregations under protection which had united into a changed religious organization according to their better ideas, without, however, hindering others who wish to remain in the order. But to unite in a permanent religious institution which is not to be subject to doubt before the public even in the lifetime of one man, and thereby to make a period of time fruitless in the progress of mankind toward improvement, thus working to the disadvantage of posterity—that is absolutely forbidden. For himself (and only for a short time) a man can postpone enlightenment in what he ought to know, but to renounce it for himself and even more to renounce it for posterity is to injure and trample on the rights of mankind.

And what a people may not decree for itself can even less be decreed for them by a monarch, for his lawgiving authority rests on his uniting the general public will in his own. If he only sees to it that all true or alleged improvement stands together with civil order, he can leave it to his subjects to do what they find necessary for their spiritual welfare. This is not his concern, though it is incumbent on him to prevent one of them from violently hindering another in determining and promoting this welfare to the best of his ability. To meddle in these matters lowers his own majesty, since by the writings in which his subjects seek to present their views he may evaluate his own governance. He can do this when, with deepest understanding, he lays upon himself the reproach, *Caesar non est supra grammaticos.*[2] Far more does he injure his own majesty when he degrades his supreme power by supporting the ecclesiastical despotism of some tyrants in his state over his other subjects.

If we are asked, "Do we now live in an *enlightened age?*" the answer is, "No," but we do live in an *age of enlightenment.* As things now stand, much is lacking which prevents men from being, or easily becoming, capable of correctly using their own reason in religious matters with assurance and free from outside direction. But, on the other hand, we have clear indications that the field has now been opened wherein men may freely deal with these things and that the obstacles to general enlightenment or the release from self-imposed tutelage are gradually being reduced. In this respect, this is the age of enlightenment, or the century of Frederick.

---

[2] *Caesar non est supra grammaticos.* "Caesar is not above the grammarians." Grammarians are scholars who study the rules and principles of an art or a science.

A prince who does not find it unworthy of himself to say that he holds it to be his duty to prescribe nothing to men in religious matters but to give them complete freedom while renouncing the haughty name of *tolerance,* is himself enlightened and deserves to be esteemed by the grateful world and posterity as the first, at least from the side of government, who divested the human race of its tutelage and left each man free to make use of his reason in matters of conscience. Under him venerable ecclesiastics are allowed, in the role of scholars, and without infringing on their official duties, freely to submit for public testing their judgments and views which here and there diverge from the established symbol. And an even greater freedom is enjoyed by those who are restricted by no official duties. This spirit of freedom spreads beyond this land, even to those in which it must struggle with external obstacles erected by a government which misunderstands its own interest. For an example gives evidence to such a government that in freedom there is not the least cause for concern about public peace and the stability of the community. Men work themselves gradually out of barbarity if only intentional artifices are not made to hold them in it.

I have placed the main point of enlightenment—the escape of men from their self-incurred tutelage—chiefly in matters of religion because our rulers have no interest in playing the guardian with respect to the arts and sciences and also because religious incompetence is not only the most harmful but also the most degrading of all. But the manner of thinking of the head of a state who favors religious enlightenment goes further, and he sees that there is no danger to his lawgiving in allowing his subjects to make public use of their reason and to publish their thoughts on a better formulation of his legislation and even their open-minded criticisms of the laws already made. Of this we have a shining example wherein no monarch is superior to him whom we honor.

But only one who is himself enlightened, is not afraid of shadows, and has a numerous and well-disciplined army to assure public peace can say: "Argue as much as you will, and about what you will, only obey!" A republic could not dare say such a thing. Here is shown a strange and unexpected trend in human affairs in which almost everything, looked at in the large, is paradoxical. A greater degree of civil freedom appears advantageous to the freedom of mind of the people, and yet it places inescapable limitations upon it; a lower degree of civil freedom, on the contrary, provides the mind with room for each man to extend himself to his full capacity. As nature has uncovered from under this hard shell the seed for which she most tenderly cares—the propensity and vocation to free thinking—this gradually works back upon the character of the people, who thereby gradually become capable of managing freedom; finally, it affects the principles of government, which finds it to its advantage to treat men, who are now more than machines, in accordance with their dignity.

Questions for Critical Thinking

1. Is Kant's essay a subversive work? Explain.

2. Do you think we are living in an Age of Enlightenment today? Explain.

DAVID HUME
Selections from *A Treatise of Human Nature*

A Treatise of Human Nature is a classic of Western philosophy, but it was not considered as such when first published in 1738–1740. Its author, the Scotsman David Hume (1711–1776), lamented that it "fell stillborn from the press." Hume later revised and republished its two themes, the first on knowledge, in *Enquiries: Concerning Human Understanding* (1748), and the second on ethics, in *Concerning Principles of Morals* (1751). These works made Hume the greatest philosophical mind of his day. However, his skepticism undermined the Enlightenment's optimistic rationalism which encouraged the rise of romanticism (see Rousseau's *Confessions*). Today, *A Treatise of Human Nature* is recognized as a revolutionary work of ideas.

Hume's goal, in this treatise, is to create a science of human nature, equivalent to that emerging in the sciences during the Enlightenment. Following the English thinker John Locke, Hume bases his reasoning about human nature purely on experience. Like Locke, Hume reasons that what we know is first in the senses, as either "impressions" or "ideas." But Hume parts ways with Locke over the nature of the "ideas" in the mind. Hume rejects Locke's claim that "ideas" are formed by innate workings of the mind, such as memory, comparison, and contrast. For Hume, the mind is a receptacle, collecting impressions and the mental images inspired by them. In other words, human nature is not fixed, but a continuously shifting pattern of images for each individual. Since nothing can be known apart from the senses, Hume's empiricism collapses into solipsism—the belief that all that can be known is one's own mental world. Hume's quest also leads to a twofold skepticism: the subjective world, though knowable, contains no certainty of its objective truth, and the external world, while able to be perceived, is viewed and interpreted only through the unreliable human mind. Hume's skepticism has proven to be a serious challenge to later thinkers.

Reading the Selection

This selection from Book I of *A Treatise of Human Nature* deals with the topic of reason and shows Hume's empirical/skeptical method in action. Like other thinkers of the day, he wanted philosophy to achieve the same level of truth as was done in the sciences, namely, "rules [that] are certain and infallible." He then demonstrated the uncertainty of reason and claimed "all knowledge degenerates into probability." Thus, there is no truth, only skepticism.

Skepticism did not lead Hume to despair. Rather, he claimed to live in ignorance of his theory: "[N]either I, nor any other person was ever sincerely and constantly of that [skeptical] opinion." Elsewhere, Hume makes it clear that his theorizing did not interfere with his own happiness: "I dine, I play a game of back-gammon [a board game with checkers], I converse, and am merry with my friends; and when . . . I would return to these speculations, they appear so cold, and strain'd, and ridiculous, that I cannot find in my heart to enter into them any further."

∽

Book I, Of the Understanding
Part IV, Of the Sceptical and Other Systems of Philosophy

Sect. I

OF SCEPTICISM WITH REGARD TO REASON

In all demonstrative sciences the rules are certain and infallible; but when we apply them, our fallible and uncertain faculties are very apt to depart from them, and fall into error. We must, therefore, in every reasoning form a new judgment, as a check or controul on our first judgment or belief; and must enlarge our view to comprehend a kind of history of all the instances, wherein our understanding has deceiv'd us, compar'd with those, wherein its testimony was just and true. Our reason must be consider'd as a kind of cause, of which truth is the natural effect; but such-a-one as by the irruption of other causes, and by the inconstancy of our mental powers, may frequently be prevented. By this means all knowledge degenerates into probability; and this probability is greater or less, according to our experience of the veracity or deceitfulness of our understanding, and according to the simplicity or intricacy of the question.

There is no Algebraist[3] nor Mathematician so expert in his science, as to place entire confidence in any truth immediately upon his discovery of it, or regard it as any thing, but a mere probability. Every time he runs over his proofs, his confidence encreases; but still more by the approbation of his friends; and is rais'd to its utmost perfection by the universal assent and applauses of the learned world. Now 'tis evident, that this gradual encrease of assurance is nothing but the addition of new probabilities, and is deriv'd from the constant union of causes and effects, according to past experience and observation.

_____

[3] **Algebraist** A person skilled in algebra.

In accompts[4] of any length or importance, Merchants seldom trust to the infallible certainty of numbers for their security; but by the artificial structure of the accompts, produce a probability beyond what is deriv'd from the skill and experience of the accomptant.[5] For that is plainly of itself some degree of probability; tho' uncertain and variable, according to the degrees of his experience and length of the accompt. Now as none will maintain, that our assurance in a long numeration exceeds probability, I may safely affirm, that there scarce is any proposition concerning numbers, of which we can have a fuller security. For 'tis easily possible, by gradually diminishing the numbers, to reduce the longest series of addition to the most simple question, which can be form'd, to an addition of two single numbers; and upon this supposition we shall find it impracticable to shew the precise limits of knowledge and of probability, or discover that particular number, at which the one ends and the other begins. But knowledge and probability are of such contrary and disagreeing natures, that they cannot well run insensibly into each other, and that because they will not divide, but must be either entirely present, or entirely absent. Besides, if any single addition were certain, every one wou'd be so, and consequently the whole or total sum; unless the whole can be different from all its parts. I had almost said, that this was certain; but I reflect, that it must reduce *itself,* as well as every other reasoning, and from knowledge, degenerate into probability.

Since therefore all knowledge resolves itself into probability, and becomes at last of the same nature with that evidence, which we employ in common life, we must now examine this latter species of reasoning, and see on what foundation it stands.

In every judgment, which we can form concerning probability, as well as concerning knowledge, we ought always to correct the first judgment, deriv'd from the nature of the object, by another judgment, deriv'd from the nature of the understanding. 'Tis certain a man of solid sense and long experience ought to have, and usually has, a greater assurance in his opinions, than one that is foolish and ignorant, and that our sentiments have different degrees of authority, even with ourselves, in proportion to the degrees of our reason and experience. In the man of the best sense and longest experience, this authority is never entire; since even such-a-one must be conscious of many errors in the past, and must still dread the like for the future. Here then arises a new species of probability to correct and regulate the first, and fix its just standard and proportion. As demonstration is subject to the controul of probability, so is probability liable to a new correction by a reflex act of the mind, wherein the nature of our understanding, and our reasoning from the first probability become our objects.

Having thus found in every probability, beside the original uncertainty inherent in the subject, a new uncertainty deriv'd from the weakness of that faculty, which judges, and having adjusted these two together, we are oblig'd by our reason to add a new doubt deriv'd from the possibility of error in the estimation we make of the truth and fidelity of our faculties. This is a doubt, which immediately occurs to us, and of which, if we wou'd closely pursue our reason, we cannot avoid giving a decision. But this decision, tho' it shou'd be favourable to our preceeding judgement, being founded only on probability, must weaken still further our first evidence, and must itself be weaken'd by a fourth doubt of the same kind, and so on *in infinitum*[6] till at last there remain nothing of the original probability, however great we may suppose it to have been, and however small the diminution by every new uncertainty. No finite object can subsist under a decrease repeated *in infinitum;* and even the vastest quantity, which can enter into human imagination, must in this manner be reduc'd to nothing. Let our first belief be never so strong, it must infallibly perish by passing thro' so many new examinations, of which each diminishes somewhat of its force and vigour. When I reflect on the natural fallibility of my judgment, I have less confidence in my opinions, than when I only consider the objects concerning which I reason; and when I proceed still farther, to turn the scrutiny against every successive estimation I make of my faculties, all the rules of logic require a continual diminution, and at last a total extinction of belief and evidence.

Shou'd it here be ask'd me, whether I sincerely assent to this argument, which I seem to take such pains to inculcate, and whether I be really one of those sceptics, who hold that all is uncertain, and that our judgment is not in *any* thing possest of *any* measures of truth and falshood; I shou'd reply, that this question is entirely superfluous, and that neither I, nor any other person was ever sincerely and constantly of that opinion. Nature, by an absolute and uncontroulable necessity has determin'd us to judge as well as to breathe and feel; nor can we any more forbear viewing certain objects in a stronger and fuller light, upon account of their customary connexion with a present impression, than we can hinder ourselves from thinking as long as we are awake, or seeing the surrounding bodies, when we turn our eyes towards them in broad sunshine. Whoever has taken the pains to refute the cavils[7] of this *total* scepticism, has really disputed without an antagonist, and endeavour'd by arguments to establish a faculty, which nature has antecedently implanted in the mind, and render'd unavoidable.

My intention then in displaying so carefully the arguments of that fantastic sect,[8] is only to make the reader sensible of the truth of my hypothesis, *that all our reasonings concerning causes and effects are deriv'd from nothing but custom; and that belief is more properly an act of the sensitive*[9] *than of the cogitative*[10] *part of our natures.*

---

[4] **accompts** Accounts.
[5] **accomptant** Accountant.

[6] *in infinitum* Latin, "forever."
[7] **cavils** Petty objections.
[8] **fantastic sect** Hume's rhetorical term for "total skeptics."
[9] **sensitive** Having to do with the senses.
[10] **cogitative** Having to do with the mind.

. . .

Sect. VI

OF PERSONAL IDENTITY

There are some philosophers,[11] who imagine we are every moment intimately conscious of what we call our SELF; that we feel its existence and its continuance in existence; and are certain, beyond the evidence of a demonstration, both of its perfect identity and simplicity. The strongest sensation, the most violent passion, say they, instead of distracting us from this view, only fix it the more intensely, and make us consider their influence on *self* either by their pain or pleasure. To attempt a farther proof of this were to weaken its evidence; since no proof can be deriv'd from any fact, of which we are so intimately conscious; nor is there any thing, of which we can be certain, if we doubt of this.

Unluckily all these positive assertions are contrary to that very experience, which is pleaded for them, nor have we any idea of *self*, after the manner it is here explain'd. For from what impression cou'd this idea be deriv'd?[12] This question 'tis impossible to answer without a manifest contradiction and absurdity; and yet 'tis a question, which must necessarily be answer'd, if we wou'd have the idea of self pass for clear and intelligible. It must be some one impression, that gives rise to every real idea. But self or person is not any one impression, but that to which our several impressions and ideas are suppos'd to have a reference. If any impression gives rise to the idea of self, that impression must continue invariably the same, thro' the whole course of our lives; since self is suppos'd to exist after that manner. But there is no impression constant and invariable. Pain and pleasure, grief and joy, passions and sensations succeed each other, and never all exist at the same time. It cannot, therefore, be from any of these impressions, or from any other, that the idea of self is deriv'd; and consequently there is no such idea.

But farther, what must become of all our particular perceptions upon this hypothesis? All these are different, and distinguishable, and separable from each other, and may be separately and have no need of any thing to support their existence. After what manner, therefore, do they belong to self; and how are they connected with it? For my part, when I enter most intimately into what I call *myself*, I always stumble on some particular perception or other, of heat or cold, light or shade, love or hatred, pain or pleasure. I never can catch *myself* at any time without a perception, and never can observe any thing but the perception. When my perceptions are remov'd for any time, as by sound-sleep; so long am I insensible of *myself*, and may truly be said not to exist. And were all my perceptions remov'd by death, and cou'd I neither think, nor feel, nor see, nor love, nor hate after the dissolution of my body, I shou'd be entirely annihilated, nor do I conceive what is farther requisite to make me a perfect non-entity. If any one upon serious and unprejudic'd reflection, thinks he has a different notion of *himself*, I must confess I can reason no longer with him. All I can allow him is, that he may be in the right as well as I, and that we are essentially different in this particular. He may perhaps, perceive something simple and continu'd, which he calls *himself*; tho' I am certain there is no such principle in me.

But setting aside some metaphysicians of this kind, I may venture to affirm of the rest of mankind, that they are nothing but a bundle or collection of different perceptions, which succeed each other with an inconceivable rapidity, and are in a perpetual flux and movement. Our eyes cannot turn in their sockets without varying our perceptions. Our thought is still more variable than our sight, and all our other senses and faculties contribute to this change; nor is there any single power of the soul, which remains unalterably the same, perhaps for one moment. The mind is a kind of theatre, where several perceptions successively make their apperance; pass, re-pass, glide away, and mingle in an infinite variety of postures and situations. There is properly no *simplicity* in it at one time, nor *identity* in different; whatever natural propension we may have to imagine that simplicity and identity. The comparison of the theatre must not mislead us. They are the successive perceptions only, that constitute the mind; nor have we the most distant notion of the place, where these scenes are represented, or of the materials, of which it is compos'd.[13]

---

[11] **philosophers** Such as Plato, Aristotle, the Stoics, and the Epicureans.

[12] **For from what . . . deriv'd?** This a key point in Hume's argument. How does the idea of *self* get into the mind? Hume maintains that it must come from a sense impression, which is a "manifest contradiction and absurdity." Thus, there is no continuously existing self.

---

[13] **The mind is a kind of theatre . . . of which it is compos'd.** Hume's theater metaphor is reminiscent of Plato's "Allegory of the Cave" (see *The Republic* in Chapter 3, Volume I), but Hume and Plato reach opposite conclusions about ultimate truth and reality.

∞

Questions for Critical Thinking

1. How does Hume explain causality, that is, cause and effect? Does his explanation make sense to you? Explain.

2. What role do the senses play in Hume's philosophy? Explain the role of the senses and the concept of "the self," in Hume's point of view.

MARY WOLLSTONECRAFT
Selection from *A Vindication of the Rights of Woman*

A Vindication of the Rights of Woman (1792) is a key text of feminism. Its author, Mary Wollstone-craft, was not the first feminist, for this cause began with Christine de Pizan (see *The Book of the City of Ladies* in Chapter 11, Volume I) in the 1400s, when it was called the "Woman Question." Wollstonecraft, however, gave feminism its modern focus (see Beauvoir's *The Second Sex* in Chapter 22) as she made women's rights part of the struggle for human rights in general.

Human rights was the defining issue of the Enlightenment, but no thinker before Woll-stonecraft, including Voltaire (see *Candide*), Rousseau (see *Confessions*), and Jefferson (see *The Declaration of Independence* in Chapter 18), even considered applying the concept of rights to women. In her treatise she forever changed the character of the debate on rights by arguing that men and women alike shared in the rights bestowed by nature. For her, the rights of liberty and equality applied to both men and women, and if fraternity made all men brothers, then men must accept that they had sisters as well.

Wollstonecraft stood in Rousseau's shadow, but she rejected his argument that the "duties" of women are "to please, to be useful to [men], to make [men] love and esteem them, to educate [men] when young, and take care of [men] when grown up, to advise, to console [men], and to render [men's] lives easy and agreeable." Although admitting that Rousseau accurately re-flected existing society, she found his view morally wrong. She argued that women, as rational creatures, should be treated like men—that is, educated for virtue. Society's goal should be the full, free expression of both sexes.

The feminism of Mary Wollstonecraft (1759–1797) sprang from her marginal status. Born into genteel poverty in England, she made her way in the world only with great difficulty. A failed career in teaching taught her the pain of being female and poor, without respect or inde-pendence. With her intellectual gifts, she was drawn into progressive circles where Enlighten-ment ideas flourished. When revolution broke out in France, she traveled to Paris, where she shared with French militants their hopes for a new society free of oppression. Back in London, she joined the radicals grouped around William Godwin (1756–1836), an ex-minister and novel-ist. When she was made pregnant by Godwin, they secretly married, fearing to offend radical friends by the disclosure of their wedding. She died in childbirth in 1797, giving life to the child later known as Mary Wollstonecraft Shelley, the author of *Frankenstein* (see Chapter 18).

Reading the Selection

This selection—the treatise's introduction—offers a summary of Wollstonecraft's views. Like Rousseau, she accepts that men are physically stronger than women; unlike Rousseau, however, she maintains that men use this fact as a pretext to impose a greater inequality than nature allows, thus keeping women in "perpetual childhood."

According to her, men keep women in their place by treating them as "alluring mis-tresses," or sex objects. To this end, men have created a vocabulary in praise of feminine virtues, such as "soft phrases . . . [and] delicacy of sentiments." These, rather than being words of praise, are in reality words of subjection to man's demands, from a love of power. She con-demns women for going along with men, in thinking themselves the "weaker vessels." Only when women can freely choose between reason and the passions, just as men do, will they become "affectionate wives and rational mothers"—the goal of this early feminist tract.

∾

Introduction

After considering the historic page, and viewing the living world with anxious solicitude, the most melancholy emotions of sorrowful indignation have depressed my spirits, and I have sighed when obliged to confess, that either nature has made a great difference between man and man, or that the civilization which has hitherto taken place in the world has been very partial. I have turned over various books written on the subject of education, and patiently observed the conduct of parents and the management of schools; but what has been the result?—a profound conviction that the neglected education of my fellow-creatures is the grand source of the misery I deplore; and that women, in particular, are rendered weak and wretched by a variety of concurring causes, originating from one hasty conclusion. The conduct and manners of women, in fact, evidently prove that their minds are not in a healthy state; for, like flowers which are planted in too rich a soil, strength and usefulness are sacrificed to beauty; and the flaunting leaves, after having pleased a fastidious eye, fade, disregarded on the stalk, long before the season when they ought to have arrived at maturity.—One cause of this barren blooming I attribute to a false system of education, gathered from the books written on this subject by men who, considering females rather as women than human creatures, have been more anxious to make them alluring mistresses than affectionate wives and rational mothers; and the understanding of the sex has been so bubbled by this specious homage, that the civilized women of the present century, with a few exceptions, are only anxious to inspire love, when they ought to cherish a nobler ambition, and by their abilities and virtues exact respect.

In a treatise, therefore, on female rights and manners, the works which have been particularly written for their improvement must not be overlooked; especially when it is asserted, in direct terms, that the minds of women are enfeebled by false refinement; that the books of instruction, written by men of genius, have had the same tendency as more frivolous productions; and that, in the true style of Mahometanism,[14] they are treated as a kind of subordinate beings, and not as a part of the human species, when improveable reason is allowed to be the dignified distinction which raises men above the brute creation, and puts a natural sceptre in a feeble hand.

Yet, because I am a woman, I would not lead my readers to suppose that I mean violently to agitate the contested question respecting the equality or inferiority of the sex; but as the subject lies in my way, and I cannot pass it over without subjecting the main tendency of my reasoning to misconstruction, I shall stop a moment to deliver, in a few words, my opinion.—In the government of the physical world it is observable that the female in point of strength is, in general, inferior to the male. This is the law of nature; and it does not appear to be suspended or abrogated in favour of women. A degree of physical superiority cannot, therefore, be denied—and it is a noble prerogative! But not content with this natural pre-eminence, men endeavour to sink us still lower, merely to render us alluring objects for a moment; and women, intoxicated by the adoration which men, under the influence of their senses, pay them, do not seek to obtain a durable interest in their hearts, or to become the friends of the fellow creatures who find amusement in their society.

I am aware of an obvious inference:—from every quarter have I heard exclamations against masculine women; but where are they to be found? If by this appellation men mean to inveigh against their ardour in hunting, shooting, and gaming, I shall most cordially join in the cry; but if it be against the imitation of manly virtues, or, more properly speaking, the attainment of those talents and virtues, the exercise of which ennobles the human character, and which raise females in the scale of animal being, when they are comprehensively termed mankind;—all those who view them with a philosophic eye must, I should think, wish with me, that they may every day grow more and more masculine.

This discussion naturally divides the subject. I shall first consider women in the grand light of human creatures, who, in common with men, are placed on this earth to unfold their faculties; and afterwards I shall more particularly point out their peculiar designation.

I wish also to steer clear of an error which many respectable writers have fallen into; for the instruction which has hitherto been addressed to women, has rather been applicable to *ladies,* if the little indirect advice, that is scattered through Sandford and Merton,[15] be excepted; but, addressing my sex in a firmer tone, I pay particular attention to those in the middle class, because they appear to be in the most natural state. Perhaps the seeds of false-refinement, immorality, and vanity, have ever been shed by the great. Weak, artificial beings, raised above the common wants and affections of their race, in a premature unnatural manner, undermine the very foundation of virtue, and spread corruption through the whole mass of society! As a class of mankind they have the strongest claim to pity; the education of the rich tends to render them vain and helpless, and the unfolding mind is not strengthened by the practice of those duties which dignify the human

---

[14] **Mahometanism** A variation of the spelling of *Mohammedanism,* or the Muslim religion, Islam.

[15] **Sandford and Merton** Thomas Day's *The History of Sandford and Merton* (1783–1789) was an attempt to explain through fiction Jean-Jacques Rousseau's ideas and doctrines on education and naturalism. Rousseau, the French *philosophe* and writer, generated many debates in the late eighteenth century. Wollstonecraft believed that Day's book had been more direct in discussing issues concerning women than most works.

character.—They only live to amuse themselves, and by the same law which in nature invariably produces certain effects, they soon only afford barren amusement.

But as I propose taking a separate view of the different ranks of society, and of the moral character of women, in each, this hint is, for the present, sufficient; and I have only alluded to the subject, because it appears to me to be the very essence of an introduction to give a cursory account of the contents of the work it introduces.

My own sex, I hope, will excuse me, if I treat them like rational creatures, instead of flattering their *fascinating* graces, and viewing them as if they were in a state of perpetual childhood, unable to stand alone. I earnestly wish to point out in what true dignity and human happiness consists—I wish to persuade women to endeavour to acquire strength, both of mind and body, and to convince them that the soft phrases, susceptibility of heart, delicacy of sentiment, and refinement of taste, are almost synonymous with epithets of weakness, and that those beings who are only the objects of pity and that kind of love, which has been termed its sister, will soon become objects of contempt.

Dismissing then those pretty feminine phrases, which the men condescendingly use to soften our slavish dependence, and despising that weak elegancy of mind, exquisite sensibility, and sweet docility of manners, supposed to be the sexual characteristics of the weaker vessel, I wish to shew that elegance is inferior to virtue, that the first object of laudable ambition is to obtain a character as a human being, regardless of the distinction of sex; and that secondary views should be brought to this simple touchstone.

This is a rough sketch of my plan; and should I express my conviction with the energetic emotions that I feel whenever I think of the subject, the dictates of experience and reflection will be felt by some of my readers. Animated by this important object, I shall disdain to cull my phrases or polish my style;—I aim at being useful, and sincerity will render me unaffected; for, wishing rather to persuade by the force of my arguments, than dazzle by the elegance of my language, I shall not waste my time in rounding periods, or in fabricating the turgid bombast of artificial feelings, which, coming from the head, never reach the heart.—I shall be employed about things, not words!—and, anxious to render my sex more respectable members of society, I shall try to avoid that flowery diction which has slided from essays into novels, and from novels into familiar letters and conversation.

These pretty superlatives, dropping glibly from the tongue, vitiate the taste, and create a kind of sickly delicacy that turns away from simple unadorned truth, and a deluge of false sentiments and overstretched feelings, stifling the natural emotions of the heart, render the domestic pleasures insipid, that ought to sweeten the exercise of those severe duties, which educate a rational and immortal being for a nobler field of action.

The education of women has, of late, been more attended to than formerly; yet they are still reckoned a frivolous sex, and ridiculed or pitied by the writers who endeavour by satire or instruction to improve them. It is acknowledged that they spend many of the first years of their lives in acquiring a smattering of accomplishments; meanwhile strength of body and mind are sacrificed to libertine notions of beauty, to the desire of establishing themselves,—the only way women can rise in the world,—by marriage. And this desire making mere animals of them, when they marry they act as such children may be expected to act—they dress; they paint, and nickname God's creatures.—Surely these weak beings are only fit for a seraglio[16]!—Can they be expected to govern a family with judgment, or take care of the poor babes whom they bring into the world?

If then it can be fairly deduced from the present conduct of the sex, from the prevalent fondness for pleasure which takes place of ambition and those nobler passions that open and enlarge the soul; that the instruction which women have hitherto received has only tended, with the constitution of civil society, to render them insignificant objects of desire—mere propagators of fools!—if it can be proved that in aiming to accomplish them, without cultivating their understandings, they are taken out of their sphere of duties, and made ridiculous and useless when the short-lived bloom of beauty is over, I presume that *rational* men will excuse me for endeavouring to persuade them to become more masculine and respectable.

Indeed the word masculine is only a bugbear: there is little reason to fear that women will acquire too much courage or fortitude; for their apparent inferiority with respect to bodily strength, must render them, in some degree, dependent on men in the various relations of life, but why should it be increased by prejudices that give a sex to virtue, and confound simple truths with sensual reveries?

Women are, in fact, so much degraded by mistaken notions of female excellence, that I do not mean to add a paradox when I assert, that this artificial weakness produces a propensity to tyrannize, and gives birth to cunning, the natural opponent of strength, which leads them to play off those contemptible infantine airs that undermine esteem even whilst they excite desire. Let men become more chaste and modest, and if women do not grow wiser in the same ratio, it will be clear that they have weaker understandings. It seems scarcely necessary to say, that I now speak of the sex in general. Many individuals have more sense than their male relatives; and, as nothing preponderates where there is a constant struggle for an equilibrium, without it has naturally more gravity, some women govern their husbands without degrading themselves, because intellect will always govern.

---

[16] **seraglio** Harem.

Questions for Critical Thinking

1. How does Wollstonecraft explain the position of women in her own day?

2. What is Wollstonecraft's vision of true relations between the sexes? Compare and contrast her views with the situation today.

DENIS DIDEROT
Selections from *Encyclopédie*

In France the *Encyclopédie,* issued between 1751 and 1772, expressed the ideals and vision of the Enlightenment—the eighteenth-century movement that was devoted to a critical reexamination of accepted doctrines and institutions from the point of view of rationalism (as defined by Francis Bacon, René Descartes, and John Locke) and Newtonian science. In twenty-eight volumes, of which seventeen were text and eleven were plates and illustrations, this vast work was perhaps the most ambitious publishing venture of its day. Embracing the Enlightenment ideal that knowledge is useful, the *Encyclopédie* covered practical knowledge (explaining the arts, crafts, and technology, and most especially, how things are manufactured, traded, and used) and philosophical knowledge (describing existing institutions and beliefs and critiquing their underlying rationales). This project engaged the talents of more than 160 writers, who, although not always in agreement, were deeply committed to freeing their age from the ignorance and prejudices of the past. These *philosophes,* as the encyclopedists were also known, shared a vision that reason and science, when applied to human affairs, would have a progressive effect on individuals and society. Applicable to all races and classes, this vision called for a universal standard of moral behavior, assuring a sense of dignity to everyone based on a uniform code of civil rights.

The *Encyclopédie*'s editor was Denis Diderot (1713–1784), who performed heroically under fire. Sharing chores with Diderot was the eloquent and scientific-minded Jean Le Rond d'Alembert (1717–1783), who took charge of the essays on mathematics and physics. Nevertheless, Diderot was the project's guiding spirit. For more than twenty years, he fought and outmaneuvered the French censors, confronted printed attacks by Catholic leaders, most notably the Jesuits, and still kept the presses running, by means of subterfuge when they were officially shut by the state. At the same time, he was managing the project's financial affairs, meeting deadlines, writing many of the essays himself, and most difficult of all, soothing the egos of his famous contributors, such as Voltaire (who wrote over forty essays), Rousseau, and Montesquieu. Besides editing the *Encyclopédie,* Diderot wrote plays, novels, and critical essays on art, the latter helping to establish the field of art history. He was later befriended by Russia's Catherine the Great (r. 1762–1796), at whose court he spent one of his last years.

Reading the Selections

"Encyclopedia" and "Intolerance" were written by Diderot, and both reflect his faith in the moral value of learning. In "Encyclopedia," he first defines an encyclopedia's purpose: to collect and preserve all knowledge to the end that future generations will be "more virtuous and happier." He next expresses the hope that posterity will honor the encyclopedists for their efforts to improve human life. He then pleads for full examination of "all things," "without exception and without regard for anyone's feelings," so that the arts and sciences will be widely understood and thus benefit all people, rather than the current few.

The second selection concerns intolerance, which Diderot defines as "a violent emotion inciting people to hate and persecute individuals with erroneous notions." His hatred of intolerance is based on the philosophes' view that centuries of privilege and arrogance enjoyed by the church and its leaders have resulted in the institutionalization of intolerance. Perhaps to avoid the wrath of the church censors, Diderot focuses on secular intolerance, in both its passive form—the breaking of social ties—and its violent form—persecution by all sorts of means. Calling for tolerance, he invokes the words of St. Paul, the church fathers, and Jesus Christ. He asks that the intolerant open their eyes to the cruelty resulting from their feelings, and he calls for the tolerant to join in destroying the "atrocious system" of bigotry that is an "injustice in the eyes of God and man." Diderot's impassioned request for tolerance is as relevant today as it was when he wrote this essay.

ENCYCLOPEDIA, f. n. *(Philosophy)*. This word means the [1] *interrelation of all knowledge;* it is made up of the Greek prefix *en,* in, and the noun *kyklos,* circle, and *paideia,* instruction, science, knowledge. In truth, the aim of an *encyclopedia* is to collect all the knowledge scattered over the face of the earth, to present its general outlines and structure to the men with whom we live, and to transmit this to those who will come after us, so that the work of past centuries may be useful to the following centuries, that our children, by becoming more educated, may at the same time become more virtuous and happier, and that we may not die without having deserved well of the human race.

. . .

We have seen that our *Encyclopedia* could only have been the endeavor of a philosophical century; that this age has dawned, and that fame, while raising to immortality the names of those who will perfect man's knowledge in the future, will perhaps not disdain to remember our own names. We have been heartened by the ever so consoling and agreeable idea that people may speak to one another about us, too, when we shall no longer be alive; we have been encouraged by hearing from the mouths of a few of our contemporaries a certain voluptuous murmur that suggests what may be said of us by those happy and educated men in whose interests we have sacrificed ourselves, whom we esteem and whom we love, even though they have not yet been born. We have felt within ourselves the development of those seeds of emulation which have moved us to renounce the better part of ourselves to accomplish our task, and which have ravished away into the void the few moments of our existence of which we are genuinely proud. Indeed, man reveals himself to his contemporaries and is seen by them for what he is: a peculiar mixture of sublime attributes and shameful weaknesses. But our weaknesses follow our mortal remains into the tomb and disappear with them; the same earth covers them both, and there remains only the total result of our attributes immortalized in the monuments we raise to ourselves or in the memorials that we owe to public

respect and gratitude—honors which a proper awareness of our own deserts enables us to enjoy in anticipation, an enjoyment that is as pure, as great, and as real as any other pleasure and in which there is nothing imaginary except, perhaps, the titles on which we base our pretensions. Our own claims are deposited in the pages of this work, and posterity will judge them.

I have said that it could only belong to a philosophical age to attempt an *encyclopedia;* and I have said this because such a work constantly demands more intellectual daring than is commonly found in ages of pusillanimous taste. All things must be examined, debated, investigated without exception and without regard for anyone's feelings. . . . We must ride roughshod over all these ancient puerilities, overturn the barriers that reason never erected, give back to the arts and sciences the liberty that is so precious to them. . . . We have for quite some time needed a reasoning age when men would no longer seek the rules in classical authors but in nature, when men would be conscious of what is false and true about so many arbitrary treatises on aesthetics: and I take the term *treatise on aesthetics* in its most general meaning, that of a system of given rules to which it is claimed that one must conform in any genre whatsoever in order to succeed.

. . .

INTOLERANCE, f. n. *(Ethics)*. It is generally understood [1] that intolerance is a violent emotion inciting people to hate and persecute individuals with erroneous notions. For the sake of clarity let us first distinguish between ecclesiastic and secular forms of *intolerance.*

Ecclesiastic *intolerance* consists in regarding as false all other religions except one's own and in demonstrating or shouting this true religion from the rooftops without being stopped by any form of terror, sense of decency, or even the risk of death. This article will not be concerned with the particular heroism that created so many martyrs in the long history of the Church.

Secular *intolerance* consists in breaking off all relations with those people who have a different conception and way of worshiping God and in persecuting them by all sorts of violent means.

A few extracts from Holy Scripture, the Fathers of the Church, and various ecclesiastic councils will be sufficient to show that the *intolerant* person, according to the second definition, is an evil man, a bad Christian, a dangerous individual, a bad politician, and a bad citizen.

Before we begin to quote from some of these most re- 5 spectable authorities, we must give credit to our Catholic theologians because several of them have endorsed the following opinions without any reservations.

Tertullian[17] said (*Apolog. ad Scapul*): *Humani juris et naturalis potestatis est unicuique quod putaverit, colere; nec alii obest aut prodest alterius religio. Sed nec religionis est cogere religionem quae sponte suscipi debeat, non vi; cum et hostiae ab animo lubenti expostulentur.*

This is what the weak and persecuted Christians pointed out to the idolaters who forced them to kneel at their altars.

It is impious to expose religion to the odious charges of being tyrannical, severe, unjust, and unsociable, even with the intent of bringing back to the fold those people who have unfortunately strayed.

The mind can only consent to what seems true, the heart can only love what appears good. Force will make a hypocrite out of a weak man, but a martyr out of a courageous one. Whether weak or courageous, he will feel the injustice of persecution and become indignant.

Education, persuasion, and prayer are the only legiti- 10 mate means of spreading religious faith.

Any method that produces hatred, indignation, and contempt is impious.

Any method that arouses the passions and supports selfish interests is impious.

Any method that weakens the natural bonds of the family and alienates fathers from their children, brothers from brothers, and sisters from sisters is impious.

Any method that would tend to stir up men, to arm nations, and to soak the earth with blood is impious.

It is impious to want to impose laws upon man's con- 15 science: this is a universal rule of conduct. People must be enlightened and not constrained.

Men who are sincerely mistaken are to be pitied, never to be punished.

Neither sincere nor dishonest men should be tormented: they should be abandoned to the judgment of God.

If you break off all bonds of friendship with an individual who is considered impious, then you will also break off all ties with those people who are considered miserly, immodest, ambitious, irascible, and vicious. You will soon advise your friends to break off relations with these people, and three or four *intolerant* individuals will be sufficient to destroy an entire society.

If you can pull out a hair from the head of a person who thinks differently than we do, then his head is also at your disposal, because there are no limits set for injustice. Either profit or fanaticism, the moment or the circumstance will decide whether the greater or the lesser evil will be allowed.

If a prince who is an unbeliever were to ask the mis- 20 sionaries of an *intolerant* religion how they treat those who do not believe in their faith, they would have to acknowledge an odious thing, lie, or remain shamefully silent.

What did Christ recommend to his disciples when he sent them among the Gentiles? Was it to kill or to die? Was it to persecute or to suffer?

Saint Paul wrote to the Thessalonians: *If someone should come among you proclaiming another Christ or another Holy Ghost and preaching another Gospel, you will suffer his presence.*—Intolerant people! Is it in this fashion that you treat those who have nothing to propose, nothing to announce, and nothing to preach?

Furthermore, he wrote: *Do not look on any man as an enemy because he does not share our views; only warn him as a brother. Intolerant people!* Is this the way you act?

If your opinions entitle you to hate me, why will not my opinions also entitle me to hate you?

If you cry out that the truth is on your side, I will cry 25 out as loudly that I have the truth on my side, but I will add: it does not matter who is mistaken, provided that there is peace among us. If I am blind, must you strike a blind person in the face?

If an *intolerant* person were to explain clearly what he is, which corner of the earth would not be closed to him? And where is the sensible man who would dare to approach the country where this *intolerant* person lives?

You can read in Origen, in Minutius Felix, and in the Fathers of the Church[18] during the first three centuries the following comments: *Religion persuades, and does not command. Man must have a free choice in the form of his worship; the persecutor causes his God to be hated; the persecutor slanders his own religion.* Tell me if it was ignorance or deception that created these maxims?

In an *intolerant* state the prince would only be a torturer in the pay of the priest. The prince is the universal father of his subjects; and his apostolate is to make them all happy.

---

[17] **Tertullian** Second- and third-century Christian writer who, as a convert, became a teacher and later a hermit. He led a small band of Christians who left the church and founded their own sect. He wrote many treatises on morals and discipline and attacked his critics in his other works.

Tertullian's Latin passage "It is a fundamental human right and a law of nature that any and every man should worship in accordance with his own views, for the beliefs of one are of no value to another. Moreover, it is not consistent with the essence of religious belief to force itself on anyone, for it should be received of one's own free will: even sacrificial victims are demanded in a pleasant manner."

---

[18] **Origen, Minutius Felix, and the Fathers of the Church** Origen, the third-century Greek Christian leader, wrote a book on the Old Testament, on prayer, and a strong defense of Christianity against pagan philosophers. Minutius Felix, better known as Minucius Felix, converted to Christianity in the third century. He wrote a dialogue between a Christian and a pagan in which the Christian defended his faith and refuted all the arguments of his adversary. The Fathers of the Church refers to the early Christian leaders and writers, including St. Augustine, St. Jerome, and St. Ambrose.

If one had to proclaim a law in order to treat people in a severe manner, there would not be any tyrants.

On some occasions we are as strongly persuaded by error as by truth. This fact can only be contested by those individuals who were never sincerely mistaken. [30]

If your truth ostracizes me, then my error that I take for the truth will likewise ostracize you.

Stop being violent, or stop reproaching pagans and Muslims for their violence.

Is it the spirit of God that moves you to hate your brother and preach hatred to your neighbor?

Christ said: *My kingdom is not of this world.* And you, his disciple, you want to tyrannize the world!

He said: *I am gentle and lowly in heart.* Are you gentle and lowly in heart? [35]

He said: *Blessed are the meek, the peacemakers, and the merciful.* Examine your conscience and see if you deserve this blessing; are you meek, peacemakers, and merciful?

He said: *I am the lamb who was led to the slaughter without complaining.* And you are quite ready to take the butcher's knife and cut the throat of the one for whom the blood of the lamb was shed.

He said: *When they persecute you, flee.* And you chase those who will let you speak and who do not ask for anything more than to live peacefully by your side.

He said: *You would like me to send down the wrath of heaven upon your enemies; you do not know what spirit moves you.* And I repeat for you His very words: *intolerant* people, you do not know what spirit moves you.

Listen to Saint John: *My children, love one another.* [40]

Saint Athanasius:[19] *If they persecute you, this alone is clear proof that they are neither pious nor do they fear God. It is the very nature of piety not to constrain but to persuade, in imitation of our Lord who allowed everyone the freedom to follow him. As for the devil, since he does not possess the truth, he comes with hatchets and axes.*

Saint John Chrysostom:[20] *Jesus Christ asked his disciples if they also want to go away in peace, for this must be the attitude of the person who does not do violence to anyone.*

Salvien:[21] *These men are deluded, but they do not know it. In our company they are mistaken, but with their own kind they are not mistaken. They consider themselves such good Catholics that they call us heretics. What they are in our eyes, we are in theirs. They are misguided but have good intentions. What will be their fate? Only the Great Judge knows. Until the final judgment He tolerates them.*

Saint Augustine:[22] *Let those people abuse you, who know not how difficult it is to find the truth and not be deceived. Let those people abuse you, who know not how extraordinary and painful it is to master the fantasms of the flesh. Let those people abuse you, who know not that it is necessary to moan and sigh to understand something from God. Let those people abuse you, who have not fallen into error.*

Saint Hilary:[23] *You use constraint in a cause where only reason is necessary; you employ force where only understanding is necessary.* [45]

The Constitutions of the Holy Pope Clement I: *The Lord left to men the use of their free will, not punishing them with a temporal death but summoning them into the other world to account for their actions.*

The Fathers of a council of Toledo: *Do no violence of any kind to people in order to lead them back to the faith, for God is merciful or severe to whomever He chooses.*

We could fill volumes with these frequently forgotten quotations from the Christians of our day.

Saint Martin[24] repented his entire life for having communicated with the persecutors of heretics.

All wise men have disapproved the violence committed against the Samaritans by Emperor Justinian.[25] [50]

Writers who have advised penal laws against disbelief have been detested.

Recently the apologist of the Revocation of the Edict of Nantes[26] was considered a bloody creature with whom it was advisable not to share the same roof.

Which is the true voice of humanity, the persecutor who strikes or the persecuted who moans?

If an unbelieving prince has an undeniable right to demand obedience from his subject, does not an infidel subject have an undeniable right to demand the protection of his prince? It is a reciprocal obligation.

If the prince says that the infidel subject does not deserve to live, is it not to be feared that the subject might say that the infidel prince does not deserve to rule? *Intolerant people,* men of blood, see the consequences of your principles and shudder. Men of good will, whatever your beliefs, it is for you that I have collected these thoughts, and I beg you to meditate upon them. If you do so, then you will renounce an atrocious system that is not proper for an honest mind and a kind heart. [55]

Effect your own salvation. Pray for mine, and believe that everything that you allow yourself beyond this is an abominable injustice in the eyes of God and man.

—(DIDEROT)

---

[19] **St. Athanasius** Fourth-century Greek theologian who became embroiled in many disputes in the early years of the church. His views eventually became orthodox.
[20] **Saint John Chrysostom** Fourth-century Syrian church leader. Called *Chrysostom*, or "Golden Mouth," because of his sermons and preaching. Author of many homilies and commentaries.
[21] **Salvien** Salvianus, a fifth-century German priest who wrote books on Christian doctrines.
[22] **Saint Augustine** Fourth- and early-fifth-century Christian leader and author who formulated many orthodox positions and doctrines that still guide the Roman Catholic Church.

[23] **Saint Hilary** Fourth-century French church leader who wrote several works and a book of hymns.
[24] **Saint Martin** Fourth-century French prelate and leader of church. A protégé of St. Hilary, he became a monk and founded a monastery. Patron saint of France.
[25] **Emperor Justinian** Sixth-century ruler of the Eastern Roman Empire whose armies conquered many lands.
[26] **Revocation of the Edict of Nantes** The Edict of Nantes of 1598 guaranteed religious freedom to a group of French Protestants known as the Huguenots, but Louis XIV revoked the Edict in 1685. Many Huguenots left France and settled in other parts of Europe and the New World.

Questions for Critical Thinking

1. What function does Diderot think that an encyclopedia serves? What is the source of Diderot's optimism?

2. What are Diderot's views on intolerance in both ecclesiastical and secular forms? Compare and contrast his views with the situation in today's world.

ADAM SMITH

Selections from *An Inquiry into the Nature and Causes of the Wealth of Nations*

Adam Smith (1723–1790), the Scottish social philosopher and political economist, was a major figure of the Age of Reason. Although he wrote on moral philosophy (the study of human conduct and values), he is most famous for his study of political economy or economics and produced what was the first and, in many ways, the most influential study of the then-emerging capitalistic system. Over the past two centuries *The Wealth of Nations*, as it is now called, has become the bible of industrial capitalism.

Little is known of Smith's early life. He came from a modest but secure background and received a standard elementary education. He entered the University of Glasgow at age fourteen (not unusual in the eighteenth century) where he studied moral philosophy—in today's terms, philosophy, ethics, theology, jurisprudence, sociology, history, and economics. Upon graduation in 1740, Smith matriculated at Oxford University, where he read (the English term for *studied*) literature and the classics. He then returned to Scotland and, in 1752, was appointed professor of moral philosophy at the University of Glasgow. He lectured and wrote essays and tracts on moral philosophy and published his first book, which quickly established his reputation: *The Theory of the Moral Sentiments,* a treatise on human nature. During these years he formed a close and lasting friendship with the Scottish philosopher David Hume (see A *Treatise of Human Nature*). A turning point came in Smith's life, in 1764, when he became the private tutor of the young Duke of Buccleuch and spent the next two years in Europe. While in Europe, Smith visited Voltaire (see *Candide*) and, in Paris, met the French physiocrats, a group of social and economic reformers who were attempting to revitalize their nation's economy. From 1767 to 1776, he divided his time between London and Scotland, working on *The Wealth of Nations,* which was published in 1776. His book was an instant success—going through five editions in his lifetime. Moreover, Smith's argument justifying what later came to be called laissez-faire capitalism immediately began to change opinions on how the economy worked, and furnished English businessmen the rationale they needed to justify their actions. Smith returned to Scotland to become the commissioner of customs in Edinburgh (1778), where he was treated as an intellectual celebrity until his death in 1790.

Adam Smith was not interested in providing entrepreneurs with a justification to make money; indeed, he often criticized their motives and purposes. He was, as a product of the Enlightenment, concerned with larger and more profound issues. As the full title of his book states, Smith's intention was to inquire, that is, to investigate, the nature of why and how nations gained wealth. In the broader context of his earlier work on moral philosophy, Smith wanted to explore, from a historical point of view, how was it that some societies generated and accumulated wealth and others did not. After examining several economic models, Smith concluded that a free-market system founded on private property created the most wealth for the greatest number of individuals as long as the process was held in check by certain forces, including what he called the "invisible hand" and the "law" of supply and demand. At a more fundamental level, he was also concerned about the nature of human behavior and what motivated humans to act as they did in a civil society. Rather than making a set of assumptions or having a predetermined outcome in mind, as was the way most scholars then approached their subjects, Smith applied empirical data and historical evidence and observed the world around him to inquire into his topic. By these innovative research methods Smith inadvertently helped establish modern economic studies.

Reading the Selections

The "Introduction and Plan of the Work" lays out what Smith will discuss in the five "books" in the *Wealth of Nations*. In this overview Smith makes it clear that he believes that labor, not wages or rent, generates wealth and, thus, fosters the well-being of a society or nation. Chapter I of Book I, on the division of labor, is Smith's famous demonstration of how, in the making of pins, all manufacturing can be made more efficient and profitable, and he discusses how the cultivation of land and the use of labor produces certain crops, such as corn (wheat or grain in American English), silk, and wool. Chapter II examines two topics: self-interest, one of the basic motives of human behavior and how self-interest works to the good of society; and the role of "natural talent." In the third selection, from Book V, Smith explains the necessity, purposes, and characteristics of taxes.

∞

Introduction and Plan of the Work

The annual labour of every nation is the fund which originally supplies it with all the necessaries and conveniences of life which it annually consumes, and which consist always either in the immediate produce of that labour, or in what is purchased with that produce from other nations.

According therefore as this produce, or what is purchased with it, bears a greater or smaller proportion to the number of those who are to consume it, the nation will be better or worse supplied with all the necessaries and conveniences for which it has occasion.

But this proportion must in every nation be regulated by two different circumstances; first, by the skill, dexterity, and judgment with which its labour is generally applied; and, secondly, by the proportion between the number of those who are employed in useful labour, and that of those who are not so employed. Whatever be the soil, climate, or extent of territory of any particular nation, the abundance or scantiness of its annual supply must, in that particular situation, depend upon those two circumstances.

The abundance or scantiness of this supply, too, seems to depend more upon the former of those two circumstances than upon the latter. Among the savage nations of hunters and fishers, every individual who is able to work, is more or less employed in useful labour, and endeavours to provide, as well as he can, the necessaries and conveniences of life, for himself, of such of his family or tribe as are either too old, or too young, or too infirm to go a hunting and fishing. Such nations, however, are so miserably poor that, from mere want, they are frequently reduced, or, at least, think themselves reduced, to the necessity sometimes of directly destroying, and sometimes of abandoning their infants, their old people, and those afflicted with lingering diseases, to perish with hunger, or to be devoured by wild beasts. Among civilised and thriving nations, on the contrary, though a great number of people do not labour at all, many of whom consume the produce of ten times, frequently of a hundred times more labour than the greater part of those who work; yet the produce of the whole labour of the society is so great that all are often abundantly supplied, and a workman, even of the lowest and poorest order, if he is frugal and industrious, may enjoy a greater share of the necessaries and conveniences of life than it is possible for any savage to acquire.

The causes of this improvement, in the productive powers of labour, and the order, according to which its produce is naturally distributed among the different ranks and conditions of men in the society, make the subject of the first book of this Inquiry.

Whatever be the actual state of the skill, dexterity, and judgment with which labour is applied in any nation, the abundance or scantiness of its annual supply must depend, during the continuance of that state, upon the proportion between the number of those who are annually employed in useful labour, and that of those who are not so employed. The number of useful and productive labourers, it will hereafter appear, is everywhere in proportion to the quantity of capital stock which is employed in setting them to work, and to the particular way in which it is so employed. The second book, therefore, treats of the nature of capital stock, of the manner in which it is gradually accumulated, and of the different quantities of labour which it puts into motion, according to the different ways in which it is employed.

Nations tolerably well advanced as to skill, dexterity, and judgment, in the application of labour, have followed very different plans in the general conduct or direction of it; and those plans have not all been equally favourable to the greatness of its produce. The policy of some nations has given extraordinary encouragement to the industry of the country; that of others to the industry of towns. Scarce any nation has dealt equally and impartially with every sort of industry. Since the downfall of the Roman empire, the policy of Europe has been more favourable to arts, manufactures, and commerce, the industry of towns, than to agriculture, the industry of the country. The circumstances which seem to have introduced and established this policy are explained in the third book.

Though those different plans were, perhaps, first introduced by the private interests and prejudices of particular orders of men, without any regard to, or foresight of, their consequences upon the general welfare of the society; yet they have given occasion to very different theories of political economy; of which some magnify the importance of that industry which is carried on in towns, others of that which is carried on in the country. Those theories have had a considerable influence, not only upon the opinions of men of learning, but upon the public conduct of princes and sovereign states. I have endeavoured, in the fourth book, to explain, as fully and distinctly as I can, those different theories, and the principal effects which they have produced in different ages and nations.

To explain in what has consisted the revenue of the great body of the people, or what has been the nature of those funds which, in different ages and nations, have supplied their annual consumption, is the object of these four first books. The fifth and last book treats of the revenue of the sovereign, or commonwealth. In this book I have endeavoured to show, first, what are the necessary expenses of the sovereign, or commonwealth; which of those expenses ought to be defrayed by the general contribution of the whole society; and which of them by that of some particular part only, or of some particular members of it: secondly, what are the different methods in which the whole society may be made to contribute towards defraying the expenses incumbent on the whole society, and what are the principal advantages and inconveniences of each of those methods: and, thirdly and lastly, what are the reasons and causes which have induced almost all modern governments to mortgage some part of this revenue, or to contract debts, and what have been the effects of those debts upon the real wealth, the annual produce of the land and labour of the society.

Book I

Of the Causes of Improvement in the Productive Powers of Labour, and of the Order According to Which Its Produce Is Naturally Distributed among the Different Ranks of the People

Chapter I

OF THE DIVISION OF LABOUR

The greatest improvement in the productive powers of labour, and the greater part of the skill, dexterity, and judgment with which it is anywhere directed, or applied, seem to have been the effects of the division of labour.

The effects of the division of labour, in the general business of society, will be more easily understood by considering in what manner it operates in some particular manufactures. It is commonly supposed to be carried furthest in some very trifling ones; not perhaps that it really is carried further in them than in others of more importance; but in those trifling manufactures which are destined to supply the small wants of but a small number of people, the whole number of workmen must necessarily be small; and those employed in every different branch of the work can often be collected into the same workhouse, and placed at once under the view of the spectator. In those great manufactures, on the contrary, which are destined to supply the great wants of the great body of the people, every different branch of the work employs so great a number of workmen that it is impossible to collect them all into the same workhouse. We can seldom see more, at one time, than those employed in one single branch. Though in such manufactures, therefore, the work may really be divided into a much greater number of parts than in those of a more trifling nature, the division is not near so obvious, and has accordingly been much less observed.

To take an example, therefore, from a very trifling manufacture; but one in which the division of labour has been very often taken notice of, the trade of the pinmaker; a workman not educated to this business (which the division of labour has rendered a distinct trade), not acquainted with the use of the machinery employed in it (to the invention of which the same division of labour has probably given occasion), could scarce, perhaps, with his utmost industry, make one pin in a day, and certainly could not make twenty. But in the way in which this business is now carried on, not only the whole work is a peculiar trade, but it is divided into a number of branches, of which the greater part are likewise peculiar trades. One man draws out the wire, another straights it, a third cuts it, a fourth points it, a fifth grinds it at the top for receiving the head; to make the head requires two or three distinct operations; to put it on is a peculiar business, to whiten the pins is another; it is even a trade by itself to put them into the paper; and the important business of making a pin is, in this manner, divided into about eighteen distinct operations, which, in some manufactories, are all performed by distinct hands, though in others the same man will sometimes perform two or three of them. I have seen a small manufactory of this kind where ten men only were employed, and where some of them consequently performed two or three distinct operations. But though they were very poor, and therefore but indifferently accommodated with the necessary machinery, they could, when they exerted themselves, make among them about twelve pounds of pins in a day. There are in a pound upwards of four thousand pins of a middling size. Those ten persons, therefore, could make among them upwards of forty-eight thousand pins in a day. Each person, therefore, making a tenth part of forty-eight thousand pins, might be considered as making four thousand eight hundred pins in a day. But if they had all wrought separately and independently, and without any of them having been educated to this peculiar business, they certainly could not each of them have made twenty, perhaps not one pin in a day; that is, certainly, not the two hundred and fortieth, perhaps not the four thousand eight hundredth part of what they are at present capable of performing, in consequence of a proper division and combination of their different operations.

In every other art and manufacture, the effects of the division of labour are similar to what they are in this very trifling one; though, in many of them, the labour can neither be so much subdivided, nor reduced to so great a simplicity of operation. The division of labour, however, so far as it can be introduced, occasions, in every art, a proportionable increase of the productive powers of labour. The separation of different trades and employments from one another seems to have taken place in consequence of this advantage. This separation, too, is generally carried furthest in those countries which enjoy the highest degree of industry and improvement; what is the work of one man in a rude state of society being generally that of several in an improved one. In every improved society, the farmer is generally nothing but a farmer; the manufacturer, nothing but a manufacturer. The labour, too, which is necessary to produce any one complete manufacture is almost always divided among a great number of hands. How many different trades are employed in each branch of the linen and woollen manufactures from the growers of the flax and the wool, to the bleachers and smoothers of the linen, or to the dyers and dressers of the cloth! The nature of agriculture, indeed, does not admit of so many subdivisions of labour, nor of so complete a separation of one business from another, as manufactures. It is impossible to separate so entirely the business of the grazier from that of the corn-farmer as the trade of the carpenter is commonly separated from that of the smith. The spinner

is almost always a distinct person from the weaver; but the ploughman, the harrower, the sower of the seed, and the reaper of the corn, are often the same. The occasions for those different sorts of labour returning with the different seasons of the year, it is impossible that one man should be constantly employed in any one of them. This impossibility of making so complete and entire a separation of all the different branches of labour employed in agriculture is perhaps the reason why the improvement of the productive powers of labour in this art does not always keep pace with their improvement in manufactures. The most opulent nations, indeed, generally excel all their neighbours in agriculture as well as in manufactures; but they are commonly more distinguished by their superiority in the latter than in the former. Their lands are in general better cultivated, and having more labour and expense bestowed upon them, produce more in proportion to the extent and natural fertility of the ground. But this superiority of produce is seldom much more than in proportion to the superiority of labour and expense. In agriculture, the labour of the rich country is not always much more productive than that of the poor; or, at least, it is never so much more productive as it commonly is in manufactures. The corn of the rich country, therefore, will not always, in the same degree of goodness, come cheaper to market than that of the poor. The corn of Poland, in the same degree of goodness, is as cheap as that of France, notwithstanding the superior opulence and improvement of the latter country. The corn of France is, in the corn provinces, fully as good, and in most years nearly about the same price with the corn of England, though, in opulence and improvement, France is perhaps inferior to England. The corn-lands of England, however, are better cultivated than those of France, and the corn-lands of France are said to be much better cultivated than those of Poland. But though the poor country, notwithstanding the inferiority of its cultivation, can, in some measure, rival the rich in the cheapness and goodness of its corn, it can pretend to no such competition in its manufacturers; at least if those manufactures suit the soil, climate, and situation of the rich country. The silks of France are better and cheaper than those of England, because the silk manufacture, at least under the present high duties upon the importation of raw silk, does not so well suit the climate of England as that of France. But the hardware and the coarse woollens of England are beyond all comparison superior to those of France, and much cheaper too in the same degree of goodness. In Poland there are said to be scarce any manufactures of any kind, a few of those coarser household manufactures excepted, without which no country can well subsist.

This great increase of the quantity of work which, in 5 consequence of the division of labour, the same number of people are capable of performing, is owing to three different circumstances; first, to the increase of dexterity in every particular workman; secondly, to the saving of the time which is commonly lost in passing from one species of work to another; and lastly, to the invention of a great number of machines which facilitate and abridge labour, and enable one man to do the work of many.

. . .

Chapter II

OF THE PRINCIPLE WHICH GIVES OCCASION
TO THE DIVISION OF LABOUR

This division of labour, from which so many advantages 1
are derived, is not originally the effect of any human wisdom, which foresees and intends that general opulence to
which it gives occasion. It is the necessary, though very
slow and gradual consequence of a certain propensity in
human nature which has in view no such extensive utility; the propensity to truck, barter, and exchange one
thing for another.

Whether this propensity be one of those original
principles in human nature of which no further account
can be given; or whether, as seems more probable, it be
the necessary consequence of the faculties of reason and
speech, it belongs not to our present subject to inquire. It
is common to all men, and to be found in no other race of
animals, which seem to know neither this nor any other
species of contracts. Two greyhounds, in running down
the same hare, have sometimes the appearance of acting
in some sort of concert. Each turns her towards his companion or endeavours to intercept her when his companion turns her towards himself. This, however, is not the
effect of any contract, but of the accidental concurrence of
their passions in the same object at that particular time.
Nobody ever saw a dog make a fair and deliberate exchange of one bone for another with another dog. Nobody
ever saw one animal by its gestures and natural cries signify to another, this is mine, that yours; I am willing to
give this for that. When an animal wants to obtain something either of a man or of another animal, it has no other
means of persuasion but to gain the favour of those whose
service it requires. A puppy fawns upon its dam,[27] and a
spaniel endeavours by a thousand attractions to engage
the attention of its master who is at dinner, when it wants
to be fed by him. Man sometimes uses the same arts with
his brethren, and when he has no other means of engaging
them to act according to his inclinations; endeavours by
every servile and fawning attention to obtain their good
will. He has not time, however, to do this upon every occasion. In civilised society he stands at all times in need of
the cooperation and assistance of great multitudes, while
his whole life is scarce sufficient to gain the friendship of
a few persons. In almost every other race of animals each
individual, when it is grown up to maturity, is entirely
independent, and in its natural state has occasion for the
assistance of no other living creature. But man has almost
constant occasion for the help of his brethren, and it is in
vain for him to expect it from their benevolence only. He
will be more likely to prevail if he can interest their self-
love in his favour, and show them that it is for their own
advantage to do for him what he requires of them. Whoever offers to another a bargain of any kind, proposes to
do this. Give me that which I want, and you shall have this
which you want, is the meaning of every such offer; and

it is in this manner that we obtain from one another the
far greater part of those good offices which we stand in
need of. It is not from the benevolence of the butcher, the
brewer, or the baker that we expect our dinner, but from
their regard to their own interest. We address ourselves,
not to their humanity but to their self-love, and never talk
to them of our own necessities but of their advantages.
Nobody but a beggar chooses to depend chiefly upon the
benevolence of his fellow-citizens. Even a beggar does
not depend upon it entirely. The charity of well-disposed
people, indeed, supplies him with the whole fund of his
subsistence. But though this principle ultimately provides
him with all the necessaries of life which he has occasion
for, it neither does nor can provide him with them as he
has occasion for them. The greater part of his occasional
wants are supplied in the same manner as those of other
people, by treaty, by barter, and by purchase. With the
money which one man gives him he purchases food. The
old clothes which another bestows upon him he exchanges
for other old clothes which suit him better, or for lodging,
or for food, or for money, with which he can buy either
food, clothes, or lodging, as he has occasion.

As it is by treaty, by barter, and by purchase that we
obtain from one another the greater part of those mutual
good offices which we stand in need of, so it is this same
trucking disposition which originally gives occasion to
the division of labour. In a tribe of hunters or shepherds
a particular person makes bows and arrows, for example,
with more readiness and dexterity than any other. He frequently exchanges them for cattle or for venison with his
companions; and he finds at last that he can in this manner get more cattle and venison than if he himself went
to the field to catch them. From a regard to his own interest, therefore, the making of bows and arrows grows to
be his chief business, and he becomes a sort of armourer.
Another excels in making the frames and covers of their
little huts or movable houses. He is accustomed to be of
use in this way to his neighbours, who reward him in
the same manner with cattle and with venison, till at last
he finds it his interest to dedicate himself entirely to this
employment, and to become a sort of house-carpenter. In
the same manner a third becomes a smith or a brazier,[28] a
fourth a tanner or dresser of hides or skins, the principal
part of the clothing of savages. And thus the certainty of
being able to exchange all that surplus part of the produce
of his own labour, which is over and above his own consumption, for such parts of the produce of other men's labour as he may have occasion for, encourages every man
to apply himself to a particular occupation, and to culti-
vate and bring to perfection whatever talent or genius he
may possess for that particular species of business.

The difference of natural talents in different men is, in
reality, much less than we are aware of; and the very different genius which appears to distinguish men of different professions, when grown up to maturity, is not upon
many occasions so much the cause as the effect of the
division of labour. The difference between the most dissimilar characters, between a philosopher and a common

---

[27] **dam** Dog-mother.

[28] **brazier** A worker in brass.

street porter, for example, seems to arise not so much from nature as from habit, custom, and education. When they came into the world, and for the first six or eight years of their existence, they were perhaps very much alike, and neither their parents nor playfellows could perceive any remarkable difference. About that age, or soon after, they come to be employed in very different occupations. The difference of talents comes then to be taken notice of, and widens by degrees, till at last the vanity of the philosopher is willing to acknowledge scarce any resemblance. But without the disposition to truck, barter, and exchange, every man must have procured to himself every necessary and conveniency of life which he wanted. All must have had the same duties to perform, and the same work to do, and there could have been no such difference of employment as could alone give occasion to any great difference of talents.

As it is this disposition which forms that difference 5 of talents, so remarkable among men of different professions, so it is this same disposition which renders that difference useful. Many tribes of animals acknowledged to be all of the same species derive from nature a much more remarkable distinction of genius, than what, antecedent to custom and education, appears to take place among men. By nature a philosopher is not in genius and disposition half so different from a street porter, as a mastiff is from a greyhound, or a greyhound from a spaniel, or this last from a shepherd's dog. Those different tribes of animals, however, though all of the same species, are of scarce any use to one another. The strength of the mastiff is not, in the least, supported either by the swiftness of the greyhound, or by the sagacity of the spaniel, or by the docility of the shepherd's dog. The effects of those different geniuses and talents, for want of the power or disposition to barter and exchange, cannot be brought into a common stock, and do not in the least contribute to the better accommodation and conveniency of the species. Each animal is still obliged to support and defend itself, separately and independently, and derives no sort of advantage from that variety of talents with which nature has distinguished its fellows. Among men, on the contrary, the most dissimilar geniuses are of use to one another; the different produces of their respective talents, by the general disposition to truck, barter, and exchange, being brought, as it were, into a common stock, where every man may purchase whatever part of the produce of other men's talents he has occasion for.

. . .

∞

Book V

Of the Revenue of the Sovereign or Commonwealth

Chapter II, Part 2

OF TAXES

The private revenue of individuals, it has been shown in 1 the first book of this Inquiry, arises ultimately from three different sources: Rent, Profit, and Wages. Every tax must finally be paid from some one or other of those three different sorts of revenue, or from all of them indifferently. I shall endeavour to give the best account. I can, first, of those taxes which, it is intended, should fall upon rent; secondly, of those which, it is intended, should fall upon profit; thirdly, of those which, it is intended, should fall upon wages; and, fourthly, of those which, it is intended, should fall indifferently upon all those three different sources of private revenue. The particular consideration of each of these four different sorts of taxes will divide the second part of the present chapter into four articles, three of which will require several other subdivisions. Many of those taxes, it will appear from the following review, are not finally paid from the fund, or source of revenue, upon which it was intended they should fall.

Before I enter upon the examination of particular taxes, it is necessary to premise the four following maxims with regard to taxes in general.

I. The subjects of every state ought to contribute towards the support of the government, as nearly as possible, in proportion to their respective abilities; that is, in proportion to the revenue which they respectively enjoy under the protection of the state. The expense of government to the individuals of a great nation is like the expense of management to the joint tenants of a great estate, who are all obliged to contribute in proportion to their respective interests in the estate. In the observation or neglect of this maxim consists what is called the equality or inequality of taxation. Every tax, it must be observed once for all, which falls finally upon one only of the three sorts of revenue above mentioned, is necessarily unequal in so far as it does not affect the other two. In the following examination of different taxes I shall seldom take much further notice of this sort of inequality, but shall, in most cases, confine my observations to that inequality which is occasioned by a particular tax falling unequally even upon that particular sort of private revenue which is affected by it.

II. The tax which each individual is bound to pay ought to be certain, and not arbitrary. The time of payment, the manner of payment, the quantity to be paid, ought all to be clear and plain to the contributor, and to every other person. Where it is otherwise, every person subject to the tax is put more or less in the power of the tax-gatherer, who can either aggravate the tax upon any obnoxious contributor, or extort, by the terror of such aggravation, some present or perquisite to himself. The uncertainty of taxation encourages the insolence and favours the corruption of an order of men who are naturally un-popular, even where they are neither insolent nor corrupt. The certainty of what each individual ought to pay is, in taxation, a matter of so great importance that a very considerable degree of inequality, it appears, I believe, from the experience of all nations, is not near so great an evil as a very small degree of uncertainty.

III. Every tax ought to be levied at the time, or in the manner, in which it is most likely to be convenient for the contributor to pay it. A tax upon the rent of land or of houses, payable at the same term at which such rents are usually paid, is levied at the time when it is most likely to be convenient for the contributor to pay; or, when he is most likely to have wherewithal to pay. Taxes upon such consumable goods as are articles of luxury are all finally paid by the consumer, and generally in a manner that is very convenient for him. He pays them by little and little, as he has occasion to buy the goods. As he is at liberty, too, either to buy, or not to buy, as he pleases, it must be his own fault if he ever suffers any considerable inconveniency from such taxes.

IV. Every tax ought to be so contrived as both to take out and to keep out of the pockets of the people as little as possible over and above what it brings into the public treasury of the state. A tax may either take out or keep out of the pockets of the people a great deal more than it brings into the public treasury, in the four following ways. First, the levying of it may require a great number of officers, whose salaries may eat up the greater pair of the produce of the tax, and whose perquisites may impose another additional tax upon the people. Secondly, it may obstruct the industry of the people, and discourage them from applying to certain branches of business which might give

maintenance and employment to great multitudes. While it obliges the people to pay, it may thus diminish, or perhaps destroy, some of the funds which might enable them more easily to do so. Thirdly, by the forfeitures and other penalties which those unfortunate individuals incur who attempt unsuccessfully to evade the tax, it may frequently ruin them, and thereby put an end to the benefit which the community might have received from the employment of their capitals. An injudicious tax offers a great temptation to smuggling. But the penalties of smuggling must rise in proportion to the temptation. The law, contrary to all the ordinary principles of justice, first creates the temptation, and then punishes those who yield to it; and it commonly enhances the punishment, too, in proportion to the very circumstance which ought certainly to alleviate it, the temptation to commit the crime. Fourthly, by subjecting the people to the frequent visits and the odious examination of the tax-gatherers, it may expose them to much unnecessary trouble, vexation, and oppression; and though vexation is not, strictly speaking, expense, it is certainly equivalent to the expense at which every man would be willing to redeem himself from it. It is in some one or other of these four different ways that taxes are frequently so much more burdensome to the people than they are beneficial to the sovereign.

The evident justice and utility of the foregoing maxims have recommended them more or less to the attention of all nations. All nations have endeavoured, to the best of their judgment, to render their taxes as equal as they could contrive; as certain, as convenient to the contributor, both in the time and in the mode of payment, and, in proportion to the revenue which they brought to the prince, as little burdensome to the people.

Questions for Critical Thinking

1. According to Smith, why is the division of labor important for the well-being of society?

2. Discuss the role of self-interest in Smith's theory. Is self-interest natural or acquired? Explain.

JEAN-JACQUES ROUSSEAU
Selection from *Confessions*

Voltaire (see *Candide*) dominated the Age of Reason, but from today's vantage point, he takes second place to the Swiss thinker Rousseau, whose literary works significantly reshaped the West. Rousseau's works were often greeted with cries for his exile or arrest, but most of his causes are now familiar parts of the modern landscape. For example, he is often credited with the "discovery" of childhood; for in *Émile* (1761), he was one of the first to urge school reform based on graded stages of child development. In *The New Heloise* (1762) he pioneered the idea that marriages should be based on love and not simply be arranged, and in *The Social Contract* (1762) he established the principles of modern direct democracy. His spirit foreshadowed the romantic cultural movement, notably in *The Reveries of the Solitary Walker* (1792), a veritable anthology of what later became romantic clichés about God in Nature. Finally, he was a Marxist before Marx, calling property the root of social inequality (*The Second Discourse*, 1755).

Jean-Jacques Rousseau (1712–1778) seemed to have his finger on the pulse of Western culture, perhaps because he was guided by his inner voice. That voice, contradictory and passionate, may still be heard speaking from the pages of his autobiography, *Confessions* (1781). Like almost everything Rousseau touched, the autobiography left a revolution in its wake. Other writers had taken themselves as subjects, most notably Augustine (see *Confessions*, Chapter 7, Volume I) and Montaigne (see *Essays*, Chapter 14), but no one before Rousseau had written with such uncensored frankness. Rousseau's work pointed the way for modern confessional writing in both autobiography and fiction; it inspired writers to search their childhoods for patterns that shaped their maturity (see Wordsworth's "Tintern Abbey," Chapter 18).

Reading the Selection

This selection from *Confessions* covers Rousseau's life from birth to seven years of age. It is memorable for establishing Rousseau's unique voice. The voice is obsessive, as shown by seventeen instances of "I," "me," "my," or "myself" in the first seven sentences; self-pitying, as in the story of his birth that "cost my mother her life"; and emotional in both language ("cry," "groan," "romantic") and behavior (his exaggerated love of novels). The voice is also self-dramatizing, convinced that the world is listening, as when he imagines the Last Judgment with "numberless . . . men gather[ed] round me, [to] hear my confessions."

Rousseau presents himself as a "judge-penitent"; that is, he confesses to a moral weakness and then turns around and judges himself better than others for having exposed his own failing. In effect, he aims at moral power by revealing his sins. This pattern is in the Last Judgment fantasy, when he admits to "depravities" and then says that no witness to his recital can say, "'I was a better man than he.'" This behavior, an outgrowth of his Calvinist faith, is the central motif of *Confessions*. It leads him to reveal sexual hang-ups, religious vacillation, and a decision to place his five offspring in an orphanage as soon as each was born. The "judge-penitent" motif is confirmed at the end when he warns that anyone who doubts his honor, "even if he has not read my writings . . . deserves to be stifled."

Book I
1712–1719

I have resolved on an enterprise which has no precedent, and which, once complete, will have no imitator. My purpose is to display to my kind a portrait in every way true to nature, and the man I shall portray will be myself.

Simply myself. I know my own heart and understand my fellow man. But I am made unlike any one I have ever met; I will even venture to say that I am like no one in the whole world. I may be no better, but at least I am different. Whether Nature did well or ill in breaking the mould in which she formed me, is a question which can only be resolved after the reading of my book.

Let the last trump sound when it will, I shall come forward with this work in my hand, to present myself before my Sovereign Judge, and proclaim aloud: "Here is what I have done, and if by chance I have used some immaterial embellishment it has been only to fill a void due to a defect of memory. I may have taken for fact what was no more than probability, but I have never put down as true what I knew to be false. I have displayed myself as I was, as vile and despicable when my behaviour was such, as good, generous, and noble when I was so. I have bared my secret soul as Thou thyself hast seen it, Eternal Being! So let the numberless legion of my fellow men gather round me, and hear my confessions. Let them groan at my depravities, and blush for my misdeeds. But let each one of them reveal his heart at the foot of Thy throne with equal sincerity, and may any man who dares, say 'I was a better man than he.'"

I was born at Geneva in 1712, the son of Isaac Rousseau, a citizen of that town, and Susanne Bernard, his wife. My father's inheritance, being a fifteenth part only of a very small property which had been divided among as many children, was almost nothing, and he relied for his living entirely on his trade of watchmaker, at which he was very highly skilled. My mother was the daughter of a minister of religion and rather better-off. She had besides both intelligence and beauty, and my father had not found it easy to win her. Their love had begun almost with their birth; at eight or nine they would walk together every evening along La Treille, and at ten they were inseparable. Sympathy and mental affinity strengthened in them a feeling first formed by habit. Both, being affectionate and sensitive by nature, were only waiting for the moment when they would find similar qualities in another; or rather the moment was waiting for them, and both threw their affections at the first heart that opened to receive them. Fate, by appearing to oppose their passion, only strengthened it. Unable to obtain his mistress, the young lover ate out his heart with grief, and she counselled him to travel and forget her. He travelled in vain, and returned more in love than ever, to find her he loved still faithful and fond. After such a proof, it was inevitable that they should love one another for all their lives. They swore to do so, and Heaven smiled on their vows.

Gabriel Bernard, one of my mother's brothers, fell in love with one of my father's sisters, and she refused to marry him unless her brother could marry my mother at the same time. Love overcame all obstacles, and the two pairs were wedded on the same day. So it was that my uncle married my aunt, and their children became my double first cousins. Within a year both couples had a child, but at the end of that time each of them was forced to separate.

My uncle Bernard, who was an engineer, went to serve in the Empire and Hungary under Prince Eugène,[29] and distinguished himself at the siege and battle of Belgrade. My father, after the birth of my only brother, left for Constantinople, where he had been called to become watchmaker to the Sultan's Seraglio.[30] While he was away my mother's beauty, wit, and talents brought her admirers, one of the most pressing of whom was M. de la Closure, the French Resident in the city. His feelings must have been very strong, for thirty years later I have seen him moved when merely speaking to me about her. But my mother had more than her virtue with which to defend herself; she deeply loved my father, and urged him to come back. He threw up everything to do so, and I was the unhappy fruit of his return. For ten months later I was born, a poor and sickly child, and cost my mother her life. So my birth was the first of my misfortunes.

5

---

[29] **Prince Eugène** Prince Eugène of Savoy fought for the Austrian Empire in the War of Spanish Succession against Louis XIV of France and won many battles. He was a brilliant field general and an inspiring leader.
[30] **Seraglio** A harem or the sultan's palace.

I never knew how my father stood up to his loss, but I know that he never got over it. He seemed to see her again in me, but could never forget that I had robbed him of her; he never kissed me that I did not know by his sighs and his convulsive embrace that there was a bitter grief mingled with his affection, a grief which nevertheless intensified his feeling for me. When he said to me, "Jean-Jacques, let us talk of your mother," I would reply: "Very well, father, but we are sure to cry." "Ah," he would say with a groan; "Give her back to me, console me for her, fill the void she has left in my heart! Should I love you so if you were not more to me than a son?" Forty years after he lost her he died in the arms of a second wife, but with his first wife's name on his lips, and her picture imprinted upon his heart.

Such were my parents. And of all the gifts with which Heaven endowed them, they left me but one, a sensitive heart. It had been the making of their happiness, but for me it has been the cause of all the misfortunes in my life.

I was almost born dead, and they had little hope of saving me. I brought with me the seed of a disorder which has grown stronger with the years, and now gives me only occasional intervals of relief in which to suffer more painfully in some other way. But one of my father's sisters, a nice sensible woman, bestowed such care on me that I survived; and now, as I write this, she is still alive at the age of eighty, nursing a husband rather younger than herself but ruined by drink. My dear aunt, I pardon you for causing me to live, and I deeply regret that I cannot repay you in the evening of your days all the care and affection you lavished on me at the dawn of mine. My nurse Jacqueline is still alive too, and healthy and strong. Indeed the fingers that opened my eyes at birth may well close them at my death.

I felt before I thought: which is the common lot of man, though more pronounced in my case than in another's. I know nothing of myself till I was five or six. I do not know how I learnt to read. I only remember my first books and their effect upon me; it is from my earliest reading that I date the unbroken consciousness of my own existence. My mother had possessed some novels, and my father and I began to read them after our supper. At first it was only to give me some practice in reading. But soon my interest in this entertaining literature became so strong that we read by turns continuously, and spent whole nights so engaged. For we could never leave off till the end of the book. Sometimes my father would say with shame as we heard the morning larks: "Come, let us go to bed. I am more a child than you are."

In a short time I acquired by this dangerous method, not only an extreme facility in reading and expressing myself, but a singular insight for my age into the passions. I had no idea of the facts, but I was already familiar with every feeling. I had grasped nothing; I had sensed everything. These confused emotions which I experienced one after another, did not warp my reasoning powers in any way, for as yet I had none. But they shaped them after a special pattern, giving me the strangest and most romantic notions about human life, which neither experience nor reflection has ever succeeded in curing me of.

10

Questions for Critical Thinking

1. Summarize the confessions Rousseau makes in this brief passage. Does he inspire sympathy in you? Explain.

2. Rousseau has been accused of helping create a "confessional culture." Considering today's world of movies, television, Internet, electronic games, novels, plays, music, politics, and celebrity culture, do you think we live in a "confessional age"? Explain.

VOLTAIRE
Selections from *Candide*

Voltaire's *Candide* was the most popular novel of the Age of Reason. It is a delightful, sometimes bawdy tale that satirizes the follies of the Western world of the time. Presumably because of fear that the sharp satire might give offense in certain quarters, Voltaire is nowhere identified as the book's author. Instead, its title page says simply, "Translated from the German by Dr. Ralph"—a disguise that fooled no one, as readers recognized Voltaire's biting wit and deft touch. After two hundred years, *Candide* survives as one of the best-loved fictional works in the world.

That Voltaire's novel survives is surprising, since it is a satire on topical events, and such satires are thought to grow stale as quickly as today's newspaper. What saves it from the dustbin of history is its glowing style—lighthearted, worldly, and sly—and the fact that most modern Westerners see the world much as Voltaire did. Who today does not share Voltaire's hatred of slavery, war, snobbery, religious persecution, and crooked clergy, or his skepticism about divine kings and utopian societies? Of course, not all of the satire works today, as in the anti-Semitic jokes and the portrayal of women as fickle. Still, the novel charms most readers as it pays homage to humanity's unsinkable spirit.

Candide (1759) is the story of the education of its naive hero, Candide, as he moves from Westphalia, a province in Prussia, across much of the Western world, including South America. What drives Candide's odyssey is the hope of marrying the lovely Cunégonde, a Westphalian baroness who keeps slipping from his grasp. Despite Candide's love for Cunégonde, the novel is not a love story, since their troubles are treated as comedy. Instead, it is a novel of ideas whose characters, except for Candide, show little or no growth and simply express Voltaire's point of view.

The novel is subtitled *Optimism,* and it was facile optimism that aroused Voltaire's anger. Facile optimism, derived from the German thinker Leibniz, denies that evil exists and insists that the world is basically good. In the novel, Leibniz is represented by Pangloss (from Greek, "all tongue"), who, faced with constant trials, offers this advice: "This is the best of all possible worlds." Pangloss's opposite is Martin, a facile pessimist who thinks all happens for the worst. In the end, Candide rejects both rival philosophies, opting instead for pragmatism: "We must go and work in the garden."

Voltaire (1694–1778) (born François Marie Arouet) dominated his age unlike any writer before or since. A universal genius, he wrote tragedies, poems, essays, novels, histories, dictionaries, letters, memoirs, philosophical treatises, and a work popularizing science. Very little of this vast work is widely read today, except for *Candide.* Voltaire's spirit survives in the term *Voltarean,* meaning a skeptic yet one who tolerates all religious points of view.

Reading the Selections

Included here are Chapters I through VI and Chapter XXX, the conclusion to the novel. The opening chapters cover Candide's travel from Westphalia, his homeland, to Lisbon, Portugal, where he barely survives an *auto-da-fé*—an "act of faith" in which heretics are persecuted. As calamities rain down on Candide, faithful Pangloss offers his optimistic bromides. Pangloss's litany quickly becomes absurd, though not to Candide.

After Chapter VI, Candide and Pangloss are rescued and join Candide's long-lost love, Cunégonde, and others in a series of adventures that takes them from Portugal to South America and back to Europe. In the last chapter, Voltaire reunites the main characters on Candide's farm in Turkey, where they continue to debate the meaning of life. A Turkish neighbor, satisfied with his simple farm life, advises them to work to eliminate the evils of boredom, vice, and poverty. Taking the Turkish farmer's advice to heart, Candide and his friends settle down and tend to their farm.

∞

Chapter I

How Candide Was Brought Up in a Beautiful Country House, and How He Was Driven Away

There lived in Westphalia,[31] at the country seat of Baron Thunder-ten-tronckh, a young lad blessed by nature with the most agreeable manners. You could read his character in his face. He combined sound judgment with unaffected simplicity; and that, I suppose, was why he was called Candide. The old family servants suspected that he was the son of the Baron's sister by a worthy gentleman of that neighbourhood, whom the young lady would never agree to marry because he could only claim seventy-one quarterings, the rest of his family tree having suffered from the ravages of time.

The Baron was one of the most influential noblemen in Westphalia, for his house had a door and several windows and his hall was actually draped with tapestry. Every dog in the courtyard was pressed into service when he went hunting, and his grooms acted as whips. The village curate was his private chaplain. They all called him Your Lordship, and laughed at his jokes.

The Baroness, whose weight of about twenty-five stone[32] made her a person of great importance, entertained with a dignity which won her still more respect. Her daughter, Cunégonde, was a buxom girl of seventeen with a fresh, rosy complexion; altogether seductive. The Baron's son was in every way worthy of his father. His tutor, Pangloss, was the recognised authority in the household on all matters of learning, and young Candide listened to his teaching with that unhesitating faith which marked his age and character.

Pangloss taught metaphysico-theologo-cosmolonigology. He proved incontestably that there is no effect without a cause, and that in this best of all possible worlds, his lordship's country seat was the most beautiful of mansions and her ladyship the best of all possible ladyships.

"It is proved," he used to say, "that things cannot be other than they are, for since everything was made for a purpose, it follows that everything is made for the best purpose. Observe: our noses were made to carry spectacles, so we have spectacles. Legs were clearly intended for breeches, and we wear them. Stones were meant for carving and for building houses, and that is why my lord has a most beautiful house; for the greatest baron in Westphalia ought to have the noblest residence. And since pigs were made to be eaten, we eat pork all the year round. It follows that those who maintain that all is right talk nonsense; they ought to say that all is for the best."

Candide listened attentively, and with implicit belief; for he found Lady Cunégonde extremely beautiful, though he never had the courage to tell her so. He decided that the height of good fortune was to have been born Baron Thunder-ten-Tronckh and after that to be Lady Cunégonde. The next was to see her every day, and failing that to listen to his master Pangloss, the greatest philosopher in Westphalia, and consequently the greatest in all the world.

One day Cunégonde was walking near the house in a little coppice, called "the park," when she saw Dr. Pangloss behind some bushes giving a lesson in experimental physics to her mother's waiting-woman, a pretty little brunette who seemed eminently teachable. Since Lady Cunégonde took a great interest in science, she watched the experiments being repeated with breathless fascination. She saw clearly the Doctor's "sufficient reason," and took note of cause and effect. Then, in a disturbed and

---

[31] **Westphalia** Westphalia, a small Prussian state, was considered very unattractive and provincial by the educated classes.
[32] **stone** British unit of measurement. Twenty-five stone equals 350 pounds.

thoughtful state of mind, she returned home filled with a desire for learning, and fancied that she could reason equally well with young Candide and he with her.

On her way home she met Candide, and blushed. Candide blushed too. Her voice was choked with emotion as she greeted him, and Candide spoke to her without knowing what he said. The following day, as they were leaving the dinner table, Cunégonde and Candide happened to meet behind a screen. Cunégonde dropped her handkerchief, and Candide picked it up. She quite innocently took his hand, he as innocently kissed hers with singular grace and ardour. Their lips met, their eyes flashed, their knees trembled, and their hands would not keep still. Baron Thunder-ten-tronckh, happening to pass the screen at that moment, noticed both cause and effect, and drove Candide from the house with powerful kicks on the backside. Cunégonde fainted, and on recovering her senses was boxed on the ears by the Baroness. Thus consternation reigned in the most beautiful and delightful of all possible mansions.

Chapter II

What Happened to Candide amongst the Bulgars

After being turned out of this earthly paradise, Candide wandered off without thinking which way he was going. As he plodded along he wept, glancing sometimes towards heaven, but more often in the direction of the most beautiful of houses, which contained the loveliest of barons' daughters. He lay down for the night in the furrow of a ploughed field with snow falling in thick flakes; and, to make matters worse, he had nothing to eat. Next day, perished with cold and hunger, and without a penny in his pocket, he dragged his weary limbs to a neighbouring town called Waldberghoff-trarbk-dikdorff, where he stopped at an inn and cast a pathetic glance towards the door.

Two men in blue noticed him.

"There's a well-made young fellow, chum," said one to the other, "and just the height we want."

They went up to Candide and politely asked him to dine with them.

"Gentlemen," said Candide modestly, "I deeply appreciate the honour, but I haven't enough money to pay my share."

"People of your appearance and merit, Sir, never pay anything," said one of the men in blue; "aren't you five feet five inches tall?"

"Yes, gentlemen, that is my height," said Candide, with a bow.

"Very well, Sir, sit down; we'll pay your share, and what's more we shall not allow a man like you to go short of money. That's what men are for, to help each other."

"You are quite right," said Candide; "for that is what Mr. Pangloss used to tell me. I am convinced by your courteous behaviour that all is for the best."

His new companions then asked him to accept a few shillings. Candide took them gratefully and wanted to give a receipt; but his offer was brushed aside, and they all sat down to table.

"Are you not a devoted admirer . . . ?" began one of the men in blue.

"Indeed I am," said Candide earnestly, "I am a devoted admirer of Lady Cunégonde."

"No doubt," replied the man; "but what we want to know is whether you are a devoted admirer of the King of the Bulgars."

"Good Heavens, no!" said Candide; "I've never seen him."

"Oh, but he is the most amiable of kings and we must drink his health."

"By all means, gentlemen," replied Candide, and emptied his glass.

"That's enough," they cried. "You are now his support and defender, and a Bulgar hero into the bargain. Your fortune is made. Go where glory waits you."

And with that they clapped him into irons and hauled him off to the barracks. There he was taught "right turn," "left turn," and "quick march," "slope arms," and "order arms," how to aim and how to fire, and was given thirty strokes of the "cat." Next day his performance on parade was a little better, and he was given only twenty strokes. The following day he received a mere ten and was thought a prodigy by his comrades.

The bewildered Candide was still rather in the dark about his heroism. One fine spring morning he took it into his head to decamp and walked straight off, thinking it a privilege common to man and beast to use his legs when he wanted. But he had not gone six miles before he was caught, bound, and thrown into a dungeon by four other six-foot heroes. At the court martial he was graciously permitted to choose between being flogged thirty-six times by the whole regiment or having twelve bullets in his brain. It was useless to declare his belief in Free Will and say he wanted neither; he had to make his choice. So, exercising that divine gift called Liberty, he decided to run the gauntlet thirty-six times, and survived two floggings. The regiment being two thousand strong, he received four thousand strokes, which exposed every nerve and muscle from the nape of his neck to his backside. The course had been set for the third heat, but Candide could endure no more and begged them to do him the kindness of beheading him instead. The favour was granted, his eyes were bandaged, and he was made to kneel down. The King of the Bulgars passed by at that moment and asked what crime the culprit had committed. Since the King was a man of great insight, he recognised from what he was told about Candide that here was a young philosopher utterly ignorant of the way of the world, and granted him a pardon, an exercise of mercy which will be praised in every newspaper and in every age. Candide was cured in three weeks by a worthy surgeon with ointments originally prescribed by Dioscorides; and he had just enough skin on his feet to walk, when the King of the Bulgars joined battle with the King of the Abars.[33]

---

[33] **Bulgars, Abars** *Bulgars,* another name for Bulgarians, lived in the Balkans and were known for bloodthirsty raids and wars. The *Abars,* or Avars (their usual name), overran Russia and eastern Europe in the fifth and sixth centuries. Charlemagne (768–815), king of the Franks, subdued them, and they disappeared from history. Like the Bulgars, they were considered to be fierce and cruel.

∞

Chapter III

How Candide Escaped from the Bulgars, and What Happened to Him Afterwards

Those who have never seen two well-trained armies drawn up for battle, can have no idea of the beauty and brilliance of the display. Bugles, fifes, oboes, drums, and salvoes of artillery produced such a harmony as Hell itself could not rival. The opening barrage destroyed about six thousand men on each side. Rifle-fire which followed rid this best of worlds of about nine or ten thousand villains who infested its surface. Finally, the bayonet provided "sufficient reason" for the death of several thousand more. The total casualties amounted to about thirty thousand. Candide trembled like a philosopher, and hid himself as best he could during this heroic butchery.

When all was over and the rival kings were celebrating their victory with Te Deums in their respective camps, Candide decided to find somewhere else to pursue his reasoning into cause and effect. He picked his way over piles of dead and dying, and reached a neighbouring village on the Abar side of the border. It was now no more than a smoking ruin, for the Bulgars had burned it to the ground in accordance with the terms of international law. Old men, crippled with wounds, watched helplessly the death-throes of their butchered women-folk, who still clasped their children to their bloodstained breasts. Girls who had satisfied the appetites of several heroes lay disembowelled in their last agonies. Others, whose bodies were badly scorched, begged to be put out of their misery. Whichever way he looked, the ground was strewn with the legs, arms, and brains of dead villagers.

Candide made off as quickly as he could to another village. This was in Bulgar territory, and had been treated in the same way by Abar heroes. Candide walked through the ruins over heaps of writhing bodies and at last left the theatre of war behind him. He had some food in his knapsack, and his thoughts still ran upon Lady Cunégonde. His provisions were exhausted by the time he reached Holland, but as he had heard that everyone in that country was rich and all were Christians, he had no doubt that he would be treated as kindly as he had been at Castle Thunder-ten-tronckh before Lady Cunégonde's amorous glances caused his banishment.

He appealed for alms from several important-looking people, who all told him that if he persisted in begging he would be sent to a reformatory to be taught how to earn his daily bread.

At last he approached a man who had just been addressing a big audience for a whole hour on the subject of charity. The orator peered at him, and said:

"What is your business here? Do you support the Good Old Cause?"

"There is no effect without a cause," replied Candide modestly. "All things are necessarily connected and arranged for the best. It was my fate to be driven from Lady Cunégonde's presence and made to run the gauntlet, and now I have to beg my bread until I can earn it. Things could not have happened otherwise."

"Do you believe that the Pope is Antichrist, my friend?" said the minister.

"I have never heard anyone say so," replied Candide; "but whether he is or he isn't, I want some food."

"You don't deserve to eat," said the other. "Be off with you, you villain, you wretch! Don't come near me again or you'll suffer for it."

The minister's wife looked out of the window at that moment, and seeing a man who was not sure that the Pope was Antichrist, emptied over his head a pot full of . . . , which shows to what lengths ladies are driven by religious zeal.

A man who had never been christened, a worthy Anabaptist[34] called James, had seen the cruel and humiliating treatment of his brother man, a creature without wings but with two legs and a soul; he brought him home and washed him, gave him some bread and beer and a couple of florins, and even offered to apprentice him to

---

[34] **Anabaptist** The Anabaptists, founded in the early sixteenth century during the Protestant Reformation, were a small Christian sect that had been subject to persecutions and had found refuge in Holland by the eighteenth century.

his business of manufacturing those Persian silks that are made in Holland. Candide almost fell at his feet.

"My tutor, Pangloss, was quite right," he exclaimed, "when he told me that all is for the best in this world of ours, for your generosity moves me much more than the harshness of that gentleman in the black gown and his wife."

While taking a walk the next day, Candide met a beggar covered with sores. His eyes were lifeless, the end of his nose had rotted away, his mouth was all askew and his teeth were black. His voice was sepulchral, and a violent cough tormented him, at every bout of which he spat out a tooth.

∞

Chapter IV

How Candide Met His Old Tutor, Dr. Pangloss, and What Came of It

Candide was moved more by compassion than by horror at the sight of this ghastly scarecrow, and gave him the two florins he had received from James, the honest Anabaptist. The apparition looked at him intently and, with tears starting to his eyes, fell on the young man's neck. Candide drew back in terror.

"Does this mean," said one wretch to the other, "that you don't recognise your dear Pangloss any more?"

"Pangloss!" cried Candide. "Can this be my beloved master in such a shocking state? What misfortune has befallen you? What has driven you from the most lovely of mansions? What has happened to Lady Cunégonde, that pearl among women, the masterpiece of nature?"

"My breath fails me," murmured Pangloss.

At this Candide quickly led him to the Anabaptist's stable, where he made him eat some bread, and as soon as he had revived, said to him:

"You mentioned Cunégonde?"

"She is dead," replied the other.

At these words Candide fainted, but his friend restored him to his senses with a little sour vinegar which happened to be in the stable. Candide opened his eyes.

"Cunégonde is dead!" said he. "Oh, what has become of the best of worlds? . . . But what did she die of? No doubt it was grief at seeing me sent flying from her father's lovely mansion at the point of a jack-boot?"

"No," said Pangloss. "She was disembowelled by Bulgar soldiers after being ravished as much as a poor woman could bear. When my lord tried to defend her, they broke his head. Her ladyship was cut into small pieces, and my poor pupil treated in precisely the same way as his sister. As for the house, not one stone was left standing on another; not a barn was left, not a sheep, not a duck, not a tree. But we have been amply avenged, for the Abars did just the same in a neighbouring estate which belonged to a Bulgar nobleman."

At this tale Candide fainted once more. When he recovered his senses, he first said all that was called for, and then enquired into cause and effect, and into the "sufficient reason" that had reduced Pangloss to such a pitiable state.

"I fear it is love," said his companion; "love, the comforter of humanity, the preserver of the universe, the soul of all living beings; tender love!"

"I know what this love is," said Candide, with a shake of his head, "this sovereign of hearts and quintessence of our souls: my entire reward has been a kiss and twenty kicks on the backside. But how could such a beautiful cause produce so hideous an effect upon you?"

"My dear Candide," replied Pangloss, "you remember Pacquette, that pretty girl who used to wait on our noble lady. In her arms I tasted the delights of Paradise, and they produced these hellish torments by which you see me devoured. She was infected, and now perhaps she is dead. Pacquette was given this present by a learned Franciscan, who had traced it back to its source. He had had it from an old countess, who had had it from a cavalry officer, who was indebted for it to a marchioness. She took it from her page, and he had received it from a Jesuit who, while still a novice, had had it in direct line from one of the companions of Christopher Columbus. As for me, I shall not give it to anyone, for I am a dying man."

"What a strange genealogy, Pangloss!" exclaimed Candide. "Isn't the devil at the root of it?"

"Certainly not," replied the great man. "It is indispensable in this best of worlds. It is a necessary ingredient. For if Columbus, when visiting the West Indies, had not caught this disease, which poisons the source of generation, which frequently even hinders generation, and is clearly opposed to the great end of Nature, we should have neither chocolate nor cochineal.[35] We see, too, that to this very day the disease, like religious controversy, is peculiar to us Europeans. The Turks, the Indians, the Persians, the Chinese, the Siamese, the Japanese as yet have no knowledge of it; but there is a 'sufficient reason' for their experiencing it in turn in the course of a few centuries. Meanwhile, it has made remarkable progress amongst us, and most of all in these huge armies of honest, well-trained mercenaries, who decide the destinies of nations. It can safely be said that when thirty thousand men are ranged against an army of equal numbers, there will be about twenty thousand infected with pox on each side."

"I could listen to you for ever," said Candide; "but you must be cured."

---

[35] **cochineal** A red dyestuff made from the dried bodies of the female cochineal insect, used today as a biological stain. Voltaire may be satirizing it when comparing it to chocolate, which was a very popular drink in his day.

"How can I be cured?" said Pangloss. "I haven't a penny, my dear friend, and there is not a doctor in all this wide world who will bleed you, or purge you without a fee."

This last remark decided Candide. He hurried to James, the charitable Anabaptist, and, falling at his feet, painted so moving a picture of the state to which his friend had been reduced that the good man did not hesitate to take Dr. Pangloss in and had him cured at his own expense. During treatment, Pangloss lost only an eye and an ear. He still wrote well and had a perfect command of arithmetic, so the Anabaptist appointed him his accountant. Two months later he was obliged to go to Lisbon on business and set sail in his own ship, taking the two philosophers with him. On the voyage Pangloss explained to him how all was designed for the best. James did not share this view.

"Men," he said, "must have somewhat altered the course of nature; for they were not born wolves, yet they have become wolves. God did not give them twenty-four-pounders or bayonets, yet they have made themselves bayonets and guns to destroy each other. In the same category I place not only bankruptcies, but the law which carries off the bankrupts' effects, so as to defraud their creditors."

"More examples of the indispensable!" remarked the one-eyed doctor. "Private misfortunes contribute to the general good, so that the more private misfortunes there are, the more we find that all is well."

While he was pursuing his argument the sky became overcast, the winds blew from the four corners of the earth, and the ship was caught in a most terrible storm in sight of the port of Lisbon.

∞

Chapter V

Describing Tempest, Shipwreck, and Earthquake, and What Happened to Dr. Pangloss, Candide, and James, the Anabaptist

Half the passengers were at the last gasp of nervous and physical exhaustion from the pitching and tossing of the vessel, and were so weak that they had no strength left to realise their danger. The other half uttered cries of alarm and said their prayers, for the sails were torn, the masts were broken, and the ship was splitting. Work as they might, all were at sixes and sevens, for there was no one to take command. The Anabaptist gave what help he could in directing the ship's course, and was on the poop when a madly excited sailor struck him a violent blow, which laid him at full length on the deck. The force of his blow upset the sailor's own balance, and he fell head first overboard; but, in falling, he was caught on a piece of the broken mast and hung dangling over the ship's side. The worthy James ran to his assistance and helped him to climb on board again. The efforts he made were so strenuous, however, that he was pitched into the sea in full view of the sailor, who left him to perish without taking the slightest notice. Candide was in time to see his benefactor reappear above the surface for one moment before being swallowed up for ever. He wanted to throw himself into the sea after the Anabaptist, but the great philosopher, Pangloss, stopped him by proving that Lisbon harbour was made on purpose for this Anabaptist to drown there. Whilst he was proving this from first principles, the ship split in two and all perished except Pangloss, Candide, and the brutal sailor who had been the means of drowning the honest Anabaptist. The villain swam successfully to shore; and Pangloss and Candide, clinging to a plank, were washed up after him.

When they had recovered a little of their strength, they set off towards Lisbon, hoping they had just enough money in their pockets to avoid starvation after escaping the storm.

Scarcely had they reached the town, and were still mourning their benefactor's death, when they felt the earth tremble beneath them. The sea boiled up in the harbour and broke the ships which lay at anchor. Whirlwinds of flame and ashes covered the streets and squares. Houses came crashing down. Roofs toppled on to their foundations, and the foundations crumbled. Thirty thousand men, women, and children were crushed to death under the ruins.

The sailor chuckled:

"There'll be something worth picking up here," he remarked with an oath.

"What can be the 'sufficient reason' for this phenomenon?" said Pangloss.

"The Day of Judgment has come," cried Candide.

The sailor rushed straight into the midst of the debris and risked his life searching for money. Having found some, he ran off with it to get drunk; and after sleeping off the effects of the wine, he bought the favours of the first girl of easy virtue he met amongst the ruined houses with the dead and dying all around. Pangloss pulled him by the sleeve and said:

"This will never do, my friend; you are not obeying the universal rule of Reason; you have misjudged the occasion."

"Bloody hell," replied the other. "I am a sailor and was born in Batavia. I have had to trample on the crucifix four times in various trips I've been to Japan.[36] I'm not the man for your Universal Reason!"

---

[36] **I have had . . . been to Japan.** The sailor is referring to actions denouncing his Christian faith in order to survive and live in a non-Christian society.

Candide had been wounded by splinters of flying masonry and lay helpless in the road, covered with rubble.

"For Heaven's sake," he cried to Pangloss, "fetch me some wine and oil! I am dying!"

"This earthquake is nothing new," replied Pangloss; "the town of Lima in America experienced the same shocks last year. The same causes produce the same effects. There is certainly a vein of sulphur running under the earth from Lima to Lisbon."

"Nothing is more likely," said Candide; "but oil and wine, for pity's sake!"

"Likely!" exclaimed the philosopher. "I maintain it's proved!"

Candide lost consciousness, and Pangloss brought him a little water from a fountain close by.

The following day, while creeping amongst the ruins, they found something to eat and recruited their strength. They then set to work with the rest to relieve those inhabitants who had escaped death. Some of the citizens whom they had helped gave them as good a dinner as could be managed after such a disaster. The meal was certainly a sad affair, and the guests wept as they ate; but Pangloss consoled them with the assurance that things could not be otherwise:

"For all this," said he, "is a manifestation of the rightness of things, since if there is a volcano at Lisbon it could not be anywhere else. For it is impossible for things not to be where they are, because everything is for the best."

A little man in black, an officer of the Inquisition, who was sitting beside Pangloss, turned to him and politely said:

"It appears, Sir, that you do not believe in original sin; for if all is for the best, there can be no such thing as the fall of Man and eternal punishment."

"I most humbly beg your Excellency's pardon," replied Pangloss, still more politely, "but I must point out that the fall of Man and eternal punishment enter, of Necessity, into the scheme of the best of all possible worlds."

"Then you don't believe in Free Will, Sir?" said the officer.

"Your Excellency must excuse me," said Pangloss; "Free Will is consistent with Absolute Necessity, for it was ordained that we should be free. For the Will that is Determined . . ."

Pangloss was in the middle of his sentence when the officer nodded to his henchman, who was pouring him out a glass of port wine.

Chapter VI

How a Magnificent Auto-da-fé Was Staged to Prevent Further Earthquakes, and How Candide Was Flogged

The University of Coimbra had pronounced that the sight of a few people ceremoniously burned alive before a slow fire was an infallible prescription for preventing earthquakes; so when the earthquake had subsided after destroying three-quarters of Lisbon, the authorities of that country could find no surer means of avoiding total ruin than by giving the people a magnificent auto-da-fé.

They therefore seized a Basque, convicted of marrying his godmother, and two Portuguese Jews who had refused to eat bacon with their chicken; and after dinner Dr. Pangloss and his pupil, Candide, were arrested as well, one for speaking and the other for listening with an air of approval. Pangloss and Candide were led off separately and closeted in exceedingly cool rooms, where they suffered no inconvenience from the sun, and were brought out a week later to be dressed in sacrificial cassocks and paper mitres.[37] The decorations on Candide's mitre and cassock were penitential in character, inverted flames and devils without tails or claws; but Pangloss's devils had tails and claws,

and his flames were upright. They were then marched in procession, clothed in these robes, to hear a moving sermon followed by beautiful music in counterpoint. Candide was flogged in time with the anthem; the Basque and the two men who refused to eat bacon were burnt; and Pangloss was hanged, though that was not the usual practice on those occasions. The same day another earthquake occurred and caused tremendous havoc.

The terrified Candide stood weltering in blood and trembling with fear and confusion.

"If this is the best of all possible worlds," he said to himself, "what can the rest be like? Had it only been a matter of flogging, I should not have questioned it, for I have had that before from the Bulgars. But when it comes to my dear Pangloss being hanged—the greatest of philosophers—I must know the reason why. And was it part of the scheme of things that my dear Anabaptist (the best of men!) should be drowned in sight of land? And Lady Cunégonde, that pearl amongst women! Was it really necessary for her to be disembowelled?"

He had been preached at, flogged, absolved, and blessed, and was about to stagger away, when an old woman accosted him and said:

"Pull yourself together, young man, and follow me."

---

[37] **sacrificial cassocks and paper mitres** Sacrificial cassocks were decorated sackcloth garments worn by those who were condemned to die in a Spanish *auto-da-fé*, or public burning. Mitres, or miters, are liturgical headdresses worn by church officials. Here the victims wear paper mitres.

∞

Chapter XXX
Conclusion

At the bottom of his heart, Candide had no wish to marry   1
Cunégonde, but the Baron's intransigence determined
him to go through with the match; and besides, Cunégonde was pressing him so strongly that he could not
retract. He consulted Pangloss, Martin, and the faithful
Cacambo. Pangloss compiled a beautiful memorandum
in which he proved that the Baron had no rights over his
sister, and that in accordance with Imperial law she could
give Candide her left hand in marriage.[38] Martin recommended throwing the Baron into the sea, while Cacambo
decided that he must be given back to the Levantine captain and replaced in the galleys, after which he should be
sent to Rome to the Father General by the very first ship.
Cacambo's advice seemed the most sensible, and was approved by the old woman, but nothing was said to Cunégonde about the plan. It was carried out at little cost, and
they enjoyed the double pleasure of overreaching a Jesuit
and punishing the pride of a German baron.

It would be natural to suppose that, after so many disasters, Candide should lead the most pleasing life imaginable, married at last to his mistress, and living with
the philosophical Pangloss, the philosophical Martin, the
prudent Cacambo, and the old woman, especially as he
had brought away so many diamonds from the country
once occupied by the Incas. But he had been so badly
cheated by the Jews, that he had nothing left beyond his
little farm. His wife daily grew uglier, and became more
and more cantankerous and insufferable. The old woman
was now quite infirm, and had developed an even worse
temper than Cunégonde's. Cacambo, whose job was
to work in the garden and sell vegetables in Constantinople, was quite worn out with toil, and cursed his lot.
Pangloss was vexed to think that he was not the master
spirit in some German university. As for Martin, he was
firmly persuaded that a man is badly off wherever he is,
so he suffered in patience. Candide, Martin, and Pangloss
sometimes discussed metaphysics and morals. From the
windows of the farmhouse boats were often seen passing, crowded with Turkish statesmen, military governors,
and judges, bound for exile in Lemnos, Mytilene, or Erzerum,[39] and other judges, governors, and statesmen were
seen coming to take the place of the banished, only to be
banished in their turn. Heads, too, were to be seen, decently impaled for display at the Sublime Porte. Sights

such as these made the philosophers renew their dispu-
tations; and when there was no discussion, the boredom
was so intolerable that the old woman was provoked one
day to remark:

"I should like to know which is the worst, to be ravished a hundred times by negro pirates, to have one but-
tock cut off, to run the gauntlet of a Bulgar regiment, to be
whipped and hanged at an auto-da-fé, to be dissected, to
row in the galleys—in fact, to experience all the miseries
through which we have passed—or just to stay here with
nothing to do?"

"That's a difficult question," said Candide.

The old woman's speech produced fresh reflections.   5
Martin's conclusion was that man was born to suffer from
the restlessness of anxiety or from the lethargy of boredom. Candide did not agree, but he admitted nothing.
Pangloss allowed that his sufferings had been uniformly
horrible; but as he had once maintained that everything
would turn out right in some marvellous way, he still
maintained it would, however little he believed it.

One day an incident occurred which confirmed Martin in his detestable views, and at the same time embarrassed Pangloss and made Candide more dubious than
ever. It was the arrival of Pacquette and Brother Giroflée
at the little farm in the utmost distress. They had soon got
through their three thousand piastres, and had parted
company only to be reconciled and to quarrel once again.
They had been in prison and had escaped, and Brother
Giroflée had at last turned Turk. Pacquette had continued
to practise her profession but without a shadow of profit
to herself.

"I knew quite well," said Martin to Candide, "that
your presents would soon be spent and would leave them
much worse off than before. You've squandered millions
of piastres, you and Cacambo between you, and you are
no happier than Brother Giroflée and Pacquette."

"My dear child," cried Pangloss to Pacquette, "so
Heaven has brought you back to us at last! Do you realise
that you cost me an eye, an ear, and the end of my nose?
What a state you are in! What a world this is!"

This fresh adventure drove them back to their discussions with redoubled ardour.

There lived in the neighbourhood a famous dervish,   10
who was reputed to be the greatest philosopher in Turkey.
They went to consult him, and chose Pangloss as their
spokesman.

"Master," said he, "we have come to ask a favour. Will
you kindly tell us why such a strange animal as man was
ever made?"

"What has that got to do with you?" said the dervish.
"Is it your business?"

"But surely, reverend father," said Candide, "there is
a great deal of evil in the world."

---

[38] **left hand in marriage** A left-handed, or *morganatic*, marriage
occurs when the party of the lower or inferior rank remains in
his or her rank and the children of the marriage do not inherit
any titles or property. Obviously, Candide, in this arrangement,
would be second to his Cunégonde and gain nothing, since she
was of noble birth.

[39] **Lemnos, Mytilene, or Erzerum** Lemnos and Mytilene are islands in the Aegean Sea. Erzerum is a province in western Turkey.

"And what if there is?" said the dervish. "When His Highness sends a ship to Egypt, do you suppose he worries whether the ship's mice are comfortable or not?"

"What ought to be done, then?" said Pangloss.

"Keep your mouth shut!" said the dervish.

"I had been looking forward," said Pangloss, "to a little discussion with you about cause and effect, the best of all possible worlds, the origin of evil, the nature of the soul, and pre-established harmony."

At these words the dervish got up and slammed the door in their faces.

During this conversation, news had spread that two cabinet ministers and a judge had been strangled at Constantinople, and that several of their friends had been impaled. This catastrophe kept people talking for several hours. On their way back to the little farm, Pangloss, Candide, and Martin noticed an old man of patriarchal appearance sitting at his door under an arbour of orange-trees enjoying the fresh air. Pangloss, who liked gossip as much as argument, asked the old fellow the name of the judge who had been strangled.

"I have no idea," he replied. "I could not tell you the name of any judge or any minister. I am utterly ignorant of what you have been talking about. I suppose it's true that those who enter politics sometimes come to a miserable end, and deserve it; but I never bother myself about what happens in Constantinople. I send my garden stuff to be sold there, and that's enough for me."

With these words, he invited the strangers into his house, where his two sons and daughters offered them several kinds of sherbet which they had made themselves, as well as drinks flavoured with candied lemon peel, oranges, lemons, citrons, pineapples, and pistachios, and pure Mocha coffee unmixed with the bad coffee you get from Batavia and the West Indies. After this refreshment the worthy Mussulman's two daughters perfumed the beards of the three visitors.

"You must have a magnificent estate," said Candide to the Turk.

"Only twenty acres," replied the Turk; "my children help me to farm it, and we find that the work banishes those three great evils, boredom, vice, and poverty."

As he walked back to the farm, Candide reflected on what the Turk had said. "That old fellow," said he, turning to Pangloss and Martin, "seemed to me to have done much better for himself than those six kings we had the honour of supping with."

"High estate," said Pangloss, "is always dangerous, as every philosopher knows. For Eglon, King of Moab, was assassinated by Ehud, and Absalom was hanged by his hair and stabbed with three spears; King Nadab, the son of Jeroboam, was killed by Baasha; King Elah by Zimri; Joram by Jehu; Athaliah by Jehoiada; and King Jehoiakim, King Jehoiachin, and King Zedekiah all became slaves. You know the miserable fate of Croesus, Astyages, Darius, Dionysius of Syracuse, Pyrrhus, Perseus, Hannibal, Jugurtha, Ariovistus, Caesar, Pompey, Nero, Otho, Vitellius, Domitian, Richard II of England, Edward II, Henry VI, Richard III, Mary Queen of Scots, Charles I, the three Henrys of France, and the Emperor Henry IV? You know . . . ?"

"I also know," said Candide, "that we must go and work in the garden."

"You are quite right," said Pangloss. "When man was placed in the Garden of Eden, he was put there 'to dress it and to keep it,' to work, in fact; which proves that man was not born to an easy life."

"We must work without arguing," said Martin; "that is the only way to make life bearable."

The entire household agreed to this admirable plan, and each began to exercise his talents. Small as the estate was, it bore heavy crops. There was no denying that Cunégonde was decidedly ugly, but she soon made excellent pastry. Pacquette was clever at embroidery, and the old woman took care of the linen. No one refused to work, not even Brother Giroflée, who was a good carpenter, and thus became an honest man. From time to time Pangloss would say to Candide:

"There is a chain of events in this best of all possible worlds; for if you had not been turned out of a beautiful mansion at the point of a jackboot for the love of Lady Cunégonde, and if you had not been involved in the Inquisition, and had not wandered over America on foot, and had not struck the Baron with your sword, and lost all those sheep you brought from Eldorado, you would not be here eating candied fruit and pistachio nuts."

"That's true enough," said Candide; "but we must go and work in the garden."

Questions for Critical Thinking

1. What is optimism according to Voltaire? Show how *Candide* satirizes this philosophy. At the end of the novel, Voltaire concludes, "we must go and work in the garden." Explain this conclusion.

2. Discuss the varied topics—besides optimism—that Voltaire ridicules or mocks in this broad social satire.

ALEXANDER POPE
Selections from *An Essay on Man*

The poet and essayist Alexander Pope (1688–1744) lived during one of the great eras in English letters, the Augustan Age (ca. 1660–1760). This period's authors drew inspiration from the first Augustan Age—that is, the reign of Emperor Augustus (27 BCE–14 CE)—when many fine writers flourished, notably Virgil, Horace, and Ovid. Imitating the style of the Roman heritage, Pope and the rest of these latter-day Augustans transformed their period into a time of harmony, decorum ("good taste"), and proportion. The Augustan ideal was correctness, and writers were under some moral and aesthetic obligation to instruct as well as to please. From the vantage of European letters, the Augustan Age was part of the neoclassical movement then sweeping across the West, whose writers believed that the classical authors had set the literary standards for all time.

Early in his career, Alexander Pope, ever sensitive to the spirit of classicism, developed a European-wide reputation and made himself financially secure with his translation of Homer's *Iliad* and *Odyssey*. He cemented his high literary position with his later works, such as poems, satires, epistles (letters in verse), and collected prose letters. Nowhere was his devotion to classicism so evident as in his poetry, where he wrote in heroic couplets—a verse form nearly always in iambic pentameter rhymed in pairs, *aa, bb, cc, dd,* and so on, with ten syllables in each line.

Pope's life was beset with misfortune. A Roman Catholic at a time when Protestantism, under King William and Queen Mary, reached new heights of popularity, he as a youth was barred from England's best educational institutions, its public (meaning "private") schools. Thus he was tutored by several Catholic priests, studied at two private schools, and after age thirteen, taught himself at home. Pope was never physically strong, being subject to a tubercular infection that left him small in stature and with curvature of the spine. He also was forced to endure his critics' bitter attacks on his writings, though he gave as good as he got, as for example in *The Dunciad* (1728), a satire against the bad poets ("dunces") of his period. Nonetheless, he persevered to become a dominant voice of the Augustan Age.

Reading the Selections

Pope considered *An Essay on Man* (1733–1734) one of his most important works. To thwart his critics and gain the best possible reception for this long work, he published two poems that his enemies attacked while he then anonymously issued the *Essay on Man,* which was highly praised. Typically, the *Essay* is composed in heroic couplets.

Addressed to Pope's patron, Henry St. John Bolingbroke ("St. John," line 1), the *Essay* comprises four epistles on the favorite topic of neoclassical writers, man and his activities: "The proper study of mankind is man." Epistle 1 deals with man in the cosmos; Epistle 2 analyzes man as an individual; Epistle 3 examines man in society; and Epistle 4 explores the theme of happiness, concluding that personal and social happiness are the same.

Pope's basic conservatism, though not in a negative sense, is shown in the following excerpts from the *Essay.* In Epistle 1 he advocates the seemingly fatalistic principle that "Whatever is, is right," but in Epistle 2 he encourages the study of man and his environment, with the end goal of fitting into the moral order.

∾

To Henry St. John, Lord Bolingbroke

Epistle 1. Of the Nature and State of Man with Respect to the Universe

Awake, my St. John! leave all meaner things   1
To low ambition, and the pride of kings.
Let us (since life can little more supply
Than just to look about us and to die)
Expatiate free o'er all this scene of man;
A mightly maze! but not without a plan;
A wild, where weeds and flowers promiscuous shoot,
Or garden, tempting with forbidden fruit.
Together let us beat this ample field,
Try what the open, what the covert yield;   10
The latent tracts, the giddy heights, explore
Of all who blindly creep, or sightless soar;
Eye Nature's walks, shoot folly as it flies,
And catch the manners living as they rise;
Laugh where we must, be candid where we can;
But vindicate the ways of God to man.

    1. Say first, of God above, or man below,
What can we reason, but from what we know?
Of man, what see we but his station here,
From which to reason, or to which refer?   20
Through worlds unnumbered though the God be known,
'Tis ours to trace him only in our own.
He, who through vast immensity can pierce,
See worlds on worlds compose one universe,
Observe how system into system runs,
What other planets circle other suns,
What varied being peoples every star,
May tell why Heaven has made us as we are.
But of this frame the bearings, and the ties,
The strong connections, nice dependencies,   30
Gradations just, has thy pervading soul
Looked through? or can a part contain the whole?
    Is the great chain, that draws all to agree,
And drawn supports, upheld by God, or thee?

    2. Presumptuous man! the reason wouldst thou find,
Why formed so weak, so little, and so blind?
First, if thou canst, the harder reason guess,
Why formed no weaker, blinder, and no less!
Ask of thy mother earth, why oaks are made
Taller or stronger than the weeds they shade?   40
Or ask of yonder argent fields above,
Why Jove's satellites are less than Jove[40]?
    Of systems possible, if 'tis confessed
That Wisdom Infinite must form the best,
Where all must full or not coherent be,

And all that rises, rise in due degree;
Then, in the scale of reasoning life, 'tis plain,
There must be, somewhere, such a rank as man:
And all the question (wrangle e'er so long)
Is only this, if God has placed him wrong?   50
    Respecting man, whatever wrong we call,
May, must be right, as relative to all.
In human works, though labored on with pain,
A thousand movements scarce one purpose gain;
In God's, one single can its end produce;
Yet serves to second too some other use.
So man, who here seems principal alone,
Perhaps acts second to some sphere unknown,
Touches some wheel, or verges to some goal;
'Tis but a part we see, and not a whole.   60
    When the proud steed shall know why man restrains
His fiery course, or drives him o'er the plains;
When the dull ox, why now he breaks the clod,
Is now a victim, and now Egypt's god:
Then shall man's pride and dullness comprehend
His actions', passions', being's use and end;
Why doing, suffering, checked, impelled; and why
This hour a slave, the next a deity.
    Then say not man's imperfect, Heaven in fault;
Say rather, man's as perfect as he ought;   70
His knowledge measured to his state and place,
His time a moment, and a point his space.
If to be perfect in a certain sphere,
What matter, soon or late, or here or there?
The blest today is as completely so,
As who began a thousand years ago.

    3. Heaven from all creatures hides the book of Fate,
All but the page prescribed, their present state:
From brutes what men, from men what spirits know:
Or who could suffer being here below?   80
The lamb thy riot dooms to bleed today,
Had he thy reason, would he skip and play?
Pleased to the last, he crops the flowery food,
And licks the hand just raised to shed his blood.
O blindness to the future! kindly given,
That each may fill the circle marked by Heaven:
Who sees with equal eye, as God of all,
A hero perish, or a sparrow fall,
Atoms or systems into ruin hurled,
And know a bubble burst, and now a world.   90
    Hope humbly then; with trembling pinions soar;
Wait the great teacher Death, and God adore!
What future bliss, he gives not thee to know,
But gives that hope to be thy blessing now.
Hope springs eternal in the human breast:
Man never is, but always to be blest:
The soul, uneasy and confined from home,
Rests and expatiates in a life to come.

---

[40] **Jove** Another name for Jupiter; here the planet and its satellites.

Lo! the poor Indian, whose untutored mind
Sees God in clouds, or hears him in the wind; 100
His soul proud Science never taught to stray
Far as the solar walk, or milky way;
Yet simple Nature to his hope has given,
Behind the cloud-topped hill, an humbler heaven;
Some safer world in depth of woods embraced,
Some happier island in the watery waste,
Where slaves once more their native land behold,
No fiends torment, no Christians thirst for gold!
To be, contents his natural desire,
He asks no angel's wing, no seraph's[41] fire; 110
But thinks, admitted to that equal sky,
His faithful dog shall beat him company.

4. Go, wiser thou! and, in thy scale of sense,
Weigh thy opinion against Providence;
Call imperfection what thou fancy'st such,
Say, here he gives too little, there too much;
Destroy all creatures for thy sport or gust,
Yet cry, if man's unhappy, God's unjust;
If man alone engross not Heaven's high care,
Alone made perfect here, immortal there: 120
Snatch from his hand the balance and the rod,[42]
Rejudge his justice, be the God of God!
In pride, in reasoning pride, our error lies;
All quit their sphere, and rush into the skies.
Pride still is aiming at the blest abodes,
Men would be angels, angels would be gods.
Aspiring to be gods, if angels fell,
Aspiring to be angels, men rebel:
And who but wishes to invert the laws
Of order, sins against the Eternal Cause. 130

5. Ask for what end the heavenly bodies shine,
Earth for whose use? Pride answers, " 'Tis for mine:
For me kind Nature wakes her genial power,
Suckles each herb, and spreads out every flower;
Annual for me, the grape, the rose renew
The juice nectareous, and the balmy dew;
For me, the mine a thousand treasures brings;
For me, health gushes from a thousand springs;
Seas roll to waft me, suns to light me rise;
My footstool earth, my canopy the skies." 140

But errs not Nature from this gracious end,
From burning suns when livid deaths descend,
When earthquakes swallow, or when tempests sweep
Towns to one grave, whole nations to the deep?
"No," 'tis replied, "the first Almighty Cause
Acts not by partial, but by general laws;
The exceptions few; some change since all began,
And what created perfect?"—Why then man?
If the great end be human happiness,
Then Nature deviates; and can man do less? 150
As much that end a constant course requires

Of showers and sunshine, as of man's desires;
As much eternal springs and cloudless skies,
As men forever temperate, calm, and wise.
If plagues or earthquakes break not Heaven's design,
Why then a Borgia, or a Catiline[43]?
Who knows but he whose hand the lightning forms,
Who heaves old ocean, and who wings the storms,
Pours fierce ambition in a Caesar's mind,
Or turns young Ammon[44] loose to scourge mankind? 160
From pride, from pride, our very reasoning springs;
Account for moral, as for natural things:
Why charge we Heaven in those, in these acquit?
In both, to reason right is to submit.

Better for us, perhaps, it might appear,
Were there all harmony, all virtue here;
That never air or ocean felt the wind;
That never passion discomposed the mind:
But ALL subsists by elemental strife;
And passions are the elements of life. 170
The general ORDER, since the whole began,
Is kept in Nature, and is kept in man.

6. What would this man? Now upward will he soar,
And little less than angel, would be more;
Now looking downwards, just as grieved appears
To want the strength of bulls, the fur of bears.
Made for his use all creatures if he call,
Say what their use, had he the powers of all?
Nature to these, without profusion, kind,
The proper organs, proper powers assigned; 180
Each seeming want compénsated of course,
Here with degrees of swiftness, there of force;
All in exact proportion to the state;
Nothing to add, and nothing to abate.
Each beast, each insect, happy in its own;
Is Heaven unkind to man, and man alone?
Shall he alone, whom rational we call,
Be pleased with nothing, if not blessed with all?
The bliss of man (could pride that blessing find)
Is not to act or think beyond mankind; 190
No powers of body or of soul to share,
But what his nature and his state can bear.
Why has not man a microscopic eye?
For this plain reason, man is not a fly.
Say what the use, were finer optics given,
To inspect a mite, not comprehend the heaven?
Or touch, if tremblingly alive all o'er,
To smart and agonize at every pore?
Or quick effluvia darting through the brain,
Die of a rose in aromatic pain? 200
If nature thundered in his opening ears,
And stunned him with the music of the spheres,

---

[41] **seraph** One of the orders of angels who stand in the presence of God.
[42] **the balance and the rod** Symbols of justice and office or power.

---

[43] **a Borgia, or a Catiline** References to the Borgias, who were a ruthless ruling family during the Renaissance, and to a first-century BCE Roman official who plotted to overthrow the government.
[44] **Ammon** In the Old Testament, son of Lot. Ammon was the founder of the Ammonites, who were enemies of the Hebrews. They flourished from the thirteenth to the eighth century BCE.

How would he wish that Heaven had left him still
The whispering zephyr, and the purling rill?
Who finds not Providence all good and wise,
Alike in what it gives, and what denies?

7. Far as creation's ample range extends,
The scale of sensual, mental powers ascends:
Mark how it mounts, to man's imperial race,
From the green myriads in the peopled grass: 210
What modes of sight betwixt each wide extreme,
The mole's dim curtain, and the lynx's beam:
Of smell, the headlong lioness between,
And hound sagacious on the tainted green:
Of hearing, from the life that fills the flood,
To that which warbles through the vernal wood:
The spider's touch, how exquisitely fine!
Feels at each thread, and lives along the line:
In the nice bee, what sense so subtly true
From poisonous herbs extracts the healing dew: 220
How instinct varies in the groveling swine,
Compared, half-reasoning elephant, with thine!
'Twixt that, and reason, what a nice barrier,
Forever separate, yet forever near!
Remembrance and reflection how allied;
What thin partitions sense from thought divide:
And middle natures, how they long to join,
Yet never pass the insuperable line!
Without this just gradation, could they be
Subjected, these to those, or all to thee?   230
The powers of all subdued by thee alone,
Is not thy reason all these powers in one?

8. See, through this air, this ocean, and this earth,
All matter quick, and bursting into birth.
Above, how high progressive life may go!
Around, how wide! how deep extend below!
Vast Chain of Being! which from God began,
Natures ethereal, human, angel, man,
Beast, bird, fish, insect, what no eye can see,
No glass can reach! from Infinite to thee,   240
From thee to nothing.—On superior powers
Were we to press, inferior might on ours:
Or in the full creation leave a void,
Where, one step broken, the great scale's destroyed:
From Nature's chain whatever link you strike,
Tenth or ten thousandth, breaks the chain alike.
And, if each system in gradation roll
Alike essential to the amazing Whole,
The least confusion but in one, not all
That system only, but the Whole must fall.   250
Let earth unbalanced from her orbit fly,
Planets and suns run lawless through the sky,
Let ruling angels from their spheres be hurled,
Being on being wrecked, and world on world,
Heaven's whole foundations to their center nod,
And Nature tremble to the throne of God:
All this dread order break—for whom? for thee?
Vile worm!—oh, madness, pride, impiety!

9. What if the foot, ordained the dust to tread,
Or hand, to toil, aspired to be the head?   260
What if the head, the eye, or ear repined
To serve mere engines to the ruling Mind?
Just as absurd, to mourn the tasks or pains,
The great directing MIND of ALL ordains.
All are but parts of one stupendous whole,
Whose body Nature is, and God the soul;
That, changed through all, and yet in all the same,
Great in the earth, as in the ethereal frame,
Warms in the sun, refreshes in the breeze,
Glows in the stars, and blossoms in the trees,   270
Lives through all life, extends through all extent,
Spreads undivided, operates unspent,
Breathes in our soul, informs our mortal part,
As full, as perfect, in a hair as heart;
As full, as perfect, in vile man that mourns,
As the rapt seraph that adores and burns;
To him no high, no low, no great, no small;
He fills, he bounds, connects, and equals all.

10. Cease then, nor ORDER imperfection name:
Our proper bliss depends on what we blame.   280
Know thy own point: this kind, this due degree
Of blindness, weakness, Heaven bestows on thee.
Submit—In this, or any other sphere,
Secure to be as blest as thou canst bear:
Safe in the hand of one disposing Power,
Or in the natal, or the mortal hour.
All Nature is but art, unknown to thee;
All chance, direction, which thou canst not see;
All discord, harmony not understood;
All partial evil, universal good: 290
And, spite of pride, in erring reason's spite,
One truth is clear: Whatever IS, is RIGHT.

Epistle 2. Of the Nature and State of Man with Respect to Himself, as an Individual

1. Know then thyself, presume not God to scan;   1
The proper study of mankind is Man.
Placed on this isthmus of a middle state,
A being darkly wise, and rudely great:
With too much knowledge for the skeptic side,
With too much weakness for the Stoic's pride,
He hangs between; in doubt to act, or rest,
In doubt to deem himself a god, or beast;
In doubt his mind or body to prefer,
Born but to die, and reasoning but to err;   10
Alike in ignorance, his reason such,
Whether he thinks too little, or too much:
Chaos of thought and passion, all confused;
Still by himself abused, or disabused;
Created half to rise, and half to fall;
Great lord of all things, yet a prey to all;
Sole judge of truth, in endless error hurled:
The glory, jest, and riddle of the world!

.   .   .

Questions for Critical Thinking

1. Explain Pope's view on the place of humans in the universe. What role does the Great Chain of Being play in his thinking? Do you agree with Pope? Explain.

2. "The proper study of mankind is Man." What does Pope mean in this famous line?

18

REVOLUTION, REACTION, AND CULTURAL RESPONSE
1760–1830

THOMAS JEFFERSON
Selection from *The Declaration of Independence*

The American writer and statesman Thomas Jefferson (1743–1826) personified the liberal and rational ideals of the Age of Reason. In *The Declaration of Independence,* the document that severed ties between the American colonies and Britain, and which Jefferson chiefly wrote, he translated this age's values into ringing phrases still echoed around the world. In his distinguished career, he worked to bring to fruition this era's vision. He held many public offices, both appointive and elective, including member of the Virginia House of Burgesses, delegate to the Continental Congress, ambassador to France, secretary of state, vice president, and president.

Jefferson, a plantation owner, was born into the gentry of colonial Virginia, which assured him a comfortable life, the best available education, and opportunities for leadership when war with Britain came. In college, he studied the classics, Shakespeare, Milton, and above all three figures whose knowledge of science, human nature, and politics greatly influenced his thinking: Newton, Bacon (see *Essays* in Chapter 16), and Locke (see *Second Treatise of Civil Government* in Chapter 16). A member of the third generation of Enlightenment thinkers, Jefferson developed a philosophy geared to the improvement of life for individuals and society; it was inspired by faith in education and natural law theory. In the debates leading up to the American Revolution, he was guided by this philosophy and made a name for himself as an outspoken defender of free speech, free thought, and liberty of religious conscience. Thus it was perhaps inevitable that in Philadelphia in 1776, as the delegates to the Continental Congress inched their way toward making a break with the British crown, they should appoint a committee to draw up a declaration of independence, and the committee would select Jefferson to draft the document.

Reading the Selection

The Declaration of Independence contains four sections. The first section echoed in plain and firm language what Jefferson called "the harmonizing sentiments of the day." These ideas were part of a set of beliefs shared by the members of the Continental Congress; they could be traced back to Locke and had found recent voice in the colonists' writings leveled against the

British. The second part is a specific bill of twenty-seven accusations against King George III's policies toward the American colonies. In the third section, the delegates maintain that they have, in vain, petitioned the British government many times to redress their grievances. In the fourth part, they conclude that the Congress has no alternative but to declare the colonies "free and independent," calling on the "Protection of divine Providence" as they pledge their lives, fortunes, and honor to each other in support of the declaration.

Jefferson, who spent the better part of a month drafting and polishing the document, later asserted that it was intended to be "an expression of the American mind." He drew on long-standing principles: equal rights for all citizens as based on the laws of nature, popular sovereignty, and limited, constitutional government. He chose his words with great care. In particular, the phrase "life, liberty and the pursuit of happiness," which, unlike Locke's wording ("life, liberty and property"), expressed Jefferson's own Enlightenment philosophy: that society has more noble goals than the protection of citizens' worldly possessions.

∞

When in the course of human events, it becomes necessary for one people to dissolve the political bands which have connected them with another, and to assume among the powers of the earth, the separate and equal station to which the Law of Nature and of Nature's God entitle them, a decent respect to the opinions of mankind requires that they should declare the causes which impel them to the separation.

We hold these truths to be self-evident, that all men are created equal, that they are endowed by their Creator with certain unalienable[1] rights, that among these are life, liberty and the pursuit of happiness. That to secure these rights, governments are instituted among men, deriving their just powers from the consent of the governed. That whenever any form of government becomes destructive of these ends, it is the right of the people to alter or to abolish it, and to institute new government, laying its foundation on such principles and organizing its powers in such form, as to them shall seem most likely to effect their safety and happiness. Prudence, indeed, will dictate that governments long established should not be changed for light and transient causes; and accordingly all experience hath shown, that mankind are more disposed to suffer, while evils are sufferable, than to right themselves by abolishing the forms to which they are accustomed. But when a long train of abuses and usurpations,[2] pursuing invariably the same object, evinces a design to reduce them under absolute despotism, it is their right, it is their duty, to throw off such government, and to provide new guards for their future security. Such has been the patient sufferance of these Colonies; and such is now the necessity which constrains them to alter their former systems of government. This history of the present King of Great Britain[3] is a history of repeated injuries and usurpations, all having in direct object the establishment of an absolute tyranny over these States. . . .

_____

[1] **unalienable** Inalienable, not able to be alienated, surrendered, or transferred. In property law, "alienate" means transfer by an action rather than the due course of law.

[2] **usurpations** The taking or making use of things without right or proper authority.

[3] **King of Great Britain** George III (r. 1760–1820).

∞

Questions for Critical Thinking

1. For what purpose is *The Declaration of Independence* written?

2. How is the act of independence justified? What benefits are claimed through the proclamation of independence?

Declaration of the Rights of Man and Citizen

Like the American *Declaration of Independence,* which it resembles in its call for an end to tyranny and the establishment of a new political order, the French *Declaration of the Rights of Man and Citizen* reflected the ideals of the Age of Reason. These included the natural rights theory of Locke (see the *Second Treatise of Civil Government* in Chapter 16) and the constitutional principles of the English political settlement of 1688. But this French document was firmly rooted in French history, for it meant to wipe out centuries of feudal privilege founded on tradition, blood, and wealth. At the same time, it assured French citizens of their natural and inalienable rights of liberty, property, security, and resistance to oppression, denied under the old regime.

In contrast to the American document, which appeared at the start of a revolution to justify future events, the French document was drafted after the French Revolution began and became one of a number of important pieces of legislation approved by the National Assembly in the summer of 1789. By the time the National Assembly passed the *Declaration of the Rights of Man and Citizen* on August 27, 1789, the revolution was in full swing. The Bastille, the symbolic prison of royal tyranny, had fallen on July 14; on August 3, the French aristocrats representing their Estate in the Assembly had risen, noble by noble, to renounce their feudal rights. When the declaration of August 27 was passed, the way was cleared to deal with suffrage, taxes, the Catholic Church, and the drafting of a constitution setting up a limited monarchy.

Reading the Selection

The founding document of the French Revolution has stood the test of time, outlasting the Reign of Terror (1793–1794), the Napoleonic empire, later revolutions, constitutional crises, and five republics. After a brief preamble in which the past is blamed for the ills of the present and a rationale is presented justifying the presentation of these natural and civil rights, there follows a list of seventeen "rights of man and citizen."

The concepts of rights and law are linked in many ways in the document. Law is referred to in nine of the seventeen articles. The committee that drafted the declaration felt that since French law had been abused so often under the old regime, it must now specify how the law was to protect citizens from arbitrary arrests, unfair trials, and *ex post facto* legislation. Law, as explained by the thinker Rousseau, expressed the general will that was embodied in representative government. Thus citizens became eligible for public office according to their talents and not, as with past practice, because of their class position. This is a revolutionary idea: it transforms people from subjects to be acted on into citizens who are self-governing.

The declaration proclaimed that all citizens would be taxed, a correction of an abuse from the old regime in which the rich were exempt from paying taxes. A "public force," or army, was still deemed necessary; however, it was not to be operated by the privileged few—once more, a reference to the past when army officers were uniformly of the nobility. Finally, the declaration asserted that the free circulation of ideas was a "precious" right—a provision meant to remove the censorship that had muzzled society in the past.

∞

The representatives of the French people, organized in National Assembly,[4] considering that ignorance, forgetfulness, or contempt of the rights of man are the sole causes of public misfortunes and of the corruption of governments, have resolved to set forth in a solemn declaration the natural, inalienable,[5] and sacred rights of man, in order that such declaration, continually before all members of the social body, may be a perpetual reminder of their rights and duties; in order that the acts of the legislative power and those of the executive power may constantly be compared with the aim of every political institution and may accordingly be more respected; in order that the demands of the citizens, founded henceforth upon simple and incontestable principles, may always be directed towards the maintenance of the Constitution and the welfare of all.

Accordingly, the National Assembly recognizes and proclaims, in the presence and under the auspices of the Supreme Being,[6] the following rights of man and citizen.

1. Men are born and remain free and equal in rights; social distinctions may be based only upon general usefulness.
2. The aim of every political association is the preservation of the natural and inalienable rights of man; these rights are liberty, property, security, and resistance to oppression.
3. The source of all sovereignty resides essentially in the nation; no group, no individual may exercise authority not emanating expressly therefrom.
4. Liberty consists of the power to do whatever is not injurious to others; thus the enjoyment of the natural rights of every man has for its limits only those that assure other members of society the enjoyment of those same rights; such limits may be determined only by law.
5. The law has the right to forbid only actions which are injurious to society. Whatever is not forbidden by law may not be prevented, and no one may be constrained to do what it does not prescribe.
6. Law is the expression of the general will; all citizens have the right to concur personally, or through their representatives, in its formation; it must be the same for all,

whether it protects or punishes. All citizens, being equal before it, are equally admissible to all public offices, positions, and employments, according to their capacity, and without other distinction than that of virtues and talents.
7. No man may be accused, arrested, or detained except in the cases determined by law, and according to the forms prescribed thereby. Whoever solicit, expedite, or execute arbitrary[7] orders, or have them executed, must be punished; but every citizen summoned or apprehended in pursuance of the law must obey immediately; he renders himself culpable by resistance.
8. The law is to establish only penalties that are absolutely and obviously necessary; and no one may be punished except by virtue of a law established and promulgated prior to the offence and legally applied.
9. Since every man is presumed innocent until declared guilty, if arrest be deemed indispensable, all unnecessary severity for securing the person of the accused must be severely repressed by law.
10. No one is to be disquieted because of his opinions, even religious, provided their manifestation does not disturb the public order established by law.
11. Free communication of ideas and opinions is one of the most precious of the rights of man. Consequently, every citizen may speak, write, and print freely, subject to responsibility for the abuse of such liberty in the cases determined by law.
12. The guarantee of the rights of man and citizen necessitates a public force; such a force, therefore, is instituted for the advantage of all and not for the particular benefit of those to whom it is entrusted.
13. For the maintenance of the public force and for the expenses of administration a common tax is indispensable; it must be assessed equally on all citizens in proportion to their means.
14. Citizens have the right to ascertain, by themselves or through their representatives, the necessity of the public tax, to consent to it freely, to supervise its use, and to determine its quota, assessment, payment, and duration.
15. Society has the right to require of every public agent an accounting of his administration.
16. Every society in which the guarantee of rights is not assured or the separation of powers not determined has no constitution at all.
17. Since property is a sacred and inviolable right, no one may be deprived thereof unless a legally established public necessity obviously requires it, and upon condition of a just and previous indemnity.

---

[4] **National Assembly** In 1789, France's Estates General regrouped itself as the National Assembly and, until 1791, acted as a constituent assembly, drafting a new constitution and governing day by day.
[5] **inalienable** Not able to be alienated, surrendered, or transferred. In property law, "alienate" means transfer by an action rather than the due course of law.
[6] **Supreme Being** God. As the revolution progressed, the Roman Catholic Church was stripped of its privileged position in France, and an unsuccessful attempt was made, in 1794, to institute a cult of the Supreme Being.

---

[7] **arbitrary** Depending on individual discretion (as of a judge) and not by law.

Questions for Critical Thinking

1. What rights are claimed as coming from nature? What rights are claimed as citizens? What is the difference between natural rights and civil rights?

2. How do property rights balance with democratic rights in this *Declaration*? Is there, or is there not, an inherent conflict between them? Explain.

JANE AUSTEN
Selections from *Pride and Prejudice*

Jane Austen (1775–1817), England's first great woman novelist, published her first work, *Sense and Sensibility*, in 1811. A comic novel about middle-class, provincial life, this work staked out a part of the literary world that she soon made her own. Austen knew this terrain intimately, for she spent her life in small towns far from London. When *Sense and Sensibility* found an admiring public, there followed five more novels: *Pride and Prejudice* (1813); *Mansfield Park* (1814); *Emma* (1816); *Northanger Abbey,* and *Persuasion,* issued jointly (1818). Of these, *Pride and Prejudice* is the best known.

Pride and Prejudice was written during the Napoleonic era (1799–1815), when England was nearly always fighting France. The novel, however, contains no hint of these wars, except that a soldier like Mr. Wickham appears as an eligible bachelor. Nor is there mention of the Industrial Revolution, which was changing England for the worse. The novel's world is rustic towns and unspoiled countryside with well-kept estates and tidy farms. Austen focused on a vanishing society whose smallest unit was the family and whose major problems involved shifting social relationships.

Pride and Prejudice has a simple plot: the Bennets—a shabby-genteel family of the middle class—look for suitable husbands for their five daughters. Austen turns this plot into an intriguing story through clear writing, subtle irony, and most notably, precise dissection of the manners and rituals of middle-class life: the balls, the letters and gossip, the visits back and forth, and the unexpected calamities, such as a social snub, an elopement, a betrayed secret, or a broken engagement. She was especially aware of society's constraints on women, as in the depiction of the dilemma of Charlotte Lucas, who weighs her future husband's ugly character against the social position he offers.

Austen composed *Pride and Prejudice* in the neoclassical style, which had dominated English writing in the 1700s. This style's stress on decorum and orthodox morals suited Austen's purposes very well. Neither romantic nor sentimental but with great insight, she showed people of varied temperaments dealing with social conventions.

Reading the Selections

Pride and Prejudice's first three chapters show Austen's skillful handling of the characters and her good ear for dialogue. Chapter I deftly lays out the dynamics in the Bennet family: Mrs. Bennet is a social climber, eager to provide rich husbands for her daughters; she is vulgar in comparison to Mr. Bennet, who is beleaguered by his wife's prattling yet does not stop her scheming. Mr. Bennet is partial to daughter Lizzy—Elizabeth—the high-spirited heroine, as it turns out, of this delightful novel.

In Chapter II, Mr. Bennet reveals his social call on Mr. Bingley, a potential suitor for his daughters. Four daughters are introduced, and they begin to assert their individual natures.

Chapter III presents the last Bennet daughter, Jane; the wealthy Mr. Bingley; and the haughty Mr. Darcy. Thereafter Darcy and Elizabeth give the novel its focus: proud Darcy and equally proud Elizabeth must endure mutual slights and disagreements before love can dissolve their prejudices against one another.

∞

Chapter I

It is a truth universally acknowledged, that a single man in possession of a good fortune, must be in want of a wife.

However little known the feelings or views of such a man may be on his first entering a neighbourhood, this truth is so well fixed in the minds of the surrounding families, that he is considered as the rightful property of some one or other of their daughters.

"My dear Mr Bennet," said his lady to him one day, "have you heard that Netherfield Park is let at last?"

Mr Bennet replied that he had not.

"But it is," returned she; "for Mrs Long has just been here, and she told me all about it."

Mr Bennet made no answer.

"Do not you want to know who has taken it?" cried his wife impatiently.

"*You* want to tell me, and I have no objection to hearing it."

This was invitation enough.

"Why, my dear, you must know, Mrs Long says that Netherfield is taken by a young man of large fortune from the north of England; that he came down on Monday in a chaise and four to see the place, and was so much delighted with it that he agreed with Mr Morris immediately; that he is to take possession before Michaelmas,[8] and some of his servants are to be in the house by the end of next week."

"What is his name?"

"Bingley."

"Is he married or single?"

"Oh! single my dear, to be sure! A single man of large fortune; four or five thousand a year.[9] What a fine thing for our girls!"

"How so? how can it affect them?"

"My dear Mr Bennet," replied his wife, "how can you be so tiresome! You must know that I am thinking of his marrying one of them."

"Is that his design in settling here?"

"Design! nonsense, how can you talk so! But it is very likely that he *may* fall in love with one of them, and therefore you must visit him as soon as he comes."

"I see no occasion for that. You and the girls may go, or you may send them by themselves, which perhaps will be still better, for as you are as handsome as any of them, Mr Bingley might like you the best of the party."

"My dear, you flatter me. I certainly *have* had my share of beauty, but I do not pretend to be any thing extraordinary now. When a woman has five grown up daughters, she ought to give over thinking of her own beauty."

"In such cases, a woman has not often much beauty to think of."

"But, my dear, you must indeed go and see Mr Bingley when he comes into the neighborhood."

"It is more than I engage for, I assure you."

"But consider your daughters. Only think what an establishment it would be for one of them. Sir William and Lady Lucus are determined to go, merely on that account, for in general you know they visit no new comers. Indeed you must go, for it will be impossible for *us* to visit him, if you do not."

"You are over scrupulous surely. I dare say Mr Bingley will be very glad to see you; and I will send a few lines by you to assure him of my hearty consent to his marrying which ever he chuses[10] of the girls; though I must throw in a good word for my little Lizzy."

"I desire you will do no such thing. Lizzy is not a bit better than the others; and I am sure she is not half so handsome as Jane, nor half so good humored as Lydia. But you are always giving *her* the preference."

"They have none of them much to recommend them," replied he; "they are all silly and ignorant like other girls; but Lizzy has something more of quickness than her sisters."

"Mr Bennet, how can you abuse your own children in such a way? You take delight in vexing me. You have no compassion on my poor nerves."

"You mistake me, my dear. I have a high respect for your nerves. They are my old friends. I have heard you mention them with consideration these twenty years at least."

"Ah! you do not know what I suffer."

"But I hope you will get over it, and live to see many young men of four thousand a year come into the neighbourhood."

---

[8] **Michaelmas** Literally, "Michael's Mass," the festival of St. Michael the Archangel, on September 29.

[9] **four or five thousand a year** Annual income; roughly $250,000 purchasing power in today's American dollars.

---

[10] **chuses** Chooses.

"It will be no use to us, if twenty such should come since you will not visit them."

"Depend upon it, my dear, that when there are twenty, I will visit them all."

Mr Bennet was so odd a mixture of quick parts, sarcastic humour, reserve, and caprice, that the experience of three and twenty years had been sufficient to make his wife understand his character. *Her* mind was less difficult to develop. She was a woman of mean understanding, little information, and uncertain temper. When she was discontented she fancied herself nervous. The business of her life was to get her daughters married; its solace was visiting and news.

Chapter II

Mr Bennet was among the earliest of those who waited on Mr Bingley. He had always intended to visit him, though to the last always assuring his wife that he should not go; and till the evening after the visit was paid, she had no knowledge of it. It was then disclosed in the following manner. Observing his second daughter employed in trimming a hat, he suddenly addressed her with,

"I hope Mr Bingley will like it, Lizzy."

"We are not in a way to know *what* Mr Bingley likes," said her mother resentfully, "since we are not to visit."

"But you forget, mama," said Elizabeth, "that we shall meet him at the assemblies,[11] and that Mrs Long has promised to introduce him."

"I do not believe Mrs Long will do any such thing. She has two nieces of her own. She is a selfish, hypocritical woman, and I have no opinion of her."

"No more have I," said Mr Bennet; "and I am glad to find that you do not depend on her serving you."

Mrs Bennet deigned not to make any reply; but unable to contain herself, began scolding one of her daughters.

"Don't keep coughing so, Kitty, for heaven's sake! Have a little compassion on my nerves. You tear them to pieces."

"Kitty has no discretion in her coughs," said her father; "she times them ill."

"I do not cough for my own amusement," replied Kitty fretfully.

"When is your next ball to be, Lizzy?"

"To-morrow fortnight."

"Aye, so it is," cried her mother, "and Mrs Long does not come back till the day before; so, it will be impossible for her to introduce him, for she will not know him herself."

"Then, my dear, you may have the advantage of your friend, and introduce Mr Bingley to *her*."

"Impossible, Mr Bennet, impossible, when I am not acquainted with him myself; how can you be so teazing[12]?"

"I honour your circumspection. A fortnight's acquaintance is certainly very little. One cannot know what a man really is by the end of a fortnight. But if *we* do not venture, somebody else will; and after all, Mrs Long and her nieces must stand their chance; and therefore, as she will think it an act of kindness, if you decline the office, I will take it on myself."

The girls stared at their father. Mrs Bennet said only, "Nonsense, nonsense!"

"What can be the meaning of that emphatic exclamation?" he cried. "Do you consider the forms of introduction, and the stress that is laid on them, as nonsense? I cannot quite agree with you *there*. What say you, Mary? for you are a young lady of deep reflection I know, and read great books, and make extracts."

Mary wished to say something very sensible, but knew not how.

"While Mary is adjusting her ideas," he continued, "let us return to Mr Bingley."

"I am sick of Mr Bingley," cried his wife.

"I am sorry to hear *that*; but why did you not tell me so before? If I had known as much this morning, I certainly would not have called on him. It is very unlucky; but as I have actually paid the visit, we cannot escape the acquaintance now."

The astonishment of the ladies was just what he wished; that of Mrs Bennet perhaps surpassing the rest; though when the first tumult of joy was over, she began to declare that it was what she had expected all the while.

"How good it was in you, my dear Mr Bennet! But I knew I should persuade you at last. I was sure you loved your girls too well to neglect such an acquaintance. Well, how pleased I am! and it is such a good joke, too, that you should have gone this morning, and never said a word about it till now."

"Now, Kitty, you may cough as much as you chuse," said Mr Bennet; and, as he spoke, he left the room, fatigued with the raptures of his wife.

"What an excellent father you have, girls," said she, when the door was shut. "I do not know how you will ever make him amends for his kindness; or me either, for that matter. At our time of life, it is not so pleasant I can tell you, to be making new acquaintance every day; but for your sakes, we would do any thing. Lydia, my love, though you *are* the youngest, I dare say Mr Bingley will dance with you at the next ball."

"Oh!" said Lydia stoutly, "I am not afraid; for though I *am* the youngest, I'm the tallest."

The rest of the evening was spent in conjecturing how soon he would return Mr Bennet's visit, and determining when they should ask him to dinner.

---

[11] **assemblies** Social gatherings; a popular term dating from the eighteenth century.
[12] **teazing** Teasing.

❧

Chapter III

Not all that Mrs Bennet, however, with the assistance of her five daughters, could ask on the subject was sufficient to draw from her husband any satisfactory description of Mr Bingley. They attacked him in various ways; with barefaced questions, ingenious suppositions, and distant surmises; but he eluded the skill of them all; and they were at last obliged to accept the second-hand intelligence of their neighbour Lady Lucas. Her report was highly favourable. Sir William had been delighted with him. He was quite young, wonderfully handsome, extremely agreeable, and to crown the whole, he meant to be at the next assembly with a large party. Nothing could be more delightful! To be fond of dancing was a certain step towards falling in love; and very lively hopes of Mr Bingley's heart were entertained.

"If I can but see one of my daughters happily settled at Netherfield," said Mrs Bennet to her husband, "and all the others equally well married, I shall have nothing to wish for."

In a few days Mr Bingley returned Mr Bennet's visit, and sat about ten minutes with him in his library. He had entertained hopes of being admitted to a sight of the young ladies, of whose beauty he had heard much; but he saw only the father. The ladies were somewhat more fortunate, for they had the advantage of ascertaining from an upper window, that he wore a blue coat and rode a black horse.

An invitation to dinner was soon afterwards dispatched; and already had Mrs Bennet planned the courses that were to do credit to her housekeeping, when an answer arrived which deferred it all. Mr Bingley was obliged to be in town the following day, and consequently unable to accept the honour of their invitation, &c. Mrs Bennet was quite disconcerted. She could not imagine what business he could have in town so soon after his arrival in Hertfordshire;[13] and she began to fear that he might be always flying about from one place to another, and never settled at Netherfield as he ought to be. Lady Lucas quieted her fears a little by starting the idea of his being gone to London only to get a large party for the ball; and a report soon followed that Mr Bingley was to bring twelve ladies and seven gentlemen with him to the assembly. The girls grieved over such a number of ladies; but were comforted the day before the ball by hearing, that instead of twelve, he had brought only six with him from London, his five sisters and a cousin. And when the party entered the assembly room, it consisted of only five altogether; Mr Bingley, his two sisters, the husband of the eldest, and another young man.

Mr Bingley was good looking and gentlemanlike; he had a pleasant countenance, and easy, unaffected manners. His sisters were fine women, with an air of decided fashion. His brother-in-law, Mr Hurst, merely looked the gentleman; but his friend Mr Darcy soon drew the attention of the room by his fine, tall person, handsome features, noble mien; and the report which was in general circulation within five minutes after his entrance, of his having ten thousand a year. The gentlemen pronounced him to be a fine figure of a man, the ladies declared he was much handsomer than Mr Bingley, and he was looked at with great admiration for about half the evening, till his manners gave a disgust which turned the tide of his popularity; for he was discovered to be proud, to be above his company, and above being pleased; and not all his large estate in Derbyshire[14] could then save him from having a most forbidding, disagreeable countenance, and being unworthy to be compared with his friend.

Mr Bingley had soon made himself acquainted with all the principal people in the room; he was lively and unreserved, danced every dance, was angry that the ball closed so early, and talked of giving one himself at Netherfield. Such amiable qualities must speak for themselves. What a contrast between him and his friend! Mr Darcy danced only once with Mrs Hurst and once with Miss Bingley, declined being introduced to any other lady, and spent the rest of the evening in walking about the room, speaking occasionally to one of his own party. His character was decided. He was the proudest, most disagreeable man in the world, and every body hoped that he would never come there again. Amongst the most violent against him was Mrs Bennet, whose dislike of his general behaviour, was sharpened into particular resentment, by his having slighted one of her daughters.

Elizabeth Bennet had been obliged, by the scarcity of gentlemen, to sit down for two dances; and during part of that time, Mr Darcy had been standing near enough for her to overhear a conversation between him and Mr Bingley, who came from the dance for a few minutes, to press his friend to join it.

"Come, Darcy," said he, "I must have you dance. I hate to see you standing about by yourself in this stupid manner. You had much better dance."

"I certainly shall not. You know how I detest it, unless I am particularly acquainted with my partner. At such an assembly as this, it would be insupportable. Your sisters are engaged, and there is not another woman in the room, whom it would not be a punishment to me to stand up with."

"I would not be so fastidious as you are," cried Bingley, "for a kingdom! Upon my honour, I never met with so many pleasant girls in my life, as I have this evening; and there are several of them you see uncommonly pretty."

---

[13] **Hertfordshire** The county of Hertford, in southeast England.

[14] **Derbyshire** The county of Derby, in north central England.

"*You* are dancing with the only handsome girl in the room," said Mr Darcy, looking at the eldest Miss Bennet.

"Oh! She is the most beautiful creature I ever beheld! But there is one of her sisters sitting down just behind you, who is very pretty, and I dare say, very agreeable. Do let me ask my partner to introduce you."

"Which do you mean?' and turning round, he looked for a moment at Elizabeth, till catching her eye, he withdrew his own and coldly said, "She is tolerable; but not handsome enough to tempt *me*; and I am in no humour at present to give consequence to young ladies who are slighted by other men. You had better return to your partner and enjoy her smiles, for you are wasting your time with me."

Mr Bingley followed his advice. Mr Darcy walked off; and Elizabeth remained with no very cordial feelings towards him. She told the story however with great spirit among her friends; for she had a lively, playful disposition, which delighted in any thing ridiculous.

The evening altogether passed off pleasantly to the whole family. Mrs Bennet had seen her eldest daughter much admired by the Netherfield party. Mr Bingley had danced with her twice, and she had been distinguished by his sisters. Jane was as much gratified by this, as her mother could be, though in a quieter way. Elizabeth felt Jane's pleasure. Mary had heard herself mentioned to Miss Bingley as the most accomplished girl in the neighbourhood; and Catherine and Lydia had been fortunate enough to be never without partners, which was all that they had yet learnt to care for at a ball. They returned therefore in good spirits to Longbourn, the village where they lived, and of which they were the principal inhabitants. They found Mr Bennet still up. With a book he was regardless of time; and on the present occasion he had a good deal of curiosity as to the event of an evening which had raised such splendid expectations. He had rather hoped that all his wife's views on the stranger would be disappointed; but he soon found that he had a very different story to hear.

"Oh! my dear Mr Bennet," as she entered the room, "we have had a most delightful evening, a most excellent ball. I wish you had been there. Jane was so admired, nothing could be like it. Every body said how well she looked; and Mr Bingley thought her quite beautiful, and danced with her twice. Only think of *that* my dear; he actually danced with her twice; and she was the only creature in the room that he asked a second time. First of all, he asked Miss Lucas. I was so vexed to see him stand up with her; but, however, he did not admire her at all: indeed, nobody can, you know; and he seemed quite struck with Jane as she was going down the dance. So, he enquired who she was, and got introduced, and asked her for the two next. Then, the two third he danced with Miss King, and the two fourth with Maria Lucas, and the two fifth with Jane again, and the two sixth with Lizzy, and the Boulanger—"

"If he had had any compassion for *me*," cried her husband impatiently, "he would not have danced half so much! For God's sake, say no more of his partners. Oh! that he had sprained his ankle in the first dance!"

"Oh! my dear," continued Mrs Bennet, "I am quite delighted with him. He is so excessively handsome! and his sisters are charming women. I never in my life saw any thing more elegant than their dresses. I dare say the lace upon Mrs Hurst's gown—"

Here she was interrupted again. Mr Bennet protested against any description of finery. She was therefore obliged to seek another branch of the subject, and related, with much bitterness of spirit and some exaggeration, the shocking rudeness of Mr Darcy.

"But I can assure you," she added, "that Lizzy does not lose much by not suiting *his* fancy; for he is a most disagreeable, horrid man, not at all worth pleasing. So high and so conceited that there was no enduring him! He walked here, and he walked there, fancying himself so very great! Not handsome enough to dance with! I wish you had been there, my dear, to have given him one of your set downs. I quite detest the man."

Questions for Critical Thinking

1. Show—using quotations from the selection—how Austen's novel represents the neoclassical literary style: stress on social decorum and orthodox morals.

2. Speculate as to why *Pride and Prejudice*—set deep in the provinces, infused with rural values, and focused on the minutiae of daily life—has survived so long and continued to attract readers today.

WILLIAM WORDSWORTH
Lines Composed a Few Miles above Tintern Abbey

Wordsworth's poem "Lines Composed a Few Miles above Tintern Abbey" represents a turning point in English letters. Before it appeared, poetry was dominated by the neoclassical style (1660–1798), which was characterized by correctness in language and moral sentiments supportive of the existing social order. Neoclassical poets revered the classical authors, especially the Romans, using their literary genres as models and sources of rules (see Pope's *An Essay on Man* in Chapter 17). With the appearance of Wordsworth's poem (1798), poetry fell under the sway of the romantic style, which was marked by rejection of the ideals and rules of classicism and neoclassicism. Romantic poets advocated the free, subjective expression of passion and personal feelings.

"Tintern Abbey" was one of the poems in *Lyrical Ballads* by William Wordsworth (1770–1850) and Samuel Taylor Coleridge (1772–1834). The poems in this collection were revolutionary in form, replacing what the two poets termed the artificial style of the neoclassicists with a more natural verse. For Coleridge, this meant ballad forms; for Wordsworth, simple lyrics voiced in the common language of the "middle and lower classes." This desire to reproduce customary speech, a reflection of the age's democratic revolutions, became henceforth a prominent motif in Western letters, even after the formal end of the romantic period in 1848 (see Hurston's *Their Eyes Were Watching God* in Chapter 21).

Wordsworth may have been a rebel in aesthetics, but he was a conservative in his social and political views, except for a brief flirtation with liberal ideas at the dawn of the French Revolution. From *Lyrical Ballads* onward, he used his poetry to express fears of the emerging modern world, such as teeming cities, mass democracy, and lack of community. He made the unspoiled countryside his symbol for the disappearing world of village England, under siege by the Industrial Revolution. For him, rural equaled good, urban equaled evil. His love for rural values was, at bottom, an attempt to revive the structures and symbols of the Middle Ages.

Reading the Selection

"Tintern Abbey" reflects Wordsworth's lifelong (religious) love affair with nature, which he conceives in pantheistic terms. Indeed, it is a classic expression of pantheism (Greek, "all gods"), the doctrine that identifies God with the forces and workings of nature. To this end, he describes nature in terms usually reserved for God, such as finding peace of mind in nature and calling the natural world "The anchor of my purest thoughts, the nurse, / The guide, the guardian of my heart, and soul / Of all my moral being."

The poem is a conversation, albeit one-sided, in which the poet speaks directly to his sister Dorothy ("My dear, dear Sister!"). Its conversational tone is established by the blank verse—a Renaissance verse form often used by poets in the romantic era—and the informal speech. Its theme is the cult of nature, about which, Wordsworth explains to Dorothy, his feelings have changed since he, "like a roe [deer]," roamed this spot five years before. Sadder but wiser, he now finds himself less exalted in mood, "but hearing . . . / The still, sad music of humanity." He tries to describe his younger self but finally gives up: "I cannot paint / What then I was." He, however, recognizes in his sister his old feelings ("in thy voice I catch / The language of my former heart"), hence his lecture on nature's moral power. Sharing nature in the company of a loved one, as seen in "Tintern Abbey," became a familiar theme in later romantic poetry and art.

Five years have past; five summers, with the length   1
Of five long winters! and again I hear
These waters,[15] rolling from their mountain-springs
With a soft inland murmur.—Once again
Do I behold these steep and lofty cliffs,
That on a wild secluded scene impress
Thoughts of more deep seclusion; and connect
The landscape with the quiet of the sky.
The day is come when I again repose
Here, under this dark sycamore, and view   10
These plots of cottage-ground, these orchard-tufts,[16]
Which at this season, with their unripe fruits,
Are clad in one green hue and lose themselves
'Mid groves and copses.[17] Once again I see
These hedge-rows, hardly hedge-rows, little lines
Of sportive wood run wild: these pastoral farms,
Green to the very door; and wreaths of smoke
Sent up, in silence, from among the trees!
With some uncertain notice, as might seem
Of vagrant dwellers in the houseless woods,   20
Or of some Hermit's cave, where by his fire
The Hermit sits alone.

          These beauteous forms,
Through a long absence, have not been to me
As is a landscape to a blind man's eye:
But oft, in lonely rooms, and 'mid the din[18]
Of towns and cities, I have owed to them
In hours of weariness, sensations sweet,
Felt in the blood, and felt along the heart
And passing even into my purer mind,   30
With tranquil restoration:—feelings too
Of unremembered pleasure: such, perhaps,
As have no slight or trivial influence
On that best portion of a good man's life,
His little, nameless, unremembered, acts
Of kindness and of love. Nor less, I trust,
To them I may have owed another gift,
Of aspect more sublime; that blessed mood,
In which the burthen[19] of the mystery,
In which the heavy and the weary weight   40
Of all this unintelligible world,
Is lightened:—that serene and blessed mood,
In which the affections gently lead us on,—
Until, the breath of this corporeal frame[20]
And even the motion of our human blood
Almost suspended, we are laid asleep

In body, and become a living soul:
While with an eye made quiet by the power
Of harmony, and the deep power of joy,
We see into the life of things.   50

          If this
Be but a vain belief, yet, oh! how oft—
In darkness and amid the many shapes
Of joyless daylight; when the fretful stir
Unprofitable, and the fever of the world,
Have hung upon the beatings of my heart—
How oft, in spirit, have I turned to thee,
O sylvan[21] Wye! thou wanderer thro' the woods,
How often has my spirit turned to thee!

      And now, with gleams of half-extinguished thought,   60
With many recognitions dim and faint,
And somewhat of a sad perplexity,
The picture of the mind revives again:
While here I stand, not only with the sense
Of present pleasure, but with pleasing thoughts
That in this moment there is life and food
For future years. And so I dare to hope,
Though changed, no doubt, from what I was when first
I came among these hills; when like a roe
I bounded o'er the mountains, by the sides   70
Of the deep rivers, and the lonely streams,
Wherever nature led: more like a man
Flying from something that he dreads, than one
Who sought the thing he loved. For nature then
(The coarser pleasures of my boyish days,
And their glad animal movements all gone by)
To me was all in all.—I cannot paint
What then I was. The sounding cataract[22]
Haunted me like a passion: the tall rock,
The mountain, and the deep and gloomy wood,   80
Their colours and their forms, were then to me
An appetite; a feeling and a love,
That had no need of a remoter charm,
By thought supplied, nor any interest
Unborrowed from the eye.—That time is past,
And all its aching joys are now no more,
And all its dizzy raptures. Not for this
Faint I, nor mourn nor murmur; other gifts
Have followed; for such loss, I would believe,
Abundant recompense. For I have learned   90
To look on nature, not as in the hour
Of thoughtless youth; but hearing oftentimes
The still, sad music of humanity,
Nor harsh nor grating, though of ample power
To chasten and subdue. And I have felt
A presence that disturbs me with the joy
Of elevated thoughts; a sense sublime

---

[15] **waters** Wye River. The Wye, rising in East Wales, flows west across the English border and then south into the estuary of the Severn River. The ruins of Tintern Abbey are on the banks of the Wye.
[16] **orchard-tufts** Orchard with clumps of trees.
[17] **copse** Thicket.
[18] **din** Noise.
[19] **burthen** Burden.
[20] **corporeal frame** Human body.

---

[21] **sylvan** From Latin, *silva*, "wood." Wooded.
[22] **cataract** Waterfall.

Of something far more deeply interfused,
Whose dwelling is the light of setting suns,
And the round ocean and the living air,   100
And the blue sky, and in the mind of man:
A motion and a spirit, that impels
All thinking things, all objects of all thought,
And rolls through all things. Therefore am I still
A lover of the meadows and the woods,
And mountains; and of all that we behold
From this green earth; of all the mighty world
Of eye, and ear,—both what they half create,
And what perceive; well pleased to recognise
In nature and the language of the sense,   110
The anchor of my purest thoughts, the nurse,
The guide, the guardian of my heart, and soul
Of all my moral being.

              Nor perchance,
If I were not thus taught, should I the more
Suffer my genial spirits to decay:
For thou[23] art with me here upon the banks
Of this fair river; thou my dearest Friend,
My dear, dear Friend; and in thy voice I catch
The language of my former heart, and read   120
My former pleasures in the shooting lights
Of thy wild eyes. Oh! yet a little while
May I behold in thee what I was once,
My dear, dear Sister! and this prayer I make,
Knowing that Nature never did betray
The heart that loved her; 'tis her privilege,

Through all the years of this our life, to lead
From joy to joy: for she can so inform
The mind that is within us, so impress
With quietness and beauty, and so feed   130
With lofty thoughts, that neither evil tongues,
Rash judgments, nor the sneers of selfish men,
Nor greetings where no kindness is, nor all
The dreary intercourse of daily life,
Shall e'er prevail against us, or disturb
Our cheerful faith, that all which we behold
Is full of blessings. Therefore let the moon
Shine on thee in thy solitary walk;
And let the misty mountain-winds be free
To blow against thee: and, in after years,   140
When these wild ecstasies shall be matured
Into a sober pleasure; when thy mind
Shall be a mansion for all lovely forms,
Thy memory be as a dwelling-place
For all sweet sounds and harmonies; oh! then,
If solitude, or fear, or pain, or grief,
Should be thy portion, with what healing thoughts
Of tender joy wilt thou remember me,
And these my exhortations! Nor, perchance—
If I should be where I no more can hear   150
Thy voice, nor catch from thy wild eyes these gleams
Of past existence—will thou then forget
That on the banks of this delightful stream
We stood together; and that I, so long
A worshipper of Nature, hither came
Unwearied in that service; rather say
With warmer love—oh! with far deeper zeal
Of holier love. Nor wilt thou then forget,
That after many wanderings, many years
Of absence, these steep woods and lofty cliffs,   160
And this green pastoral landscape, were to me
More dear, both for themselves and for thy sake!

---

[23] **thou** Dorothy Wordsworth (1771–1855), sister and constant companion of William Wordsworth. She shared a home with him before and after his marriage and kept journals about him and his circle—*Alfoxden Journal* (1798) and *Grasmere Journal* (1800–1803).

                  ∞

Questions for Critical Thinking

1. Show how Wordsworth's poem embodies the romantic literary style. Be specific in your use of examples.

2. Discuss the persistence of the romantic "cult of Nature" in today's culture.

JOHANN WOLFGANG VON GOETHE
Selection from *Faust*, Part I

Goethe [GUHR-tuh] is generally acknowledged as Germany's greatest author, and *Faust* is considered his masterpiece. A play in verse, *Faust* is the most popular drama in Germany, where hardly a day passes without its being performed on some stage. Outside Germany, it is better known as a work to be read. This play's appeal is in its portrait of Faust as archetypal rebel, ready to trade his soul for forbidden knowledge. Some read a more sinister meaning into its appeal, making the Faustian quest a metaphor for what they perceive to be the West's drive for world dominion and mastery of nature.

Goethe's play merits comparison with Christopher Marlowe's *Dr. Faustus* (1604), since both were based on the same legend. Where Marlowe's ending is morally ambiguous—Is his Faust a noble martyr who played God or a sinner meant to warn others?—Goethe's Faust, despite his mistakes, is ultimately saved by God. Notwithstanding the clarity of its ending, Goethe introduced a new dimension of ambiguity into this work: *why* God rescues the wayward hero is not made clear.

Goethe recognized the moral uncertainty of his approach. Unable to finish the play, he first presented it to the world with the hero Faust left alive and in despair. Subtitled Part I, this portion of *Faust* was issued in 1808. For the rest of his life Goethe wrestled with Part II, finishing it before he died in 1832.

Despite the unresolved ending, Part I is Goethe's finest work. Faust is presented in this era's romantic language, which rejected historic religion but believed there was a mystery at the core of life. Thus Faust is revealed as obsessed with human ignorance ("nobody knows . . . the tiniest crumb / Which is why I feel completely undone"). Disappointed in science, he calls up the devil Mephistopheles "to enlarge my soul to encompass all humanity." Faust, joined by Mephistopheles, then goes through a series of adventures in quest of life's elusive meaning. At the end of Part I, Faust's quest, rather than bringing knowledge, has brought despair; he prays, "I wish I had never been born."

In Part II, Goethe further muddles the play's moral. It ends with Faust ironically yielding his soul to Mephistopheles, thinking he is doing it for the good of humanity. Faust's motive is pure, but his act rests on an illusion: Mephistopheles has tricked him into a meaningless death. And yet, by saving Faust from hell, Goethe seems to say that to God, dreams count more than deeds.

The middle-class Johann Wolfgang von Goethe (1749–1832) was one of the West's last universal men. Besides being a dramatist, he was also an essayist, author of lyric verse, novelist, lawyer, and scientist, writing on botany, anatomy, and the theory of color. No ivory-tower intellectual, he was for many years a bureaucrat in Weimar, capital of the petty duchy of Saxe-Weimar-Eisenach.

Reading the Selection

This selection contains most of *Faust*'s first scene. Introduced here are the two scholars, Wagner and Faust, who symbolize rival paths to truth: sense or sensibility, Enlightenment or romanticism. Wagner is sense, dedicated to reason and determined "to improve [my] mind so, / I'd stay up all night gladly." Faust, bored with Wagner, is sensibility, so devoted to feeling that he is paradoxically prepared to commit suicide to calm his soul. During the rest of Part I, Faust's commitment to romantic feeling brings destruction in its wake. Perhaps because of destruction's link with feeling, Goethe later condemned romanticism as "unhealthy."

⚬

Night

In a narrow, high-vaulted Gothic[24] room, FAUST, *seated restlessly in an armchair at his desk.*

FAUST: I've studied, alas, philosophy,   1
  Law and medicine, recto[25] and verso,[26]
  And how I regret it, theology also,
  Oh God, how hard I've slaved away,
  With what result? Poor fool that I am,
  I'm no whit wiser than when I began!
  I've got a Master of Arts degree,
  On top of that a Ph.D.,
  For ten long years, around and about,
  Upstairs, downstairs, in and out,   10
  I've led my students by the nose
  To what conclusion?—that nobody knows,
  Or ever can know, the tiniest crumb!
  Which is why I feel completely undone.
    Of course I'm cleverer than these stuffed shirts,
  These Doctors, Masters, Jurists,[27] Priests;
  I'm not bothered by a doubt or a scruple,
  I'm not afraid of Hell or the Devil—
  But the consequence is, my mirth's all gone
  No longer can I fool myself   20
  I am able to teach men
  How to be better, love true worth
  I've got no money or property,
  Worldly honors or celebrity
  A dog wouldn't put up with this life!
  Which is why I've turned to magic,
  Seeking to know, by ways occult,
  From ghostly mouths, many a secret
  So I no longer need to sweat
  Painfully explaining what   30
  I don't know anything about
  So I may penetrate the power
  That holds the universe together,
  Behold the source whence all proceeds
  And deal no more in words, words, words.

  O full moon, melancholy-bright,
  Friend I've watched for, many a night,
  Till your quiet-shining face
  Appeared above my high-piled desk—
  If this were only the last time   40
  You looked down on my pain!
  If only I might stray at will
  Beneath your light, high on the hill,

Haunt with spirits upland hollows,
Fade with you in dim-lit meadows,
And soul no longer gasping in
The stink of learning's midnight lamp,
Bathe in your dews till well again!

But oh, unhappy man that I am,
Isn't this your familiar prison?   50
Damned musty-smelling hole in the wall
Where even the golden light of Heaven
Must struggle hard to force its way through
The dim panes of the stained-glass window.[28]
Yes, here you sit walled in by books
Stacked up to the shadowy vault,
Books worm-eaten, covered with dust,
With rolls of paper, all smoke-blackened,
Pushed and wedged and stuck between them,
With vessels, flasks, retorts, and beakers[29]   60
Filling all the shelves and drawers,
And adding to the dense confusion
Your family's ancient furnishings.
Call this a world, this world you live in?

Can you still wonder why your heart
Should tighten in your breast so anxiously?
Why your every impulse is stopped short
By an inexplicable misery?
Instead of the living house of Nature
God created man to dwell in,   70
Dust, mold, they are what surround you,
Dog's bones, a human skeleton.

Escape outdoors! Breathe the fresh air!
And this strange book of secret lore
By Nostradamus'[30] own hand—
What better help to master the secrets
Of how the stars turn in their orbits,
From Nature learn to understand
The spirits' power to speak to spirits.

---

[24] **Gothic** Love for all things associated with the Middle Ages, such as the **Gothic** style, was a defining aspect of the romantic movement.

[25] **recto** From Latin, the right-hand page. The page of a manuscript to be read first.

[26] **verso** From Latin, the page being turned. The page of a manuscript to be read second.

[27] **Jurists** Lawyers.

[28] **stained-glass window** A defining feature of **Gothic** architecture.

[29] **vessels, flasks, retorts, and beakers** Assorted laboratory containers, which suggest that Faust is practicing alchemy, a medieval pseudoscience that sought to transform base metal into gold, discover a universal cure for disease, and uncover the secret of human life.

[30] **book . . . by Nostradamus'** Nostradamus (1503–1566), or Michel De Notredame, was a French astrologer, doctor, and prophet, most famously the author of *Centuries*, a work in ten volumes. Written in rhyming four-line verses, *Centuries* is divided into sets of one hundred verses, with each set called a century. This work is highly ambiguous because the text freely mixes words from French, Spanish, Latin, and Hebrew, and the prophecies take the forms of riddles, puns, anagrams, and epigrams. Devotees of the occult have studied the work since its publication in 1558. In 1781 the Inquisition condemned it.

Sitting here and racking your brains   80
To puzzle out the sacred signs—
What a sterile, futile business!
Spirits, I feel your presence around me:
Announce yourselves if you hear me!

[*He opens the book and his eye encounters the sign of the Macrocosm.*[31]]

The pure bliss[32] flooding all my senses
Seeing this! Through every nerve and vein
I feel youth's fiery, fresh spirit race again.
Was it a god marked out these signs
By which my agitated bosom's stilled,
By which my bleak heart's filled with joy,   90
By whose mysterious agency
The powers of Nature all around me stand revealed?
Am *I* a god? All's bright as day!
By these pure brush strokes I can see,
At my soul's feet, great Nature unconcealed.
And the sage's words—I understand them, finally:
"The spirit world is not barred shut,
It's your own mind, your dead heart!
Stand up unappalled, my scholar,
And bathe your breast in the rose of Aurora[33]!"   100

[*He contemplates the sign.*]

How all is woven one, uniting,
Each in the other living, working!
How Heavenly Powers rise, descend,
Passing gold vessels from hand to hand!
On wings that scatter sweet-smelling blessings,
Everywhere they post in earth
And make a universal harmony sound forth!
Oh, what a sight! But a sight, and no more!
How seize you and hold you, infinite Nature?
Find the life-giving fountains, your breasts,   110
      that sustain
Both the earth and the heavens, breasts at which
      my breast,
So dried up, a desert, is yearning to nurse—
You flow, *overflow*, yet I go on thirsting in vain.

[*Morosely,*[34] *he turns the pages of the book and comes on the sign of the Spirit of Earth.*[35]]

What a different effect this sign has on me!
You, Spirit of Earth, are closer to me,
Already fresh lifeblood pours through every vein,
Already I glow as if from new wine—
Now I have the courage to dare
To go out into the world and bear
The ill and well of life, to battle   120
Storms, and when the ship splits, not to tremble.

How the air grows thick overhead—
The moon's put out her light,
The lamp flame looks like dying.
Vapors eddy and drift—
Red flashes, leaping, dazzle—
Fear, shuddering down from the vault,
Seizes me by the throat!
Spirit I have invoked, hovering near:
Reveal yourself!   130
How all my senses fumble toward, founder in
Never-experienced feelings!
Spirit, I feel I am yours, body and breath!
Appear! Oh, you must! Though it costs me my life!

[*He seizes the book and pronounces the Spirit's mystic spell.*[36] *A red flame flashes, in the midst of which the Spirit appears.*]

SPIRIT: Who's calling?
FAUST: [*Averting his face*] Overpowering! Dreadful!
SPIR.: Potently you've drawn me here,
      A parched mouth sucking at my sphere.
      And now—?
FAUST: Oh, you're unbearable!   140
SPIR.: You're breathless from your implorations
      To see my face, to hear me speak,
      I've yielded to your supplications
      And here I am.—Well, in a funk
      I find the superman[37]! I come at your bidding
      And you're struck dumb! Is this the mind
      That builds a whole interior world, doting
      On its own creation, puffed to find
      Itself quite on a par, the equal,
      Of us spirits? Wherever is that Faust   150
      Who urged himself just now with all
      His strength on me, made such a fuss?
      You're Faust? The one who at my breath's
      Least touch, shudders to his depths,
      A worm who wriggles away in terror?
FAUST: *I* shrink back from you, abject and fearful?
      Yes, I'm called so, called Faust—your equal!
SPIR.: I surge up and down
      In the tides of being,
      Drive forward and back   160
      In the shocks of men's striving!
      I am birth and the grave,
      An eternal ocean,
      A web changing momently,

---

[31] *sign of the Macrocosm* Occult symbol that represents the universe, usually depicted as a series of concentric circles surrounding the earth, with the circles serving as orbits of the sun, moon, planets, and stars. In occult science, scholars sought to understand the influence of the Macrocosm on the Microcosm (individual human being).
[32] **bliss** Faust at first has a transcendental moment as he contemplates the **sign of the Macrocosm,** but the ecstasy quickly passes and he becomes **morose.**
[33] **Aurora** Dawn. Aurora was the Roman goddess of dawn.
[34] *Morosely* Faust comes to earth as his mood changes (see footnote 32).
[35] *the sign of the Spirit of Earth* Occult symbol that represents the **Earth Spirit,** which, in turn, speaks for and controls the earth. Faust initially feels rejuvenated when he contemplates this sign ("I glow as if from new wine"), but his mood soon changes to fear.

---

[36] *pronounces . . . spell* Faust speaks the mantra—mystical formula—that invokes the **Earth Spirit.**
[37] **superman** The **Earth Spirit** speaks ironically, mocking Faust for being afraid of him.

A life burning hotly.
Thus seated at time's whirring loom
I weave the Godhead's living gown.
FAUST: We're equals, I know! I feel so close to you, near,
You busy spirit ranging everywhere!
SPIR.: It's your idea of me you're equal to,   170
Not me! [*Vanishes.*]
FAUST: [*Deflated*] Not you?
Then who?
Me, made in God's own image,
Not even equal to you?

[*A knocking*]

Death! My famulus[38]—I know that knock.
Finis[39] my supremest moment—worse luck!
That visions richer than I could have guessed
Should be scattered by a shuffling Dryasdust[40]!

[WAGNER *in dressing gown and nightcap, carrying a lamp.*
FAUST *turns around impatiently.*]

WAGNER: Excuse me, sir, but wasn't that   180
Your voice I heard declaiming? A Greek tragedy,
I'm sure. Well, that's an art that comes in handy
Nowadays. I'd love to master it.
People say, how often I have heard it,
Actors could really give lessons to the clergy.
FAUST: Yes, when clergymen go in for acting—
Something I have seen in more than one case.
WAG.: Oh dear, to be so shut up in one's study,
Seeing the world only now and then, on holiday,
And only from far off, as if through a spyglass—   190
How can one ever teach it what's the right way?
FAUST: You can't—unless you speak with feeling's own
True voice, unless your words are from
The soul and by their spontaneous power,
Seize with delight the soul of your hearer.
But no! Stick in your seats, you fellows!
Paste bits and pieces together, cook up
A beggar's stew from others' leftovers,
Over a flame you've sweated to coax up
From your own little heap of smoldering ashes,   200
Filling with wonder all the jackasses,
If that's the kind of stuff your taste favors—
But you'll never get heart to cleave to heart
Unless you speak from your own heart.
WAG.: Still and all, a good delivery is what
Makes the orator. I'm far behind in that art.
FAUST: Advance yourself in an honest way.
Don't try to be a performing ape!
Good sense, good understanding, they
Are quite enough, they are their own art.   210
When you have something serious
To say, what need is there to hunt
Around for fancy words and phrases?
All those speeches polished up

With bits and pieces collected out
Of every tongue and race, are about
As bracing as the foggy autumnal breeze
Swaying the last leaves on the trees.
WAG.: Dear God, but art is long
And our life—lots shorter.[41]   220
Often in the middle of my labor
My confidence and courage falter.
How hard it is to master all the stuff
For dealing with each and every source.
And before you've traveled half the course,
Poor devil, you have gone and left this life.
FAUST: Parchment,[42] tell me—that's the sacred fount
You drink out of, to slake your eternal thirst?
The only true refreshment that exists
You get from where? Yourself—where all things   230
start.
WAG.: But sir, it's such a pleasure, isn't it,
To enter into another age's spirit,
To see what thinkers long before us thought
And measure how far since then we have got.
FAUST: As far as to the stars, no doubt!
Your history, why, it's a joke
Bygone times are a seven-sealed book.[43]
The thing you call the spirit of the past,[44]
What is it? Nothing but your own poor spirit
With the past reflected in it.   240
And it's pathetic, what's to be seen in your mirror!
One look and I have to beat a quick retreat—
A trash can, strewn attic, junk-filled cellar,
At best it is a blood-and-thunder thriller
Improved with the most high-minded sentiments
Exactly suited for mouthing by marionettes.
WAG.: But the world we're in! The hearts and minds
of men!
Surely all of us want to know about them.
FAUST: Yes, know as the world knows knowing!
Who wants to know the real truth, tell me?   250
Those few with vision, feeling, understanding,
Who failed to stand guard, most unwisely,
Over their tongues, speaking their minds and hearts
For the mob to hear—you know what's been
their fate:
They were crucified, burnt, torn to bits.
But we must break off, friend, it's getting late.
WAG.: I love serious conversation; to improve
One's mind so, I'd stay up all night gladly.
But it's Easter Sunday, sir, in the morning,

---

[38] **famulus** Attendant.
[39] **finis** Latin, "thus ends."
[40] **Dryasdust** Faust's negative nickname for his colleague
Wagner.

---

[41] **art is long and our life—lots shorter** Wagner muddles the
ancient Latin proverb, *ars longa, vita brevis,* "art is long, life is
short." The proverb is attributed variously to Horace, Seneca,
and Hippocrates.
[42] **parchment** Book manuscripts. With ill-concealed scorn, Faust
asks Wagner if books are his source of knowledge.
[43] **seven-sealed book** Revelation 6 describes a book with seven
seals, whose opening of the seals coincides with the apocalypse.
[44] **spirit of the past** Faust ridicules Wagner's reliance on history.
"Spirit of the past" is meant sarcastically, in contrast to Faust's
earlier summoning of the **Earth Spirit.**

And perhaps I may ask you a question or two then,   260
   if you're willing?
I've studied hard, yes, studied diligently,
I know a lot, but still, I aim at knowing everything.

[*Exit.*]

FAUST: [*Alone*] How such fellows keep their hopes up is a
   wonder!
   Their attention forever occupied with trivialities,
   Digging greedily in the ground for treasure,
   And when they've turned a worm up—what
      ecstasies!

That banal, commonplace human accents
Should fill air just now filled with spirits' voices!
Still, this one time you've earned my thanks,
You sorriest of human specimens.[45]   270
You snatched me out of the grip of a dejection
So profound, I was nearly driven off
My head. So gigantic was the apparition,
It made me feel no bigger than a dwarf—

Me, the one made in the very image of God,
Fully persuaded the mirror of eternal truth
At last lay in his reach, already basking in
The heavenly light and glory, all earthliness cast off
Me, higher placed than the cherubim,[46] imagining
His own strength already poured freely,   280
Divinely creative, through Nature's great body!
      Well, now
I must pay for it: a thunderous word and I am
   laid low.

No, I can't claim we are equals, presumptuously!
Though I was strong enough to draw you[47] down
   to me,
Holding on to you was another matter entirely.
In that exalted-humbling moment of pure delight
I felt myself at once both small and great.
And then you thrust me remorselessly back
Into uncertainty, which is all of humanity's fate.   290
Who'll teach me what to seek, what to shun?
Yield, should I, to that burning desire of mine?
Alas, what we do as much as what's done to us
Cramps and obstructs our entire life's progress.

The noblest thoughts our minds are able to entertain
Are undermined by a corrupting grossness;
When we've managed a bit of the good of this world
   for ourselves
Then the better's dismissed as a fairy tale or confi-
   dence game
Those radiant sentiments which were once life itself
   to us
Grow pale and expire in the glare of the world's   300
   busyness.

There was a time when bold imagination
Pitched her flight as high as God's own station,
But now that everything I took such joy in
Has shipwrecked for me in time's maelstrom,
She's quite content to cower in a narrow space.
In our heart of hearts Care has her nesting place
And there she does her worst,
Dithering nervously, poisoning pleasure and peace,
Masking herself as genuine concern
For house and home, for wife and children,   310
In fear of fire and flood, violence and mayhem
You shrink back in terror from imagined blows
And weep over losing what you never in fact lose.

Oh no, I'm no god, only too well do I know it!
A worm's what I am, wriggling through the dust
And finding his nourishment in it,
Whom the wayfarer treads underfoot.

These high walls with their shelves and niches—
Dust is what shrinks them to a stifling cell;
This moth-eaten world with its trash and its   320
   trinkets—
It is the reason I feel shut up in jail.
And here I'll discover the things I most lack?
Devour thousands of books so as to learn, shall I,
Mankind has always been stretched on the rack,
With now and then somebody, somewhere, who's
   happy?
You, empty skull there, smirking so, I know why!
Your brain, once as whirling as mine is,
Seeking the bright day, longing for truth,
Blundered about, lost in onerous darkness, just as
   wretchedly.
And all that apparatus—how I feel you are   330
   mocking me,
With your wheels and cylinders, cams, and
   ratchets[48]!
I stood at the door, certain you were the key
But the key, though cut intricately, couldn't
   unlatch it.
Great Nature, so mysterious even in broad day,
Doesn't let you unveil her, plead how you may.
And if she won't allow you one glimpse of her
   mystery,
You'll never compel her with all your machinery.

Old instruments I've never touched,
You're here, and why?—because my father[49]
   used you.
And you, old scrolls, have gathered soot   340
For as long as the lamp's smoked on this table.
Much better to have squandered the little I've got
Than find myself sweating under its weight.

---

[45] **You . . . specimens** Wagner.
[46] **cherubim** One of the nine orders of angels.
[47] **you** The **Earth Spirit.**

[48] **wheels and cylinders, cams, and ratchets** Apparatus used in alchemy (see footnote 29).
[49] **father** Faust has followed in his father's footsteps as an alchemist.

It's from our fathers, what we inherit,
To make it ours truly, we've got to earn it.
What's never used weighs like lead
What's useful responds to a living need.

But why do I find I must stare in that corner,
Is that bottle[50] a magnet enchanting my sight?
Why is everything all at once lovely and luminous,   350
Like woods when the moon's up and floods them
          with light?

Vial,[51] I salute you, O rare, O precious!
And reverently bring you down from the shelf,
Honoring in you man's cunning and craft.
Quintessence of easeful sleeping potions,
Pure distillation of subtle poisons,
Do your master the kindness that lies in your power!
One look at you and my agony lessens,
One touch and my feverish straining grows calmer
And my tight-stretched spirit bit by bit slackens.   360
The glassy waters glitter before me,
My way is clear—into Ocean's immensity,
A new day is dawning, a new shore beckons.

A fiery chariot, bird-winged, swoops down on me,
I am ready to follow new roads through the ether,
Aloft into new spheres of purest activity.
An existence so exalted, a rapture so godlike—
Does the worm of a minute ago deserve it?
No matter. Resolution! Turn your back bravely
On the sunlight, sweet sunlight, of our earth forever!   370
Fling wide open those dark gates, defiantly,

Which the whole world skulks past with averted
          heads!
The time has come to disprove by deeds,
Because the gods are great, man's a derision,
To cringe back no more from that black pit[52]
Whose unspeakable tortures are your own
          invention,
To struggle toward that narrow gate
Around which all Hellfire's darkly flaming,
To take resolutely the last step,
Even at the risk of utter extinction.   380

And now let me take this long forgotten
Crystal wine cup down from its case.
Once it shone at our family feasts,
Making the solemn guests' faces brighten
When it went round with the lively toasts.
The figures artfully cut in the crystal,
Which it was the duty of all at the table,
In turn, to make up rhymes about,
Then drain the cup at a single draught—
How they recall many nights of my youth!   390
But now there's no passing you on to my neighbor
Or thinking up rhymes to parade my quick wit;
Here is a juice that is quick too—to intoxicate,
A brownish liquid, see, filling the beaker,
Chosen by me, by me mixed together,
My last drink! Which now I lift up in festive greeting
To the bright new day I can see dawning!

[*He raises the cup to his lips. Bells peal,*[53] *a choir bursts into song.*]

---

[50] **bottle** Perhaps of laudanum, a mixture of opium and alcohol. Laudanum was used in the early 1800s as a sedative; however, an overdose could cause death.
[51] **Vial** Bottle of laudanum.

---

[52] **black pit** Hell.
[53] ***Bells peal*** A melodramatic moment: The church bells of Easter morning stop Faust as he prepares to drink the potion—thus saving him from his suicide attempt.

Questions for Critical Thinking

1. Characterize the Faustian spirit, as revealed in this selection. Use the text for your examples.

2. Do you think that Western culture is Faustian? Explain.

PERCY BYSSHE SHELLEY
Poems

Today, Percy Bysshe Shelley (1792–1822) is regarded as a great romantic poet; in his own day, however, his works were not widely known. Of about 450 poems, only 70 or so were in print when he died. Poems issued during his life, such as *Queen Mab* (1813), gave him a reputation for atheism and radicalism. Moreover, his scandalous life cast a shadow over his poetry and obscured its true meaning.

When Shelley fled England in 1818, he left behind a legend of bohemianism and rebellion dating from early youth. As a student at Oxford, he was expelled for refusing to disown an atheistic pamphlet he had written. This expulsion led to a break with his wealthy father, who later disinherited him. After university, he offended middle-class norms by sharing households with like-minded friends, including unattached women. Both of his marriages began as elopements. The second elopement hastened the suicide of his first wife; her family then obtained a court order denying him access to his children. The second marriage, to Mary Wollstonecraft Godwin, was more stable; still, the Shelleys fled England for the continent, both because of debts and for the not unreasonable fear that their children might also be taken away.

Shelley's last four years, wandering in Italy, brought maturity and some of his best poems, including *Prometheus Unbound* (1820), the story of the Titan persecuted by divine forces for his efforts to help humanity—a work whose subtext was Shelley's own trials. Back home, the legend of "Shelley-the-Monster" grew so that few mourned Shelley's drowning in Italy a month before his thirtieth birthday.

Recent critics have discovered a Shelley much different from the one of legend. He is a Platonist who advocated (1) the doctrine of Platonic love, which holds that physical beauty is secondary to intellectual beauty, and (2) the idea that the poet is an inspired person ("the unacknowledged legislator of the world"). He is also considered a reformer today and less of a revolutionary, because he was repelled by violence of all kinds; and his causes, such as nonviolence, democracy, free speech, and vegetarianism, have entered the mainstream.

Reading the Selections

"Ozymandias" (1817) and "England in 1819" (1819) are Shelley's most splendid sonnets. "Ozymandias" grew out of romantic Hellenism, which made Greece into an imaginary world where hearts troubled by the present sought nourishment from the glorious past. Shelley's inspiration was a Greek writer's record of an inscription honoring Ozymandias, another name for Egypt's Ramses II. Shelley used the inscription (lines 10–11) to underscore the Platonic theme that human achievement is illusory. In "England in 1819," written during this exile, he described his country in the grip of post-Napoleonic reaction, though he ended with the prediction of a new day.

"Ode to the West Wind" (1820) is one of Shelley's most famous poems. It marked a personal crisis, following the death of a child in Italy, and savage reviews of new poems in England. In form, it comprises five sonnets, each built of three *terza rima* verses in the style of Dante (see *The Divine Comedy* in Chapter 10, Volume I) plus an end-couplet. The ode builds in emotional power as it moves along. The images of the first three sonnets—the leaf, the cloud, and the wave—are folded into the fourth sonnet with the words "If I were . . . ." In the fifth sonnet, the poem changes to become a prayer. Typically, the poem ends on a hopeful note: "If Winter comes, can Spring be far behind?"

∞

Ozymandias

I met a traveler from an antique land   The hand that mocked them, and the heart that fed:
Who said: Two vast and trunkless legs of stone   And on the pedestal these words appear:
Stand in the desert . . . Near them, on the sand,   "My name is Ozymandias, king of kings: 10
Half sunk, a shattered visage lies, whose frown,   Look on my works, ye Mighty, and despair!"
And wrinkled lip, and sneer of cold command,   Nothing beside remains. Round the decay
Tell that its sculptor well those passions read   Of that colossal wreck, boundless and bare
Which yet survive, stamped on these lifeless things,   The lone and level sands stretch far away.

∞

England in 1819[54]

An old, mad, blind, despised, and dying King[55];   Through public scorn,—mud from a muddy spring;
Princes,[56] the dregs of their dull race, who flow   Rulers who neither see nor feel nor know,
                                                                         But leechlike to their fainting country cling
                                                                         Till they drop, blind in blood, without a blow.
                                                                         A people starved and stabbed in th' untilled field;
                                                                         An army, whom liberticide[57] and prey
                                                                         Makes as a two-edged sword to all who wield;
                                                                         Golden and sanguine[58] laws which tempt and slay;   10
                                                                         Religion Christless, Godless—a book sealed;
                                                                         A senate, Time's worst statute, unrepealed[59]—
                                                                         Are graves from which a glorious Phantom may
                                                                         Burst, to illumine our tempestuous day.

---

[54] **1819** A dark year in the history of England, following the end of the Napoleonic era in 1815. The abrupt shift from wartime to peace brought about a prolonged depression, high food prices, and social unrest, particularly in the industrialized North, culminating in the Peterloo Massacre on August 16, 1819. The "massacre" was the violent dispersal by armed cavalry of a protest meeting conducted on St. Peter's Fields in Manchester. More than sixty thousand protesters had assembled, expressing their lack of confidence in the Tory government and demanding parliamentary reform. Tory leaders overreacted and sent in troops to break up the meeting, with the result that eleven people were killed and more than five hundred injured. Shelley's poem reflects his support for the protesters and his radical politics.
[55] **King** George III (r. 1760–1820). Four times, George III experienced episodes of mental illness, until, in 1811, he became permanently deranged. He also became blind.
[56] **Princes** The four sons of George III included (1) the Prince Regent, later George IV (r. 1811–1820, 1820–1830), a notorious dandy and libertine; first marriage (1785–1795) to Mrs. Maria Anne Fitzherbert (1756–1837), a commoner, declared invalid because he was underage and she a Catholic; second marriage (1795–1820) to Princess Caroline of Brunswick (1768–1821) was disastrous, ending in separation (1814) and divorce; (2) William, Duke of Clarence, later William IV (r. 1830–1837), served in Royal Navy (1778–1790), numerous love affairs, father of ten illegitimate children, second in line to throne, after 1817; married Princess Adelaide of Saxe-Meiningen in 1818; (3) Earnest, Duke of Cumberland (1799), King of Hanover, an unpopular figure because of his conservative views; and (4) Edward, Duke of Kent (1767–1820), soldier, married Princess Mary Louisa Victoria of Saxe-Coburg-Gotha (1818), father of Queen Victoria (1837–1901).

---

[57] **liberticide** The murder of liberty.
[58] **sanguine** Bloody.
[59] **unrepealed** Shelley supported parliamentary reform. *Senate* means "parliament."

∞

Ode to the West Wind

I

O wild West Wind, thou breath of Autumn's being,   Yellow, and black, and pale, and hectic red,
Thou, from whose unseen presence the leaves dead   Pestilence-stricken multitudes: O thou,
Are driven, like ghosts from an enchanter fleeing,   Who chariotest to their dark wintry bed

The wingéd seeds, where they lie cold and low,
Each like a corpse within its grave, until
Thine azure sister of the Spring shall blow

Her clarion o'er the dreaming earth, and fill   10
(Driving sweet buds like flocks to feed in air)
With living hues and odors plain and hill:

Wild Spirit, which art moving everywhere
Destroyer and preserver; hear, oh, hear!

II

Thou on whose stream, mid the steep sky's commotion,
Loose clouds like earth's decaying leaves are shed,
Shook from the tangled boughs of Heaven and Ocean,

Angels of rain and lightning: there are spread
On the blue surface of thine aery surge,[60]
Like the bright hair uplifted from the head   20

Of some fierce Maenad,[61] even from the dim verge
Of the horizon to the zenith's height,
The locks of the approaching storm. Thou dirge

Of the dying year, to which this closing night
Will be the dome of a vast sepulcher,[62]
Vaulted with all thy congregated might

Of vapors, from whose solid atmosphere
Black rain, and fire, and hail will burst: oh, hear!

III

Thou who didst waken from his summer dreams
The blue Mediterranean, where he lay,   30
Lulled by the coil of his crystálline streams,

Beside a pumice[63] isle in Baiae's bay[64]
And saw in sleep old palaces and towers
Quivering within the wave's intenser day,

All overgrown with azure moss and flowers
So sweet, the sense faints picturing them! Thou
For whose path the Atlantic's level powers

---

[60] **aery surge** Airy surge, i.e., the turbulent clouds.
[61] **Maenad** Female participant in the orgiastic revels of the god Dionysus; the hair of Maeneds, in Greek art, was represented as wild and unruly.
[62] **sepulcher** Tomb.
[63] **pumice** Volcanic stone, made of glass.
[64] **Baiae's bay** Baiae, in ancient Rome, was a famous resort town near Naples, home to the wealthy, including Julius Caesar and Emperor Nero.

Cleave themselves into chasms, while far below
The sea-blooms and the oozy woods which wear
The sapless foliage of the ocean, know   40

Thy voice, and suddenly grow gray with fear,
And tremble and despoil themselves; oh, hear!

IV

If I were a dead leaf thou mightest bear;
If I were a swift cloud to fly with thee;
A wave to pant beneath thy power, and share

The impulse of thy strength, only less free
Than thou, O uncontrollable! If even
I were as in my boyhood, and could be

The comrade of thy wanderings over Heaven,
As then, when to outstrip thy skyey speed   50
Scarce seemed a vision; I would ne'er have striven

As thus with thee in prayer in my sore need.
Oh, lift me as a wave, a leaf, a cloud!
I fall upon the thorns of life! I bleed!

A heavy weight of hours has chained and bowed
One too like thee: tameless, and swift, and proud.

V

Make me thy lyre,[65] even as the forest is:
What if my leaves are falling like its own!
The tumult of thy mighty harmonies

Will take from both a deep, autumnal tone,   60
Sweet though in sadness. Be thou, Spirit fierce,
My spirit! Be thou me, impetuous one!

Drive my dead thoughts over the universe
Like withered leaves to quicken a new birth!
And, by the incantation of this verse,

Scatter, as from an unextinguished hearth
Ashes and sparks, my words among mankind!
Be through my lips to unawakened earth

The trumpet of a prophecy! O Wind,
If Winter comes, can Spring be far behind?   70

---

[65] **Make me thy lyre** A lyre is a handheld stringed instrument. As Homer asked the Muse to sing through him, so Shelley asks Nature to "make me thy lyre." Both poets claimed to submerge their own personalities and become conduits for the divine.

Questions for Critical Thinking

1. What is the moral message of the poem "Ozymandias"?

2. Discuss the mixture of personal and public themes in Shelley's three poems. Show how these themes help classify Shelley as a romantic poet.

MARY SHELLEY
Selections from *Frankenstein*

Shelley's *Frankenstein* (1818) is a neglected classic, for fewer people have read the novel than know the story. This neglect began soon after publication, when the novel became the basis of a popular drama. The story's appeal grew in the twentieth century, inspiring countless movies, television films, cartoons, and even a musical. Success transformed the basic story, in the Nuclear Age, into a myth of humanity's foolish attempts to unlock the secrets of nature.

Shelley's original work deserves to be read, for it is both richer and more complex than the popular tale. It belongs to the genre of epistolary novel, or novel in the form of letters and diary entries—a popular eighteenth-century form. At the core of her novel is the story of Victor Frankenstein, a Swiss scientist who discovers the secret of life and creates a being from raw materials salvaged from graves, butcher shops, and dissecting rooms.

This creature with no name—thus adding to his inhuman traits—is of such loathsome appearance that all who see him are filled with horror and disgust. Innately kind, the creature is transformed by personal loneliness and encounters with fearful humans into a monster whose rage is directed toward Frankenstein and his family. Pursuit becomes the novel's theme as the monster chases his creator across pitiless, ice-filled seas to a grim conclusion.

Frankenstein's tale is framed within a second story that concerns Robert Walton, an English sailor who seeks fame by making "a voyage of discovery towards the north pole." It is during this voyage that Walton meets Frankenstein, takes him on board ship, and hears his strange story. Walton's letters report his own exploits and those of Frankenstein and the monster, each in his own words.

Shelley intended *Frankenstein* to be a morality fable about unbridled ambition, as indicated by the subtitle, *The Modern Prometheus*. In Greek myth, Prometheus was a Titan who created the first man and woman and brought them mixed gifts, fire and sorrows. The novel's Prometheus is both Frankenstein and Walton. Together they symbolize knowledge pursued regardless of cost. This moral reflected Europe's reactionary mood in post-Napoleonic times, a period marked by economic depression and political repression.

Mary Wollstonecraft Shelley (1797–1851) had excellent literary ties, and this may have inspired her to become a writer. The daughter of the novelist William Godwin and the feminist Mary Wollstonecraft, she eloped with the poet Percy Bysshe Shelley, causing a scandal. She began *Frankenstein* in Switzerland in the summer of 1817 while recovering from the birth of her second child. The novel was sparked by an evening of ghost stories told by the poets Shelley and Lord Byron. Mary Shelley was then only twenty years old.

Reading the Selections

The selections from Chapters IV and V of *Frankenstein* give Frankenstein's story—as recorded by Walton—of the "birth" of the monster. In telling his story, the doctor knows it is too late for himself—he accepts his ultimate death at the hands of the monster—but he wants Walton to avoid a similar fate by adopting a new moral code: stifle ambition if it weakens natural feelings. If ambition were to be controlled, he reasoned, then "America would have been discovered more gradually, and the empires of Mexico and Peru had not been destroyed." Frankenstein—and Shelley—thus make a plea for a global family united by mutual ties of affection.

∞

Chapter IV

. . .

One of the phaenomena which had peculiarly attracted my attention was the structure of the human frame, and indeed, any animal endued with life. Whence, I often asked myself, did the principle of life proceed? It was a bold question, and one which has ever been considered as a mystery: yet with how many things are we upon the brink of becoming acquainted, if cowardice or carelessness did not restrain our enquiries. I revolved these circumstances in my mind and determined thenceforth to apply myself more particularly to those branches of natural philosophy which relate to physiology. Unless I had been animated by an almost supernatural enthusiasm, my application to this study would have been irksome and almost intolerable. To examine the causes of life, we must first have recourse to death. I became acquainted with the science of anatomy, but this was not sufficient; I must also observe the natural decay and corruption of the human body. In my education my father had taken the greatest precautions that my mind should be impressed with no supernatural horrors. I do not ever remember to have trembled at a tale of superstition or to have feared the apparition of a spirit. Darkness had no effect upon my fancy, and a churchyard was to me merely the receptacle of bodies deprived of life, which, from being the seat of beauty and strength, had become food for the worm. Now I was led to examine the cause and progress of this decay and forced to spend days and nights in vaults and charnel-houses.[66] My attention was fixed upon every object the most insupportable to the delicacy of the human feelings. I saw how the fine form of man was degraded and wasted; I beheld the corruption of death succeed to the blooming cheek of life; I saw how the worm inherited the wonders of the eye and brain. I paused, examining and analysing all the minutiae of causation, as exemplified in the change from life to death, and death to life, until from the midst of this darkness a sudden light broke in upon me—a light so brilliant and wondrous, yet so simple, that while I became dizzy with the immensity of the prospect which it illustrated, I was surprized that among so many men of genius who had directed their enquiries towards the same science, that I alone should be reserved to discover so astonishing a secret.

Remember, I am not recording the vision of a madman. The sun does not more certainly shine in the heavens than that which I now affirm is true. Some miracle might have produced it, yet the stages of the discovery were distinct and probable. After days and nights of incredible labour and fatigue, I succeeded in discovering the cause of generation and life; nay, more, I became myself capable of bestowing animation upon lifeless matter.

The astonishment which I had at first experienced on this discovery soon gave place to delight and rapture. After so much time spent in painful labour, to arrive at once at the summit of my desires was the most gratifying consummation of my toils. But this discovery was so great and overwhelming that all the steps by which I had been progressively led to it were obliterated, and I beheld only the result. What had been the study and desire of the wisest men since the creation of the world was now within my grasp. Not that, like a magic scene, it all opened upon me at once: the information I had obtained was of a nature rather to direct my endeavours so soon as I should point them towards the object of my search than to exhibit that object already accomplished. I was like the Arabian who had been buried with the dead and found a passage to life, aided only by one glimmering and seemingly ineffectual light.[67]

I see by your eagerness and the wonder and hope which your eyes express, my friend, that you expect to be informed of the secret with which I am acquainted; that cannot be; listen patiently until the end of my story, and you will easily perceive why I am reserved upon that subject. I will not lead you on, unguarded and ardent as I then was, to your destruction and infallible misery. Learn from me, if not by my precepts, at least by my example, how dangerous is the acquirement of knowledge and how much happier that man is who believes his native town to

---

[66] **charnel-houses** Buildings housing dead bodies.

[67] **the Arabian . . . ineffectual light** The story is in Sinbad's Fourth Voyage in *The Arabian Nights*.

be the world, than he who aspires to become greater than his nature will allow.

When I found so astonishing a power placed within my hands, I hesitated a long time concerning the manner in which I should employ it. Although I possessed the capacity of bestowing animation,[68] yet to prepare a frame for the reception of it, with all its intricacies of fibres, muscles, and veins, still remained a work of inconceivable difficulty and labour. I doubted at first whether I should attempt the creation of a being like myself, or one of simpler organization; but my imagination was too much exalted by my first success to permit me to doubt of my ability to give life to an animal as complex and wonderful as man. The materials at present within my command hardly appeared adequate to so arduous an undertaking, but I doubted not that I should ultimately succeed. I prepared myself for a multitude of reverses; my operations might be incessantly baffled, and at last my work be imperfect; yet when I considered the improvement which every day takes place in science and mechanics, I was encouraged to hope my present attempts would at least lay the foundations of future success. Nor could I consider the magnitude and complexity of my plan as any argument of its impracticability. It was with these feelings that I began the creation of a human being. As the minuteness of the parts formed a great hindrance to my speed, I resolved, contrary to my first intention, to make the being of a gigantic stature; that is to say, about eight feet in height, and proportionately large. After having formed this determination and having spent some months in successfully collecting and arranging my materials, I began.

No one can conceive the variety of feelings which bore me onwards, like a hurricane, in the first enthusiasm of success. Life and death appeared to me ideal bounds, which I should first break through, and pour a torrent of light into our dark world. A new species would bless me as its creator and source; many happy and excellent natures would owe their being to me. No father could claim the gratitude of his child so completely as I should deserve theirs. Pursuing these reflections, I thought that if I could bestow animation upon lifeless matter, I might in process of time (although I now found it impossible) renew life where death had apparently devoted the body to corruption.

These thoughts supported my spirits, while I pursued my undertaking with unremitting ardour. My cheek had grown pale with study, and my person had become emaciated with confinement. Sometimes, on the very brink of certainty, I failed; yet still I clung to the hope which the next day or the next hour might realize. One secret which I alone possessed was the hope to which I had dedicated myself; and the moon gazed on my midnight labours, while, with unrelaxed and breathless eagerness, I pursued nature to her hiding-places. Who shall conceive the horrors of my secret toil as I dabbled among the unhallowed damps of the grave or tortured the living animal to animate the lifeless clay? My limbs now tremble, and my eyes swim with the remembrance; but then a resistless and almost frantic impulse urged me forward; I seemed to have lost all soul or sensation but for this one pursuit. It was indeed but a passing trance, that only made me feel with renewed acuteness so soon as, the unnatural stimulus ceasing to operate, I had returned to my old habits. I collected bones from charnel-houses and disturbed, with profane fingers, the tremendous secrets of the human frame. In a solitary chamber, or rather cell, at the top of the house, and separated from all the other apartments by a gallery and staircase, I kept my workshop of filthy creation: my eyeballs were starting from their sockets in attending to the details of my employment. The dissecting room and the slaughter-house furnished many of my materials; and often did my human nature turn with loathing from my occupation, whilst, still urged on by an eagerness which perpetually increased, I brought my work near to a conclusion.

The summer months passed while I was thus engaged, heart and soul, in one pursuit. It was a most beautiful season; never did the fields bestow a more plentiful harvest or the vines yield a more luxuriant vintage: but my eyes were insensible to the charms of nature. And the same feelings which made me neglect the scenes around me caused me also to forget those friends who were so many miles absent, and whom I had not seen for so long a time. I knew my silence disquieted them, and I well remembered the words of my father: "I know that while you are pleased with yourself you will think of us with affection, and we shall hear regularly from you. You must pardon me if I regard any interruption in your correspondence as a proof that your other duties are equally neglected."

I knew well therefore what would be my father's feelings, but I could not tear my thoughts from my employment, loathsome in itself, but which had taken an irresistible hold of my imagination. I wished, as it were, to procrastinate all that related to my feelings of affection until the great object, which swallowed up every habit of my nature, should be completed.

I then thought that my father would be unjust if he ascribed my neglect to vice or faultiness on my part, but I am now convinced that he was justified in conceiving that I should not be altogether free from blame. A human being in perfection ought always to preserve a calm and peaceful mind and never to allow passion or a transitory desire to disturb his tranquility. I do not think that the pursuit of knowledge is an exception to this rule. If the study to which you apply yourself has a tendency to weaken your affections and to destroy your taste for those simple pleasures in which no alloy can possibly mix, then that study is certainly unlawful, that is to say, not befitting the human mind. If this rule were always observed; if no man allowed any pursuit whatsoever to interfere with the tranquility of his domestic affections, Greece[69] had not been enslaved,

---

[68] **animation** Life.

[69] **Greece** Conquered by Rome and became part of the Roman Empire in 146 BCE.

Caesar[70] would have spared his country, America would have been discovered more gradually, and the empires of Mexico[71] and Peru[72] had not been destroyed.

But I forget that I am moralizing in the most interesting part of my tale, and your looks remind me to proceed.

My father made no reproach in his letters and only took notice of my silence by enquiring into my occupations more particularly than before. Winter, spring, and summer passed away during my labours; but I did not watch the blossom or the expanding leaves—sights which

---

[70] **Caesar** Julius Caesar plunged the Roman Republic into civil war in 49 BCE and quickly assumed control of the government; he was murdered by a band of nobles in 44 BCE.
[71] **Mexico** Conquered by Spanish soldiers led by Hernán Cortés, 1519–1521.
[72] **Peru** Conquered by Spanish soldiers led by Pizarro, in 1533.

before always yielded me supreme delight—so deeply was I engrossed in my occupation. The leaves of that year had withered before my work drew near to a close, and now every day showed me more plainly how well I had succeeded. But my enthusiasm was checked by my anxiety, and I appeared rather like one doomed by slavery to toil in the mines, or any other unwholesome trade than an artist occupied by his favourite employment. Every night I was oppressed by a slow fever, and I became nervous to a most painful degree; the fall of a leaf startled me, and I shunned my fellow creatures as if I had been guilty of a crime. Sometimes I grew alarmed at the wreck I perceived that I had become; the energy of my purpose alone sustained me: my labours would soon end, and I believed that exercise and amusement would then drive away incipient disease; and I promised myself both of these when my creation should be complete.

Chapter V

It was on a dreary night of November that I beheld the accomplishment of my toils. With an anxiety that almost amounted to agony, I collected the instruments of life around me, that I might infuse a spark of being into the lifeless thing that lay at my feet. It was already one in the morning; the rain pattered dismally against the panes, and my candle was nearly burnt out, when, by the glimmer of the half-extinguished light, I saw the dull yellow eye of the creature open; it breathed hard, and a convulsive motion agitated its limbs.

How can I describe my emotions at this catastrophe, or how delineate the wretch whom with such infinite pains and care I had endeavoured to form? His limbs were in proportion, and I had selected his features as beautiful. Beautiful! Great God! His yellow skin scarcely covered the work of muscles and arteries beneath; his hair was of a lustrous black, and flowing; his teeth of pearly whiteness; but these luxuriances only formed a more horrid contrast with his watery eyes, that seemed almost of the same colour as the dun-white sockets in which they were set, his shrivelled complexion and straight black lips.

The different accidents of life are not so changeable as the feelings of human nature. I had worked hard for nearly two years, for the sole purpose of infusing life into an inanimate body. For this I had deprived myself of rest and health. I had desired it with an ardour that far exceeded moderation; but now that I had finished, the beauty of the dream vanished, and breathless horror and disgust filled my heart. Unable to endure the aspect of the being I had created, I rushed out of the room and continued a long time traversing my bedchamber, unable to compose my mind to sleep. At length lassitude succeeded to the tumult I had before endured, and I threw myself on the bed in my clothes, endeavouring to seek a few moments of

forgetfulness. But it was in vain; I slept, indeed, but I was disturbed by the wildest dreams. I thought I saw Elizabeth,[73] in the bloom of health, walking in the streets of Ingolstadt.[74] Delighted and surprised, I embraced her, but as I imprinted the first kiss on her lips, they became livid with the hue of death; her features appeared to change, and I thought that I held the corpse of my dead mother in my arms; a shroud enveloped her form, and I saw the grave-worms crawling in the folds of the flannel. I started from my sleep with horror; a cold dew covered my forehead, my teeth chattered, and every limb became convulsed; when, by the dim and yellow light of the moon, as it forced its way through the window shutters, I beheld the wretch—the miserable monster whom I had created. He held up the curtain of the bed; and his eyes, if eyes they may be called, were fixed on me. His jaws opened, and he muttered some inarticulate sounds, while a grin wrinkled his cheeks. He might have spoken, but I did not hear; one hand was stretched out, seemingly to detain me, but I escaped and rushed downstairs. I took refuge in the courtyard belonging to the house which I inhabited, where I remained during the rest of the night, walking up and down in the greatest agitation, listening attentively, catching and fearing each sound as if it were to announce the approach of the daemoniacal corpse to which I had so miserably given life.

Oh! No mortal could support the horror of that countenance. A mummy again endued with animation could

---

[73] **Elizabeth** Young peasant girl, adopted into the Frankenstein household; intended as the bride of Victor Frankenstein, the doctor who created the monster.
[74] **Ingolstadt** City in Bavaria, Germany.

not be so hideous as that wretch. I had gazed on him while unfinished; he was ugly then, but when those muscles and joints were rendered capable of motion, it became a thing such as even Dante could not have conceived.

I passed the night wretchedly. Sometimes my pulse 5 beat so quickly and hardly that I felt the palpitation of every artery; at others, I nearly sank to the ground through languor and extreme weakness. Mingled with this horror, I felt the bitterness of disappointment; dreams that had been my food and pleasant rest for so long a space were now become a hell to me; and the change was so rapid, the overthrow so complete! . . .

Questions for Critical Thinking

1. Describe the "birth" of Dr. Frankenstein's monster, as described in this selection. What does this "birth" symbolize?

2. Discuss elements of the romantic literary style in this selection by Mary Shelley.

GEORG WILHELM FRIEDRICH HEGEL
Selection from *Reason in History*

Hegelianism, the philosophy of the German Georg Wilhelm Friedrich Hegel (1770–1831), dominated Western thought from his time until World War I. Nationalists and conservatives on the right and socialists and communists (see Marx and Engels, *The Communist Manifesto* in Chapter 19) on the left all claimed him as their own. Hegel's appeal sprang from many sources. He was a genius at borrowing from others, including Plato (see *The Republic* in Chapter 3, Volume I) and the German philosopher Immanuel Kant (1724–1804) (see "Answer to the Question: What Is Enlightenment?" in Chapter 17), to forge a compelling system meant to supersede older philosophies. He also garnered support because he harmonized the era's main currents of thought, the rationalism of the Enlightenment and the emotionalism of romanticism. Most important, his philosophical arguments offered an alternative to Judeo-Christian beliefs that were under siege from science and biblical criticism.

The rationalist Hegel approached philosophy in the spirit of medieval mysticism. Obsessed with uncovering the final nature and meaning of the universe and human history, he constructed an all-encompassing metaphysical system that has become fabled for complexity and obscurity. The guiding force of his system is the World Spirit, also known as Reason, Logic, Idea, and Absolute. In his system, philosophy and history are virtually indistinguishable, so that each is the expression of the other though in different guises. Thus history is created by the World Spirit, and at the same time the World Spirit reaches self-awareness through the unfolding of historical events.

Hegel was not the first to employ dialectical reasoning—the belief that growth occurs through the clash of opposites. That honor belongs to the ancient Greek thinker Heraclitus (fl. 500 BCE). But Hegel's version of the dialectic is the one best known in modern times. In his philosophy, Hegel uses the dialectic to explain how the World Spirit operates. However, the World Spirit, unable to act independently, enters and guides the masses to its own ends without their awareness, thereby making them part of the dialectical process. On the philosophic level, the dialectic manifests itself as a clash between an idea (thesis) and its adversary (antithesis); in some cases, a resolution (synthesis) may emerge that preserves the best of the opposing forces and thus represents a new and higher stage of life. In contrast, on the history level, the dialectic constitutes a "slaughter bench" on which mortal armies, incarnating opposing ideas of the World Spirit, fight to the death. Because struggle embodies the World Spirit, Hegel praised warfare for its benefits to society.

Reading the Selection

This selection from Hegel's *Reason in History,* also called *Lectures on the Philosophy of History,* was published posthumously in 1837. The text represents Hegel's lecture notes delivered at the University of Berlin, where he became professor in 1818. The lectures have been supplemented and clarified by students' notes. As a professor, Hegel was so revered by state officials that enemies viewed him as the mouthpiece of Prussia's reactionary monarchy. In fairness, however, he was a moderate liberal, supporting constitutional government but preferring monarchy to democracy and opposing individualism.

Several key Hegelian ideas appear here:

1. Reason considered as Idea, Nature, and Spirit
2. Three main phases of world history: Asiatic, rule by absolute monarch; Greco-Roman, with freedom for the few; and Germanic-European, typified by nation-states devoted to freedom for all under the law
3. Freedom, or obedience to law, as the goal of history
4. The passions as the driving force in history—a Romantic idea
5. The State as the realization of the divine Idea

∞

III. The Idea of History and Its Realization

The question of how Reason is determined in itself and what its relation is to the world coincides with the question, *What is the ultimate purpose of the world?* This question implies that the purpose is to be actualized and realized. Two things, then, must be considered: first, the content of this ultimate purpose, the determination as such, and secondly, its realization.

To begin with, we must note that world history goes on within the realm of Spirit. The term "world" includes both physical and psychical[75] nature. Physical nature does play a part in world history, and from the very beginning we shall draw attention to the fundamental natural relations thus involved. But Spirit, and the course of its development, is the substance of history. We must not contemplate nature as a rational system in itself, in its own particular domain, but only in its relation to Spirit.

[After the creation of nature appears Man. He constitutes the antithesis to the natural world; he is the being that lifts itself up to the second world. We have in our universal consciousness two realms, the realm of Nature and the realm of Spirit. The realm of Spirit consists in what is produced by man. One may have all sorts of ideas about the Kingdom of God; but it is always a realm of Spirit to be realized and brought about in man.

The realm of Spirit is all-comprehensive; it includes everything that ever has interested or ever will interest man. Man is active in it; whatever he does, he is the creature within which

the Spirit works. Hence it is of interest, in the course of history, to learn to know spiritual nature in its existence, that is, the point where Spirit and Nature unite, namely, human nature. In speaking of human nature we mean something permanent. The concept of human nature must fit all men and all ages, past and present. This universal concept may suffer infinite modifications; but actually the universal is one and the same essence in its most various modifications. Thinking reflection disregards the variations and adheres to the universal, which under all circumstances is active in the same manner and shows itself in the same interest. The universal type appears even in what seems to deviate from it most strongly; in the most distorted figure we can still discern the human. . . .*

This kind of reflection abstracts from the content, the purpose of human activity. . . . But the cultured human mind cannot help making distinctions between inclinations and desires as they manifest themselves in small circumstances and as they appear in the struggle of world-wide historical interests. Here appears an objective interest, which impresses us in two aspects, that of the universal aim and that of the individual who represents this aim. It is this which makes history so fascinating. These are the aims and individuals whose loss and decline we mourn. When we have before us the struggle of the Greeks against the Persians[76] or Alexander's mighty dominion,[77] we know very well

---

[75] **psychical** Immaterial, moral, or spiritual in origin.

[76] *the Greeks against the Persians* Persian Wars, first half of the fifth century BCE.
[77] *Alexander's . . . dominion* Alexander the Great (356–323 BCE) conquered and founded an empire, starting in 336 BCE

what interests us. We want to see the Greeks saved from barbarism, we want the Athenian state preserved, and we are interested in the ruler under whose leadership the Greeks subjugated Asia.[78] If it were only a matter of human passion, we would not feel any loss in imagining that Alexander would have failed in his enterprise. We could very well content ourselves in seeing here a mere play of passions, but we would not feel satisfied. We have here a substantial, an objective interest. . . .

In contemplating world history we must thus consider its ultimate purpose. This ultimate purpose is what is willed in the world itself. We know of God that He is the most perfect; He can will only Himself and what is like Him. God and the nature of His will are one and the same; these we call philosophically, the Idea. Hence, it is the Idea in general, in its manifestation as human spirit, which we have to contemplate. More precisely it is the idea of human freedom. The purest form in which the Idea manifests itself is Thought itself. In this aspect the Idea is treated in Logic. Another form is that of physical Nature.[79] The third form, finally is that of Spirit in general.] Spirit, on the stage on which we observe it, that of world history, is in its most concrete reality. But nevertheless—or rather in order to understand also the general idea of this concrete existence of Spirit—we must set forth, first, some general definition of the *nature of Spirit.* But this can only be done here as a mere assertion; this is not the place to develop the idea of Spirit through philosophical speculation. As was mentioned above, what can be said in an introduction can be taken only historically—as an assumption to be explained and proved elsewhere or to be verified by the science of history itself.

We have therefore to indicate here:

1. The abstract characteristics of the nature of Spirit.
2. The means Spirit uses in order to realize its Idea.
3. The form which the complete realization of Spirit assumes in existence—the State.

1. The Idea of Freedom

The nature of Spirit may be understood by a glance at its direct opposite—Matter. The essence of matter is gravity, the essence of Spirit—its substance—is Freedom. It is immediately plausible to everyone that, among other properties, Spirit also possesses Freedom. But philosophy teaches us that *all* the properties of Spirit exist only through Freedom. All are but means of attaining Freedom; all seek and produce this and this alone. It is an insight of speculative philosophy that Freedom is the sole truth of Spirit. Matter possesses gravity by virtue of its tendency toward a central point; it is essentially composite, consisting of parts that exclude each other. It seeks its unity and thereby its own abolition; it seeks its opposite. If it would attain this it would be matter no longer, but would have perished. It strives toward ideality, for in unity it exists ideally. Spirit, on the contrary, is that which has its center in itself. It does

not have unity outside of itself but has found it: it is in itself and with itself. Matter has its substance outside of itself; Spirit is Being-within-itself (self-contained existence). But this, precisely, is Freedom. For when I am dependent, I refer myself to something else which I am not; I cannot exist independently of something external. I am free when I am within myself. This self-contained existence of Spirit is self-consciousness, consciousness of self.

Two things must be distinguished in consciousness, first, *that* I know and, secondly, *what* I know. In self-consciousness the two coincide, for Spirit knows itself. It is the judgment of its own nature and, at the same time, the operation of coming to itself, to produce itself, to make itself (actually) into that which it is in itself (potentially). Following this abstract definition it may be said that world history is the exhibition of spirit striving to attain knowledge of its own nature. As the germ bears in itself the whole nature of the tree, the taste and shape of its fruit, so also the first traces of Spirit virtually contain the whole of history. Orientals do not yet know that Spirit—Man as such—is free. And because they do not know it, they are not free. They only know that *one* is free; but for this very reason such freedom is mere caprice, ferocity, dullness of passion, or, perhaps, softness and tameness of desire—which again is nothing but an accident of nature and thus, again, caprice. This *one* is therefore only a despot, not a free man. The consciousness of freedom first arose among the Greeks, and therefore they were free. But they, and the Romans likewise, only knew that some are free—not man as such. This not even Plato[80] and Aristotle[81] knew. For this reason the Greeks not only had slavery, upon which was based their whole life and the maintenance of their splendid liberty, but their freedom itself was partly an accidental, transient, and limited flowering and partly a severe thralldon of human nature. Only the Germanic peoples came, through Christianity, to realize that man as man is free and that freedom of Spirit is the very essence of man's nature. This realization first arose in religion, in the innermost region of spirit; but to introduce it in the secular world was a further task which could only be solved and fulfilled by a long and severe effort of civilization. Thus slavery did not cease immediately with the acceptance of the Christian religion. Liberty did not suddenly predominate in states nor reason in governments and constitutions. The application of the principle to secular conditions, the thorough molding and interpenetration of the secular world by it, is precisely the long process of history. I have already drawn attention to this distinction between a principle as such and its application, its introduction and execution in the actuality of life and spirit. This is a fundamental fact in our science and must be kept constantly in mind. Just as we noted it in the Christian principle of self-consciousness and freedom, so it shows itself in the principle of freedom

---

[78] *Asia* Conquered much of Asia Minor to the Indus River.
[79] *Nature* In this aspect the Idea is treated in the Philosophy of Nature [Hegel's note].

[80] **Plato** (ca. 428–348 BCE), Greek philosopher, author of *The Republic* (q.v.).
[81] **Aristotle** (384–322 BCE), Greek philosopher, author of the *Politics*.

in general. World history is the progress of the consciousness and freedom—a progress whose necessity we have to investigate.

The preliminary statement given above of the various grades in the consciousness of freedom—that the Orientals knew only that *one* is free, the Greeks and Romans that *some* are free, while we know that *all* men absolutely, that is, as men, are free—is at the same time the natural division of world history and the manner in which we shall treat it. But this is only mentioned in passing; first, we must explain some other concepts.

. . .

2. The Means of Realization

(A) THE IDEA AND THE INDIVIDUAL

The question of the *means* whereby Freedom develops itself into a world leads us directly to the phenomenon of history. Although Freedom as such is primarily an internal idea, the means it uses are the external phenomena which in history present themselves directly before our eyes. The first glance at history convinces us that the actions of men spring from their needs, their passions, their interests, their characters, and their talents. Indeed, it appears as if in this drama of activities these needs, passions, and interests are the sole springs of action and the main efficient cause. It is true that this drama involves also universal purposes, benevolence, or noble patriotism. But such virtues and aims are insignificant on the broad canvas of history. We may, perhaps, see the ideal of Reason actualized in those who adopt such aims and in the spheres of their influence; but their number is small in proportion to the mass of the human race and their influence accordingly limited. Passions, private aims, and the satisfaction of selfish desires are, on the contrary, tremendous springs of action. Their power lies in the fact that they respect none of the limitations which law and morality would impose on them; and that these natural impulses are closer to the core of human nature than the artificial and troublesome discipline that tends toward order, self-restraint, law, and morality.

When we contemplate this display of passions and the consequences of their violence, the unreason which is associated not only with them, but even—rather we might say *especially*—with *good* designs and righteous aims; when we see arising therefrom the evil, the vice, the ruin that has befallen the most flourishing kingdoms which the mind of man ever created, we can hardly avoid being filled with sorrow at this universal taint of corruption. And since this decay is not the work of mere nature, but of human will, our reflections may well lead us to a moral sadness, a revolt of the good will (spirit)—if indeed it has a place within us. Without rhetorical exaggeration, a simple, truthful account of the miseries that have overwhelmed the noblest of nations and polities and the finest exemplars of private virtue forms a most fearful picture and excites emotions of the profoundest and most hopeless sadness, counter-balanced by no consoling result. We can endure it and strengthen ourselves against it only by thinking that this is the way it had to be—it is fate; nothing can be done.

And at last, out of the boredom with which this sorrowful reflection threatens us, we draw back into the vitality of the present, into our aims and interests of the moment; we retreat, in short, into the selfishness that stands on the quiet shore and thence enjoys in safety the distant spectacle of wreckage and confusion.

. . .

3. The State

(A) THE STATE AS REALIZATION OF THE IDEA

The third point, then, concerns the end to be attained by these means, that is, the form it assumes in the realm of the actual. We have spoken of means; but the carrying out of a subjective, limited aim also requires a *material* element, either already present or to be procured or to serve this actualization. Thus the question would arise: What is the material in which the final end of Reason is to be realized? It is first of all the subjective agent itself, human desires, subjectivity in general. In human knowledge and volition, as its material basis, the rational attains existence. We have considered subjective volition with its purpose, namely, the truth of reality, insofar as moved by a great world-historical passion. As a subjective will in limited passions it is dependent; it can gratify its particular desires only within this dependence. But the subjective will has also a substantial life, a reality where it moves in the region of essential being and has the essential itself as the object of its existence. This essential being is the union of the subjective with the rational will; it is the moral whole, the *State*. It is that actuality in which the individual has and enjoys his freedom, but only as knowing, believing, and willing the universal. This must not be understood as if the subjective will of the individual attained its gratification and enjoyment through the common will and the latter were a means for it—as if the individual limited his freedom among the other individuals, so that this common limitation, the mutual constraint of all, might secure a small space of liberty for each. (This would only be negative freedom.) Rather, law, morality, the State, and they alone, are the positive reality and satisfaction of freedom. The caprice of the individual is not freedom. It is this caprice which is being limited, the license of particular desires.

The subjective will, passion, is the force which actualizes and realizes. The Idea is the interior; the State is the externally existing, genuinely moral life. It is the union of the universal and essential with the subjective will, and as such it is *Morality*. The individual who lives in this unity has a moral life, a value which consists in this substantiality alone. Sophocles' Antigone[82] says: "The divine commands are not of yesterday nor of today; no, they have an infinite existence, and no one can say whence they came." The laws of ethics are not accidental, but are rationality itself. It is the end of the State to make the substantial

---

[82] **Sophocles' Antigone** The heroine of the Greek tragedy of the same name by Sophocles (ca. 496–ca. 406 BCE). Claiming to speak for the divine will of the gods, Antigone refused to bow to the law of the state, which represented (in the play) the will of the king.

prevail and maintain itself in the actual doings of men and in their convictions. It is the absolute interest of Reason that this moral whole exist; and herein lies the justification and merit of heroes who have founded states, no matter how crude.

. . .

[The state] is the realization of Freedom, of the absolute, final purpose, and exists for its own sake. All the value man has, all the spiritual reality, he has only through the state. For his spiritual reality is the knowing presence to him of his own essence, of rationality, of its objective, immediate actuality present in and for him. Only thus is he truly a consciousness, only thus does he partake in morality, in the legal and moral life of the state. For the True is the unity of the universal and particular will. And the universal in the state is in its laws, its universal and rational provisions. The state is the divine Idea as it exists on earth.

Thus the State is the definite object of world history proper. In it freedom achieves its objectivity and lives in the enjoyment of this objectivity. For law is the objectivity of Spirit; it is will in its true form. Only the will that obeys the law is free, for it obeys itself and, being in itself, is free. In so far as the state, our country, constitutes a community of existence, and as the subjective will of man subjects itself to the laws, the antithesis of freedom and necessity disappears. The rational, like the substantial, is necessary. We are free when we recognize it as law and follow it as the substance of our own being. The objective and the subjective will are then reconciled and form one and the same harmonious whole. For the ethos of the state is not of the moral, the reflective kind in which one's own conviction rules supreme. This latter is rather the peculiarity of the modern world. The true and antique morality is rooted in the principle that everybody stands in his place of duty. An Athenian citizen did what was required of him, as it were from instinct. But if I reflect on the object of my activity, I must have the consciousness that my will counts. Morality, however, is the duty, the substantial law, the second nature, as it has been rightly called; for the first nature of man is his immediate, animalic existence.

Questions for Critical Thinking

1. Define *dialectic*. Show, using three separate examples, how the dialectic operates in Hegel's theory.

2. "The State is the realization of Freedom." Explain this key idea of Hegel.

19

THE TRIUMPH OF THE BOURGEOISIE
1830–1871

KARL MARX AND FRIEDRICH ENGELS
Selection from *The Communist Manifesto*

Not all of Marxist ideology is to be found in *The Communist Manifesto*, but this short pamphlet of barely fifty pages, with its striking phrases and call to revolution, is the best introduction available to the ideas of Karl Marx (1818–1883) and Friedrich Engels (1820–1895), his close friend and collaborator. This work shows how Marxism interprets the unfolding of history, provides a practical plan to change the existing social system, and predicts the future. Labeled by the first communists as their "confession of faith," the *Manifesto* constitutes the most inspiring, yet precise and practical, document for the followers of the "religion" of Marxism. A secular gospel, this document offers true believers a materialistic, scientific analysis of the past, complete with unquestioned dogmas and a call to arms for a new heaven on earth—a communist society free of class conflict and with justice for all.

Marx and Engels coauthored the *Manifesto*, but Engels was always modest in his own claims, accepting without protest that the world called their philosophy Marxism, not Engelism. Thus Marx is usually the focus of discussions of Marxism. Nonetheless, Engels's contribution was significant, and it should be noted that the two authors had much in common. Both were born middle-class but with a difference: Their families were assimilated German Jews, a source of prejudice toward them because of lingering anti-Semitism. As youths, both spent time among left-wing Hegelians (see *Reason in History* in Chapter 18) who were atheistic and communistic (Marx as a university student in Bonn, Berlin, and Jena, and Engels as a visitor). Both came to identify with the proletariat, or working class, as the revolutionary hope for the future, substantiated by Marx's contacts with the downtrodden in Paris and by Engels's experience with factory workers in industrially advanced England.

These founders of communism first met in the early 1840s, when Marx was writer for and then editor of the *Rheinische Zeitung (Rhineland Times)* and Engels was the self-educated son of a wealthy Rhineland industrialist. Marx, having completed a doctorate in philosophy, was in journalism only because his radical politics had effectively blocked him from a post at one of the German universities. Politics inevitably cost Marx the job at the newspaper, and he moved to Paris, then alive with intellectual ferment, especially by socialists intent on remodeling the world. In Paris, in 1844, he cemented his friendship with Engels, and in what was to become a lifelong pattern, Engels gave Marx financial aid. After managing his father's textile factory in Manchester, England, Engels had just written his first major work, *The Condition of the Working Class in England in 1844* (1845), a damning indictment of industrialism.

For the rest of Marx's life, he and Engels were a team, with Engels, who never married, providing financial, intellectual, and emotional sustenance to Marx. When French authorities, prodded by the Prussians, invited Marx to move to Belgium in 1845, Engels joined him there and they collaborated on three books, including *The Communist Manifesto* (1848). Marx and his family settled permanently in England in 1849, and Engels was there to provide him with support upon the deaths of two children and the birth of an illegitimate one. Research has uncovered the fact that Engels wrote about one-fourth of the articles supposedly written by Marx and collaborated in several others that were published in the New York *Tribune* between 1851 and 1862. Engels, by means of financial gifts, also eased the Marx family's poverty, especially in the early London years.

The Communist Manifesto was written in Belgium at the request of a group of exiled German workers called the Communist League. Marx's major contribution to this work, according to Engels, was the "truly original idea" that culture is an outgrowth of prevailing economic conditions—in other words, economic determinism. Engels's primary role was to supply first-hand knowledge of the workers, showing how the factory system had turned them into wage slaves and stripped them of their dignity and humanity. Together, Marx and Engels devised a dialectical approach to history, based on a marriage of economic determinism with the Hegelian dialectic. In the Marxist dialectic, the driving force is class struggle, in which the haves (thesis) and have-nots (antithesis) battle endlessly, with the occasional emergence of a new and dominant class (synthesis) when economic conditions permit. Marx and Engels envisioned an end to class struggle only with the destruction of the bourgeoisie and the capitalist system by their enemies, the proletariat, who would then set up a classless society under a communist economy.

Reading the Selection

The opening paragraphs of *The Communist Manifesto* have been repeated so often that they have become a cliché, but when read by fresh minds, they still raise hope for those who see themselves as victims of economic and social repression. After discussing the causes for the rise of the bourgeoisie, Marx and Engels detail the ways this class controls the modes of production and society. They then explain the relationship between the communists and the proletariat, noting that the former will join the latter in its struggle for freedom and justice. At the end of this section, the authors catalog the measures needed to ensure the establishment of proletariat rule, in which "the free development of each is the condition for the free development of all"—a classic expression of the humanitarian thinking of these writers. The concluding call to arms—"Workingmen of all countries, unite!"—opposes the bourgeois period's nationalism and represents the belief (which turned out to be false) that a country's workers have more in common with foreign workers than they do with their middle-class oppressors at home.

❧

A specter[1] is haunting Europe—the specter of communism. All the powers of old Europe have entered into a holy alliance[2] to exorcise this specter: Pope[3] and Czar,[4] Metternich[5] and Guizot,[6] French Radicals[7] and German police spies.[8]

---

[1] **specter** Ghost.

[2] **holy alliance** The Holy Alliance was formed at the Congress of Vienna, in 1815, by the politically conservative rulers of Russia, Prussia, and Austria, to protect the Christian faith. Virtually all of Europe's rulers eventually joined this group, except for the pope, the Ottoman sultan, and the British king. Short-lived and ineffectual, the alliance supported repressive and authoritarian regimes.

[3] **Pope** The popes did not belong to the **Holy Alliance,** but they nevertheless were identified with repressive governments. At the time Marx and Engels were writing, the pope was the liberal Pius IX (pope 1846–1878), who quickly abandoned his progressive ideas in the wake of the failures of the revolutions of 1848.

[4] **Czar** Also spelled Tsar; Russian for "Caesar." The title of the emperor of Russia. An allusion to Nicholas I (r. 1825–1855), a despot who opposed all social and liberal reform.

[5] **Metternich** Prince Klemens Metternich (1773–1859), Austrian statesman, who controlled Austria and opposed liberal reforms and nationalistic movements across Europe. He was Austria's court chancellor and chancellor of state, 1821–1848.

[6] **Guizot** François Guizot (1787–1874), French historian and statesman. A moderate monarchist, he served King Louis Philippe (r. 1830–1848) as leader of the government, 1840–1848. A doctrinaire liberal, he opposed democratic and social reforms.

[7] **French Radicals** A political party opposing Louis Philippe (see footnote 6); called for a republic, a constitution, popular sovereignty, and nationalist public policies; represented by the newspaper *La Reforme* and the radical leader Alphonse Lamartine (1790–1869).

[8] **German police spies** The period from 1815 to 1848 was rich in secret societies, revolutionary plots, and undercover police. Marx writes from personal experience, as the Prussian authorities kept close account of his activities.

Where is the party in opposition that has not been decried as communistic by its opponents in power? Where the Opposition that has not hurled back the branding reproach of communism, against the more advanced opposition parties, as well as against its reactionary adversaries?

Two things result from this fact:

I. Communism is already acknowledged by all European powers to be itself a power.

II. It is high time that Communists should openly, in the face of the whole world, publish their views, their aims, their tendencies, and meet this nursery tale of the specter of communism with a manifesto of the party itself.

To this end, Communists of various nationalities have assembled in London, and sketched the following manifesto, to be published in the English, French, German, Italian, Flemish, and Danish languages. . . .

The bourgeoisie has played a most revolutionary role in history.

The bourgeoisie, wherever it has got the upper hand, has put an end to all feudal, patriarchal, idyllic relations. It has pitilessly torn asunder the motley feudal ties that bound man to his "natural superiors," and has left no other bond between man and man than naked self-interest, than callous "cash payment."[9] It has drowned the most heavenly ecstasies of religious fervor, of chivalrous enthusiasm, of philistine sentimentalism, in the icy water of egotistical calculation.[10] It has resolved personal worth into exchange value, and in place of the numberless indefeasible[11] chartered freedoms,[12] has set up that single, unconscionable freedom—Free Trade.[13] In one word, for exploitation, veiled by religious and political illusions, it has substituted naked, shameless, direct, brutal exploitation.

The bourgeoisie has stripped of its halo every occupation hitherto honored and looked up to with reverent awe. It has converted the physician, the lawyer, the priest, the poet, the man of science, into its paid wage-laborers.

The bourgeoisie has torn away from the family its sentimental veil, and has reduced the family relation to a mere money relation.

The bourgeoisie has disclosed how it came to pass that the brutal display of vigor in the Middle Ages, which reactionaries so much admire, found its fitting complement in the most slothful indolence. It has been the first to show what man's activity can bring about. It has accomplished wonders far surpassing Egyptian pyramids, Roman aqueducts, and Gothic cathedrals; it has conducted expeditions that put in the shade all former migrations of nations and crusades.

The bourgeoisie cannot exist without constantly revolutionizing the instruments of production, and thereby the relations of production, and with them the whole relations of society. Conservation of the old modes of production in unaltered form was, on the contrary, the first condition of existence for all earlier industrial classes. Constant revolutionizing of production, uninterrupted disturbance of all social conditions, everlasting uncertainty and agitation distinguish the bourgeois epoch from all earlier ones. All fixed, fast-frozen relations, with their train of ancient and venerable prejudices and opinions, are swept away, all new-formed ones become antiquated before they can ossify.[14] All that is solid melts into air, all that is holy is profaned, and man is at last compelled to face with sober senses his real conditions of life and his relations with his kind.

The need of a constantly expanding market for its products chases the bourgeoisie over the whole surface of the globe. It must nestle everywhere, settle everywhere, establish connections everywhere.

The bourgeoisie has through its exploitation of the world market given a cosmopolitan character to production and consumption in every country. To the great chagrin of reactionaries, it has drawn from under the feet of industry the national ground on which it stood. All old-established national industries have been destroyed or are daily being destroyed. They are dislodged by new industries, whose introduction becomes a life and death question for all civilized nations, by industries that no longer work up indigenous raw material, but raw material drawn from the remotest zones; industries whose products are consumed, not only at home, but in every quarter of the globe. In place of the old wants, satisfied by the production of the country, we find new wants, requiring for their satisfaction the products of distant lands and climes. In place of the old local and national seclusion and self-sufficiency, we have intercourse in every direction, universal interdependence of nations. And as in material, so also in intellectual production. The intellectual creations of individual nations become common property. National one-sidedness and narrow-mindedness become more and more impossible, and from the numerous national and local literatures there arises a world literature. . . .

We have seen above, that the first step in the revolution by the working class, is to raise the proletariat to the position of ruling class, to establish democracy.

The proletariat will use its political supremacy to wrest, by degrees, all capital from the bourgeoisie, to centralize all instruments of production in the hands of the

---

[9] **"cash payment"** A term derived from the Scottish essayist and historian Thomas Carlyle (1795–1881). In his 1839 pamphlet "Chartism," Carlyle referred to "Cash payment . . . the universal sole nexus [from the Latin, "to bind"] of man to man."

[10] **egotistical calculation** Utilitarianism, the philosophy of the British thinker Jeremy Bentham (1748–1832), which advocated laws, morality, and other actions be based on "the greatest happiness of the greatest number."

[11] **indefeasible** Not able to be annulled or voided or undone.

[12] **chartered freedoms** In medieval Europe, charters for towns, guilds, universities, and other groups listed specific freedoms and immunities enjoyed by the members of the chartered group, thus providing protection against despotism by the central government.

[13] **Free Trade** A policy of free flow of goods between countries. The classic case for Free Trade was that of the Scottish thinker Adam Smith in *Wealth of Nations* (1776; see Chapter 17). Great Britain, the country that originated the Industrial Revolution, became the leading advocate for Free Trade, in 1846, with the repeal of the Corn Laws. The Corn Laws were tariffs and duties on the movement of various grains.

[14] **ossify** Become rigid.

state, *i.e.*, of the proletariat organized as the ruling class; and to increase the total of productive forces as rapidly as possible.

Of course, in the beginning, this cannot be effected except by means of despotic inroads on the rights of property, and on the conditions of bourgeois production; by means of measures, therefore, which appear economically insufficient and untenable, but which, in the course of the movement, outstrip themselves, necessitate further inroads upon the old social order, and are unavoidable as a means of entirely revolutionizing the mode of production.

These measures will of course be different in different countries.

Nevertheless in the most advanced countries, the following will be pretty generally applicable.

1. Abolition of property in land and application of all rents of land to public purposes.
2. A heavy progressive or graduated income tax.
3. Abolition of all right of inheritance.
4. Confiscation of the property of all emigrants and rebels.
5. Centralization of credit in the hands of the state, by means of a national bank with state capital and an exclusive monopoly.
6. Centralization of the means of communication and transport in the hands of the state.
7. Extension of factories and instruments of production owned by the state; the bringing into cultivation of waste lands, and the improvement of the soil generally in accordance with a common plan.
8. Equal obligation of all to work. Establishment of industrial armies, especially for agriculture.
9. Combination of agriculture with manufacturing industries; gradual abolition of the distinction between town and country, by a more equable distribution of the population over the country.
10. Free education for all children in public schools. Abolition of child factory labor in its present form. Combination of education with industrial production, etc.

When, in the course of development, class distinctions have disappeared, and all production has been concentrated in the hands of a vast association of the whole nation, the public power will lose its political character. Political power, properly so called, is merely the organized power of one class for oppressing another. If the proletariat during its contest with the bourgeoisie is compelled, by the force of circumstances, to organize itself as a class; if, by means of a revolution, it makes itself the ruling class, and, as such sweeps away by force the old conditions of production, then it will, along with these conditions, have swept away the conditions for the existence of class antagonisms, and of classes generally, and will thereby have abolished its own supremacy as a class.

In place of the old bourgeois society, with its classes and class antagonisms, we shall have an association, in which the free development of each is the condition for the free development of all. . . .

The Communists fight for the attainment of the immediate aims, for the enforcement of the momentary interests of the working class; but in the movement of the present, they also represent and take care of the future of that movement. In France the Communists ally themselves with the Social-Democrats,[15] against the conservative and radical bourgeoisie, reserving, however, the right to take up a critical position in regard to phrases and illusions traditionally handed down from the great Revolution.

In Switzerland they support the Radicals,[16] without losing sight of the fact that this party consists of antagonistic elements, partly of Democratic Socialists,[17] in the French sense, partly of radical bourgeois.

In Poland they support the party that insists on an agrarian revolution as the prime condition for national emancipation, that party which fomented the insurrection of Cracow in 1846.[18]

In Germany they fight with the bourgeoisie whenever it acts in a revolutionary way against the absolute monarchy,[19] the feudal squirearchy,[20] and the petty bourgeoisie.[21]

But they never cease, for a single instant, to instill into the working class the clearest possible recognition of the hostile antagonism between bourgeoisie and proletariat, in order that the German workers may straightway use, as so many weapons against the bourgeoisie, the social and political conditions that the bourgeoisie must necessarily introduce along with its supremacy, and in order that, after the fall of the reactionary classes in Germany, the fight against the bourgeoisie itself may immediately begin.

The Communists turn their attention chiefly to Germany,[22] because that country is on the eve of a bourgeois

---

[15] **France . . . Social-Democrats** A left-wing political coalition, composed of secular and Catholic supporters, that pursued socialist goals along with constitutional methods and some aspects of capitalism; typified by the socialist Louis Blanc (1811–1882).

[16] **Switzerland . . . Radicals** A left-wing political party, composed mainly of Protestants, that advocated the expulsion of the Jesuits, the founding of a public school system, and the introduction of a democratic constitution modeled on that of the United States. In 1847, the Radicals fought and won a civil war against a Conservative grouping composed mainly of Catholics. In 1848, the Radicals imposed a new federal constitution on their country, which led to their political hegemony, until 1891.

[17] **Democratic Socialists** A Swiss fringe group that advocated socialist aims along with a democratic constitution and some aspects of capitalism.

[18] **insurrection of Cracow in 1846** Also spelled Krakow, a Polish city. In 1815, Krakow became independent, as the republic of Krakow, and the rest of Poland was divided among Prussia, Austria, and Russia. In 1846, when Polish nationalists launched a liberation movement, the revolt was quelled, and Krakow became part of Austria.

[19] **Germany . . . monarchy** Headed by Frederick William IV (r. 1840–1861), king of Prussia, a staunch conservative.

[20] **the feudal squirearchy** Junkers, Prussian landowners based on large estates, mainly to the east of the Elbe River. Prussia's civil servants and army officers were exclusively from this class.

[21] **petty bourgeoisie** Lower middle class. Marx and Engels heap scorn on this class for its political conservatism.

[22] **Germany** Two major failures of Marx's and Engels's prophecies were that the next great revolution would occur in Germany (not in Russia, as actually happened), and the revolution would be led by the bourgeoisie (not by the proletariat, as was the case).

revolution that is bound to be carried out under more advanced conditions of European civilization and with a much more developed proletariat than what existed in England in the 17th[23] and in France in the 18th century,[24] and because the bourgeois revolution in Germany will be but the prelude to an immediately following proletarian revolution.

In short, the Communists everywhere support every revolutionary movement against the existing social and political order of things.

In all these movements they bring to the front, as the leading question in each case, the property question, no matter what its degree of development at the time.

Finally, they labor everywhere for the union and agreement of the democratic parties of all countries.

The Communists disdain to conceal their views and aims. They openly declare that their ends can be attained only by the forcible overthrow of all existing social conditions. Let the ruling classes tremble at a Communist revolution. The proletarians have nothing to lose but their chains. They have a world to win.

Workingmen of all countries, unite!

---

[23] **England in the 17th (century)** The source of the belief that England's Civil War (1640–1660) was an uprising of the bourgeoisie, an idea explored by Marxist historians.
[24] **France in the 18th century** The source of the belief that France's Great Revolution (1789–1795) was an uprising of the bourgeoisie, an idea explored by Marxist historians.

Questions for Critical Thinking

1. Define *dialectic*. Show, using three separate examples, how the dialectic operates in Marx and Engels's theory.

2. According to Marx and Engels, what is the ultimate goal of history? Describe. Compare and contrast Marx and Engels's communism with modern examples of communist regimes.

CHARLES DARWIN
Selection from *The Descent of Man*

Charles Darwin's *The Descent of Man* (1871) is one of the West's most explosive books. In two volumes, the first limited to man and the second given to the role of sexual selection in evolution, it is written in matter-of-fact prose and backed by masses of scientific data. Darwin argues that evolution—the idea that all life began with a common ancestor, an amoeba-like being—is not a hypothesis, as had been claimed when this notion first appeared in Greek thought; rather, it is a principle of biology operating throughout nature. In other words, viewed over the course of millennia, the plant, animal, and human worlds constitute a vast cousinhood. Thus Darwin's book destroyed the biblical view of human genesis, or creationism—Adam and Eve were the first parents, having been created by God after he had made the plant and animal kingdoms— an idea that had dominated Western thought since Christianity became the religion of Rome in about 400 CE. Darwin replaced it with the principle of evolution. The full meaning of evolution, that humans are creatures without souls and that life is without purpose, remains a controversial topic even today.

The Descent of Man, while controversial, did not raise the firestorm of criticism that had greeted his earlier work, *The Origin of Species* (1859). It was in the 1859 work that Darwin first advanced the principle of evolution, but he had not included the human species in his discussion of animal species, though he hinted at it. *The Origin of Species* sold out on the first day of publication, but it also made him and his ideas notorious, a distressing turn of events for one of the most staid men in the Victorian Age—a period obsessed with respectability. (Darwin even became seriously ill when confronted with unpleasant ideas.) At the same time, he was the quintessential expression of the period's realism, a pure scientist, totally disinterested in theory and devoted solely to facts. It was only after amassing incontrovertible data, collected between 1831 and 1836 on his voyage to South America with the British ship *Beagle,* and in the 1850s in his investigation of orchids, that he was prepared to publish his research. By 1871 the principle of evolution, proven by Darwin's documentation, had won over his fellow scientists, so that when *The Descent of Man* appeared, despite the explosive theme, it was soon adopted into the worldview of most educated people.

The blind force "guiding" Darwinian evolution is natural selection, the notion that favorable variations within a species tend to be preserved, while unfavorable variations are destroyed; the result is the formation of new species. The variations occur randomly, without design on the part of a divine creator or desire on the part of the organism. Darwin claimed that the idea of natural selection was inspired by his reading of Thomas Malthus's essay *On Population* (1797). The idea, however, was also explicitly stated in Herbert Spencer's *Population* (1852), where it was called "survival of the fittest." It was Spencer's term that Darwin appropriated and made his own.

Reading the Selection

This passage is taken from the last chapter of *The Descent of Man.* Darwin praises man's intellectual ("godlike intellect") and moral faculties ("sympathy . . . for the most debased," and "benevolence . . . to other men [and] living creature[s]"), claiming them to be the result of natural selection instead of divine origin.

· · ·

The main conclusion arrived at in this work, and now held by many naturalists who are well competent to form a sound judgment, is that man is descended from some less highly organized form. The grounds upon which this conclusion rests will never be shaken, for the close similarity between man and the lower animals in embryonic[25] development, as well as in innumerable points of structure and constitution, both of high and of the most trifling importance—the rudiments which he retains, and the abnormal reversions to which he is occasionally liable—are facts which cannot be disputed. They have long been known, but until recently they told us nothing with respect to the origin of man. Now when viewed by the light of our knowledge of the whole organic world, their meaning is unmistakable. The great principle of evolution stands up clear and firm, when these groups of facts are considered in connection with others, such as the mutual affinities of the members of the same group, their geographical distribution in past and present times, and their geological succession. It is incredible that all these facts should speak falsely. He who is not content to look, like a savage, at the phenomena of nature as disconnected cannot any longer believe that man is the work of a separate act of creation. He will be forced to admit that the close resemblance of the embryo of man to that, for instance, of a dog—the construction of his skull, limbs, and whole frame, independently of the uses to which the parts may be put, on the same plan with that of other mammals—the occasional reappearance of various structures, for instance of several distinct muscles, which man does not normally possess, but which are common to the Quadrumana[26]—and a crowd of analogous facts—all point in the plainest manner to the conclusion that man is the codescendant with other mammals of a common progenitor.

· · ·

The main conclusion arrived at in this work, namely that man is descended from some lowly-organized form, will, I regret to think, be highly distasteful to many persons. But there can hardly be a doubt that we are descended from barbarians. The astonishment which I felt on first seeing a

---

[25] **embryonic** Within the fetus, during the earliest stages of development; for humans, during the first six weeks from conception.

[26] **Quadrumana** From Latin, "four hands." Primates, excluding humans, which are distinguished by hand-shaped feet. The term was coined in 1819.

party of Fuegians[27] on a wild and broken shore will never be forgotten by me, for the reflection at once rushed into my mind—such were our ancestors. These men were absolutely naked and bedaubed with paint, their long hair was tangled, their mouths frothed with excitement, and their expression was wild, startled, and distrustful. They possessed hardly any arts, and like wild animals lived on what they could catch; they had no government, and were merciless to everyone not of their own small tribe. He who has seen a savage in his native land will not feel much shame, if forced to acknowledge that the blood of some more humble creature flows in his veins. For my own part I would as soon be descended from that heroic little monkey, who braved his dreaded enemy in order to save the life of his keeper; or from that old baboon, who, descending from the mountains, carried away in triumph his young comrade from a crowd of astonished dogs—as from a savage who delights to torture his enemies, offers

up bloody sacrifices, practices infanticide[28] without remorse, treats his wives like slaves, knows no decency, and is haunted by the grossest superstitions.

Man may be excused for feeling some pride at having risen, though not through his own exertions, to the very summit of the organic scale; and the fact of his having thus risen, instead of having been aboriginally placed there, may give him hopes for a still higher destiny in the distant future. But we are not here concerned with hopes or fears, only with the truth as far as our reason allows us to discover it. I have given the evidence to the best of my ability; and we must acknowledge, as it seems to me, that man with all his noble qualities, with sympathy which feels for the most debased, with benevolence which extends not only to other men but to the humblest living creature, with his godlike intellect which has penetrated into the movements and constitution of the solar system— with all these exalted powers—Man still bears in his bodily frame the indelible stamp of his lowly origin.

---

[27] **Fuegians** Inhabitants of Tierra del Fuego, the large island and the archipelago of islands in the Strait of Magellan off South America. Darwin visited the island in 1832, when the H.M.S. *Beagle,* on which he served as naturalist, made a stopover there, as reported in his *Journal of Researches on the Voyage of the Beagle* (1839).

[28] **infanticide** The killing of an infant soon after birth. In Tierra del Fuego, Darwin observed the Yahgan Indians and reported an instance of infanticide (see footnote 27). Later scholars who studied this tribe say that infanticide among the tribe members was rare.

Questions for Critical Thinking

1. "Man is descended from some lowly-organized form." Why is Darwin's conclusion so controversial?

2. Define *survival of the fittest.* Explain how humans would acquire "noble qualities" and "godlike intellect" in Darwin's view of evolution.

EMILY DICKINSON
Poems

Emily Dickinson (1830–1886) was America's first great woman poet, but she was virtually unknown when she died. She published only three poems while living, and their original style doomed her to obscurity. Her world was New England, and though Puritan values were in decline, a literary career for a woman then was hard to manage. She nonetheless pioneered the way for other female writers.

For the most part, Dickinson lived in Amherst, Massachusetts, where her father, Edward Dickinson, was treasurer of Amherst College for forty years. She is known to have made only two forays from Amherst—the first in 1847–1848 when she was a student at Mount Holyoke Female Seminary, and the second in 1854 when she visited her father in Washington, D.C., where he was a congressman. After 1862 she became a recluse in her father's house, devoting her time to writing a "letter to the world"—the 1,775 poems that constitute her legacy. These poems, which she asked to be destroyed at her death, were saved for posterity by her sister Lavinia. Aided by Thomas Wentworth Higginson, a minor literary figure who had been Dickinson's sole tie with the wider literary world, and Mabel Todd Loomis, the gifted wife of an Amherst professor, Lavinia produced the first selection of Emily's poems in 1891. It was not until the 1920s, with the appearance of a rebellious generation, that Dickinson's works found a welcoming audience. Since World War II, especially with the rise of feminism, her reputation has grown exponentially. Today this literary star is deemed of the magnitude of Henry David Thoreau (see "On the Duty of Civil Disobedience") and Walt Whitman (see "Song of Myself"), who, with Dickinson, helped to create a unique American style of writing.

Dickinson's poems were characterized by discordant metaphors drawn from flowers, village life, the Bible, the law, and the mechanical and domestic arts. Compressed and elusive, her works prefigure Modernism, the ruling style from 1870 to 1970, which used rich metaphors; yet, at the same time, they reflect late romanticism, with their claustrophobic images and sexual disturbance.

Reading the Selections

As life passed her by, Dickinson grew ever more eccentric. Dressed in white, she became a village legend; some thought her half-demented. Death became a near obsession, as reflected in five poems printed here. "There's a certain Slant of light" (ca. 1861) shows her thoughts wandering to death, inspired surprisingly by the normally optimistic images of sunlight and church hymns. "I felt a Funeral, in my Brain" (ca. 1861) presents the unusual metaphor of a parade of persons trampling up and down her brain as corresponding to her state of disillusion; the poem is unfinished, a typical feature. "I heard a Fly buzz—when I died—" (ca. 1862) calls up a disturbed sexual image of the poet seated, the air moved only by the buzz of a fly— perhaps a metaphor of Dickinson's fate of life in death. "Because I could not stop for Death—" (ca. 1863) speaks to her feeling that death too soon ends life's little pleasures, such as "the School, where Children strove at Recess."

The third of the five poems, "Much Madness is divinest Sense—," reveals Dickinson as a rebel, as she joins the "mad" against the sensible majority; the word *Chain* evokes a sense of being imprisoned.

∞

There's a certain Slant of light

There's a certain Slant of light, Winter Afternoons— That oppresses, like the Heft[29] Of Cathedral Tunes— Heavenly Hurt, it gives us— We can find no scar, But internal difference, Where the Meanings, are—	None may teach it—Any— 'Tis the Seal Despair— An imperial affliction Sent us of the Air— When it comes, the Landscape lister Shadows—hold their breath— When it goes, 'tis like the Distance On the look of Death—

1   10

---

[29] **Heft** Weight; power.

I felt a Funeral, in my Brain

I felt a Funeral, in my Brain,   1
And Mourners to and fro
Kept treading—treading—till it seemed
That Sense was breaking through—

And when they all were seated,
A Service, like a Drum—
Kept beating—beating—till I thought
My Mind was going numb—

And then I heard them lift a Box
And creak across my Soul   10

With those same Boots of Lead, again,
Then Space—began to toll,

As all the Heavens were a Bell,
And Being, but an Ear,
And I, and Silence, some strange Race
Wrecked, solitary, here—

And then a Plank in Reason, broke,
And I dropped down, and down—
And hit a World, at every plunge,
And Finished knowing—then—   20

Much Madness is divinest Sense—

Much Madness is divinest Sense—   1
To a discerning Eye—
Much Sense—the starkest Madness—
'Tis the Majority

In this, as All, prevail—
Assent—and you are sane—
Demur—you're straightway dangerous—
And handled with a Chain—

I heard a Fly buzz—when I died—

I heard a Fly buzz—when I died—   1
The Stillness in the Room
Was like the Stillness in the Air—
Between the Heaves of Storm—

The Eyes around—had wrung them dry—
And Breaths were gathering firm
For that last Onset—when the King
Be witnessed—in the Room—

I willed my Keepsakes—Signed away
What portion of me be   10
Assignable—and then it was
There interposed a Fly—

With Blue—uncertain stumbling Buzz—
Between the light—and me—
And then the Windows failed—and then
I could not see to see—

Because I could not stop for Death—

Because I could not stop for Death—   1
He kindly stopped for me—
The Carriage held but just Ourselves—
And Immortality.

We slowly drove—He knew no haste
And I had put away
My labor and my leisure too,
For His Civility—

We passed the School, where Children strove
At Recess—in the Ring—
We passed the Fields of Gazing Grain—
We passed the Setting Sun—   10

Or rather—He passed Us—
The Dews drew quivering and chill—
For only Gossamer, my Gown—
My Tippet[30]—only Tulle[31]—

We paused before a House that seemed
A Swelling of the Ground—
The Roof was scarcely visible—
The Cornice—in the Ground—   20

Since then—'tis Centuries—and yet
Feels shorter than the Day
I first surmised the Horses' Heads
Were toward Eternity—

_____
[30] **Tippet** A shoulder-covering, usually made of fur.
[31] **Tulle** Soft, silk netting used in veils and hats.

Questions for Critical Thinking

1. Characterize Dickinson's literary style as revealed in these five poems.

2. Compose a short poem in the style of Dickinson. Justify your choice of theme, language, and layout.

WALT WHITMAN
Selections from "Song of Myself"

Walt Whitman (1819–1892), America's first world-class poet, was also America's most American poet. Unlike any poet before or after, he made his own country the subject of his lifelong project. The poem group titled *Leaves of Grass* (first edition, 1855; ninth or deathbed edition, 1891–1892) is a hymn celebrating the whole life of the nation, with the poet identifying himself with male and female, young and old, white and black, slave and free, healthy and handicapped—and animals, too. Speaking in a mystical, biblical voice, Whitman sang of the body and the soul, of night, earth, and sea, of vice and virtue. *Leaves of Grass* was a living work that evolved in structure over thirty-seven years, with almost constant revision, reordering, additions, and subtractions, starting with 12 and expanding to 383 poems in the deathbed edition. It was meant to represent the growth of his country, to give voice to "a composite, electric, democratic personality," to embody America's soul—the mystical reality of national consciousness.

   Leaves of Grass, innovative in form, style, and subject, helped free American poetry from European tradition. At the same time, it opened up European writing to fresh voices in the ever-widening global culture. Whitman's work attracted admirers among England's writers, who charged that Americans did not fully appreciate him. Though Whitman was not neglected at home (Emerson, then dean of American letters, welcomed *Leaves of Grass* with these words: "I greet you at the beginning of a great career. . . ."), it is true that Whitman had to deal with the criticism that *Leaves of Grass* was an immoral book because of sexual overtones in certain poems. Indeed, because of this work, he was fired from a government clerkship after serving less than six months.

   Whitman's reputation has grown since the late 1950s, when he was rediscovered by America's beat generation—a group of writers who were repulsed by society's materialism and militarism. The leading beat poet, Allen Ginsberg, found a kindred spirit in Whitman; they shared not only a contempt for elegant writing, but also homosexual feelings, a beard, and an unkempt appearance. Both, too, shared a decided preference for society's rejects, called "beats" by Ginsberg but "roughs" by Whitman (a poem in *Leaves of Grass* introduced "Walt Whitman, an American, one of the roughs, a kosmos"). The bohemian Whitman was only one phase of his life, the time prior to the Civil War. After working during the war as a nurse to Northern and Southern soldiers in Army hospitals in Washington, D.C., he settled down into a new persona that he kept to the end: the "good gray poet," living quietly and receiving visitors.

Reading the Selections

"Song of Myself," with its sensual, even erotic language, is the heart of Whitman's *Leaves of Grass.* In these lyrical verses, filled with romantic images, Whitman sings of love of self, of man, of woman, of nature, of country, of the world, of the gift of life itself. The voice that speaks is exuberant, as if the words can scarcely be uttered, so complete is the zest for living. Scholars who have analyzed the poem, however, conclude that the poetical structure is artfully crafted so as to give the impression of spontaneity. Originally published as a single poem, without divisions, "Song of Myself" took up more than half the space of the first edition of *Leaves of Grass.* In the deathbed edition the poem, now divided into fifty-two sections, occupied only a small portion of the whole. The poem's first twelve sections are included here.

1

I celebrate myself, and sing myself,
And what I assume you shall assume,
For every atom belonging to me as good belongs to you.

I loafe and invite my soul,
I lean and loafe at my ease observing a spear of summer
    grass.
My tongue, every atom of my blood, form'd from this
    soil, this air,
Born here of parents born here from parents the same,
    and their parents the same,
I, now thirty-seven years old in perfect health begin,
Hoping to cease not till death.

Creeds and schools in abeyance,
Retiring back a while sufficed at what they are, but never
    forgotten,
I harbor for good or bad, I permit to speak at every
    hazard,
Nature without check with original energy.

2

Houses and rooms are full of perfumes, the shelves are
    crowded with perfumes,
I breathe the fragrance myself and know it and like it,
The distillation would intoxicate me also, but I shall not
    let it.

The atmosphere is not a perfume, it has no taste of the
    distillation, it is odorless,
It is for my mouth forever, I am in love with it,
I will go to the bank by the wood and become
    undisguised and naked,
I am mad for it to be in contact with me.
The smoke of my own breath,
Echoes, ripples, buzz'd whispers, love-root, silk-thread,
    crotch and vine,
My respiration and inspiration, the beating of my heart,
    the passing of blood and air through my lungs,
The sniff of green leaves and dry leaves, and of the shore
    and dark-color'd sea-rocks, and of hay in the barn,
The sound of the belch'd words of my voice loos'd to the
    eddies of the wind,
A few light kisses, a few embraces, a reaching around of
    arms,
The play of shine and shade on the trees as the supple
    boughs wag,
The delight alone or in the rush of the streets, or along
    the fields and hill-sides,
The feeling of health, the full-noon trill, the song of me
    rising from bed and meeting the sun.

Have you reckon'd a thousand acres much? have you
    reckon'd the earth much?
Have you practis'd so long to learn to read?
Have you felt so proud to get at the meaning of poems?

Stop this day and night with me and you shall possess
    the origin of all poems,

You shall possess the good of the earth and sun, (there
    are millions of suns left,)
You shall no longer take things at second or third hand,
    nor look through the eyes of the dead, nor feed on
    the spectres[32] in books,
You shall not look through my eyes either, nor take
    things from me,
You shall listen to all sides and filter them from your self.

3

I have heard what the talkers were talking, the talk of the
    beginning and the end,
But I do not talk of the beginning or the end.

There was never any more inception than there is now,   40
Nor any more youth or age than there is now,
And will never be any more perfection than there is now,
Nor any more heaven or hell than there is now.
Urge and urge and urge,
Always the procreant[33] urge of the world.

Out of the dimness opposite equals advance, always
    substance and increase, always sex,
Always a knit of identity, always distinction, always a
    breed of life.

To elaborate is no avail, learn'd and unlearn'd feel that it
    is so.

Sure as the most certain sure, plumb in the uprights, well
    entretied, braced in the beams,[34]
Stout as a horse, affectionate, haughty, electrical,   50
I and this mystery here we stand.

Clear and sweet is my soul, and clear and sweet is all that
    is not my soul.

Lack one lacks both, and the unseen is proved by the
    seen,
Till that becomes unseen and receives proof in its turn.
Showing the best and dividing it from the worst age
    vexes age,
Knowing the perfect fitness and equanimity of things,
    while they discuss I am silent, and go bathe and
    admire myself.

Welcome is every organ and attribute of me, and of any
    man hearty and clean,
Not an inch nor a particle of an inch is vile, and none
    shall be less familiar than the rest.

I am satisfied—I see, dance, laugh, sing;
As the hugging and loving bed-fellow sleeps at my side   60
    through the night, and withdraws at the peep of the
    day with stealthy tread,
Leaving me baskets cover'd with white towels swelling
    the house with their plenty,
Shall I postpone my acceptation and realization and
    scream at my eyes,
That they turn from gazing after and down the road,
And forthwith cipher[35] and show me to a cent,
Exactly the value of one and exactly the value of two, and
    which is ahead?

4

Trippers[36] and askers[37] surround me,
People I meet, the effect upon me of my early life or the
    ward and city I live in, or the nation,
The latest dates, discoveries, inventions, societies, authors
    old and new,
My dinner, dress, associates, looks, compliments, dues,
The real or fancied indifference of some man or woman   70
    I love,
The sickness of one of my folks or of myself, or ill-
    doing or loss or lack of money, or depressions or
    exaltations,
Battles, the horrors of fratricidal[38] war, the fever of
    doubtful news, the fitful events;
These come to me days and nights and go from me again,
But they are not the Me myself.

Apart from the pulling and hauling stands what I am,
Stands amused, complacent, compassionating, idle,
    unitary,
Looks down, is erect, or bends an arm on an impalpable
    certain rest,
Looking with side-curved head curious what will come
    next,
Both in and out of the game and watching and
    wondering at it.

Backward I see in my own days where I sweated through   80
    fog with linguists and contenders,
I have no mockings or arguments, I witness and wait.

5

I believe in you my soul, the other I am must not abase
    itself to you,
And you must not be abased to the other.

---

[32] **spectres** Ghosts.
[33] **procreant** Producing offspring.
[34] **plumb ... entretied ... braced in the beams** Carpenter's
terms, each signifying "well made." *Plumb* means "exactly in the
center"; *entretied* means "cross-braced, as between two joists or
walls"; and *braced* means "strengthened with iron or lumber."

[35] **cipher** Work out by means of arithmetic.
[36] **Trippers** People going about their daily chores.
[37] **askers** People asking questions.
[38] **fratricidal** Having to do with the killing of one's own brothers and sisters; a term often used to describe the American Civil
War.

Loafe with me on the grass, loose the stop[39] from your
    throat,
Not words, not music or rhyme I want, not custom or
    lecture, not even the best,
Only the lull I like, the hum of your valvèd voice.

I mind how once we lay such a transparent summer
    morning,
How you settled your head athwart my hips and gently
    turn'd over upon me,
And parted the shirt from my bosom-bone, and plunged
    your tongue to my bare-stript heart,
And reach'd till you felt my beard, and reach'd till you   90
    held my feet.

Swiftly arose and spread around me the peace and
    knowledge that pass all the argument of the earth,
And I know that the hand of God is the promise of my own,
And I know that the spirit of God is the brother of my own,
And that all the men ever born are also my brothers, and
    the women my sisters and lovers,
And that a kelson[40] of the creation is love,
And limitless are leaves stiff or drooping in the fields,
And brown ants in the little wells beneath them,
And mossy scabs of the worm fence, heap'd stones, elder,
    mullein[41] and poke-weed.[42]

6

A child said *What is the grass?* fetching it to me with full
    hands;
How could I answer the child? I do not know what it is   100
    any more than he.

I guess it must be the flag of my disposition, out of
    hopeful green stuff woven.

Or I guess it is the handkerchief of the Lord,
A scented gift and remembrancer designedly dropt,
Bearing the owner's name someway in the corners, that
    we may see and remark, and say *Whose?*
Or I guess the grass is itself a child, the produced babe of
    the vegetation.

Or I guess it is a uniform hieroglyphic,
And it means, Sprouting alike in broad zones and narrow
    zones,
Growing among black folks as among white,

Kanuck,[43] Tuckahoe,[44] Congressman, Cuff,[45] give them the
    same, I receive them the same.
And now it seems to me the beautiful uncut hair of   110
    graves.

Tenderly will I use you curling grass,
It may be you transpire from the breasts of young men,
It may be if I had known them I would have loved them,
It may be you are from old people, or from offspring
    taken soon out of their mothers' laps,
And here you are the mothers' laps.

This grass is very dark to be from the white heads of old
    mothers,
Darker than the colorless beards of old men,
Dark to come from under the faint red roofs of mouths.

O I perceive after all so many uttering tongues,
And I perceive they do not come from the roofs of   120
    mouths for nothing.

I wish I could translate the hints about the dead young
    men and women,
And the hints about old men and mothers, and the
    offspring taken soon out of their laps.

What do you think has become of the young and old men?
And what do you think has become of the women and
    children?

They are alive and well somewhere,
The smallest sprout shows there is really no death,
And if ever there was it led forward life, and does not
    wait at the end to arrest it,
And ceas'd the moment life appear'd.
All goes onward and outward, nothing collapses,
And to die is different from what any one supposed, and   130
    luckier.

7

Has any one supposed it lucky to be born?
I hasten to inform him or her it is just as lucky to die, and
    I know it.

I pass death with the dying and birth with the new-
    wash'd babe, and am not contain'd between my hat
    and boots,
And peruse manifold objects, no two alike and every one
    good,
The earth good and the stars good, and their adjuncts all
    good.

---

[39] **stop** In an organ, a knob for regulating the volume and quality of the sounds.
[40] **kelson** From Old Norse. Variant of *keelson*, a nautical term.
A timber or girder fastened above and parallel to the keel of a
ship, to give additional strength.
[41] **mullein** A plant with wooly leaves and yellow flowers; a
member of the snapdragon family.
[42] **poke-weed** An American plant, with white flowers and
purple berries, used in emetics and purgatives.

---

[43] **Kanuck** Also Canuck. Slang for French Canadian.
[44] **Tuckahoe** Native American from tidewater Virginia who eats
"tuckahoe," an edible rootstock of an underground fungus.
[45] **Cuff** African American.

I am not an earth nor an adjunct of an earth,
I am the mate and companion of people, all just as
    immortal and fathomless as myself,
(They do not know how immortal, but I know.)

Every kind for itself and its own, for me mine male and
    female,
For me those that have been boys and that love women,   140
For me the man that is proud and feels how it stings to be
    slighted,
For me the sweet-heart and the old maid, for me mothers
    and the mothers of mothers,
For me lips that have smiled, eyes that have shed tears,
For me children and the begetters of children.

Undrape! you are not guilty to me, nor stale nor
    discarded,
I see through the broadcloth and gingham whether or no,
And am around, tenacious, acquisitive, tireless, and
    cannot be shaken away.

8

The little one sleeps in its cradle,
I lift the gauze and look a long time, and silently brush
    away flies with my hand.

The youngster and the red-faced girl turn aside up the   150
    bushy hill,
I peeringly view them from the top.

The suicide sprawls on the bloody floor of the bedroom,
I witness the corpse with its dabbled hair, I note where
    the pistol has fallen.

The blab of the pave, tires of carts, sluff of boot-soles,[46]
    talk of the promenaders,
The heavy omnibus, the driver with his interrogating
    thumb, the clank of the shod horses on the granite
    floor,
The snow-sleighs, clinking, shouted jokes, pelts of
    snowballs,
The hurrahs for popular favorites, the fury of rous'd
    mobs,
The flap of the curtain'd litter,[47] a sick man inside borne
    to the hospital,
The meeting of enemies, the sudden oath, the blows
    and fall,
The excited crowd, the policeman with his star quickly   160
    working his passage to the centre of the crowd,
The impassive stones that receive and return so many
    echoes,

What groans of over-fed or half-starv'd who fall
    sunstruck or in fits,
What exclamations of women taken suddenly who hurry
    home and give birth to babes,
What living and buried speech is always vibrating here,
    what howls restrain'd by decorum,
Arrests of criminals, slights, adulterous offers made,
    acceptances, rejections with convex lips,
I mind them or the show or resonance of them—I come
    and I depart.

9

The big doors of the country barn stand open and ready,
The dried grass of the harvest-time loads the slow-drawn
    wagon,
The clear light plays on the brown gray and green
    intertinged,
The armfuls are pack'd to the sagging mow.   170

I am there, I help, I came stretch'd atop of the load,
I felt its soft jolts, one leg reclined on the other,
I jump from the cross-beams and seize the clover and
    timothy,[48]
And roll head over heels and tangle my hair full of
    wisps.

10

Alone far in the wilds and mountains I hunt,
Wandering amazed at my own lightness and glee,
In the late afternoon choosing a safe spot to pass the
    night,
Kindling a fire and broiling the fresh-kill'd game,
Falling asleep on the gather'd leaves with my dog and
    gun by my side.

The Yankee clipper is under her sky-sails, she cuts the   180
    sparkle and scud,[49]
My eyes settle the land, I bend at her prow or shout
    joyously from the deck.

The boatmen and clam-diggers arose early and stopt for
    me,
I tuck'd my trowser-ends in my boots and went and had
    a good time;
You should have been with us that day round the
    chowder-kettle.

I saw the marriage of the trapper in the open air in the
    far west, the bride was a red girl,[50]

---

[46] **blab ... pave ... tires ... boot-soles** Idle sounds made on
the pavement by cart wheels and boot soles. *Sluff,* also spelled
slough, means "droppings."
[47] **litter** A couch secluded by curtains and carried on men's
shoulders or by beasts of burden.

[48] **timothy** A grass grown for hay.
[49] **sparkle and scud** "Sparkle" alludes to the play of sunlight
on water; "scud" is a sailing term meaning "to run before the
wind."
[50] **red girl** Young Native American woman.

Her father and his friends sat near cross-legged and
    dumbly smoking, they had moccasins to their
    feet and large thick blankets hanging from their
    shoulders,
On a bank lounged the trapper, he was drest mostly in
    skins, his luxuriant beard and curls protected his
    neck, he held his bride by the hand,
She had long eyelashes, her head was bare, her coarse
    straight locks descended upon her voluptuous limbs
    and reach'd to her feet.[51]

The runaway slave came to my house and stopt outside,
I heard his motions crackling the twigs of the woodpile,   190
Through the swung half-door of the kitchen I saw him
    limpsy[52] and weak,
And went where he sat on a log and led him in and
    assured him,
And brought water and fill'd a tub for his sweated body
    and bruis'd feet,
And gave him a room that enter'd from my own, and
    gave him some coarse clean clothes,
And remember perfectly well his revolving eyes and his
    awkwardness,
And remember putting plasters on the galls[53] of his neck
    and ankles;
He staid with me a week before he was recuperated and
    pass'd north,
I had him sit next me at table, my fire-lock[54] lean'd in the
    corner.

11

Twenty-eight young men bathe by the shore,
Twenty-eight young men and all so friendly;   200
Twenty-eight years of womanly life and all so lonesome.

She owns the fine house by the rise of the bank,
She hides handsome and richly drest aft the blinds of the
    window.

Which of the young men does she like the best?
Ah the homeliest of them is beautiful to her.

Where are you off to, lady? for I see you,
You splash in the water there, yet stay stock still in your
    room.
Dancing and laughing along the beach came the twenty-
    ninth bather,
The rest did not see her, but she saw them and loved them.

The beards of the young men glisten'd with wet, it ran   210
    from their long hair,
Little streams pass'd all over their bodies.
An unseen hand also pass'd over their bodies,
It descended tremblingly from their temples and ribs.

The young men float on their backs, their white bellies
    bulge to the sun, they do not ask who seizes fast to
    them,
They do not know who puffs and declines with pendant
    and bending arch,
They do not think whom they souse with spray.

12

The butcher-boy puts off his killing-clothes, or sharpens
    his knife at the stall in the market,
I loiter enjoying his repartee and his shuffle and
    break-down.
Blacksmiths with grimed and hairy chests environ the
    anvil,
Each has his main-sledge, they are all out, there is a great   220
    heat in the fire.
From the cinder-strew'd threshold I follow their
    movements,
The lithe sheer of their waists plays even with their
    massive arms,
Overhand the hammers swing, overhand so slow,
    overhand so sure,
They do not hasten, each man hits in his place.

. . . .

---

[51] **feet** Whitman's description of the marriage in this verse is based on "The Trapper's Bride," a painting by the Baltimore artist Alfred Jacob Miller (1810–1874).
[52] **limpsy** Poetic, limp; without energy or will.
[53] **galls** Sores caused by chafing.
[54] **fire-lock** A gun outfitted with a lock that requires a slow match to ignite the powder charge.

Questions for Critical Thinking

1. In this selection, identify seven of the different "selves" to which Whitman gives voice. What is the point of these varied impersonations?

2. Show how Whitman's poem expresses the romantic literary style.

GUSTAVE FLAUBERT
Selection from *Madame Bovary*

Flaubert's *Madame Bovary* (1857) is considered the greatest novel in the French language. Its heroine, Emma Bovary, is the first of a line of unhappy middle-class wives, such as the Russian writer Leo Tolstoy's Anna Karenina, who appear in modern fiction. Flaubert's story of Emma's revolt against marriage led officials to prosecute him (unsuccessfully) for "immorality." Such a charge is ludicrous today, partly because morals are more relaxed, and partly because studies of sexuality (see Freud's *Civilization and Its Discontents* in Chapter 20; Beauvoir's *The Second Sex* in Chapter 22) have made Emma's adultery more understandable. Hence Flaubert's novel is a pioneering work in the literature of female consciousness.

Although published in 1857, when France was undergoing rapid change fueled by the rise of the railroad, telegraph, and newspaper, *Madame Bovary* was set in a slightly earlier, more stable period, before new technologies destroyed old ways of life. The novel's general subject is provincial culture (the subtitle was *Moeurs de province*, "provincial life"), which Flaubert despised with a vehemence akin to Marx's (see *The Communist Manifesto*). Unlike Marx, he remained a loyal member of the middle class, but he used this novel to portray the narrowness, mediocrity, and hypocrisy of small-town culture. This culture he expressed in the imaginary towns of Tostes and Yonville, in cultural artifacts (a keepsake album, a medical journal, and a shop ledger), speech patterns (everyone speaks in clichés), and social events (a local ball and an opera performance).

The novel's specific subject is Emma Bovary, whose personal tragedy is inevitable, given Flaubert's dark vision of provincial life. Convent-educated, innately sensual, and addicted to romantic novels, Emma is also a stupid, vulgar, and cruel woman. She marries Charles Bovary, a physician, who is good-hearted but insensitive, and within weeks she says, "Oh, why, dear God, did I marry him?" Bored with her husband, she allows herself to be seduced by Rodolphe Boulanger, a wealthy landowner and sexual libertine. She plunges into a downward spiral of pleasure seeking, all of which ends in further disappointment. Beset by debt and despair, she takes arsenic and dies. Charles, now penniless, dies soon after.

Gustave Flaubert (1821–1880) practically invented the realistic-style novel with this work. Its setting and characters were true to his world near Rouen, where he, the son of a doctor, lived on a private income (he left Rouen for three years to study law in Paris and for eighteen months to tour the Near East). Its meticulously prosaic language reflected the banal speech that he heard in Rouen (he kept a "Dictionary of Received Ideas" to collect choice examples of overheard clichés). Emma Bovary, he claimed, was patterned after himself: "Madame Bovary, c'est moi!" ("I am Madame Bovary!")

Reading the Selection

This selection from Chapter VIII of *Madame Bovary* takes place on the day of Yonville's agricultural show. Flaubert's account is cinematic, shifting back and forth between fragments of Rodolphe's seduction of Emma, which takes place upstairs in the Town Hall, and fragments of the town official Lieuvain's speech, which occurs out of doors. Emma sits mesmerized by Rodolphe's smooth whisperings ("I am yours!"), just as Yonville's citizens listen transfixed by Lieuvain's oratory ("Persevere! listen neither to the suggestions of routine, nor to the over-hasty councils of a rash empiricism."). Hence, in Flaubert's vision, there is no escape from this provincial world, either through love or through material progress. Both are illusions.

Chapter VIII

"Madame Bovary!" exclaimed Homais.[55] "I must go at once and pay her my respects. Perhaps she'll be pleased to have a seat in the enclosure under the peristyle." And, without heeding Madame Lefrançois,[56] who was calling him back for more gossip, the pharmacist walked off rapidly with a smile on his face and his walk jauntier than ever, bowing copiously to right and left, and taking up much room with the large tails of his frock-coat that fluttered behind him in the wind.

Rodolphe having caught sight of him from afar, quickened his pace, but Madame Bovary couldn't keep up; so he walked more slowly, and, smiling at her, said roughly:

"It's only to get away from that fat fellow, you know, the pharmacist."

She nudged him with her elbow.

"How shall I understand that?" he asked himself.

And, walking on, he looked at her out of the corner of his eyes.

Her profile was so calm that it revealed nothing.

It stood out in the light from the oval of her hat that was tied with pale ribbons like waving rushes. Her eyes with their long curved lashes looked straight before her, and though wide open, they seemed slightly slanted at the cheek-bones, because of the blood pulsing gently under the delicate skin. A rosy light shone through the partition between her nostrils. Her head was bent upon her shoulder, and the tips of her teeth shone through her lips like pearls.

"Is she making fun of me?" thought Rodolphe.

Emma's gesture, however, had only been meant for a warning; for Monsieur Lheureux was accompanying them, and spoke now and again as if to enter into the conversation.

"What a beautiful day! Everybody is outside! The wind is from the east!"

Neither Madame Bovary nor Rodolphe answered him, but their slightest movement made him draw near saying, "I beg your pardon!" and raising his hat.

When they reached the blacksmith's house, instead of following the road up to the fence, Rodolphe suddenly turned down a path, drawing Madame Bovary with him. He called out:

"Good evening, Monsieur Lheureux! We'll see you soon!"

"How you got rid of him!" she said, laughing.

"Why," he went on, "allow oneself to be intruded upon by others? And as to-day I have the happiness of being with you . . ."

Emma blushed. He did not finish his sentence. Then he talked of the fine weather and of the pleasure of walking on the grass. A few daisies had sprung up again.

"Here are some pretty Easter daisies," he said, "and enough to provide oracles for all the lovers in the vicinity."

He added,

"Shall I pick some? What do you think?"

"Are you in love?" she asked, coughing a little.

"H'm, h'm! who knows?" answered Rodolphe.

The meadow was beginning to fill up, and the housewives were hustling about with their great umbrellas, their baskets, and their babies. One often had to make way for a long file of country girls, servant-maids with blue stockings, flat shoes and silver rings, who smelt of milk when one passed close to them. They walked along holding one another by the hand, and thus they spread over the whole field from the row of open trees to the banquet tent. But this was the judging time, and the farmers one after the other entered a kind of enclosure formed by ropes supported on sticks.

The beasts were there, their noses turned toward the rope, and making a confused line with their unequal rumps. Drowsy pigs were burrowing in the earth with their snouts, calves were lowing and bleating; the cows, one leg folded under them stretched their bellies on the grass, slowly chewing their cud, and blinking their heavy eyelids at the gnats that buzzed around them. Ploughmen with bare arms were holding by the halter prancing stallions that neighed with dilated nostrils looking in the direction of the mares. These stood quietly, stretching out their heads and flowing manes, while their foals rested in their shadow, or sucked them from time to time. And above the long undulation of these crowded bodies one saw some white mane rising in the wind like a wave, or some sharp horns sticking out, and the heads of men running about. Apart, outside the enclosure, a hundred paces off, was a large black bull, muzzled, with an iron ring in its nostrils, and who moved no more than if he had been in bronze. A child in rags was holding him by a rope.

Between the two lines the committee-men were walking with heavy steps, examining each animal, then consulting one another in a low voice. One who seemed of more importance now and then took notes in a book as he walked along. This was the president of the jury, Monsieur Derozerays[57] de la Panville. As soon as he recognised Rodolphe he came forward quickly, and smiling amiably, said:

"What! Monsieur Boulanger, you are deserting us?"

Rodolphe protested that he would come. But when the president had disappeared:

"To tell the truth," he said, "I shall not go. Your company is better than his."

And while poking fun at the show, Rodolphe, to move about more easily, showed the gendarme his blue card, and even stopped now and then in front of some fine beast, which Madame Bovary did not at all admire. He noticed

---

[55] **Homais** The village pharmacist, the focus of much of Flaubert's satire.
[56] **Madame Lefrançois** Innkeeper of the village hostelry, the Lion d'Or (French, "Golden Lion").

[57] **Monsieur Derozerays** Chairman of the jury that awards prizes at the Yonville agricultural fair.

this, and began jeering at the Yonville ladies and their dresses; then he apologised for his own casual attire. It had the inconsistency of things at once commonplace and refined which enchants or exasperates the ordinary man because he suspects that it reveals an unconventional existence, a dubious morality, the affectations of the artist, and above all, a certain contempt for established conventions. The wind, blowing up his batiste[58] shirt with pleated cuffs revealed a waistcoat of grey linen, and his broad-striped trousers disclosed at the ankle nankeen[59] boots with patent leather gaiters. These were so polished that they reflected the grass. He trampled on horse's dung, one hand in the pocket of his jacket and his straw hat tilted on one side.

"Anyway," he added, "when one lives in the country . . ."

"Nothing is worth while," said Emma.

"That is true," replied Rodolphe. "To think that not one of these people is capable of understanding even the cut of a coat!"

Then they talked about provincial mediocrity, of the lives it stifles, the lost illusions.

"No wonder," said Rodolphe, "that I am more and more sinking in gloom."

"You!" she said in astonishment; "I thought you very lighthearted."

"Oh, yes, it seems that way because I know how to wear a mask of mockery in society, and yet, how many a time at the sight of a cemetery by moonlight have I not asked myself whether it were not better to join those sleeping there!"

"Oh! and your friends?" she said. "How can you forget them."

"My friends! What friends? Have I any? Who cares about me?" And he followed up the last words with a kind of hissing whistle.

They were obliged to separate because of a great pile of chairs that a man was carrying behind them. He was so overladen that one could only see the tips of his wooden shoes and the ends of his two outstretched arms. It was Lestiboudois, the gravedigger, who was carrying the church chairs about amongst the people. Alive to all that concerned his interests, he had hit upon this means of turning the agricultural show to his advantage, and his idea was succeeding, for he no longer knew which way to turn. In fact, the villagers, who were tired and hot, quarrelled for these seats, whose straw smelt of incense, and they leant against the thick backs, stained with the wax of candles, within a certain veneration.

Madame Bovary again took Rodolphe's arm; he went on as if speaking to himself:

"Yes, I have missed so many things. Always alone! Ah! if I had some aim in life, if I had met some love, if I had found some one! Oh, how I would have spent all the energy of which I am capable, surmounted everything, overcome everything!"

"Yet it seems to me," said Emma, "that you are not to be pitied."

"Ah! you think so?" said Rodolphe.

"For after all," she went on, "you are free . . ."

She hesitated.

"Rich . . ."

"Don't mock me," he replied.

And she protested that she was not mocking him, when the sound of a cannon was heard; immediately all began crowding one another towards the village.

It was a false alarm. The prefect[60] seemed not to be coming, and the members of the jury felt much embarrassed, not knowing if they ought to begin the meeting or wait longer.

At last, at the end of the Place a large hired landau[61] appeared, drawn by two thin horses, generously whipped by a coachman in a white hat. Binet[62] had only just time to shout, "Present arms!" and the colonel to imitate him. There was a rush towards the guns; every one pushed forward. A few even forgot their collars.

But the prefectural coach seemed to sense the trouble, for the two yoked nags, dawdling in their harness, came at a slow trot in front of the townhall at the very moment when the National Guard and firemen deployed, beating time with their boots.

"Present arms!" shouted Binet.

"Halt!" shouted the colonel. "By the left flank, march!"

And after presenting arms, during which the clang of the band, letting loose, rang out like a brass kettle rolling downstairs, all the guns were lowered.

Then was seen stepping down from the carriage a gentleman in a short coat with silver braiding, with bald brow, and wearing a tuft of hair at the back of his head, of a sallow complexion and the most benign of aspects. His eyes, very large and covered by heavy lids, were half-closed to look at the crowd, while at the same time he raised his sharp nose, and forced a smile upon his sunken mouth. He recognised the mayor by his scarf, and explained to him that the prefect was not able to come. He[63] himself was a councillor at the prefecture; then he added a few apologies. Monsieur Tuvache reciprocated with polite compliments, humbly acknowledged by the other; and they remained thus, face to face, their foreheads almost touching, surrounded by members of the jury, the municipal council, the notable personages, the National Guard and the crowd. The councillor pressing his little cocked hat to his breast repeated his greetings, while Tuvache, bent like a bow, also smiled, stammered, tried to say something, protested his devotion to the monarchy and the honor that was being done to Yonville.

[58] **batiste** French; a fine linen or cotton cloth.
[59] **nankeen** From Nanking (modern Nanjing, China). A hard-wearing, brownish-yellow cotton fabric, first loomed by hand in China.
[60] **prefect** From Latin, *praefectus*. French governmental official, chief administrative officer of the prefecture, which included the village of Yonville.
[61] **landau** From German. A four-wheeled carriage with an enclosed compartment for passengers and a raised seat outside for the driver; the front cover is removable, and the back cover may be raised or lowered.
[62] **Binet** The village tax-collector and captain of the volunteer fire brigade.
[63] **He** Monsieur Lieuvain, the prefectural councilor.

Hippolyte, the groom from the inn, took the head of the horses from the coachman, and limping along with his clubfoot, led them to the door of the "Lion d'Or" where a number of peasants collected to look at the carriage. The drum beat, the howitzer thundered, and the gentlemen one by one mounted the platform, where they sat down in red utrecht velvet arm-chairs that had been lent by Madame Tuvache.

All these people looked alike. Their fair flabby faces, somewhat tanned by the sun, were the color of sweet cider, and their puffy whiskers emerged from stiff collars, kept up by white cravats with broad bows. All the waistcoats were of velvet, double-breasted; all the watches had, at the end of a long ribbon, an oval seal; all rested their two hands on their thighs, carefully stretching the stride of their trousers, whose unspunged glossy cloth shone more brilliantly than the leather of their heavy boots.

The ladies of the company stood at the back under the porch between the pillars, while the common herd was opposite, standing up or sitting on chairs. Lestiboudois had brought there all the chairs that he had moved from the field, and he even kept running back every minute to fetch others from the church. He caused such confusion with this piece of business that one had great difficulty in getting to the small steps of the platform.

"I think," said Monsieur Lheureux to the pharmacist who was heading for his seat, "that they ought to have put up two Venetian masts with something rather severe and rich for ornaments; it would have been a very pretty sight."

"Certainly," replied Homais; "but what can you expect? The mayor took everything on his own shoulders. He hasn't much taste. Poor Tuvache! he is completely devoid of what is called the genius of art." 60

Meanwhile, Rodolphe and Madame Bovary had ascended to the first floor of the townhall, to the "councilroom," and, as it was empty, he suggested that they could enjoy the sight there more comfortably. He fetched three chairs from the round table under the bust of the monarch, and having carried them to one of the windows, they sat down together.

There was commotion on the platform, long whisperings, much parleying. At last the councillor got up. It was known by now that his name was Lieuvain, and in the crowd the name was now passing from lip to lip. After he had reshuffled a few pages, and bent over them to see better, he began:

"Gentlemen! May I be permitted first of all (before addressing you on the object of our meeting to-day, and this sentiment will, I am sure, be shared by you all), may I be permitted, I say, to pay a tribute to the higher administration, to the government, to the monarch, gentlemen, our sovereign, to that beloved king, to whom no branch of public or private prosperity is a matter of indifference, and who directs with a hand at once so firm and wise the chariot of the state amid the incessant perils of a stormy sea,[64]

knowing, moreover, how to make peace respected as well as war, industry, commerce, agriculture, and the fine arts."

"I ought," said Rodolphe, "to get back a little further."

"Why?" said Emma. 65

But at this moment the voice of the councillor rose to an extraordinary pitch. He declaimed—

"This is no longer the time, gentlemen, when civil discord made blood flow in our market squares, when the landowner, the businessman, the working-man himself, lying down to peaceful sleep, trembled lest he should be awakened suddenly by the noise of alarming tocsins,[65] when the most subversive doctrines audaciously sapped foundations . . ."

"Well, some one down there might see me," Rodolphe resumed, "then I should have to invent excuses for a fortnight; and with my bad reputation . . ."

"Oh, you are slandering yourself," said Emma.

"No! It is dreadful, I assure you." 70

"But, gentlemen," continued the councillor, "if, banishing from my memory the remembrance of these sad pictures, I carry my eyes back to the present situation of our dear country, what do I see there? Everywhere commerce and the arts are flourishing; everywhere new means of communication, like so many new arteries in the body politic, establish within it new relations. Our great industrial centers have recovered all their activity; religion, more consolidated, smiles in all hearts; our ports are full, confidence is born again, and France breathes once more! . . . ."

"Besides," added Rodolphe, "perhaps from the world's point of view they are right."

"How so?" she asked.

"What!" said he. "Don't you know that there are souls constantly tormented? They need by turns to dream and to act, the purest passions and the most turbulent joys, and thus they fling themselves into all sorts of fantasies, of follies."

Then she looked at him as one looks at a traveler who 75 has voyaged over strange lands, and went on:

"We have not even this distraction, we poor women!"

"A sad distraction, for happiness isn't found in it."

"But is it ever found?" she asked.

"Yes; one day it comes," he answered.

"And this is what you have understood," said the 80 councillor. "You, farmers, agricultural laborers! you pacific pioneers of a work that belongs wholly to civilisation! you, men of progress and morality, you have understood, I say, that political storms are even more redoubtable than atmospheric disturbances!"

"A day comes," repeated Rodolphe, "one is near despair. Then the horizon expands; it is as if a voice cried, 'It is here!' You feel the need of confiding the whole of your life, of giving everything, sacrificing everything to

---

[64] **monarch . . . directs with a hand . . . stormy sea** Ironic allusion to King Louis Philippe (r. 1830–1848), whose reign was marked by political corruption, judicial misbehavior, and restricted voting rights. The novel covers the period 1827–1846.

[65] **tocsins** Alarm bells.

this person. There is no need for explanations; one understands each other, having met before in dreams!" (And he looked at her.) "At last, here it is, this treasure so sought after, here before you. It glitters, it flashes; yet one still doubts, one does not believe it; one remains dazzled, as if one went out from darkness into light."

And as he ended, Rodolphe suited the action to the word. He passed his hand over his face, like a man about to faint. Then he let it fall on Emma's. She drew hers back. But the councillor was still reading.

"And who would be surprised at it, gentlemen? He only who was so blind, so imprisoned (I do not fear to say it), so imprisoned by the prejudices of another age as still to misunderstand the spirit of our rural populations. Where, indeed, is more patriotism to be found than in the country, greater devotion to the public welfare, in a word, more intelligence? And, gentlemen, I do not mean that superficial intelligence, vain ornament of idle minds, but rather that profound and balanced intelligence that applies itself above all else to useful objects, thus contributing to the good of all, to the common amelioration and to the support of the state, born of respect for law and the practice of duty . . ."

"Ah! again!" said Rodolphe. "Always 'duty.' I am sick of the word. They are a lot of old jackasses in woolen vests and old bigots with foot-warmers and rosaries who constantly drone into our ears 'Duty, duty!' Ah! by Jove! as if one's real duty were not to feel what is great, cherish the beautiful, and not accept all the conventions of society with the hypocrisy it forces upon us."

"Yet . . . yet . . ." objected Madame Bovary.

"No, no! Why cry out against the passions? Are they not the one beautiful thing on earth, the source of heroism, of enthusiasm, of poetry, music, the arts, in a word, of everything?"

"But one must," said Emma, "to some extent bow to the opinion of the world and accept its morality."

"Ah, but there are two moralities," he replied, "the petty one, the morality of small men that constantly keeps changing, but yells itself hoarse; crude and loud like the crowd of imbeciles that you see down there. But the other, the eternal, that is about us and above, like the landscape that surrounds us, and the blue heavens that give us light."

Monsieur Lieuvain had just wiped his mouth with a pocket-handkerchief. He continued:

"It would be presumptuous of me, gentlemen, to point out to you the uses of agriculture. Who supplies our wants, who provides our means of subsistence, if not the farmer? It is the farmer, gentlemen, who sows with laborious hand the fertile furrows of the country, brings forth the wheat, which, being ground, is made into a powder by means of ingenious machinery, issues from there under the name of flour, and is then transported to our cities, soon delivered to the baker, who makes it into food for poor and rich alike. Again, is it not the farmer who fattens his flocks in the pastures in order to provide us with warm clothing? For how should we clothe or nourish ourselves

without his labor? And, gentlemen, is it even necessary to go so far for examples? Who has not frequently reflected on all the momentous things that we get out of that modest animal, the ornament of poultry-yards, that provides us at once with a soft pillow for our bed, with succulent flesh for our tables, and eggs? But I should never end if I were to enumerate one after the other all the different products which the earth, well cultivated, like a generous mother, lavishes upon her children. Here it is the vine; elsewhere apple trees for cider; there colza;[66] further, cheeses; and flax; gentlemen, let us not forget flax, which has made such great strides forward these last years and to which I call your special attention!"

He had no need to call it, for all the mouths of the multitude were wide open, as if to drink in his words. Tuvache by his side listened to him with staring eyes. Monsieur Derozerays from time to time softly closed his eyelids, and farther on the pharmacist, with his son Napoleon between his knees, put his hand behind his ear in order not to lose a syllable. The chins of the other members of the jury nodded slowly up and down in their waistcoats in sign of approval. The firemen at the foot of the platform rested on their bayonets; and Binet, motionless, stood with out-turned elbows, the point of his sabre in the air. Perhaps he could hear, but he certainly couldn't see a thing, for the visor of his helmet fell down on his nose. His lieutenant, the youngest son of Monsieur Tuvache, had an even bigger one; it was so large that he could hardly keep it on, in spite of the cotton scarf that peeped out from underneath. He wore a smile of childlike innocence, and his thin pale face, dripping with sweat, expressed satisfaction, some exhaustion and sleepiness.

The square was crowded up to the houses. People were leaning on their elbows at all the windows, others were standing on their doorsteps, and Justin, in front of the pharmacy, seemed fascinated by the spectacle. In spite of the silence Monsieur Lieuvain's voice was lost in the air. It reached you in fragments of phrases, interrupted here and there by the creaking of chairs in the crowd; then the long bellowing of an ox would suddenly burst forth from behind, or else the bleating of the lambs, who answered one another from street to street. Even the cowherds and shepherds had driven their beasts this far, and one could hear their lowing from time to time, while with their tongues they tore down some scrap of foliage that hung over their muzzles.

Rodolphe had drawn nearer to Emma, and was whispering hurriedly in her ear:

"Doesn't this conspiracy of society revolt you? Is there a single sentiment it does not condemn? The noblest instincts, the purest feelings are persecuted, slandered; and if at length two poor souls do meet, all is organized in such a way as to keep them from becoming one. Yet they will try, they will call to each other. Not in vain, for sooner or later, be it in six or ten years, they will come together in love; for fate has decreed it, and they are born for each other."

---

[66] **colza** A forage plant used as food for livestock; its seeds are a source of oil.

His arms were folded across his knees, and thus 95
lifting his face at her from close by, he looked fixedly at
her. She noticed in his eyes small golden lines radiating
from the black pupils; she even smelt the perfume of the
pomade that made his hair glossy. Then something gave
way in her; she recalled the Viscount[67] who had waltzed
with her at Vaubyessard, and whose beard exhaled a similar scent of vanilla and lemon, and mechanically she half-
closed her eyes the better to breathe it in. But in making
this movement, as she leant back in her chair, she saw in
the distance, right on the line of the horizon, the old diligence[68] the "Hirondelle," that was slowly descending the
hill of Leux, dragging after it a long trail of dust. It was
in this yellow carriage that Léon had so often come back
to her, and by this route down there that he had gone for
ever. She fancied she saw him opposite at his window;
then all grew confused; clouds gathered; it seemed to her
that she was again turning in the waltz under the light
of the lustres on the arm of the Viscount, and that Léon
was not far away, that he was coming . . . and yet all the
time she was conscious of Rodolphe's head by her side.
The sweetness of this sensation revived her past desires,
and like grains of sand under a gust of wind, they swirled
around in the subtle breath of the perfume that diffused
over her soul. She breathed deeply several times to drink
in the freshness of the ivy round the columns. She took off
her gloves and wiped her hands; then she fanned her face
with her handkerchief while she kept hearing, through
the throbbing of her temples, the murmur of the crowd
and the voice of the councillor intoning his phrases.

He was saying:

*"Persevere! listen neither to the suggestions of routine,
nor to the over-hasty councils of a rash empiricism.* Apply
yourselves, above all, to the amelioration of the soil, to
good manures, to the development of the breeds, whether
equine, bovine, ovine, or porcine. May these shows be to
you pacific arenas, where the victor in leaving will hold
forth a hand to the vanquished, and will fraternise with
him in the hope of even greater success. And you, aged
servants! humble helpers, whose hard labor no Government up to this day has taken into consideration, receive
the reward of your silent virtues, and be assured that the
state henceforward has its eye upon you; that it encourages you, protects you; that it will accede to your just
demands, and alleviate as much as possible the heavy
burden of your painful sacrifices."

Monsieur Lieuvain sat down; Monsieur Derozerays
got up, beginning another speech. His was not perhaps so
florid as that of the councillor, but it stood out by a more
direct style, that is to say, by more specific knowledge and
more elevated considerations. Thus the praise of the Government took up less space; religion and agriculture more.
He showed the relation between both, and how they had

always contributed to civilisation. Rodolphe was talking
dreams, forebodings, magnetism[69] with Madame Bovary.
Going back to the cradle of society, the orator painted
those fierce times when men lived on acorns in the heart
of woods. Then they had left off the skins of beasts, had
put on cloth, tilled the soil, planted the vine. Was this a
good, or wasn't there more harm than good in this discovery? That was the problem to which Monsieur Derozerays
addressed himself. From magnetism little by little Rodolphe had come to affinities, and while the president was
citing Cincinnatus and his plough,[70] Diocletian planting
his cabbages,[71] and the emperors of China inaugurating
the year by the sowing of seed,[72] the young man was explaining to the young woman that these irresistible attractions find their cause in some previous state of existence.

"Take us, for instance," he said, "how did we happen
to meet? What chance willed it? It was because across infinite distances, like two streams uniting, our particular
inclinations pushed us toward one another."

And he seized her hand; she did not withdraw it. 100

"First prize for general farming!" announced the
president.

"—Just now, for example, when I went to your
home . . ."

"To Mr. Bizat of Quincampoix."

"—Did I know I would accompany you?"

"Seventy francs!" 105

"—A hundred times I tried to leave; yet I followed
you and stayed . . ."

"For manures!"

"—As I would stay to-night, to-morrow, all other
days, all my life!"

"To Monsieur Caron of Argueil, a gold medal!"

"—For I have never enjoyed anyone's company so 110
much."

"To Monsieur Bain of Givry-Saint-Martin."

"—And I will never forget you."

---

[67] **Viscount** The son or younger brother of a count. An allusion
to an unnamed aristocrat, about whom Emma Bovary developed a romantic fantasy after the two danced together at a ball
at Vaubyessard.
[68] **diligence** A stagecoach.

[69] **magnetism** Animal magnetism, a theory developed by the
Austrian physician Franz Anton Mesmer (1734–1815), claimed
that the movement of the planets affected human health by
influencing an invisible fluid in the human body and throughout nature. Branded pseudoscience by the medical profession,
Mesmer's experiments with trancelike states opened the way for
the modern practice of hypnosis.
[70] **Cincinnatus and his plough** Lucius Quinctius Cincinnatus
(ca. 519–438 BCE), a hero of the early Roman Republic. His life
was romanticized by the historian Livy: Cincinnatus, a farmer,
was "called from the plow" to fight for the republic and, after
victory over Rome's enemies was secured, returned to his
plowing.
[71] **Diocletian planting his cabbages** The speaker, M. Derozerays, is confused. Diocletian (r. 284–305) was a Roman emperor.
Derozerays should have said Diogenes (ca. 325 BCE), the Greek
philosopher who founded the Cynic (from Greek, *kyon*, "dog")
school. Diogenes claimed that natural needs (in the manner of
a dog) were all one needed for human happiness. Accordingly,
Diogenes lived in a tub and ate only cabbages.
[72] **emperors . . . sowing of seed** A tradition dating from the
third millennium BCE, in which a rice ritual was held annually at sowing time, with the ruler casting the first seeds. This
tradition evolved into a day dedicated to the enjoyment of rice,
as part of the extended New Year's festivities.

"For a merino ram . . ."

"—Whereas you will forget me; I'll pass through your life as a mere shadow . . ."

"To Monsieur Belot of Notre-Dame."   115

"—But no, tell me there can be a place for me in your thoughts, in your life, can't there?"

"Hog! first prize equally divided between Mssrs. Lehérissé and Cullembourg, sixty francs!"

Rodolphe was holding her hand on his; it was warm and quivering like a captive dove that wants to fly away; perhaps she was trying to take it away or perhaps she was answering his pressure, at any rate, she moved her fingers; he exclaimed

"Oh, thank you! You do not repulse me! You are kind! You understand that I am yours! Let me see you, let me look at you!"

A gust of wind that blew in at the window ruffled the   120
cloth on the table, and in the square below all the large bonnets rose up like the fluttering wings of white butterflies.

"Use of oil-cakes!" continued the president.

He was hurrying now: "Flemish manure, flax-growing, drainage, long term leases . . . domestic service."

Rodolphe was no longer speaking. They looked at each other. As their desire increased, their dry lips trembled and languidly, effortlessly, their fingers intertwined. . . .

Questions for Critical Thinking

1. Summarize Flaubert's social criticism of provincial life, based on this selection.

2. Discuss the realist literary style as revealed in this selection from *Madame Bovary*.

CHARLES DICKENS
Selection from *Hard Times*

Charles Dickens's (1812–1870) prolific and frenetic career made him the most popular and most successful author of the Victorian Age, perhaps second only to Shakespeare in popularity in the whole of English letters. Discovering his literary gift, Dickens rose from poverty (his father and family were in debtors' prison at one time). He became, first, a court transcriber; next, a reporter in Parliament; and then a recorder of the human comedy, with his *Sketches by Boz* serialized in popular magazines. His reputation grew with the *Pickwick Papers,* which he followed with a stream of novels and a lecture tour of America, where he was lionized as the greatest author of the age. In the 1850s he founded his own magazine and embraced many social causes that became themes in his writings. By the mid-1860s, having written fourteen novels, published a magazine, and acted in amateur plays, his strenuous life began to undermine his health. When he died in 1870, he received national honors and was buried in Westminster Abbey.

Dickens was England's leading exponent of realism, which had risen in part as a reaction against both classicism and romanticism. Rejecting the elegant writing ideal of classicism and the sentimentality of romanticism, the realists believed literature should serve a purpose and not be judged alone on its aesthetic merits. They were concerned with the world around them, not only with daily events but also with political and social issues, and they believed life should be portrayed as it was, neither idealized nor romanticized. Realism came to be defined as a bold and honest treatment of the human condition with specific details.

Reading the Selection

In *Hard Times* (1851–1854), Dickens addressed three current topics: class struggle, education, and utilitarianism (the doctrine set forth in the social theory of Jeremy Bentham that the goal of society is "the greatest good for the greatest number"). Through the characters representing management (Gradgrind) and labor (Sissy's father) in Coketown (probably based on the factory town of Preston), Dickens publicized the class struggle that was being called in the 1840s the "Condition of England question." In Chapter V, "The Key-note," the central idea is caught in the vivid picture of Coketown, its ugly buildings, polluted river, and ill-dressed inhabitants; the middle class's contempt for workers is seen in Gradgrind and Bounderby's hasty opinions. Gradgrind and Bounderby's prejudices flare up in the exchange with the working-class youths, Bitzer and Sissy, who are judged disrespectful; Sissy's father, the object of Gradgrind and Bounderby's excursion into this rundown section of Coketown, is assumed to be a lazy drunk.

Prior to Chapter V, Dickens satirized the utilitarian approach to schooling with its unrelenting emphasis on "facts, facts, facts." In this selection, the reference to M'Choakumchild's school further registers his contempt for the period's style of education, with its use of corporal punishment as a necessary aid to learning.

Chapter V: The Key-note

Coketown, to which Messrs Bounderby and Gradgrind now walked, was a triumph of fact; it had no greater taint of fancy in it than Mrs Gradgrind herself. Let us strike the key-note, Coketown, before pursuing our tune.

It was a town of red brick, or of brick that would have been red if the smoke and ashes had allowed it; but, as matters stood it was a town of unnatural red and black like the painted face of a savage. It was a town of machinery and tall chimneys, out of which interminable serpents of smoke trailed themselves for ever and ever, and never got uncoiled. It had a black canal in it, and a river that ran purple with ill-smelling dye, and vast piles of building full of windows where there was a rattling and a trembling all day long, and where the piston of the steam-engine worked monotonously up and down, like the head of an elephant in a state of melancholy madness. It contained several large streets all very like one another, and many small streets still more like one another, inhabited by people equally like one another, who all went in and out at the same hours, with the same sound upon the same pavements, to do the same work, and to whom every day was the same as yesterday and tomorrow, and every year the counterpart of the last and the next.

These attributes of Coketown were in the main inseparable from the work by which it was sustained; against them were to be set off, comforts of life which found their way all over the world, and elegancies of life which made, we will not ask how much of the fine lady, who could scarcely bear to hear the place mentioned. The rest of its features were voluntary, and they were these.

You saw nothing in Coketown but what was severely workful. If the members of a religious persuasion built a chapel there—as the members of eighteen religious persuasions had done—they made it a pious warehouse of red brick, with sometimes (but this only in highly ornamented examples) a bell in a bird-cage on the top of it. The solitary exception was the New Church; a stuccoed edifice with a square steeple over the door, terminating in four short pinnacles like florid wooden legs. All the public inscriptions in the town were painted alike, in severe characters of black and white. The jail might have been the infirmary, the infirmary might have been the jail, the townhall might have been either, or both, or anything else, for anything that appeared to the contrary in the graces of their construction. Fact, fact, fact, everywhere in the material aspect of the town; fact, fact, fact, everywhere in the immaterial. The M'Choakumchild school was all fact, and the school of design was all fact, and the relations between master and man were all fact, and everything was fact between the lying-in hospital and the cemetery, and what you couldn't state in figures, or show to be purchaseable in the cheapest market and saleable in the dearest,[73] was not, and never should be, world without end, Amen.

A town so sacred to fact, and so triumphant in its assertion, of course got on well? Why no, not quite well. No? Dear me!

No. Coketown did not come out of its own furnaces, in all respects like gold that had stood the fire. First, the perplexing mystery of the place was, Who belonged to the eighteen denominations? Because, whoever did, the labouring people did not. It was very strange to walk through the streets on a Sunday morning, and note how few of *them* the barbarous jangling of bells that was

---

[73] **purchaseable . . . dearest** The foundation of classical economics and a perspective adopted by nineteenth-century British industrialists, a target of Dickens's satire.

driving the sick and nervous mad, called away from their own quarter, from their own close rooms, from the corners of their own streets, where they lounged listlessly, gazing at all the church and chapel going, as at a thing with which they had no manner of concern. Nor was it merely the stranger who noticed this, because there was a native organization in Coketown itself, whose members were to be heard of in the House of Commons every session, indignantly petitioning for acts of parliament that should make these people religious by main force. Then, came the Teetotal Society, who complained that these same people *would* get drunk, and showed in tabular statements that they did get drunk, and proved at tea parties that no inducement, human or Divine (except a medal), would induce them to forego their custom of getting drunk. Then, came the chemist and druggist, with other tabular statements, showing that when they didn't get drunk, they took opium. Then, came the experienced chaplain of the jail, with more tabular statements, outdoing all the previous tabular statements, and showing that the same people *would* resort to low haunts, hidden from the public eye, where they heard low singing and saw low dancing, and mayhap joined in it; and where A. B., aged twenty-four next birthday, and committed for eighteen months' solitary, had himself said (not that he had ever shown himself particularly worthy of belief) his ruin began, as he was perfectly sure and confident that otherwise he would have been a tip-top moral specimen. Then, came Mr Gradgrind and Mr Bounderby, the two gentlemen at this present moment walking through Coketown, and both eminently practical, who could, on occasion, furnish more tabular statements derived from their own personal experience, and illustrated by cases they had known and seen, from which it clearly appeared—in short it was the only clear thing in the case—that these same people were a bad lot altogether, gentlemen; that do what you would for them they were never thankful for it, gentlemen; that they were restless, gentlemen; that they never knew what they wanted; that they lived upon the best, and bought fresh butter, and insisted on Mocha coffee, and rejected all but prime parts of meat, and yet were eternally dissatisfied and unmanageable. In short it was the moral of the old nursery fable:

> *There was an old woman, and what do you think?*
> *She lived upon nothing but victuals and drink;*
> *Victuals and drink were the whole of her diet,*
> *And yet this old woman would* NEVER *be quiet.*

Is it possible, I wonder, that there was any analogy between the case of the Coketown population and the case of the little Gradgrinds? Surely, none of us in our sober senses and acquainted with figures, are to be told at this time of day, that one of the foremost elements in the existence of the Coketown working people had been for scores of years, deliberately set at nought? That there was any Fancy in them demanding to be brought into healthy existence instead of struggling on in convulsions? That exactly in the ratio as they worked long and monotonously, the craving grew within them for some physical

relief—some relaxation, encouraging good humour and good spirits, and giving them a vent—some recognized holiday, though it were but for an honest dance to a stirring band of music—some occasional light pie in which even M'Choakumchild had no finger—which craving must and would be satisfied aright, or must and would inevitably go wrong, until the laws of the Creation were repealed?

"This man lives at Pod's End, and I don't quite know Pod's End," said Mr Gradgrind. "Which is it, Bounderby?"

Mr Bounderby knew it was somewhere down town, but knew no more respecting it. So they stopped for a moment, looking about.

Almost as they did so, there came running round the [10] corner of the street at a quick pace and with a frightened look, a girl whom Mr Gradgrind recognized. "Halloa!" said he. "Stop! Where are you going? Stop!" Girl number twenty stopped then, palpitating, and made him a curtsey.

"Why are you tearing about the streets," said Mr Gradgrind, "in this improper manner?"

"I was—I was run after, sir," the girl panted, "and I wanted to get away."

"Run after?" repeated Mr Gradgrind. "Who would run after *you?*"

The question was unexpectedly and suddenly answered for her, by the colourless boy, Bitzer, who came round the corner with such blind speed and so little anticipating a stoppage on the pavement, that he brought himself up against Mr Gradgrind's waistcoat, and rebounded into the road.

"What do you mean, boy?" said Mr Gradgrind. "What [15] are you doing? How dare you dash against—everybody—in this manner?"

Bitzer picked up his cap, which the concussion had knocked off; and backing, and knuckling his forehead, pleaded that it was an accident.

"Was this boy running after you, Jupe?" asked Mr Gradgrind.

"Yes, sir," said the girl reluctantly.

"No, I wasn't, sir!" cried Bitzer. "Not till she run away from me. But the horse-riders never mind what they say, sir; they're famous for it. You know the horse-riders are famous for never minding what they say," addressing Sissy. "It's as well known in the town as—please, sir, as the multiplication table isn't known to the horse-riders." Bitzer tried Mr Bounderby with this.

"He frightened me so," said the girl, "with his cruel [20] faces!"

"Oh!" cried Bitzer. "Oh! An't you one of the rest! An't you a horse-rider! I never looked at her, sir. I asked her if she would know how to define a horse tomorrow, and offered to tell her again, and she ran away, and I ran after her, sir, that she might know how to answer when she was asked. You wouldn't have thought of saying such mischief if you hadn't been a horse-rider!"

"Her calling seems to be pretty well known among 'em," observed Mr Bounderby. "You'd have had the whole school peeping in a row, in a week."

"Truly, I think so," returned his friend. "Bitzer, turn you about and take yourself home. Jupe, stay here a moment. Let me hear of your running in this manner any more, boy, and you will hear of me through the master of the school. You understand what I mean. Go along."

The boy stopped in his rapid blinking, knuckled his forehead again, glanced at Sissy, turned about, and retreated.

"Now, girl," said Mr Gradgrind, "take this gentleman ²⁵ and me to your father's; we are going there. What have you got in that bottle you are carrying?"

"Gin," said Mr Bounderby.

"Dear, no sir! It's the nine oils."

"The what?" cried Mr Bounderby.

"The nine oils, sir. To rub father with." Then, said Mr Bounderby, with a loud, short laugh, "What the devil do you rub your father with nine oils for?"

"It's what our people always use, sir, when they get ³⁰ any hurts in the ring," replied the girl, looking over her shoulder, to assure herself that her pursuer was gone. "They bruise themselves very bad sometimes."

"Serve 'em right," said Mr Bounderby, "for being idle." She glanced up at his face, with mingled astonishment and dread.

"By George!" said Mr Bounderby, "when I was four or five years younger than you, I had worse bruises upon me than ten oils, twenty oils, forty oils, would have rubbed off. I didn't get 'em by posture-making, but by being banged about. There was no rope-dancing for me; I danced on the bare ground and was larruped with the rope."

Mr Gradgrind, though hard enough, was by no means so rough a man as Mr Bounderby. His character was not unkind, all things considered; it might have been a very kind one indeed, if he had only made some round mistake in the arithmetic that balanced it, years ago. He said, in what he meant for a reassuring tone, as they turned down a narrow road, "And this is Pod's End; is it, Jupe?"

"This is it, sir, and—if you wouldn't mind, sir—this is the house."

She stopped, at twilight, at the door of a mean little ³⁵ public house,⁷⁴ with dim red lights in it. As haggard and as shabby, as if, for want of custom, it had itself taken to drinking, and had gone the way all drunkards go, and was very near the end of it.

"It's only crossing the bar, sir, and up the stairs, if you wouldn't mind, and waiting there for a moment till I get a candle. If you should hear a dog, sir, it's only Merrylegs, and he only barks."

"Merrylegs and nine oils, eh!" said Mr Bounderby, entering last with his metallic laugh. "Pretty well this, for a self-made man!"

---

⁷⁴ **public house** British, tavern.

Questions for Critical Thinking

1. Describe Coketown, a nineteenth-century factory town, as seen through Dickens's eyes.

2. Show how this selection from *Hard Times* represents the realist literary style. Does this style still persist in today's cultural landscape? Explain.

FREDERICK DOUGLASS

Selections from *Narrative of the Life of Frederick Douglass, an American Slave*

Frederick Douglass's autobiography reflects the maturity of the trend toward globalization of the world's culture, which began about 1500. From then on, Europe exported peoples, technology, religions, and ideas to colonies in Asia, Africa, and the Americas; in return, Europe received slaves and servants, foodstuffs, raw materials, religions, and ideas. Central to this process in the New World was the uprooting and transportation of Africans to work as slaves. The faint contours of a global literary culture were first visible in the 1600s, when European writers began to draw on colonial life. Spanish and English America now gave birth to colonial literatures, though at first heavily indebted to Europe. Hence the appearance in 1845 of *Narrative of the*

Life of Frederick Douglass, an American Slave was a literary milestone. It introduced a unique literary genre, the slave narrative, thus loosening America's dependency on European models. Also, it was one of the first great books in the West since the fall of Rome to be written by a person of color; thus, it pointed toward a unified world literature freed from the racial segregation that had so far characterized the varied literatures of the world since the Middle Ages. Douglass's later life also furthered globalization, as he was America's first ambassador (1889–1895) to Haiti, the Western Hemisphere's first black-ruled state.

Douglass's slave narrative is the most famous and the most superbly crafted of the thousands of representative examples of the slave experiences of African Americans that were published between the founding of the United States of America and the outbreak of its Civil War. These works, many of which sold by the thousands and some of which were translated into Dutch, German, and Celtic, made converts for abolitionism, the antislavery movement that began in the late eighteenth century. Abolitionism was concentrated in New England and helped prepare the moral ground for the Civil War. By focusing on the psychic wounds of slavery, the writers of slave narrative forced readers, then and now, to recognize that attempts to forge an American national identity would have to come to grips with the country's slave past.

Reading the Selections

Frederick Douglass (ca. 1818–1895) was born on a Maryland plantation, the son of a slave woman and a white man, perhaps his master. Caught in his first bid for freedom, he finally slipped slavery's chains in 1838 when he rode the train (the "upperground" railroad [his term]) from Baltimore to New York. He married Anna Murray, a Baltimore freewoman who had helped him escape, and they moved to Massachusetts, living as respected members of the black community. Becoming an advocate of abolitionism, he wrote his life story in 1845, partly to satisfy a creative need and partly to silence critics who thought him too eloquent to have ever been a slave.

The selections from Frederick Douglass's slave narrative include two parts: Chapters 1 and 7. In Chapter 1, Douglass sets forth the circumstances of his birth into slavery on a Maryland plantation, to a black woman, Harriet Bailey, who was a field slave. In contrast to house slaves, who were comparatively better off, field slaves were treated as "a drove of human cattle" [the words of a British observer, James Stirling, in 1857]. Douglass's account corroborates the inhumane treatment of field slaves, but most important, it provides details about the casual cruelty of slave life in general, including the forcible separation of slave children from their mothers, the inability of slaves to sustain family life, the opportunity for white masters to become sexual predators on their slave property, and the use of corporal punishment to keep the slaves in their place.

Chapter 7 covers Douglass's youth in the Baltimore household of his then master, Hugh Auld. Douglass describes his efforts to learn to read and write and the sense of empowerment conveyed by being literate. It is a heroic story in which he moves from "mental darkness" to the light of knowledge, overcoming private and social obstacles erected by white society to keep slaves ignorant of their rights. Possessing literacy placed Douglass within the context of this period's reformers who made education the universal panacea—a legacy of the Age of Reason.

Chapter 1

I was born in Tuckahoe, near Hillsborough, and about twelve miles from Easton, in Talbot county, Maryland. I have no accurate knowledge of my age, never having seen any authentic record containing it. By far the larger part of the slaves know as little of their ages as horses know of theirs, and it is the wish of most masters within my knowledge to keep their slaves thus ignorant. I do not remember to have ever met a slave who could tell of his birthday. They seldom come nearer to it than planting-time, harvest-time, cherry-time, spring-time, or fall-time. A want of information concerning my own was a source of unhappiness to me even during childhood. The white children could tell their ages. I could not tell why I ought to be deprived of the same privilege. I was not allowed to make any inquiries of my master concerning it. He deemed all such inquiries on the part of a slave improper and impertinent, and evidence of a restless spirit. The nearest estimate I can give makes me now between twenty-seven and twenty-eight years of age. I come to this, from hearing my master say, some time during 1835, I was about seventeen years old.

My mother was named Harriet Bailey. She was the daughter of Isaac and Betsey Bailey, both colored, and quite dark. My mother was of a darker complexion than either my grandmother or grandfather.

My father was a white man. He was admitted to be such by all I ever heard speak of my parentage. The opinion was also whispered that my master was my father; but of the correctness of this opinion, I know nothing; the means of knowing was withheld from me. My mother and I were separated when I was but an infant—before I knew her as my mother. It is a common custom, in the part of Maryland from which I ran away, to part children from their mothers at a very early age. Frequently, before the child has reached its twelfth month, its mother is taken from it, and hired out on some farm a considerable distance off, and the child is placed under the care of an old woman, too old for field labor. For what this separation is done, I do not know, unless it be to hinder the development of the child's affection toward its mother, and to blunt and destroy the natural affection of the mother for the child. This is the inevitable result.

I never saw my mother, to know her as such, more than four or five times in my life; and each of those times was very short in duration, and at night. She was hired by a Mr. Stewart, who lived about twelve miles from my home. She made her journeys to see me in the night, travelling the whole distance on foot, after the performance of her day's work. She was a field hand, and a whipping is the penalty of not being in the field at sunrise, unless a slave has special permission from his or her master to the contrary—a permission which they seldom get, and one that gives to him that gives it the proud name of being a kind master. I do not recollect of ever seeing my mother by the light of day. She was with me in the night. She would lie down with me, and get me to sleep, but long before I waked she was gone. Very little communication ever took place between us. Death soon ended what little we could have while she lived, and with it her hardships and suffering. She died when I was about seven years old, on one of my master's farms, near Lee's Mill. I was not allowed to be present during her illness, at her death, or burial. She was gone long before I knew any thing about it. Never having enjoyed, to any considerable extent, her soothing presence, her tender and watchful care, I received the tidings of her death with much the same emotions I should have probably felt at the death of a stranger.

Called thus suddenly away, she left me without the slightest intimation of who my father was. The whisper that my master was my father, may or may not be true; 5

and, true or false, it is of but little consequence to my purpose whilst the fact remains, in all its glaring odiousness, that slaveholders have ordained, and by law established, that the children of slave women shall in all cases follow the condition of their mothers; and this is done too obviously to administer to their own lusts, and make a gratification of their wicked desires profitable as well as pleasurable; for by this cunning arrangement, the slaveholder, in cases not a few, sustains to his slaves the double relation of master and father.

I know of such cases; and it is worthy of remark that such slaves invariably suffer greater hardships, and have more to contend with, than others. They are, in the first place, a constant offence to their mistress. She is ever disposed to find fault with them; they can seldom do any thing to please her; she is never better pleased than when she sees them under the lash, especially when she suspects her husband of showing to his mulatto children favors which he withholds from his black slaves. The master is frequently compelled to sell this class of his slaves, out of deference to the feelings of his white wife; and, cruel as the deed may strike any one to be, for a man to sell his own children to human flesh-mongers, it is often the dictate of humanity for him to do so; for, unless he does this, he must not only whip them himself, but must stand by and see one white son tie up his brother, of but few shades darker complexion than himself, and ply the gory lash to his naked back; and if he lisp one word of disapproval, it is set down to his parental partiality, and only makes a bad matter worse, both for himself and the slave whom he would protect and defend.

Every year brings with it multitudes of this class of slaves. It was doubtless in consequence of a knowledge of this fact, that one great statesman of the south predicted the downfall of slavery by the inevitable laws of population.[75] Whether this prophecy is ever fulfilled or not, it is nevertheless plain that a very different-looking class of people are springing up at the south, and are now held in slavery, from those originally brought to this country from Africa; and if their increase will do no other good, it will do away the force of the argument, that God cursed Ham,[76] and therefore American slavery is right. If the lineal

---

[75] **statesman . . . population** The statesman is unidentified; the rationale for the collapse of slavery being that as the numbers of slaves with white blood increased, white masters would eventually abandon slavery, rather than keep their own offspring in servitude.

[76] **Ham** The youngest son of Noah. Genesis 9:18–27 recounts a post-flood story of Noah and his sons, Shem, Japheth, and Ham. When a drunken Noah was lying naked in his tent, Ham reported this fact to his brothers, while they, averting their gaze, covered their father's nakedness. For Ham's lack of respect, Noah cursed Ham's son Canaan, saying Canaan would be "a slave of slaves . . . to his brothers." Scholars later interpreted the sons of Noah to be the progenitors of the races of the earth (Shem of Semitic people, Ham of Hamitic people, and Japheth of the rest), and the skin color of Ham and his descendants was supposedly black—the visible symbol of Noah's curse. The curse on Ham's descendants was also used to justify slavery and other racist practices in the nineteenth century.

descendants of Ham are alone to be scripturally enslaved, it is certain that slavery at the south must soon become unscriptural; for thousands are ushered into the world, annually, who, like myself, owe their existence to white fathers, and those fathers most frequently their own masters.

I have had two masters. My first master's name was Anthony. I do not remember his first name. He was generally called Captain Anthony—a title which, I presume, he acquired by sailing a craft on the Chesapeake Bay. He was not considered a rich slaveholder. He owned two or three farms, and about thirty slaves. His farms and slaves were under the care of an overseer. The overseer's name was Plummer. Mr. Plummer was a miserable drunkard, a profane swearer, and a savage monster. He always went armed with a cowskin and a heavy cudgel.[77] I have known him to cut and slash the women's heads so horribly, that even master would be enraged at his cruelty, and would threaten to whip him if he did not mind himself. Master, however, was not a humane slaveholder. It required extraordinary barbarity on the part of an overseer to affect him. He was a cruel man, hardened by a long life of slaveholding. He would at times seem to take great pleasure in whipping a slave. I have often been awakened at the dawn of day by the most heart-rending shrieks of an own aunt of mine, whom he used to tie up to a joist,[78] and whip upon her naked back till she was literally covered with blood. No words, no tears, no prayers, from his gory victim, seemed to move his iron heart from its bloody purpose. The louder she screamed, the harder he whipped; and where the blood ran fastest, there he whipped longest. He would whip her to make her scream, and whip her to make her hush; and not until overcome by fatigue, would he cease to swing the blood-clotted cowskin. I remember the first time I ever witnessed this horrible exhibition. I was quite a child, but I well remember it. I never shall forget it whilst I remember any thing. It was the first of a long series of such outrages, of which I was doomed to be a witness and a participant. It struck me with awful force. It was the blood-stained gate, the entrance to the hell of slavery, through which I was about to pass. It was a most terrible spectacle. I wish I could commit to paper the feelings with which I beheld it.

This occurrence took place very soon after I went to live with my old master, and under the following circumstances. Aunt Hester went out one night,—where or for what I do not know,—and happened to be absent when my master desired her presence. He had ordered her not to go out evenings, and warned her that she must never let him catch her in company with a young man, who was paying attention to her belonging to Colonel Lloyd. The young man's name was Ned Roberts, generally called Lloyd's Ned. Why master was so careful of her, may be safely left to conjecture. She was a woman of noble form, and of graceful proportions, having very few equals, and fewer superiors, in personal appearance, among the colored or white women of our neighborhood.

Aunt Hester had not only disobeyed his orders in going out, but had been found in company with Lloyd's Ned; which circumstance, I found, from what he said while whipping her, was the chief offence. Had he been a man of pure morals himself, he might have been thought interested in protecting the innocence of my aunt; but those who knew him will not suspect him of any such virtue. Before he commenced whipping Aunt Hester, he took her into the kitchen, and stripped her from neck to waist, leaving her neck, shoulders, and back, entirely naked. He then told her to cross her hands, calling her at the same time a d—d b—h.[79] After crossing her hands, he tied them with a strong rope, and led her to a stool under a large hook in the joist, put in for the purpose. He made her get upon the stool, and tied her hands to the hook. She now stood fair for his infernal purpose. Her arms were stretched up at their full length, so that she stood upon the ends of her toes. He then said to her, "Now, you d—d b—h, I'll learn you how to disobey my orders!" and after rolling up his sleeves, he commenced to lay on the heavy cowskin, and soon the warm, red blood (amid heart-rending shrieks from her, and horrid oaths from him) came dripping to the floor. I was so terrified and horror-stricken at the sight, that I hid myself in a closet, and dared not venture out till long after the bloody transaction was over. I expected it would be my turn next. It was all new to me. I had never seen any thing like it before. I had always lived with my grandmother on the outskirts of the plantation, where she was put to raise the children of the younger women. I had therefore been, until now, out of the way of the bloody scenes that often occurred on the plantation.

---

[77] **cudgel** A short heavy club.
[78] **joist** An overhead support beam, connecting two walls.

---

[79] **d—d b—h** "Damned bitch." The blanked-out letters are from the original book, reflecting the prevailing censorship of the nineteenth century.

∽

Chapter 7

I lived in Master Hugh's family about seven years. During this time, I succeeded in learning to read and write. In accomplishing this, I was compelled to resort to various stratagems. I had no regular teacher. My mistress, who had kindly commenced to instruct me, had, in compliance with the advice and direction of her husband, not only ceased to instruct, but had set her face against my being instructed by any one else. It is due, however, to my mistress to say of her, that she did not adopt this course of treatment immediately. She at first lacked the depravity indispensable to shutting me up in mental darkness. It was at least necessary for her to have some training in the exercise of irresponsible power, to make her equal to the task of treating me as though I were a brute.

My mistress was, as I have said, a kind and tender-hearted woman; and in the simplicity of her soul she commenced, when I first went to live with her, to treat me as she supposed one human being ought to treat another. In entering upon the duties of a slaveholder, she did not seem to perceive that I sustained to her the relation of a mere chattel, and that for her to treat me as a human being was not only wrong, but dangerously so. Slavery proved as injurious to her as it did to me. When I went there, she was a pious, warm, and tender-hearted woman. There was no sorrow or suffering for which she had not a tear. She had bread for the hungry, clothes for the naked, and comfort for every mourner that came within her reach. Slavery soon proved its ability to divest her of these heavenly qualities. Under its influence, the tender heart became stone, and the lamblike disposition gave way to one of tiger-like fierceness. The first step in her downward course was in her ceasing to instruct me. She now commenced to practise her husband's precepts. She finally became even more violent in her opposition than her husband himself. She was not satisfied with simply doing as well as he had commanded; she seemed anxious to do better. Nothing seemed to make her more angry than to see me with a newspaper. She seemed to think that here lay the danger. I have had her rush at me with a face made all up of fury, and snatch from me a newspaper, in a manner that fully revealed her apprehension. She was an apt woman; and a little experience soon demonstrated, to her satisfaction, that education and slavery were incompatible with each other.

From this time I was most narrowly watched. If I was in a separate room any considerable length of time, I was sure to be suspected of having a book, and was at once called to give an account of myself. All this, however, was too late. The first step had been taken. Mistress, in teaching me the alphabet, had given me the *inch*, and no precaution could prevent me from taking the *ell*.[80]

The plan which I adopted, and the one by which I was most successful, was that of making friends of all the little white boys whom I met in the street. As many of these as I could, I converted into teachers. With their kindly aid, obtained at different times and in different places, I finally succeeded in learning to read. When I was sent on errands, I always took my book with me, and by doing one part of my errand quickly, I found time to get a lesson before my return. I used also to carry bread with me, enough of which was always in the house, and to which I was always welcome; for I was much better off in this regard than many of the poor white children in our neighborhood. This bread I used to bestow upon the hungry little urchins, who, in return, would give me that more valuable bread of knowledge. I am strongly tempted to give the names of two or three of those little boys, as a testimonial of the gratitude and affection I bear them; but prudence forbids;—not that it would injure me, but it might embarrass them; for it is almost an unpardonable offence to teach slaves to read in this Christian country. It is enough to say of the dear little fellows, that they lived on Philpot Street, very near Durgin and Bailey's shipyard. I used to talk this matter of slavery over with them. I would sometimes say to them, I wished I could be as free as they would be when they got to be men. "You will be free as soon as you are twenty-one, *but I am a slave for life!* Have not I as good a right to be free as you have?" These words used to trouble them; they would express for me the liveliest sympathy, and console me with the hope that something would occur by which I might be free.

I was now about twelve years old, and the thought of being *a slave for life* began to bear heavily upon my heart. Just about this time, I got hold of a book entitled "The Columbian Orator."[81] Every opportunity I got, I used to read this book. Among much of other interesting matter, I found in it a dialogue between a master and his slave. The slave was represented as having run away from his master three times. The dialogue represented the conversation which took place between them, when the slave was retaken the third time. In this dialogue, the whole argument in behalf of slavery was brought forward by the master, all of which was disposed of by the slave. The slave was made to say some very smart as well as impressive things in reply to his master—things which had the desired though unexpected effect; for the conversation resulted in the voluntary emancipation of the slave on the part of the master.

In the same book, I met with one of Sheridan's mighty speeches on and in behalf of Catholic emancipation.[82] These were choice documents to me. I read them over and over again with unabated interest. They gave tongue to interesting thoughts of my own soul, which had frequently flashed through my mind, and died away for want of utterance. The moral which I gained from the dialogue was the power of truth over the conscience of even a slave-holder. What I got from Sheridan was a bold

---

[80] *ell* An old measure of length, about 45 inches. The modern equivalent is "Give an inch, take a mile."

[81] **"The Columbian Orator"** Full title: *The Columbian Orator: Containing a Variety of Original and Selected Pieces Together with Rules, Which Are Calculated to Improve Youth and Others,* edited by an American textbook author, Caleb Bingham (1757–1817), first published in 1797—the book used by Douglass in teaching himself to read.

[82] **Sheridan's . . . Catholic Emancipation** Richard Brinsley Sheridan (1751–1816), Irish playwright and politician, author of *The Rivals* (1775) and *School for Scandal* (1777), served as a Whig M.P. in the English Parliament, 1780–1812, held office in various Whig governments, supported voting rights for Catholics (**Catholic Emancipation**), and was noted for his electrifying speaking style. In Sheridan's day, Ireland was a colony of Great Britain, with its own legislature, until 1801, when the United Kingdom of Great Britain and Ireland was formed, uniting the countries legislatively. Although Catholics formed about 80 percent of the Irish population, Catholics were only granted the right to vote in 1829.

denunciation of slavery, and a powerful vindication of human rights. The reading of these documents enabled me to utter my thoughts, and to meet the arguments brought forward to sustain slavery; but while they relieved me of one difficulty, they brought on another even more painful than the one of which I was relieved. The more I read, the more I was led to abhor and detest my enslavers. I could regard them in no other light than a band of successful robbers, who had left their homes, and gone to Africa, and stolen us from our homes, and in a strange land reduced us to slavery. I loathed them as being the meanest as well as the most wicked of men. As I read and contemplated the subject, behold! that very discontentment which Master Hugh had predicted would follow my learning to read had already come, to torment and sting my soul to unutterable anguish. As I writhed under it, I would at times feel that learning to read had been a curse rather than a blessing. It had given me a view of my wretched condition, without the remedy. It opened my eyes to the horrible pit, but to no ladder upon which to get out. In moments of agony, I envied my fellow-slaves for their stupidity. I have often wished myself a beast. I preferred the condition of the meanest reptile to my own. Any thing, no matter what, to get rid of thinking! It was this everlasting thinking of my condition that tormented me. There was no getting rid of it. It was pressed upon me by every object within sight or hearing, animate or inanimate. The silver trump of freedom had roused my soul to eternal wakefulness. Freedom now appeared, to disappear no more forever. It was heard in every sound, and seen in every thing. It was ever present to torment me with a sense of my wretched condition. I saw nothing without seeing it, I heard nothing without hearing it, and felt nothing without feeling it. It looked from every star, it smiled in every calm, breathed in every wind, and moved in every storm.

I often found myself regretting my own existence, and wishing myself dead; and but for the hope of being free, I have no doubt but that I should have killed myself, or done something for which I should have been killed. While in this state of mind, I was eager to hear any one speak of slavery. I was a ready listener. Every little while, I could hear something about the abolitionists. It was some time before I found what the word meant. It was always used in such connections as to make it an interesting word to me. If a slave ran away and succeeded in getting clear, or if a slave killed his master, set fire to a barn, or did any thing very wrong in the mind of a slaveholder, it was spoken of as the fruit of *abolition.* Hearing the word in this connection very often, I set about learning what it meant. The dictionary afforded me little or no help. I found it was "the act of abolishing"; but then I did not know what was to be abolished. Here I was perplexed. I did not dare to ask any one about its meaning, for I was satisfied that it was something they wanted me to know very little about. After a patient waiting, I got one of our city papers, containing an account of the number of petitions from the north, praying for the abolition of slavery in the District of Columbia, and of the slave trade between the States. From this time I understood the words *abolition* and *abolitionist,* and always drew near when that word was spoken, expecting to hear something of importance

to myself and fellow-slaves. The light broke in upon me by degrees. I went one day down on the wharf of Mr. Waters; and seeing two Irishmen unloading a scow[83] of stone, I went, unasked, and helped them. When we had finished, one of them came to me and asked me if I were a slave. I told him I was. He asked, "Are ye a slave for life?" I told him that I was. The good Irishman seemed to be deeply affected by the statement. He said to the other that it was a pity so fine a little fellow as myself should be a slave for life. He said it was a shame to hold me. They both advised me to run away to the north; that I should find friends there, and that I should be free. I pretended not to be interested in what they said, and treated them as if I did not understand them; for I feared they might be treacherous. White men have been known to encourage slaves to escape, and then, to get the reward, catch them and return them to their masters. I was afraid that these seemingly good men might use me so; but I nevertheless remembered their advice, and from that time I resolved to run away. I looked forward to a time at which it would be safe for me to escape. I was too young to think of doing so immediately; besides, I wished to learn how to write, as I might have occasion to write my own pass. I consoled myself with the hope that I should one day find a good chance. Meanwhile, I would learn to write.

The idea as to how I might learn to write was suggested to me by being in Durgin and Bailey's ship-yard, and frequently seeing the ship carpenters, after hewing, and getting a piece of timber ready to use, write on the timber the name of that part of the ship for which it was intended. When a piece of timber was intended for the larboard[84] side, it would be marked thus—"L." When a piece was for the starboard[85] side, it would be marked thus—"S." A piece for the larboard side forward, would be marked thus—"L. F." When a piece was for starboard side forward, it would be marked thus—"S. F." For larboard aft,[86] it would be marked thus—"L. A." For starboard aft, it would be marked thus—"S. A." I soon learned the names of these letters, and for what they were intended when placed upon a piece of timber in the ship-yard. I immediately commenced copying them, and in a short time was able to make the four letters named. After that, when I met with any boy who I knew could write, I would tell him I could write as well as he. The next word would be, "I don't believe you. Let me see you try it." I would then make the letters which I had been so fortunate as to learn, and ask him to beat that. In this way I got a good many lessons in writing, which it is quite possible I should never have gotten in any other way. During this time, my copy-book was the board fence, brick wall, and pavement; my pen and ink was a lump of chalk. With these, I learned mainly how to write. I then commenced and continued copying the Italics in Webster's Spelling Book, until I could make them all without looking on the book. By this time, my

---

[83] **scow** A flat-bottomed boat used for transferring goods from a ship to the wharf or from a ship to a ship.
[84] **larboard** Also called port. Left side (looking forward) of a boat or ship.
[85] **starboard** Right side (looking forward) of a boat or ship.
[86] **aft** At or near the stern or tail of a boat or ship.

little Master Thomas had gone to school, and learned how to write, and had written over a number of copy-books. These had been brought home, and shown to some of our near neighbors, and then laid aside. My mistress used to go to class meeting[87] at the Wilk Street meetinghouse every Monday afternoon, and leave me to take care of the house. When left thus, I used to spend time in writing in the spaces left in Master Thomas's copy-book, copying what he had written. I continued to do this until I could write a hand very similar to that of Master Thomas. Thus, after a long, tedious effort for years, I finally succeeded in learning how to write.

---

[87] **class meeting** An idea pioneered by John Wesley (1703–1791), the English founder of Methodism. Class meetings had two aims: to nurture new converts—via Bible reading, public confession, and financial gifts—in their Christian faith, and to train church leaders.

Questions for Critical Thinking

1. Summarize the conditions of slavery in early-nineteenth-century Maryland, as shown in this selection from Frederick Douglass's slave narrative.

2. How did Frederick Douglass become literate? Why was literacy an important ingredient in helping bring about the end of slavery?

SOJOURNER TRUTH
"Ain't I a Woman?"

The African American woman Sojourner Truth (1795–1883) was an original voice who was a force for vital change in the nineteenth century. She made her mark both as a writer and as a supporter of progressive causes. As author of *Narrative of Sojourner Truth* (1850), the first classic by an African American woman writer, she made it possible for other African American women (see Zora Neale Hurston in Chapter 21 and Toni Morrison in Chapter 23) to speak their minds in print; thus, she contributed to the ongoing process of redefining Western culture. She was an advocate of women's rights, spiritualism, temperance, hydrotherapy (the use of water in treating disease), perfectionism (the belief that humans can achieve moral perfection on earth), Grahamism (the ideas of Sylvester Graham [1794–1851], an American vegetarian who urged dietary reform), and, especially, antislavery. She aligned herself with advanced thinkers who envisioned a utopian society in the New World, free of the corruption of old Europe. Relatively unknown between 1900 and 1950, she was restored to her rightful place in history with the civil rights movement.

Sojourner Truth was not her birth name but an adopted name meant to erase her slave origins. Born Isabella, or "Bell," she originally shared her master's last name, Hardenberg; when she was sold to a man named Dumont, she took his last name. In 1843 mystical "voices" instructed her to change her name and pursue the life of an itinerant preacher. Thereafter her mission was to "sojourn" America and speak God's "truth." She was active in New England in the 1840s, and in 1850 she shifted headquarters to Salem, Ohio, operating out of the office of the *Anti-Slavery Bugle*. In 1857 she moved permanently to Battle Creek, Michigan.

Sojourner Truth's career as an antislave advocate resembled that of Frederick Douglass (see *Narrative of the Life of Frederick Douglass, an American Slave*), for both were famous abolitionists and both published widely read slave narratives. She differed from Douglass in two major ways: She experienced slavery in the North, and she never learned to read or write. As an ex-slave from New York (she bolted to freedom in 1827, the year slavery was abolished there), she could bear witness to the evils of Northern slavery, even in the case of "kindly" masters. As an illiterate, she spoke for the African Americans of her day, most of whom also could not read or write. The literate Douglass, whom she met in 1844, termed her "a genuine specimen of the uncultured [N]egro." Scholars today regard Sojourner Truth in many ways as the more authentic African American voice of the two; Douglass, by becoming literate, is seen by some as a black European. Faithful to her roots, Sojourner Truth's *Narrative,* dictated to Olive Gilbert, represents the collective memory and vision of previously disenfranchised black America.

Reading the Selection

The "Ain't I a Woman?" speech is the record of Sojourner Truth's address at the 1851 Women's Rights Convention in Akron, Ohio. This version was written from memory by the feminist Frances Gage, but its accuracy is questionable. (A more accurate record of the speech is the on-the-scene report printed in the *Anti-Slavery Bugle.*) Gage's version nonetheless was widely read and contributed to the image of Sojourner Truth as a nimble-witted, gifted orator. The speech, homespun and rich in biblical allusions, blends the themes of racial equality and women's rights—the two causes to which Sojourner Truth was most devoted.

∞

Well, children, where there is so much racket there must be something out of kilter. I think that 'twixt the negroes of the South and the women at the North, all talking about rights, the white men will be in a fix pretty soon. But what's all this here talking about?

That man over there says that women need to be helped into carriages, and lifted over ditches, and to have the best place everywhere. Nobody ever helps me into carriages, or over mud-puddles, or gives me any best place! And ain't I a woman? Look at me! Look at my arm! I have ploughed and planted, and gathered into barns, and no man could head me! And ain't I a woman? I could work as much and eat as much as a man—when I could get it—and bear the lash as well! And ain't I a woman? I have borne thirteen children, and seen them most all sold off to slavery, and when I cried out with my mother's grief, none but Jesus heard me! And ain't I a woman?

Then they talk about this thing in the head; what's this they call it? (Intellect, someone whispers.) That's it,

honey. What's that got to do with women's rights or ne-gro's rights? If my cup won't hold but a pint, and yours holds a quart, wouldn't you be mean not to let me have my little half-measure full?

Then that little man in black there, he says women can't have as much rights as men, 'cause Christ wasn't a woman! Where did your Christ come from? Where did your Christ come from? From God and a woman! Man had nothing to do with Him.

If the first woman God ever made was strong enough to turn the world upside down all alone, these women together ought to be able to turn it back, and get it right side up again! And now they is asking to do it, the men better let them.

Obliged to you for hearing me, and now old Sojourner ain't got nothing more to say.

∞

Questions for Critical Thinking

1. What is the message of Sojourner Truth's speech?

2. Summarize, from this brief speech, the various arguments Truth uses to make her case for racial equality and women's rights.

HENRY DAVID THOREAU
Selection from "On the Duty of Civil Disobedience"

Henry David Thoreau (1817–1862) was a nineteenth-century nonconformist whose messages of self-communion, harmony with nature, and a "higher law" fell on deaf ears in his own day. Educated in classical and English literature at Harvard College and inspired by America's reigning philosopher, Ralph Waldo Emerson (1803–1882), Thoreau gave up a teaching career to devote his life to lecturing and writing. Under Emerson's influence, he became a voice for the transcendental movement that attracted many New England writers and ministers prior to the Civil War. Rejecting the empiricism of Francis Bacon and John Locke, the transcendentalists believed that the ultimate truth could not be found through the senses but could be attained only from intuitive sources, especially mystical, transcendent states.

Over a period of seventeen years (1845–1862), Thoreau published a small body of works, mainly essays, including "On the Duty of Civil Disobedience" and "A Plea for Captain John Brown," and two books, *A Week on the Concord and Merrimack Rivers* and *Walden*. These works reflected his growing disenchantment with America—its democratic government, industrial system, institution of slavery, and cult of success. When he died in 1862, the literary world barely mourned, for he was considered—if thought about at all—as an inferior disciple of Emerson and a minor literary figure.

During the twentieth century, Thoreau's reputation grew as his alienated point of view attracted many supporters. His retreat from civilization, his disapproval of materialism, and his condemnation of government's increased power over the individual provoked sympathetic responses in many people disenchanted with modern life. So great is his prestige today that he is generally accepted as one of the greats of Western thought and literature.

A defining moment in Thoreau's life occurred in March 1845 when he moved to Walden Pond, near Concord, Massachusetts, where he built a wooden hut and lived simply until September 1847. *Walden or, Life in the Woods* is an outgrowth of the writer's two years spent at the pond, though he wrote and polished the work over many years, incorporating entries from wide-ranging dates in his *Journals*—a fourteen-volume diary of his daily jottings. Largely ignored when published in 1854, *Walden* is now recognized as a classic of English prose and as a key text for environmentalists.

While at Walden Pond, Thoreau was arrested and jailed in 1846 for refusing to pay a tax. Although he spent only one night in jail, this incident sparked his most significant literary work. In 1848 he first focused on this incident in "The Rights and Duties of the Individual in Relations to Government," a lecture justifying his actions. In 1849 the lecture became an essay, "Resistance to Civil Government," which was later retitled "On the Duty of Civil Disobedience." Under this last title, the essay became the bible for Mohandas K. Gandhi's (known as Mahatma Gandhi) passive-resistance campaign in India from the 1920s to the 1940s and the handbook of underground groups opposed to Nazi occupation of Europe during World War II. Through Gandhi's example, Thoreau's message influenced Martin Luther King Jr. (see "Letter from a Birmingham Jail" in Chapter 22) and the civil rights movement of the 1950s and 1960s.

Reading the Selection

In this selection from "Civil Disobedience," Thoreau addresses the broader issues raised by his refusal to pay taxes: the growing power of government, the wrongful power exercised by the majority over the minority, the manipulation of voters by political leaders, and the acquiescence of citizens to their government's actions, whether legitimate or not. His basic argument is that there is a higher law—a transcendental concept—that supersedes the laws made by human devising. Thus, laws should be obeyed only when they are just—that is, in accord with the higher law. Unjust laws, such as those in support of slavery, have no validity and should be resisted by the citizenry. He also asserts that governments have no power over individuals or their property, except what is conceded by each person. In effect, the individual is a "higher and independent power," superior to the state. He predicts that a free and enlightened government will never exist so long as the state dominates its citizens.

Thoreau also offers a brief account of his night in jail for refusing to pay a tax (very minor by today's standards) that he thought was unjust. Using vivid and detailed language, he describes the sense of liberation he felt and the moral authority he gained from this experience. Having viewed the world from jail, he believed he could never see things the same way again—a perspective similar to those who have had an existential experience (see Sartre, *The Humanism of Existentialism*, in Chapter 22).

∞

. . .

Unjust laws exist: shall we be content to obey them, or shall we endeavor to amend them, and obey them until we have succeeded, or shall we transgress them at once? Men generally, under such a government as this, think that they ought to wait until they have persuaded the majority to alter them. They think that, if they should resist, the remedy would be worse than the evil. But it is the fault of the government itself that the remedy *is* worse than the evil. *It* makes it worse. Why is it not more apt to anticipate and provide for reform? Why does it not cherish its wise minority? Why does it cry and resist before it is hurt? Why does it not encourage its citizens to be on the alert to point out its faults, and *do* better than it would have them? Why does it always crucify Christ, and excommunicate Copernicus[88] and Luther,[89] and pronounce Washington and Franklin rebels?

One would think, that a deliberate and practical denial of its authority was the only offence never contemplated by government; else, why has it not assigned its definite, its suitable and proportionate penalty? If a man who has no property refuses but once to earn nine shillings[90] for the State, he is put in prison for a period unlimited by any law that I know, and determined only by the discretion of those who placed him there; but if he should steal ninety times nine shillings from the State, he is soon permitted to go at large again.

If the injustice is part of the necessary friction of the machine of government, let it go, let it go: perchance it will wear smooth,—certainly the machine will wear out.

If the injustice has a spring, or a pulley, or a rope, or a crank, exclusively for itself, then perhaps you may consider whether the remedy will not be worse than the evil; but if it is of such a nature that it requires you to be the agent of injustice to another, then, I say, break the law. Let your life be a counter friction to stop the machine. What I have to do is to see, at any rate, that I do not lend myself to the wrong which I condemn.

As for adopting the ways which the State has provided for remedying the evil, I know not of such ways. They take too much time, and a man's life will be gone. I have other affairs to attend to. I came into this world, not chiefly to make this a good place to live in, but to live in it, be it good or bad. A man has not every thing to do, but something; and because he cannot do *every thing*, it is not necessary that he should do *something* wrong. It is not my business to be petitioning the governor or the legislature any more than it is theirs to petition me; and, if they should not hear my petition, what should I do then? But in this case the State has provided no way: its very Constitution is the evil. This may seem to be harsh and stubborn and unconciliatory; but it is to treat with the utmost kindness and consideration the only spirit that can appreciate or deserves it. So is all change for the better, like birth and death which convulse the body.

I do not hesitate to say, that those who call themselves abolitionists should at once effectually withdraw their support, both in person and property, from the government of Massachusetts, and not wait till they constitute a majority of one, before they suffer the right to prevail through them. I think that it is enough if they have God on their side, without waiting for that other one. Moreover, any man more right than his neighbors, constitutes a majority of one already. . . . If a plant cannot live according to its nature, it dies; and so a man.

The night in prison was novel and interesting enough. The prisoners in their shirt-sleeves were enjoying a chat and the evening air in the door-way, when I entered. But the jailer said, "Come, boys, it is time to lock up;" and so they dispersed, and I heard the sound of their steps returning into the hollow apartments. My room-mate was introduced

---

[88] **Copernicus** Nicolaus Copernicus (1473–1543), Polish astronomer, advocate of the heliocentric system, which triumphed over the Ptolemaic system during the Scientific Revolution; he was not excommunicated, but his book *Revolutions of the Heavenly Bodies* was banned by the Catholic Church from 1616 until 1824.
[89] **Luther** Martin Luther (1483–1546), German founder of the Reformation and of Protestant Christianity. Excommunicated by the Catholic Church in 1521.
[90] **shilling** British coin, worth about 23 cents in 1849 and about $6.60 in 2012.

to me by the jailer, as "a first-rate fellow and a clever man." When the door was locked, he showed me where to hang my hat, and how he managed matters there. The rooms were whitewashed once a month; and this one, at least, was the whitest, most simply furnished, and probably the neatest apartment in the town. He naturally wanted to know where I came from, and what brought me there; and, when I had told him, I asked him in my turn how he came there, presuming him to be an honest man, of course; and, as the world goes, I believe he was. "Why," said he, "they accuse me of burning a barn; but I never did it." As near as I could discover, he had probably gone to bed in a barn when drunk, and smoked his pipe there; and so a barn was burnt. He had the reputation of being a clever man, had been there some three months waiting for his trial to come on, and would have to wait as much longer; but he was quite domesticated and contented, since he got his board for nothing, and thought that he was well treated.

He occupied one window, and I the other; and I saw, that if one stayed there long, his principal business would be to look out the window. I had soon read all the tracts that were left there, and examined where former prisoners had broken out, and where a grate had been sawed off, and heard the history of the various occupants of that room; for I found that even here there was a history and a gossip which never circulated beyond the walls of the jail. Probably this is the only house in the town where verses are composed, which are afterward printed in a circular form, but not published. I was shown quite a long list of verses which were composed by some young men who had been detected in an attempt to escape, who avenged themselves by singing them.

I pumped my fellow-prisoner as dry as I could, for fear I should never see him again; but at length he showed me which was my bed, and left me to blow out the lamp.

It was like travelling into a far country, such as I had never expected to behold, to lie there for one night. It seemed to me that I never had heard the town-clock strike before, nor the evening sounds of the village; for we slept with the windows open, which were inside the grating. It was to see my native village in the light of the middle ages, and our Concord was turned into a Rhine[91] stream, and visions of knights and castles passed before me. They were the voices of old burghers that I heard in the streets. I was an involuntary spectator and auditor of whatever was done and said in the kitchen of the adjacent village-inn,—a wholly new and rare experience to me. It was a closer view of my native town. I was fairly inside of it. I never had seen its institutions before. This is one of its peculiar institutions; for it is a shire[92] town. I began to comprehend what its inhabitants were about.

In the morning, our breakfasts were put through the hole in the door, in small oblong-square tin pans, made to fit, and holding a pint of chocolate, with brown bread,

and an iron spoon. When they called for the vessels again, I was green enough to return what bread I had left; but my comrade seized it, and said that I should lay that up for lunch or dinner. Soon after, he was let out to work at haying in a neighboring field, whither he went every day, and would not be back till noon; so he bade me good-day, saying that he doubted if he should see me again.

When I came out of prison,—for some one[93] interfered, and paid the tax,—I did not perceive that great changes had taken place on the common, such as he observed who went in a youth, and emerged a tottering and gray-headed man; and yet a change had to my eyes come over the scene,—the town, and State, and country,—greater than any that mere time could effect. I saw yet more distinctly the State in which I lived. I saw to what extent the people among whom I lived could be trusted as good neighbors and friends; that their friendship was for summer weather only; that they did not greatly purpose to do right; that they were a distinct race from me by their prejudices and superstitions, as the Chinamen and Malays are; that, in their sacrifices to humanity, they ran no risks, not even to their property; that, after all, they were not so noble but they treated the thief as he had treated them, and hoped, by a certain outward observance and a few prayers, and by walking in a particular straight though useless path from time to time, to save their souls. This may be to judge my neighbors harshly; for I believe that most of them are not aware that they have such an institution as the jail in their village.

It was formerly the custom in our village, when a poor debtor came out of jail, for his acquaintances to salute him, looking through their fingers, which were crossed to represent the grating of a jail window, "How do ye do?" My neighbors did not thus salute me, but first looked at me, and then at one another, as if I had returned from a long journey. I was put into jail as I was going to the shoemaker's to get a shoe which was mended. When I was let out the next morning, I proceeded to finish my errand, and, having put on my mended shoe, joined a huckleberry party, who were impatient to put themselves under my conduct; and in half an hour,—for the horse was soon tackled,[94]—was in the midst of a huckleberry field, on one of our highest hills, two miles off; and then the State was nowhere to be seen.

This is the whole history of "My Prisons."[95]

No man with a genius for legislation has appeared in America. They are rare in the history of the world. There are orators, politicians, and eloquent men, by the thousand; but the speaker has not yet opened his mouth to speak, who is capable of settling the much-vexed questions of the day. We love eloquence for its own sake, and not for any truth which it may utter, or any heroism it may inspire. Our legislators have not yet learned the comparative value of free-trade and of freedom, of union, and of rectitude, to

---

[91] **Rhine** River in western Europe, rising in Switzerland and flowing northward to the North Sea. Prominent in German legend and history.
[92] **shire** County seat.

[93] **one** Perhaps Thoreau's aunt, Maria Thoreau, paid the tax.
[94] **tackled** Harnessed.
[95] **"My Prisons"** A reference to a now-forgotten work, *Le Mie Prigioni*, by an Italian patriot, Silvio Pellico (1789–1854).

a nation. They have no genius or talent for comparatively humble questions of taxation and finance, commerce and manufactures and agriculture. If we were left solely to the wordy wit of legislators in Congress for our guidance, uncorrected by the seasonable experience and the effectual complaints of the people, America would not long retain her rank among the nations. For eighteen hundred years, though perchance I have no right to say it, the New Testament has been written; yet where is the legislator who has wisdom and practical talent enough to avail himself of the light which it sheds on the science of legislation?

The authority of government, even such as I am willing to submit to,—for I will cheerfully obey those who know and can do better than I, and in many things even those who neither know nor can do so well,—is still an impure one: to be strictly just, it must have the sanction and consent of the governed. It can have no pure right over my person and property but what I concede to it. The progress from an absolute to a limited monarchy, from a limited monarchy to a democracy, is a progress toward a true respect for the individual. Is a democracy, such as we know it, the last improvement possible in government? Is it not possible to take a step further towards recognizing and organizing the rights of man? There will never be a really free and enlightened State, until the State comes to recognize the individual as a higher and independent power, from which all its own power and authority are derived, and treats him accordingly. I please myself with imagining a State at last which can afford to be just to all men, and to treat the individual with respect as a neighbor; which even would not think it inconsistent with its own repose, if a few were to live aloof from it, not meddling with it, nor embraced by it, who fulfilled all the duties of neighbors and fellow-men. A State which bore this kind of fruit, and suffered it to drop off as fast as it ripened, would prepare the way for a still more perfect and glorious State, which also I have imagined, but not yet anywhere seen.

❧

Questions for Critical Thinking

1. Explain what Thoreau means by the "Duty of Civil Disobedience."

2. In Thoreau's mind, which is more important, the individual or the State? Explain. What do you think of this basic idea of Thoreau's?

---❧---

FYODOR DOSTOYEVSKY
Selection from *Notes from Underground*

The Russian novelist Fyodor Dostoyevsky (1821–1881), a master of nineteenth-century realism, is acclaimed today as both a giant of world literature and a prophet of modernism. Much of his fame stems from his uncanny insight into the motives of his tormented heroes—like Raskalnikov in *Crime and Punishment* (1864) and Ivan and Dmitri in *The Brothers Karamazov* (1879–1880); he lays bare the latent violence in their souls, thus anticipating the findings of depth psychology. He is equally known for his political wisdom, for he predicted the ultimate failure of liberalism and socialism, the rival theories that claimed to hold the key to the West's future. In contrast to these godless theories, which saw humanity as good and rational, Dostoyevsky believed mankind was depraved, irrational, and rebellious—thus incapable of self-rule. He concluded that the whole point of life is to seek salvation through suffering and love, a belief based on his mystical Orthodox Christian faith.

Dostoyevsky did not always have such a gloomy outlook. When he began to write in 1844, after giving up a military career, he was a "Westernizer," a term for Russians who thought their country should model itself on France and England, then Europe's leading progressive states. As a Westernizer, he believed socialism would help alleviate the suffering of Russia's masses. His novels, such as *Poor Folk* (1846), reflected this hope and were written in the sentimental romantic style then popular in the West. Events in 1848–1849 changed his point of view forever. He was arrested by the police on a charge of subversion (he belonged to a young socialist cell). Jailed and taken out to be shot, he was reprieved at the last minute, as part of a carefully orchestrated plan, and was sentenced to prison in Siberia. In prison he had his eyes opened to cruelty by the behavior of both jailers and inmates. When he returned from Siberia in 1859, he was a Slavophile—a Russian who thought that his country should keep true to its Slavic roots—and claimed that Russians were God's chosen people. His writings thereafter expressed his hatred of Europe and were written in a realistic style, which dwelt on suffering, with no hope of redemption except in heaven, if then.

Reading the Selection

The first three episodes of Part One of *Notes from Underground* (1862) (there are only two parts) introduce the "Mousehole Man," the unnamed social "dropout" who narrates the novel. In form, the novel is the Mousehole Man's monologue protesting his age's advanced ideas— liberalism, democracy, socialism, and science—each of which saw enlightened self-interest as the key to human happiness. His protest springs from his conviction that human whims and wishes are bound to clash with what is socially useful—an idea Freud later made popular (see *Civilization and Its Discontents* in Chapter 20). The narrator calls himself an "anti-hero," the first mention of this concept so central to twentieth-century literature (see Kafka's *The Trial* in Chapter 20). Bitter, self-mocking, and ironic, he speaks with Dostoyevsky's own "nasty" voice, a fact confirmed by those who knew the author. A mountain of hate, he cannot decide which to loathe more: the West's dream of a well-fed, happy society, symbolized by the Crystal Palace (the 1851 London exhibition, the first world's fair), or his fellow Russians' enthusiasm for French socialists like Charles Fourier (1772–1837), whose ideas Dostoyevsky once shared and who now seemed foolish and shallow.

∞

Part One

Underground

I

I am a sick man . . . I am a spiteful man. I am an unpleas- 1 ant man. I think my liver is diseased. However, I don't know beans about my disease, and I am not sure what is bothering me. I don't treat it and never have, though I respect medicine and doctors. Besides, I am extremely superstitious, let's say sufficiently so to respect medicine. (I am educated enough not to be superstitious, but I am.) No, I refuse to treat it out of spite. You probably will not understand that. Well, but *I* understand it. Of course, I can't explain to you just whom I am annoying in this case by my spite. I am perfectly well aware that I cannot "get even" with the doctors by not consulting them. I know better than anyone that I thereby injure only myself and no one else. But still, if I don't treat it, it is out of spite. My liver is bad, well then—let it get even worse!

I have been living like that for a long time now— twenty years. I am forty now. I used to be in the civil service, but no longer am. I was a spiteful official. I was rude and took pleasure in being so. After all, I did not accept bribes, so I was bound to find a compensation in that, at least. (A bad joke but I will not cross it out. I wrote it thinking it would sound very witty; but now that I see myself that I only wanted to show off in a despicable way, I will purposely not cross it out!) When petitioners would come to my desk for information I would gnash my teeth at them, and feel intense enjoyment when I succeeded in distressing some one. I was almost always successful. For the most part they were all timid people—of course, they were petitioners. But among the fops there was one officer in particular I could not endure. He simply would not be humble, and clanked his sword in a disgusting way. I carried on a war with him for eighteen months over that sword. At last I got the better of him. He left off clanking it. However, that happened when I was still young. But do you know, gentlemen, what the real point of my spite was? Why, the whole trick, the real vileness of it lay in the fact that continually, even in moments of the worst spleen, I was inwardly conscious with shame that I was not only not spiteful but not even an embittered man, that I was simply frightening sparrows at random and amusing myself by it. I might foam at the mouth, but bring me some kind of toy, give me a cup of tea with sugar, and I would be appeased. My heart might even be touched, though probably I would gnash my teeth at myself afterward and lie awake at night with shame for months after. That is the way I am.

I was lying when I said just now that I was a spiteful official. I was lying out of spite. I was simply indulging myself with the petitioners and with the officer, but I could never really become spiteful. Every moment I was conscious in myself of many, very many elements completely opposite to that. I felt them positively teeming in me, these opposite elements. I knew that they had been teeming in me all my life, begging to be let out, but I would not let them, would not let them, purposely would not let them out. They tormented me till I was ashamed; they drove me to convulsions, and finally, they bored me, how they bored me! Well, are you not imagining, gentlemen, that I am repenting for something now, that I am asking your forgiveness for something? I am sure you are imagining that. However, I assure you it does not matter to me if you are.

Not only could I not become spiteful, I could not even become anything: neither spiteful nor kind, neither a rascal nor an honest man, neither a hero nor an insect. Now, I am living out my life in my corner, taunting myself with the spiteful and useless consolation that an intelligent man cannot seriously become anything and that only a fool can become something. Yes, an intelligent man in the nineteenth century must and morally ought to be preeminently a characterless creature; a man of character, an active man, is preeminently a limited creature. That is the conviction of my forty years. I am forty years old now, and forty years, after all, is a whole lifetime; after all, that is extreme old age. To live longer than forty years is bad manners; it is vulgar, immoral. Who does live beyond forty? Answer that, sincerely and honestly. I will tell you who do: fools and worthless people do. I tell all old men that to their face, all those respectable old men, all those silver-haired and reverend old men! I tell the whole world that to its face. I have a right to say so, for I'll go on living to sixty myself. I'll live till seventy! Till eighty! Wait, let me catch my breath.

No doubt you think, gentlemen, that I want to amuse ⁵ you. You are mistaken in that, too. I am not at all such a merry person as you imagine, or as you may imagine; however, if irritated by all this babble (and I can feel that you are irritated) you decide to ask me just who I am—then my answer is, I am a certain low-ranked civil servant. I was in the service in order to have something to eat (but only for that reason), and when last year a distant relation left me six thousand roubles⁹⁶ in his will I immediately retired from the service and settled down in my corner. I used to live in this corner before, but now I have settled down in it. My room is a wretched, horrid one on the outskirts of town. My servant is an old country-woman, spiteful out of stupidity, and, moreover, she always smells bad. I am told that the Petersburg climate is bad for me, and that with my paltry means it is very expensive to live in Petersburg. I know all that better than all these sage

---

⁹⁶ **rouble** Variation of ruble; the chief monetary unit of Russia.

and experienced counsellors and monitors. But I am going to stay in Petersburg. I will not leave Petersburg! I will not leave because . . . Bah, after all it does not matter in the least whether I leave or stay.

But incidentally, what can a decent man speak about with the greatest pleasure?

Answer: About himself.

Well, then, I will talk about myself.

II

Now I want to tell you, gentlemen, whether you care to hear it or not, why I could not even become an insect. I tell you solemnly that I wanted to become an insect many times. But I was not even worthy of that. I swear to you, gentlemen, that to be hyperconscious is a disease, a real positive disease. Ordinary human consciousness would be too much for man's everyday needs, that is, half or a quarter of the amount which falls to the lot of a cultivated man of our unfortunate nineteenth century, especially one who has the particular misfortune to inhabit Petersburg, the most abstract and intentional city in the whole world. (There are intentional and unintentional cities.) It would have been quite enough, for instance, to have the consciousness by which all so-called straightforward persons and men of action live. I'll bet you think I am writing all this to show off, to be witty at the expense of men of action; and what is more, that out of ill-bred showing-off, I am clanking a sword, like my officer. But, gentlemen, whoever can pride himself on his diseases and even show off with them?

However, what am I talking about? Everyone does ¹⁰ that. They do pride themselves on their diseases, and I, perhaps, more than any one. There is no doubt about it: my objection was absurd. Yet just the same, I am firmly convinced not only that a great deal of consciousness, but that any consciousness is a disease. I insist on it. Let us drop that, too, for a minute. Tell me this: why did it happen that at the very, yes, at the very moment when I was most capable of recognizing every refinement of "all the sublime and beautiful," as we used to say at one time, I would, as though purposely, not only feel but do such hideous things, such that—well, in short, such as everyone probably does but which, as though purposely, occurred to me at the very time when I was most conscious that they ought not to be done. The more conscious I was of goodness, and of all that "sublime and beautiful," the more deeply I sank into my mire and the more capable I became of sinking into it completely. But the main thing was that all this did not seem to occur in me accidentally, but as though it had to be so. As though it were my most normal condition, and not in the least disease or depravity, so that finally I even lost the desire to struggle against this depravity. It ended by my almost believing (perhaps actually believing) that probably this was really my normal condition. But at first, in the beginning, that is, what agonies I suffered in that struggle! I did not believe that others went through the same things, and therefore I hid this fact about myself as a secret all my life. I was ashamed (perhaps I am even ashamed now). I reached the point of feeling a sort of secret abnormal, despicable enjoyment in returning home to my corner on some disgusting Petersburg night, and being acutely conscious that that day I had again done something loathsome, that what was done could never be undone, and secretly, inwardly gnaw, gnaw at myself for it, nagging and consuming myself till at last the bitterness turned into a sort of shameful accursed sweetness, and finally into real positive enjoyment! Yes, into enjoyment, into enjoyment! I insist upon that. And that is why I have started to speak, because I keep wanting to know for a fact whether other people feel such an enjoyment. Let me explain: the enjoyment here consisted precisely in the hyperconsciousness of one's own degradation; it was from feeling oneself that one had reached the last barrier, that it was nasty, but that it could not be otherwise; that you no longer had an escape; that you could never become a different person; that even if there remained enough time and faith for you to change into something else you probably would not want to change; or if you did want to, even then you would do nothing; because perhaps in reality there was nothing for you to change into. And the worst of it, and the root of it all, was that it all proceeded according to the normal and fundamental laws of hyperconsciousness, and with the inertia that was the direct result of those laws, and that consequently one could not only not change but one could do absolutely nothing. Thus it would follow, as the result of hyperconsciousness, that one is not to blame for being a scoundrel, as though that were any consolation to the scoundrel once he himself has come to realize that he actually is a scoundrel. But enough. Bah, I have talked a lot of nonsense, but what have I explained? Can this enjoyment be explained? But I will explain it! I will get to the bottom of it! That is why I have taken up my pen.

To take an instance, I am terribly vain. I am as suspicious and touchy as a hunchback or a dwarf. But to tell the truth, there have been moments when if someone had happened to slap my face I would, perhaps, have even been glad of that. I say, very seriously, that I would probably have been able to discover a peculiar sort of enjoyment even in that—the enjoyment, of course, of despair; but in despair occur the most intense enjoyments, especially when one is very acutely conscious of one's hopeless position. As for the slap in the face—why then the consciousness of being beaten to a pulp would positively overwhelm one. The worst of it is, no matter how I tried, it still turned out that I was always the most to blame in everything, and what is most humiliating of all, to blame for no fault of my own but, so to say, through the laws of nature. In the first place, to blame because I am cleverer than any of the people surrounding me. (I have always considered myself cleverer than any of the people surrounding me, and sometimes, would you believe it, I have even been ashamed of that. At any rate, all my life, I have, as it were, looked away and I could never look people straight in the eye.) To blame, finally, because even if I were magnanimous, I would only have suffered more from the consciousness of all its uselessness. After all, I would probably never have been able to do anything with my magnanimity—neither to forgive, for my assailant may have slapped me because of the laws of nature, and one cannot forgive the laws of nature; nor to forget, for even if it were the laws of nature, it is insulting all the same. Finally, even if I had wanted to be anything but magnanimous, had desired on the contrary to revenge myself on the man who insulted me, I could not have revenged myself on anyone nor anything because I would certainly never have made up my mind to do anything, even if I had been able to. Why would I not have made up my mind? I want to say a few words about that in particular.

III

After all, people who know how to revenge themselves and to take care of themselves in general, how do they do it? After all, when they are possessed, let us suppose, by the feeling of revenge, then for the time there is nothing else but that feeling left in their whole being. Such a man simply rushes straight toward his object like an infuriated bull with its horns down, and nothing but a wall will stop him. (By the way: facing the wall, such people—that is, the straightforward persons and men of action—are genuinely nonplussed. For them a wall is not an evasion, as for example for us people who think and consequently do nothing; it is not an excuse for turning aside, an excuse for which our kind is always very glad, though we scarcely believe in it ourselves, usually. No, they are nonplussed in all sincerity. The wall has for them something tranquilizing, morally soothing, final—maybe even something mysterious . . . but of the wall later.) Well, such a direct person I regard as the real normal man, as his tender mother nature wished to see him when she graciously brought him into being on the earth. I envy such a man till I am green in the face. He is stupid. I am not disputing that, but perhaps the normal man should be stupid, how do you know? Perhaps it is very beautiful, in fact. And I am all the more convinced of that suspicion, if one can call it so, by the fact that if, for instance, you take the antithesis of the normal man, that is, the hyperconscious man, who has come, of course, not out of the lap of nature but out of a retort (this is almost mysticism, gentlemen, but I suspect this, too), this retort-made man is sometimes so nonplussed in the presence of his antithesis that with all his hyperconsciousness he genuinely thinks of himself as a mouse and not a man. It may be a hyperconscious mouse, yet it is a mouse, while the other is a man, and therefore, etc. And the worst is, he himself, his very own self, looks upon himself as a mouse. No one asks him to do so. And that is an important point. Now let us look at this mouse in action. Let us suppose, for instance, that it feels insulted, too (and it almost always does feel insulted), and wants to revenge itself too. There may even be a greater accumulation of spite in it than in *l'homme de la nature et de la vérité*.[97] The base, nasty desire to repay with spite whoever has offended it, rankles perhaps even more nastily in it than in *l'homme de la nature et de la vérité*, because *l'homme de la nature et de la vérité* through his innate stupidity looks upon his revenge as justice pure

---

[97] *l'homme de la nature et de la vérité* French, "the natural and truthful man."

and simple; while in consequence of his hyperconsciousness the mouse does not believe in the justice of it. To come at last to the deed itself, to the very act of revenge. Apart from the one fundamental nastiness the unfortunate mouse succeeds in creating around it so many other nastinesses in the form of doubts and questions, adds to the one question so many unsettled questions, that there inevitably works up around it a sort of fatal brew, a stinking mess, made up of its doubts, agitations and lastly of the contempt spat upon it by the straightforward men of action who stand solemnly about it as judges and arbitrators, laughing at it till their healthy sides ache. Of course the only thing left for it is to dismiss all that with a wave of its paw, and, with a smile of assumed contempt in which it does not even believe itself, creep ignominiously into its mouse-hole. There, in its nasty, stinking, underground home our insulted, crushed and ridiculed mouse promptly becomes absorbed in cold, malignant and, above all, everlasting spite. For forty years together it will remember its injury down to the smallest, most shameful detail, and every time will add, of itself, details still more shameful, spitefully teasing and irritating itself with its own imagination. It will be ashamed of its own fancies, but yet it will recall everything, it will go over it again and again, it will invent lies against itself pretending that those things might have happened, and will forgive nothing. Maybe it will begin to revenge itself, too, but, as it were, piecemeal, in trivial ways, from behind the stove, incognito, without believing either in its own right to vengeance, or in the success of its revenge, knowing beforehand that from all its efforts at revenge it will suffer a hundred times more than he on whom it revenges itself, while he, probably will not even feel it. On its deathbed it will recall it all over again, with interest accumulated over all the years. But it is just in that cold, abominable half-despair, half-belief, in that conscious burying oneself alive for grief in the underworld for forty years, in that hyperconsciousness and yet to some extent doubtful hopelessness of one's position, in that hell of unsatisfied desires turned inward, in that fever of oscillations, of resolutions taken for ever and regretted again a minute later—that the savor of that strange enjoyment of which I have spoken lies. It is so subtle, sometimes so difficult to analyze consciously, that somewhat limited people, or simply people with strong nerves, will not understand anything at all in it. "Possibly," you will add on your own account with a grin, "people who have never received a slap in the face will not understand it either," and in that way you will politely hint to me that I, too, perhaps, have been slapped in the face in my life, and so I speak as an expert. I'll bet that you are thinking that. But set your minds at rest, gentlemen, I have not received a slap in the face, though it doesn't matter to me at all what you may think about it. Possibly, I even myself regret that I have given so few slaps in the face during my life. But enough, not another word on the subject of such extreme interest to you.

I will continue calmly about people with strong nerves who do not understand a certain refinement of enjoyment.

Though in certain circumstances these gentlemen bellow their loudest like bulls, though this, let us suppose, does them the greatest honor, yet, as I have already said, confronted with the impossible they at once resign themselves. Does the impossible mean the stone wall? What stone wall? Why, of course, the laws of nature, the conclusions of natural science, of mathematics. As soon as they prove to you, for instance, that you are descended from a monkey,[98] then it is no use scowling, accept it as a fact. When they prove to you that in reality one drop of your own fat must be dearer to you than a hundred thousand of your fellow creatures, and that this conclusion is the final solution of all so-called virtues and duties and all such ravings and prejudices, then you might as well accept it, you can't do anything about it, because two times two is a law of mathematics.[99] Just try refuting it.

"But really," they will shout at you, "there is no use protesting; it is a case of two times two makes four! Nature does not ask your permission, your wishes, and whether you like or dislike her laws does not concern her. You are bound to accept her as she is, and consequently also all her conclusions. A wall, you see, is a wall—etc. etc." Good God! but what do I care about the laws of nature and arithmetic, when, for some reason, I dislike those laws and the fact that two times two makes four? Of course I cannot break through a wall by battering my head against it if I really do not have the strength to break through it, but I am not going to resign myself to it simply because it is a stone wall and I am not strong enough.

As though such a stone wall really were a consolation, and really did contain some word of conciliation, if only because it is as true as two times two makes four. Oh, absurdity of absurdities! How much better it is to understand it all, to be conscious of it all, all the impossibilities and the stone walls, not to resign yourself to a single one of those impossibilities and stone walls if it disgusts you to resign yourself; to reach, through the most inevitable, logical combinations, the most revolting conclusions on the everlasting theme that you are yourself somehow to blame even for the stone wall, though again it is as clear as day you are not to blame in the least, and therefore grinding your teeth in silent impotence sensuously to sink into inertia, brooding on the fact that it turns out that there is even no one for you to feel vindictive against, that you have not, and perhaps never will have, an object for your spite, that it is a sleight-of-hand, a bit of juggling, a cardsharper's trick, that it is simply a mess, no knowing what and no knowing who, but in spite of all these uncertainties, and jugglings, still there is an ache in you, and the more you do not know, the worse the ache.

---

[98] **you are descended from a monkey** An allusion to Darwin's *Origin of the Species,* published in 1859, three years before *Notes from Underground.*
[99] **two times two is a law of mathematics** A satiric version of English utilitarianism; the emphasis on facts and statistics echoes the English historian Henry Thomas Buckle (1821–1862), in his *History of Civilization in England* (1857–1861).

∽

Questions for Critical Thinking

1. Compare and contrast Dostoyevsky's "Mousehole Man" with the prevailing culture of Western Europe.

2. The "Mousehole Man" calls himself "an anti-hero." Compare and contrast Dostoyevsky's character with a typical hero of fiction. Speculate as to why such a character as "Mousehole Man" would appear in the mid–nineteenth century.

20

THE AGE OF EARLY MODERNISM
1871–1914

FRIEDRICH NIETZSCHE
Selection from *Thus Spake Zarathustra*

The German thinker Friedrich Nietzsche (1844–1900) is a key, though paradoxical, figure in Western thought. Supremely influential on the diverse minds of his own day and those of succeeding generations (see Freud, Sartre, and Beauvoir), he nonetheless felt an extreme psychological isolation from European culture. He eventually slipped into a paralyzing madness (perhaps the result of syphilis) for the last eleven years of his life. Even so, in his writings he registered his poignantly ambivalent vision of the emerging nihilism—belief in nothing— that has characterized the West since 1900. He was a prophet of modernism, the century-long movement (1870–1970) that sought to wipe the cultural slate clean of both the Judeo-Christian and Greco-Roman traditions, as well as a prophet of postmodernism, modernism's successor starting around 1970. Postmodernism aims at an open-ended, indeterminate set of attitudes democratically embracing the contributions, tastes, and ideas of many groups of people of all races and all countries, past and present.

Nietzsche is also one of the most passionate and misunderstood writers in the West, in part because German Nazis in the 1930s made him their favorite philosopher and linked him to their campaign against the Jews and in favor of Aryan superiority. He is also misunderstood through his own doing, for Nietzsche's thought is clouded by an excess of adolescent emotion and his writing style is filled with aphorisms, or pithy sayings, that are easily misinterpreted when quoted out of context. Today Nietzsche's linkage to Nazism has been exposed as false, since his writings repeatedly ridicule anti-Semites and German nationalists. Nietzsche's linkage to Nazism is now viewed as a joint fabrication by Nazis who twisted his ideas to support their cause and by his sister, a Nazi sympathizer and his literary executor, who edited his works to make this connection. As to interpretive problems arising from his style, that remains a central concern for all readers of this challenging writer.

Reading the Selection

This selection from *Thus Spake Zarathustra* (1883) offers an example of Nietzsche's striking, biblical-sounding prose. Two themes dominate here: uncompromising hostility to religion and emphatic support of the idea of the Will to Power. He was the first major Western thinker to break completely with religion ("God is dead") and deny the truth of all transcendent belief. Much of his thought, such as radical perspectivism and rejection of universal values, was simply an attempt to come to terms with the full meaning of a godless world.

❦

Part I

3

When Zarathustra came into the next town, which lies on the edge of the forest, he found many people gathered together in the market place; for it had been promised that there would be a tightrope walker. And Zarathustra spoke thus to the people:

"*I teach you the overman.* Man is something that shall be overcome. What have you done to overcome him?

"All beings so far have created something beyond themselves; and do you want to be the ebb of this great flood and even go back to the beasts rather than overcome man? What is the ape to man? A laughingstock or a painful embarrassment. And man shall be just that for the overman: a laughingstock or a painful embarrassment. You have made your way from worm to man, and much in you is still worm. Once you were apes, and even now, too, man is more ape than any ape.

"Whoever is the wisest among you is also a mere conflict and cross between plant and ghost. But do I bid you become ghosts or plants?

"Behold, I teach you the overman. The overman is the meaning of the earth. Let your will say: the overman *shall be* the meaning of the earth! I beseech you, my brothers, *remain faithful to the earth,* and do not believe those who speak to you of otherworldly hopes! Poison-mixers are they, whether they know it or not. Despisers of life are they, decaying and poisoned themselves, of whom the earth is weary: so let them go.

"Once the sin against God was the greatest sin; but God died, and these sinners died with him. To sin against the earth is now the most dreadful thing, and to esteem the entrails of the unknowable higher than the meaning of the earth.

"Once the soul looked contemptuously upon the body, and then this contempt was the highest: she wanted the body meager, ghastly, and starved. Thus she hoped to escape it and the earth. Oh, this soul herself was still meager, ghastly, and starved: and cruelty was the lust of this soul. But you, too, my brothers, tell me: what does your body proclaim of your soul? Is not your soul poverty and filth and wretched contentment?

"Verily, a polluted stream is man. One must be a sea to be able to receive a polluted stream without becoming unclean. Behold, I teach you the overman: he is this sea; in him your **great** contempt can go under.

"What is the greatest experience you can have? It is the hour of the great contempt. The hour in which your happiness, too, arouses your disgust, and even your reason and your virtue.

"The hour when you say, 'What matters my happiness? It is poverty and filth and wretched contentment. But my happiness ought to justify existence itself.'

"The hour when you say, 'What matters my reason? Does it crave knowledge as the lion his food? It is poverty and filth and wretched contentment.'

"The hour when you say, 'What matters my virtue? As yet it has not made me rage. How weary I am of my good and my evil! All that is poverty and filth and wretched contentment.'

"The hour when you say, 'What matters my justice? I do not see that I am flames and fuel. But the just are flames and fuel.'

"The hour when you say, 'What matters my pity? Is not pity the cross on which he is nailed who loves man? But my pity is no crucifixion.'

"Have you yet spoken thus? Have you yet cried thus? Oh, that I might have heard you cry thus!

"Not your sin but your thrift cries to heaven; your meanness even in your sin cries to heaven.

"Where is the lightning to lick you with its tongue? Where is the frenzy with which you should be inoculated?

"Behold, I teach you the overman: he is this lightning, he is this frenzy."

When Zarathustra had spoken thus, one of the people cried: "Now we have heard enough about the tightrope walker; now let us see him too!" And all the people laughed at Zarathustra. But the tightrope walker, believing that the word concerned him, began his performance.

· · ·

5

When Zarathustra had spoken these words he beheld the people again and was silent. "There they stand," he said to his heart; "there they laugh. They do not understand me; I am not the mouth for these ears. Must one smash their ears before they learn to listen with their eyes? Must one clatter like kettledrums and preachers of repentance? Or do they believe only the stammerer?

"They have something of which they are proud. What do they call that which makes them proud? Education they call it; it distinguishes them from goatherds. That is why they do not like to hear the word 'contempt' applied to them. Let me then address their pride. Let me speak to them of what is most contemptible: but that is the *last man*."

And thus spoke Zarathustra to the people: "The time has come for man to set himself a goal. The time has come for man to plant the seed of his highest hope. His soil is still rich enough. But one day this soil will be poor and domesticated, and no tall tree will be able to grow in it. Alas, the time is coming when man will no longer shoot the arrow of his longing beyond man, and the string of his bow will have forgotten how to whir!

"I say unto you: one must still have chaos in oneself to be able to give birth to a dancing star. I say unto you: you still have chaos in yourselves.

"Alas, the time is coming when man will no longer 5 give birth to a star. Alas, the time of the most despicable man is coming, he that is no longer able to despise himself. Behold, I show you the *last man*.

"'What is love? What is creation? What is longing? What is a star?' thus asks the last man, and he blinks.

"The earth has become small, and on it hops the last man, who makes everything small. His race is as ineradicable as the flea-beetle; the last man lives longest.

"'We have invented happiness,' say the last men, and they blink. They have left the regions where it was hard to live, for one needs warmth. One still loves one's neighbor and rubs against him, for one needs warmth.

"Becoming sick and harboring suspicion are sinful to them: one proceeds carefully. A fool, whoever still stumbles over stones or human beings! A little poison now and then: that makes for agreeable dreams. And much poison in the end, for an agreeable death.

"One still works, for work is a form of entertainment. 10 But one is careful lest the entertainment be too harrowing.

One no longer becomes poor or rich: both require too much exertion. Who still wants to rule? Who obey? Both require too much exertion.

"No shepherd and one herd! Everybody wants the same, everybody is the same: whoever feels different goes voluntarily into a madhouse.

"'Formerly, all the world was mad,' say the most refined, and they blink.

"One is clever and knows everything that has ever happened: so there is no end of derision. One still quarrels, but one is soon reconciled—else it might spoil the digestion.

"One has one's little pleasure for the day and one's little pleasure for the night: but one has a regard for health.

"'We have invented happiness,' say the last men, and 15 they blink."

And here ended Zarathustra's first speech, which is also called "the Prologue"; for at this point he was interrupted by the clamor and delight of the crowd. "Give us this last man, O Zarathustra," they shouted. "Turn us into these last men! Then we shall make you a gift of the overman!" And all the people jubilated and clucked with their tongues.

But Zarathustra became sad and said to his heart: "They do not understand me: I am not the mouth for these ears. I seem to have lived too long in the mountains; I listened too much to brooks and trees: now I talk to them as to goatherds. My soul is unmoved and bright as the mountains in the morning. But they think I am cold and I jeer and make dreadful jests. And now they look at me and laugh: and as they laugh they even hate me. There is ice in their laughter."

∞

Questions for Critical Thinking

1. Define the "overman," as Zarathustra labels him in Part I, 3.

2. Define Zarathustra's "last man," in Part I, 5. Compare and contrast the "overman" and "last man," as part of Nietzsche's criticism of Western culture.

SIGMUND FREUD
Selection from *Civilization and Its Discontents*

The Austrian physician and psychologist Sigmund Freud (1856–1939), like the English biologist Darwin, was a pioneer of modernist thought. Indeed, it may be said that Freud began where Darwin (see *The Descent of Man* in Chapter 19) left off. Darwin claimed that life was not the result of a divine plan set up at the dawn of time by a benevolent God; rather, it was the outcome of millennia of purposeless and random changes in an endless competition of survival of the fittest, so that the one thing that remains true for the human enterprise is the constancy of struggle. From this starting point, Freud argued that endless struggle, both within each individual and between the individual and society, is the basic nature of the human condition.

The founder of psychoanalysis—that is, the probing of the mind through the "free association" of ideas buried in it—Freud was one of the first to map out the subconscious, as he sought to prove that each person's self is a battle zone. The results of this probing into depth psychology led him to conclude that below the surface of human consciousness (ego) lurks a set of innate drives (id). The id is mainly sexual and aggressive, engaged in a continual war with the individual's socially acquired standards of right and wrong, called conscience (superego). Whether the ego can successfully negotiate the continual conflict between the id and the superego has dramatic meaning, resulting in either happiness or self-destructive behavior. With this reasoning, Freud insisted on the primacy of the unconscious mind in helping to shape the self and thereby laid to rest the psychology of John Locke, which had claimed that human consciousness is molded exclusively by the environment.

Near the end of his life as he was suffering from cancer of the mouth, Freud wrote *Civilization and Its Discontents* (1929), in which he applied his new insights to the field of history. Written in the shadow of the rise of totalitarian states of both the right and the left across Europe, and perhaps tinged with a sense of his own impending death, this book offers a gloomy philosophy of history. Freud argues that humanity collectively is locked in a never-ending conflict between the aggressive drives of the collective id (Thanatos, the death instinct) and the sexual drives (Eros, the pleasure principle)—a macrocosmic version of the private war inside each person. The book ends with a question added in 1931 when the menace of the Nazi leader Hitler was becoming apparent, and it is expressive of Freud's ambiguous hopes—"Who can foresee [the] result?"

Reading the Selection

Chapter V, one of the eight short chapters in this monograph, focuses on the conflict between private sexual drives and the demands of civilization for cooperation. For Freud, this conflict is unresolvable, partly because love relationships at their height exclude all interest in other people, and partly because civilization is relentless in demanding that all members of society bond together in strong ties of friendship. Aggravating the conflict between sexuality and civilization is the aggressive drive, a force that civilization must hold in check in order to survive.

Freud next discusses one of the powerful ideologies of the time, communism, whose basic premise—human nature is wholly good until corrupted by private property—contradicts his ruling idea that humans are innately aggressive. To him, communism is an "untenable illusion" because it teaches that the abolition of private property will eliminate ill will and bring forth a golden age. Instead, he asserts that aggressiveness is endemic in history, as demonstrated by several examples. At the end of the day, Freud sides with civilization in imposing controls on aggressiveness and sexuality. This solution inevitably makes people unhappy, but of greater worth, it provides security for communal life.

In the last paragraph, Freud casts his gaze critically on American society, thinking it perhaps too successful in forging a collective identity—an allusion to "the masses," a key political theme when he wrote. The danger in the American experience, he notes, is that its leaders fail to lead, as they become mouthpieces of an ignorant group. Having raised the topic, he quickly drops it, thinking it sufficient to point out this potential problem.

∞

Chapter V

Psycho-analytic work has shown us that it is precisely 1 these frustrations of sexual life which people known as neurotics cannot tolerate. The neurotic creates substitutive satisfactions for himself in his symptoms, and these either cause him suffering in themselves or become sources of suffering for him by raising difficulties in his relations with his environment and the society he belongs to. The latter fact is easy to understand; the former presents us with a new problem. But civilization demands other sacrifices besides that of sexual satisfaction.

We have treated the difficulty of cultural development as a general difficulty of development by tracing it to the inertia of the libido, to its disinclination to give up an old position for a new one. We are saying much the same thing when we derive the antithesis between civilization and sexuality from the circumstance that sexual love is a relationship between two individuals in which a third can only be superfluous or disturbing, whereas civilization depends on relationships between a considerable number of individuals. When a love-relationship is at its height there is no room left for any interest in the environment; a pair of lovers are sufficient to themselves, and do not even need the child they have in common to make them happy. In no other case does Eros so clearly betray the core of his being, his purpose of making one out of more than one; but when he has achieved this in the proverbial way through the love of two human beings, he refuses to go further.

So far, we can quite well imagine a cultural community consisting of double individuals like this, who, libidinally satisfied in themselves, are connected with one another through the bonds of common work and common interests. If this were so, civilization would not have to withdraw any energy from sexuality. But this desirable state of things does not, and never did, exist. Reality shows us that civilization is not content with the ties we have so far allowed it. It aims at binding the members of the community together in a libidinal way as well and employs every means to that end. It favours every path by which strong identifications can be established between the members of the community, and it summons up aim-inhibited libido on the largest scale so as to strengthen the communal bond by relations of friendship. In order for these aims to be fulfilled, a restriction upon sexual life is unavoidable. But we are unable to understand what the necessity is which forces civilization along this path and which causes its antagonism to sexuality. There must be some disturbing factor which we have not yet discovered.

The clue may be supplied by one of the ideal demands, as we have called them, of civilized society. It runs: "Thou shalt love thy neighbour as thyself." It is known throughout the world and is undoubtedly older than Christianity, which puts it forward as its proudest claim. Yet it is certainly not very old; even in historical times it was still strange to mankind. Let us adopt a naïve attitude towards it, as though we were hearing it for the first time; we shall be unable then to suppress a feeling of surprise and bewilderment. Why should we do it? What good will it do us? But, above all, how shall we achieve it? How can it be possible? My love is something valuable to me which I ought not to throw away without reflection. It imposes duties on me for whose fulfilment I must be ready to make sacrifices. If I love someone, he must deserve it in some way. (I leave out of account the use he may be to me, and also his possible significance for me as a sexual object, for neither of these two kinds of relationship comes into question where the precept to love my neighbour is concerned.) He deserves it if he is so like me in important ways that I can love myself in him; and he deserves it if he is so much more perfect than myself that I can love my ideal of my own self in him. Again, I have to love him if he is my friend's son, since the pain my friend would feel if any harm came to him would be my pain too—I should have to share it. But if he is a stranger to me and if he cannot attract me by any worth of his own or any significance that he may already have acquired for my emotional life, it will be hard for me to love him. Indeed, I should be wrong to do so, for my love is valued by all my own people as a sign of my preferring them, and it is an injustice to them if I put a stranger on a par with them. But if I am to love him (with this universal love) merely because he, too, is an inhabitant of this earth, like an insect, an earth-worm or a grass-snake, then I fear that only a small modicum of my love will fall to his share—not by any possibility as much as, by the judgement of my reason, I am entitled to retain for myself. What is the point of a precept enunciated with so much solemnity if its fulfilment cannot be recommended as reasonable?

On closer inspection, I find still further difficulties. 5 Not merely is this stranger in general unworthy of my love; I must honestly confess that he has more claim to my hostility and even my hatred. He seems not to have the least trace of love for me and shows me not the slightest consideration. If it will do him any good he has no hesitation in injuring me, nor does he ask himself whether the amount of advantage he gains bears any proportion to the extent of the harm he does to me. Indeed, he need not even obtain an advantage; if he can satisfy any sort of desire by it, he thinks nothing of jeering at me, insulting me, slandering me and showing his superior power; and the more secure he feels and the more helpless I am, the more certainly I can expect him to behave like this to me. If he behaves differently, if he shows me consideration and forbearance as a stranger, I am ready to treat him in the same way, in any case and quite apart from any precept. Indeed, if this grandiose commandment had run "Love thy neighbour as thy neighbor loves thee," I should not take exception to it. And there is a second commandment, which seems to me even more incomprehensible and arouses still stronger opposition in me. It is "Love thine enemies." If I think it over, however, I see that I am wrong in treating it as a greater imposition. At bottom it is the same thing. . . .

The existence of this inclination to aggression, which we can detect in ourselves and justly assume to be present in others, is the factor which disturbs our relations with our neighbour and which forces civilization into such a high expenditure [of energy]. In consequence of this primary mutual hostility of human beings, civilized society is perpetually threatened with disintegration. The interest of work in common would not hold it together; instinctual passions are stronger than reasonable interests. Civilization has to use its utmost efforts in order to set limits to man's aggressive instincts and to hold the manifestations of them in check by psychical reaction-formations. Hence, therefore, the use of methods intended to incite people into identifications and aim-inhibited relationships of love, hence the restriction upon sexual life, and hence too the ideal's commandment to love one's neighbour as oneself—a commandment which is really justified by the fact that nothing else runs so strongly counter to the original nature of man. In spite of every effort, these endeavours of civilization have not so far achieved very much. It hopes to prevent the crudest excesses of brutal violence by itself assuming the right to use violence against criminals, but the law is not able to lay hold of the more cautious and refined manifestations of human aggressiveness. The time comes when each one of us has to give up as illusions the expectations which, in his youth, he pinned upon his fellow-men, and when he may learn how much difficulty and pain has been added to his life by their ill-will. At the same time, it would be unfair to reproach civilization with trying to eliminate strife and competition from human activity. These things are undoubtedly indispensable. But opposition is not necessarily enmity; it is merely misused and made an *occasion* for enmity.

The communists believe that they have found the path to deliverance from our evils. According to them, man is wholly good and is well-disposed to his neighbour; but the institution of private property has corrupted his nature. The ownership of private wealth gives the individual power, and with it the temptation to ill-treat his neighbour; while the man who is excluded from possession is bound to rebel in hostility against his oppressor. If private property were abolished, all wealth held in common, and everyone allowed to share in the enjoyment of it, ill-will and hostility would disappear among men. Since everyone's needs would be satisfied, no one would have any reason to regard another as his enemy; all would willingly undertake the work that was necessary. I have no concern with any economic criticisms of the communist system; I cannot enquire into whether the abolition of private property is expedient or advantageous. But I am able to recognize that the psychological premises on which the system is based are an untenable illusion. In abolishing private property we deprive the human love of aggression of one of its instruments, certainly a strong one, though certainly not the strongest; but we have in no way altered the differences in power and influence which are misused by aggressiveness, nor have we altered anything in its nature. Aggressiveness was not created by property. It reigned almost without limit in primitive times, when property was still very scanty, and it already shows itself in the nursery almost before property has given up its primal, anal form; it forms the basis of every relation of affection and love among people (with the single exception, perhaps, of the mother's relation to her male child). If we do away with personal rights over material wealth, there still remains prerogative in the field of sexual relationships, which is bound to become the source of the strongest dislike and the most violent hostility among men who in other respects are on an equal footing. If we were to remove this factor, too, by allowing complete freedom of sexual life and thus abolishing the family, the germ-cell of civilization, we cannot, it is true, easily foresee what new paths the development of civilization could take; but one thing we can expect, and that is that this indestructible feature of human nature will follow it there.

It is clearly not easy for men to give up the satisfaction of this inclination to aggression. They do not feel comfortable without it. The advantage which a comparatively small cultural group offers of allowing this instinct an outlet in the form of hostility against intruders is not to be despised. It is always possible to bind together a considerable number of people in love, so long as there are other people left over to receive the manifestations of their aggressiveness. I once discussed the phenomenon that it is precisely communities with adjoining territories, and related to each other in other ways as well, who are engaged in constant feuds and in ridiculing each other—like the Spaniards and Portuguese, for instance, the North Germans and South Germans, the English and Scotch, and so on. I gave this phenomenon the name of "the narcissism of minor differences," a name which does not do much to explain it. We can now see that it is a convenient and relatively harmless satisfaction of the inclination to aggression, by means of which cohesion between the members of the community is made easier. In this respect the Jewish people, scattered everywhere, have rendered most useful services to the civilizations of the countries that have been their hosts; but unfortunately all the massacres of the Jews in the Middle Ages did not suffice to make that period more peaceful and secure for their Christian fellows. When once the Apostle Paul had posited universal love between men as the foundation of his Christian community, extreme intolerance on the part of Christendom towards those who remained outside it became the inevitable consequence. To the Romans, who had not founded their communal life as a State upon love, religious intolerance was something foreign, although with them religion was a concern of the State and the State was permeated by religion. Neither was it an unaccountable chance that the dream of a Germanic world-dominion called for antisemitism as its complement; and it is intelligible that the attempt to establish a new, communist civilization in Russia should find its psychological support in the persecution of the bourgeois. One only wonders, with concern, what the Soviets will do after they have wiped out their bourgeois.

If civilization imposes such great sacrifices not only on man's sexuality but on his aggressivity, we can understand better why it is hard for him to be happy in that civilization. In fact, primitive man was better off in knowing no restrictions of instinct. To counterbalance this, his prospects of enjoying this happiness for any length of time were very slender. Civilized man has exchanged a portion of his possibilities of happiness for a portion of security. We must not forget, however, that in the primal family only the head of it enjoyed this instinctual freedom; the rest lived in slavish suppression. In that primal period of civilization, the contrast between a minority who enjoyed the advantages of civilization and a majority who were robbed of those advantages was, therefore, carried to extremes. As regards the primitive peoples who exist to-day, careful researches have shown that their instinctual life is by no means to be envied for its freedom. It is subject to restrictions of a different kind but perhaps of greater severity than those attaching to modern civilized man.

When we justly find fault with the present state of our civilization for so inadequately fulfilling our demands for a plan of life that shall make us happy, and for allowing the existence of so much suffering which could probably be avoided—when, with unsparing criticism, we try to uncover the roots of its imperfection, we are undoubtedly exercising a proper right and are not showing ourselves enemies of civilization. We may expect gradually to carry through such alterations in our civilization as will better satisfy our needs and will escape our criticisms. But perhaps we may also familiarize ourselves with the idea that there are difficulties attaching to the nature of civilization which will not yield to any attempt at reform. Over and above the tasks of restricting the instincts, which we are prepared for, there forces itself on our notice the danger of a state of things which might be termed "the psychological poverty of groups." This danger is most threatening where the bonds of a society are chiefly constituted by the identification of its members with one another, while individuals of the leader type do not acquire the importance that should fall to them in the formation of a group. The present cultural state of America would give us a good opportunity for studying the damage to civilization which is thus to be feared. But I shall avoid the temptation of entering upon a critique of American civilization; I do not wish to give an impression of wanting myself to employ American methods.

Questions for Critical Thinking

1. Is Freud optimistic or pessimistic about the future for humanity? Explain. Do you agree or disagree with Freud? Explain.

2. Show how Freud adapted his theory of the self to explain how society itself works. Do you think this is a valid type of reasoning? Explain.

KATE CHOPIN
"The Story of an Hour"

Kate Chopin (born Catherine O'Flaherty, 1851–1904) was an important American writer around 1900, but her work was neglected for most of the twentieth century. Famed as a local colorist, she wrote about Creole and Cajun life in Louisiana (in two collections of stories, *Bayou Folk* [1894] and *A Night in Acadie* [1897], and in a novel, *At Fault* [1890]). It was a world she knew well from her twelve-year marriage to a Creole planter and merchant. Ultimately, she set in motion events that abruptly ended her literary career when she published *The Awakening* (1899), her masterpiece. A tale of adulterous passion about a woman who awakens to find the man she loves is not her husband (inevitably called the American equivalent of Gustave Flaubert's *Madame Bovary;* see Chapter 19), this novel unleashed a firestorm of public criticism when it first appeared. Libraries across the nation banned it, and in her hometown of St. Louis, the Fine Arts Club denied her membership, despite her obvious distinction. Sensitive to the cry raised against the novel, Chopin was stunned into silence and never wrote again. When she died, her name and works passed from memory until rediscovered in the 1960s, prompted by the burgeoning feminist movement. Today her reputation has been restored to the literary pantheon, and she is regarded as a pioneer of postmodernism, with her keen interest in marginal people and feminist themes.

Reading the Selection

Chopin's "The Story of an Hour" is actually little more than an anecdote. In the Middle Ages, it would have been a moral fable that delivered a religious message. In Chopin's hands, however, it became a story meant to surprise with its ironic twist at the end—a type of tale pioneered by the then-popular writer O. Henry (1862–1910), the pen name of William Sydney Porter. Chopin's story recounts the ironic fate of Louise Mallard, who secretly welcomes the news of her husband Brently's unexpected death in a railroad disaster; then she discovers that he is still very much alive, having "been far from the scene of the accident," at which point she falls down dead, the victim of "heart disease."

Chopin manages to make several points with this sad little tale. She has Louise condemn the institution of marriage because it allows "men and women [to] believe that they have a right to impose a private will upon a fellow-creature." Indeed, Louise's initial joy on hearing of Brently's death is that she is finally free of him: "Free! Body and soul free!" Chopin also understands the human heart, as in her description of Louise's kaleidoscopic emotions: from weeping, to locking herself in her room, to listening to life in the square, to stifling a sob, and ultimately, to accepting her true feelings.

What makes the story especially intriguing is that it has an autobiographical aspect, though to what degree is not clear. Chopin heard the news of her husband's unexpected death just as Louise did here; however, whereas Louise is "killed by joy," Chopin was left at age thirty-two with six children to support. One wonders if, given such a great material burden, Chopin's husband's death allowed her to "live for herself," Louise's wish.

∞

Knowing that Mrs. Mallard was afflicted with a heart trouble, great care was taken to break to her as gently as possible the news of her husband's death.

It was her sister Josephine who told her, in broken sentences; veiled hints that revealed in half concealing. Her husband's friend Richards was there, too, near her. It was he who had been in the newspaper office when intelligence of the railroad disaster was received, with Brently Mallard's name leading the list of "killed." He had only taken the time to assure himself of its truth by a second telegram, and had hastened to forestall any less careful, less tender friend in bearing the sad message.

She did not hear the story as many women have heard the same, with a paralyzed inability to accept its significance. She wept at once, with sudden, wild abandonment, in her sister's arms. When the storm of grief had spent itself she went away to her room alone. She would have no one follow her.

There stood, facing the open window, a comfortable, roomy armchair. Into this she sank, pressed down by a physical exhaustion that haunted her body and seemed to reach into her soul.

She could see in the open square before her house the tops of trees that were all aquiver with the new spring life. The delicious breath of rain was in the air. In the street below a peddler was crying his wares. The notes of a distant song which some one was singing reached her faintly, and countless sparrows were twittering in the eaves.

There were patches of blue sky showing here and there through the clouds that had met and piled one above the other in the west facing her window.

She sat with her head thrown back upon the cushion of the chair, quite motionless, except when a sob came up into her throat and shook her, as a child who has cried itself to sleep continues to sob in its dreams.

She was young, with a fair, calm face, whose lines bespoke repression and even a certain strength. But now there was a dull stare in her eyes, whose gaze was fixed away off yonder on one of those patches of blue sky. It was not a glance of reflection, but rather indicated a suspension of intelligent thought.

There was something coming to her and she was waiting for it, fearfully. What was it? She did not know; it was too subtle and elusive to name. But she felt it, creeping out of the sky, reaching toward her through the sounds, the scents, the color that filled the air.

Now her bosom rose and fell tumultuously. She was 10 beginning to recognize this thing that was approaching to possess her, and she was striving to beat it back with her will—as powerless as her two white slender hands would have been.

When she abandoned herself a little whispered word escaped her slightly parted lips. She said it over and over under her breath: "free, free, free!" The vacant stare and the look of terror that had followed it went from her eyes. They stayed keen and bright. Her pulses beat fast, and the coursing blood warmed and relaxed every inch of her body.

She did not stop to ask if it were or were not a monstrous joy that held her. A clear and exalted perception enabled her to dismiss the suggestion as trivial.

She knew that she would weep again when she saw the kind, tender hands folded in death; the face that had never looked save with love upon her, fixed and gray and dead. But she saw beyond that bitter moment a long procession of years to come that would belong to her absolutely. And she opened and spread her arms out to them in welcome.

There would be no one to live for her during those coming years; she would live for herself. There would be no powerful will bending hers in that blind persistence with which men and women believe they have a right to impose a private will upon a fellow-creature. A kind intention or a cruel intention made the act seem no less a crime as she looked upon it in that brief moment of illumination.

And yet she had loved him—sometimes. Often she 15 had not. What did it matter! What could love, the unsolved mystery, count for in face of this possession of self-assertion which she suddenly recognized as the strongest impulse of her being!

"Free! Body and soul free!" she kept whispering.

Josephine was kneeling before the closed door with her lips to the keyhole, imploring for admission. "Louise, open the door! I beg; open the door—you will make yourself ill. What are you doing, Louise? For heaven's sake open the door."

"Go away. I am not making myself ill." No; she was drinking in a very elixir of life through that open window.

Her fancy was running riot along those days ahead of her. Spring days, and summer days, and all sorts of days that would be her own. She breathed a quick prayer that life might be long. It was only yesterday she had thought with a shudder that life might be long.

She arose at length and opened the door to her sis- 20 ter's importunities. There was a feverish triumph in her eyes, and she carried herself unwittingly like a goddess of Victory. She clasped her sister's waist, and together they descended the stairs. Richards stood waiting for them at the bottom.

Some one was opening the front door with a latchkey. It was Brently Mallard who entered, a little travel-stained, composedly carrying his gripsack and umbrella. He had been far from the scene of accident, and did not even know there had been one. He stood amazed at Josephine's piercing cry; at Richards' quick motion to screen him from the view of his wife.

But Richards was too late.

When the doctors came they said she had died of heart disease—of joy that kills.

❦

Questions for Critical Thinking

1. Summarize the plot of this story. What is Chopin's moral?

2. Summarize the steps of grief that Louise, the story's heroine, undergoes after hearing of her spouse's sudden death. Do you think this psychological portrait is credible? Explain.

FRANZ KAFKA
Selection from *The Trial*

The Austrian Franz Kafka (1883–1924) is generally described as one of the founders of modernist fiction, but scholars are divided over the meaning of his art. One school of thought labels Kafka a prophet of modern life and emphasizes his triple alienation: a German-speaking Jew from the Czech-speaking and Protestant section of largely Roman Catholic Austria. This school further claims that Kafka, a deeply self-aware writer, used his own plight to create literary heroes—each a modern Everyman often named "K."—who were victims of forces beyond their control. Thus, in this view, Kafka's works may be interpreted variously as existentialist parables about meaning in a godless age, or as religious allegories about the retreat of the divine in modern times, or as satires on modern bureaucracy and its oppression of the individual (Kafka was a lifelong civil servant).

Downplaying Kafka as a prophet, another school of thought stresses the autobiographical in his works. Impressed by the soul-searching revealed in his *Diaries* (2 vols., 1948–1949), this school claims that Kafka was tormented by conflict with his father: Kafka, the frail, sensitive, and intellectual son, was dominated by his physically fit, no-nonsense, businessman father. Indeed, Kafka once asserted that all his works were about his father. Thus, in this view, Kafka was always writing about his own condition.

As usual, the true meaning of Kafka probably lies between the two rival views, part visionary, part anguished son. Whatever the view, his works inspired the term "Kafkaesque," a self-absorbed style marked by feelings of guilt and paranoid helplessness.

Despite present fame, Kafka in his own day doubted the worth of his literary efforts. When *Metamorphosis and Other Stories* (1915) and *The Penal Colony* (1919) met with little critical acclaim, he planned to have the rest of his work destroyed at his death. His literary executor frustrated this wish and (happily) arranged for these remaining works to be published: *The Trial* (1925), *The Castle* (1926), and *Amerika* (1927)—all classics of modernist literature.

Reading the Selection

Kafka's *Trial* begins with a thunderclap, at least metaphorically speaking. The hero, Joseph K., a mild-mannered bank clerk, is arrested "one fine morning" and his world suddenly falls apart. Strange men, dressed in vaguely identifiable uniforms, push into his boardinghouse and take him prisoner. Nosy neighbors gawk at the spectacle unfolding outside their window. A cat-and-mouse game ensues between Joseph K. and the intruders. But nothing makes sense. No criminal charge is made. No one is identified as K.'s accuser. Yet, K. remains under arrest or, at least, a form of surveillance. From this ominous opening, the novel proceeds as Joseph K. tries to understand and escape from the process that has taken over his life. After many twists and turns, climaxing with the famous trial of the novel's title, K. is murdered by men wearing top hats and left for dead in a field—the reason for his death still a mystery.

Readers and critics have discovered many theories to explain the plight of Joseph K., from religious (original sin), to political (totalitarianism), to personal (Kafka's own tormented family history), to structural (the bureaucratization of modern life). And, perhaps, it is just that calculated ambiguity which helps explain the continuing regard of *The Trial* as one of the masterpieces of modernist fiction.

∞

Chapter One

The Arrest

Someone must have been telling lies about Joseph K., for without having done anything wrong he was arrested one fine morning. His landlady's cook, who always brought him his breakfast at eight o'clock, failed to appear on this occasion. That had never happened before. K. waited for a little while longer, watching from his pillow the old lady opposite, who seemed to be peering at him with a curiosity unusual even for her, but then, feeling both put out and hungry, he rang the bell. At once there was a knock at the door and a man entered whom he had never seen before in the house. He was slim and yet well knit, he wore a closely fitting black suit furnished with all sorts of pleats, pockets, buckles, and buttons, as well as a belt, like a tourist's outfit, and in consequence looked eminently practical, though one could not quite tell what actual purpose it served. "Who are you?" asked K., half raising himself in bed. But the man ignored the question, as though his appearance needed no explanation, and merely said: "Did you ring?" "Anna is to bring me my breakfast," said K., and then studied the fellow, silently and carefully, trying to make out who he could be. The man did not submit to this scrutiny for very long, but turned to the door and opened it slightly so as to report to someone who was evidently standing just behind it: "He says Anna is to bring him his breakfast." A short guffaw from the next room came in answer; and it rather sounded as if several people had joined in. Although the strange man could not have learned anything from it that he did not know already, he now said to K., as if passing on a statement: "It can't be done." "This is news indeed," cried K., springing out of bed and quickly pulling on his trousers. "I must see what people these are next door, and how Frau Grubach can account to me for such behavior." Yet it occurred to him at once that he should not have said this aloud and that by doing so he had in a way admitted the stranger's right to superintend his actions; still, that did not seem important to him at the moment. The stranger, however, took his words in some such sense, for he asked: "Hadn't you better stay here?" "I shall neither stay here nor let you address me until you have introduced yourself." "I meant well enough," said the stranger, and then of his own accord threw the door open. In the next room, which K. entered more slowly than he had intended, everything looked at first glance almost as it had the evening before. It was Frau Grubach's living room; perhaps among all the furniture, rugs, china, and photographs with which it was crammed there was a little more free space than usual, yet one did not perceive that at first, especially as the main change consisted in the presence of a man who was sitting at the open window reading a book, from which he now glanced up. "You should have stayed in your room! Didn't Franz tell you that?" "Yes, but what are you doing here?" asked K., looking from his new acquaintance to the man called Franz, who was still standing by the door, and

then back again. Through the open window he had another glimpse of the old woman, who with truly senile inquisitiveness had moved along to the window exactly opposite, in order to go on seeing all that could be seen. "I'd better get Frau Grubach—" said K., as if wrenching himself away from the two men (though they were standing at quite a distance from him) and making as if to go out. "No," said the man at the window, flinging the book down on the table and getting up. "You can't go out, you are arrested." "So it seems," said K. "But what for?" he added. "We are not authorized to tell you that. Go to your room and wait there. Proceedings have been instituted against you, and you will be informed of everything in due course. I am exceeding my instructions in speaking freely to you like this. But I hope nobody hears me except Franz, and he himself has been too free with you, against his express instructions. If you continue to have as good luck as you have had in the choice of your warders,[1] then you can be confident of the final result." K. felt he must sit down, but now he saw that there was no seat in the whole room except the chair beside the window. "You'll soon discover that we're telling you the truth," said Franz, advancing toward him simultaneously with the other man. The latter overtopped K. enormously and kept clapping him on the shoulder. They both examined his nightshirt and said that he would have to wear a less fancy shirt now, but that they would take charge of this one and the rest of his underwear and, if his case turned out well, restore them to him later. "Much better give these things to us than hand them over to the depot," they said, "for in the depot there's lots of thieving, and besides they sell everything there after a certain length of time, no matter whether your case is settled or not. And you never know how long these cases will last, especially these days. Of course you would get the money out of the depot in the long run, but in the first place the prices they pay you are always wretched, for they sell your things to the best briber, not the best bidder, and anyhow it's well known that money dwindles a lot if it passes from hand to hand from one year to another." K. paid hardly any attention to this advice. Any right to dispose of his own things which he might possess he did not prize very highly; far more important to him was the necessity to understand his situation clearly; but with these people beside him he could not even think. The belly of the second warder—for they could only be warders—kept butting against him in an almost friendly way, yet if he looked up he caught sight of a face which did not in the least suit that fat body, a dry, bony face with a great nose, twisted to one side, which seemed to be consulting over his head with the other warder. Who could these men be? What were they talking about? What authority could they

---

[1] **warder** A guard.

represent? K. lived in a country with a legal constitution, there was universal peace, all the laws were in force; who dared seize him in his own dwelling? He had always been inclined to take things easily, to believe in the worst only when the worst happened, to take no care for the morrow even when the outlook was threatening. But that struck him as not being the right policy here, one could certainly regard the whole thing as a joke, a rude joke which his colleagues in the Bank had concocted for some unknown reason, perhaps because this was his thirtieth birthday, that was of course possible, perhaps he had only to laugh knowingly in these men's faces and they would laugh with him, perhaps they were merely porters from the street corner—they looked very like it—nevertheless his very first glance at the man Franz had decided him for the time being not to give away any advantage that he might possess over these people. There was a slight risk that later on his friends might possibly say he could not take a joke, but he had in mind—though it was not usual with him to learn from experience—several occasions, of no importance in themselves, when against all his friends' advice he had behaved with deliberate recklessness and without the slightest regard for possible consequences, and had had in the end to pay dearly for it. That must not happen again, at least not this time; if this was a comedy he would insist on playing it to the end.

But he was still free. "Allow me," he said, passing quickly between the warders to his room. "He seems to have some sense," he heard one of them saying behind him. When he reached his room he at once pulled out the drawer of his desk. Everything lay there in perfect order, but in his agitation he could not find at first the identification papers for which he was looking. At last he found his bicycle license and was about to start off with it to the warders, but then it seemed too trivial a thing, and he searched again until he found his birth certificate. As he was re-entering the next room the opposite door opened and Frau Grubach showed herself. He saw her only for an instant, for no sooner did she recognize him than she was obviously overcome by embarrassment, apologized for intruding, vanished, and shut the door again with the utmost care. "Come in, do," he would just have had time to say. But he merely stood holding his papers in the middle of the room, looking at the door, which did not open again, and was only recalled to attention by a shout from the warders, who were sitting at a table by the open window and, as he now saw, devouring his breakfast. "Why didn't she come in?" he asked. "She isn't allowed to," said the tall warder, "since you're under arrest." "But how can I be under arrest? And particularly in such a ridiculous fashion?" "So now you're beginning it all over again?" said the warder, dipping a slice of bread and butter into the honey-pot. "We don't answer such questions." "You'll have to answer them," said K. "Here are my papers, now show me yours, and first of all your warrant for arresting me." "Oh, good Lord," said the warder. "If you would only realize your position, and if you wouldn't insist on uselessly annoying us two, who probably mean better by you and stand closer to you than any other people in the world." "That's so, you can believe that," said Franz, not

raising to his lips the coffee cup he held in his hand, but instead giving K. a long, apparently significant, yet incomprehensible look. Without wishing it K. found himself decoyed into an exchange of speaking looks with Franz, none the less he tapped his papers and repeated: "Here are my identification papers." "What are your papers to us?" cried the tall warder. "You're behaving worse than a child. What are you after? Do you think you'll bring this fine case of yours to a speedier end by wrangling with us, your warders, over papers and warrants? We are humble subordinates who can scarcely find our way through a legal document and have nothing to do with your case except to stand guard over you for ten hours a day and draw our pay for it. That's all we are, but we're quite capable of grasping the fact that the high authorities we serve, before they would order such an arrest as this, must be quite well informed about the reasons for the arrest and the person of the prisoner. There can be no mistake about that. Our officials, so far as I know them, and I know only the lowest grades among them, never go hunting for crime in the populace, but, as the Law decrees, are drawn toward the guilty and must then send out us warders. That is the Law. How could there be a mistake in that?" "I don't know this Law," said K. "All the worse for you," replied the warder. "And it probably exists nowhere but in your own head," said K.; he wanted in some way to enter into the thoughts of the warders and twist them to his own advantage or else try to acclimatize himself to them. But the warder merely said in a discouraging voice: "You'll come up against it yet." Franz interrupted; "See, Willem, he admits that he doesn't know the Law and yet he claims he's innocent." "You're quite right, but you'll never make a man like that see reason," replied the other. K. gave no further answer; Must I, he thought, let myself be confused still worse by the gabble of those wretched hirelings?— they admit themselves that's all they are. They're talking of things, in any case, which they don't understand. Plain stupidity is the only thing that can give them such assurance. A few words with a man on my own level of intelligence would make everything far clearer than hours of talk with these two. He walked up and down a few times in the free part of the room; at the other side of the street he could still see the old woman, who had now dragged to the window an even older man, whom she was holding round the waist. K. felt he must put an end to this farce. "Take me to your superior officer," he said. "When he orders me, not before," retorted the warder called Willem. "And now I advise you," he went on, "to go to your room, stay quietly there, and wait for what may be decided about you. Our advice to you is not to let yourself be distracted by vain thoughts, but to collect yourself, for great demands will be made upon you. You haven't treated us as our kind advances to you deserved, you have forgotten that we, no matter who we may be, are at least free men compared to you; that is no small advantage. All the same, we are prepared, if you have any money, to bring you a little breakfast from the coffeehouse across the street."

Without replying to this offer K. remained standing where he was for the moment. If he were to open the door of the next room or even the door leading to the hall, perhaps the two of them would not dare to hinder him, perhaps that would be the simplest solution of the whole business, to bring it to a head. But perhaps they might seize him after all, and if he were once down, all the superiority would be lost which in a certain sense he still retained. Accordingly, instead of a quick solution he chose that certainty which the natural course of things would be bound to bring, and went back to his room without another word having been said by him or by the warders.

He flung himself on his bed and took from the washstand a fine apple which he had laid out the night before for his breakfast. Now it was all the breakfast he would have, but in any case, as the first few bites assured him, much better than the breakfast from the filthy night café would have been, which the grace of his warders might have secured him. He felt fit and confident, he would miss his work in the Bank that morning, it was true, but that would be easily overlooked, considering the comparatively high post he held there. Should he give the real reason for his absence? He considered doing so. If they did not believe him, which in the circumstances would be understandable, he could produce Frau Grubach as a witness, or even the two odd creatures over the way, who were now probably meandering back again to the window opposite his room. K. was surprised, at least he was surprised considering the warders' point of view, that they had sent him to his room and left him alone there, where he had abundant opportunities to take his life. Though at the same time he also asked himself, looking at it from his own point of view, what possible ground he could have to do so. Because two warders were sitting next door and had intercepted his breakfast? To take his life would be such a senseless act that, even if he wished, he could not bring himself to do it because of its very senselessness. If the intellectual poverty of the warders were not so manifest, he might almost assume that they too saw no danger in leaving him alone, for the very same reason. They were quite at liberty to watch him now while he went to a wall-cupboard where he kept a bottle of good brandy, while he filled a glass and drank it down to make up for his breakfast, and then drank a second to give him courage, the last one only as a precaution, for the improbable contingency that it might be needed.

Then a shout came from the next room which made him start so violently that his teeth rattled against the glass. "The Inspector wants you," was its tenor. It was merely the tone of it that startled him, a curt, military bark with which we would never have credited the warder Franz. The command itself was actually welcome to him. "At last," he shouted back, closing the cupboard and hurrying at once into the next room. There the two warders were standing, and, as if that were a matter of course, immediately drove him back into his room again. "What are you thinking of?" they cried. "Do you imagine you can appear before the Inspector in your shirt? He'll have you well thrashed, and us too." "Let me alone, damn you," cried K., who by now had been forced back to his wardrobe. "If you grab me out of bed, you can't expect to find me all dressed up in my best suit." "That can't be helped," said the warders, who as soon as K. raised his

voice always grew quite calm, indeed almost melancholy, and thus contrived either to confuse him or to some extent bring him to his senses. "Silly formalities!" he growled, but immediately lifted a coat from a chair and held it up for a little while in both hands, as if displaying it to the warders for their approval. They shook their heads. "It must be a black coat," they said. Thereupon K. flung the coat on the floor and said—he did not himself know in what sense he meant the words—"But this isn't the capital charge yet." The warders smiled, but stuck to their: "It must be a black coat." "If it's to dispatch my case any quicker, I don't mind," replied K., opening the wardrobe, where he searched for a long time among his many suits, chose his best black one, a lounge suit which had caused almost a sensation among his acquaintances because of its elegance, then selected another shirt and began to dress with great care. In his secret heart he thought he had managed after all to speed up the proceedings, for the warders had forgotten to make him take a bath. He kept an eye on them to see if they would remember the ducking, but of course it never occurred to them, yet on the other hand Willem did not forget to send Franz to the Inspector with the information that K. was dressing.

When he was fully dressed he had to walk, with Willem treading on his heels, through the next room, which was now empty, into the adjoining one, whose double doors were flung open. This room, as K. knew quite well, had recently been taken by a Fräulein Bürstner, a typist, who went very early to work, came home late, and with whom he had exchanged little more than a few words in passing. Now the night table beside her bed had been pushed into the middle of the floor to serve as a desk, and the Inspector was sitting behind it. He had crossed his legs, and one arm was resting on the back of the chair.

In a corner of the room three young men were standing looking at Fräulein Bürstner's photographs, which were stuck into a mat hanging on the wall. A white blouse dangled from the latch of the open window. In the window over the way the two old creatures were again stationed, but they had enlarged their party, for behind them, towering head and shoulders above them, stood a man with a shirt open at the neck and a reddish, pointed beard, which he kept pinching and twisting with his fingers. "Joseph K.?" asked the Inspector, perhaps merely to draw K.'s roving glance upon himself, K. nodded. "You are presumably very much surprised at the events of this morning?" asked the Inspector, with both hands rearranging the few things that lay on the night table, a candle and a matchbox, a book and a pincushion, as if they were objects which he required for his interrogation. "Certainly," said K., and he was filled with pleasure at having encountered a sensible man at last, with whom he could discuss the matter. "Certainly, I am surprised, but I am by no means very much surprised." "Not very much surprised?" asked the Inspector, setting the candle in the middle of the table and then grouping the other things round it. "Perhaps you misunderstand me," K. hastened to add. "I mean"—here K. stopped and looked round him for a chair. "I suppose I may sit down?" he asked. "It's not usual," answered the Inspector. "I mean," said K. without further parley, "that

I am very much surprised, of course, but when one has lived for thirty years in this world and had to fight one's way through it, as I have had to do, one becomes hardened to surprises and doesn't take them too seriously. Particularly the one this morning." "Why particularly the one this morning?" "I won't say that I regard the whole thing as a joke, for the preparations that have been made seem too elaborate for that. The whole staff of the boarding-house would have to be involved, as well as all you people, and that would be past a joke. So I don't say that it's a joke." "Quite right," said the Inspector, looking to see how many matches there were in the matchbox. "But on the other hand," K. went on, turning to everybody there—he wanted to bring in the three young men standing beside the photographs as well—"on the other hand, it can't be an affair of any great importance either. I argue this from the fact that though I am accused of something, I cannot recall the slightest offense that might be charged against me. But that even is of minor importance, the real question is, who accuses me? What authority is conducting these proceedings? Are you officers of the law? None of you has a uniform, unless your suit"—here he turned to Franz—"is to be considered a uniform, but it's more like a tourist's outfit. I demand a clear answer to these questions, and I feel sure that after an explanation we shall be able to part from each other on the best of terms." The Inspector flung the matchbox down on the table. "You are laboring under a great delusion," he said. "These gentlemen here and myself have no standing whatever in this affair of yours, indeed we know hardly anything about it. We might wear the most official uniforms and your case would not be a penny the worse. I can't even confirm that you are charged with an offense, or rather I don't know whether you are. You are under arrest, certainly, more than that I do not know. Perhaps the warders have given you a different impression, but they are only irresponsible gossips. However, if I can't answer your questions, I can at least give you a piece of advice; think less about us and of what is going to happen to you, think more about yourself instead. And don't make such an outcry about your feeling innocent, it spoils the not unfavorable impression you make in other respects. Also you should be far more reticent, nearly everything you have just said could have been implied in your behavior with the help of a word here and there, and in any case does not redound particularly to your credit."

K. stared at the Inspector. Was he to be taught lessons in manners by a man probably younger than himself? To be punished for his frankness by a rebuke? And about the cause of his arrest and about its instigator was he to learn nothing?

He was thrown into a certain agitation, and began to walk up and down—nobody hindered him—pushed back his cuffs, fingered his shirt-front, ruffled his hair, and as he passed the three young men said: "This is sheer nonsense!" Whereupon they turned toward him and regarded him sympathetically but gravely; at last he came to a stand before the Inspector's table. "Hasterer, the lawyer, is a personal friend of mine," he said. "May I telephone to him?" "Certainly," replied the Inspector, "but I don't see what sense there would be in that, unless you have some private business of your own to consult him about." "What sense would there be in that?" cried K., more in amazement than exasperation. "What kind of man are you, then? You ask me to be sensible and you carry on in the most senseless way imaginable yourself! It's enough to sicken the dogs. People first fall upon me in my own house and then lounge about the room and put me through my paces for your benefit. What sense would there be in telephoning to a lawyer when I'm supposed to be under arrest? All right, I won't telephone." "But do telephone if you want to," replied the Inspector, waving an arm toward the entrance hall, where the telephone was, "please do telephone." "No, I don't want to now," said K., going over to the window. Across the street the party of three was still on the watch, and their enjoyment of the spectacle received its first slight check when K. appeared at the window. The two old people moved as if to get up, but the man at the back pacified them. "Here's a fine crowd of spectators!" cried K. in a loud voice to the Inspector, pointing at them with his finger. "Go away," he shouted across. The three of them immediately retreated a few steps, the two ancients actually took cover behind the younger man, who shielded them with his massive body and to judge from the movements of his lips was saying something which, owing to the distance, could not be distinguished. Yet they did not remove themselves altogether, but seemed to be waiting for the chance to return to the window again unobserved. "Officious, inconsiderate wretches!" said K. as he turned back to the room again. The Inspector was possibly of the same mind, K. fancied, as far as he could tell from a hasty sideglance. But it was equally possible that the Inspector had not even been listening, for he had pressed one hand firmly on the table and seemed to be comparing the length of his fingers. The two warders sat on a chest draped with an embroidered cloth, rubbing their knees. The three young men were looking aimlessly round them with their hands on their hips. It was as quiet as in some deserted office. "Come, gentlemen," cried K.— it seemed to him for the moment as if he were responsible for all of them— "from the look of you this affair of mine seems to be settled. In my opinion the best thing now would be to bother no more about the justice or injustice of your behavior and settle the matter amicably by shaking hands on it. If you are of the same opinion, why, then—" and he stepped over to the Inspector's table and held out his hand. The Inspector raised his eyes, bit his lips, and looked at K.'s hand stretched out to him; K. still believed he was going to close with the offer. But instead he got up, seized a hard round hat lying on Fräulein Bürstner's bed, and with both hands put it carefully on his head, as if he were trying it on for the first time. "How simple it all seems to you!" he said to K. as he did so, "You think we should settle the matter amicably, do you? No, no, that really can't be done. On the other hand I don't mean to suggest that you should give up hope. Why should you? You are only under arrest, nothing more. I was requested to inform you of this. I have done so, and I have also observed your reactions. That's enough for today, and we can say good-by, though only for the time being, naturally. You'll be going to the Bank now, I suppose?" "To the Bank?" asked K. "I thought I was under arrest?" K. asked the question with a certain defiance, for though his offer to shake hands had been ignored, he felt more and more independent of all these people, especially now that the Inspector had risen to his feet. He was playing with them. He considered the idea of running after them to the front door as they left and challenging them to take him prisoner. So he said again: "How can I go to the Bank, if I am under arrest?" "Ah, I see," said the Inspector, who had already reached the door. "You have misunderstood me. You are under arrest, certainly, but that need not hinder you from going about your business. Nor will you be prevented from leading your ordinary life." "Then being arrested isn't so very bad," said K., going up to the Inspector. "I never suggested that it was," said the Inspector. "But in that case it would seem there was no particular necessity to tell me about it," said K., moving still closer. The others had drawn near too. They were all gathered now in a little space beside the door. "It was my duty," said the Inspector. "A stupid duty," said K. inflexibly. "That may be," replied the Inspector, "but we needn't waste our time with such arguments. I was assuming that you would want to go to the Bank. As you are such a quibbler over words, let me add that I am not forcing you to go to the Bank, I was merely assuming that you would want to go. And to facilitate that, and render your arrival at the Bank as unobtrusive as possible, I have detained these three gentlemen here, who are colleagues of yours, to be at your disposal." "What?" cried K., gaping at the three of them. These insignificant anemic young men, whom he had observed only as a group standing beside the photographs, were actually clerks in the Bank, not colleagues of his— that was putting it too strongly and indicated a gap in the omniscience of the Inspector—but they were subordinate employees of the Bank all the same. How could he have failed to notice that? He must have been very much taken up with the Inspector and the warders not to recognize these three young men. The stiff Rabensteiner swinging his arms, the fair Kullich with the deep-set eyes, and Kaminer with his insupportable smile, caused by a chronic muscular twitch. "Good morning!" said K. after a pause, holding out his hand to the three politely bowing figures. "I didn't recognize you. Well, shall we go to our work now, eh?" The young men nodded, smilingly and eagerly, as if they had been waiting all the time merely for this, but when K. turned to get his hat, which he had left in his room, they all fled one after the other to fetch it, which

seemed to indicate a certain embarrassment. K. stood still and watched them through the two open doors; the languid Rabensteiner, naturally, brought up the rear, for he merely minced along at an elegant trot. Kaminer handed over the hat and K. had to tell himself expressly, as indeed he had often to do in the Bank, that Kaminer's smile was not intentional, that the man could not smile intentionally if he tried. Then Frau Grubach, who did not appear to be particularly conscious of any guilt, opened the front door to let the whole company out, and K. glanced down, as so often before, at her apron string, which made such an unreasonably deep cut in her massive body. Down below he decided, his watch in his hand, to take a taxi so as to save any further delay in reaching the Bank, for he was already half an hour late. Kaminer ran to the corner to get a taxi, the other two were obviously doing their best to distract K., when suddenly Kullich pointed to the opposite house door, where the tall man with the reddish, pointed beard was emerging into sight, and immediately, a little embarrassed at showing himself in his full height, retreated against the wall and leaned there. The old couple must be still coming down the stairs. K. was annoyed at Kullich for drawing his attention to the man, whom he had already identified, indeed whom he had actually expected to see. "Don't look across," he said hurriedly, without noticing how strange it must seem to speak in that fashion to grown-up men. But no explanation proved necessary, for at that moment the taxi arrived, they took their seats and drove off. Then K. remembered that he had not noticed the Inspector and the warders leaving, the Inspector had usurped his attention so that he did not recognize the three clerks, and the clerks in turn had made him oblivious of the Inspector. That did not show much presence of mind, and K. resolved to be more careful in this respect. Yet in spite of himself he turned round and craned from the back of the car to see if he could perhaps catch sight of the Inspector and the warders. But he immediately turned away again and leaned back comfortably in the corner without even having attempted to distinguish one of them. Unlikely as it might seem, this was just the moment when he would have welcomed a few words from his companions, but the others seemed to be suddenly tired: Rabensteiner gazed out to the right, Kullich to the left, and only Kaminer faced him with his nervous grin, which, unfortunately, on grounds of humanity could not be made a subject of conversation.

Questions for Critical Thinking

1. Summarize the events that disrupt Joseph K.'s "fine morning."

2. Who do you think Joseph K. represents? Explain.

21

THE AGE OF THE MASSES
AND THE ZENITH OF MODERNISM
1914–1945

ELIE WIESEL
Selection from *Night*

Of all the moral dilemmas raised by World War II, including America's dropping of atomic bombs on nonstrategic cities and both Allied and Axis air attacks on civilian populations, the dominant issue in the postwar world has been the Holocaust—Nazi Germany's master plan. Termed by its leaders the Final Solution, it was intended to eliminate the Jewish people, which involved the murder of 6 million Jews out of a population of 9 million, along with perhaps 6 million other people deemed undesirable, including gypsies, the handicapped and disabled, and homosexuals. In a sense it was the German people who provided the terrifying vision of the Holocaust. Race paranoia, especially anti-Semitism, or hatred of Jews, was deeply embedded in German culture, fostered by generations of nationalist-minded intellectuals since the dawn of the romantic era in about 1800. It was only during World War II, as part of a national response to war, that the Nazis provided the means to carry out this colossal crime.

Since World War II, in an effort to come to terms with these senseless killings, a vast Holocaust literature has emerged. Novels, short stories, plays, essays, memoirs, histories, anthropological studies, sociological analyses, and theological treatises, as well as countless films and TV productions, deal in part or in whole with this theme. The Hungarian writer Elie Wiesel (b. 1928), a survivor of a Nazi death camp, has been in the forefront of Holocaust literature. As a writer of international stature, Wiesel has kept the world's attention focused unflinchingly on the Holocaust, lest it be forgotten and history repeat itself.

Wiesel was first interned by the Nazis in 1944 at Auschwitz, Poland, where his mother and youngest sister were killed in gas chambers; his two older sisters were taken elsewhere and killed. He and his father were then moved to the camp in Buchenwald, Germany, where his father died from hunger and disease. Wiesel survived to be freed by American troops during the war's final days. After the war, he became part of the homeless refugee population called displaced persons, or "D.P.'s," roaming over Europe, until he settled in Paris to study philosophy and literature. From Paris he traveled to Asia, where he shifted his interest to comparative mysticism, a subject that led him to make the Holocaust his lifelong literary project. He became a U.S. citizen in 1963 and was awarded the Nobel Peace Prize in 1986.

Reading the Selection

Wiesel's novel *Night* (1960) belongs to Holocaust literature, the genre whose central concern is the question of how a beneficent God could have allowed the Final Solution. One of the first and in many ways the most powerful of the Holocaust's accounts, it not only chronicles the atrocities inflicted on the Jews but also raises the question of God's apparent indifference to human suffering.

In *Night*, prior to this selection: The time is near the end of World War II, when Russian invaders appeared to have the Germans on the run. The scholarly narrator, living in an isolated village, tells of the disruption of his biblical study. A fellow Jew, fleeing from the Nazis, warns him and the rest of the village about mass killings. The villagers fail to heed this warning, only to fall victim to a last-ditch Nazi effort that results in shipping the entire village to a death camp. In the following selection, the Holocaust's horror is personalized in scenes of humiliation, deprivation, and murder. In the end, the narrator's spirit is crushed, as he questions God's existence.

∞

THE BELOVED OBJECTS that we had carried with us from 1
place to place were now left behind in the wagon and,
with them, finally, our illusions.

Every few yards, there stood an SS[1] man, his machine
gun trained on us. Hand in hand we followed the throng.

An SS came toward us wielding a club. He
commanded:

"Men to the left! Women to the right!"

Eight words spoken quietly, indifferently, without 5
emotion. Eight simple, short words. Yet that was the moment when I left my mother. There was no time to think,
and I already felt my father's hand press against mine:
we were alone. In a fraction of a second I could see my
mother, my sisters, move to the right. Tzipora was holding Mother's hand. I saw them walking farther and farther away; Mother was stroking my sister's blond hair, as
if to protect her. And I walked on with my father, with the
men. I didn't know that this was the moment in time and
the place where I was leaving my mother and Tzipora forever. I kept walking, my father holding my hand.

Behind me, an old man fell to the ground. Nearby, an
SS man replaced his revolver in its holster.

My hand tightened its grip on my father. All I could
think of was not to lose him. Not to remain alone.

The SS officers gave the order.

"Form ranks of fives!"

There was a tumult. It was imperative to stay together. 10

"Hey, kid, how old are you?"

The man interrogating me was an inmate. I could not
see his face, but his voice was weary and warm.

"Fifteen."

"No. You're eighteen."

"But I'm not," I said. "I'm fifteen." 15

"Fool. Listen to what *I* say."

Then he asked my father, who answered:

"I'm fifty."

"No." The man now sounded angry. "Not fifty. You're
forty. Do you hear? Eighteen and forty."

He disappeared into the darkness. Another inmate 20
appeared. unleashing a stream of invectives:

"Sons of bitches, why have you come here: Tell
me, why?"

Someone dared to reply:

"What do you think? That we came here of our own
free will? That we asked to come here?"

The other seemed ready to kill him:

"Shut up, you moron, or I'll tear you to pieces! You 25
should have hanged yourselves rather than come here.
Didn't you know what was in store for you here in
Auschwitz? You didn't know? In 1944?"

True. We didn't know. Nobody had told us. He
couldn't believe his ears. His tone became even harsher:

"Over there. Do you see the chimney over there? Do
you see it? And the flames, do you see them?" (Yes, we
saw the flames.) "Over there, that's where they will take
you. Over there will be your grave. You still don't understand? You sons of bitches. Don't you understand anything? You will be burned! Burned to a cinder! Turned
into ashes!"

His anger changed into fury. We stood stunned, petrified. Could this be just a nightmare? An unimaginable
nightmare?

I heard whispers around me:

"We must do something. We can't let them kill us like 30
that, like cattle in the slaughterhouse. We must revolt."

There were, among us, a few tough young men. They
actually had knives and were urging us to attack the
armed guards. One of them was muttering:

"Let the world learn about the existence of Auschwitz.
Let everybody find out about it while they still have a
chance to escape . . ."

But the older men begged their sons not to be foolish:

"We mustn't give up hope, even now as the sword
hangs over our heads. So taught our sages . . ."

---

[1] **SS** Abbreviation of *Schutzstaffel* (German, "Protection Squad"),
the elite black-shirted troops of the Nazi Party. Founded in 1925
as Hitler's personal bodyguards, the SS amassed vast military
and police power in Nazi Germany.

The wind of revolt died down. We continued to walk until we came to a crossroads. Standing in the middle of it was, though I didn't know it then, Dr. Mengele, the notorious Dr. Mengele.[2] He looked like the typical SS officer: a cruel, though not unintelligent, face, complete with monocle. He was holding a conductor's baton and was surrounded by officers. The baton was moving constantly, sometimes to the right, sometimes to the left.

In no time, I stood before him.

"Your age?" he asked, perhaps trying to sound paternal.

"I'm eighteen." My voice was trembling.

"In good health?"

"Yes."

"Your profession?"

Tell him that I was a student?

"Farmer." I heard myself saying.

This conversation lasted no more than a few seconds. It seemed like an eternity.

The baton pointed to the left. I took half a step forward. I first wanted to see where they would send my father. Were he to have gone to the right, I would have run after him.

The baton, once more, moved to the left. A weight lifted from my heart.

We did not know, as yet, which was the better side, right or left, which road led to prison and which to the crematoria. Still, I was happy, I was near my father. Our procession continued slowly to move forward.

Another inmate came over to us:

"Satisfied?"

"Yes," someone answered.

"Poor devils, you are heading for the crematorium."

He seemed to be telling the truth. Not far from us, flames, huge flames, were rising from a ditch. Something was being burned there. A truck drew close and unloaded its hold: small children. Babies! Yes, I did see this, with my own eyes . . . children thrown into the flames. (Is it any wonder that ever since then, sleep tends to elude me?)

So that was where we were going. A little farther on, there was another, larger pit for adults.

I pinched myself: Was I still alive? Was I awake? How was it possible that men, women, and children were being burned and that the world kept silent? No. All this could not be real. A nightmare perhaps . . . Soon I would wake up with a start, my heart pounding, and find that I was back in the room of my childhood, with my books.

My father's voice tore me from my daydreams:

"What a shame, a shame that you did not go with your mother . . . I saw many children your age go with their mothers . . ."

His voice was terribly sad. I understood that he did not wish to see what they would do to me. He did not wish to see his only son go up in flames.

My forehead was covered with cold sweat. Still, I told him that I could not believe that human beings were being burned in our times, the world would never tolerate such crimes . . .

"The world? The world is not interested in us. Today, everything is possible, even the crematoria . . ." His voice broke.

"Father," I said." If that is true, then I don't want to wait. I'll run into the electrified barbed wire. That would be easier than a slow death in the flames."

He didn't answer. He was weeping. His body was shaking. Everybody around us was weeping. Someone began to recite Kaddish, the prayer for the dead. I don't know whether, during the history of the Jewish people, men have ever before recited Kaddish for themselves.

"*Yisgadal veyiskadash shmey raba*. . . . May His name be celebrated and sanctified . . ." whispered my father.

For the first time, I felt anger rising within me. Why should I sanctify His name? The Almighty, the eternal and terrible Master of the Universe, chose to be silent. What was there to thank Him for.

We continued our march. We were coming closer and closer to the pit, from which an infernal heat was rising. Twenty more steps. If I was going to kill myself, this was the time. Our column had only some fifteen steps to go. I bit my lips so that my father would not hear my teeth chattering. Ten more steps. Eight. Seven. We were walking slowly, as one follows a hearse, our own funeral procession. Only four more steps. Three. There it was now, very close to us, the pit and its flames. I gathered all that remained of my strength in order to break rank and throw myself onto the barbed wire. Deep down, I was saying good-bye to my father, to the whole universe, and, against my will, I found myself whispering the words: "*Yisgadal veyiskadash shmey raba*. . . . May His name be exalted and sanctified . . ." My heart was about to burst. There, I was face-to-face with the Angel of Death . . .

No. Two steps from the pit, we were ordered to turn left and herded into barracks.

I squeezed my father's hand. He said:

"Do you remember Mrs. Schächter, in the train?"

NEVER SHALL I FORGET that night, the first night in camp, that turned my life into one long night seven times sealed.

Never shall I forget that smoke.

Never shall I forget the small faces of the children whose bodies I saw transformed into smoke under a silent sky.

Never shall I forget those flames that consumed my faith forever.

Never shall I forget the nocturnal silence that deprived me for all eternity of the desire to live.

Never shall I forget those moments that murdered my God and my soul and turned my dreams to ashes.

Never shall I forget those things, even were I condemned to live as long as God Himself.

Never.

THE BARRACK we had been assigned to was very long. On the roof, a few bluish skylights. I thought: This is what the antechamber of hell must look like. So many crazed men, so much shouting, so much brutality.

---

[2] **Mengele** Josef Mengele (1911–1979), Nazi doctor at Auschwitz (1943–1945), who determined the fate of prisoners, selecting some for the gas chambers and others for medical experiments.

Dozens of inmates were there to receive us, sticks in hand, striking anywhere, anyone, without reason. The orders came:

"Strip! Hurry up! *Raus!* Hold on only to your belt and your shoes . . ."

Our clothes were to be thrown on the floor at the back of the barrack. There was a pile there already. New suits, old ones, torn overcoats, rags. For us it meant true equality: nakedness. We trembled in the cold.

A few SS officers wandered through the room, look- 80 ing for strong men. If vigor was that appreciated, perhaps one should try to appear sturdy? My father thought the opposite. Better not to draw attention. (We later found out that he had been right. Those who were selected that day were incorporated into the Sonder-Kommando, the Kommando working in the crematoria. Béla Katz, the son of an important merchant of my town, had arrived in Birkenau with the first transport, one week ahead of us. When he found out that we were there, he succeeded in slipping us a note. He told us that having been chosen because of his strength, he had been forced to place his own father's body into the furnace.)

The blows continued to rain on us:

"To the barber!"

Belt and shoes in hand, I let myself be dragged along to the barbers. Their clippers tore out our hair, shaved every hair on our bodies. My head was buzzing; the same thought surfacing over and over: not to be separated from my father.

Freed from the barbers' clutches, we began to wander about the crowd, finding friends, acquaintances. Every encounter filled us with joy—yes, joy: Thank God! You are still alive!

Some were crying. They used whatever strength they 85 had left to cry. Why had they let themselves be brought here? Why didn't they die in their beds? Their words were interspersed with sobs.

Suddenly someone threw his arms around me in a hug: Yehiel, the Sigheter rebbe's[3] brother. He was weeping bitterly. I thought he was crying with joy at still being alive.

"Don't cry, Yehiel," I said. "Don't waste your tears . . ."

"Not cry? We're on the threshold of death. Soon, we shall be inside . . . Do you understand? Inside. How could I not cry?"

I watched darkness fade through the bluish skylights in the roof. I no longer was afraid. I was overcome by fatigue.

The absent no longer entered our thoughts. One spoke 90 of them—who knows what happened to them?—but their fate was not on our minds. We were incapable of thinking. Our senses were numbed, everything was fading into a fog. We no longer clung to anything. The instincts of self-preservation, of self-defense, of pride, had all deserted us. In one terrifying moment of lucidity, I thought of us

as damned souls wandering through the void, souls condemned to wander through space until the end of time, seeking redemption, seeking oblivion, without any hope of finding either.

AROUND FIVE O'CLOCK in the morning, we were expelled from the barrack. The Kapos[4] were beating us again, but I no longer felt the pain. A glacial wind was enveloping us. We were naked, holding our shoes and belts. An order:

"Run!" And we ran. After a few minutes of running, a new barrack.

A barrel of foul-smelling liquid stood by the door. Disinfection. Everybody soaked in it. Then came a hot shower. All very fast. As we left the showers, we were chased outside. And ordered to run some more. Another barrack: the storeroom. Very long tables. Mountains of prison garb. As we ran, they threw the clothes at us: pants, jackets, shirts . . .

In a few seconds, we had ceased to be men. Had the situation not been so tragic, we might have laughed. We looked pretty strange! Meir Katz, a colossus, wore a child's pants, and Stern, a skinny little fellow, was floundering in a huge jacket. We immediately started to switch.

I glanced over at my father. How changed he looked! 95 His eyes were veiled. I wanted to tell him something, but I didn't know what.

The night had passed completely. The morning star shone in the sky. I too had become a different person. The student of Talmud,[5] the child I was, had been consumed by the flames. All that was left was a shape that resembled me. My soul had been invaded—and devoured—by a black flame.

So many events had taken place in just a few hours that I had completely lost all notion of time. When had we left our homes? And the ghetto? And the train? Only a week ago? One night? *One single night?*

How long had we been standing in the freezing wind? One hour? A single hour? Sixty minutes?

Surely it was a dream.

NOT FAR FROM US, prisoners were at work. Some were 100 digging holes, others were carrying sand. None as much as glanced at us. We were withered trees in the heart of the desert. Behind me, people were talking. I had no desire to listen to what they were saying, or to know who was speaking and what about. Nobody dared raise his voice, even though there was no guard around. We whispered. Perhaps because of the thick smoke that poisoned the air and stung the throat.

We were herded into yet another barrack, inside the Gypsy camp. We fell into ranks of five.

"And now, stop moving!"

---

[3] **Sigheter rebbe** Sigheter, during World War II, was a town in Hungary (today, in Romania). A rebbe is a charismatic leader; part of Hasidic Judaism.

---

[4] **Kapos** From Latin *capo,* head. A term for any functionary in Auschwitz.

[5] **Talmud** The authoritative collection of Jewish traditions of the Oral Law, which is in contrast to the Written Law or *The Holy Scriptures.* It includes commentaries and elaborations dating back to the second century CE.

There was no floor. A roof and four walls. Our feet sank into the mud.

Again, the waiting. I fell asleep standing up. I dreamed of a bed, of my mother's hand on my face. I woke: I was standing, my feet in the mud. Some people collapsed, sliding into the mud. Others shouted:

"Are you crazy? We were told to stand. Do you want 105 to get us all in trouble?"

As if all the troubles in the world were not already upon us.

Little by little, we all sat down in the mud. But we had to get up whenever a Kapo came in to check if, by chance, somebody had a new pair of shoes. If so, we had to hand them over. No use protesting: the blows multiplied and, in the end, one still had to hand them over.

I had new shoes myself. But as they were covered with a thick coat of mud, they had not been noticed. I thanked God, in an improvised prayer, for having created mud in His infinite and wondrous universe.

Suddenly, the silence became more oppressive. An SS officer had come in and, with him, the smell of the Angel of Death.[6] We stared at his fleshy lips. He harangued us from the center of the barrack:

"You are in a concentration camp. In Auschwitz . . ." 110

A pause. He was observing the effect his words had produced. His face remains in my memory to this day. A tall man, in his thirties, crime written all over his forehead and his gaze. He looked at us as one would a pack of leprous dogs clinging to life.

"Remember," he went on. "Remember it always, let it be graven in your memories. You are in Auschwitz. And Auschwitz is not a convalescent home. It is a concentration camp. Here, you must work. If you don't you will go straight to the chimney. To the crematorium. Work or crematorium—the choice is yours."

We had already lived through a lot that night. We thought that nothing could frighten us anymore. But his harsh words sent shivers through us. The word "chimney" here was not an abstraction: it floated in the air, mingled with the smoke. It was, perhaps, the only word that had a real meaning in this place. He left the barrack. The Kapos arrived, shouting:

"All specialists—locksmiths, carpenters, electricians, watchmakers—one step forward!"

The rest of us were transferred to yet another bar- 115 rack, this one of stone. We had permission to sit down. A Gypsy inmate was in charge.

---

[6] **Death** SS members wore caps with death's-head symbols (see footnote 1).

My father suddenly had a colic attack. He got up and asked politely, in German, "Excuse me . . . Could you tell me where the toilets are located?"

The Gypsy stared at him for a long time, from head to toe. As if he wished to ascertain that the person addressing him was actually a creature of flesh and bone, a human being with a body and a belly. Then, as if waking from a deep sleep, he slapped my father with such force that he fell down and then crawled back to his place on all fours.

I stood petrified. What had happened to me? My father had just been struck, in front of me, and I had not even blinked. I had watched and kept silent. Only yesterday, I would have dug my nails into this criminal's flesh. Had I changed that much? So fast? Remorse began to gnaw at me. All I could think was: I shall never forgive them for this. My father must have guessed my thoughts, because he whispered in my ear:

"It doesn't hurt." His cheek still bore the red mark of the hand.

"EVERYBODY outside!"   120

A dozen or so Gypsies had come to join our guard. The clubs and whips were cracking around me. My feet were running on their own. I tried to protect myself from the blows by hiding behind others. It was spring. The sun was shining.

"Fall in, five by five!"

The prisoners I had glimpsed that morning were working nearby. No guard in sight, only the chimney's shadow . . . Lulled by the sunshine and my dreams, I felt someone pulling at my sleeve. It was my father: "Come on, son."

We marched. Gates opened and closed. We continued to march between the barbed wire. At every step, white signs with black skulls looked down on us. The inscription: WARNING! DANGER OF DEATH. What irony. Was there here a single place where one was *not* in danger of death?

The Gypsies had stopped next to a barrack. They 125 were replaced by SS men, who encircled us with machine guns and police dogs.

The march had lasted half an hour. Looking around me, I noticed that the barbed wire was behind us. We had left the camp.

It was a beautiful day in May. The fragrances of spring were in the air. The sun was setting.

But no sooner had we taken a few more steps than we saw the barbed wire of another camp. This one had an iron gate with the overhead inscription: ARBEIT MACHT FREI. Work makes you free.

Auschwitz.

Questions for Critical Thinking

1. Summarize the scene depicted in this selection—the Wiesel family as it enters the Auschwitz camp.

2. What lessons of survival does the young Elie quickly learn? What is Wiesel's message for his readers?

VIRGINIA WOOLF
Selections from *A Room of One's Own*

Virginia Woolf (1882–1941) was a major force in the modernist project of dethroning the past and establishing the reign of newness everywhere. Much of her power as a catalyst sprang from her role in the Bloomsbury group, the coterie of writers who lived between the wars in the Bloomsbury area of London and had a strong impact on letters, art, and philosophy. A founder of the Hogarth Press, she influenced what people of this period read, publishing writers such as T. S. Eliot (see "The Love Song of J. Alfred Prufrock"), who shared her modernist outlook. Through her essays, she assisted in the triumph of new art, as, for example, in her 1910 piece welcoming the first London exhibit of the postimpressionist school. A tough-minded critic (*The Common Reader,* 2 vols., 1925, 1932), she interpreted and made popular the era's new writings. Beyond all this, she was a novelist trying new narrative methods.

Woolf's novels reflected distaste for realism, the style favored by late-nineteenth-century writers who focused on the surface of life while ignoring the mind's intersection with the external world. Woolf thought such intersections crucial, for it was there that readers achieved insight by understanding not only facts but their symbolic import. To this end, she adopted the stream-of-consciousness method, pioneered by the Irish writer James Joyce, to explore how different characters in her novels reacted and felt about each other and their environment. For example, in *Mrs. Dalloway* (1925) she skillfully showed her upper-class heroine's complexity beneath a conventional exterior by presenting in a single day all the lives that touched hers, near or far, even unseen. Partly modeled on herself (Woolf was the daughter of Leslie Stephen, a famous man of letters in nineteenth-century London), Mrs. Dalloway was the society woman Woolf might have become had she not pursued a literary career.

Reading the Selections

Virginia Woolf wrote *A Room of One's Own* (1929) after her reputation had been established as an innovative and successful novelist. She uses her experiences as a woman writer to clarify her own opinions on the intellectual subjection of women, examines the role of female writers in history and literature, and calls for changes in society to allow more women to express themselves in a variety of ways. Her essay's impact went beyond the literary world, as it helped rekindle the feminist movement, which had died down once British women won the right to vote in 1918. Today, advocates for women's rights still refer to *A Room of One's Own* as one of the most persuasive and influential works in women's literature.

A Room of One's Own is a monograph expanded from two lectures Woolf delivered at Cambridge University. Its conversational style and her references to the audience set a casual tone. Woolf's mastery of imagery and illustrations of everyday events enliven what otherwise might have been a numbing and polemic discussion on the rights of women. A fictional figure, Mary Beton, who is Woolf's voice, becomes the vehicle for the author's personal experiences and the mouthpiece for her main arguments. However, Woolf, at the end of the work, speaks directly to her audience and encourages her readers to take advantage of the recent changes in society to better their lives and expand their careers.

Through the narrative of Mary Beton's fictitious life and adventures, Woolf lays out her arguments forcefully and clearly. She asserts that women have not been able to succeed because they are poor, and they are poor because they have been burdened with so many children. Women have also been the victims of distractions that society places upon them, and these conditions have prevented them from creating works of literature. Furthermore, she observes, men, in what is a patriarchal world, have written the histories and the great literary works—and from their point of view. Woolf, after a quick survey of women writers, concludes that very few women have contributed to the field of literature. Having noted the reasons that women have not been successful writers, Woolf then offers her formula for women to succeed. Women, she argues, need a certain amount of money or financial support, education, a corps of women professionals as models, and a tradition of women writers. What is required, then, is a room of one's own to write, to create, and to allow the genius within to flourish.

◈

Chapter One

But, you may say, we asked you to speak about women and fiction—what has that got to do with a room of one's own? I will try to explain. When you asked me to speak about women and fiction I sat down on the banks of a river and began to wonder what the words meant. They might mean simply a few remarks about Fanny Burney; a few more about Jane Austen; a tribute to the Brontës and a sketch of Haworth Parsonage under snow; some witticisms if possible about Miss Mitford; a respectful allusion to George Eliot; a reference to Mrs. Gaskell[7] and one would have done. But at second sight the words seemed not so simple. The title women and fiction might mean, and you may have meant it to mean, women and what they are like; or it might mean women and the fiction that they write; or it might mean women and the fiction that is written about them; or it might mean that somehow all three are inextricably mixed together and you want me to consider them in that light. But when I began to consider the subject in this last way, which seemed the most interesting. I soon saw that it had one fatal drawback. I should never be able to come to a conclusion. I should never be able to fulfil what is, I understand, the first duty of a lecturer—to hand you after an hour's discourse a nugget of pure truth to wrap up between the pages of your notebooks and keep on the mantel-piece for ever. All I could do was to offer you an opinion upon one minor point—a woman must have money and a room of her own if she is to write fiction; and that, as you will see, leaves the great problem of the true nature of woman and the true nature of fiction unsolved. I have shirked the duty of coming to a conclusion upon these two questions—women and fiction remain, so far as I am concerned, unsolved problems. But in order to make some amends I am going to do what I can to show you how I arrived at this opinion about the room and the money. I am going to develop in your presence as fully and freely as I can the train of thought which led me to think this. Perhaps if I lay bare the ideas, the prejudices, that lie behind this statement you will find that they have some bearing upon women and some upon fiction. At any rate, when a subject is highly controversial—and any question about sex is that—one cannot hope to tell the truth. One can only show how one came to hold whatever opinion one does hold. One can only give one's audience the chance of drawing their own conclusions as they observe the limitations, the prejudices, the idiosyncrasies of the speaker. Fiction here is likely to contain more truth than fact. Therefore I propose, making use of all the liberties and licences of a novelist, to tell you the story of the two days that preceded my coming here—how, bowed down by the weight of the subject which you have laid upon my shoulders, I pondered it, and made it work in and out of my daily life. I need not say that what I am about to describe has no existence; Oxbridge is an invention; so is Fernham[8]; "I" is only a convenient term for somebody who has no real being. Lies will flow from my lips, but there may perhaps be some truth mixed up with them; it is for you to seek out this truth and to decide whether any part of it is worth keeping. If not, you will of course throw the whole of it into the wastepaper basket and forget all about it. . . .

---

[7] **Fanny Burney, Jane Austen, the Brontës, Miss Mitford, George Eliot, Mrs. Gaskell** English women writers whose novels and works won wide audiences in their own times; many of their books remain popular, and some are now considered classics. Fanny Burney was one of the first of these writers; she lived in the late eighteenth and early nineteenth centuries. Jane Austen was a prolific novelist of the early nineteenth century whose books are still read. The Brontës refer to the three sisters—Charlotte, Emily, and Anne—who wrote novels in the first part of the nineteenth century. Miss Mitford was Mary Russell Mitford, an early-nineteenth-century novelist and dramatist. George Eliot was the pen name of Mary Ann Evans, a nineteenth-century novelist. Mrs. Gaskill was Elizabeth Gaskell, who wrote novels in the nineteenth century.

---

[8] **Oxbridge, Fernham** Oxbridge, as an invention of Woolf's, represents Oxford University and Cambridge University. Fernham, also a figment of Woolf's writings, is one of the women's colleges at Oxbridge.

Chapter Two

The scene, if I may ask you to follow me, was now changed. The leaves were still falling, but in London now, not Oxbridge; and I must ask you to imagine a room, like many thousands, with a window looking across people's hats and vans and motor-cars to other windows, and on the table inside the room a blank sheet of paper on which was written in large letters WOMEN AND FICTION, but no more. The inevitable sequel to lunching and dining at Oxbridge seemed, unfortunately, to be a visit to the British Museum. One must strain off what was personal and accidental in all these impressions and so reach the pure fluid, the essential oil of truth. For that visit to Oxbridge and the luncheon and the dinner had started a swarm of questions. Why did men drink wine and women water? Why was one sex so prosperous and the other so poor? What effect has poverty on fiction? What conditions are necessary for the creation of works of art?—a thousand questions at once suggested themselves. But one needed answers, not questions; and an answer was only to be had by consulting the learned and the unprejudiced, who have removed themselves above the strife of tongue and the confusion of body and issued the result of their reasoning and research in books which are to be found in the British Museum. If truth is not to be found on the shelves of the British Museum, where, I asked myself, picking up a notebook and a pencil, is truth?

Thus provided, thus confident and enquiring, I set out in the pursuit of truth. The day, though not actually wet, was dismal, and the streets in the neighborhood of the Museum were full of open coal-holes, down which sacks were showering; four-wheeled cabs were drawing up and depositing on the pavement corded boxes containing, presumably, the entire wardrobe of some Swiss or Italian family seeking fortune or refuge or some other desirable commodity which is to be found in the boarding-houses of Bloomsbury in the winter. The usual hoarse-voiced men paraded the streets with plants on barrows. Some shouted; others sang. London was like a workshop. London was like a machine. We were all being shot backwards and forwards on this plain foundation to make some pattern. The British Museum was another department of the factory. The swing-doors swung open; and there one stood under the vast dome, as if one were a thought in the huge bald forehead which is so splendidly encircled by a band of famous names. One went to the counter; one took a slip of paper; one opened a volume of the catalogue, and . . . . . the five dots here indicate five separate minutes of stupefaction, wonder and bewilderment. Have you any notion how many books are written about women in the course of one year? Have you any notion how many are written by men? Are you aware that you are, perhaps, the most discussed animal in the universe? Here had I come with a notebook and a pencil proposing to spend a morning reading, supposing that at the end of the morning I should have transferred the truth to my notebook. But I

should need to be a herd of elephants, I thought, and a wilderness of spiders, desperately referring to the animals that are reputed longest lived and most multitudinously eyed, to cope with all this. I should need claws of steel and beak of brass even to penetrate the husk. How shall I ever find the grains of truth embedded in all this mass of paper, I asked myself, and in despair began running my eye up and down the long list of titles. Even the names of the books gave me food for thought. Sex and its nature might well attract doctors and biologists; but what was surprising and difficult of explanation was the fact that sex—woman, that is to say—also attracts agreeable essayists, light-fingered novelists, young men who have taken the M.A. degree; men who have taken no degree; men who have no apparent qualification save that they are not women. Some of these books were, on the face of it, frivolous and facetious; but many, on the other hand, were serious and prophetic, moral and hortatory. Merely to read the titles suggested innumerable schoolmasters, innumerable clergymen mounting their platforms and pulpits and holding forth with a loquacity which far exceeded the hour usually allotted to such discourse on this one subject. It was a most strange phenomenon; and apparently—here I consulted the letter M—one confined to male sex. Women do not write books about men—a fact that I could not help welcoming with relief, for if I had first to read all that men have written about women, then all that women have written about men, the aloe that flowers once in a hundred years would flower twice before I could set pen to paper. So, making a perfectly arbitrary choice of a dozen volumes or so, I sent my slips of paper to lie in the wire tray, and waited in my stall, among the other seekers for the essential oil of truth.

What could be the reason, then, of this curious disparity, I wondered, drawing cart-wheels on the slips of paper provided by the British taxpayer for other purposes. Why are women, judging from this catalogue, so much more interesting to men than men are to women? A very curious fact it seemed, and my mind wandered to picture the lives of men who spend their time in writing books about women; whether they were old or young, married or unmarried, red-nosed or hump-backed—anyhow, it was flattering, vaguely, to feel oneself the object of such attention, provided that it was not entirely bestowed by the crippled and the infirm—so I pondered until all such frivolous thoughts were ended by an avalanche of books sliding down on to the desk in front of me. Now the trouble began. The student who has been trained in research at Oxbridge has no doubt some method of shepherding his question past all distractions till it runs into its answer as a sheep runs into its pen. The student by my side, for instance, who was copying assiduously from a scientific manual was, I felt sure, extracting pure nuggets of the essential ore every ten minutes or so. His little grunts of satisfaction indicated so much. But if, unfortunately, one has had no training in a university, the question far from being shepherded to its pen flies like a frightened flock hither and thither, helter-skelter, pursued by a whole pack of hounds. Professors, schoolmasters, sociologists, clergymen, novelists, essayists, journalists, men who had no qualification save that they were not women, chased my simple and single question—Why are women poor?—until it became fifty questions; until the fifty questions leapt frantically into mid-stream and were carried away. Every page in my notebook was scribbled over with notes. . . .

Chapter Three

It was disappointing not to have brought back in the evening some important statement, some authentic fact. Women are poorer than men because—this or that. Perhaps now it would be better to give up seeking for the truth, and receiving on one's head an avalanche of opinion hot as lava, discoloured as dish-water. It would be better to draw the curtains; to shut out distractions; to light the lamp; to narrow the enquiry and to ask the historian, who records not opinions but facts, to describe under what conditions women lived, not throughout the ages, but in England, say in the time of Elizabeth.

For it is a perennial puzzle why no woman wrote a word of that extraordinary literature when every other man, it seemed, was capable of song or sonnet. What were the conditions in which women lived, I asked myself; for fiction, imaginative work that is, is not dropped like a pebble upon the ground, as science may be; fiction is like a spider's web, attached ever so lightly perhaps, but still attached to life at all four corners. Often the attachment is scarcely perceptible; Shakespeare's plays, for instance, seem to hang there complete by themselves. But when the web is pulled askew, hooked up at the edge, torn in the middle, one remembers that these webs are not spun in mid-air by incorporeal creatures, but are the work of suffering human beings, and are attached to grossly material things, like health and money and the houses we live in.

I went, therefore, to the shelf where the histories stand and took down one of the latest, Professor Trevelyan's *History of England*.[9] Once more I looked up Women, found "position of," and turned to the pages indicated. "Wife-beating," I read, "was a recognised right of man, and was practised without shame by high as well as low . . . . Similarly," the historian goes on, "the daughter who refused to marry the gentleman of her parents' choice was liable to be locked up, beaten and flung about the room, without any shock being inflicted on public opinion. Marriage was not an affair of personal affection, but of family avarice, particularly in the 'chivalrous' upper classes. . . . Betrothal often took place while one or both of the parties was in the cradle, and marriage when they were scarcely out of the nurses' charge." That was about 1470, soon after Chaucer's time. The next reference to the position of women is some two hundred years later, in the time of the Stuarts. "It was still the exception for women of the upper and middle class to choose their own husbands, and when the husband had been assigned, he was lord and master, so far at least as law and custom could make him. Yet even so," Professor Trevelyan concludes, "neither Shakespeare's women nor those of authentic seventeenth-century memoirs, like the Verneys and the Hutchinsons, seem wanting in personality and character." Certainly,[10] if we consider it, Cleopatra must have had a way with her; Lady Macbeth, one would suppose, had a will of her own; Rosalind, one might conclude, was an attractive girl. Professor Trevelyan is speaking no more than the truth when he remarks that Shakespeare's women do not seem wanting in personality and character. Not being a historian, one might go even further and say that women have burnt like beacons in all the works of all the poets from the beginning of time—Clytemnestra, Antigone, Cleopatra, Lady Macbeth, Phèdre, Cressida, Rosalind, Desdemona, the Duchess of Malfi, among the dramatists; then among the prose writers: Millamant, Clarissa, Becky Sharp, Anna Karenina, Emma Bovary, Madame de Guermantes—the names flock to mind, nor do they recall women "lacking in personality and character." Indeed, if woman had no existence save in the fiction written by men, one would imagine her a person of the utmost importance; very various; heroic and mean; splendid and sordid; infinitely beautiful and

---

[9] **Professor Trevelyan's *History of England*** George Macaulay Trevelyan was a distinguished historian at Cambridge University whose *History of England* had been published in 1926, three years before Woolf wrote *A Room of One's Own*.

[10] "It remains a strange and almost inexplicable fact that in Athena's city, where women were kept in almost Oriental suppression as odalisques or drudges, the stage should yet have produced figures like Clytemnestra and Cassandra, Atossa and Antigone, Phèdre and Medea, and all the other heroines who dominate play after play of the 'misogynist' Euripides. But the paradox of this world where in real life a respectable woman could hardly show her face alone in the street, and yet on the stage woman equals or surpasses man, has never been satisfactorily explained. In modern tragedy the same predominance exists. At all events, a very cursory survey of Shakespeare's work (similarly with Webster, though not with Marlowe or Jonson) suffices to reveal how this dominance, this initiative of women, persists from Rosalind to Lady Macbeth. So too in Racine; six of his tragedies bear their heroines' names; and what male characters of his shall we set against Hermione and Andromaque, Bérénice and Roxane, Phèdre and Athalie? So again with Ibsen; what men shall we match with Solveig and Nora, Hedda and Hilda Wangel and Rebecca West?"—F. L. Lucas, *Tragedy*, pp. 114–15. (Author's Footnote)

hideous in the extreme; as great as a man, some think even greater. But this is woman in fiction. In fact, as Professor Trevelyan points out, she was locked up, beaten and flung about the room.

A very queer, composite being thus emerges. Imaginatively she is of the highest importance; practically she is completely insignificant. She pervades poetry from cover to cover; she is all but absent from history. She dominates the lives of kings and conquerors in fiction; in fact she was the slave of any boy whose parents forced a ring upon her finger. Some of the most inspired words, some of the most profound thoughts in literature fall from her lips; in real life she could hardly read, could scarcely spell, and was the property of her husband. . . .

∽

Chapter Six

Next day the light of the October morning was falling in dusty shafts through the uncurtained windows, and the hum of traffic rose from the street. London then was winding itself up again; the factory was astir; the machines were beginning. It was tempting, after all this reading, to look out of the window and see what London was doing on the morning of the twenty-sixth of October 1928. And what was London doing? Nobody, it seemed, was reading *Antony and Cleopatra.* London was wholly indifferent, it appeared, to Shakespeare's plays. Nobody cared a straw—and I do not blame them—for the future of fiction, the death of poetry or the development by the average woman of a prose style completely expressive of her mind. If opinions upon any of these matters had been chalked on the pavement, nobody would have stooped to read them. The nonchalance of the hurrying feet would have rubbed them out in half an hour. Here came an errand-boy; here a woman with a dog on a lead. The fascination of the London street is that no two people are ever alike; each seems bound on some private affair of his own. There were the business-like, with their little bags; there were the drifters rattling sticks upon area railings; there were affable characters to whom the streets serve for clubroom, hailing men in carts and giving information without being asked for it. Also there were funerals to which men, thus suddenly reminded of the passing of their own bodies, lifted their hats. And then a very distinguished gentleman came slowly down a doorstep and paused to avoid collision with a bustling lady who had, by some means or other, acquired a splendid fur coat and a bunch of Parma violets. They all seemed separate, self-absorbed, on business of their own.

At this moment, as so often happens in London, there was a complete lull and suspension of traffic. Nothing came down the street; nobody passed. A single leaf detached itself from the plane tree at the end of the street, and in that pause and suspension fell. Somehow it was like a signal falling, a signal pointing to a force in things which one had overlooked. It seemed to point to a river, which flowed past, invisibly, round the corner, down the street, and took people and eddied them along, as the stream at Oxbridge had taken the undergraduate in his boat and the dead leaves. Now it was bringing from one side of the street to the other diagonally a girl in patent leather boots, and then a young man in a maroon overcoat; it was also bringing a taxi-cab; and it brought all three together at a point directly beneath my window; where the taxi stopped; and the girl and the young man stopped; and they got into the taxi; and then the cab glided off as if it were swept on by the current elsewhere.

The sight was ordinary enough; what was strange was the rhythmical order with which my imagination had invested it; and the fact that the ordinary sight of two people getting into a cab had the power to communicate something of their own seeming satisfaction. The sight of two people coming down the street and meeting at the corner seems to ease the mind of some strain, I thought, watching the taxi turn and make off. Perhaps to think, as I had been thinking these two days, of one sex as distinct from the other is an effort. It interferes with the unity of the mind. Now that effort had ceased and that unity had been restored by seeing two people come together and get into a taxi-cab. The mind is certainly a very mysterious organ, I reflected, drawing my head in from the window, about which nothing whatever is known, though we depend upon it so completely. Why do I feel that there are severances and oppositions in the mind, as there are strains from obvious causes on the body? What does one mean by "the unity of the mind," I pondered, for clearly the mind has so great a power of concentrating at any point at any moment that it seems to have no single state of being. It can separate itself from the people in the street, for example, and think of itself as apart from them, at an upper window looking down on them. Or it can think with other people spontaneously, as, for instance, in a crowd waiting to hear some piece of news read out. It can think back through its fathers or through its mothers, as I have said that a woman writing thinks back through her mothers. Again if one is a woman one is often surprised by a sudden splitting off of consciousness, say in walking down Whitehall, when from being the natural inheritor of that civilisation, she becomes, on the contrary, outside of it, alien and critical. Clearly the mind is always altering its focus, and bringing the world into different perspectives. But some of these states of mind seem, even if adopted spontaneously, to be less comfortable than others. In order to keep oneself continuing in them one is unconsciously holding something back, and gradually the repression becomes an effort. But there may be some state of mind in which one could continue without effort because nothing is required to be held back. And this perhaps, I thought, coming in from the window, is one of them. For certainly when I saw the couple get into the taxi-cab the mind felt as if, after being divided, it had come together again in a natural fusion. The obvious reason would be that it is natural for the sexes to cooperate. One has a profound, if irrational, instinct in favour of the theory that the union of man and woman makes for the greatest satisfaction, the most complete happiness. But the sight of the two people getting into the taxi and the satisfaction it gave me made me also ask whether there are two sexes in the mind corresponding to the two sexes in the body, and whether they also require to be united in order to get complete satisfaction and happiness. And I went on amateurishly to sketch a plan of the soul so that in each of us two powers preside, one male, one female; and in the man's brain, the man predominates over the woman, and in the woman's brain, the woman predominates over the man. The normal and comfortable state of being is that when the two live in harmony together, spiritually cooperating. If one is a man, still the woman part of the brain must have effect; and a woman also must have intercourse with the man in her. Coleridge perhaps meant this when he said that a great mind is androgynous. It is when this fusion takes place that the mind is fully fertilised and uses all its faculties. Perhaps a mind that is purely masculine cannot create, any more than a mind that is purely feminine, I thought. But it would be well to test what one meant by man-womanly, and conversely by woman-manly, by pausing and looking at a book or two.

Coleridge certainly did not mean, when he said that a great mind is androgynous, that it is a mind that has any special sympathy with women; a mind that takes up their cause or devotes itself to their interpretation. Perhaps the androgynous mind is less apt to make these distinctions than the single-sexed mind. He meant, perhaps, that the androgynous mind is resonant and porous; that it transmits emotion without impediment; that it is naturally creative, incandescent and undivided. In fact one goes back to Shakespeare's mind as the type of the androgynous, of the man-womanly mind, though it would be impossible to say what Shakespeare thought of women. And if it be true that it is one of the tokens of the fully developed mind that it does not think specially or separately of sex, how much harder it is to attain that condition now than ever before. Here I came to the books by living writers, and there paused and wondered if this fact were not at the root of something that had long puzzled me. No age can ever have been as stridently sex-conscious as our own; those innumerable books by men about women in the British Museum are a proof of it. The Suffrage campaign[11] was no doubt to blame. It must have roused in men an extraordinary desire for self-assertion; it must have made them lay an emphasis upon their own sex and its characteristics which they would not have troubled to think about had they not been challenged. And when one is challenged, even by a few women in black bonnets, one retaliates, if one has never been challenged before, rather excessively. That perhaps accounts for some of the characteristics that I remember to have found here, I thought, taking down a new novel by Mr. A, who is in the prime of life and very well thought of, apparently, by the reviewers. I opened it. Indeed, it was delightful to read a man's writing again. It was so direct, so straightforward after the writing of women. It indicated such freedom of mind, such liberty of person, such confidence in himself. One had a sense of physical well-being in the presence of this well-nourished, well-educated, free mind, which had never been thwarted or opposed, but had had full liberty from birth to stretch itself in whatever way it liked. All this was admirable. But after reading a chapter or two a shadow seemed to lie across the page. It was a straight dark bar, a shadow shaped something like the letter "I." One began dodging this way and that to catch a glimpse of the landscape behind it. Whether that was indeed a tree or a woman walking I was not quite sure. Back one was always hailed to the letter "I." One began to be tired of "I." Not but what this "I" was a most respectable "I"; honest and logical; as hard as a nut, and polished for centuries by good teaching and good feeding. I respect and admire that "I" from the bottom of my heart. But—here I turned a page or two, looking for something or other—the worst of it is that in the shadow of the letter "I" all is shapeless as mist. Is that a tree? No, it is a woman. But . . . she has not a bone in her body, I thought, watching Phoebe, for that was her name, coming across the beach. Then Alan got up and the shadow of Alan at once obliterated Phoebe. For Alan had views and Phoebe was quenched in the flood of his views. And then Alan, I thought, has passions; and here I turned page after page very fast, feeling that the crisis was approaching, and so it was. It took place on the beach under the sun. It was done very openly. It was done very vigorously. Nothing could have been more indecent. But . . . I had said "but" too often. One cannot go on saying "but." One must finish the sentence somehow, I rebuked myself. Shall I finish it, "But—I am bored!" But why was I bored? Partly because of the dominance of the letter "I" and the aridity, which, like the giant beech tree, it casts within its shade. Nothing will grow there. And partly for some more obscure reason. There seemed to be some obstacle, some impediment of Mr. A's mind which blocked the fountain of creative energy and shored it within narrow limits. . . .

How can I further encourage you to go about the business of life? Young women, I would say, and please attend, for the peroration is beginning, you are, in my opinion, disgracefully ignorant. You have never made a discovery of any sort of importance. You have never shaken an empire or led an army into battle. The plays of Shakespeare are not by you, and you have never introduced a barbarous race to the blessings of civilisation. What is your excuse? It is all very well for you to say, pointing to the streets and squares and forests of the globe swarming with black and white and coffee-coloured inhabitants, all busily engaged in traffic and enterprise and love-making,

5

---

[11] **The Suffrage campaign** The early-twentieth-century political and protest campaign in Britain to gain the right to vote for women. Many women, in their protest, destroyed public and private property, were arrested, and were inhumanely treated in prison. Their tactics and their subsequent imprisonment became contentious public issues and often divided the country.

we have had other work on our hands. Without our do-ing, those seas would be unsailed and those fertile lands a desert. We have borne and bred and washed and taught, perhaps to the age of six or seven years, the one thousand six hundred and twenty-three million human beings who are, according to statistics, at present in existence, and that, allowing that some had help, takes time.

There is truth in what you say—I will not deny it. But at the same time may I remind you that there have been at least two colleges for women in existence in England since the year 1866; that after the year 1880 a married woman was allowed by law to possess her own property; and that in 1919—which is a whole nine years ago—she was given

a vote? May I also remind you that most of the professions have been open to you for close on ten years now? When you reflect upon these immense privileges and the length of time during which they have been enjoyed, and the fact that there must be at this moment some two thousand women capable of earning over five hundred a year in one way or another, you will agree that the excuse of lack of opportunity, training, encouragement, leisure and money no longer holds good. Moreover, the economists are tell-ing us that Mrs. Seton has had too many children. You must, of course, go on bearing children, but, so they say, in twos and threes, not in tens and twelves. . . .

Questions for Critical Thinking

1. Explain Woolf's title *A Room of One's Own.*

2. Summarize what Woolf's fictitious "I"—Mary Beton— discovers during her visit to the British Museum. Is Woolf's fictional character a successful literary device for setting forth her views? Explain.

WILLIAM FAULKNER
Selection from *The Sound and the Fury*

The Sound and the Fury (1929), a novel about the American South, is one of the classics of mod-ernism. With its stream-of-consciousness narrative, adopted from James Joyce and Virginia Woolf, this novel introduced European-style experimentation into American letters and made William Faulkner (1897–1962) a force in world literature. By 1939, for example, translations of *The Sound and the Fury* and five other novels by Faulkner were available to French writers, such as Albert Camus, who imitated their "interior monologue" technique. Largely neglected in the 1940s, Faulkner reemerged onto the international stage in 1950 when he received the Nobel Prize in Literature, a recognition of his heroic achievement.

Faulkner belonged to that species of writer who finds the world in a grain of sand, metaphorically speaking. His "grain of sand" was Yoknapatawpha, the fictional Mississippi county—based on Faulkner's own Lafayette County—whose history he wrote in the series of sixteen novels beginning with *Sartoris* (1929) and ending with *The Reivers* (1962). These novels deal with the period mainly between the end of the Civil War and the time Faulkner was writ-ing. An old social order characterized by a gentleman's code of behavior was passing away, defeated from within, and a new social pattern expressed in a code of "everyone looking out for number one" was being born. In some novels this changing order is represented through, respectively, the Sartoris family, who are gentry in decline, and the money-grubbing Snopes clan, who are "poor whites" on the make. White society is usually the foreground, but black life, providing an element of stability, is always present, represented by black servants who hold white families together. Racism is sometimes a theme (*Light in August*, 1932), and when it is, Faulkner portrays black victims with sympathy. Yoknapatawpha functions as a symbol of the entire South, but it also stands for any place where there is a decline in old ways.

Reading the Selection

This passage—the first few pages of *The Sound and the Fury*—shows Faulkner blending "local color" with experimental method. Tough going for a first-time Faulkner reader, the passage begins to make sense only with great difficulty. The speaker is Benjamin, the thirty-three-year-old idiot son of the Compsons, the Yoknapatawpha family gone to seed, whose history is the focus of the novel. This opening gambit, as well as the novel's title, is derived from Shakespeare's famous line in *Macbeth,* Act V, Scene v: "Life's . . . a tale / Told by an idiot, full of sound and fury, / Signifying nothing." Benjamin's untrustworthy monologue runs for almost one hundred pages.

The novel is about the dissolution of the Compson family, but this theme is clouded initially because Benjamin is the narrator, and in his disordered mind, reality and memory are merged. The full tragedy of the Compsons comes into view only later in the novel when other family members tell their stories. When the novel opens, Benjamin is watching a golf game while being looked after by Luster, the fourteen-year-old son of Dilsey, the black cook. At the same time, the past asserts itself in Benjamin's memories of Caddy, or Candace, his sister and protector when he was a child. Only gradually is it learned that the family has banished the adult Candace for reasons of sexual promiscuity, and her daughter, Quentin, who lives with the Compsons, may be a child of incest.

∞

April Seventh, 1928.

Through the fence, between the curling flower spaces, I could see them hitting. They were coming toward where the flag was and I went along the fence. Luster was hunting in the grass by the flower tree. They took the flag out, and they were hitting. Then they put the flag back and they went to the table, and he hit and the other hit. Then they went on, and I went along the fence. Luster came away from the flower tree and we went along the fence and they stopped and we stopped and I looked through the fence while Luster was hunting in the grass.

"Here, caddie." He hit. They went away across the pasture. I held to the fence and watched them going away.

"Listen at you, now." Luster said. "Aint you something, thirty three years old, going on that way. After I done went all the way to town to buy you that cake. Hush up that moaning. Aint you going to help me find that quarter so I can go to the show tonight."

They were hitting little, across the pasture. I went back along the fence to where the flag was. It flapped on the bright grass and the trees.

"Come on." Luster said. "We done looked there. They aint no more coming right now. Les go down to the branch and find that quarter before them niggers finds it."

It was red, flapping on the pasture. Then there was a bird slanting and tilting on it. Luster threw. The flag flapped on the bright grass and the trees. I held to the fence.

"Shut up that moaning." Luster said. "I cant make them come if they aint coming, can I. If you dont hush up, mammy aint going to have no birthday for you. If you dont hush, you know what I going to do. I going to eat that cake all up. Eat them candles, too. Eat all them thirty three candles. Come on, les go down to the branch. I got to find my quarter. Maybe we can find one of they balls. Here. Here they is. Way over yonder. See." He came to the fence and pointed his arm. "See them. They aint coming back here no more. Come on."

We went along the fence and came to the garden fence, where our shadows were. My shadow was higher than Luster's on the fence. We came to the broken place and went through it.

"Wait a minute." Luster said. "You snagged on that nail again. Cant you never crawl through here without snagging on that nail."

Caddy uncaught me and we crawled through. Uncle Maury said to not let anybody see us, so we better stoop over, Caddy said. Stoop over, Benjy. Like this, see. We stooped over and crossed the garden, where the flowers rasped and rattled against us. The ground was hard. We climbed the fence, where the pigs were grunting and snuffing. I expect they're sorry because one of them got killed today, Caddy said. The ground was hard, churned and knotted.

Keep your hands in your pockets, Caddy said. Or they'll get froze. You don't want your hands froze on Christmas, do you.

"It's too cold out there." Versh said. "You dont want to go out doors."

"What is it now." Mother said.

"He want to go out doors." Versh said.

"Let him go." Uncle Maury said.

"It's too cold." Mother said. "He'd better stay in. Benjamin. Stop that, now."

"It wont hurt him." Uncle Maury said.

"You, Benjamin." Mother said. "If you don't be good, you'll have to go to the kitchen."

"Mammy say keep him out the kitchen today." Versh said. "She say she got all that cooking to get done."

"Let him go, Caroline." Uncle Maury said. "You'll worry yourself sick over him."

"I know it." Mother said. "It's a judgment on me. I sometimes wonder."

"I know, I know." Uncle Maury said. "You must keep your strength up. I'll make you a toddy."

"It just upsets me that much more." Mother said. "Dont you know it does."

"You'll feel better." Uncle Maury said. "Wrap him up good, boy, and take him out for a while."

Uncle Maury went away. Versh went away.

"Please hush." Mother said. "We're trying to get you out as fast as we can. I dont want you to get sick."

Versh put my overshoes and overcoat on and we took my cap and went out. Uncle Maury was putting the bottle away in the sideboard in the diningroom.

"Keep him out about half an hour, boy." Uncle Maury said. "Keep him in the yard, now."

"Yes, sir." Versh said. "We dont never let him get off the place."

We went out doors. The sun was cold and bright.

"Where you heading for." Versh said. "You dont think you going to town, does you." We went through the rattling leaves. The gate was cold. "You better keep them hands in your pockets." Versh said. "You get them froze onto that gate, then what you do. Whyn't you wait for them in the house." He put my hands into my pockets. I could hear him rattling in the leaves. I could smell the cold. The gate was cold.

"Here some hickeynuts. Whooey. Git up that tree. Look here at this squirl, Benjy."

I couldn't feel the gate at all, but I could smell the bright cold.

"You better put them hands back in your pockets."

Caddy was walking. Then she was running, her booksatchel swinging and jouncing behind her.

"Hello, Benjy." Caddy said. She opened the gate and came in and stooped down. Caddy smelled like leaves. "Did you come to meet me." she said. "Did you come to meet Caddy. What did you let him get his hands so cold for, Versh."

"I told him to keep them in his pockets." Versh said. "Holding on to that ahun gate."

"Did you come to meet Caddy." she said, rubbing my hands. "What is it. What are you trying to tell Caddy." Caddy smelled like trees and like when she says we were asleep.

What are you moaning about, Luster said. You can watch them again when we get to the branch. Here. Here's you a jimson weed. He gave me the flower. We went through the fence, into the lot.

"What is it." Caddy said. "What are you trying to tell Caddy. Did they send him out, Versh."

"Couldn't keep him in." Versh said. "He kept on until they let him go and he come right straight down here, looking through the gate."

"What is it." Caddy said. "Did you think it would be Christmas when I came home from school. Is that what you thought. Christmas is the day after tomorrow. Santy Claus, Benjy. Santy Claus. Come on, let's run to the house and get warm." She took my hand and we ran through the bright rustling leaves. We ran up the steps and out of the bright cold, into the dark cold. Uncle Maury was putting the bottle back in the sideboard. He called Caddy. Caddy said,

"Take him in to the fire, Versh. Go with Versh." she said. "I'll come in a minute."

We went to the fire. Mother said,

"Is he cold, Versh."

"Nome." Versh said.

"Take his overcoat and overshoes off." Mother said. "How many times do I have to tell you not to bring him into the house with his overshoes on."

"Yessum." Versh said. "Hold still, now." He took my overshoes off and unbuttoned my coat. Caddy said,

"Wait, Versh. Cant he go out again, Mother. I want him to go with me."

"You'd better leave him here." Uncle Maury said. "He's been out enough today."

"I think you'd both better stay in." Mother said. "It's getting colder, Dilsey says."

"Oh, Mother." Caddy said.

"Nonsense." Uncle Maury said. "She's been in school all day. She needs the fresh air. Run along, Candace."

"Let him go, Mother." Caddy said. "Please. You know he'll cry."

"Then why did you mention it before him." Mother said. "Why did you come in here. To give him some excuse to worry me again. You've been out enough today. I think you'd better sit down here and play with him."

"Let them go, Caroline." Uncle Maury said. "A little cold wont hurt them. Remember, you've got to keep your strength up."

"I know." Mother said. "Nobody knows how I dread Christmas. Nobody knows. I am not one of these women who can stand things. I wish for Jason's and the children's sakes I was stronger."

"You must do the best you can and not let them worry you." Uncle Maury said. "Run along, you two. But dont stay out long, now. Your mother will worry."

"Yes, sir." Caddy said. "Come on, Benjy. We're going out doors again." She buttoned my coat and we went toward the door.

"Are you going to take that baby out without his overshoes." Mother said. "Do you want to make him sick, with the house full of company."

"I forgot." Caddy said. "I thought he had them on."

We went back. "You must think." Mother said. *Hold still now* Versh said. He put my overshoes on. "Someday I'll be gone, and you'll have to think for him." *Now stomp* Versh said. "Come here and kiss Mother, Benjamin."

Caddy took me to Mother's chair and Mother took my face in her hands and then she held me against her.

"My poor baby." she said. She let me go. "You and Versh take good care of him, honey."

"Yessum." Caddy said. We went out. Caddy said,

"You needn't go, Versh. I'll keep him for a while."

"All right." Versh said. "I aint going out in that cold for no fun." He went on and we stopped in the hall and Caddy knelt and put her arms around me and her cold bright face against mine. She smelled like trees.

"You're not a poor baby. Are you. Are you. You've got your Caddy. Haven't you got your Caddy."

Cant you shut up that moaning and slobbering, Luster said. Aint you shamed of yourself, making all this racket. We passed the carriage house, where the carriage was. It had a new wheel.

"Git in, now, and set still until your maw come." Dilsey said. She shoved me into the carriage. T. P. held the reins. "Clare I don't see how come Jason wont get a new surrey." Dilsey said. "This thing going to fall to pieces under you all some day. Look at them wheels."

Mother came out, pulling her veil down. She had some flowers.

"Where's Roskus." she said.

"Roskus cant lift his arms, today." Dilsey said. "T. P. can drive all right."

"I'm afraid to." Mother said. "It seems to me you all could furnish me with a driver for the carriage once a week. It's little enough I ask, Lord knows."

"You know just as well as me that Roskus got the rheumatism too bad to do more than he have to, Miss Cahline." Dilsey said. "You come on and get in, now. T. P. can drive you just as good as Roskus."

"I'm afraid to." Mother said. "With the baby."

Dilsey went up the steps. "You calling that thing a baby." she said. She took Mother's arm. "A man big as T. P. Come on, now, if you going."

"I'm afraid to." Mother said. They came down the steps and Dilsey helped Mother in. "Perhaps it'll be the best thing, for all of us." Mother said.

"Aint you shamed, talking that way." Dilsey said. "Dont you know it'll take more than a eighteen year old nigger to make Queenie run away. She older than him and Benjy put together. And dont you start no projecking with Queenie, you hear me. T. P. If you dont drive to suit Miss Cahline, I going to put Roskus on you. He aint too tied up to do that."

"Yessum." T. P. said.

"I just know something will happen." Mother said. "Stop, Benjamin."

"Give him a flower to hold." Dilsey said. "That what he wanting." She reached her hand in.

"No, no." Mother said. "You'll have them all scattered."

"You hold them." Dilsey said. "I'll get him one out." She gave me a flower and her hand went away.

"Go on now, fore Quentin see you and have to go too." Dilsey said.

"Where is she." Mother said.

"She down to the house playing with Luster." Dilsey said. "Go on, T. P. Drive that surrey like Roskus told you, now."

"Yessum." T. P. said. "Hum up, Queenie."

"Quentin." Mother said. "Dont let "

"Course I is." Dilsey said.

The carriage jolted and crunched on the drive. "I'm afraid to go and leave Quentin." Mother said. "I'd better not go. T. P." We went through the gate, where it didn't jolt anymore. T. P. hit Queenie with the whip.

"You, T. P." Mother said.

"Got to get her going." T. P. said. "Keep her wake up till we get back to the barn."

"Turn around." Mother said. "I'm afraid to go and leave Quentin."

"Cant turn here." T. P. said. Then it was broader.

"Cant you turn here." Mother said.

"All right." T. P. said. We began to turn.

"You, T. P." Mother said, clutching me.

"I got to turn around some how." T. P. said. "Whoa, Queenie." We stopped.

"You'll turn us over." Mother said.

"What you want to do, then." T. P. said.

"I'm afraid for you to try to turn around." Mother said.

"Get up, Queenie." T. P. said. We went on.

"I just know Dilsey will let something happen to Quentin while I'm gone." Mother said. "We must hurry back."

"Hum up, there." T. P. said. He hit Queenie with the whip.

"You, T. P." Mother said, clutching me. I could hear Queenie's feet and the bright shapes went smooth and steady on both sides, the shadows of them flowing across Queenie's back. They went on like the bright tops of wheels. Then those on one side stopped at the tall white post where the soldier was. But on the other side they went on smooth and steady, but a little slower.

"What do you want." Jason said. He had his hands in his pockets and a pencil behind his ear.

"We're going to the cemetery." Mother said.

"All right." Jason said. "I dont aim to stop you, do I. Was that all you wanted with me, just to tell me that."

"I know you wont come." Mother said. "I'd feel safer if you would."

"Safe from what." Jason said. "Father and Quentin cant hurt you."

Mother put her handkerchief under her veil. "Stop it, Mother." Jason said. "Do you want to get that damn looney to bawling in the middle of the square. Drive on, T. P."

"Hum up, Queenie." T. P. said.

"It's a judgment on me." Mother said. "But I'll be gone too, soon."

"Here." Jason said.

"Whoa." T. P. said. Jason said,

"Uncle Maury's drawing on you for fifty. What do you want to do about it."

"Why ask me." Mother said. "I dont have any say so. I try not to worry you and Dilsey. I'll be gone soon, and then you."

"Go on, T. P." Jason said.

"Hum up, Queenie." T. P. said. The shapes flowed on. The ones on the other side began again, bright and fast and smooth, like when Caddy says we are going to sleep.

Cry baby, Luster said. Aint you shamed. We went through the barn. The stalls were all open. You aint got no spotted pony to ride now, Luster said. The floor was dry and dusty. The roof was falling. The slanting holes were full of spinning yellow. What do you want to go that way, for. You want to get your head knocked off with one of them balls.

"Keep your hands in your pockets." Caddy said. "Or they'll be froze. You dont want your hands froze on Christmas, do you."

We went around the barn. The big cow and the little one were standing in the door, and we could hear Prince and Queenie and Fancy stomping inside the barn. "If it wasn't so cold, we'd ride Fancy." Caddy said. "But it's too cold to hold on today." Then we could see the branch, where the smoke was blowing. "That's where they are killing the pig." Caddy said. "We can come back by there and see them." We went down the hill.

"You want to carry the letter." Caddy said. "You can carry it." She took the letter out of her pocket and put it in mine. "It's a Christmas present." Caddy said. "Uncle Maury is going to surprise Mrs Patterson with it. We got to give it to her without letting anybody see it. Keep your hands in your pockets good, now." We came to the branch.

"It's froze." Caddy said. "Look." She broke the top of the water and held a piece of it against my face. "Ice. That means how cold it is." She helped me across and we went up the hill. "We cant even tell Mother and Father. You know what I think it is. I think it's a surprise for Mother and Father and Mr Patterson both, because Mr Patterson sent you some candy. Do you remember when Mr Patterson sent you some candy last summer."

There was a fence. The vine was dry, and the wind rattled in it.

"Only I dont see why Uncle Maury didn't send Versh." Caddy said. "Versh wont tell." Mrs Patterson was looking out the window. "You wait here." Caddy said. "Wait right here, now. I'll be back in a minute. Give me the letter." She took the letter out of my pocket. "Keep your hands in your pockets." She climbed the fence with the letter in her hand and went through the brown, rattling flowers. Mrs Patterson came to the door and opened it and stood there.

Mr Patterson was chopping in the green flowers. He stopped chopping and looked at me. Mrs Patterson came across the garden, running. When I saw her eyes I began to cry. You idiot, Mrs Patterson said, I told him never to send you alone again. Give it to me. Quick. Mr Patterson came fast, with the hoe. Mrs Patterson leaned across the fence, reaching her hand. She was trying to climb the fence. Give it to me, she said. Give it to me. Mr Patterson climbed the fence. I saw her eyes again and I ran down the hill.

"They aint nothing over yonder but houses." Luster said. "We going down to the branch."

They were washing down at the branch. One of them   130
was singing. I could smell the clothes flapping, and the smoke blowing across the branch. . . .

Questions for Critical Thinking

1. Summarize the scene that unfolds in this selection from *The Sound and the Fury*.

2. Define stream-of-consciousness narrative. Show, using specific examples, how Faulkner makes this technique work in this passage.

WILLIAM BUTLER YEATS
Poems

The poet and dramatist William Butler Yeats (1865–1939) is one of the most highly regarded literary figures of the twentieth century. Renowned as both a founder of the Irish Literary Renaissance and a pioneer of literary modernism, he was awarded the Nobel Prize in Literature in 1923, and since his death, his life and works have remained the objects of intense scholarly study. Highly gifted, he had a genius not so much for inspiration in the manner of romantic writers, such as Lord Byron, as for the patient editing of a manuscript. Yeats's usual approach for writing a poem was to begin with a simple idea, develop it into a working text, and then polish the wording until the final poem emerged. The finished poem was often a work in which every word felt spontaneous and inevitable, unlike the prosaic original idea. In a term often used to describe poetic writing, his verses are "lapidary"—that is, of an elegance suitable for carving on a monument. Many of his poems, including "The Second Coming" and "Sailing to Byzantium," are now part of the modernist canon, celebrated for both their crisp, fresh diction and haunting images that stick in the mind.

A restless figure, reminiscent of other geniuses of modernism, such as the painter Picasso, Yeats was constantly reshaping the style and content of his writing in response to personal circumstances and the changing political environment, especially the rise of Irish nationalism climaxed by the founding of the Irish Free State in 1922. Although a member of the Irish Protestant minority, Yeats nevertheless joined forces with Irish Catholic writers as they tried to rid their country of the influence of English literature and searched their heritage for myths, legends, and a "lost" golden age. Yeats's earliest writings were Gaelic tales and Celtic folklore, especially the collection of Celtic folktales in *The Celtic Twilight* (1893), one of the two or three major works of the Irish literary revival. Yeats's title "Celtic twilight," evocative of a dreamy, heroic Irish past, became an alternative name for this literary movement. Yeats also helped create an Irish literary theater, taking the lead in founding Dublin's Abbey or National Theatre Society in 1901. Today, the Abbey Theatre is recognized as one of Ireland's foremost cultural landmarks.

After 1910 Yeats stripped his verses of folkloric imagery and adopted a new artistic credo that he explained in a 1912 poem as "walking naked" before the world. This credo meant focusing more on the personal, especially giving voice to inner feelings. Still, even with the new credo of "nakedness," he continued to believe in the occult and the relevance of myth. He also remained attuned to unfolding events in Ireland, particularly after the failed Easter Rebellion of 1916. Most scholars consider Yeats's finest works the later poems, especially those written between 1919 and 1930, in which the personal and the political are virtually inseparable.

Reading the Selections

"The Second Coming" (1919) is probably Yeats's most famous poem. This poem reflects Yeats's pessimistic thoughts for the future, triggered by two signal events in world history: the "blood-dimmed tide" caused by the warring armies of World War I and the "mere anarchy" unleashed by the revolutionary communists in Russia in 1917. A visionary work, "The Second Coming" also owes much to the writings of Friedrich Nietzsche (see *Thus Spake Zarathustra* in Chapter 20), including the prophetic tone and the idea of impending apocalypse. Surveying the past twenty centuries, the poem forecasts a basic change in the human condition. This change is not the "second coming" of Jesus predicted by Christians but instead is the advent of a new age, an age of violence and barbarism, which will be ushered in by the birth of a new religion whose horrific nature can only be imagined. Two key motifs in this poem, and in Yeats's writing generally, are *Spiritus Mundi* and gyre. *Spiritus Mundi*, or "spirit of the world," an occult term, is the repository from which Yeats draws certain powerful images and symbols. *Gyre*, also an occult term, means the spiraling movement in history whereby two stages of development, which stand in opposition to one another, interact and regularly exchange places every 2,000 years.

"Sailing to Byzantium" (1927) is one of Yeats's most admired works. Composed when the poet was sixty-two years old, this poem has as its theme the coming of age: "That is no country for old men," the speaker complains in the opening line. The speaker views the world as aflame with erotic activity, "the young in one another's arms." Distracted by incessant lovemaking, the young have no time or need for art. Faced with such neglect, the speaker, who is also a poet, proposes to set sail for Byzantium, the ancient city, fabled for luxury, learning, and brilliant arts—a metaphor for a perfect world where beauty and art are eternally honored. There, in this poetic Byzantium, the speaker imagines himself transformed into a bird, crafted of "gold and gold enamelling," eternally singing before the imperial court.

∽

The Second Coming

Turning and turning in the widening gyre[12]
The falcon cannot hear the falconer;
Things fall apart; the centre cannot hold;
Mere anarchy is loosed upon the world,
The blood-dimmed tide is loosed, and everywhere
The ceremony of innocence is drowned;
The best lack all conviction, while the worst
Are full of passionate intensity.

Surely some revelation is at hand;
Surely the Second Coming is at hand.
The Second Coming! Hardly are those words out

When a vast image out of *Spiritus Mundi*[13]
Troubles my sight: somewhere in sands of the desert
A shape with lion body and the head of a man,
A gaze blank and pitiless as the sun,
Is moving its slow thighs, while all about it
Reel shadows of the indignant desert birds.
The darkness drops again; but now I know
That twenty centuries of stony sleep
Were vexed to nightmare by a rocking cradle,
And what rough beast, its hour come round at last,
Slouches towards Bethlehem to be born?

———————

[13] *Spiritus Mundi*   The World Spirit or Spirit of the World; identified in ancient, medieval, and Renaissance philosophy as the
fifth element and the highest element in nature; associated with
the substance composing the heavenly bodies.

———————

[12] **gyre**   A circular or spiral motion.

∽

Sailing to Byzantium

I

That is no country for old men. The young
In one another's arms, birds in the trees,
—Those dying generations—at their song,
The salmon-falls, the mackerel-crowded seas,
Fish, flesh, or fowl, commend all summer long
Whatever is begotten, born, and dies.
Caught in that sensual music all neglect
Monuments of unageing intellect.

II

An aged man is but a paltry thing,
A tattered coat upon a stick, unless
Soul clap its hands and sing, and louder sing
For every tatter in its mortal dress,
Nor is there singing school but studying
Monuments of its own magnificence;
And therefore I have sailed the seas and come
To the holy city of Byzantium.

III

O sages standing in God's holy fire
As in the gold mosaic of a wall,
Come from the holy fire, perne in a gyre,[14]
And be the singing-masters of my soul.
Consume my heart away; sick with desire
And fastened to a dying animal
It knows not what it is; and gather me
Into the artifice of eternity.

IV

Once out of nature I shall never take
My bodily form from any natural thing,
But such a form as Grecian goldsmiths make
Of hammered gold and gold enamelling
To keep a drowsy Emperor awake;
Or set upon a golden bough to sing
To lords and ladies of Byzantium
Of what is past, or passing, or to come.

———————

[14] **perne in a gyre**   A honey buzzard or bee hawk flying in a
circle. The bird feeds on the larvae of bees.

Questions for Critical Thinking

1. In "The Second Coming," explain Yeats's metaphor "And what rough beast . . . / Slouches towards Bethlehem to be born?"

2. In "Sailing to Byzantium," what does Yeats mean when he writes: "That is no country for old men"?

T. S. ELIOT
"The Love Song of J. Alfred Prufrock"

Eliot's "The Love Song of J. Alfred Prufrock" (1915) is one of the first great works of modernist poetry, which flourished from about 1904 until about 1939. Modernist poetry continued to be written after 1939, but its zenith was reached in the earlier time. Its aim was typical of modernism in general, to make a radical break with the nineteenth century and establish a new style more in keeping with the kaleidoscopic changes taking place today.

Modernist poetry, first of all, is not Victorian, for it is opposed to the sentimentality of romanticism, the fine writing of neoclassicism, and the illustration of realism—the leading styles of the Victorian Age. Modernist poetry also offers neither a moral lesson nor a popular message; instead, it is deliberately difficult. Its difficulty springs from its dense writing, its rich allusiveness (quotations from other literary works), and its high intellectual tone. Though antitraditional, it is the heir of the Hellenistic (see Theocritus's *Idylls* in Chapter 4, Volume I) and the metaphysical poets, both of whom specialized in difficult and learned works. Modernist poetry is often composed in free verse, which has no regular meter or line length and relies on natural speech and the variation of stressed and unstressed syllables, a type of poetry perfected by Walt Whitman (see "Song of Myself" in Chapter 18).

The Anglo-American T. S. Eliot (1888–1965, born Thomas Stearns Eliot), the pioneer of modernist poetry, grew up in a middle-class St. Louis family, studied at Harvard, and earned a Ph.D. in philosophy. He migrated to England on the eve of World War I, marrying a genteel English woman who later became psychotic and whom he divorced and put in an insane asylum. Although he never held an academic post, choosing to support himself first as a banker and later as a publisher—particularly of modernist works—he became the dominant poet of his day and a powerbroker of modernist literature. He was also one of this period's leading critics, helping to develop what came to be called the New Criticism, which was ideally suited to interpreting modernist poetry. It advocated "close reading" and detailed textual analysis of the work rather than an interest in the mind and personality of the poet, the sources, the history of ideas, and the political and social implications.

Reading the Selection

To read "The Love Song of J. Alfred Prufrock" in terms of New Criticism is not to read it as the work of T. S. Eliot, but to study it as the expression of J. Alfred Prufrock, whoever he may be. He indeed may be Eliot's alter ego, but that is irrelevant. The reader has, in effect, been given an intellectual puzzle—to figure out Prufrock and his loves. The epigraph, the opening quotation from Dante's *Inferno*, establishes that Prufrock is shy about revealing himself, just as is the character in Dante. Drawing the reader into the text, "Let us go then, you and I," Prufrock takes the reader on a walk through a seedy neighborhood where the image of yellow fog and smoke engulfs everything. Shyly, Prufrock reveals himself, his lack of self-confidence, his hesitancy to do anything, his sad confession that his life is measured with coffee spoons. He lacks the courage to make an overture to a woman whose bare arms and perfume haunt his memory. Confused, he fears failure and the onset of age ("I grow old") and wonders what he will be like as an old man. At the end, the imagery shifts to seductive mermaids who lure him ever onward into another world, or perhaps to his destruction.

∞

S'io credesse che mia risposta fosse
A persona che mai tornasse al mondo,
Questa fiamma staria senza più scosse.
Ma per ciò che giammai di questo fondo
Non tornò vivo alcun, s'i'odo il vero,
Senza tema d'infamia ti rispondo.[15]

Let us go then, you and I,   1
When the evening is spread out against the sky
Like a patient etherized upon a table;
Let us go, through certain half-deserted streets,
The muttering retreats
Of restless nights in one-night cheap hotels
And sawdust restaurants with oyster-shells:
Streets that follow like a tedious argument
Of insidious intent
To lead you to an overwhelming question . . .   10
Oh, do not ask, "What is it?"
Let us go and make our visit.

In the room the women come and go
Talking of Michelangelo.

The yellow fog that rubs its back upon the window-panes
The yellow smoke that rubs its muzzle on the window-
        panes
Licked its tongue into the corners of the evening,
Lingered upon the pools that stand in drains,
Let fall upon its back the soot that falls from chimneys,
Slipped by the terrace, made a sudden leap,   20
And seeing that it was a soft October night,
Curled once about the house, and fell asleep.

And indeed there will be time
For the yellow smoke that slides along the street,
Rubbing its back upon the window-panes;

There will be time, there will be time
To prepare a face to meet the faces that you meet;
There will be time to murder and create,
And time for all the works and days of hands
That lift and drop a question on your plate;   30
Time for you and time for me,
And time yet for a hundred indecisions,
And for a hundred visions and revisions,
Before the taking of a toast and tea.

In the room the women come and go
Talking of Michelangelo.

And indeed there will be time
To wonder, "Do I dare?" and, "Do I dare?"
Time to turn back and descend the stair,
With a bald spot in the middle of my hair—   40
[They will say: "How his hair is growing thin!"]
My morning coat, my collar mounting firmly to the chin,
My necktie rich and modest, but asserted by a simple pin—
[They will say: "But how his arms and legs are thin!"]
Do I dare
Disturb the universe?
In a minute there is time
For decisions and revisions which a minute will reverse.

For I have known them all already, known them all:
Have known the evenings, mornings, afternoons,   50
I have measured out my life with coffee spoons;
I know the voices dying with a dying fall
Beneath the music from a farther room.
    So how should I presume?

And I have known the eyes already, known them all—
The eyes that fix you in a formulated phrase,
And when I am formulated, sprawling on a pin,
When I am pinned and wriggling on the wall,
Then how should I begin
To spit out all the butt-ends of my days and ways?   60
    And how should I presume?

---

[15] *S'io credesse che . . . ti rispondo.* Epigraph from Dante's *Inferno,* Canto XXVII, 61–66: "If I thought my answer were given to anyone who could ever return to the world, this flame would shake no more; but since none ever did return above from this depth, if what I hear is true, without fear of infamy, I answer thee." This response is given by Guido da Montefeltro when he is asked who he is. The Montefeltro family ruled Urbino, a small province in late medieval Italy. In Dante's opinion, Guido deserved to be placed in hell. During the Renaissance, the family created one of the most splendid courts of the arts and the new learning.

And I have known the arms already, known them all—
Arms that are braceleted and white and bare
[But in the lamplight, downed with light brown hair!]
Is it perfume from a dress
That makes me so digress?
Arms that lie along a table, or wrap about a shawl.
    And should I then presume?
    And how should I begin?

.   .   .

Shall I say, I have gone at dusk through narrow streets   70
And watched the smoke that rises from the pipes
Of lonely men in shirt-sleeves, leaning out of
        windows? . . .

I should have been a pair of ragged claws
Scuttling across the floors of silent seas.

.   .   .

And the afternoon, the evening, sleeps so peacefully!
Smoothed by long fingers,
Asleep . . . tired . . . or it malingers,
Stretched on the floor, here beside you and me.
Should I, after tea and cakes and ices,
Have the strength to force the moment to its crisis?   80
But though I have wept and fasted, wept and prayed,
Though I have seen my head [grown slightly bald]
        brought in upon a platter,
I am no prophet—and here's no great matter;
I have seen the moment of my greatness flicker,
And I have seen the eternal Footman[16] hold my coat, and
        snicker,
And in short, I was afraid.

And would it have been worth it, after all,
After the cups, the marmalade, the tea,
Among the porcelain, among some talk of you and me,
Would it have been worth while,   90
To have bitten off the matter with a smile,
To have squeezed the universe into a ball
To roll it toward some overwhelming question,
To say: "I am Lazarus,[17] come from the dead,

_____

[16] **the eternal Footman** A footman is a servant who waits upon his master, often assisting in his private life and accompanying him on trips. In this case, he is Death.
[17] **Lazarus** The man whom Jesus raised from the dead. Lazarus was the brother of Mary and Martha of Bethany and a friend of Jesus. See John 11:1–44.

Come back to tell you all, I shall tell you all"—
If one, settling a pillow by her head,
    Should say: "That is not what I meant at all.
    That is not it, at all."

And would it have been worth it, after all,
Would it have been worth while,   100
After the sunsets and the dooryards and the sprinkled
        streets,
After the novels, after the teacups, after the skirts that
        trail along the floor—
And this, and so much more?—
It is impossible to say just what I mean!
But as if a magic lantern threw the nerves in patterns on
        a screen:
Would it have been worth while
If one, settling a pillow or throwing off a shawl,
And turning toward the window, should say:
    "That is not it at all,
    That is not what I meant, at all."   110

.   .   .

No! I am not Prince Hamlet, nor was meant to be;
Am an attendant lord, one that will do
To swell a progress, start a scene or two,
Advise the prince; no doubt, an easy tool,
Deferential, glad to be of use,
Politic, cautious, and meticulous;
Full of high sentence, but a bit obtuse;
At times, indeed, almost ridiculous—
Almost, at times, the Fool.

I grow old . . . I grow old . . .   120
I shall wear the bottoms of my trousers rolled.

Shall I part my hair behind? Do I dare to eat a peach?
I shall wear white flannel trousers, and walk upon the
        beach.
I have heard the mermaids singing, each to each.

I do not think that they will sing to me.

I have seen them riding seaward on the waves
Combing the white hair of the waves blown back
When the wind blows the water white and black.

We have lingered in the chambers of the sea
By sea-girls wreathed with seaweed red and brown   130
Till human voices wake us, and we drown.

∞

Questions for Critical Thinking

1. Explain the image in the opening three lines, which compare "the evening" to a "patient etherized upon a table." What mood is set with this image? Explain.

2. Compose a ten-line poem, in T. S. Eliot's style, to be titled "On My First Reading 'The Love Song of J. Alfred Prufrock.'"

LANGSTON HUGHES
Poems

Langston Hughes (1902–1967) is one of the first great African American poets and the most published black writer of his era. Altogether he wrote sixteen books of poetry, two novels, seven books of short stories, two autobiographies, five works of nonfiction, and nine books for children. He also edited nine anthologies, translated several Haitian and Spanish writers, and wrote about thirty plays. Reviewed widely in mainstream journals by mainstream writers and acquainted with leading artists and writers at home and abroad, Hughes was sometimes described during his lifetime as the "poet laureate of the American Negro" or as "Shakespeare in Harlem."

Hughes was a web of paradoxes that largely reflected his anguish as a black man in a white world. The son of a black middle-class family in Joplin, Missouri (his father was a businessman and his mother was a schoolteacher), he came to speak for America's poor black masses. Passionate about writing, yet distant and difficult to know, Hughes was apparently a very lonely man who never seemed to have any deep or long-standing love affairs. Familiar with standard English, having studied at Columbia University in New York (1921–1922) and graduated from Lincoln University in Pennsylvania (1929), he made his literary task the creation of a body of works based on vernacular speech of the black working and rural classes. This innovation succeeded, since many subsequent black writers followed his lead. A citizen of the world, fluent in French and Spanish and widely traveled in Europe, Asia, Africa, and Mexico, he never wavered in his commitment to black vernacular culture.

Hughes, mainly through his poetry, soared to fame in the Harlem Renaissance, the 1920s cultural revival centered in the black area of New York City called Harlem. Jazz, blues, and folk ballads went mainstream, and Hughes was one of the first black writers to recognize the genius of this music and incorporate it into his works. He appropriated the cadences of jazz and the moods and themes of blues and folk ballads to create a soulful poetry.

Resisting the temptation encouraged by the period's growing and mobile black middle class to write in a Europeanized style, Hughes wrote primarily about blackness. His poems often concerned the struggle of black artists to be true to their race and, at the same time, to be Americans. In 1927 he wrote, "American standardization [requires us] to be as little Negro and as much American as possible." He gradually came to see poetry as a kind of salvation, for it allowed him to speak in his African American voice and yet identify with America's heritage; for example, he claimed kinship with the reclusive poet Emily Dickinson.

Reading the Selections

"The Negro Speaks of Rivers" (1921) is Hughes's best-known poem, written when he was nineteen and a student at Columbia. This poem was inspired by a quarrel with his father, who apparently hated his own race, but it is surprisingly free of rancor on Hughes's part. The poem celebrates black history, linking it to storied rivers—the Euphrates, the Congo, the Nile, and the Mississippi.

"Harlem" (1951) continues Hughes's project of integrating the black experience into American letters. It should be noted that this poem contains the phrase "a raisin in the sun," made even more memorable later when it became the title of a Pulitzer Prize play written by the African American playwright Lorraine Hansberry.

The Negro Speaks of Rivers

I've known rivers: 1
I've known rivers ancient as the world and older than the
   flow of human blood in human veins.

My soul has grown deep like the rivers.

I bathed in the Euphrates when dawns were young.
I built my hut near the Congo and it lulled me to sleep.
I looked upon the Nile and raised the pyramids above it.

I heard the singing of the Mississippi when Abe Lincoln
   went down to New Orleans, and I've seen its muddy
   bosom turn all golden in the sunset.

I've known rivers:
Ancient, dusky rivers.

My soul has grown deep like the rivers.   10

Harlem

What happens to a dream deferred?   1

Does it dry up
like a raisin in the sun?
Or fester like a sore—
And then run?
Does it stink like rotten meat?

Or crust and sugar over—
like a syrupy sweet?

Maybe it just sags
like a heavy load.   10

Or does it explode?

Questions for Critical Thinking

1. What is Hughes's message in "The Negro Speaks of Rivers"?

2. In "Harlem," what does Hughes mean by "a dream deferred"?

ZORA NEALE HURSTON
Selection from *Their Eyes Were Watching God*

The African American writer Zora Neale Hurston (1891–1960) is probably the most widely read black woman writer in schools and colleges today, but her literary reputation, like her life, has been a roller coaster. She once exulted, "I have been in Sorrow's kitchen and licked out all the pots. Then I have stood on the peaky mountain wrapped in rainbows, with a harp and a sword in my hands."

Born in Florida, poor and subjected to racism, Hurston moved north, where she shone as one of the most original voices of the Harlem Renaissance. From 1925 to 1945, she was a widely acclaimed writer, author of three novels (*Jonah's Gourd Vine*, 1934; *Their Eyes Were Watching God*,

1937; and *Moses, Man of the Mountain,* 1939); two books of folklore (*Mules and Men,* 1935, and *Tell My Horse,* 1938); an autobiography (*Dust Tracks on a Road,* 1942); and many short stories, essays, and plays. After 1945, she continued to write, publishing a fourth novel (*Seraph on the Suwanee,* 1948) and a few stories and essays, but her audience lost interest and she fell into oblivion. In 1950 she worked as a maid, and when she died in a welfare home, she had all but been forgotten. That changed when growing interest in black culture led scholars to rediscover her works and restore her to a preeminent place in American letters.

Hurston's literary task resembled that of Langston Hughes (see "The Negro Speaks of Rivers"), her contemporary, in that both wrote about being black in a white-dominated world, expressed themselves in black vernacular speech, and drew on jazz, blues, and folktales. Also like Hughes, Hurston was educated; she studied at Howard University in Washington, D.C. (1921–1924), and graduated from Barnard College, New York City, in 1928. She then spent some years in Columbia University's graduate program in anthropology (her books on folklore are based on research in the American South, Jamaica, Haiti, and Bermuda). Still, when compared with Hughes, Hurston was doubly disadvantaged, for as a black and a woman writer, she had to contend with both racism and sexism. In the 1930s, most black male writers dismissed her on the grounds that her writing sounded like a minstrel show. Even Hughes, while admiring her works, found her personally too ingratiating to whites: "In her youth she was always getting scholarships and things from wealthy white people, some of whom simply paid her to sit around and represent the Negro race for them, she did it in such a racy fashion." "Representing the Negro race for whites" was of course the goal of the Harlem Renaissance, and Hurston's genius was that in her writings, she did it better than anyone else.

Reading the Selection

Hurston's novel *Their Eyes Were Watching God* may be classified as a *bildungsroman* (German, "a novel of formation"). Despite the lofty-sounding name, this type of novel is simply a "coming-of-age" story, a long account that traces the social, psychological, and sexual development of a hero or heroine from youth to mature understanding. Hurston's *Their Eyes Were Watching God* focuses on Janie Starks, an African American woman cut from the same irreverent mold as the author.

The selection (chapter 1) begins at the end of Janie's journey, as she returns home to Eatonville, Florida, Hurston's home, as well as the home of Janie's youthful exploits. Forty-year-old Janie's homecoming is watched over disapprovingly by the "Mouth Almighty" (Janie's term)—the Greek chorus of nosy black women who observe from their perch on a nearby porch. Janie tells her story to a friend, Phoeby Watson, who listens enviously, because she is constitutionally unable to lead such a daring life. Told in flashback, the remainder of the novel recounts Janie's successes and failures, her husbands and lovers, and births and deaths of those close to her, before returning home. Sadder and wiser, yet more in tune with the rhythm of life, Janie is at peace at last, with herself, nature, and the world.

&

Chapter 1

Ships at a distance have every man's wish on board. For some they come in with the tide. For others they sail forever on the horizon, never out of sight, never landing until the Watcher turns his eyes away in resignation, his dreams mocked to death by Time. That is the life of men.

Now, women forget all those things they don't want to remember, and remember everything they don't want to forget. The dream is the truth. Then they act and do things accordingly.

So the beginning of this was a woman and she had come back from burying the dead. Not the dead of sick and ailing with friends at the pillow and the feet. She had come back from the sodden and the bloated; the sudden dead, their eyes flung wide open in judgment.

The people all saw her come because it was sundown. The sun was gone, but he had left his footprints in the sky. It was the time for sitting on porches beside the road. It was the time to hear things and talk. These sitters had been tongueless, earless, eyeless conveniences all day long. Mules and other brutes had occupied their skins. But now, the sun and the bossman were gone, so the skins felt powerful and human. They became lords of sounds and lesser things. They passed nations through their mouths. They sat in judgment.

Seeing the woman as she was made them remember the envy they had stored up from other times. So they chewed up the back parts of their minds and swallowed with relish. They made burning statements with questions, and killing tools out of laughs. It was mass cruelty. A mood come alive. Words walking without masters; walking altogether like harmony in a song.

"What she doin' coming back here in dem overhalls? Can't she find no dress to put on?—Where's dat blue satin dress she left here in?—Where all dat money her husband took and died and left her?—What dat ole forty year ole 'oman doin' wid her hair swingin' down her back lak some young gal?—Where she left dat young lad of a boy she went off here wid?—Thought she was going to marry?—Where he left *her*?—What done wid all her money?—Betcha he off wid some gal so young she ain't even got no hairs—why she don't stay in her class?—"

When she got to where they were she turned her face on the bander log and spoke. They scrambled a noisy "good evenin'" and left their mouths setting open and their ears full of hope. Her speech was pleasant enough, but she kept walking straight on to her gate. The porch couldn't talk for looking.

The men noticed her firm buttocks like she had grape fruits in her hip pockets; the great rope of black hair swinging to her waist and unraveling in the wind like a plume; then her pugnacious breasts trying to bore holes in her shirt. They, the men, were saving with the mind what they lost with the eye. The women took the faded shirt and muddy overalls and laid them away for remembrance. It was a weapon against her strength and if it turned out of no significance, still it was a hope that she might fall to their level some day.

But nobody moved, nobody spoke, nobody even thought to swallow spit until after her gate slammed behind her.

Pearl Stone opened her mouth and laughed real hard because she didn't know what else to do. She fell all over Mrs. Sumpkins while she laughed. Mrs. Sumpkins snorted violently and sucked her teeth.

"Humph! Y'all let her worry yuh. You ain't like me. Ah ain't got her to study 'bout. If she ain't got manners enough to stop and let folks know how she been makin' out, let her g'wan!"

"She ain't even worth talkin' after," Lulu Moss drawled through her nose. "She sits high, but she looks low. Dat's what Ah say 'bout dese ole women runnin' after young boys."

Pheoby Watson hitched her rocking chair forward before she spoke. "Well, nobody don't know if it's anything to tell or not. Me, Ah'm her best friend, and *Ah* don't know."

"Maybe us don't know into things lak you do, but we all know how she went 'way from here and us sho seen her come back. 'Tain't no use in your tryin' to cloak no ole woman lak Janie Starks, Pheoby, friend or no friend."

"At dat she ain't so ole as some of y'all dat's talking."

"She's way past forty to my knowledge, Pheoby."

"No more'n forty at de outside."

"She's 'way too old for a boy like Tea Cake."

"Tea Cake ain't been no boy for some time. He's round thirty his ownself."

"Don't keer what it was, she could stop and say a few words with us. She act like we done done something to her," Pearl Stone complained. "She de one been doin' wrong."

"You mean, you mad 'cause she didn't stop and tell us all her business. Anyhow, what you ever know her to do so bad as y'all make out? The worst thing Ah ever knowed her to do was taking a few years offa her age and dat ain't never harmed nobody. Y'all makes me tired. De way you talkin' you'd think de folks in dis town didn't do nothin' in de bed 'cept praise de Lawd. You have to 'scuse me, 'cause Ah'm bound to go take her some supper." Pheoby stood up sharply.

"Don't mind us," Lulu smiled, "just go right ahead, us can mind yo' house for you till you git back. Mah supper is done. You bettah go see how she feel. You kin let de rest of us know."

"Lawd," Pearl agreed, "Ah done scorched-up dat lil meat and bread too long to talk about. Ah kin stay 'way from home long as Ah please. Mah husband ain't fussy."

"Oh, er, Pheoby, if youse ready to go, Ah could walk over dere wid you," Mrs. Sumpkins volunteered. "It's sort of duskin' down dark. De booger man might ketch yuh."

"Naw, Ah thank yuh. Nothin' couldn't ketch me dese few steps Ah'm goin'. Anyhow mah husband tell me say no first class booger would have me. If she got anything to tell yuh, you'll hear it."

Pheoby hurried on off with a covered bowl in her hands. She left the porch pelting her back with unasked questions. They hoped the answers were cruel and strange. When she arrived at the place, Pheoby Watson didn't go in by the front gate and down the palm walk to the front door. She walked around the fence corner and went in the intimate gate with her heaping plate of mulatto rice. Janie must be round that side.

She found her sitting on the steps of the back porch with the lamps all filled and the chimneys cleaned.

"Hello, Janie, how you comin'?"

"Aw, pretty good, Ah'm tryin' to soak some uh de tiredness and de dirt outa mah feet." She laughed a little.

"Ah see you is. Gal, you sho looks *good*. You looks like youse yo' own daughter." They both laughed. "Even wid dem overhalls on, you shows yo' womanhood."

"G'wan! G'wan! You must think Ah brought yuh somethin'. When Ah ain't brought home a thing but mahself."

"Dat's a gracious plenty. Yo' friends wouldn't want nothin' better."

"Ah takes dat flattery offa you, Pheoby, 'cause Ah know it's from de heart." Janie extended her hand. "Good Lawd, Pheoby! ain't you never goin' tuh gimme dat lil rations you brought me? Ah ain't had a thing on mah stomach today exceptin' mah hand." They both laughed easily. "Give it here and have a seat."

"Ah knowed you'd be hongry. No time to be huntin' stove wood after dark. Mah mulatto rice ain't so good dis time. Not enough bacon grease, but Ah reckon it'll kill hongry."

"Ah'll tell you in a minute," Janie said, lifting the cover. ₃₅ "Gal, it's *too* good! you switches a mean fanny round in a kitchen."

"Aw, dat ain't much to eat, Janie. But Ah'm liable to have something sho nuff good tomorrow, 'cause you done come."

Janie ate heartily and said nothing. The varicolored cloud dust that the sun had stirred up in the sky was settling by slow degrees.

"Here, Pheoby, take yo' ole plate. Ah ain't got a bit of use for a empty dish. Dat grub sho come in handy."

Pheoby laughed at her friend's rough joke. "Youse just as crazy as you ever was."

"Hand me dat wash-rag on dat chair by you, honey. ₄₀ Lemme scrub mah feet." She took the cloth and rubbed vigorously. Laughter came to her from the big road.

"Well, Ah see Mouth-Almighty is still sittin' in de same place. And Ah reckon they got *me* up in they mouth now."

"Yes indeed. You know if you pass some people and don't speak tuh suit 'em dey got tuh go way back in yo' life and see whut you ever done. They know mo' 'bout yuh than you do yo' self. An envious heart makes a treacherous ear. They done 'heard' 'bout you just what they hope done happened."

"If God don't think no mo' 'bout 'em then Ah do, they's a lost ball in de high grass."

"Ah hears what they say 'cause they just will collect round mah porch 'cause it's on de big road. Mah husband git so sick of 'em sometime he makes 'em all git for home."

"Sam is right too. They just wearin' out yo' sittin' ₄₅ chairs."

"Yeah, Sam say most of 'em goes to church so they'll be sure to rise in Judgment. Dat's de day dat every secret is s'posed to be made known. They wants to be there and hear it *all*."

"Sam is *too* crazy! You can't stop laughin' when youse round him."

"Uuh hunh. He says he aims to be there hisself so he can find out who stole his corn-cob pipe."

"Pheoby, dat Sam of your'n just won't quit! Crazy thing!"

"Most of dese zigaboos is so het up over yo' business ₅₀ till they liable to hurry theyself to Judgment to find out about you if they don't soon know. You better make haste and tell 'em 'bout you and Tea Cake gittin' married, and if he taken all yo' money and went off wid some young gal, and where at he is now and where at is all yo' clothes dat you got to come back here in overhalls."

"Ah don't mean to bother wid tellin' 'em nothin', Pheoby. 'Tain't worth de trouble. You can tell 'em what Ah

say if you wants to. Dat's just de same as me 'cause mah tongue is in mah friend's mouf."

"If you so desire Ah'll tell 'em what you tell me to tell 'em."

"To start off wid, people like dem wastes up too much time puttin' they mouf on things they don't know nothin' about. Now they got to look into me loving Tea Cake and see whether it was done right or not! They don't know if life is a mess of corn-meal dumplings, and if love is a bed-quilt!"

"So long as they get a name to gnaw on they don't care whose it is, and what about, 'specially if they can make it sound like evil."

"If they wants to see and know, why they don't come ₅₅ kiss and be kissed? Ah could then sit down and tell 'em things. Ah been a delegate to de big 'ssociation of life. Yessuh! De Grand Lodge, de big convention of livin' is just where Ah been dis year and a half y'all ain't seen me."

They sat there in the fresh young darkness close together. Pheoby eager to feel and do through Janie, but hating to show her zest for fear it might be thought mere curiosity. Janie full of that oldest human longing—self revelation. Pheoby held her tongue for a long time, but she couldn't help moving her feet. So Janie spoke.

"They don't need to worry about me and my overhalls long as Ah still got nine hundred dollars in de bank. Tea Cake got me into wearin' 'em—following behind him. Tea Cake ain't wasted up no money of mine, and he ain't left me for no young gal, neither. He give me every consolation in de world. He's tell 'em so too, if he was here. If he wasn't gone."

Pheoby dilated all over with eagerness, "Tea Cake gone?"

"Yeah, Pheoby, Tea Cake is gone. And dat's de only reason you see me back here—cause Ah ain't got nothing to make me happy no more where Ah was at. Down in the Everglades there, down on the muck."

"It's hard for me to understand what you mean, de ₆₀ way you tell it. And then again Ah'm hard of understandin' at times."

"Naw, 'tain't nothin' lak you might think. So 'tain't no use in me telling you somethin' unless Ah give you de understandin' to go 'long wid it. Unless you see de fur, a mink skin ain't no different from a coon hide. Looka heah, Pheoby, is Sam waitin' on you for his supper?"

"It's all ready and waitin'. If he ain't got sense enough to eat it, dat's his hard luck."

"Well then, we can set right where we is and talk. Ah got the house all opened up to let dis breeze get a little catchin'."

"Pheoby, we been kissin'-friends for twenty years, so Ah depend on you for a good thought. And Ah'm talking to you from dat standpoint."

Time makes everything old so the kissing, young dark- ₆₅ ness became a monstropolous old thing while Janie talked.

Questions for Critical Thinking

1. Write a character sketch of Janie Starks, based on this selection.

2. A constant theme in Hurston's prose was the difficulty African Americans faced in the first half of the twentieth century because of white oppression and racism. What evidence do you see for this theme in this selection?

GERTRUDE STEIN
Selection from *The Autobiography of Alice B. Toklas*

The American expatriate Gertrude Stein (1874–1946) was a maddeningly original genius. Her apartment in Paris was for more than forty years a meeting place for the avant-garde, and her experimental writings helped define modernism. Misunderstood in her own day because of the impenetrability of her prose, she earned the title of America's best-known unread author. What was known about her was sufficient to make her a legendary character, part fraud, part genius. Stein fueled this image with her enigmatic sayings, as in this comment about America, "There is no there there," and in her most famous remark, "A rose is a rose is a rose is a rose." Now, more than sixty years after her death, she is a classic, and her works, back in print, are studied in college classrooms.

A rarity in her time, Stein was an independent woman who lived her life as she pleased. Born to a wealthy Jewish family in San Francisco and trained at the Johns Hopkins University in medicine, she passed up a medical career and instead moved to Paris in 1902. There she set up house in 1910 with Alice B. Toklas (1877–1967), a fellow San Franciscan who became her lifelong companion. Their personalities balanced one another, so that when they entertained, the male "geniuses" sat with Stein and the "wives" were relegated to the side with Toklas. Stein, avid for life, pursued cultural lions (Pablo Picasso and Ernest Hemingway) and anyone else who amused her; she dreamed of becoming a cultural lion herself ("think of the bible and Homer, think of Shakespeare and think of me"). In contrast, Toklas ran the domestic sphere (there is an *Alice B. Toklas Cookbook*, 1954) and seemed delighted to bask in Stein's reflected glory. During their lives, the Stein-Toklas household was the focus for the American love affair with France.

Stein's literary experiments bore little resemblance to Virginia Woolf's "interior monologues." Stein's literary project was to be abstract, as in cubism. Wanting to break with all literary tradition, she slowly got rid of narrative, punctuation, logic, forms or genres, even meanings in any normal sense. She achieved a fully abstract style in *Tender Buttons* (1914), a work divided into three sections called "Objects," "Food," and "Room," marked by repetition and obscurity ("chicken"; "Alas a dirty word, alas a dirty third alas a dirty third, alas a dirty bird"). Earlier, in *Three Lives* (1909), about servant women in 1900 Baltimore, Stein was still a realist, though experimenting with modernist effects—especially repetition and unfocused narrative structure.

Reading the Selection

Who would have thought of writing the life of a cherished companion and passing it off as an autobiography? Yet, this is just what Stein did, perhaps as a stunt to make money, perhaps as just another eccentric gesture to call attention to herself. Setting aside for the moment her own abstract style, Stein wrote in a deliberate imitation of Tolkas's deadpan, slightly sour speech pattern. The popular and critical success of the book was so unexpected that Stein was unable to write for a year.

The passage "Stein on Picasso and Matisse," from *The Autobiography of Alice B. Toklas* (1933), is typical of the work, in the name-dropping, the provocative portraits of the famous, the highly opinionated judgments ("And so cubism is spanish"), and above all, the centrality of Stein. In most ways, this book is a double autobiography of this eccentric couple.

<hr/>

Stein on Picasso and Matisse

. . .

But to return to the beginning of my life in Paris. It was [1] based upon the rue de Fleurus and the Saturday evenings and it was like a kaleidoscope slowly turning.

What happened in those early years. A great deal happened.

As I said when I became an habitual visitor at the rue de Fleurus the Picassos were once more together, Pablo and Fernande. That summer they went again to Spain and he came back with some spanish landscapes and one may say that these landscapes, two of them still at the rue de Fleurus and the other one in Moscow in the collection that Stchoukine[18] founded and that is now national property, were the beginning of cubism. In these there was no african sculpture influence. There was very evidently a strong Cézanne influence, particularly the influence of the late Cézanne water colours, the cutting up the sky not in cubes but in spaces.

But the essential thing, the treatment of the houses was essentially spanish and therefore essentially Picasso. In these pictures he first emphasised the way of building in spanish villages, the line of the houses not following the landscape but cutting across and into the landscape, becoming undistinguishable in the landscape by cutting across the landscape. It was the principle of the camouflage of the guns and the ships in the war. The first year of the war, Picasso and Eve, with whom he was living then, Gertrude Stein and myself, were walking down the boulevard Raspail a cold winter evening. There is nothing in the world colder than the Raspail on a cold winter evening, we used to call it the retreat from Moscow. All of a

sudden down the street came some big cannon, the first any of us had seen painted, that is camouflaged. Pablo stopped, he was spell-bound. C'est nous qui avons fit ça, he said, it is we that have created that, he said. And he was right, he had. From Cézanne through him they had come to that. His foresight was justified.

But to go back to the three landscapes. When they [5] were first put up on the wall naturally everybody objected. As it happened he and Fernande had taken some photographs of the villages which he had painted and he had given copies of these photographs to Gertrude Stein. When people said that the few cubes in the landscapes looked like nothing but cubes, Gertrude Stein would laugh and say, if you had objected to these landscapes as being too realistic there would be some point in your objection. And she would show them the photographs and really the pictures as she rightly said might be declared to be too photographic a copy of nature. Years after Elliot Paul[19] at Gertrude Stein's suggestion had a photograph of the painting by Picasso and the photographs of the village reproduced on the same page in transition and it was extraordinarily interesting. This then was really the beginning of cubism. The colour too was characteristically spanish, the pale silver yellow with the faintest suggestion of green, the colour afterwards so well known in Picasso's cubist pictures, as well as in those of his followers.

Gertrude Stein always says that cubism is a purely spanish conception and only spaniards can be cubists and that the only real cubism is that of Picasso and Juan Gris.[20] Picasso created it and Juan Gris permeated it with his clarity and his exaltation. To understand this one has only

<hr/>

[18] **Stchoukine** (or Shchukin) Sergei Ivanovich Shchukin (1854–1936), Russian merchant who assembled a world-class collection of modern art in the early 1900s. These works were confiscated during the Russian Revolution. Today the collection is divided between the Hermitage Museum in St. Petersburg and the Pushkin Museum in Moscow.

[19] **Elliot Paul** (1891–1958), American writer who served as coeditor (in the 1920s) of *transition*, the highly influential avant-garde literary journal, based in Paris.
[20] **Juan Gris** Pseudonym of Jose Victoriano Gonzalez (1887–1927), Spanish artist, working in Paris and associated with Picasso and Braque (see footnote 21), who helped develop cubism.

to read the life and death of Juan Gris by Gertrude Stein, written upon the death of one of her two dearest friends, Picasso and Juan Gris, both spaniards.

She always says that americans can understand spaniards. That they are the only two western nations that can realise abstraction. That in americans it expresses itself by disembodiedness, in literature and machinery, in Spain by ritual so abstract that it does not connect itself with anything but ritual.

I always remember Picasso saying disgustedly apropos of some germans who said they liked bull-fights, they would, he said angrily, they like bloodshed. To a spaniard it is not bloodshed, it is ritual.

Americans, so Gertrude Stein says, are like spaniards, they are abstract and cruel. They are not brutal they are cruel. They have no close contact with the earth such as most europeans have. Their materialism is not the materialism of existence, of possession, it is the materialism of action and abstraction. And so cubism is spanish.

We were very much struck, the first time Gertrude Stein and I went to Spain, which was a year or so after the beginning of cubism, to see how naturally cubism was made in Spain. In the shops in Barcelona instead of post cards they had square little frames and inside it was placed a cigar, a real one, a pipe, a bit of handkerchief etcetera, all absolutely the arrangement of many a cubist picture and helped out by cut paper representing other objects. That is the modern note that in Spain had been done for centuries.

Picasso in his early cubist pictures used printed letters as did Juan Gris to force the painted surface to measure up to something rigid, and the rigid thing was the printed letter. Gradually instead of using the printed thing they painted the letters and all was lost, it was only Juan Gris who could paint with such intensity a printed letter that it still made the rigid contrast. And so cubism came little by little but it came.

It was in these days that the intimacy between Braque[21] and Picasso grew. It was in these days that Juan Gris, a raw rather effusive youth came from Madrid to Paris and began to call Picasso cher maître to Picasso's great annoyance. It was apropos of this that Picasso used to address Braque as cher maître, passing on the joke, and I am sorry to say that some foolish people have taken this joke to mean that Picasso looked up to Braque as a master.

But I am once more running far ahead of those early Paris days when I first knew Fernande and Pablo.

In those days then only the three landscapes had been painted and he was beginning to paint some heads that seemed cut out in planes, also long loaves of bread.

At this time Matisse, the school still going on, was really beginning to be fairly well known, so much so that to everybody's great excitement Bernheim jeune, a very middle class firm indeed, was offering him a contract to take all his work at a very good price. It was an exciting moment.

This was happening because of the influence of a man named Fénéon. Il est très fin,[22] said Matisse, much impressed by Fénéon. Fénéon was a journalist, a french journalist who had invented the thing called a feuilleton en deux lignes, that is to say he was the first one to hit off the news of the day in two lines. He looked like a caricature of Uncle Sam made french and he had been painted standing in front of a curtain in a circus picture by Toulouse-Lautrec.

And now the Bernheims, how or wherefor I do not know, taking Fénéon into their employ, were going to connect themselves with the new generation of painters.

Something happened, at any rate this contract did not last long, but for all that it changed the fortunes of Matisse. He now had an established position. He bought a house and some land in Clamart[23] and he started to move out there. Let me describe the house as I saw it.

This home in Clamart was very comfortable, to be sure the bath-room, which the family much appreciated from long contact with americans, although it must be said that the Matisses had always been and always were scrupulously neat and clean, was on the ground floor adjoining the dining room. But that was alright, and is and was a french custom, in french houses. It gave more privacy to a bath-room to have it on the ground floor. Not so long ago in going over the new house Braque was building the bath-room was again below, this time underneath the dining room. When we said, but why, they said because being nearer the furnace it would be warmer.

The grounds at Clamart were large and the garden was what Matisse between pride and chagrin called un petit Luxembourg. There was also a glass forcing house for flowers. Later they had begonias in them that grew smaller and smaller. Beyond were lilacs and still beyond a big demountable studio. They liked it enormously. Madame Matisse with simple recklessness went out every day to look at it and pick flowers, keeping a cab waiting for her. In those days only millionaires kept cabs waiting and then only very occasionally.

They moved out and were very comfortable and soon the enormous studio was filled with enormous statues and enormous pictures. It was that period of Matisse. Equally soon he found Clamart so beautiful that he could not go home to it, that is when he came into Paris to his hour of sketching from the nude, a thing he had done every afternoon of his life ever since the beginning of things, and he came in every afternoon. His school no longer existed, the government had taken over the old convent to make a Lycée of it and the school had come to an end.

These were the beginning of very prosperous days for the Matisses. They went to Algeria and they went to Tangiers and their devoted german pupils gave them Rhine wines and a very fine black police dog, the first of the breed that any of us had seen.

And then Matisse had a great show of his pictures in Berlin. I remember so well one spring day, it was a lovely

[21] **Braque** Georges Braque (1882–1963), French artist who, along with Picasso, is generally credited wth the invention of cubism.

[22] **Il est très fin** French, "He is very clever."
[23] **Clamart** A suburb of Paris, south of the city.

day and we were to lunch at Clamart with the Matisses. When we got there they were all standing around an enormous packing case with its top off. We went up and joined them and there in the packing case was the largest laurel wreath that had ever been made, tied with a beautiful red ribbon. Matisse showed Gertrude Stein a card that had been in it. It said on it, To Henri Matisse, Triumphant on the Battlefield of Berlin, and was signed Thomas Whittemore. Thomas Whittemore was a bostonian archeologist and professor at Tufts College, a great admirer of Matisse and this was his tribute. Said Matisse, still more rueful, but I am not dead yet. Madame Matisse, the shock once over said, but Henri look, and leaning down she plucked a leaf and tasted it, it is real laurel, think how good it will be in soup. And,

said she still further brightening, the ribbon will do wonderfully for a long time as a hair ribbon for Margot.

The Matisses stayed in Clamart more or less until the war. During this period they and Gertrude Stein were seeing less and less of each other. Then after the war broke out they came to the house a good deal. They were lonesome and troubled, Matisse's family in Saint-Quentin, in the north, were within the german lines and his brother was a hostage. It was Madame Matisse who taught me how to knit woollen gloves. She made them wonderfully neatly and rapidly and I learned to do so too. Then Matisse went to live in Nice and in one way and another, although remaining perfectly good friends, Gertrude Stein and the Matisses never see each other. . . .

Questions for Critical Thinking

1. Characterize Stein's literary style in this selection. Be specific in your use of examples. How would you classify it: romantic, or realist, or modernist, or stream-of-consciousness, or what?

2. Compare and contrast briefly Stein's views of Picasso and Matisse. Do you find her portraits helpful in understanding these painters? Explain.

THOMAS MANN
Selection from *The Magic Mountain*

Thomas Mann's (1875–1955) *The Magic Mountain* is one of the most admired novels of the twentieth century, admired for its fierce intelligence, sophisticated wit, and brilliant style. A masterpiece of high modernism, the novel avoids the flashier experimental hijinks of this period's style, while it knowingly embraces—sometimes with a wink—the radical changes coursing across the West's wider culture. Published in 1924—at the midpoint in Mann's sixty-year literary career—*The Magic Mountain* burnished the author's reputation and contributed to his being awarded the 1929 Nobel Prize in Literature. Besides novels, Mann's literary works include short stories, plays, essays, and literary criticism. So great is Mann's reputation today that he is often ranked alongside Goethe as one of the leading writers in the German language.

Set in the halcyon days before World War I began in 1914, *The Magic Mountain* is a stew of literary genres: a coming-of-age story of naïve Hans Castorp, a German Everyman (in German, "Hans" is a generic name, similar to "John" in English); a novel of ideas, as key modernist intellectual trends are presented, such as depth psychology, secular humanism, totalitarian thinking, and a sprinkling of Nietzschean teachings ("life affirmation" and "strength through ordeal"); and, finally, a tragic-comic allegory of Europe's fevered dream as it moved inexorably to war. The *mountain* of the title is in the Swiss Alps, overlooking the town of Davos. There, in a sanatorium at a high altitude, various patients, suffering from tuberculosis and other respiratory ills, are partaking of the "magical" open-air cure promised by the age's medical avant-garde. Mann's cast of characters form a veritable microcosm of European society, as they undergo treatment and interact with one another.

Mann's ironic approach sets the novel's tone. Most especially, the titular *magic mountain*, which reaches for the sky, can be read as the inverse of Dante's Hell, which extends to the center of the earth (see Dante's *The Divine Comedy*, Chapter 10, Volume I). This connection is made clear in the passage (not included below) when a patient, on being introduced to Hans, asks, "Where did Minos assign you in the sanatorium?" Hans is flummoxed by the query. The patient is mockingly referring to the head of the sanatorium. But students of Dante know: Minos was the mythic judge presiding over the circles of lower Hell.

Reading the Selection

"Arrival" is the opening chapter of *The Magic Mountain*. The youthful Hans from Hamburg, Germany, is introduced, as he arrives by train at Davos-Platz, Switzerland. There, he plans a visit with his tubercular cousin, Joachim Ziemssen, a patient at the International Sanatorium Berghof. Hans' immaturity is made clear, as he is peppered with a stream of jocular remarks by his cousin. This opening scene echoes Thomas Mann's own life experience, for, in 1912, Mann watched over his wife, Katia, as she was treated in various Swiss sanatoriums.

The Magic Mountain reflects influences from earlier styles, especially romanticism, as in the vivid description of nature, but Mann's heart ultimately belongs to modernism. A central modernist theme emerges in the opening section: a critique of bourgeois society. This critique is evident in the class-conscious voice of the narrator; in Hans's strict adherence to social protocol and proper ways of speaking; and in Joachim's easy adoption of the looser habits of the patient community. Mann's view reflects the reality of the early 1920s: the German Empire is no more, having been replaced by the Weimar Republic, a democratic regime that Mann supported. Thus, *The Magic Mountain's* hermetic sanatorium is a metaphor for European society on the verge of destruction.

∞

Arrival

An ordinary young man was on his way from his hometown of Hamburg to Davos-Platz in the canton of Graubünden. It was the height of summer, and he planned to stay for three weeks.

It is a long trip, however, from Hamburg to those elevations—too long, really, for so short a visit. The journey leads through many a landscape, uphill and down, descends from the high plain of southern Germany to the shores of Swabia's sea, and proceeds by boat across its skipping waves, passing over abysses once thought unfathomable.

From there the path, which until now has followed grand, direct routes, turns choppy. There are stopovers and formalities. At Rorschach, a town in Swiss territory, you reboard a train that takes you only as far as Landquart, a small station in the Alps, where you must change trains again. After standing for a while in the wind, gazing at a rather uncharming landscape, you climb aboard a narrow-gauge train, and the moment the small, but uncommonly sturdy engine pulls out, the real adventure begins, a steep and dogged ascent that will never end, it

seems. The station at Landquart lies at a relatively low altitude; but now your route takes you on a wild ride up into real mountains, along tracks that squeeze their way between walls of rock.

Hans Castorp—that is the young man's name—found himself alone in a small compartment upholstered in gray; with him he had an alligator valise, a present from his uncle and foster father—Consul Tienappel, since we are naming names here—a rolled-up plaid blanket, and his winter coat, swinging on its hook. The window was open beside him, but the afternoon was turning cooler and cooler, and, being the coddled scion of the family, he turned up the silk-lined collar of his fashionably loose summer overcoat. On the seat beside him lay a paper-bound book entitled *Ocean Steamships*, which he had perused from time to time earlier on his trip, but which now lay neglected, the cover dirtied by soot drifting in with the steam of the heavily puffing locomotive.

Two days of travel separate this young man (and young he is, with few firm roots in life) from his everyday world, especially from what he called his duties, interests, worries, and prospects—separate him far more than he had dreamed possible as he rode to the station in a hansom cab. Space, as it rolls and tumbles away between him and his native soil, proves to have powers normally ascribed only to time; from hour to hour, space brings about changes very like those time produces, yet surpassing them in certain ways. Space, like time, gives birth to forgetfulness, but does so by removing an individual from all relationships and placing him in a free and pristine state—indeed, in but a moment it can turn a pedant and philistine into something like a vagabond. Time, they say, is water from the river Lethe[24], but alien air is a similar drink; and if its effects are less profound, it works all the more quickly.

And Hans Castorp experienced much the same thing. He had not planned to take this trip particularly seriously, to become deeply involved in it. His intention had been, rather, to put it behind him quickly, simply because that was how things had to be, to return quite the same person he had been at departure, and to pick up his life again where he had been forced to leave it lying for the moment. Only yesterday he had been totally caught up in his normal train of thought, preoccupied with what had just occurred, his exams, and with what was about to occur, his joining the firm of Tunder and Wilms (dockyards, machine works, and boilers), and looking well beyond these next three weeks with as much impatience as his nature allowed. But now it seemed to him that present circumstances demanded his full attention and that it was inappropriate to shrug them off. Being lifted like this into regions whose air he had never breathed before and whose sparse and meager conditions were, as he well knew, both unfamiliar and peculiar—it all began to excite him, to fill him with a certain anxiety. Home and a settled life not only lay far behind, but also, and more importantly, they lay fathoms below him, and he was still climbing. Hovering between home and the unknown ahead, he asked himself how he would do up there. Was it unwise and unhealthy, perhaps, for him, born only a few feet above sea level and accustomed to breathing that air, to be suddenly transported to such extreme regions without spending at least a few days someplace in between? He wished he had already reached his goal, because once you were up there, he thought, you lived just as people did everywhere, instead of having the climb constantly remind you of how unsuitable these precincts were. He looked out—the train was winding through a narrow pass; you could see the forward cars and the laboring engine, emitting great straggling tatters of brown, green, and black smoke. Water roared in the deep ravine on his right; dark pines on his left struggled up between boulders toward a stony gray sky. There were pitch-black tunnels, and when daylight returned, vast chasms were revealed, with a few villages far below. These views closed again, too, and were followed by new passes with patches of snow left in clefts and crevices. The train pulled into dingy little stations and

backed out again on the same set of tracks, confusing your sense of direction until you no longer knew whether you were heading north or south. Magnificent vistas opened onto regions toward which they were slowly climbing, a world of ineffable, phantasmagoric Alpine peaks, soon lost again to awestruck eyes as the tracks took another curve. Hans Castorp thought about how he had left hardwood forests far below him, and songbirds, too, he presumed; and the idea that such things could cease, the sense of a world made poorer without them, brought on a slight attack of dizziness and nausea, and he covered his eyes with his hand for a second or two. This passed. He realized that their climb was coming to an end, that they had taken the crest. The train was now rolling more comfortably along the level floor of a valley.

It was almost eight o'clock, but sill daylight. A lake appeared in the distant landscape; its surface was gray and from its shores black pine forests climbed the surrounding slopes, grew thinner toward the top, and gave way at last to bare, fog-enshrouded rock. They stopped at a little station, Davos-Dorf, as Hans Castorp learned when someone outside shouted the name—he would be at journey's end shortly. And suddenly, right beside him, he heard his cousin Joachim Ziemssen saying in an easygoing Hamburg voice, "Hello there. This is where you get off." And when he looked out, there on the platform below his window stood Joachim, wearing a brown ulster but no hat of any sort, and looking healthier than ever. He laughed and said again, "Come on, get off, don't be shy."

"But I'm not there yet," Hans Castorp said, dumbfounded, keeping his seat.

"Sure you are. This is Davos-Dorf. The sanatorium's closer from here. I've got a carriage. Hand me your things."

And with a laugh that betrayed his confusion and excitement at having arrived and seeing his cousin again, Hans Castorp lifted out his valise and winter coat, his plaid blanket roll plus cane and umbrella, and finally *Ocean Steamships*. Then he ran along the narrow corridor and jumped down onto the platform for a proper and more or less personal greeting, though this was done without any exuberance, as is fitting between people who are cool and reserved by custom. Strangely enough, they had always avoided calling one another by their first names, purely out of fear of showing too much warmth of emotion. And since they could not very well address one another by their last names, they confined themselves to the use of familiar pronouns—now a deeply rooted habit between the two cousins.

They quickly shook hands with some embarrassment—young Ziemssen never losing his military bearing—watched all the while by a man in livery with a braided cap, who then approached and asked Hans Castorp for his baggage ticket; this was the concierge of the International Sanatorium Berghof, and he proved quite willing to fetch the guest's large trunk from the station at Davos-Platz while the gentlemen themselves drove on ahead to dinner. The man had an obvious limp, and so the first thing that Hans Castorp asked Joachim Ziemssen was, "Is he a war veteran? Is that why he limps so badly?"

---

[24]**Lethe** In Greek mythology, the river of forgetfulness.

"Right! A war veteran," Joachim replied, somewhat sarcastically. "He's got it in the knee—or had it, that is, now that he's had his kneecap removed."

Hans Castorp mulled this over as rapidly as possible. "Oh, I see," he said, lifting his head and hastily looking back as they walked on. "But you're not going to try to tell me that you still have anything like that, are you? You look as if you've already received your commission and were just home from maneuvers." And he gave his cousin a sidelong glance.

Joachim was taller than he, with broader shoulders, the picture of youthful vigor, a man made for a uniform. He was very dark-haired, a type not all that uncommon in his blond hometown, and his naturally dark complexion was now tanned almost bronze. With his large black eyes and dark little moustache above full, finely chiseled lips, he would have been downright handsome, if his ears had not stood out so badly. For most of his life, they had been his one great sorrow, his only care. Now he had other worries. "You will be coming back down with me, won't you?" Hans Castorp went on. "I really see nothing standing in your way."

"Back down with you?" his cousin asked, turning to 15 him with large eyes that had always had a gentle look, but that in the last five months had taken on a weary, indeed sad expression. "When do you mean?"

"Why, in three weeks."

"Oh, I see—you're already thinking about heading back home," Joachim replied. "Well, wait and see, you've only just arrived. Three weeks are almost nothing for us up here, of course, but for you, just here on a visit and planning to stay a grand total of three weeks, for you that's a long time. Acclimatize yourself first—and you'll learn that's not all that easy. Besides, the climate's not the only unusual thing about us. You'll see quite a few new sights here, just watch. And as for what you've said about me—well, I'm not in such fine feather as all that, my friend. 'Home in three weeks,' that's a notion from down below. I'm nicely tanned, of course, but that's mostly from the snow and doesn't mean much, as Behrens is always saying, and at my last regular checkup he said that it's fairly certain it will be another six months yet."

"Six months? Are you crazy?" Hans Castorp cried. They were taking their seats on the hard cushions of a yellow cabriolet[25] that had stood waiting for them on the gravel apron in front of the station, itself not much more than a shed; and as the pair of bays began to pull, Hans Castorp spun around now in vexation. "Six months? You've already been here for almost that long! We don't have that much time in life!"

"Ah yes, time," Joachim said, nodding to himself several times, paying no attention to his cousin's honest indignation. "You wouldn't believe how fast and loose they play with people's time around here. Three weeks are the same as a day to them. You'll see. You have all that to

─────────
[25] **cabriolet** A small two-wheeled carriage with a hood, drawn by a horse or team of horses.

learn," he said, and then he added, "A man changes a lot of his ideas here."

Hans Castorp gazed steadily at his profile. "But you 20 really have made a splendid recovery," he said, shaking his head.

"Do you think so?" Joachim replied. "It's true, isn't it? I think so, too!" he said, sitting up taller against the cushioned back, but immediately slumping again a little to one side. "I am feeling better," he explained, "but I'm not yet entirely well, either. The upper left lobe, where the rattling used to be, there's only a little roughness there now, it's not so bad, but the lower lobe is still *very* rough, and there are also sounds in the second intercostal."

"How learned you've become," Hans Castorp said.

"Yes, a fine sort of learning, God knows. I would gladly have unlearned it all on active duty," Joachim retorted. "But I still have sputum," he said with a nonchalant, but somehow vehement shrug that did not suit him at all; and now he pulled something halfway out of the nearer side pocket of his ulster, showed it to his cousin, and put it away again at once—a curved, flattened bottle of bluish glass with a metal cap. "Most of us up here have one," he said. "We even have a name for it, a kind of nickname, a joke really. Having a look at the scenery, are you?"

And indeed that was what Hans Castorp was doing, 25 and he exclaimed, "Magnificent!"

"You think so, do you?! Joachim asked.

They had first taken a street that was faced by an irregular pattern of buildings and ran along the railroad tracks, following the valley's axis, but then turned left and crossed the narrow tracks and a brook; and they were now trotting up a gently rising road in the direction of wooded slopes and a low, outcropping meadow where an elongated building stood, its façade turned to the southwest, topped by a copper cupola, and arrayed with so many balconies that, from a distance as the first lights of evening were being lit, it looked as pockmarked and porous as a sponge. Dusk was falling fast. A pale red sunset that had enlivened the generally overcast sky faded now, leaving nature under the transient sway of the lackluster, lifeless, and mournful light that immediately precedes nightfall. Lights were coming up in the long, meandering, populous valley, dotting its floor and the slopes on both sides—particularly on the swelling rise to the right, where buildings ascended a series of terraces. Paths led up the meadowed hills on their left, but were soon lost to sight in the dull black of pine forests. Behind them, the mountains in the more distant background, where the valley tapered to an end, were a sober slate blue. Now that the wind had picked up, the evening had turned noticeably cooler.

"No, to be quite frank, I don't find it that overwhelming," Hans Castorp said. "Where are the glaciers and snowcapped, towering peaks? Seems to me, the ones here aren't all that high."

"Oh, they're high all right," Joachim replied. "You can see the tree line almost everyhere, it's really quite clearly defined; the pines come to an end, then everything else—the end, then rocks, as you can see. And over there, to the right of the Schwarzhorn, on that jagged peak there, is a glacier for you—can you see the blue? It's not that big, but it's a textbook glacier, the Scaletta Glacier. And there's Piz Micel and Tinzenhorn in that gap—you can't see them from here, but they're always snowcovered year-round."

"Eternal snow," Hans Castorp said.

"Right, eternal, if you like. And they're all very high. 30 But we're dreadfully high up ourselves, keep that in mind. Five thousand three hundred feet above sea level. So you don't notice the difference in height that much."

"Yes, it was quite a climb. Certainly had me scared, let me tell you. Five thousand three hundred feet. Why, that's over a mile high. I've never been this far up in my whole life." And in his curiosity, Hans Castorp took a deep breath, testing the alien air. It was fresh—that was all. It lacked odor, content, moisture, it went easily into the lungs and said nothing to the soul.

"Excellent!" he remarked politely.

"Yes, the air is famous. But the landscape is not showing itself to its best advantage this evening. It can look better, especially in the snow. But you soon get your fill of staring at it. Believe me, all of us up here have definitely had our fill of it," Joachim said, and his mouth wrenched in an expression of disgust that seemed both exaggerated and out of control—and once again it did not suit him.

"You're talking so strangely," Hans Castorp said.

"Strangely, am I?!" Joachim asked, turning to his 35 cousin and looking worried somehow.

"No, no, beg your pardon, it just seemed that way to me for a moment or so," Hans Castorp hastened to say. But what he really meant was that the phrase "us up here," which Joachim had used three or four times already, somehow made him feel anxious and queer.

"Our sanatorium lies at a higher altitude than the village, as you can see," Joachim continued. "A hundred fifty feet. The brochure says 'three hundred,' but it's only half that. The highest of the sanatoriums is Schatzalp, across the way, you can't see it now. They have to transport the bodies down by bobsled in the winter, because the roads are impassable."

"The bodies? Oh, I see. You don't say!" Hans Castorp cried. And suddenly he burst into laughter, a violent, overpowering laugh that shook his chest and twisted his face, stiffened by the cool wind, into a slightly painful grimace. "On bobsleds! And you can sit there and tell me that so calm and cool! You've become quite the cynic in the last five months."

"That's not cynical at all," Joachim replied with a shrug. "Why do you say that? It doesn't matter to the bodies. All the same, it may well be that we do get cynical up here. Behrens is an old cynic himself—a regular brick, by the way, an old fraternity man and a brilliant surgeon, you'll like him, seems to me. And then there's Krokowski, his assistant—a very savvy character. They make special note of his services in the brochure. He dissects the patients' psyches."

"He what! Dissects their psyches? That's disgusting!" 40 Hans Castorp cried, and now hilarity got the better of him. He could no longer control it. Psychic dissection had finished the job, and he bent over and laughed so hard that the tears ran out from under the hand with which he had covered his eyes. Joachim laughed heartily, too—it seemed to do him good. And so the two young men were in fine good humor as they climbed down from their carriage, which had borne them at a slow trot up the steep loop of the driveway to the portal of the International Sanatorium Berghof.

Questions for Critical Thinking

1. In this opening scene, what are the signs of Hans Castorp's immature worldview and what new technology and ideas confront him?

2. As a student, what new technology and ideas confront you, as you prepare to meet the world?

22

THE AGE OF ANXIETY
AND LATE MODERNISM
1945–1970

PAUL TILLICH
Selections from *The Courage to Be*

The Courage to Be is one of the exemplary texts of the Age of Anxiety. Published in 1952 by the German-American theologian Paul Tillich (1886–1965), it recognized the period's prevailing mood of despair and, at the same time, sought to counteract that mood by offering a theological ray of hope. With this book, Tillich, already a formidable force in the inner workings of the American Protestant mainstream, became a "public intellectual," an eminent thinker whose views on various topics were sought by the popular media. Other religious figures of the era commanded a larger public following, such as the revivalist Billy Graham (b. 1918) with his globe-circling crusades. But Tillich, an "ivory tower" intellectual, stood alone. His teachings appealed to educated laypeople, of both a religious and secular bent, as he confronted the leading philosophies of modernity. In 1959, *Time,* the newsmagazine, placed Tillich on the cover, in recognition of his status as one of America's foremost thinkers and cultural theorists.

    The Courage to Be originated as a series of lectures Tillich delivered at Yale University, with the charge to consider "religion in the light of science and philosophy." In the resulting book, which took the literary form of cultural history, he sought to interpret the religious crisis then gripping the West. For Tillich, the old prescientific worldview that had reigned from antiquity until about 1700 was finished, undermined by the Scientific Revolution (see Galileo, *Dialogue Concerning the Two Chief World Systems—Ptolemaic and Copernican* in Chapter 16) and such modern theories as those of Darwin (see *The Descent of Man* in Chapter 19), Marx (see *The Communist Manifesto* in Chapter 19), and Freud (see *Civilization and Its Discontents* in Chapter 20). With the ancient pieties under assault, Tillich conceived the contemporary world as a "boundary" period, marked by skepticism, fear of death, and despair. Tillich's cultural analysis, up to this point, agrees with that of the atheistic existentialists, including the French thinker Jean-Paul Sartre (see *The Humanism of Existentialism*). However, Tillich rejected Sartre's conclusion that there is no transcendental dimension to human life—*No Exit* was the portentous title of one of Sartre's plays. Instead, Tillich taught that at the precise moment in which everything seems hopeless, it is then that God—the God above God—appears. And with God's emergence in the face of anxious doubt, meaning and purpose once again become possible.

    Tillich's theology was forged in turbulent times. He served as chaplain to German troops in World War I. In 1933, he fled Germany for the United States, the first non-Jew to be expelled by the Nazis from a university teaching post. In America, he taught at prestigious schools for

the rest of his life, observing the defeat of the Nazi regime in World War II and creating a body
of theological works—for example, *Systematic Theology* (1951–1963), in three volumes—that rank
with the best of the twentieth century.

Reading the Selection

In the first paragraph, Tillich explains the choice of "courage" as the subject of his book. For
him, faced with the wreckage of modern civilization, the question becomes, how do people
have the courage to create meaning and purpose in their lives?

In the section titled "Theism Transcended," Tillich offers a three-part definition of theism, the belief in the existence of god or gods. Next, he asserts that theism, in its many guises,
including "biblical religion and historical Christianity," must be abandoned in order to make
contact with the "God above God." He concludes that it is the God of Theism that has been
made irrelevant by the philosophies of modernity.

The last section, titled "The God Above God and the Courage to Be," provides Tillich's
panacea for would-be believers: *"The courage to be is rooted in the God who appears when God has
disappeared in the anxiety of doubt."* This message is a spiritual paradox, a point of view often
expressed by earlier Christian mystics. Tillich, no mystic himself, maintains that the one true
God, independent of dogma and history, will be revealed only when a person reaches the spiritual lowest depths.

∞

Chapter 1 Being and Courage
Courage and Fortitude

· · ·

The title of this book, *The Courage to Be*, unites both mean- 1
ings of the concept of courage, the ethical and the ontological.[1] Courage as a human act, as a matter of valuation, is
an ethical concept. Courage as the universal and essential

self-affirmation of one's being is an ontological concept.
The courage to be is the ethical act in which man affirms
his own being in spite of those elements of his existence
which conflict with his essential self-affirmation.

· · ·

∞

Chapter 6 Courage and Transcendence
Theism Transcended

The courage to take meaninglessness into itself presup- 1
poses a relation to the ground of being which we have
called "absolute faith." It is without a *special* content, yet it
is not without content. The content of absolute faith is the
"God above God." Absolute faith and its consequence, the

courage that takes the radical doubt, the doubt about God,
into itself, transcends the theistic idea of God.[2]

Theism can mean the unspecified affirmation of God.
Theism in this sense does not say what it means if it uses

---

[2] **the courage that takes . . . transcends the theistic idea of God**
This paragraph summarizes Tillich's argument in *The Courage
to Be*, along with introducing three key terms: **"absolute faith"**
(the faith that emerges from despair), **"God above God"** (God
that cannot be defined in human terms), and **theism** (the God of
historic religion).

---

[1] **ontological** Having to do with the nature of being.

the name of God. Because of the traditional and psychological connotations of the word God such an empty theism can produce a reverent mood if it speaks of God. Politicians, dictators, and other people who wish to use rhetoric to make an impression on their audience like to use the word God in this sense. It produces the feeling in their listeners that the speaker is serious and morally trustworthy. This is especially successful if they can brand their foes as atheistic. On a higher level people without a definite religious commitment like to call themselves theistic, not for special purposes but because they cannot stand a world without God, whatever this God may be. They need some of the connotations of the word God and they are afraid of what they call atheism. On the highest level of this kind of theism the name of God is used as a poetic or practical symbol, expressing a profound emotional state or the highest ethical idea. It is a theism which stands on the boundary[3] line between the second type of theism and what we call "theism transcended." But it is still too indefinite to cross this boundary line. The atheistic negation of this whole type of theism is as vague as the theism itself. It may produce an irreverent mood and angry reaction of those who take their theistic affirmation seriously. It may even be felt as justified against the rhetorical-political abuse of the name God, but it is ultimately as irrelevant as the theism which it negates. It cannot reach the state of despair any more than the theism against which it fights can reach the state of faith.

Theism can have another meaning, quite contrary to the first one: it can be the name of what we have called the divine-human encounter. In this case it points to those elements in the Jewish-Christian tradition which emphasize the person-to-person relationship with God. Theism in this sense emphasizes the personalistic passages in the Bible and the Protestant creeds, the personalistic image of God, the word as the tool of creation and revelation, the ethical and social character of the kingdom of God, the personal nature of human faith and divine forgiveness, the historical vision of the universe, the idea of a divine purpose, the infinite distance between creator and creature, the absolute separation between God and the world, the conflict between holy God and sinful man, the person-to-person character of prayer and practical devotion. Theism in this sense is the nonmystical side of biblical religion and historical Christianity. Atheism from the point of view of this theism is the human attempt to escape the divine-human encounter. It is an existential—not a theoretical—problem.

Theism has a third meaning, a strictly theological one. Theological theism is, like every theology, dependent on the religious substance which it conceptualizes. It is dependent on theism in the first sense insofar as it tries to prove the necessity of affirming God in some way; it usually develops the so-called arguments for the "existence" of God. But it is more dependent on theism in the second

sense insofar as it tries to establish a doctrine of God which transforms the person-to-person encounter with God into a doctrine about two persons who may or may not meet but who have a reality independent of each other.

Now theism in the first sense must be transcended because it is irrelevant, and theism in the second sense must be transcended because it is one-sided. But theism in the third sense must be transcended because it is wrong. It is bad theology. This can be shown by a more penetrating analysis. The God of theological theism is a being beside others and as such a part of the whole of reality. He certainly is considered its most important part, but as a part and therefore as subjected to the structure of the whole. He is supposed to be beyond the ontological elements and categories which constitute reality. But every statement subjects him to them. He is seen as a self which has a world, as an ego which is related to a thou, as a cause which is separated from its effect, as having a definite space and an endless time. He is a being, not being-itself. As such he is bound to the subject-object structure of reality, he is an object for us as subjects. At the same time we are objects for him as a subject. And this is decisive for the necessity of transcending theological theism. For God as a subject makes me into an object which is nothing more than an object. He deprives me of my subjectivity because he is all-powerful and all-knowing. I revolt and try to make *him* into an object, but the revolt fails and becomes desperate. God appears as the invincible tyrant, the being in contrast with whom all other beings are without freedom and subjectivity. He is equated with the recent tyrants who with the help of terror try to transform everything into a mere object, a thing among things, a cog in the machine they control. He becomes the model of everything against which Existentialism revolted. This is the God Nietzsche[4] [see *Thus Spake Zarathustra* in Chapter 20] said had to be killed because nobody can tolerate being made into a mere object of absolute knowledge and absolute control. This is the deepest root of atheism. It is an atheism which is justified as the reaction against theological theism and its disturbing implications. It is also the deepest root of the Existentialist despair[5] and the widespread anxiety of meaninglessness in our period.

Theism in all its forms is transcended in the experience we have called absolute faith.[6] It is the accepting of the acceptance without somebody or something that accepts. It is the power of being-itself that accepts and gives the courage to be. This is the highest point to which our analysis has brought us. It cannot be described in the way the God of all forms of theism can be described. It cannot be described in mystical terms either. It transcends both mysticism and personal encounter, as it transcends both the courage to be as a part and the courage to be as oneself.

---

[3] **boundary** A word that reflects Tillich's belief that he was living on the threshold of a new period in history; one of his frequently used terms.

[4] **Nietzsche** Friedrich Nietzsche (1844–1900), the German philosopher, who claimed: "God is dead."
[5] **Existentialist despair** See Jean-Paul Sartre, *The Humanism of Existentialism.*
[6] **absolute faith** See footnote 2.

The God Above God and the Courage to Be

The ultimate source of the courage to be is the "God above God"; this is the result of our demand to transcend theism. Only if the God of theism is transcended can the anxiety of doubt and meaninglessness be taken into the courage to be. The God above God is the object of all mystical longing, but mysticism also must be transcended in order to reach him. Mysticism does not take seriously the concrete and the doubt concerning the concrete. It plunges directly into the ground of being[7] and meaning, and leaves the concrete, the world of finite values and meanings, behind. Therefore it does not solve the problem of meaninglessness.[8] In terms of the present religious situation this means that Eastern mysticism is not the solution of the problems of Western Existentialism, although many people attempt this solution. The God above the God of theism is not the devaluation of the meanings which doubt has thrown into the abyss of meaninglessness; he is their potential restitution. Nevertheless absolute faith agrees with the faith implied in mysticism in that both transcend the theistic objectivation of a God who is a being. For mysticism such a God is not more real than any finite being, for the courage to be such a God has disappeared in the abyss of meaninglessness with every other value and meaning.

The God above the God of theism is present, although hidden, in every divine-human encounter. Biblical religion as well as Protestant theology are aware of the paradoxical character of this encounter. They are aware that if God encounters man God is neither object nor subject and is therefore above the scheme into which theism has forced him. They are aware that personalism with respect to God is balanced by a transpersonal presence of the divine. They are aware that forgiveness can be accepted only if the power of acceptance is effective in man—biblically speaking, if the power of grace is effective in man. They are aware of the paradoxical character of every prayer, of speaking to somebody to whom you cannot speak because he is not "somebody," of asking somebody of whom you cannot ask anything because he gives or gives not before you ask, of saying "thou" to somebody who is nearer to the I than the I is to itself. Each of these paradoxes drives the religious consciousness toward a God above the God of theism.

The courage to be which is rooted in the experience of the God above the God of theism unites and transcends the courage to be as a part and the courage to be as oneself. It avoids both the loss of oneself by participation and the loss of one's world by individualization. The acceptance of the God above the God of theism makes us a part of that which is not also a part but is the ground of the whole. Therefore our self is not lost in a larger whole, which submerges it in the life of a limited group. If the self participates in the power of being-itself it receives itself

back. For the power of being acts through the power of the individual selves. It does not swallow them as every limited whole, every collectivism, and every conformism does. This is why the Church, which stands for the power of being-itself or for the God who transcends the God of the religions, claims to be the mediator of the courage to be. A church which is based on the authority of the God of theism cannot make such a claim. It inescapably develops into a collectivist or semicollectivist system itself.

But a church which raises itself in its message and its devotion to the God above the God of theism without sacrificing its concrete symbols can mediate a courage which takes doubt and meaninglessness into itself. It is the Church under the Cross which alone can do this, the Church which preaches the Crucified who cried to God who remained his God after the God of confidence had left him in the darkness of doubt and meaninglessness. To be as a part in such a church is to receive a courage to be in which one cannot lose one's self and in which one receives one's world.

Absolute faith, or the state of being grasped by the God beyond God, is not a state which appears beside other states of the mind. It never is something separated and definite, an event which could be isolated and described. It is always a movement in, with, and under other states of the mind. It is the situation on the boundary of man's possibilities. It *is* this boundary. Therefore it is both the courage of despair and the courage in and above every courage. It is not a place where one can live, it is without the safety of words and concepts, it is without a name, a church, a cult, a theology. But it is moving in the depth of all of them. It is the power of being, in which they participate and of which they are fragmentary expressions.

One can become aware of it in the anxiety of fate and death when the traditional symbols, which enable men to stand the vicissitudes of fate and the horror of death have lost their power. When "providence" has become a superstition and "immortality" something imaginary that which once was the power in these symbols can still be present and create the courage to be in spite of the experience of a chaotic world and a finite existence. The Stoic courage returns but not as the faith in universal reason.[9] It returns as the absolute faith which says Yes to being without seeing anything concrete which could conquer the nonbeing in fate and death.

And one can become aware of the God above the God of theism in the anxiety of guilt and condemnation when the traditional symbols that enable men to withstand the anxiety of guilt and condemnation have lost their power. When "divine judgment" is interpreted as a psychological complex and forgiveness as a remnant of the "father-image," what once was the power in those symbols can still be present and create the courage to be in spite of

---

[7] **ground of being** God; a term that reflects Tillich's indebtedness to existentialist thought.

[8] **problem of meaninglessness** In existentialism, the certainty of death renders life meaningless.

[9] **The Stoic courage . . . universal reason** Ancient Stoics faced the highs and lows of life, by trusting in universal reason. Tillich, in effect, is claiming to be a modern Stoic by having absolute faith in the God above God.

the experience of an infinite gap between what we are and what we ought to be. The Lutheran[10] courage returns but not supported by the faith in a judging and forgiving God. It returns in terms of the absolute faith which says Yes although there is no special power that conquers guilt. The courage to take the anxiety of meaninglessness upon oneself is the boundary line up to which the courage to be can go. Beyond it is mere non-being. Within it all forms of courage are re-established in the power of the God above the God of theism. *The courage to be is rooted in the God who appears when God has disappeared in the anxiety of doubt.*

---

[10] **Lutheran** Tillich emerged within the Lutheran Church, founded by Martin Luther (1483–1546); see *Ninety-Five Theses* in Chapter 14.

Questions for Critical Thinking

1. Discuss Tillich's concept: God above God.

2. "Tillich is a boundary thinker." Explain.

SIMONE DE BEAUVOIR
Selection from *The Second Sex*

Beauvoir's *The Second Sex* (1949), a treatise on female sexuality and a classic text of feminism, appeared at a time when the push for women's rights had temporarily lost forward motion. Women in most countries of the West now had voting rights (starting in Britain in 1918), thereby achieving the goal of the first phase of feminism; and no other issue drew women together as did the suffrage cause. Beauvoir's treatise did not so much offer a specific issue for women to rally around as it constituted a more general call to action—for women to rethink the way the sexes functioned and interacted. The burden of her message may be summed up in her bold line "One is not born, but rather becomes a woman." She rejected innate sexual differences and proclaimed that femaleness is learned and thus subject to revision. Her message launched a second wave of feminism, revolutionizing millions of readers who have dramatically revised the way they think and act.

Simone de Beauvoir (1908–1986), this apostle of latter-day feminism, was herself a contradictory figure. France's outstanding woman of letters from 1945 until her death, she wrote, besides *The Second Sex,* well-received novels (*She Came to Stay,* 1943; *The Mandarins,* 1954) and books of autobiography (*Memoirs of a Dutiful Daughter,* 1958; *The Prime of Life,* 1960). Yet she was content to take second place to Jean-Paul Sartre (see *The Humanism of Existentialism*), her lifelong mentor and the lover with whom she was involved in an unlicensed, open "marriage." At all stages of her life with Sartre, she readily set aside her own plans to edit, sharpen, and deliver detailed responses to his writing, duties she considered an honor. Beauvoir condemned female subservience in *The Second Sex,* but in her own life she created a myth of Sartre's genius, apparently thinking her own fame depended on his.

Reading the Selection

This selection, taken from the "Introduction" to *The Second Sex,* summarizes Beauvoir's argument for sexual equality. Two of her prime analytical tools are the concepts of "the Self" and "the Other," borrowed from the German thinker Georg Wilhelm Friedrich Hegel (1770–1831) (see *Reason in History* in Chapter 18). With these terms, she shows that in society as currently arranged, Man is the "Self," the essential being, the necessary sex; as such, Man defines Woman as "the Other," the inessential being, "the second sex." The category of "Otherness"— which, according to Beauvoir, Woman shares with the American Negro, the Jew, and the proletariat—is a primordial way of thinking in which privileged groups distinguish themselves from those they consider inferior, mysterious, and thus in need of control.

Even more than that of Hegel, the spirit of Sartre hovers over this work. Following Sartre, Beauvoir rejects preexisting social and moral categories, so that a woman is not "a feminine creature" but is instead what she wills herself to be. Beauvoir does not claim that a woman should become a masculinized female. Indeed, she recognizes that a woman has "ovaries, a uterus [and] these . . . circumscribe her within the limits of her own nature." But a woman, just as a man, must "choose" (take responsibility for) her situation, including her sex.

∞

Introduction

. . .

A man would never get the notion of writing a book on the peculiar situation of the human male. But if I wish to define myself, I must first of all say: "I am a woman"; on this truth must be based all further discussion. A man never begins by presenting himself as an individual of a certain sex; it goes without saying that he is a man. The terms *masculine* and *feminine* are used symmetrically only as a matter of form, as on legal papers. In actuality the relation of the two sexes is not quite like that of two electrical poles, for man represents both the positive and the neutral, as is indicated by the common use of *man* to designate human beings in general; whereas woman represents only the negative, defined by limiting criteria, without reciprocity. In the midst of an abstract discussion it is vexing to hear a man say: "You think thus and so because you are a woman"; but I know that my only defense is to reply: "I think thus and so because it is true," thereby removing my subjective self from the argument. It would be out of the question to reply: "And you think the contrary because you are a man," for it is understood that the fact of being a man is no peculiarity. A man is in the right in being a man; it is the woman who is in the wrong. It amounts to this: just as for the ancients there was an absolute vertical with reference to which the oblique was defined, so there is an absolute human type, the masculine. Woman has ovaries, a uterus; these peculiarities imprison her in her subjectivity, circumscribe her within the limits of her own nature. It is often said that she thinks with her glands. Man superbly ignores the fact that his anatomy also includes glands, such as the testicles, and that they secrete hormones. He thinks of his body as a direct and normal connection with the world, which he believes he apprehends objectively, whereas he regards the body of woman as a hindrance, a prison, weighed down by everything peculiar to it. "The female is a female by virtue of a certain *lack* of qualities," said Aristotle[11]; "we should regard the female nature as afflicted with a natural defectiveness." And St. Thomas[12] for his part pronounced woman to be an "imperfect man," an "incidental" being. This is symbolized in Genesis[13] where Eve is depicted as made from what Bossuet[14] called "a supernumerary bone" of Adam.

Thus humanity is male and man defines woman not in herself but as relative to him; she is not regarded as an autonomous being. Michelet[15] writes: "Woman, the relative being. . . ." And Benda[16] is most positive in his *Rapport d'Uriel:* "The body of man makes sense in itself quite apart from that of woman, whereas the latter seems wanting in significance by itself. . . . Man can think of himself without woman. She cannot think of herself without man." And she is simply what man decrees; thus she is called "the sex," by which is meant that she appears essentially to the male as a sexual being. For him she is sex—absolute sex, no less. She is defined and differentiated with reference to man and not he with reference to her; she is the incidental, the inessential as opposed to the essential. He is the Subject, he is the Absolute—she is the Other.

The category of the *Other* is as primordial as consciousness itself. In the most primitive societies, in the most ancient mythologies, one finds the expression of a duality—that of the Self and the Other. This duality was not originally attached to the division of the sexes; it was not dependent upon any empirical facts. It is revealed in such works as that of Granet on Chinese thought[17] and

---

[11] **Aristotle** (384–322 BCE), Greek philosopher whose writings dominated Western thought until the Scientific Revolution.

[12] **St. Thomas** Thomas Aquinas (1226–1274), the leading Christian thinker of the Middle Ages.

[13] **Genesis** The creation of Eve is in Genesis 2:21–23.

[14] **Bossuet** Jacques-Bénigne Bossuet (1627–1704), French bishop and supporter of the absolutist King Louis XIV.

[15] **Michelet** Jules Michelet (1798–1874), French historian, famous for romantic and nationalist prose.

[16] **Benda** Julien Benda (1867–1956), French writer and leader of antiromantic school of criticism.

[17] **Granet . . . thought** French historian Marcel Granet (1884–1940), author of *Chinese Civilization* (1930).

those of Dumézil on the East Indies and Rome.[18] The feminine element was at first no more involved in such pairs as Varuna-Mitra,[19] Uranus-Zeus,[20] Sun-Moon,[21] and Day-Night[22] than it was in the contrasts between Good and Evil, lucky and unlucky auspices,[23] right and left, God and Lucifer. Otherness is a fundamental category of human thought.

Thus it is that no group ever sets itself up as the One without at once setting up the Other over against itself. If three travelers chance to occupy the same compartment, that is enough to make vaguely hostile "others" out of all the rest of the passengers on the train. In small-town eyes all persons not belonging to the village are "strangers" and suspect; to the native of a country all who inhabit other countries are "foreigners"; Jews are "different" for the anti-Semite, Negroes are "inferior" for American racists, aborigines are "natives" for colonists, proletarians are the "lower class" for the privileged.

Lévi-Strauss,[24] at the end of a profound work on the various forms of primitive societies, reaches the following conclusion: "Passage from the state of Nature to the state of Culture is marked by man's ability to view biological relations as a series of contrasts; duality, alternation, opposition, and symmetry, whether under definite or vague forms, constitute not so much phenomena to be explained as fundamental and immediately given data of social reality." These phenomena would be incomprehensible if in fact human society were simply a *Mitsein* or fellowship based on solidarity and friendliness. Things become clear, on the contrary, if, following Hegel,[25] we find in consciousness itself a fundamental hostility toward every other consciousness; the subject can be posed only in being opposed—he sets himself up as the essential, as opposed to the other, the inessential, the object.

But the other consciousness, the other ego, sets up a reciprocal claim. The native traveling abroad is shocked to find himself in turn regarded as a "stranger" by the natives of neighboring countries. As a matter of fact, wars, festivals, trading, treaties, and contests among tribes, nations, and classes tend to deprive the concept *Other* of its absolute sense and to make manifest its relativity; willy-nilly, individuals and groups are forced to realize the reciprocity of their relations. How is it, then, that this reciprocity has not been recognized between the sexes, that one of the contrasting terms is set up as the sole essential, denying any relativity in regard to its correlative and defining the latter as pure otherness? Why is it that women do not dispute male sovereignty? No subject will readily volunteer to become the object, the inessential; it is not the Other who, in defining himself as the Other, establishes the One. The Other is posed as such by the One in defining himself as the One. But if the Other is not to regain the status of being the One, he must be submissive enough to accept this alien point of view. Whence comes this submission in the case of woman?

There are, to be sure, other cases in which a certain category has been able to dominate another completely for a time. Very often this privilege depends upon inequality of numbers—the majority imposes its rule upon the minority or persecutes it. But women are not a minority, like the American Negroes or the Jews; there are as many women as men on earth. Again, the two groups concerned have often been originally independent; they may have been formerly unaware of each other's existence, or perhaps they recognized each other's autonomy. But a historical event has resulted in the subjugation of the weaker by the stronger. The scattering of the Jews, the introduction of slavery into America, the conquests of imperialism are examples in point. In these cases the oppressed retained at least the memory of former days; they possessed in common a past, a tradition, sometimes a religion or a culture.

The parallel drawn by Bebel[26] between women and the proletariat is valid in that neither ever formed a minority or a separate collective unit of mankind. And instead of a single historical event it is in both cases a historical development that explains their status as a class and accounts for the membership of *particular individuals* in that class. But proletarians have not always existed, whereas there have always been women. They are women in virtue of their anatomy and physiology. Throughout history they have always been subordinated to men, and hence their dependency is not the result of a historical event or a social change—it was not something that *occurred*. The reason why otherness in this case seems to be an absolute is in part that it lacks the contingent or incidental nature of historical facts. A condition brought about at a certain time can be abolished at some other time, as the Negroes of Haiti[27] and others have proved; but it might seem that a natural condition is beyond the possibility of change. In truth, however, the nature of things is no more immutably given, once for

[18] **Dumézil . . . Rome** Georges Dumézil (1898–1986), French philologist and historian of religions; research focused on the cultural background shared by Indo-European peoples.

[19] **Varuna-Mitra** In Hindu mythology, Varuna and Mitra are brothers. Varuna shines at night and is related to the moon; Mitra sees by day and is related to the Sun.

[20] **Uranus-Zeus** In Greek mythology, Uranus and Zeus served as kings of the gods at different stages of early history. Uranus belonged to the first generation of gods; his reign coincided with a time of violence and injustice. Zeus belonged to the third generation of gods; his reign brought justice and order to the world.

[21] **Sun-Moon** In ancient cultures, the sun was worshiped as the source of light and heat, and hence considered a deity, usually masculine, as in the Babylonian Shamash. The moon was used to measure time and was also treated as a deity, invariably masculine until later times.

[22] **Day-Night** In Egyptian mythology, day and night were represented by the brother deities Horus and Seth, respectively, who were engaged in constant struggle.

[23] **auspices** Signs. In ancient Rome, the auspices were the priests who interpreted signs from birds, animals, or other phenomena, which were believed to foretell the future.

[24] **Lévi-Strauss** Claude Lévi-Strauss (1908–2009), French social anthropologist, author of *Les Structures élémentaires de la parenté* (*The Elementary Structures of Kinship*), first published in 1949.

[25] **Hegel** Georg Wilhelm Friedrich Hegel (1770–1831), German philosopher.

[26] **Bebel** August Bebel (1840–1913), German socialist, cofounder of the Social Democratic Party of Germany; author of *Die Frau und der Sozialismus* (*Woman and Socialism*) (1883).

[27] **Negroes of Haiti** The slave rebellion in the French colony of Santo Domingo in 1791, which created the independent black republic of Haiti, the first black-governed state in the Western Hemisphere.

all, than is historical reality. If woman seems to be the inessential which never becomes the essential, it is because she herself fails to bring about this change. Proletarians say "We"; Negroes also. Regarding themselves as subjects, they transform the bourgeois, the whites, into "others." But women do not say "We," except at some congress of feminists or similar formal demonstration; men say "women," and women use the same word in referring to themselves. They do not authentically assume a subjective attitude. The proletarians have accomplished the revolution in Russia,[28] the Negroes in Haiti, the Indo-Chinese are battling for it in Indo-China,[29] but the women's effort has never been anything more than a symbolic agitation. They have gained only what men have been willing to grant; they have taken nothing, they have only received.

The reason for this is that women lack concrete means for organizing themselves into a unit which can stand face to face with the correlative unit. They have no past, no history, no religion of their own; and they have no such solidarity of work and interest as that of the proletariat. They are not even promiscuously herded together in the way that creates community feeling among the American Negroes, the ghetto Jews, the workers of Saint-Denis,[30] or the factory hands of Renault.[31] They live dispersed among the males, attached through residence, housework, economic condition, and social standing to certain men—fathers or husbands—more firmly than they are to other women. If they belong to the bourgeoisie, they feel solidarity with men of that class, not with proletarian women; if they are white, their allegiance is to white men, not to Negro women. The proletariat can propose to massacre the ruling class, and a sufficiently fanatical Jew or Negro might dream of getting sole possession of the atomic bomb and making humanity wholly Jewish or black; but woman cannot even dream of exterminating the males. The bond that unites her to her oppressors is not comparable to any other. The division of the sexes is a biological fact, not an event in human history. Male and female stand opposed within a primordial *Mitsein*, and woman has not broken it. The couple is a fundamental unity with its two halves riveted together, and the cleavage of society along the line of sex is impossible. Here is to be found the basic trait of woman: she is the Other in a totality of which the two components are necessary to one another.

One could suppose that this reciprocity might have facilitated the liberation of woman. When Hercules sat at the feet of Omphale and helped with her spinning, his desire

for her held him captive; but why did she fail to gain a lasting power[32]? To revenge herself on Jason, Medea killed their children[33]; and this grim legend would seem to suggest that she might have obtained a formidable influence over him through his love for his offspring. In *Lysistrata* Aristophanes gaily depicts a band of women who joined forces to gain social ends through the sexual needs of their men; but this is only a play.[34] In the legend of the Sabine women, the latter soon abandoned their plan of remaining sterile to punish their ravishers.[35] In truth woman has not been socially emancipated through man's need—sexual desire and the desire for offspring—which makes the male dependent for satisfaction upon the female.

Master and slave, also, are united by a reciprocal need, in this case economic, which does not liberate the slave. In the relation of master to slave the master does not make a point of the need that he has for the other; he has in his grasp the power of satisfying this need through his own action; whereas the slave, in his dependent condition, his hope and fear, is quite conscious of the need he has for his master. Even if the need is at bottom equally urgent for both, it always works in favor of the oppressor and against the oppressed. That is why the liberation of the working class, for example, has been slow.

Now, woman has always been man's dependent, if not his slave; the two sexes have never shared the world in equality. And even today woman is heavily handicapped, though her situation is beginning to change. Almost nowhere is her legal status the same as man's, and frequently it is much to her disadvantage. Even when her rights are legally recognized in the abstract, long-standing custom prevents their full expression in the mores. In the economic sphere men and women can almost be said to make up two castes; other things being equal, the former hold the better jobs, get higher wages, and have more opportunity for success than their new competitors. In industry and politics men have a great many more positions and they monopolize the most important posts. In addition to all this, they enjoy a traditional prestige that the education of children tends in every way to support, for the present enshrines the past—and in the past all history has been made by men. At the present time, when women are beginning to take part in the affairs of the world, it is still a world that belongs to men—they have no doubt of it at all and women have scarcely any. To decline to be the Other, to refuse to be a party to the deal—this would be for women to renounce all the advantages conferred upon them by their alliance with the superior caste. Man-the-sovereign

[28] **revolution in Russia** Led by the Bolsheviks in 1917.
[29] **the Indo-Chinese . . . in Indo-China** French Indo-China, comprising the protectorates of Cambodia, Laos, Annam, and Tonkin, was founded in 1887. After World War II, the area emerged under the control of the French government. In September 1945, the Vietnamese rebel leader Ho Chi Minh carved out the area called Vietnam and proclaimed its independence from France. France's new government invaded and triggered the French Indo-China War, 1946–1954.
[30] **Saint-Denis** A working-class neighborhood in Paris.
[31] **Renault** In 1945, the Renault automobile manufacturer became Regie Nationale des Usines Renault, under the control of the French government and headquartered in Boulogne-Billancourt.

[32] **Hercules . . . power** In Greek mythology, the hero Hercules was a slave to Omphale, Queen of Lydia, for three years. During this time, Omphale wore masculine clothes, a lion skin, and Hercules dressed in a female garment.
[33] **Jason . . . children** In Euripides' play *Medea*, Jason is married to the sorceress Medea; when he attempts a more politically advantageous marriage, Medea kills their children.
[34] *Lysistrata* A Greek comedy by Aristophanes, first performed in 411 BCE.
[35] **the Sabine . . . ravishers** An ancient Roman legend. Rome's founders, lacking wives, abducted and raped the women of the Sabine people, a neighboring tribe.

will provide woman-the-liege with material protection and will undertake the moral justification of her existence; thus she can evade at once both economic risk and the metaphysical risk of a liberty in which ends and aims must be contrived without assistance. Indeed, along with the ethical urge of each individual to affirm his subjective existence, there is also the temptation to forgo liberty and become a thing. This is an inauspicious road, for he who takes it—passive, lost, ruined—becomes henceforth the creature of another's will, frustrated in his transcendence and deprived of every value. But it is an easy road; on it one avoids the strain involved in undertaking an authentic existence. When man makes of woman the *Other,* he may, then, expect her to manifest deep-seated tendencies toward complicity. Thus, woman may fail to lay claim to the status of subject because she lacks definite resources, because she feels the necessary bond that ties her to man regardless of reciprocity, and because she is often very well pleased with her role as the *Other.*

But it will be asked at once: how did all this begin? It is easy to see that the duality of the sexes, like any duality, gives rise to conflict. And doubtless the winner will assume the status of absolute. But why should man have won from the start? It seems possible that women could have won the victory; or that the outcome of the conflict might never have decided. How is it that this world has always belonged to the men and that things have begun to change only recently? Is this change a good thing? Will it bring about an equal sharing of the world between men and women?

These questions are not new, and they have often been answered. But the very fact that woman *is the Other* tends to cast suspicion upon all the justifications that men have ever been able to provide for it. These have all too evidently been dictated by men's interest. A little-known feminist of the seventeenth century, Poulain de la Barre,[36] put it this way: "All that has been written about women by men should be suspect for the men are at once judge and party to the lawsuit." Everywhere, at all times, the males have displayed their satisfaction in feeling that they are the lords of creation. "Blessed be God . . . that He did not make me a woman," say the Jews in their morning prayers,[37] while their wives pray on a note of resignation: "Blessed be the Lord, who created me according to His will." The first among the blessings for which Plato[38] thanked the gods was that he had been created free, not enslaved; the second, a man, not a woman. But the males could not enjoy this privilege fully unless they believed it to be founded on the absolute and the eternal; they sought

to make the fact of their supremacy into a right. "Being men, those who have made and compiled the laws have favored their own sex, and jurists have elevated these laws into principles," to quote Poulain de la Barre once more.

Legislators, priests, philosophers, writers, and scientists have striven to show that the subordinate position of woman is willed in heaven and advantageous on earth. The religions invented by men reflect this wish for domination. In the legends of Eve[39] and Pandora[40] men have taken up arms against women. They have made use of philosophy and theology, as the quotations from Aristotle and St. Thomas have shown. Since ancient times satirists and moralists have delighted in showing up the weaknesses of women. We are familiar with the savage indictments hurled against women throughout French literature. Montherlant,[41] for example, follows the tradition of Jean de Meung,[42] though with less gusto. This hostility may at times be well founded, often it is gratuitous; but in truth it more or less successfully conceals a desire for self-justification. As Montaigne[43] says, "It is easier to accuse one sex than to excuse the other." Sometimes what is going on is clear enough. For instance, the Roman law limiting the rights of woman cited "the imbecility, the instability of the sex" just when the weakening of family ties seemed to threaten the interests of male heirs. And in the effort to keep the married woman under guardianship, appeal was made in the sixteenth century to the authority of St. Augustine,[44] who declared that "woman is a creature neither decisive nor constant," at a time when the single woman was thought capable of managing her property. Montaigne understood clearly how arbitrary and unjust was woman's appointed lot: "Women are not in the wrong when they decline to accept the rules laid down for them, since the men make these rules without consulting them. No wonder intrigue and strife abound." But he did not go so far as to champion their cause.

It was only later, in the eighteenth century, that genuinely democratic men began to view the matter objectively. Diderot,[45] among others, strove to show that woman is, like man, a human being. Later John Stuart Mill[46] came fervently to her defense. But these philosophers displayed unusual impartiality. In the nineteenth century

15

---

[36] **Poulain de la Barre** François Poulain de la Barre (1647–1723), French scholar of women's issues, author of *De l'égalite des deux sexes (Equality of the Two Sexes)* (1673).

[37] **Jews . . . prayers** In Hebrew, *shelo asani ishah.*

[38] **Plato** (ca. 427–347 BCE), Greek philosopher. Plato's attitude toward women is a topic of vigorous debate. On the one hand, in his ideal state, he called for educated women, along with educated men, to rule as philosopher-kings, but on the other hand, he made disparaging comments about women, as in this observation in *The Republic:* "The one sex is, so to speak, far and away beaten in every field by the other."

[39] **Eve** Genesis 3:7.

[40] **Pandora** From Greek, "all gifts." In Greek legend, Pandora opened a box against the advice of the gods, thus releasing all the evils that have plagued the world ever since.

[41] **Montherlant** Henry-Marie-Joseph Millon de Montherlant (1896–1972), French writer and social critic, opposed to democratic and "feminine" values.

[42] **Jean de Meung** Jean Chopinel, known as Jean de Meun or Meung (ca. 1240–before 1305), French poet, noted for his continuation of the *Romance de la Rose,* the great medieval poem on courtly love. De Meung's verses express a coarse antifeminism.

[43] **Montaigne** Michel de Montaigne (1533–1592), French essayist.

[44] **St. Augustine** (354–430), Christian writer and church official; a father of the church.

[45] **Diderot** Denis Diderot (1713–1784), French writer and editor of the *Encyclopédie.*

[46] **John Stuart Mill** (1806–1873), English philosopher, economist, and advocate of utilitarianism; author of *The Subjection of Women* (1869), a key text of feminism.

the feminist quarrel became again a quarrel of partisans. One of the consequences of the industrial revolution was the entrance of women into productive labor, and it was just here that the claims of the feminists emerged from the realm of theory and acquired an economic basis, while their opponents became the more aggressive. Although landed property lost power to some extent, the bourgeoisie clung to the old morality that found the guarantee of private property in the solidity of the family. Woman was ordered back into the home the more harshly as her emancipation became a real menace. Even within the working class the men endeavored to restrain woman's liberation, because they began to see the women as dangerous competitors—the more so because they were accustomed to work for lower wages. . . .

So it is that many men will affirm as if in good faith that women *are* the equals of man and that they have nothing to clamor for, while *at the same time* they will say that women can never be the equals of man and that their demands are in vain. It is, in point of fact, a difficult matter for man to realize the extreme importance of social discriminations which seem outwardly insignificant but which produce in women moral and intellectual effects so profound that they appear to spring from her original nature. The most sympathetic of men never fully comprehend woman's concrete situation. And there is no reason to put much trust in the men when they rush to the defense of privileges whose full extent they can hardly measure. We shall not, then, permit ourselves to be intimidated by the number and violence of the attacks launched against women, nor to be entrapped by the self-seeking eulogies bestowed on the "true woman," nor to profit by the enthusiasm for woman's destiny manifested by men who would not for the world have any part of it. . . .

Questions for Critical Thinking

1. What does Beauvoir mean by the category of the Other? How does the concept of the Other help give shape to her argument?

2. If a woman must "choose" (take responsibility for) her situation, what does this mean for a woman, according to Beauvoir?

MALCOLM X AND ALEX HALEY
Selection from *The Autobiography of Malcolm X*

In the 1950s most African American leaders, rallying around Martin Luther King Jr., adopted the political agenda of racial integration into the American mainstream. However, more militant leaders also began to emerge—leaders who saw the future of their race as separate from white culture and society. Believing whites to be against full integration, they argued that blacks should strive to become independent from white control; to this end, they advocated the use of violence if conditions called for it. The militant agenda of these leaders appealed to the minority of blacks on the margin of black society, particularly those who had run afoul of the white justice system or who believed, for varying reasons, that black separatism was necessary.

Malcolm X (born Malcolm Little, 1925–1965) was the most charismatic of these militant black leaders of the 1950s. His ideas are enjoying a renaissance today among a large group of African Americans, his life having become the subject of a major film. Malcolm X came from a poor midwestern family who suffered at the hands of white racists, their home being burned and the father brutally murdered. Malcolm's mentally unstable mother, unable to care for eight children, allowed them to be assigned to relatives' homes and state institutions. The teenaged Malcolm wound up first in Boston and then in New York, where he became a hustler and petty thief. Prison became his school. There, he learned about the Black Muslims, an American version of the Islamic religion, which gave him a new purpose in life. His name change, from Little to X, reflected the new direction he intended to take. Released from prison in the 1950s, he became a leader of the Black Muslims, calling on African Americans, in striking and bold language, to separate themselves completely from white society. His militancy alarmed most whites and upset many black leaders at the time. However, his pleas for self-respect attracted young blacks in the 1960s. After a trip to Mecca, Malcolm X worked for closer cooperation with whites, but before he could launch his new program, he was assassinated.

Reading the Selection

The record of Malcolm X's struggle for both his own identity and that of his fellow African Americans was made possible by the patience and writing skills of Alex Haley (1921–1992). Haley was a black writer who later achieved fame with his book *Roots*, which was a search for Haley's African and slave forebears. During the writing of *The Autobiography*, Haley interviewed Malcolm X at length and accompanied him on speaking engagements where he could observe Malcolm's personality, oratorical skills, and the reactions of admirers and detractors.

    This selection from Chapter XI, "Saved," of *The Autobiography of Malcolm X* recounts Malcolm X's prison days as he began to educate himself, learning to read and studying books in the prison library. Earlier chapters detailed his criminal past, and later chapters laid out his triumphs as a black leader. Chapter XI represents the turning point of his life. In prison he studied the teachings of Elijah Muhammad (1897–1975), the founder of the Black Muslims, and learned from him that white writers leave "the black man" out of history books. This fact reinforced Malcolm's growing conviction that whites could not be trusted and that blacks must recover their own history as a first step to gaining self-respect.

Chapter XI
Saved

· · ·

I became increasingly frustrated at not being able to express what I wanted to convey in letters that I wrote, especially those to Mr. Elijah Muhammad. In the street, I had been the most articulate hustler out there—I had commanded attention when I said something. But now, trying to write simple English, I not only wasn't articulate, I wasn't even functional. How would I sound writing in slang, the way I would *say* it, something such as "Look, daddy, let me pull your coat about a cat, Elijah Muhammad—"

    Many who today hear me somewhere in person, or on television, or those who read something I've said, will think I went to school far beyond the eighth grade. This impression is due entirely to my prison studies.

    It had really begun back in the Charlestown Prison,[47] when Bimbi[48] first made me feel envy of his stock of knowl-

edge. Bimbi had always taken charge of any conversation he was in, and I had tried to emulate him. But every book I picked up had few sentences which didn't contain anywhere from one to nearly all of the words that might as well have been in Chinese. When I just skipped those words, of course, I really ended up with little idea of what the book said. So I had come to the Norfolk Prison Colony[49] still going through only book-reading motions. Pretty soon, I would have quit even these motions, unless I had received the motivation that I did.

    I saw that the best thing I could do was get hold of a dictionary—to study, to learn some words. I was lucky enough to reason also that I should try to improve my penmanship. It was sad. I couldn't even write in a straight line. It was both ideas together that moved me to request a dictionary along with some tablets and pencils from the Norfolk Prison Colony school.

---

[47] **Charlestown Prison** In Massachusetts. Malcolm X was convicted of robbery and sentenced to prison in 1946.
[48] **Bimbi** Black inmate and recruiter for the Nation of Islam. Met Malcolm X in 1947.

---

[49] **Norfolk Prison Colony** A prison, with moderate conditions, in the Massachusetts state system. Malcolm X was transferred here in 1948.

I spent two days just riffling uncertainly through ₅ the dictionary's pages. I'd never realized so many words existed! I didn't know *which* words I needed to learn. Finally, just to start some kind of action, I began copying.

In my slow, painstaking, ragged handwriting, I copied into my tablet everything printed on that first page, down to the punctuation marks.

I believe it took me a day. Then, aloud, I read back, to myself, everything I'd written on the tablet. Over and over, aloud, to myself, I read my own handwriting.

I woke up the next morning, thinking about those words—immensely proud to realize that not only had I written so much at one time, but I'd written words that I never knew were in the world. Moreover, with a little effort, I also could remember what many of these words meant. I reviewed the words whose meanings I didn't remember. Funny thing, from the dictionary first page right now, that "aardvark" springs to my mind. The dictionary had a picture of it, a long-tailed, long-eared, burrowing African mammal, which lives off termites caught by sticking out its tongue as an anteater does for ants.

I was so fascinated that I went on—I copied the dictionary's next page. And the same experience came when I studied that. With every succeeding page, I also learned of people and places and events from history. Actually the dictionary is like a miniature encyclopedia. Finally the dictionary's A section had filled a whole tablet—and I went on into the B's. That was the way I started copying what eventually became the entire dictionary. It went a lot faster after so much practice helped me to pick up handwriting speed. Between what I wrote in my tablet, and writing letters, during the rest of my time in prison I would guess I wrote a million words.

I suppose it was inevitable that as my word-base ₁₀ broadened, I could for the first time pick up a book and read and now begin to understand what the book was saying. Anyone who has read a great deal can imagine the new world that opened. Let me tell you something: from then until I left that prison, in every free moment I had, if I was not reading in the library, I was reading on my bunk. You couldn't have gotten me out of books with a wedge. Between Mr. Muhammad's teachings, my correspondence, my visitors—usually Ella[50] and Reginald[51]—and my reading of books, months passed without my even thinking about being imprisoned. In fact, up to then, I never had been so truly free in my life.

The Norfolk Prison Colony's library was in the school building. A variety of classes was taught there by instructors who came from such places as Harvard and Boston universities. The weekly debates between inmate teams were also held in the school building. You would be astonished to know how worked up convict debaters and audiences would get over subjects like "Should Babies Be Fed Milk?"

Available on the prison library's shelves were books on just about every general subject. Much of the big private

collection that Parkhurst[52] had willed to the prison was still in crates and boxes in the back of the library—thousands of old books. Some of them looked ancient: covers faded, old-time parchment-looking binding. Parkhurst, I've mentioned, seemed to have been principally interested in history and religion. He had the money and the special interest to have a lot of books that you wouldn't have in general circulation. Any college library would have been lucky to get that collection.

As you can imagine, especially in a prison where there was heavy emphasis on rehabilitation, an inmate was smiled upon if he demonstrated an unusually intense interest in books. There was a sizable number of well-read inmates, especially the popular debaters. Some were said by many to be practically walking encyclopedias. They were almost celebrities. No university would ask any student to devour literature as I did when this new world opened to me, of being able to read and *understand*.

I read more in my room than in the library itself. An inmate who was known to read a lot could check out more than the permitted maximum number of books. I preferred reading in the total isolation of my own room.

When I had progressed to really serious reading, every ₁₅ night at about ten P.M. I would be outraged with the "lights out." It always seemed to catch me right in the middle of something engrossing.

Fortunately, right outside my door was a corridor light that cast a glow into my room. The glow was enough to read by, once my eyes adjusted to it. So when "lights out" came, I would sit on the floor where I could continue reading in that glow.

At one-hour intervals the night guards paced past every room. Each time I heard the approaching footsteps, I jumped into bed and feigned sleep. And as soon as the guard passed, I got back out of bed onto the floor area of that light-glow, where I would read for another fifty-eight minutes—until the guard approached again. That went on until three or four every morning. Three or four hours of sleep a night was enough for me. Often in the years in the streets I had slept less than that.

The teachings of Mr. Muhammad stressed how history had been "whitened"—when white men had written history books, the black man simply had been left out. Mr. Muhammad couldn't have said anything that would have struck me much harder. I had never forgotten how when my class, me and all of those whites, had studied seventh-grade United States history back in Mason,[53] the history of the Negro had been covered in one paragraph, and the teacher had gotten a big laugh with his joke, "Negroes' feet are so big that when they walk, they leave a hole in the ground."

This is one reason why Mr. Muhammad's teachings spread so swiftly all over the United States, among *all* Negroes, whether or not they became followers of Mr. Muhammad. The teachings ring true—to every Negro. You

---

⁵⁰ **Ella** Ella Collins, the half sister of Malcolm X. They shared the same father, Earl Little. Ella lived in Roxbury, Massachusetts.
⁵¹ **Reginald** Reginald Little, the brother of Malcolm X.

⁵² **Parkhurst** Wealthy philanthropist who had donated a library to the Norfolk Prison.
⁵³ **Mason** A town in Michigan.

can hardly show me a black adult in America—or a white one, for that matter—who knows from the history books anything like the truth about the black man's role. In my own case, once I heard of the "glorious history of the black man," I took special pains to hunt in the library for books that would inform me on details about black history.

I can remember accurately the very first set of books [20] that really impressed me. I have since bought that set of books and have it at home for my children to read as they grow up. It's called *Wonders of the World.* It's full of pictures of archeological finds, statues that depict, usually, non-European people.

I found books like Will Durant's *Story of Civilization.*[54] I read H. G. Wells' *Outline of History.*[55] *Souls of Black Folk* by W. E. B. Du Bois[56] gave me a glimpse into the black people's history before they came to this country. Carter G. Woodson's *Negro History*[57] opened my eyes about black empires before the black slave was brought to the United States, and the early Negro struggles for freedom.

J. A. Rogers' three volumes of *Sex and Race*[58] told about race-mixing before Christ's time; about Aesop[59] being a black man who told fables; about Egypt's Pharaohs[60]; about the great Coptic Christian Empires[61]; about Ethiopia, the

earth's oldest continuous black civilization,[62] as China is the oldest continuous civilization.[63]

Mr. Muhammad's teachings about how the white man had been created led me to *Findings in Genetics* by Gregor Mendel.[64] (The dictionary's G section was where I had learned what "genetics" meant.) I really studied this book by the Austrian monk. Reading it over and over, especially certain sections, helped me to understand that if you started with a black man, a white man could be produced; but starting, with a white man, you never could produce a black man—because the white gene is recessive. And since no one disputes that there was but one Original Man, the conclusion is clear.

During the last year or so, in the *New York Times,* Arnold Toynbee[65] used the word "bleached" in describing the white man. (His words were: "White (i.e. bleached) human beings of North European origin. . . .") Toynbee also referred to the European geographic area as only a peninsula of Asia. He said there is no such thing as Europe. And if you look at the globe, you will see for yourself that America is only an extension of Asia. (But at the same time Toynbee is among those who have helped to bleach history. He has written that Africa was the only continent that produced no history. He won't write that again. Every day now, the truth is coming to light.)

I never will forget how shocked I was when I began [25] reading about slavery's total horror. It made such an impact upon me that it later became one of my favorite subjects when I became a minister of Mr. Muhammad's. The world's most monstrous crime, the sin and the blood on the white man's hands, are almost impossible to believe. Books like the one by Frederick Olmstead[66] opened my eyes to the horrors suffered when the slave was landed in the United States. The European woman, Fannie Kimball,[67] who had married a Southern white slaveowner, described how human beings were degraded. Of course I read *Uncle Tom's Cabin.*[68] In fact, I believe that's the only novel I have ever read since I started serious reading.

Parkhurst's collection also contained some bound pamphlets of the Abolitionist Anti-Slavery Society of New

---

[54] **Will Durant . . . *Civilization*** An eleven-volume work, extending from the earliest times to the end of the Napoleonic period in 1815; published between 1935 and 1967. Written by the American historians Will Durant (1885–1981) and Ariel Durant (1898–1981).
[55] **H. G. Wells . . . *History*** Herbert George Wells (1866–1946), English novelist and historian. *Outline of History* was published in 1920.
[56] ***Souls of . . . Du Bois*** William Edward Burghardt Du Bois (1868–1963), African American writer, editor, and educator; one of the founders of the National Association for the Advancement of Colored People, in 1909. Author of *The Souls of Black Folks* (1903).
[57] **Carter G. Woodson's *Negro History*** (1875–1950), African American historian, author of *The Negro in Our History* (1922) and *The Rural Negro* (1930) and other works.
[58] **J. A. Rogers' . . . *Sex and Race*** Joel Augustus Rogers (1883–1966), Jamaican American Pullman porter and historian, author of the three-volume work *Sex and Race: Negro-Caucasian Mixing in All Races and All Lands,* published between 1941 and 1944.
[59] **Aesop** (ca. 620–ca. 560 BCE), Greek writer, handicapped slave, and author of popular fables about animals. Many versions of his tales, found on Egyptian papyri, date from more than two thousand years before him. Aesop's skin color is a matter of controversy.
[60] **Pharaohs** Rulers. Egypt was ruled by a black Nubian dynasty from about 920 to 669 BCE. The Nubians lived between the First and Fourth Cataracts of the Nile River, south of Egypt. Except for the Nubian dynasty, Egypt's rulers, as well as the population, were "Mediterranean peoples, neither Sub-Saharan blacks nor Caucasian whites but peoples whose skin was adapted for life in a subtropical desert environment" (Kathryn A. Bard).
[61] **Coptic Christian Empires** The Coptic Christian Church of Egypt and Ethiopia claims to date from the first century CE, when St. Mark visited Egypt. The Coptic Church split from the rest of the church in 451, claiming a single nature for Jesus Christ, which blended the human and the divine. The kingdom of Axum in Ethiopia became Coptic Christian in the fourth century and lasted about seven hundred years. In 1270, from the ruins of Axum emerged the kingdom of Ethiopia under the Solomonic dynasty, supported by the Coptic Church. Unitary rule in Ethiopia ended in 1626, with the conversion of its kings to Roman Catholicism, though the Coptic Church continued to exist.

[62] **Ethiopia . . . civilization** Since the second century, first as Axum and then as Ethiopia (see footnote 61).
[63] **China . . . civilization** From the Qin (Ch'in) dynasty, 221–206 BCE, the concept of a unified state has prevailed in China.
[64] **Mendel** Gregor Johann Mendel (1822–1884), Austrian monk and founder of the science of genetics. He published his findings in the article "Experiment with Plant Hybrids" in 1866. The significance of his work became widely known only after 1900.
[65] **Arnold Toynbee** (1889–1975), English historian, author of a monumental survey of world cultures titled *A Study of History* (1934–1961).
[66] **Frederick Olmstead** (1822–1903), American landscape architect and opponent of slavery. In *The Cotton Kingdom* (1861), he reported on conditions in the American South, from 1852 to 1855, when he traveled there as a writer for the *New York Times.*
[67] **Fannie Kimball** Frances Anne, called Fanny, Kemble (1809–1893), English actress, who lived on her American husband's Southern plantation, 1849–1868; author of *Journal* (1835, 1863).
[68] ***Uncle Tom's Cabin*** By Harriet Beecher Stowe (1811–1896), published in 1852; an antislavery novel that sold 1.5 million copies in its first year.

England.[69] I read descriptions of atrocities, saw those illustrations of black slave women tied up and flogged with whips; of black mothers watching their babies being dragged off, never to be seen by their mothers again; of dogs after slaves, and of the fugitive slave catchers, evil white men with whips and clubs and chains and guns. I read about the slave preacher Nat Turner,[70] who put the fear of God into the white slavemaster. Nat Turner wasn't going around preaching pie-in-the-sky and "non-violent"[71] freedom for the black man. There in Virginia one night in 1831, Nat and seven other slaves started out at his master's home and through the night they went from one plantation "big house" to the next, killing, until by the next morning 57 white people were dead and Nat had about 70 slaves following him. White people, terrified for their lives, fled from their homes, locked themselves up in public buildings, hid in the woods, and some even left the state. A small army of soldiers took two months to catch and hang Nat Turner. Somewhere I have read where Nat Turner's example is said to have inspired John Brown[72] to invade Virginia and attack Harper's Ferry nearly thirty years later, with thirteen white men and five Negroes.

I read Herodotus,[73] "the father of History," or, rather, I read about him. And I read the histories of various nations, which opened my eyes gradually, then wider and wider, to how the whole world's white men had indeed acted like devils, pillaging and raping and bleeding and draining the whole world's non-white people. I remember, for instance, books such as Will Durant's story of Oriental civilization,[74] and Mahatma Gandhi's accounts of the struggle to drive the British out of India.[75]

Book after book showed me how the white man had brought upon the world's black, brown, red, and yellow peoples every variety of the sufferings of exploitation. I saw how since the sixteenth century, the so-called "Christian trader" white man began to ply the seas in his lust for Asian and African empires, and plunder, and power. I read,

I saw, how the white man never has gone among the non-white peoples bearing the Cross in the true manner and spirit of Christ's teachings—meek, humble, and Christ-like.

I perceived, as I read, how the collective white man had been actually nothing but a piratical opportunist who used Faustian[76] machinations to make his own Christianity his initial wedge in criminal conquests. First, always "religiously," he branded "heathen" and "pagan" labels upon ancient non-white cultures and civilizations. The stage thus set, he then turned upon his non-white victims his weapons of war.

I read how, entering India—half a *billion* deeply religious brown people—the British white man, by 1759, through promises, trickery and manipulations, controlled much of India through Great Britain's East India Company.[77] The parasitical British administration kept tentacling out to half of the subcontinent. In 1857, some of the desperate people of India finally mutinied[78]—and, excepting the African slave trade, nowhere has history recorded any more unnecessary bestial and ruthless human carnage than the British suppression of the non-white Indian people.

Over 115 million African blacks—close to the 1930's population of the United States—were murdered or enslaved during the slave trade. And I read how when the slave market was glutted, the cannibalistic white powers of Europe next carved up, as their colonies, the richest areas of the black continent.[79] And Europe's chancelleries for the next century played a chess game of naked exploitation and power from Cape Horn to Cairo.[80]

Ten guards and the warden couldn't have torn me out of those books. Not even Elijah Muhammad could have been more eloquent than those books were in providing indisputable proof that the collective white man had acted like a devil in virtually every contact he had with the world's collective non-white man. I listen today to the radio, and watch television, and read the headlines about the collective white man's fear and tension concerning China. When the white man professes ignorance about why the Chinese hate him so, my mind can't help flashing back to what I read, there in prison, about how the blood forebears

[69] **Abolitionist . . . England** American Anti-Slavery Society, founded in 1833 by William Lloyd Garrison (1805–1879) of Boston, Massachusetts; Garrison also edited *The Liberator*, 1831–1865, the most uncompromising of the antislavery journals.
[70] **Nat Turner** (1800–1831), African American slave who led an 1831 revolt in Southampton County, Virginia, killing fifty-seven whites before he and his group were killed.
[71] **non-violent** An allusion to the "civil disobedience" strategy advocated by Martin Luther King Jr. (see "Letter from a Birmingham Jail").
[72] **John Brown** (1800–1859), American abolitionist who led a group of whites and blacks in the capture of the federal arsenal at Harper's Ferry, Virginia, in 1859, hoping the attack would inspire a slave revolt. Two days later, American soldiers retook the arsenal, and Brown was hanged for treason and murder.
[73] **Herodotus** (ca. 484–ca. 430 BCE), Greek historian, the author of the *Histories*. (q.v.).
[74] **Will Durant's . . . civilization** *Our Oriental Heritage* (1935) (see footnote 54).
[75] **Mahatma Gandhi's accounts . . . India** Mohandas K. Gandhi (1869–1948), Indian Hindu and spiritual leader, who guided the Indian nationalists to achieving freedom for their country from Britain in 1946. The title *Mahatma*, bestowed on Gandhi by his followers, is taken from Sanskrit and means "Great Soul." Unclear what work Malcolm X was reading by Gandhi, as Gandhi left a vast legacy of more than eighty books.

[76] **Faustian** In the manner of the legendary Faust, that is, willing to traffic with the devil in exchange for human ends (see Goethe, *Faust*, Part I, in Chapter 18).
[77] **East India Company** A group of London merchants, chartered by the crown in 1600, that gradually evolved from a trading company with privileges in Asia to a territorial empire centered in India.
[78] **1857 . . . mutinied** Indian Mutiny, 1857–1858, triggered by Indian *sepoys* ("soldiers") who revolted against the East India Company. A full-scale uprising ensued, filled with atrocities on both sides. The mutiny was eventually suppressed, British control was restored, and the British crown replaced the East India Company as the ruler of India.
[79] **white powers . . . black continent** The "scramble for Africa," the rapid Europeanization of Africa, beginning with the French seizure of Tunis in 1881. By 1902, the end of the Second Boer War, most of Africa had been divided among Belgium, Britain, France, Germany, Portugal, and Spain.
[80] **Cape Horn to Cairo** Should be Cape of Good Hope (the tip of Africa) to Cairo (in Egypt); Cape Horn is the tip of South America.

of this same white man raped China at a time when China was trusting and helpless. Those original white "Christian traders" sent into China millions of pounds of opium. By 1839, so many of the Chinese were addicts that China's desperate government destroyed twenty thousand chests of opium. The first Opium War was promptly declared by the white man.[81] Imagine! Declaring *war* upon someone who objects to being narcotized! The Chinese were severely beaten, with Chinese-invented gunpowder.

The Treaty of Nanking[82] made China pay the British white man for the destroyed opium; forced open China's major ports to British trade; forced China to abandon Hong Kong; fixed China's import tariffs so low that cheap British articles soon flooded in, maiming China's industrial development.

After a second Opium War,[83] the Tientsin Treaties[84] legalized the ravaging opium trade, legalized a British-French-American control of China's customs. China tried delaying that Treaty's ratification; Peking was looted and burned.[85]

"Kill the foreign white devils!" was the 1901 Chinese war cry in the Boxer Rebellion.[86] Losing again, this time the Chinese were driven from Peking's choicest areas. The vicious, arrogant white man put up the famous signs, "Chinese and dogs not allowed."

Red China after World War II[87] closed its doors to the Western white world. Massive Chinese agricultural, scientific, and industrial efforts are described in a book that *Life*[88] magazine recently published. Some observers inside Red China have reported that the world never has known such a hate-white campaign as is now going on in this non-white country where, present birth-rates continuing, in fifty more years Chinese will be half the earth's population.[89] And it seems that some Chinese chickens will soon come home to roost, with China's recent successful nuclear tests.

Let us face reality. We can see in the United Nations a new world order being shaped, along color lines—an alliance among the non-white nations. America's U.N. Ambassador Adlai Stevenson[90] complained not long ago that in the United Nations "a skin game" was being played. He was right. He was facing reality. A "skin game" *is* being played. But Ambassador Stevenson sounded like Jesse James[91] accusing the marshal of carrying a gun. Because who in the world's history ever has played a worse "skin game" than the white man?

Mr. Muhammad, to whom I was writing daily, had no idea of what a new world had opened up to me through my efforts to document his teachings in books.

When I discovered philosophy, I tried to touch all the landmarks of philosophical development. Gradually, I read most of the old philosophers, Occidental and Oriental. The Oriental philosophers were the ones I came to prefer; finally, my impression was that most Occidental philosophy had largely been borrowed from the Oriental thinkers. Socrates,[92] for instance, traveled in Egypt. Some sources even say that Socrates was initiated into some of the Egyptian mysteries. Obviously Socrates got some of this wisdom among the East's wise men.

I have often reflected upon the new vistas that reading opened to me. I knew right there in prison that reading had changed forever the course of my life. As I see it today, the ability to read awoke inside me some long dormant craving to be mentally alive. I certainly wasn't seeking any degree, the way a college confers a status symbol upon its students. My homemade education gave me, with every additional book that I read, a little bit more sensitivity to the deafness, dumbness, and blindness that was afflicting the black race in America. Not long ago, an English writer telephoned me from London, asking questions. One was, "What's your alma mater?" I told him, "Books." You will never catch me with a free fifteen minutes in which I'm not studying something I feel might be able to help the black man.

Yesterday I spoke in London, and both ways on the plane across the Atlantic I was studying a document about how the United Nations proposes to insure the human

[81] **first Opium War . . . white man** First Opium War (1839–1842), between Britain and China. British merchants illegally imported opium from India into China. Chinese authorities confiscated the contraband opium, and the British responded with warships. The inconclusive Treaty of Nanjing, in 1842, ended the hostilities.
[82] **Treaty of Nanking** (see footnote 81).
[83] **second Opium War** Second Opium War (1856–1860), between Britain and China. The war was precipitated by the Chinese, who conducted an unauthorized search of a British ship for illegal opium. The British, joined by the French, launched a vigorous attack against the Chinese authorities. Hostilities ended with the Treaty of Tianjin, in 1860, which opened several Chinese port cities to Western trade and allowed free access to China's interior by Western merchants and missionaries.
[84] **Tientsin Treaties** (see footnotes 83 and 85).
[85] **burned** The Treaty of Tianjin was first drawn up in 1858, but China's emperor refused to ratify it. In retaliation, British and French troops seized Beijing (Peking) and burned the imperial summer palace.
[86] **Boxer Rebellion** (1899–1900), an anti-Western uprising in China, organized by the secret society of Righteous and Harmonious Fists (called "Boxers" in the West), who opposed both foreigners and the feeble Ch'ing (Manchu) dynasty. The Boxers claimed that their rituals made them impervious to bullets. In Beijing and elsewhere, attacks were launched against Western merchants, missionaries, and soldiers. Several foreign powers organized an expeditionary force to relieve Beijing, and this quelled the Boxer uprising. Punitive raids were also conducted by Western forces in the Beijing region.
[87] **Red China after World War II** The Chinese Communist Party, led by Mao Zedong (1893–1976), defeated Nationalist forces in 1949 and set up the People's Republic of China (PRC). Only in 1972 did the United States recognize the PRC as China's official government.
[88] *Life* Popular weekly picture magazine, 1936–1972.

[89] **Chinese . . . population** In 2000 the population of China was estimated as 1.2 billion and the world's population as 6 billion.
[90] **Adlai Stevenson** (1900–1965), American politician, Democratic candidate for President (1952, 1956), ambassador to the United Nations, 1961–1965.
[91] **Jesse James** (1847–1882), American outlaw and leader of a gang based in Missouri that terrorized the American heartland by robbing banks and trains.
[92] **Socrates** (ca. 470–399 BCE), Athenian philosopher, a martyr for his beliefs. He was put to death by his native city, on the charge of corrupting the youth through his teachings. Whether or not Socrates traveled in Egypt is a matter of conjecture.

rights of the oppressed minorities of the world. The American black man is the world's most shameful case of minority oppression. What makes the black man think of himself as only an internal United States issue is just a catch-phrase, two words, "civil rights." How is the black man going to get "civil rights" before first he wins his *human* rights? If the American black man will start thinking about his *human* rights, and then start thinking of himself as part of one of the world's great peoples, he will see he has a case for the United Nations.

I can't think of a better case! Four hundred years of black blood and sweat invested here in America, and the white man still has the black man begging for what every immigrant fresh off the ship can take for granted the minute he walks down the gangplank.

But I'm digressing. I told the Englishman that my alma mater was books, a good library. Every time I catch a plane, I have with me a book that I want to read—and that's a lot of books these days. If I weren't out here every

day battling the white man, I could spend the rest of my life reading, just satisfying my curiosity—because you can hardly mention anything I'm not curious about. I don't think anybody ever got more out of going to prison than I did. In fact, prison enabled me to study far more intensively than I would have if my life had gone differently and I had attended some college. I imagine that one of the biggest troubles with colleges is there are too many distractions, too much panty-raiding,[93] fraternities, and boola-boola[94] and all of that. Where else but in a prison could I have attacked my ignorance by being able to study intensely sometimes as much as fifteen hours a day? . . .

---

[93] **panty-raiding** Pranks in which male college students raided women's dormitories in search of women's undergarments, a practice that flourished in the United States in the 1950s.
[94] **boola-boola** A reference to "Boola Boola," the signature fight song of Yale University football, written in 1900. Hence, any silly college tradition.

Questions for Critical Thinking

1. Describe Malcolm X's self-education.

2. According to Malcolm X, "When white men had written history books, the black man simply had been left out." Discuss this statement, in light of your education to this point in your life.

MARTIN LUTHER KING JR.
Selection from "Letter from a Birmingham Jail"

From 1862, when President Abraham Lincoln issued the Emancipation Proclamation ending slavery, to the historic 1963 March on Washington, D.C., which culminated nearly a century of civil rights struggle, African Americans have suffered from legal and informal segregation. Barred from the mainstream of American society, they were exploited economically by capitalist forces and denied nearly all of the basic civil rights guaranteed by law and tradition to other groups, such as the waves of immigrants who came to the United States during the nineteenth and early twentieth centuries. Emerging after World War II as the leader of the so-called Free World, the United States entered a business boom (lasting to the early 1970s) that provided many opportunities for its citizens. But until the early 1960s, African Americans remained on the margins, unable to take advantage of the growing economy and shut out of the political process. In 1954 the Supreme Court in *Brown v. Board of Education* overturned the legal policy of "separate but equal" schools for the races and in effect made integration the national policy. Thereafter, African Americans, led by black leaders and often joined by many white supporters, began a series of marches, legal challenges, and political maneuverings that aimed to eliminate racial discrimination and integrate blacks into America's political, social, and economic institutions. By the early 1960s, civil rights for African Americans had become probably the central domestic issue in the United States.

In the mid-1950s, the Protestant pastor Martin Luther King Jr. (1929–1968) stepped forward to become the civil rights movement's most forceful and eloquent voice. The son of a prominent Atlanta preacher, King attended college, seminary, and graduate school before becoming pastor of a church in Montgomery, Alabama. In 1956 he led a successful boycott against the local bus company's segregated seating policy. Within three years the charismatic King, with the backing of southern black churches, was a national figure. During the Kennedy-Johnson era, he emerged as the most powerful African American leader in the nation, indeed in American history. After 1967, he headed a coalition linking the causes of poverty, the Vietnam War, and civil rights. While trying to unite his followers on these issues, he was assassinated in Memphis, Tennessee.

Reading the Selection

King's leadership was rooted in the Judeo-Christian tradition of personal salvation and social justice. Gifted with sound political instincts and a masterful command of the English language, he inspired those around him to hold to the policy of passive resistance as an agent of change, rather than resort to violence. King's tactic proved quite effective, for it won the sympathy of most Americans, white and black, as well as peoples around the world. He based his passive resistance approach on the actions of two men whom he admired—Henry David Thoreau (1817–1862) (see "On the Duty of Civil Disobedience" in Chapter 19), who defied his state government over what he deemed an immoral law, and Mohandas K. Gandhi (known as Mahatma Gandhi) (1869–1948), the Indian leader who used nonviolent civil disobedience in his drive to free India from British rule.

Jailed in Birmingham for civil disobedience in April 1963, King wrote a letter addressing his critics, in both races, who felt that he either had not suffered enough for his lawbreaking or was moving too fast in his efforts to overthrow America's segregated society. To answer the second charge, he compared the "horse and buggy pace" of the civil rights movement with the "jetlike speed" of the nations of Asia and Africa that were racing to free themselves from their imperialist oppressors. He accentuated the reason for his haste in ending segregation by listing many painful examples of racial injustice suffered by African Americans every day.

As to the charge of breaking the law when one opposes segregation, King answered his critics by appealing to the distinction between just and unjust laws. He reasoned that because segregation cannot be squared with the moral law or the law of God, it is an unjust law and thus possesses no power to coerce obedience. This argument was based on the writings of some of the best minds in Judeo-Christian thought, including the Christian thinkers Augustine (see *The City of God* in Chapter 7, Volume 1), Thomas Aquinas (see *Summa theologica* in Chapter 10, Volume I), the modern Protestant theologian Paul Tillich (see *The Courage to Be*), and the modern Jewish theologian Martin Buber.

∞

MY DEAR FELLOW CLERGYMEN,

While confined here in the Birmingham city jail, I 1 came across your recent statement calling our present activities "unwise and untimely." Seldom, if ever, do I pause to answer criticism of my work and ideas. If I sought to answer all of the criticisms that cross my desk, my secretaries would be engaged in little else in the course of the day, and I would have no time for constructive work. But since I feel that you are men of genuine good will and your criticisms are sincerely set forth, I would like to answer your statement in what I hope will be patient and reasonable terms.

I think I should give the reason for my being in Birmingham, since you have been influenced by the argument of "outsiders coming in." I have the honor of serving as president of the Southern Christian Leadership Conference, an organization operating in every southern state, with headquarters in Atlanta, Georgia.[95] We have some eighty-five affiliate organizations all across the South—one being the Alabama Christian Movement for Human

---

[95] **Southern ... Georgia** The nonsectarian civil rights organization established by Martin Luther King Jr. and his followers, in 1957.

Rights. Whenever necessary and possible we share staff, educational and financial resources with our affiliates. Several months ago our local affiliate here in Birmingham invited us to be on call to engage in a nonviolent direct-action program if such were deemed necessary. We readily consented and when the hour came we lived up to our promises. So I am here, along with several members of my staff, because we were invited here. I am here because I have basic organizational ties here.

Beyond this, I am in Birmingham because injustice is here. Just as the eighth-century prophets left their little villages and carried their "thus saith the Lord"[96] far beyond the boundaries of their hometowns; and just as the Apostle Paul left his little village of Tarsus and carried the gospel of Jesus Christ to practically every hamlet and city of the Graeco-Roman world,[97] I too am compelled to carry the gospel of freedom beyond my particular hometown. Like Paul, I must constantly respond to the Macedonian call[98] for aid.

Moreover, I am cognizant of the interrelatedness of all communities and states. I cannot sit idly by in Atlanta and not be concerned about what happens in Birmingham. Injustice anywhere is a threat to justice everywhere. We are caught in an inescapable network of mutuality, tied in a single garment of destiny. Whatever affects one directly affects all indirectly. Never again can we afford to live with the narrow, provincial "outside agitator" idea. Anyone who lives in the United States can never be considered an outsider anywhere in this country.

You deplore the demonstrations that are presently taking place in Birmingham. But I am sorry that your statement did not express a similar concern for the conditions that brought the demonstrations into being. I am sure that each of you would want to go beyond the superficial social analyst who looks merely at effects, and does not grapple with underlying causes. I would not hesitate to say that it is unfortunate that so-called demonstrations are taking place in Birmingham at this time, but I would say in more emphatic terms that it is even more unfortunate that the white power structure of this city left the Negro community with no other alternative.

In any nonviolent campaign there are four basic steps: (1) collection of the facts to determine whether injustices are alive, (2) negotiation, (3) self-purification, and (4) direct action. We have gone through all of these steps in Birmingham. There can be no gainsaying of the fact that racial injustice engulfs this community. . . .

You express a great deal of anxiety over our willingness to break laws. This is certainly a legitimate concern. Since we so diligently urge people to obey the Supreme Court's decision of 1954 outlawing segregation in public schools,[99] it is rather strange and paradoxical to find us consciously breaking laws. One may well ask, "How can you advocate breaking some laws and obeying others?" The answer is found in the fact that there are two types of laws: there are *just* and there are *unjust* laws. I would agree with Saint Augustine[100] that "An unjust law is no law at all."

Now what is the difference between the two? How does one determine when a law is just or unjust? A just law is a man-made code that squares with the moral law or the law of God. An unjust law is a code that is out of harmony with the moral law. To put it in the terms of Saint Thomas Aquinas,[101] an unjust law is a human law that is not rooted in eternal and natural law. Any law that uplifts human personality is just. Any law that degrades human personality is unjust. All segregation statutes are unjust because segregation distorts the soul and damages the personality. It gives the segregator a false sense of superiority, and the segregated a false sense of inferiority. To use the words of Martin Buber,[102] the great Jewish philosopher, segregation substitutes an "I-it" relationship for the "I-thou" relationship, and ends up relegating persons to the status of things. So segregation is not only politically, economically and sociologically unsound, but it is morally wrong and sinful. Paul Tillich[103] has said that sin is separation. Isn't segregation an existential expression of man's tragic separation, an expression of his awful estrangement, his terrible sinfulness? So I can urge men to disobey segregation ordinances because they are morally wrong. . . .

Let me give another explanation. An unjust law is a code inflicted upon a minority which that minority had no part in enacting or creating because they did not have the unhampered right to vote. Who can say that the legislature of Alabama which set up the segregation laws was democratically elected? Throughout the state of Alabama all types of conniving methods are used to prevent Negroes from becoming registered voters and there are some counties without a single Negro registered to vote despite the fact that the Negro constitutes a majority of the population. Can any law set up in such a state be considered democratically structured?

These are just a few examples of unjust and just laws. There are some instances when a law is just on its face and unjust in its application. For instance, I was arrested Friday on a charge of parading without a permit. Now there is nothing wrong with an ordinance which

---

[96] **"thus saith the Lord"** The formulaic language of prophets, to indicate that God is speaking through them. See, for example, Amos 1:3 and 1:6.

[97] **Apostle Paul . . . world** Jewish name, **Saul.** On three missionary trips, he founded churches in Asia Minor (Ephesus and Colossae), Greece (Corinth), Italy (Rome), and Macedonia (Philippi and Thessalonica), and sent them letters. Arrested in Jerusalem and later transferred to Rome. Martyred there between 62 and 68 CE.

[98] **Paul . . . Macedonian call** In Acts 16:9, Paul is called into Macedonia; i.e., he is summoned from Asia Minor into Europe, a critical step in spreading the Christian faith.

[99] **Supreme . . . 1954 . . . schools** *Brown v. Board of Education*.

[100] **Saint Augustine** (354–430), Christian writer and church official; a father of the church.

[101] **Saint Thomas Aquinas** (1226–1274), author of two great medieval *summas*; his theology is the basis of the system of official Roman Catholic beliefs.

[102] **Martin Buber** (1878–1965), Jewish philosopher, author of *Ich und Du (I and Thou)* (1923).

[103] **Paul Tillich** (1886–1965), German-American Protestant theologian, author of the highly influential *Systematic Theology* (1951–1965).

requires a permit for a parade, but when the ordinance is used to preserve segregation and to deny citizens the First Amendment privilege of peaceful assembly and peaceful protest,[104] then it becomes unjust.

I hope you can see the distinction I am trying to point out. In no sense do I advocate evading or defying the law as the rabid segregationist would do. This would lead to anarchy. One who breaks an unjust law must do it *openly, lovingly* (not hatefully as the white mothers did in New Orleans[105] when they were seen on television screaming, "nigger, nigger, nigger"), and with a willingness to accept the penalty. I submit that an individual who breaks a law that conscience tells him is unjust, and willingly accepts the penalty by staying in jail to arouse the conscience of the community over its injustice, is in reality expressing the very highest respect for law.

Of course, there is nothing new about this kind of civil disobedience. It was seen sublimely in the refusal of Shadrach, Meschach and Abednego to obey the laws of Nebuchadnezzar[106] because a higher moral law was involved. It was practiced superbly by the early Christians who were willing to face hungry lions and the excruciating pain of chopping blocks, before submitting to certain unjust laws of the Roman Empire.[107] To a degree academic freedom is a reality today because Socrates practiced civil disobedience.[108]

We can never forget that everything Hitler did in Germany[109] was "legal" and everything the Hungarian freedom fighters did in Hungary[110] was "illegal." It was "illegal" to aid and comfort a Jew in Hitler's Germany. But I am sure that if I had lived in Germany during that time I would have aided and comforted my Jewish brothers even though it was illegal. If I lived in a Communist country today where certain principles dear to the Christian faith are suppressed, I believe I would openly advocate disobeying these anti-religious laws. I must make two honest confessions to you, my Christian and Jewish brothers. First, I must confess that over the last few years I have been gravely disappointed with the white moderate. I have almost reached the regrettable conclusion that the Negro's great stumbling block in the stride toward freedom is not the White Citizens Counciler[111] or the Ku Klux Klanner,[112] but the white moderate who is more devoted to "order" than to justice; who prefers a negative peace which is the absence of tension to a positive peace which is the presence of justice; who constantly says, "I agree with you in the goal you seek, but I can't agree with your methods of direct action"; who paternalistically feels that he can set the timetable for another man's freedom; who lives by the myth of time and who constantly advised the Negro to wait until a "more convenient season." Shallow understanding from people of good will is more frustrating than absolute misunderstanding from people of ill will. Lukewarm acceptance is much more bewildering than outright rejection. . . .

Oppressed people cannot remain oppressed forever. The urge for freedom will eventually come. This is what happened to the American Negro. Something within has reminded him of his birthright of freedom; something without has reminded him that he can gain it. Consciously and unconsciously, he has been swept in by what the Germans call the *Zeitgeist*, and with his black brothers of Africa, and his brown and yellow brothers of Asia, South America and the Caribbean, he is moving with a sense of cosmic urgency toward the promised land of racial justice. Recognizing this vital urge that has engulfed the Negro community, one should readily understand public demonstrations. The Negro has many pent-up resentments and latent frustrations. He has to get them out. So let him march sometime; let him have his prayer pilgrimages to the city hall; understand why he must have sit-ins[113] and freedom rides.[114] If his repressed emotions do not come out in these nonviolent ways, they will come out in ominous expressions of violence. This is not a threat; it

---

[104] **First Amendment . . . protest** The First Amendment to the U.S. Constitution reads: "Congress shall make no law respecting an establishment of religion, or prohibiting the free exercise thereof; or abridging the freedom of speech, or of the press; or the right of the people peaceably to assemble, and to petition the government for a redress of grievances."

[105] **New Orleans** Scene of school integration efforts in the early 1960s.

[106] **Shadrach . . . Nebuchadnezzar** Daniel 1–4; Nebuchadnezzar, king of Babylon, threw three Jewish subjects—Shadrach, Meschach, and Abednego—into a fiery furnace for their refusal to worship a golden image. Because of their strong faith, God saved the three from the flames. Impressed, Nebuchadnezzar released them and worshiped their God.

[107] **early . . . Empire** Persecution of Christians was intermittent in the Roman Empire, from the reign of Nero (r. 54–68) until Constantine's Edict of Toleration in 313.

[108] **Socrates . . . civil disobedience** Charged by city authorities with corrupting the youth with his teachings, the Athenian philosopher Socrates (ca. 470–399 BCE) willingly submitted to death rather than recant his beliefs or seek exile from his beloved Athens.

[109] **Hitler . . . Germany** Adolph Hitler (1889–1945), German politician and leader of the National Socialist German Workers (or Nazi) Party. Appointed chancellor of Germany in 1933 by President Hindenberg. In the wake of the Reichstag fire, Hitler established a dictatorship and then systematically eliminated rival parties.

[110] **freedom . . . Hungary** Hungarian Revolution of 1956; an abortive uprising of the Hungarian people against the local communist regime, triggered by the presence of Soviet troops in their country. Using tanks, the Soviet troops brutally suppressed the revolt, and the Hungarian communist regime executed the rebel leaders in secret.

[111] **White Citizens Council** Starting in 1954, with its founding chapter in northern Mississippi, leading businesspeople and politicians across the Deep South formed White Citizens Councils to oppose school integration and any relaxation of white supremacy. Briefly powerful, the movement faded away after the 1960s.

[112] **Ku Klux Klan** A secret society of farmers and workers in the southern United States whose members wear white robes and hoods; founded in 1866, it used violent tactics to fight Reconstruction after the Civil War. In the 1950s, it revived and opposed the civil rights movement.

[113] **sit-ins** In the 1960s, groups of black and white protesters sat at lunch counters in the southern United States, in a direct challenge to racial discriminatory state laws.

[114] **freedom rides** In the 1960s, groups of black and white protesters chartered buses and rode through the southern states of the United States to test laws supporting racial injustice.

is a fact of history. So I have not said to my people "get rid of your discontent." But I have tried to say that this normal and healthy discontent can be channelized through the creative outlet of nonviolent direct action. Now this approach is being dismissed as extremist. I must admit that I was initially disappointed in being so categorized.

But as I continued to think about the matter I gradually gained a bit of satisfaction from being considered an extremist. Was not Jesus an extremist in love—"Love your enemies, bless them that curse you, pray for them that despitefully use you."[115] Was not Amos an extremist for justice—"Let justice roll down like waters and righteousness like a mighty stream."[116] Was not Paul an extremist for the gospel of Jesus Christ—"I bear in my body the marks of the Lord Jesus."[117] Was not Martin Luther an extremist—"Here I stand; I can do none other so help me God."[118] Was not John Bunyan an extremist—"I will stay in jail to the end of my days before I make a butchery of my

conscience."[119] Was not Abraham Lincoln an extremist—"This nation cannot survive half slave and half free."[120] Was not Thomas Jefferson an extremist—"We hold these truths to be self-evident, that all men are created equal."[121] So the question is not whether we will be extremist but what kind of extremist will we be. Will we be extremists for hate or will we be extremists for love? Will we be extremists for the preservation of injustice—or will we be extremists for the cause of justice? In that dramatic scene on Calvary's hill, three men were crucified. We must not forget that all three were crucified for the same crime—the crime of extremism. Two were extremists for immorality, and thusly fell below their environment. The other, Jesus Christ, was an extremist for love, truth and goodness, and thereby rose above his environment. So, after all, maybe the South, the nation and the world are in dire need of creative extremists.

---

[115] **"Love . . . you."** Luke 6:27–28.
[116] **"Let justice . . . stream."** Amos 5:24.
[117] **"I bear . . . Jesus."** Galatians 6:17.
[118] **"Here . . . God."** English translation of Luther's German words, spoken on June 21, 1521, before the Diet of Worms, while Luther was being examined for his religious beliefs. Probably the most memorable words spoken during the Protestant Reformation, there is some doubt as to whether Luther actually spoke them. Printed versions of his remarks include these words, but the official transcripts of the Diet's proceedings do not.

[119] **"I . . . conscience."** John Bunyan (1628–1688), English preacher and author of *Pilgrim's Progress* (1678). A Calvinist, he was imprisoned by the Anglican government for preaching without a license, 1660–1672.
[120] **Abraham . . . half free** Lincoln, American president from 1861 to 1865, spoke these words in a speech in Springfield, Illinois, June 16, 1858: "I believe this government cannot endure permanently half slave and half free."
[121] **"We hold . . . equal."** From the Declaration of Independence (q.v.).

Questions for Critical Thinking

1. How does King justify his civil disobedience campaign? Why do you think this tactic worked as well as it did?

2. Why does King single out "white moderates" as "the Negro's great stumbling block" in Negroes' drive to racial equality?

JEAN-PAUL SARTRE
Selection from *The Humanism of Existentialism*

France's Jean-Paul Sartre (1905–1980) was his era's greatest popularizer of existentialism, the individualistic philosophy that dominated Western thought for much of the twentieth century. Introduced to existentialism in the 1920s while studying with the German thinker Martin Heidegger (1889–1976), Sartre later developed his own ideas—freedom, choice, commitment, self-definition, and authenticity, centered around the principle of personal responsibility—all derived from Heidegger. Sartre's theoretical works make difficult reading for the layperson, but his novels, plays, and short stories, which are inseparable from his philosophy, are quite accessible and provide insight into existentialism in practice. In addition to direct influence, he also indirectly affected his age through other writers who adopted his ideas, as in the feminist theory of Simone de Beauvoir (see *The Second Sex*), his lifelong companion, and in the revolutionary thought of Frantz Fanon, a black disciple from Martinique.

The term "existentialism" derives from *existence,* one half of the pair of terms (the other is *essence*) coined by Aristotle. *Essence* means unchanging human nature, and *existence* denotes human aspects that are impermanent. Western thought from Plato (see *The Republic* in Chapter 3, Volume 1) to Nietzsche is essentialist, emphasizing the *essence* shared by humanity. Friedrich Nietzsche (see *Thus Spake Zarathustra* in Chapter 20) begins existentialist thought, which denies human nature and stresses the human ability to change at will.

The twentieth century embraced existentialism, partly to fill the void left by the collapse of traditional religion, but mainly as a response to the period's unfolding horrors. Helplessly watching the killing inflicted during two world wars, the evil made manifest in the Holocaust, the unyielding threat of nuclear disaster, and the cruel social problems seemingly impervious to capitalistic or socialistic solutions, many Westerners came to believe, like Nietzsche, that God was dead. Many, including Sartre, embraced existentialism as a sort of self-help panacea. For them, existentialism was a way to remain sane, by keeping a private moral sense in a world gone mad.

Reading the Selection

The Humanism of Existentialism was given first as a lecture by Sartre in 1945, as the West was beginning to recover from history's most destructive war. Spoken amid the ruins and proclaiming a message of personal responsibility, Sartre's words were seen as a sign that Europe would rise again from the ashes. Issued as an essay, these words became an instant classic and made Sartre's name formidable around the world.

In this essay, Sartre explores the full meaning of atheism, starting with the idea that there is no such thing as human nature *(essence)* "since there is no God to conceive it." He then develops the Heideggerian notion that human beings are "thrust into the world" ("appear on the scene"). Thus human beings do not choose to be born, but having been born, they "choose" (take responsibility for) their individual existence, including sex, skin color, age, economic condition, health, disposition, and personality. In what is the shakiest part of Sartre's thought, he reasons that when human beings choose themselves, "we mean that every one of us chooses all men." This "existential condition" of "legislating" for all humankind leads to "anguish," "forlornness," and "despair"—key Sartrean concepts. Nevertheless, Sartre remains optimistic, since in the final analysis, "man's destiny is within himself."

∽

. . .

Atheistic existentialism, which I represent, is . . . coherent. It states that if God does not exist, there is at least one being in whom existence precedes essence, a being who exists before he can be defined by any concept, and that this being is man, or, as Heidegger says, human reality. What is meant here by saying that existence precedes essence? It means that, first of all, man exists, turns up, appears on the scene, and, only afterwards, defines himself. If man, as the existentialist conceives him, is indefinable, it is because at first he is nothing. Only afterwards will he be something, and he himself will have made what he will be. Thus, there is no human nature, since there is no God to conceive it. Not only is man what he conceives himself to be, but he is also only what he wills himself to be after this thrust toward existence.

Man is nothing else but what he makes of himself. Such is the first principle of existentialism. It is also what is called subjectivity, the name we are labeled with when charges are brought against us. But what do we mean by this, if not that man has a greater dignity than a stone or table? For we mean that man first exists, that is, that man first of all is the being who hurls himself toward a future and who is conscious of imagining himself as being in the future. Man is at the start a plan which is aware of itself, rather than a patch of moss, a piece of garbage, or a cauliflower; nothing exists prior to this plan; there is nothing in heaven; man will be what he will have planned to be.

Not what he will want to be. Because by the word "will" we generally mean a conscious decision, which is subsequent to what we have already made of ourselves. I may want to belong to a political party, write a book, get married; but all that is only a manifestation of an earlier, more spontaneous choice that is called "will." But if existence really does precede essence, man is responsible for what he is. Thus, existentialism's first move is to make every man aware of what he is and to make the full responsibility of his existence rest on him. And when we say that a man is responsible for himself, we do not only mean that he is responsible for his own individuality, but that he is responsible for all men.

The word subjectivism has two meanings, and our opponents play on the two. Subjectivism means, on the one hand, that an individual chooses and makes himself; and, on the other, that it is impossible for man to transcend human subjectivity. The second of these is the essential meaning of existentialism. When we say that man chooses his own self, we mean that every one of us does likewise; but we also mean by that that in making this choice he also chooses all men. In fact, in creating the man that we want to be, there is not a single one of our acts which does not at the same time create an image of man as we think he ought to be. To choose to be this or that is to affirm at the same time the value of what we choose, because we can never choose evil. We always choose the good, and nothing can be good for us without being good for all.

If, on the other hand, existence precedes essence, and if we grant that we exist and fashion our image at one and the same time, the image is valid for everybody and for our whole age. Thus, our responsibility is much greater than we might have supposed, because it involves all mankind. If I am a workingman and choose to join a Christian trade-union rather than be a communist, and if by being a member I want to show that the best thing for man is resignation, that the kingdom of man is not of this world, I am not only involving my own case—I want to be resigned for everyone. As a result, my action has involved all humanity. To take a more individual matter, if I want to marry, to have children; even if this marriage depends solely on my own circumstances or passion or wish, I am involving all humanity in monogamy and not merely myself. Therefore, I am responsible for myself and for everyone else. I am creating a certain image of man of my own choosing. In choosing myself, I choose man.

This helps us understand what the actual content is ₅ of such rather grandiloquent words as anguish, forlornness, despair. As you will see, it's all quite simple.

First, what is meant by anguish? The existentialists say at once that man is anguish. What that means is this: the man who involves himself and who realizes that he is not only the person he chooses to be, but also a lawmaker who is, at the same time, choosing all mankind as well as himself, can not help escape the feeling of his total and deep responsibility. Of course, there are many people who are not anxious; but we claim that they are hiding their anxiety, that they are fleeing from it. Certainly, many people believe that when they do something, they themselves are the only ones involved, and when someone says to them, "What if everyone acted that way?" they shrug their shoulders and answer, "Everyone doesn't act that way." But really, one should always ask himself, "What would happen if everybody looked at things that way?" There is no escaping this disturbing thought except by a kind of double-dealing. A man who lies and makes excuses for himself by saying "Not everybody does that," is someone with an uneasy conscience, because the act of lying implies that a universal value is conferred upon the lie.

Anguish is evident even when it conceals itself. This is the anguish that Kierkegaard[122] called the anguish of Abraham. You know the story: an angel has ordered Abraham to sacrifice his son[123]; if it really were an angel who has come and said, "You are Abraham, you shall sacrifice your son," everything would be all right. But everyone might first wonder. "Is it really an angel, and am I really Abraham? What proof do I have?"

There was a madwoman who had hallucinations; someone used to speak to her on the telephone and give her orders. Her doctor asked her, "Who is it who talks to you?" She answered, "He says it's God." What proof did she really have that it was God? If an angel comes to me, what proof is there that it's an angel? And if I hear voices, what proof is there that they come from heaven and not from hell, or from the subconscious, or a pathological condition? What proves that they are addressed to me? What proof is there that I have been appointed to impose my choice and my conception of man on humanity? I'll never find any proof or sign to convince me of that. If a voice addresses me, it is always for me to decide that this is the angel's voice; if I consider that such an act is a good one, it is I who will choose to say that it is good rather than bad.

Now, I'm not being singled out as an Abraham, and yet at every moment I'm obliged to perform exemplary acts. For every man, everything happens as if all mankind had its eyes fixed on him and were guiding itself by what he does. And every man ought to say to himself, "Am I really the kind of man who has the right to act in such a way that humanity might guide itself by my actions?" And if he does not say that to himself, he is masking his anguish.

There is no question here of the kind of anguish which ₁₀ would lead to quietism, to inaction. It is a matter of a simple sort of anguish that anybody who has had responsibilities is familiar with. For example, when a military officer takes the responsibility for an attack and sends a certain number of men to death, he chooses to do so, and in the main he alone makes the choice. Doubtless, orders come from above, but they are too broad; he interprets them, and on this interpretation depend the lives of ten or fourteen or twenty men. In making a decision he can not help having a certain anguish. All leaders know this anguish. That doesn't keep them from acting; on the contrary, it is

---

[122] **Kierkegaard** Søren Kierkegaard (1813–1855), Danish philosopher and precursor of existentialism. In *Fear and Trembling* (1843), Kierkegaard offers several interpretations of the story of Abraham and Isaac.
[123] **Abraham . . . son** Genesis 22:1–18.

the very condition of their action. For it implies that they envisage a number of possibilities, and when they choose one, they realize that it has value only because it is chosen. We shall see that this kind of anguish, which is the kind that existentialism describes, is explained, in addition, by a direct responsibility to the other men whom it involves. It is not a curtain separating us from action, but is part of action itself.

When we speak of forlornness, a term Heidegger was fond of, we mean only that God does not exist and that we have to face all the consequences of this. The existentialist is strongly opposed to a certain kind of secular ethics which would like to abolish God with the least possible expense. About 1880, some French teachers tried to set up a secular ethics[124] which went something like this: God is a useless and costly hypothesis; we are discarding it; but, meanwhile, in order for there to be an ethics, a society, a civilization, it is essential that certain values be taken seriously and that they be considered as having an *a priori*[125] existence. It must be obligatory, *a priori*, to be honest, not to lie, not to beat your wife, to have children, etc., etc. So we're going to try a little device which will make it possible to show that values exist all the same, inscribed in a heaven of ideas, though otherwise God does not exist. In other words—and this, I believe, is the tendency of everything called reformism in France—nothing will be changed if God does not exist. We shall find ourselves with the same norms of honesty, progress, and humanism, and we shall have made of God an outdated hypothesis which will peacefully die off by itself.

The existentialist, on the contrary, thinks it very distressing that God does not exist, because all possibility of finding values in a heaven of ideas disappears along with Him; there can no longer be an *a priori* Good, since there is no infinite and perfect consciousness to think it. Nowhere is it written that the Good exists, that we must be honest, that we must not lie; because the fact is we are on a plane where there are only men. Dostoievsky said, "If God didn't exist, everything would be possible."[126] That is the very starting point of existentialism. Indeed, everything is permissible if God does not exist, and as a result man is forlorn, because neither within him nor without does he find anything to cling to. He can't start making excuses for himself.

If existence really does precede essence, there is no explaining things away by reference to a fixed and given human nature. In other words, there is no determinism, man is free, man is freedom. On the other hand, if God does not exist, we find no values or commands to turn to which legitimize our conduct. So, in the bright realm of values, we have no excuse behind us, nor justification before us. We are alone, with no excuses.

That is the idea I shall try to convey when I say that man is condemned to be free. Condemned, because he did not create himself, yet, in other respects is free; because, once thrown into the world, he is responsible for everything he does. . . .

As for despair, the term has a very simple meaning. It means that we shall confine ourselves to reckoning only with what depends upon our will, or on the ensemble of probabilities which make our action possible. When we want something, we always have to reckon with probabilities. I may be counting on the arrival of a friend. The friend is coming by rail or street-car; this supposes that the train will arrive on schedule, or that the street-car will not jump the track. I am left in the realm of possibility; but possibilities are to be reckoned with only to the point where my action comports with the ensemble of these possibilities, and no further. The moment the possibilities I am considering are not rigorously involved by my action, I ought to disengage myself from them, because no God, no scheme, can adapt the world and its possibilities to my will. When Descartes[127] said, "Conquer yourself rather than the world," he meant essentially the same thing. . . .

When all is said and done, what we are accused of, at bottom, is not our pessimism, but an optimistic toughness. If people throw up to us our works of fiction in which we write about people who are soft, weak, cowardly, and sometimes even downright bad, it's not because these people are soft, weak, cowardly, or bad; because if we were to say, as Zola did, that they are that way because of heredity, the workings of environment, society, because of biological or psychological determinism,[128] people would be reassured. They would say, "Well, that's what we're like, no one can do anything about it." But when the existentialist writes about a coward, he says that this coward is responsible for his cowardice. . . .

What the existentialist says is that the coward makes himself cowardly, that the hero makes himself heroic. There's always a possibility for the coward not to be cowardly any more and for the hero to stop being heroic. What counts is total involvement; some one particular action or set of circumstances is not total involvement.

Thus, I think we have answered a number of the charges concerning existentialism. You see that it can not be taken for a philosophy of quietism, since it defines man in terms of action; nor for a pessimistic description of man—there is no doctrine more optimistic, since man's destiny is within himself; nor for an attempt to discourage man from acting, since it tells him that the only hope is in his acting and that action is the only thing that enables a man to live. Consequently, we are dealing here with an ethics of action and involvement. . . .

---

[124] **a secular ethics** The militant republicans who controlled France under the Third Republic, 1870–1940, envisioned a citizenry whose worldview was drawn from secular values rather than religious beliefs. Thus, they reformed the university system so that its curriculum was based exclusively on science, reason, and humanism.
[125] *a priori* Logically independent of experience; given.
[126] **possible** From the novel *The Brothers Karamazov* (1879–1880), by the Russian writer Fyodor Dostoyevsky (1821–1881).

---

[127] **Descartes** René Descartes (1596–1650), French philosopher.
[128] **Zola . . . determinism** Émile Zola (1840–1902), the French novelist, believed that biology was destiny, as illustrated in his cycle of twenty novels called the *Rougon-Macquart* series (1870–1893).

The third objection is the following: "You take something from one pocket and put it into the other. That is, fundamentally, values aren't serious, since you choose them." My answer to this is that I'm quite vexed that that's the way it is; but if I've discarded God the Father, there has to be someone to invent values. You've got to take things as they are. Moreover, to say that we invent values means nothing else but this: life has no meaning *a priori*. Before you come alive, life is nothing; it's up to you to give it a meaning, and value is nothing else but the meaning that you choose. In that way, you see, there is a possibility of creating a human community. . . .

But it can not be granted that a man may make a judgment about man. Existentialism spares him from any such judgment. The existentialist will never consider man as an end because he is always in the making. Nor should we believe that there is a mankind to which we might set up a cult in the manner of Auguste Comte.[129] The cult of mankind ends in the self-enclosed humanism of Comte, and, let it be said, of fascism. This kind of humanism we can do without.

But there is another meaning of humanism. Fundamentally it is this: man is constantly outside of himself; in projecting himself, in losing himself outside of himself, he makes for man's existing; and, on the other hand, it is by pursuing transcendent goals that he is able to exist; man, being this state of passing-beyond, and seizing upon things only as they bear upon this passing-beyond, is at the heart, at the center of this passing-beyond. There is no universe other than a human universe, the universe of human subjectivity. This connection between transcendency, as a constituent element of man—not in the sense that God is transcendent, but in the sense of passing beyond—and subjectivity, in the sense that man is not closed in on himself but is always present in a human universe, is what we call existentialist humanism. Humanism, because we remind man that there is no lawmaker other than himself, and that in his forlornness he will decide by himself; because we point out that man will fulfill himself as man, not in turning toward himself, but in seeking outside of himself a goal which is just this liberation, just this particular fulfillment.

---

[129] **Auguste Comte** (1798–1857), French philosopher, founder of sociology and of positivism—a system of thought that tried to apply science to all phases of life. Comte called for a religion of humanity instead of the worship of God.

Questions for Critical Thinking

1. "Existence precedes essence." Explain how this idea relates to Sartrean existentialism.

2. Despite his rejection of God and theism, why is Sartre optimistic about human beings and their future?

DORIS LESSING
Selection from *Martha Quest*

Doris Lessing (b. 1919), writing from the vantage point of a marginal observer, has created an outstanding body of works—novels, short stories, poetry, dramas, and autobiography—to become one of the world's most important living writers. Her marginal status began at birth in Persia (now Iran) to British expatriates who later migrated to the British colony of Rhodesia (now Zimbabwe). Growing up on a farm far removed from Rhodesia's capital city, she experienced freedom from traditional female constraints. Unusual for the time and place, her father taught her to use a rifle and permitted her to wander the nearby *veldt*, or open grazing area, stalking game for the family table. This early freedom instilled in her a love of independence, which nevertheless has not prevented her from being involved with the main political and social issues of the modern world and with ideologies ranging from Marxism (see Marx and Engels's *The Communist Manifesto* in Chapter 19) to Sufism, an Islamic mystical sect (see Rumi,

Poems from the *Masnavi* in Chapter 9, Volume I). Throughout her career, however, she has kept her marginal status, refusing to be co-opted by any group or ideology for long.

Lessing's marginal status, manifested in an antiestablishment point of view, was evident from the start. In her first novel, *The Grass Is Singing* (1950), she gave a withering analysis of colonial Rhodesia, portraying the clash of value systems between white settlers and native blacks, rich and poor, and men and women. Later novels took up other adversarial themes, such as communism, the relations of women to men and each other, and the future in space. Ironically, Lessing supports women's rights, but she refuses to endorse the women's movement because she thinks women's issues should be addressed only as part of the liberation of all groups. The boldest instance of her freethinking was the announcement in 1984 that she had fooled the literary establishment by issuing two novels under the name of Jane Somers—*The Diary of a Good Neighbor* (1983) and *If the Old Could . . .* (1984). Lessing was awarded the Nobel Prize in Literature in 2007.

Reading the Selection

Martha Quest (1952) is the first of Lessing's *Children of Violence* series, a quintet of novels written in the realist style. The other volumes are *A Proper Marriage* (1954), *A Ripple from the Storm* (1958), *Landlocked* (1965), and *The Four-Gated City* (1969). According to Lessing, this series constitutes a *bildungsroman,* a type of novel that narrates the education of the protagonist. This definition indeed does apply, for the novels focus on the evolving consciousness of Martha Quest from her adolescence in Zambesia (a fictional Rhodesia) through failed marriages, mental breakdown, and nuclear disaster, to a serene death on a Scottish island.

In this selection, comprising the opening pages of *Martha Quest*, the fifteen-year-old heroine is introduced along with other major characters and images. Half-dreamy, half-rebellious, Martha is daily tormented while she ponders her future. She is repulsed by marriage and motherhood, symbolized by her mother and her mother's friend. She is attracted to, but ultimately confused by, the far-off world of culture and England, symbolized by the Cohen brothers. On a deeper level, she experiences a vision of the future (last paragraph): the four-gated city of the veldt with its gardens and fountains—a dynamic symbol of the balance between civilization and nature, races, and generations, the individual and the whole. This four-gated city represents Lessing's own hope for the future.

∞

Chapter I

Two elderly women sat knitting on that part of the veran-dah which was screened from the sun by a golden shower creeper[130]; the tough stems were so thick with flower it was as if the glaring afternoon was dammed against them in a surf of its own light made visible in the dripping, orange-coloured clusters. Inside this coloured barrier was a darkened recess, rough mud walls (the outer walls of the house itself) forming two sides, the third consisting of a bench loaded with painted petrol tins which held pink and white geraniums. The sun splashed liberal gold through the foliage, over the red cement floor, and over the ladies. They had been here since lunchtime, and would remain until sunset, talking, talking incessantly,

their tongues mercifully let off the leash. They were Mrs. Quest and Mrs. Van Rensberg[131]; and Martha Quest, a girl of fifteen, sat on the steps in full sunshine, clumsily twisting herself to keep the glare from her book with her own shadow.

She frowned, and from time to time glanced up irritably at the women, indicating that their gossip made it difficult to concentrate. But then, there was nothing to prevent her moving somewhere else; and her spasms of

---

[130] **golden shower creeper** A type of climbing or creeping plant.

[131] **Mrs. Quest and Mrs. Van Rensberg** The two women represent a study in contrasts of their respective cultures, the Englishwoman Mrs. Quest and the Afrikaner woman Mrs. Van Rensberg. An Afrikaner is a person of Dutch descent, living in Africa, who speaks Afrikaans, the language that developed from Dutch in South Africa.

resentment when she was asked a question, or her name was used in the family chronicling, were therefore unreasonable. As for the ladies, they sometimes allowed their eyes to rest on the girl with that glazed look which excludes a third person, or even dropped their voices; and at these moments she lifted her head to give them a glare of positive contempt; for they were seasoning the dull staple of their lives—servants, children, cooking—with a confinement or scandal of some kind; and since she was reading Havelock Ellis on sex,[132] and had taken good care they should know it, the dropped voices had the quality of an anomaly. Or rather, she was not actually reading it: she read a book that had been lent to her by the Cohen boys at the station,[133] while Ellis lay, like an irritant, on the top step, with its title well in view. However, there are certain rites in the talk of matrons, and Martha, having listened to such talk for a large part of her life, should have learned that there was nothing insulting, or even personal, intended. She was merely expected to play the part "young girl" against their own familiar roles.

At the other end of the verandah, on two deck chairs planted side by side and looking away over the bush[134] and the mealie fields,[135] were Mr. Quest and Mr. Van Rensberg; and they were talking about crops and the weather and the native problem. But their backs were turned on the women with a firmness which said how welcome was this impersonal talk to men who lived shut into the heated atmosphere of the family for weeks at a time, with no refuge but the farmwork. Their talk was as familiar to Martha as the women's talk; the two currents ran sleepily on inside her, like the movements of her own blood, of which she was not conscious except as an ache of irritation when her cramped position made her shift her long, bare and sunburnt legs. Then, when she heard the nagging phrases "The Government expects the farmers to . . ." and "The kaffirs[136] are losing all respect because . . . ," she sat up sharply; and the irritation overflowed into a flood of dislike for both her parents. Everything was the same; intolerable that they should have been saying the same things ever since she could remember; and she looked away from them, over the veld.

In the literature that was her tradition, the word *farm* evokes an image of something orderly, compact, cultivated; a neat farmhouse in a pattern of fields. Martha looked over a mile or so of bush to a strip of pink ploughed land; and then the bush, dark green and sombre, climbed a ridge to another patch of exposed earth, this time a clayish yellow; and then, ridge after ridge, fold after fold, the bush stretched to a line of blue kopjes.[137] The fields were

a timid intrusion on a landscape hardly marked by man; and the hawk which circled in mile-wide sweeps over her head saw the house, crouched on its long hill, the cluster of grass huts which was the native compound huddled on a lower rise half a mile away; perhaps a dozen patches of naked soil—and then nothing to disturb that ancient, down-peering eye, nothing that a thousand generations of his hawk ancestors had not seen.

The house, raised high on its eminence into the blue and sweeping currents of air, was in the centre of a vast basin, which was bounded by mountains. In front, there were seven miles to the Dumfries Hills; west, seven miles of rising ground to the Oxford Range; seven miles east, a long swelling mountain which was named Jacob's Burg. Behind, there was no defining chain of kopjes, but the land travelled endlessly, without limit, and faded into a bluish haze, like that hinterland to the imagination we cannot do without—the great declivity was open to the north.

Over it curved the cloudless African sky, but Martha could not look at it, for it pulsed with light; she must lower her eyes to the bush; and that was so familiar the vast landscape caused her only the prickling feeling of claustrophobia.

She looked down at her book. She did not want to read it; it was a book on popular science, and even the title stiffened her into a faint but unmistakable resentment. Perhaps, if she could have expressed what she felt, she would have said that the calm factual air of the writing was too distant from the uncomfortable emotions that filled her; perhaps she was so resentful of her surroundings and her parents that the resentment overflowed into everything near her. She put that book down and picked up Ellis. Now, it is hardly possible to be bored by a book on sex when one is fifteen, but she was restless because this collection of interesting facts seemed to have so little to do with her own problems. She lifted her eyes and gazed speculatively at Mrs. Van Rensberg, who had had eleven children.

She was a fat, good-natured, altogether pleasant woman in a neat flowered cotton dress, which was rather full and long, and, with the white kerchief folded at the neck, gave her the appearance of a picture of one of her own grandmothers. It was fashionable to wear long skirts and tie a scarf loosely at the neck, but in Mrs. Van Rensberg the fashion arranged itself obstinately into that other pattern. Martha saw this, and was charmed by it; but she was looking at the older woman's legs. They were large and shapeless, veined purple under the mask of sunburn, and ended in green sandals, through which her calloused feet unashamedly splayed for comfort. Martha was thinking with repugnance, Her legs are like that because she has had so many children.

Mrs. Van Rensberg was what is described as uneducated; and for this she might apologize, without seeming or feeling in the slightest apologetic, when a social occasion demanded it—for instance, when Mrs. Quest aggressively stated that Martha was clever and would have a career. That the Dutchwoman could remain calm and good-natured on such occasions was proof of considerable inner strength, for Mrs. Quest used the word "career" not in terms of something that Martha might actually do, such as doctoring, or

---

[132] **sex** Havelock Ellis (1859–1939), author of the seven-volume *Studies in the Psychology of Sex* (1897–1928), a pioneering work in sexuality.

[133] **the station** A trading post.

[134] **bush** Wild untamed area.

[135] **mealie fields** Fields of maize, or Indian corn.

[136] **kaffir** Arabic, an infidel. The Arabs originally used the term to denote non-Muslims. The British adopted it and applied it only to black Africans.

[137] **kopje** Afrikaans, small hill.

the law, but as a kind of stick to beat the world with, as if she were saying, "My daughter will be somebody, whereas yours will only be married." Mrs. Quest had been a pretty and athletic-looking English girl with light-brown hair and blue eyes as candid as spring sunshine; and she was now exactly as she would have been had she remained in England: a rather tired and disappointed but decided matron, with ambitious plans for her children.

Both ladies had been living in this farming district for many years, seventy miles from the nearest town, which was itself a backwater; but no part of the world can be considered remote these days; their homes had the radio, and newspapers coming regularly from what they respectively considered as Home—Tory[138] newspapers from England for the Quests, nationalist journals from the Union of South Africa[139] for the Van Rensbergs. They had absorbed sufficient of the spirit of the times to know that their children might behave in a way which they instinctively thought shocking, and as for the book Martha now held, its title had a clinical sound quite outside their own experience. In fact, Martha would have earned nothing but a good-natured and traditional sigh of protest, had not her remaining on the steps been in itself something of a challenge. Just as Mrs. Quest found it necessary to protest, at half-hourly intervals, that Martha would get sunstroke if she did not come into the shade, so she eventually remarked that she supposed it did no harm for girls to read that sort of book; and once again Martha directed towards them a profoundly scornful glare, which was also unhappy and exasperated; for she felt that in some contradictory way she had been driven to use this book as a means of asserting herself, and now found the weapon had gone limp and useless in her hands.

Three months before, her mother had said angrily that Epstein[140] and Havelock Ellis were disgusting. "If people dug up the remains of this civilization a thousand years hence, and found Epstein's statues and that man Ellis, they would think we were just savages." This was at the time when the inhabitants of the colony, introduced unwillingly through the chances of diplomacy and finance to what they referred to as "modern art," were behaving as if they had been severally and collectively insulted. Epstein's statues were not fit, they averred, to represent them even indirectly. Mrs. Quest took that remark from a leader in the *Zambesia*[141] *News*; it was probably the first time she had made any comment on art or literature for twenty years. Martha then had borrowed a book on Epstein from the Cohen boys at the station. Now, one of the advantages of not having one's taste formed in a particular school is that one may look at the work of an Epstein with the same excited interest as at a Michelangelo. And this is what Martha did. She felt puzzled, and took the book of reproductions

to her mother. Mrs. Quest was busy at the time, and had never found an opportunity since to tell Martha what was so shocking and disgusting in these works of art. And so with Havelock Ellis.

Now Martha was feeling foolish, even let down. She knew, too, that she was bad-tempered and boorish. She made resolutions day after day that from now on she would be quite different. And yet a fatal demon always took possession of her, so that at the slightest remark from her mother she was impelled to take it up, examine it, and hand it back, like a challenge—and by then the antagonist was no longer there; Mrs. Quest was simply not interested.

"Ach," said Mrs. Van Rensberg, after a pause, "it's not what you read that matters, but how you behave." And she looked with good-natured affection towards Martha, who was flushed with anger and with sunshine. "You'll have a headache, my girl," she added automatically; and Martha bent stubbornly to her book, without moving, and her eyes filled with tears.

The two women began discussing, as was natural, how they had behaved when young, but with reservations, for Mrs. Van Rensberg sensed that her own experience included a good deal that might shock the English lady; so what they exchanged were not the memories of their behaviour, but the phrases of their respective traditions, which sounded very similar—Mrs. Van Rensberg was a member of the Dutch Reformed Church; the Quests, Church of England. Just as they never discussed politics, so they never discussed—but what did they discuss? Martha often reflected that their years-old friendship had survived just because of what had been left out, everything of importance, that is; and the thought caused the girl the swelling dislike of her surroundings which was her driving emotion. On the other hand, since one lady was conservative British and the other conservative Afrikaans,[142] this friendship could be considered as a triumph of tact and good feeling over almost insuperable obstacles, since they were bound, by those same traditions, to dislike each other. This view naturally did not recommend itself to Martha, whose standards of friendship were so high she was still waiting for that real, that ideal friend to present himself.

"*The Friend,*" she had copied in her diary, "*is some fair floating isle of palms eluding the mariner in Pacific seas . . .*" And so down the page to the next underlined sentence: "*There goes a rumour that the earth is inhabited, but the shipwrecked mariner has not seen a footprint on the shore.*" And the next: "*Our actual friends are but distant relations of those to whom we pledged.*"[143]

And could Mrs. Van Rensberg be considered even as a *distant* relation? Clearly not. It would be a betrayal of the sacred name of friendship.

Martha listened (not for the first time) to Mrs. Van Rensberg's long account of how she had been courted by Mr. Van Rensberg, given with a humorous deprecation of everything that might be described (though not by

[138] **Tory** Another name for the British Conservative Party.
[139] **Union of South Africa** Country formed in 1910, uniting the British colonies of Cape Colony and Natal with two Boer (Dutch) republics, the Orange Free State and Transvaal. A member of the British Commonwealth until 1961.
[140] **Epstein** Sir Jacob Epstein (1880–1959), British sculptor, noted for allegorical and symbolic works.
[141] *Zambesia* Lessing's fictional name for Salisbury, Rhodesia.

[142] **Afrikaans** Usually Afrikaners (see footnote 131).
[143] *"The Friend . . . whom we pledged."* Passages from the *Journal* of Henry David Thoreau (1817–1862).

Martha, instinctively obedient to the taboos of the time) as Romance. Mrs. Quest then offered an equally humorous though rather drier account of her own engagement. These two heavily, though unconsciously, censored tales at an end, they looked towards Martha, and sighed, resignedly, at the same moment. Tradition demanded from them a cautionary moral, helpful to the young, the fruit of their sensible and respectable lives; and the look on Martha's face inhibited them both.

Mrs. Van Rensberg hesitated, and then said firmly (the firmness was directed against her own hesitation), "A girl must make men respect her." She was startled at the hatred and contempt in Martha's suddenly raised eyes, and looked for support towards Mrs. Quest.

"That's right," said Mrs. Quest, rather uncertainly. "A man will never marry a girl he does not respect."

Martha slowly sat up, closing her book as if it were [20] of no more use to her, and stared composedly at them. She was now quite white with the effort of controlling that hatred. She got up, and said in a low tight voice, "You are loathsome, bargaining and calculating and . . ." She was unable to continue. "You are *disgusting*," she ended lamely, with trembling lips. Then she marched off down the garden, and ran into the bush.

The two ladies watched her in silence. Mrs. Quest was upset, for she did not know why her daughter thought her disgusting, while Mrs. Van Rensberg was trying to find a sympathetic remark likely to be acceptable to her friend.

"She's so difficult," murmured Mrs. Quest apologetically; and Mrs. Van Rensberg said, "It's the age, my Marnie's[144] just as bad." She did not know she had failed to find the right remark: Mrs. Quest did not consider her daughter to be on a level with Marnie, whom she found in altogether bad taste, wearing grown-up clothes and lipstick at fifteen, and talking about "boys." Mrs. Van Rensberg was quite unconscious of the force of her friend's feeling. She dismissed her strictness with Martha as one of those English foibles; and besides, she knew Marnie to be potentially a sensible woman, a good wife and mother. She continued to talk about Marnie, while Mrs. Quest listened with the embarrassment due to a social *gaffe*,[145] saying "Quite" or "Exactly," thinking that her daughter's difficulty was caused by having to associate with the wrong type of child, meaning Marnie herself. But the Dutch-woman was unsnubbable, since her national pride was as deep as the Englishwoman's snobbishness, and soon their conversation drifted back to servants and cooking. That evening, each would complain to her husband—one, with the English inarticulateness over matters of class, that Mrs. Van Rensberg was "really so trying," while the other, quite frankly, said that these rooineks[146] got her down, they were all the same, they thought they owned the earth they walked on. Then, from unacknowledged guilt, they would ring each other up on the district telephone, and talk for half an hour

or so about cooking and servants. Everything would continue as usual, in fact.

In the meantime, Martha, in an agony of adolescent misery, was lying among the long grass under a tree, repeating to herself that her mother was hateful, all these old women hateful, every one of these relationships, with their lies, evasions, compromises, wholly disgusting. For she was suffering that misery peculiar to the young, that they are going to be cheated by circumstances out of the full life every nerve and instinct is clamouring for.

After a short time, she grew more composed. A self-preserving nerve had tightened in her brain, and with it her limbs and even the muscles of her face became set and hardened. It was with a bleak and puzzled look that she stared at a sunlit and glittering bush which stood at her feet; for she did not see it, she was seeing herself, and in the only way she was equipped to do this—through literature. For if one reads novels from earlier times, and if novels accurately reflect, as we hope and trust they do, the life of their era, then one is forced to conclude that being young was much easier then than it is now. Did X and Y and Z, those blithe heroes and heroines, loathe school, despise their parents and teachers who never understood them, spend years of their lives fighting to free themselves from an environment they considered altogether beneath them? No, they did not; while in a hundred years' time people will read the novels of this century and conclude that everyone (no less) suffered adolescence like a disease, for they will hardly be able to lay hands on a novel which does not describe the condition. What then? For Martha was tormented, and there was no escaping it.

Perhaps, she thought (retreating into the sour humour [25] that was her refuge at such moments), one should simply take the years from, let us say, fourteen to twenty as read, until those happier times arrive when adolescents may, and with a perfectly clear conscience, again enjoy themselves? How lucky, she thought, those coming novelists, who would be able to write cheerfully, and without the feeling that they were evading a problem: "Martha went to school in the usual way, liked the teachers, was amiable with her parents, and looked forward with confidence to a happy and well-spent life!" But then (and here she suffered a twisting spasm of spite against those cold-minded mentors who so persistently analyzed her state, and in so many volumes), what would they have to write about?

That defensive spite released her, and it was almost with confidence that she again lay back, and began to consider herself. For if she was often resentfully conscious that she was expected to carry a burden that young people of earlier times knew nothing about, then she was no less conscious that she was developing a weapon which would enable her to carry it. She was not only miserable, she could focus a dispassionate eye on that misery. This detached observer, felt perhaps as a clear-lit space situated just behind the forehead, was the gift of the Cohen boys at the station, who had been lending her books for the last two years. Joss Cohen tended towards economics and sociology, which she read without feeling personally implicated. Solly Cohen was in love (there is no other word for it) with psychology; he passionately defended everything to do

---

[144] **Marnie** Daughter of Mrs. Van Rensberg (see footnote 131).
[145] *gaffe* French, "mistake."
[146] **rooineks** Afrikaans, "red-necks." A negative term used by the Dutch against first the British and then all Europeans.

with it, even when his heroes contradicted each other. And from these books Martha had gained a clear picture of herself, from the outside. She was adolescent, and therefore bound to be unhappy; British, and therefore uneasy and defensive; in the fourth decade of the twentieth century, and therefore inescapably beset with problems of race and class; female, and obliged to repudiate the shackled women of the past. She was tormented with guilt and responsibility and self-consciousness; and she did not regret the torment, though there were moments when she saw quite clearly that in making her see herself thus the Cohen boys took a malicious delight which was only too natural. There were moments, in fact, when she hated them.

But what they perhaps had not foreseen was that this sternly objective picture of herself merely made her think, no doubt unreasonably, Well, if all this has been said, why do I have to go through with it? If we *know* it, why do we have to go through the painful business of living it? She felt, though dimly, that now it was time to move on to something new, the act of giving names to things should be enough.

Besides, the experts themselves seemed to be in doubt as to how she should see herself. There was the group which stated that her life was already determined[147] when she still crouched sightless in the womb of Mrs. Quest. She grew through phases of fish and lizard and monkey, rocked in the waters of ancient seas, her ears lulled by the rhythm of the tides. But these tides, the pulsing blood of Mrs. Quest, sang no uncertain messages to Martha, but songs of anger, or love, or fear or resentment, which sank into the passive brain of the infant, like a doom.

Then there were those who said it was the birth itself which set Martha on a fated road. It was during the long night of terror, the night of the difficult birth,[148] when the womb of Mrs. Quest convulsed and fought to expel its burden through the unwilling gates of bone (for Mrs. Quest was rather old to bear a first child), it was during that birth, from which Martha emerged shocked and weary, her face temporarily scarred purple from the forceps, that her character and therefore her life were determined for her.

And what of the numerous sects who agreed on only one thing, that it was the first five years of life which laid an unalterable basis for everything that followed[149]? During those years (though she could not remember them), events had occurred which had marked her fatally forever. For the feeling of fate, of doom, was the one message they all had in common. Martha, in violent opposition to her parents, was continually being informed that their influence on her was unalterable, and that it was much too late to change herself. She had reached the point where she could not read one of these books without feeling as exhausted as if she had just concluded one of her

arguments with her mother. When a native bearer came hastening over the veld with yet another parcel of books from the Cohen boys, she felt angry at the mere sight of them, and had to fight against a tired reluctance before she could bring herself to read them. There were, at this very moment, half a dozen books lying neglected in her bedroom, for she knew quite well that if she read them she would only be in possession of yet more information about herself, and with even less idea of how to use it.

But if to read their books made her unhappy, those occasions when she could visit them at the store were the happiest of her life. Talking to them exhilarated her, everything seemed easy. She walked over to the kaffir store when her parents made the trip into the station; sometimes she got a lift from a passing car. Sometimes, though secretly, since this was forbidden, she rode in on her bicycle. But there was always an uneasiness about this friendship, because of Mrs. Quest; only last week, she had challenged Martha. Being what she was, she could not say outright, "I don't want you to know Jewish shopkeepers." She launched into a tirade about how Jews and Greeks exploited the natives worse than anyone, and ended by saying that she did not know what to do with Martha, who seemed bent on behaving so as to make her mother as unhappy as possible. And for the first time that Martha could remember, she wept; and though her words were dishonest, her emotion was not. Martha had been deeply disturbed by those tears.

Yesterday, Martha had been on the point of getting out her bicycle in order to ride in to the station, so badly did she need to see the Cohen boys, when the thought of another scene with her mother checked her. Guiltily, she left the bicycle where it was. And now, although she wanted more than anything else to tell them about her silly and exaggerated behaviour in front of Mrs. Van Rensberg, so that they might laugh good-naturedly at it, and restore it to proportion, she could not make the effort to rise from under the big tree, let alone get out the bicycle and go secretly into the station, hoping she would not be missed. And so she remained under the tree, whose roots were hard under her back, like a second spine, and looked up through the leaves to the sky, which shone in a bronze clamour of light. She ripped the fleshy leaves between her fingers, and thought again of her mother and Mrs. Van Rensberg. She would *not* be like Mrs. Van Rensberg, a fat and earthy housekeeping woman; she would *not* be bitter and nagging and dissatisfied, like her mother. But then, who was she to be like? Her mind turned towards the heroines she had been offered, and discarded them. There seemed to be a gap between herself and the past, and so her thoughts swam in a mazed and unfed way through her mind, and she sat up, rubbing her stiffened back, and looked down the aisles of stunted trees, over a wash of pink feathery grass, to the red clods of a field which was invisible from the house.

There moved a team of oxen, a plough, a native driver with his long whip, and at the head of the team a small black child, naked except for a loincloth, tugging at the strings which passed through the nostrils of the leaders of the team. The driver she did not like—he was a harsh and

---

[147] **determined** The view of biological determinism.
[148] **the difficult birth** The view of Carl Jung (1875–1961), Swiss psychologist and psychiatrist.
[149] **first five years of life . . . that followed** The view of Sigmund Freud (1856–1939), Austrian psychologist and founder of psychoanalysis.

violent man who used that whip with too much zest; but the pity she refused herself flooded out and surrounded the black child like a protective blanket. And again her mind swam and shook, like clearing water, and now, instead of one black child, she saw a multitude, and so lapsed easily into her familiar daydream. She looked away over the ploughed land, across the veld to the Dumfries Hills, and refashioned that unused country to the scale of her imagination. There arose, glimmering whitely over the harsh scrub and the stunted trees, a noble city, set four-square and colonnaded along its falling, flower-bordered terraces. There were splashing fountains, and the sound of flutes; and its citizens moved, grave and beautiful, black and white and brown together; and these groups of elders paused, and smiled with pleasure at the sight of the children—the blue-eyed, fair-skinned children of the North playing hand in hand with the bronze-skinned, dark-eyed children of the South. Yes, they smiled and approved these many-fathered children, running and playing among the flowers and the terraces, through the white pillars and tall trees of this fabulous and ancient city . . .

Questions for Critical Thinking

1. What role does literature play in helping shape the worldview of young Martha Quest? Does Lessing have a positive or a negative view of the impact of literature on her heroine? Explain.

2. What vision does young Martha have of the future? What is the source of this vision?

ALEXANDER SOLZHENITSYN
Selections from *One Day in the Life of Ivan Denisovich*

In 1962, when the Soviet government began to publicize Joseph Stalin's widespread crimes, the writer Alexander Solzhenitsyn (1918–2008) joined those denouncing the late dictator's oppressive regime. But in 1974 he was abruptly deported because his novels were critical of life under communism. A stateless exile, he moved to the United States and continued to write novels; however, in interviews and public lectures he alternated complaints against the USSR with stinging rebukes of his host country's rampant consumerism, lack of moral courage in blocking the spread of communism, and abdication of its responsibility to be the world's advocate of human rights and personal freedom. Having lost faith in the two most powerful nations on Earth, he condemned both as morally decadent and spiritually bankrupt. With the collapse of the communist system, Solzhenitsyn regained faith in Russia, now stripped of its empire, and returned to his beloved homeland in 1994. What role he may have envisioned for himself in a postcommunist society seems never to have materialized and his voice was completely ignored.

Solzhenitsyn grew up in Rostov-on-Don, a large provincial city in European Russia near the Black Sea. Reared in poverty by his widowed mother, he excelled in school and graduated in mathematics and physics from the local university. At the same time, he finished correspondence courses in Russian and Western history and literature—his lifelong passions. When World War II came, he distinguished himself in battle and rose quickly through the ranks, becoming an artillery officer. Disaster struck just before the war ended: he was arrested and charged with crimes against the state because he had criticized Stalin in letters to a friend. He was sent to a labor camp as a political prisoner. From 1945 to 1953 Solzhenitsyn served time in a number of camps and prisons before being released and exiled to Asiatic Russia, where he taught in a secondary school. In the late 1950s the authorities allowed him to return to European Russia, and he continued to teach.

In 1962, during Premier Nikita Khrushchev's de-Stalinization campaign, when many political prisoners were freed and rehabilitated into Soviet life, Solzhenitsyn's first novel, *One Day in the Life of Ivan Denisovich,* was published with the premier's blessings. This book was perhaps the most influential book to circulate freely in the USSR since the 1917 revolution. Solzhenitsyn quickly followed it with several short stories and two novels—*The Cancer Ward,* based on his experiences as a cancer patient, and *The First Circle,* drawn from his years as a victim of Soviet prisons and state bureaucracy. The latter title, taken from Dante's *Divine Comedy,* reveals Solzhenitsyn's continuing interest in European literature.

With the fall of Khrushchev in 1964 and the rise of the more conservative Leonid Brezhnev, Solzhenitsyn came increasingly under fire from Soviet officials. His works were rejected for publication, and the all-powerful Writers' Union expelled him from membership—a blow that ended his literary career in Russia. Meanwhile, his novels were smuggled out of the USSR and published to great acclaim in the West. In 1970 he received the Nobel Prize in Literature. This award infuriated the Soviet establishment, and pressures against him continued to mount until he was forced into exile in 1974.

In terms of style, Solzhenitsyn works in the realist mode with a strong moral dimension. Considering himself an oppositional force to the existing government, he made it his task to expose, through literature, the lies and evils of the Soviet system. His novels, plays, and essays tend to reflect his own experiences, such as military service, imprisonment, state-funded research, hospital stays, and classroom teaching. These experiences are then reworked around three central themes: indignation at the exploitation of the weak by the strong; conviction that spiritual values outshine worldly concerns; and faith in human survival against all odds. The moral core of his being springs from his deep Orthodox Christian faith, a quality he shares with the great Dostoyevsky (see *Notes from Underground* in Chapter 19), the writer whom he most resembles.

Reading the Selections

One Day describes in meticulous detail a twenty-four-hour period in the life of Ivan Denisovich Shukhov, a Russian John Doe who is a political prisoner in a Siberian labor camp. The novel's time frame may be classical, based as it is on Aristotle's unity of time (see *Poetics* in Chapter 3, Volume I), but the petty horrors of camp life are unmistakable signs of totalitarian regimes in the twentieth century. Solzhenitsyn details with such vividness the most ordinary events that mark the average prisoner's day—for example, getting dressed or competing for small and tasteless morsels of food—that the reader is pulled into the camp setting and quickly identifies with Ivan Denisovich and the rest of the inmates. The novel's theme is a kind of bleak humanism in which the prisoners conspire to stay alive under intolerable conditions. Solzhenitsyn shows them working in teams to complete impossible tasks and outwitting the guards to get an extra morsel of bread or a better pair of shoes.

The first selection describes the start of the day. The second selection depicts life in the barracks after an exhausting day in the freezing cold. In the conclusion (not included here), Ivan Denisovich falls asleep, remembering fondly the day's events and counting the days remaining in his sentence.

∞

While the men tramped wordlessly one after another into the corridor, then through the entryway out onto the porch, and the foreman of No. 20, taking his cue from Tyurin,[150]

called "All out" in turn, Shukhov had managed to pull his boots over the two layers of foot rags, put his overcoat on over his jerkin, and tie a length of rope tightly around his waist. (If you arrived in a special camp with a leather belt, it was taken away from you—not allowed.)

So he was ready on time, and caught up with the last of his gang as their numbered backs were passing through

---

[150] **Tyurin** The foreman of No. 104, the work gang of which Ivan Denisovich is a member.

the door onto the porch. In single file, making no effort to keep up with each other, every man looking bulky because he was muffled up in every piece of clothing he possessed, they trudged across to the midway with not a sound except for the crunch of snow underfoot.

It was still dark, although a greenish light was brightening in the east. A thin, treacherous breeze was creeping in from the same direction.

There is no worse moment than when you turn out for work parade in the morning. In the dark, in the freezing cold, with a hungry belly, and the whole day ahead of you. You lose the power of speech. You haven't the slightest desire to talk to each other.

The junior work assigner was restlessly pacing the midway. "Come on, Tyurin, how long have we got to wait for you? Dragging your feet again, eh?"

Somebody like Shukhov might be afraid of the junior work assigner, but Tyurin wasn't. Wouldn't waste breath on him in that frost. Just tramped ahead without a word. And the whole gang tramped after him: stomp, stomp, crunch, crunch.

Tyurin must have handed over the kilo of fatback, though—because, looking at the other teams, you could see that 104 was in its old position. Some other lot, poorer and more stupid, would be shunted off to Sotsgorodok. It would be murder out there—twenty-seven below, with a mean wind blowing, no shelter, and no hope of a warm!

The foreman needed plenty of fatback—for the PPS, and to keep his own belly purring. He might not get parcels himself, but he never went short. Every man in the gang who did get a parcel gave him a present right away.

It was that or perish.

The senior work assigner was ticking off names on his board.

"One sick, Tyurin, twenty-three on parade?"

The foreman nodded. "Twenty-three."

Who was missing? Panteleyev.[151] Who said he was sick, though?

A whisper went around the gang. Panteleyev, that son of a bitch, had stayed behind in camp again. He wasn't sick at all, the security officer had kept him back. He'd be squealing on somebody again.

Nothing to stop them sending for him later in the day and keeping him for three hours if necessary. Nobody would be there to see or hear.

They could pretend he was in sick bay.

The whole midway was black with prison jackets as the gangs slowly jostled each other toward the checkpoint. Shukhov remembered that he'd meant to freshen up the number on his jerkin, and squeezed through the crowd to the other side of the road. Two or three zeks[152] were lining up for the artist already. Shukhov stood behind them. Those numbers were the plague of a zek's life. A warder could spot him a long way off. One of the guards might make a note of it: And if you didn't get it touched up in time, you were in the hole[153] for not looking after it!

There were three artists in the camp. They painted pictures for the bosses, free, and also took turns painting numbers on work parade. This time it was the old man with the little gray beard. The way his brush moved as he painted a number on a cap made you think of a priest anointing a man's forehead with holy oil. He would paint for a bit and then stop to breathe into his glove. It was a thin knitted glove, and his hand would get too numb to trace the figures.

The artist renewed the Shcha-854[154] on Shukhov's jerkin. He wasn't far from the search point, so he didn't bother to fasten his jacket but overtook the rest of the gang with his rope belt in his hand. He suddenly spotted a chance of scrounging a butt: one of the gang, Tsezar,[155] was smoking a cigarette instead of his usual pipe. Shukhov didn't ask straight out, though. Just took his stand near Tsezar, half facing him and looking past him.

He was gazing at something in the distance, trying to look uninterested, but seeing the cigarette grow shorter and the red tip creep closer to the holder every time Tsezar took an absentminded drag.

That scavenger Fetyukov[156] was there too, leeching onto Tsezar, standing right in front of him and staring hot-eyed at his mouth.

Shukhov had not a shred of tobacco left, and couldn't see himself getting hold of any before evening. He was on tenterhooks. Right then he seemed to yearn for that butt more than for freedom itself, but he wouldn't lower himself like Fetyukov, wouldn't look at Tsezar's mouth.

Tsezar was a mixture of all nationalities. No knowing whether he was Greek, Jew, or gypsy. He was still young. Used to make films, but they'd put him inside before he finished his first picture. He had a heavy black walrus mustache. They'd have shaved it off, only he was wearing it when they photographed him for the record.

Fetyukov couldn't stand it any longer. "Tsezar Markovich," he drooled. "Save me just one little drag."

His face was twitching with greed.

. . . Tsezar raised his half-closed eyelids and turned his dark eyes on Fetyukov. He'd taken to smoking a pipe to avoid this sort of thing—people barging in, begging for the last drag. He didn't grudge them the tobacco, but he didn't like being interrupted when he was thinking. He smoked to set his mind racing in pursuit of some idea. But the moment he lit a cigarette he saw "Leave a puff for me!" in several pairs of eyes.

. . . He turned to Shukhov and said, "Here you are, Ivan Denisovich."

His thumb eased the glowing butt out of the short amber holder.

That was all Shukhov had been waiting for. He sprang into action and gratefully caught hold of the butt, keeping

---

[151] **Panteleyev** A member of work gang No. 104; an informer.
[152] **zeks** Slang, "prisoners."
[153] **in the hole** Solitary confinement, with little food and water.

[154] **Shcha-854** Identifying number. "Shcha" denotes the camp's abbreviated name, and "854" is Ivan Denisovich Shukhov's personal number.
[155] **Tsezar** Also spelled Caesar. A member of work gang No. 104; a former film director.
[156] **Fetyukov** A member of work gang No. 104; weak, shameless wretch.

the other hand underneath for safety. He wasn't offended that Tsezar was too fussy to let him finish the cigarette in the holder. Some mouths are clean, others are dirty, and anyway his horny fingers could hold the glowing tip without getting burned. The great thing was that he'd cut the scavenger Fetyukov out and was now inhaling smoke, with the hot ash beginning to burn his lips. Ah, lovely. The smoke seemed to reach every part of his hungry body, he felt it in his feet as well as in his head.

But no sooner had this blissful feeling pervaded his body than Ivan Denisovich heard a rumble of protest: "They're taking our undershirts off us." [30]

A zek's life was always the same. Shukhov was used to it: relax for a minute and somebody was at your throat.

What was this about undershirts? The camp commandant had issued them himself. No, it couldn't be right.

There were only two gangs ahead waiting to be searched, so everybody in 104 got a good view: the disciplinary officer, Lieutenant Volkovoy,[157] walked over from HQ hut and barked at the warders. They had been frisking the men halfheartedly before Volkovoy appeared, but now they went mad, setting upon the prisoners like wild beasts, with the head warder yelling, "Unbutton your shirts!"

Volkovoy was dreaded not just by the zeks and the warders but, so it was said, by the camp commandant himself. God had marked the scoundrel with a name to suit his wolfish looks. He was lanky, dark, beetle-browed, quick on his feet: he would pop up when you least expected him, shouting, "Why are you all hanging around here?" There was no hiding from him. At one time he'd carried a lash, a plaited leather thing as long as your forearm. They said he thrashed people with it in the camp jail. Or else, when zeks were huddled outside the door during the evening hut search, he would creep up and slash you across the neck with it: "Why aren't you lined up properly, you scum?" The crowd would reel back like an ebbing wave. The whipped man would clutch his burning neck, wipe the blood away, and say nothing: he didn't want a spell in the hole as well.

Just lately he'd stopped carrying his lash for some reason. [35]

In frosty weather, body searches were usually less strict in the morning than in the evening; the prisoner simply undid his jacket and held its skirts away from his body. Prisoners advanced five at a time, and five warders stood ready for them. They slapped the sides of each zek's belted jerkin, and tapped the one permitted pocket on his right knee. They would be wearing gloves themselves, and if they felt something strange they didn't immediately pull it out but lazily asked what it was.

What would you expect to find on a zek in the morning? A knife? They don't carry knives out, they bring them in. Just make sure he hasn't got three kilograms of food on him, to run away with—that's all that matters in the morning. At one time they got so worried about the two hundred grams every zek took with him for dinner that

each gang was ordered to make a wooden chest to hold the lot. Why the bastards thought that would do any good was a mystery. They were probably just out to make life more miserable, give the men something extra to worry about. You took a bite and looked hard at your bread before you put it in the chest. But the pieces were still all alike, still just bread, so you couldn't help fretting all the way to work in case somebody switched rations. Men argued with each other and sometimes came to blows. Then one day three men helped themselves to a chest full of bread and escaped from a work site in a truck. The brass came to their senses, had the chests chopped up in the guardhouse, and let everybody carry his own ration again.

Another thing the searchers looked for in the morning: men wearing civilian dress under prison clothes. Never mind that everybody had been stripped of his civilian belongings long ago, and told that he'd get them back the day his sentence ended (a day nobody in that camp had yet seen).

And one other thing—prisoners carrying letters for free workers to smuggle out. Only, if you searched everybody for letters, you'd be messing about till dinnertime.

But Volkovoy only had to bawl out an order and the warders peeled off their gloves, made the prisoners unbelt the jerkins under which they were all hugging the warmth of the hut and unbutton their shirts, and set about feeling for anything hidden underneath contrary to regulations. A zek was allowed two shirts—shirt and undershirt; everything else must come off. That was the order from Volkovoy relayed from rank to rank. The teams that had gone past earlier were the lucky ones. Some of them were already through the gates, but for those left behind, it was "Open up!" All those with too much on underneath must take it off right there in the cold. [40]

. . .

By now he'd pulled his boots off, climbed up on his bunk, taken the fragment of steel out of his mitten, examined it, and made up his mind to look for a good stone next day and hone himself a cobbler's knife—work at it a bit morning and evening and in four days he'd have a great little knife with a sharp, curved blade.

For the time being, the steel had to be hidden, even at night. He could wedge it between his bedboards and one of the crossbars. While the captain[158] wasn't there for the dust to fall in his face, Shukhov turned back his heavy mattress (stuffed with sawdust, not shavings) at the pillow end, and set about hiding the blade.

His neighbors up top—Alyoshka the Baptist[159] and the two Estonian brothers[160] on the next bunk across the

[157] **Volkovoy** A lieutenant in the camp; the disciplinary officer. His name evokes the Russian word for "wolf"—*volk*.

[158] **captain** A member of work gang No. 104; a former officer in the Soviet military.
[159] **Alyoshka the Baptist** A member of work gang No. 104; an evangelical Christian. Solzhenitsyn's portrait of Alyoshka is completely positive.
[160] **two Estonian brothers** Members of work gang No. 104. Most of the work camp officials and prisoners are Russians, but the brothers belong to an ethnic minority. From 1939 to 1991, Estonia was part of the Soviet Union.

gangway—could see him, but Shukhov knew he was safe with them.

Fetyukov passed down the hut, sobbing. He was bent double. His lips were smeared with blood. He must have been beaten up again for licking out bowls. He walked past the whole team without looking at anybody, not trying to hide his tears, climbed onto his bunk, and buried his face in his mattress.

You felt sorry for him, really. He wouldn't see his time out. He didn't know how to look after himself.

At that point the captain appeared, looking happy, carrying specially brewed tea in a mess tin. There were two buckets of tea in the hut, if you could call it tea. Warm and tea-colored, all right, but like dishwater. And the bucket made it smell of moldy wood pulp. Tea for the common working man, that was. Buynovsky must have gotten a handful of real tea from Tsezar, popped it in the mess tin, and fetched hot water from the boiler. He settled down at his nightstand, mighty pleased with himself.

"Nearly scalded my fingers under the tap," he said, showing off.

Down below there, Tsezar unfolded a sheet of paper and laid things out on it. Shukhov put his mattress back in place, so he wouldn't see and get upset. But yet again they couldn't manage without him. Tsezar rose to his full height in the gangway, so that his eyes were on a level with Shukhov's, and winked: "Denisovich! Lend us your ten-day gadget."

The little folding knife, he meant. Shukhov had one hidden in his bed. Smaller than your finger crooked at the middle knuckle, but the devil would cut fatback five fingers thick. Shukhov had made a beautiful job of that knife and kept it well honed.

He felt for the knife, drew it out, and handed it over. Tsezar gave him a nod and vanished again.

The knife was another earner. Because you could land in the hole (ten days!) for keeping it. Only somebody with no conscience at all would say lend us your knife so we can cut our sausage, and don't think you're getting any.

Tsezar had put himself in debt to Shukhov again.

Now that he'd dealt with the bread and the knives, Shukhov fished out his pouch. He took from it a pinch exactly as big as that he had borrowed and held it out across the gangway to the Estonian, with a thank-you.

The Estonian's lips straightened into a smile of sorts, he muttered something to his brother, and they rolled a separate cigarette to sample Shukhov's tobacco.

Go ahead and try it, it's no worse than yours! Shukhov would have tried it himself, but the clock in his guts said it was very close to roll call. Just the time for the warders to come prowling round the huts. If he wanted a smoke he'd have to go out in the corridor quick, and he fancied it was a bit warmer up on his top bunk. It wasn't at all warm in the hut, and the ceiling was still patterned with hoarfrost. You'd get pretty chilly at night, but for the time being, it was just about bearable.

All his little jobs done, Shukhov began breaking bits from his two hundred grams. He couldn't help listening to the captain and Tsezar drinking tea and talking down below.

"Help yourself, Captain, don't be shy! Have some of this smoked fish. Have some sausage."

"Thank you, I will."

"Butter yourself a piece of this loaf! It's a real Moscow baton!"

"Dear-oh-dear-oh-dear, I just can't believe that somewhere or other batons are still being baked. This sudden abundance reminds me of something that once happened to me. It was at Sevastopol, before the Yalta Conference.[161] The town was absolutely starving and we had to show an American admiral around. So they set up a shop specially, chockful of foodstuff, but it wasn't to be opened until they saw us half a block away, so that the locals wouldn't have time to crowd the place out. Even so, the shop was half full one minute after it opened. And you couldn't ask for the wrong thing. 'Look, butter!' people were shouting, 'Real butter! And white bread!'"

Two hundred harsh voices were raising a din in their half of the hut, but Shukhov still thought he could make out the clanging on the rail. Nobody else heard, though. Shukhov also noticed that the warder they called Snub Nose—a short, red-faced young man—had appeared in the hut. He was holding a piece of paper, and this and his whole manner showed that he hadn't come to catch people smoking or drive them outside for roll call, but was looking for somebody in particular.

Snub Nose consulted his piece of paper and asked: "Where's 104?"

"Here," they answered. The Estonians concealed their cigarettes and waved the smoke away.

"Where's the foreman?"

"What do you want?" Tyurin spoke from his bed, swinging his legs over the edge so that his feet barely touched the floor.

"Have the men who were told to submit written explanations got them ready?"

"They're doing it," Tyurin said confidently.

"They should have been in by now."

"Some of my men are more or less illiterate, it's hard work for them." (Tsezar and the captain, he was talking about. He was sharp, Tyurin. Never stuck for an answer.) "We've got no pens, or ink."

"Well, you should have."

"They keep confiscating it."

"Watch it, foreman, just mind what you're saying, or I'll have you in the cell block," Snub Nose promised, mildly. "The explanatory notes will be in the warders' barracks before work parade in the morning! And you will report that all prohibited articles have been handed in to the personal-property store. Understood?"

"Understood."

("The captain's in the clear!" Shukhov thought. The captain himself was purring over his sausage and didn't hear a thing.)

---

[161] **Yalta Conference** February 4–11, 1945, a meeting of the Allied leaders of the United States (Roosevelt), Britain (Churchill), and the Soviet Union (Stalin), that settled the final efforts of World War II and set the stage for the postwar world.

"Now, then," said the warder. "Shcha-301—is he in 75 your gang?"

"I'll have to look at the list," the foreman said, pretending ignorance. "How can anybody be expected to remember these blasted numbers?" (If he could drag it out till roll call, he might save Buynovsky at least for the night.)

"Buynovsky—is he here?"

"Eh? That's me!" the captain piped up from his hiding place under Shukhov's top bunk.

The quick louse is always first on the comb.

"You, is it? Right then, Shcha-301. Get ready."   80

"To go where?"

"You know where."

The captain only sighed and groaned. Taking a squadron of torpedo boats out into a stormy sea in the pitch dark must have been easier for him than leaving his friends' company for the icy cell block.

"How many days?" he asked in a faint voice.

"Ten. Come along now, hurry it up!"   85

Just then the orderlies began yelling, "Roll call! Everybody out for roll call!"

The warder sent to call the roll must be in the hut already.

The captain looked back, wondering whether to take his overcoat. If he did, though, they'd whip it off him and leave him just his jerkin. So better go as he was. The captain had hoped for a while that Volkovoy would forget—but Volkovoy never forgot or forgave—and had made no preparations, hadn't even hidden himself a bit of tobacco in his jerkin. No good holding it in his hand—they'd take it off him the moment they frisked him.

All the same, Tsezar slipped him a couple of cigarettes while he was putting his cap on.

"Well, so long, chums," the captain said with a miserable look, nodding to his teammates, and followed the warder out of the hut.   90

Several voices called after him, "Keep smiling," "Don't let them get you down"—but there was nothing much you could say.

✹

Questions for Critical Thinking

1. Describe the early-morning routine of workers in this camp, as set forth in Solzhenitsyn's novel. What seems to be the purpose of this routine?

2. Document and discuss signs of humanity among the workers in the camp.

23

THE CONTEMPORARY WORLD
Globalization, Terrorism, and Postmodernism
1970–

TONI MORRISON
Selection from *The Song of Solomon*

Toni Morrison (b. 1931) is probably the most distinguished African American writer to have appeared thus far. Educated at Howard University, America's most prestigious black university (B.A., 1953), and Cornell University (M.A., 1955), over the course of her career Morrison has scaled the upper reaches of mainstream culture. Author of a book of literary criticism, a play, and ten novels, as well as editor of four collections of essays, she has been showered with praise and honors. *The Song of Solomon* (1977), her third novel, won two prizes, the 1978 National Book Critics Circle Award for fiction and the American Academy and Institute of Arts and Letters Award. *Beloved* (1987), her fifth novel, was given the 1988 Pulitzer Prize for fiction. Later, this novel was transformed into a film and then a video, directed by and starring Oprah Winfrey (b. 1954), thus reaching a larger audience than any of her other works. Crowning Morrison's literary achievements is the 1993 Nobel Prize in Literature, the first such award for an African American. Apart from awards, Morrison also has had a distinguished career as a university teacher. She was appointed to the Schweitzer Chair at the State University of New York at Albany from 1984 to 1989, and from 1989 to 2006, she held the Robert F. Goheen Chair, Council of the Humanities, at Princeton University. She was also the first African American woman to be featured on the cover of *Newsweek* (1981).

   In her novels, Morrison sets forth the black experience of white racism, with a special focus on black people who find their identity by accommodating themselves to white society and its values. This literary task, surprisingly, did not arise from her own early situation. Growing up in Lorain, Ohio, a steel town on Lake Erie, population about 30,000, Morrison claims that class was more of an issue than race. She admits there was racism in Lorain, but there was no black ghetto, and she seems to bear few racist scars from her upbringing. Nor was she much affected by her experience in racially divided Washington, D.C., while attending Howard University in the years immediately preceding the 1954 Supreme Court ruling against segregated schools. In an interview, reflecting on her early life, she once said: "Thinking on it now I suppose I was backward, but I never longed for social integration with white people. For a place to pee when shopping, yes, but I was prey to the racism of my early years in Lorain where the only truly interesting people to me were the black people." Probably contributing to her youthful identity was her father's often-stated belief that African people were better than Europeans because, as victims of white racism, they were made morally superior by their suffering.

Ultimately, Morrison's political consciousness was changed mainly by the civil rights struggle of the late 1950s and the 1960s. Her consciousness was further expanded by the writings of the African historian Chinweizu (b. 1943), one of whose works she edited while working at Random House. Especially influencing her views is Chinweizu's theory that European propaganda brainwashed some African peoples so thoroughly that they became filled with self-hatred. Adapting this theory to American conditions, Morrison made it a central theme in *The Bluest Eye* (1970), her first novel, in which she portrays a young black woman traumatized by her inability to live up to white standards of beauty, such as blond hair and blue eyes.

Morrison's fiction has taken a Western form—the novel—but she freely draws on elements of myth, legend, obsession, and fantasy taken from African and African American sources. Because her novels mix the realistic with the supernatural, she is sometimes grouped with magic realists. She opposes this label, claiming it denies the origins of her worldview within African American life. As to her own self-image, she asserted in a 1997 lecture that she is a religious writer working within the Western framework, a tradition embracing Homer, Dante, and Milton.

Morrison's use of names such as "Milkman" and "Pilate" in *The Song of Solomon* reflects her faith in the power of names to shape personal identity. She also believes black people should resist the identity imposed on them by white society. Instead, she urges blacks to take charge of their lives and work out identities for themselves. She heeded her own advice in the way she created her name. Born Chloe Anthony Wofford, into a marginalized family, she took the name "Toni" after graduating from Howard. "Morrison" became her married name in 1957, and she kept it after her 1964 divorce. So "Toni Morrison" represents an invented self, a new identity capable of successfully besieging the bastions of white power in America.

Reading the Selection

The Song of Solomon includes many nonrational elements, such as surrealism, supernaturalism, magic, astrology, myth, and science fiction. The novel's hero is a young black man, Milkman Dead, who spends much of the novel searching for a family legacy (gold). Milkman is a typical Morrison hero in that he has a false consciousness reflective of his adoption of white values. Milkman's outlook perpetuates the views of his father, Macon Dead, who is embarrassed by fellow blacks and seeks respect from white people only. However, Milkman lives only to party, unlike Macon, who runs a small business. Milkman, reaching manhood in the 1950s, is oblivious to the equal rights struggle being waged by African Americans. After journeying through the American South, Milkman discovers his legacy, but, before he can enjoy it, he leaps to his death. Milkman's life is thus a warning rather than an example to be emulated.

The selection, taken from Chapter 1, begins with the fatal leap from the roof of Mercy Hospital by Robert Smith, an insurance agent. Smith's leap serves to frame the novel at the beginning, just as Milkman's jump does at the end. More important, Smith's death symbolizes an auspicious event, often found in folklore, heralding the birth of a heroic figure, in this instance, Milkman Dead. After Milkman's birth, his mother Ruth breast-feeds him for years. Their close tie echoes the incestuous love between Ruth and her dead father. When the servant Freddie spies them together, he gives the boy the unfortunate nickname that becomes his identity.

Flying is a major motif in the novel. Milkman eventually learns, after freeing himself from his father's values, that he is descended from Solomon Sugarman—the father of twenty-one children and famous for being able to fly. Solomon's flying becomes celebrated in a nursery rhyme, "The Song of Solomon," and his launching site comes to be called Solomon's Leap. At the birth of Milkman, his aunt Pilate (unnamed in this selection) sings a few lines from the "Song of Solomon":

O Sugarman done fly away
Sugarman done gone
Sugarman cut across the sky
Sugarman gone home. . . .

This song is also a variation of a Gullah folk story about a black man who flew home to Africa to escape the chains of slavery. By having Milkman find his roots in the Sugarman story, Morrison stresses the African idea of identifying and paying respect to one's ancestors.

∞

Chapter 1

The North Carolina Mutual Life Insurance agent promised to fly from Mercy to the other side of Lake Superior at three o'clock. Two days before the event was to take place he tacked a note on the door of his little yellow house:

> At 3:00 p.m. on Wednesday the 18th of February, 1931, I will take off from Mercy and fly away on my own wings. Please forgive me. I loved you all.
>
> (SIGNED) ROBERT SMITH, INS. AGENT

Mr. Smith didn't draw as big a crowd as Lindbergh[1] had four years earlier—not more than forty or fifty people showed up—because it was already eleven o'clock in the morning, on the very Wednesday he had chosen for his flight, before anybody read the note. At that time of day, during the middle of the week, word-of-mouth news just lumbered along. Children were in school; men were at work; and most of the women were fastening their corsets and getting ready to go see what tails or entrails the butcher might be giving away. Only the unemployed, the self-employed, and the very young were available— deliberately available because they'd heard about it, or accidentally available because they happened to be walking at that exact moment in the shore end of Not Doctor Street, a name the post office did not recognize. Town maps registered the street as Mains Avenue, but the only colored doctor in the city had lived and died on that street, and when he moved there in 1896 his patients took to calling the street, which none of them lived in or near, Doctor Street. Later, when other Negroes moved there, and when the postal service became a popular means of transferring messages among them, envelopes from Louisiana, Virginia, Alabama, and Georgia began to arrive addressed to people at house numbers on Doctor Street. The post office workers returned these envelopes or passed them on to the Dead Letter Office. Then in 1918, when colored men were being drafted, a few gave their address at the recruitment office as Doctor Street. In that way, the name acquired a quasi-official status. But not for long. Some of the city legislators, whose concern for appropriate names and the maintenance of the city's landmarks was the principal part of their political life, saw to it that "Doctor Street" was never used in any official capacity. And since they knew that only Southside residents kept it up, they had notices posted in the stores, barbershops, and restaurants in that part of the city saying that the avenue running northerly and southerly from Shore Road fronting the lake to the junction of routes 6 and 2 leading to Pennsylvania, and also running parallel to and between Rutherford Avenue and Broadway, had always been and would always be known as Mains Avenue and not Doctor Street.

It was a genuinely clarifying public notice because it gave Southside residents a way to keep their memories alive and please the city legislators as well. They called it Not Doctor Street, and were inclined to call the charity hospital at its northern end No Mercy Hospital since it was 1931, on the day following Mr. Smith's leap from its cupola, before the first colored expectant mother was allowed to give birth inside its wards and not on its steps. The reason for the hospital's generosity to that particular woman was not the fact that she was the only child of this Negro doctor, for during his entire professional life he had never been granted hospital privileges and only two of his patients were ever admitted to Mercy, both white. Besides, the doctor had been dead a long time by 1931. It must have been Mr. Smith's leap from the roof over their heads that made them admit her. In any case, whether or not the little insurance agent's conviction that he could fly contributed to the place of her delivery, it certainly contributed to its time.

When the dead doctor's daughter saw Mr. Smith emerge as promptly as he had promised from behind the cupola, his wide blue silk wings curved forward around his chest, she dropped her covered peck[2] basket, spilling red velvet rose petals. The wind blew them about, up, down, and into small mounds of snow. Her half-grown daughters scrambled about trying to catch them, while their mother moaned and held the underside of her stomach. The rose-petal scramble got a lot of attention, but the pregnant lady's moans did not. Everyone knew the girls had spent hour after hour tracing, cutting, and stitching the costly velvet, and that Gerhardt's Department Store would be quick to reject any that were soiled.

It was nice and gay there for a while. The men joined in trying to collect the scraps before the snow soaked through them—snatching them from a gust of wind or plucking them delicately from the snow. And the very young children couldn't make up their minds whether to watch the man circled in blue on the roof or the bits of red flashing around on the ground. Their dilemma was solved when a woman[3] suddenly burst into song. The singer,

---

[1] **Lindbergh** Charles A. Lindbergh (1902–1974), the American adventurer, caught the world's attention with his 1927 flight in the monoplane, *Spirit of St. Louis,* from New York to Paris—the first solo transatlantic flight.

[2] **peck** A dry measure, equal to 2 gallons or 8 quarts.
[3] **woman** Pilate, Milkman's aunt.

standing at the back of the crowd, was as poorly dressed as the doctor's daughter was well dressed. The latter had on a neat gray coat with the traditional pregnant-woman bow at her navel, a black cloche,[4] and a pair of four-button ladies' galoshes. The singing woman wore a knitted navy cap pulled far down over her forehead. She had wrapped herself up in an old quilt instead of a winter coat. Her head cocked to one side, her eyes fixed on Mr. Robert Smith, she sang in a powerful contralto:

O Sugarman done fly away
Sugarman done gone
Sugarman cut across the sky
Sugarman gone home. . . .

A few of the half a hundred or so people gathered there nudged each other and sniggered. Others listened as though it were the helpful and defining piano music in a silent movie. They stood this way for some time, none of them crying out to Mr. Smith, all of them preoccupied with one or the other of the minor events about them, until the hospital people came.

They had been watching from the windows—at first with mild curiosity, then, as the crowd seemed to swell to the very walls of the hospital, they watched with apprehension. They wondered if one of those things that racial-uplift groups were always organizing was taking place. But when they saw neither placards nor speakers, they ventured outside into the cold: white-coated surgeons, dark-jacketed business and personnel clerks, and three nurses in starched jumpers.

The sight of Mr. Smith and his wide blue wings transfixed them for a few seconds, as did the woman's singing and the roses strewn about. Some of them thought briefly that this was probably some form of worship. Philadelphia, where Father Divine[5] reigned, wasn't all that far away. Perhaps the young girls holding baskets of flowers were two of his virgins. But the laughter of a gold-toothed man brought them back to their senses. They stopped daydreaming and swiftly got down to business, giving orders. Their shouts and bustling caused great confusion where before there had been only a few men and some girls playing with pieces of velvet and a woman singing.

One of the nurses, hoping to bring some efficiency into the disorder, searched the faces around her until she saw a stout woman who looked as though she might move the earth if she wanted to.

"You," she said, moving toward the stout woman. "Are these your children?"

The stout woman turned her head slowly, her eyebrows lifted at the carelessness of the address. Then, seeing where the voice came from, she lowered her brows and veiled her eyes.

"Ma'am?"

"Send one around back to the emergency office. Tell him to tell the guard to get over here quick. That boy there can go. That one." She pointed to a cat-eyed boy about five or six years old.

The stout woman slid her eyes down the nurse's finger and looked at the child she was pointing to.

"Guitar, ma'am."

"What?"

"Guitar."

The nurse gazed at the stout woman as though she had spoken Welsh. Then she closed her mouth, looked again at the cat-eyed boy, and lacing her fingers, spoke her next words very slowly to him.

"Listen. Go around to the back of the hospital to the guard's office. It will say 'Emergency Admissions' on the door. A-D-M-I-S-I-O-N-S. But the guard will be there. Tell him to get over here—on the double. Move now. Move!" She unlaced her fingers and made scooping motions with her hands, the palms pushing against the wintry air.

A man in a brown suit came toward her, puffing little white clouds of breath. "Fire truck's on its way. Get back inside. You'll freeze to death."

The nurse nodded.

"You left out a *s*, ma'am," the boy said. The North was new to him and he had just begun to learn he could speak up to white people. But she'd already gone, rubbing her arms against the cold.

"Granny, she left out a *s*."

"And a 'please.'"

"You reckon he'll jump?"

"A nutwagon do anything."

"Who is he?"

"Collects insurance. A nutwagon."

"Who is that lady singing?"

"That, baby, is the very last thing in pea-time." But she smiled when she looked at the singing woman, so the cat-eyed boy listened to the musical performance with at least as much interest as he devoted to the man flapping his wings on top of the hospital.

The crowd was beginning to be a little nervous now that the law was being called in. They each knew Mr. Smith. He came to their houses twice a month to collect one dollar and sixty-eight cents and write down on a little yellow card both the date and their eighty-four cents a week payment. They were always half a month or so behind, and talked endlessly to him about paying ahead—after they had a preliminary discussion about what he was doing back so soon anyway.

"You back in here already? Look like I just got rid of you."

"I'm tired of seeing your face. Really tired."

"I knew it. Soon's I get two dimes back to back, here you come. More regular than the reaper.[6] Do Hoover[7] know about you?"

They kidded him, abused him, told their children to tell him they were out or sick or gone to Pittsburgh. But

[4] **cloche** French, "bell." A woman's close-fitting, bell-shaped hat.
[5] **Father Divine** (ca. 1882–1965), African American evangelist, the founder of a cult that flourished from the 1940s until his death. He administered to the downtrodden, attracting thousands of black and a few white followers. Some considered him the living personification of God and attributed healing powers to him.

[6] **reaper** Usually, the grim reaper: death.
[7] **Hoover** Herbert C. Hoover (1874–1964), the thirty-first president of the United States, 1929–1933.

they held on to those little yellow cards as though they meant something—laid them gently in the shoe box along with the rent receipts, marriage licenses, and expired factory identification badges. Mr. Smith smiled through it all, managing to keep his eyes focused almost the whole time on his customers' feet. He wore a business suit for his work, but his house was no better than theirs. He never had a woman that any of them knew about and said nothing in church but an occasional "Amen." He never beat anybody up and he wasn't seen after dark, so they thought he was probably a nice man. But he was heavily associated with illness and death, neither of which was distinguishable from the brown picture of the North Carolina Mutual Life Building on the back of their yellow cards. Jumping from the roof of Mercy was the most interesting thing he had done. None of them had suspected he had it in him. Just goes to show, they murmured to each other, you never really do know about people.

The singing woman quieted down and, humming the tune, walked through the crowd toward the rose-petal lady, who was still cradling her stomach.

"You should make yourself warm," she whispered to her, touching her lightly on the elbow. "A little bird'll be here with the morning."

"Oh?" said the rose-petal lady. "Tomorrow morning?"

"That's the only morning coming."

"It can't be," the rose-petal lady said. "It's too soon." 40

"No it ain't. Right on time."

The women were looking deep into each other's eyes when a loud roar went up from the crowd—a kind of wavy *oo* sound. Mr. Smith had lost his balance for a second, and was trying gallantly to hold on to a triangle of wood that jutted from the cupola. Immediately the singing woman began again:

> *O Sugarman done fly*
> *O Sugarman done gone . . .*

Downtown the firemen pulled on their greatcoats, but when they arrived at Mercy, Mr. Smith had seen the rose petals, heard the music, and leaped on into the air.

The next day a colored baby was born inside Mercy for the first time. Mr. Smith's blue silk wings must have left their mark, because when the little boy discovered, at four, the same thing Mr. Smith had learned earlier—that only birds and airplanes could fly—he lost all interest in himself. To have to live without that single gift saddened him and left his imagination so bereft that he appeared dull even to the women who did not hate his mother. The ones who did, who accepted her invitations to tea and envied the doctor's big dark house of twelve rooms and the green sedan, called him "peculiar." The others, who knew that the house was more prison than palace, and that the Dodge sedan was for Sunday drives only, felt sorry for Ruth Foster and her dry daughters, and called her son "deep." Even mysterious.

"Did he come with a caul[8]?" 45

"You should have dried it and made him some tea from it to drink. If you don't he'll see ghosts."

"You believe that?"

"I don't, but that's what the old people say."

"Well, he's a deep one anyway. Look at his eyes."

And they pried pieces of baked-too-fast sunshine cake 50 from the roofs of their mouths and looked once more into the boy's eyes. He met their gaze as best he could until, after a pleading glance toward his mother, he was allowed to leave the room.

It took some planning to walk out of the parlor, his back washed with the hum of their voices, open the heavy double doors leading to the dining room, slip up the stairs past all those bedrooms, and not arouse the attention of Lena and Corinthians sitting like big baby dolls before a table heaped with scraps of red velvet. His sisters made roses in the afternoon. Bright, lifeless roses that lay in peck baskets for months until the specialty buyer at Gerhardt's sent Freddie the janitor over to tell the girls that they could use another gross. If he did manage to slip by his sisters and avoid their casual malice, he knelt in his room at the window sill and wondered again and again why he had to stay level on the ground. The quiet that suffused the doctor's house then, broken only by the murmur of the women eating sunshine cake, was only that: quiet. It was not peaceful, for it was preceded by and would soon be terminated by the presence of Macon Dead.

Solid, rumbling, likely to erupt without prior notice, Macon kept each member of his family awkward with fear. His hatred of his wife glittered and sparked in every word he spoke to her. The disappointment he felt in his daughters sifted down on them like ash, dulling their buttery complexions and choking the lilt out of what should have been girlish voices. Under the frozen heat of his glance they tripped over doorsills and dropped the salt cellar into the yolks of their poached eggs. The way he mangled their grace, wit, and self-esteem was the single excitement of their days. Without the tension and drama he ignited, they might not have known what to do with themselves. In his absence his daughters bent their necks over blood-red squares of velvet and waited eagerly for any hint of him, and his wife, Ruth, began her days stunned into stillness by her husband's contempt and ended them wholly animated by it.

When she closed the door behind her afternoon guests, and let the quiet smile die from her lips, she began the preparation of food her husband found impossible to eat. She did not try to make her meals nauseating; she simply didn't know how not to. She would notice that the sunshine cake was too haggled to put before him and decide on a rennet[9] dessert. But the grinding of the veal and beef for a meat loaf took so long she not only forgot the pork, settling for bacon drippings poured over the meat, she had no time to make a dessert at all. Hurriedly, then, she began to set the table. As she unfolded the white linen and let it billow over the fine mahogany table, she would look once more at the large water mark. She never set the table

---

[8] **caul** Remnant of the inner membrane surrounding the human fetus, found on a child's head at birth; an omen of good luck.

[9] **rennet** A foodstuff made from the stomach membrane of a calf; often used in the making of cheese.

or passed through the dining room without looking at it. Like a lighthouse keeper drawn to his window to gaze once again at the sea, or a prisoner automatically searching out the sun as he steps into the yard for his hour of exercise, Ruth looked for the water mark several times during the day. She knew it was there, would always be there, but she needed to confirm its presence. Like the keeper of the lighthouse and the prisoner, she regarded it as a mooring, a checkpoint, some stable visual object that assured her that the world was still there; that this was life and not a dream. That she was alive somewhere, inside, which she acknowledged to be true only because a thing she knew intimately was out there, outside herself.

Even in the cave of sleep, without dreaming of it or thinking of it at all, she felt its presence. Oh, she talked endlessly to her daughters and her guests about how to get rid of it—what might hide this single flaw on the splendid wood: Vaseline, tobacco juice, iodine, a sanding followed by linseed oil. She had tried them all. But her glance was nutritious; the spot became, if anything, more pronounced as the years passed.

The cloudy gray circle identified the place where the bowl filled every day during the doctor's life with fresh flowers had stood. Every day. And when there were no flowers, it held a leaf arrangement, a gathering of twigs and berries, pussy willow, Scotch pine. . . . But always something to grace the dinner table in the evening.

It was for her father a touch that distinguished his own family from the people among whom they lived. For Ruth it was the summation of the affectionate elegance with which she believed her childhood had been surrounded. When Macon married her and moved into Doctor's house, she kept up the centerpiece-arranging. Then came the time she walked down to the shore through the roughest part of the city to get some driftwood. She had seen an arrangement of driftwood and dried seaweed in the homemakers section of the newspaper. It was a damp November day, and Doctor was paralyzed even then and taking liquid food in his bedroom. The wind had lifted her skirt from around her ankles and cut through her laced shoes. She'd had to rub her feet down with warm olive oil when she got back. At dinner, where just the two of them sat, she turned toward her husband and asked him how he liked the centerpiece. "Most people overlook things like that. They see it, but they don't see anything beautiful in it. They don't see that nature has already made it as perfect as it can be. Look at it from the side. It is pretty, isn't it?"

Her husband looked at the driftwood with its lacy beige seaweed, and without moving his head, said, "Your chicken is red at the bone. And there is probably a potato dish that is supposed to have lumps in it. Mashed ain't the dish."

Ruth let the seaweed disintegrate, and later, when its veins and stems dropped and curled into brown scabs on the table, she removed the bowl and brushed away the scabs. But the water mark, hidden by the bowl all these years, was exposed. And once exposed, it behaved as though it were itself a plant and flourished into a huge suede-gray flower that throbbed like fever, and sighed like the shift of sand dunes. But it could also be still. Patient, restful, and still.

But there was nothing you could do with a mooring except acknowledge it, use it for the verification of some idea you wanted to keep alive. Something else is needed to get from sunup to sundown: a balm, a gentle touch or nuzzling of some sort. So Ruth rose up and out of her guileless inefficiency to claim her bit of balm right after the preparation of dinner and just before the return of her husband from his office. It was one of her two secret indulgences—the one that involved her son—and part of the pleasure it gave her came from the room in which she did it. A damp greenness lived there, made by the evergreen that pressed against the window and filtered the light. It was just a little room that Doctor had called a study, and aside from a sewing machine that stood in the corner along with a dress form, there was only a rocker and tiny footstool. She sat in this room holding her son on her lap, staring at his closed eyelids and listening to the sound of his sucking. Staring not so much from maternal joy as from a wish to avoid seeing his legs dangling almost to the floor.

In late afternoon, before her husband closed his office and came home, she called her son to her. When he came into the little room she unbuttoned her blouse and smiled. He was too young to be dazzled by her nipples, but he was old enough to be bored by the flat taste of mother's milk, so he came reluctantly, as to a chore, and lay as he had at least once each day of his life in his mother's arms, and tried to pull the thin, faintly sweet milk from her flesh without hurting her with his teeth.

She felt him. His restraint, his courtesy, his indifference, all of which pushed her into fantasy. She had the distinct impression that his lips were pulling from her a thread of light. It was as though she were a cauldron issuing spinning gold. Like the miller's daughter—the one who sat at night in a straw-filled room, thrilled with the secret power Rumpelstiltskin had given her: to see golden thread stream from her very own shuttle. And that was the other part of her pleasure, a pleasure she hated to give up. So when Freddie the janitor, who liked to pretend he was a friend of the family and not just their flunky as well as their tenant, brought his rent to the doctor's house late one day and looked in the window past the evergreen, the terror that sprang to Ruth's eyes came from the quick realization that she was to lose fully half of what made her daily life bearable. Freddie, however, interpreted her look as simple shame, but that didn't stop him from grinning.

"Have mercy. I be damn."

He fought the evergreen for a better look, hampered more by his laughter than by the branches. Ruth jumped up as quickly as she could and covered her breast, dropping her son on the floor and confirming for him what he had begun to suspect—that these afternoons were strange and wrong.

Before either mother or son could speak, rearrange themselves properly, or even exchange looks, Freddie had run around the house, climbed the porch steps, and was calling them between gulps of laughter.

"Miss Rufie. Miss Rufie. Where you? Where you all at?" He opened the door to the green room as though it were his now.

"I be damn, Miss Rufie. When the last time I seen that? I don't even know the last time I seen that. I mean, ain't nothing wrong with it. I mean, old folks swear by it. It's just, you know, you don't see it up here much. . . ." But his eyes were on the boy. Appreciative eyes that communicated some complicity she was excluded from. Freddie looked the boy up and down, taking in the steady but secretive eyes and the startling contrast between Ruth's lemony skin and the boy's black skin. "Used to be a lot of womenfolk nurse they kids a long time down South. Lot of 'em. But you don't see it much no more. I knew a family—the mother wasn't too quick, though—nursed hers till the boy, I reckon, was near 'bout thirteen. But that's a bit much, ain't it?" All the time he chattered, he rubbed his chin and looked at the boy. Finally he stopped, and gave a long low chuckle. He'd found the phrase he'd been searching for. "A milkman. That's what you got here, Miss Rufie. A natural milkman if ever I seen one. Look out, womens. Here he come. Huh!"

Freddie carried his discovery not only into the homes in Ruth's neighborhood, but to Southside, where he lived and where Macon Dead owned rent houses. So Ruth kept close to home and had no afternoon guests for the better part of two months, to keep from hearing that her son had been rechristened with a name he was never able to shake and that did nothing to improve either one's relationship with his father.

Macon Dead never knew how it came about—how his only son acquired the nickname that stuck in spite of his own refusal to use it or acknowledge it. It was a matter that concerned him a good deal, for the giving of names in his family was always surrounded by what he believed to be monumental foolishness. No one mentioned to him the incident out of which the nickname grew because he was a difficult man to approach—a hard man, with a manner so cool it discouraged casual or spontaneous conversation. Only Freddie the janitor took liberties with Macon Dead, liberties he purchased with the services he rendered, and Freddie was the last person on earth to tell him. So Macon Dead neither heard of nor visualized Ruth's sudden terror, her awkward jump from the rocking chair, the boy's fall broken by the tiny footstool, or Freddie's amused, admiring summation of the situation.

Without knowing any of the details, however, he guessed, with the accuracy of a mind sharpened by hatred, that the name he heard schoolchildren call his son, the name he overheard the ragman use when he paid the boy three cents for a bundle of old clothes—he guessed that this name was not clean. Milkman. It certainly didn't sound like the honest job of a dairyman, or bring to his mind cold bright cans standing on the back porch, glittering like captains on guard. It sounded dirty, intimate, and hot. He knew that wherever the name came from, it had something to do with his wife and was, like the emotion he always felt when thinking of her, coated with disgust.

This disgust and the uneasiness with which he regarded his son affected everything he did in that city. If he could have felt sad, simply sad, it would have relieved him. Fifteen years of regret at not having a son had become the bitterness of finally having one in the most revolting circumstances. 70

. . .

Questions for Critical Thinking

1. Identify African and African American elements in this selection from *The Song of Solomon*. Why is it important to Morrison's artistic vision to include such elements as these?

2. Discuss the nonnatural, or magical, features used by Morrison in this selection. Since Morrison denies that she belongs to the magic realist school, why do you think she includes these touches in her fiction?

MAXINE HONG KINGSTON
Selection from *The Woman Warrior*

Maxine Hong Kingston (b. 1940) is one of the most talented and original Chinese American writers in this nation's history. Through her critically acclaimed and popular writings, she has put the Chinese American experience into American literature. Her literary project is to "claim America," meaning to show that the Chinese have the right to belong through their labor in building the country and supporting themselves. In staking out this claim, she has been influenced by the poet William Carlos Williams (1883–1963), who envisioned an American culture distinct from Europe and built from indigenous materials and forms. On another level, she wants to combat Sinophobia, fear of the "yellow race," which has been a marked feature of American life since the first wave of Chinese immigrants in the late nineteenth century. Thus, Kingston not only celebrates Chinese achievement but she also avenges past wrongs—by calling exploitation, racism, and ignorance by their true names.

As the first-generation daughter of immigrants, Kingston uses her own life as a paradigm of Chinese American culture. A graduate of an American university and a high school teacher from 1965 to 1977, Kingston nevertheless feels a need to explore her ancestral roots. In China, both of her parents were engaged in promising careers, the father as a schoolteacher and the mother as a midwife; both left their jobs to seek their fortunes in "Gold Mountain," an overly optimistic name for California. Once in Stockton's Chinatown, they could only find work in a laundry. The parents' fall in the world plunged her father into black moods during much of Maxine's childhood. In contrast, her mother kept her good humor by telling stories in the peasant talk-story Cantonese tradition that is the heritage of most Chinese Americans.

Talk-stories are moral tales of ancient heroes and family secrets. It is these stories, reworked from those Kingston's mother told, written in an artful combination of Chinese rhythms and American slang, that provide the narrative structure of Kingston's best-known works: *The Woman Warrior: Memoirs of a Girlhood Among Ghosts* (1976), dealing with matriarchal influence, and *China Men* (1980), telling of the patriarchal side. Partly written to come to terms with her family, both books have the broader aim of describing the Chinese American predicament— being caught in a double bind between two proud, often mutually antagonistic cultures. *The Woman Warrior* won the National Book Critics Award for Nonfiction in 1976 and *China Men* won the National Book Award for Nonfiction in 1981.

Reading the Selection

"No Name Woman," the first episode in *The Woman Warrior,* is the talk-story of Kingston's paternal aunt, a "ghost" who haunts the author's past. The aunt's name is unmentionable because she disgraced the family in China by becoming pregnant—perhaps by rape—while her husband was in America. When her illegitimate baby was born, villagers destroyed the family compound. In despair, "No Name" aunt drowned herself and her child in the family well.

The talk-story of "No Name" sets the tone for *The Woman Warrior,* establishing that traditional Chinese culture has a low opinion of women. It is this oppression against which the heroic deeds of the idealized female warriors, treated in later chapters, can be judged. The "No Name" episode also reflects Kingston's self-identification as a woman warrior. Her sympathetic portrait of the aunt whom the family deliberately forgot is an act of rebellion against tradition and a vindication of the wronged relative.

∞

No Name Woman

"You must not tell anyone," my mother said, "what I am ₁ about to tell you. In China your father had a sister who killed herself. She jumped into the family well. We say that your father has all brothers because it is as if she had never been born.

"In 1924 just a few days after our village celebrated seventeen hurry-up weddings—to make sure that every young man who went 'out on the road' would responsibly come home—your father and his brothers and your grandfather and his brothers and your aunt's new husband sailed for America, the Gold Mountain. It was your grandfather's last trip. Those lucky enough to get contracts waved goodbye from the decks. They fed and guarded the stowaways and helped them off in Cuba, New York, Bali, Hawaii. 'We'll meet in California next year,' they said. All of them sent money home.

"I remember looking at your aunt one day when she and I were dressing; I had not noticed before that she had such a protruding melon of a stomach. But I did not think, 'She's pregnant,' until she began to look like other pregnant women, her shirt pulling and the white tops of her black pants showing. She could not have been pregnant, you see, because her husband had been gone for years. No one said anything. We did not discuss it. In early summer she was ready to have the child, long after the time when it could have been possible.

"The village had also been counting. On the night the baby was to be born the villagers raided our house. Some were crying. Like a great saw, teeth strung with lights, files of people walked zigzag across our land, tearing the rice. Their lanterns doubled in the disturbed black water, which drained away through the broken bunds.[10] As the villagers closed in, we could see that some of them, probably men and women we knew well, wore white masks. The people with long hair hung it over their faces. Women with short hair made it stand up on end. Some had tied white bands around their foreheads, arms, and legs.

"At first they threw mud and rocks at the house. Then 5 they threw eggs and began slaughtering our stock. We could hear the animals scream their deaths—the roosters, the pigs, a last great roar from the ox. Familiar wild heads flared in our night windows; the villagers encircled us. Some of the faces stopped to peer at us, their eyes rushing like search-lights. The hands flattened against the panes, framed heads, and left red prints.

"The villagers broke in the front and the back doors at the same time, even though we had not locked the doors against them. Their knives dripped with the blood of our animals. They smeared blood on the doors and walls. One woman swung a chicken, whose throat she had slit, splattering blood in red arcs about her. We stood together in the middle of our house, in the family hall with the pictures and tables of the ancestors around us, and looked straight ahead.

"At that time the house had only two wings. When the men came back, we would build two more to enclose our courtyard and a third one to begin a second courtyard. The villagers pushed through both wings, even your grandparents' rooms, to find your aunt's, which was also mine until the men returned. From this room a new wing for one of the younger families would grow. They ripped up her clothes and shoes and broke her combs, grinding them underfoot. They tore her work from the loom. They scattered the cooking fire and rolled the new weaving in it. We could hear them in the kitchen breaking our bowls and banging the pots. They overturned the great waist-high earthenware jugs; duck eggs, pickled fruits, vegetables burst out and mixed in acrid torrents. The old woman from the next field swept a broom through the air and loosed the spirits-of-the-broom over our heads. 'Pig.' 'Ghost.' 'Pig,' they sobbed and scolded while they ruined our house.

"When they left, they took sugar and oranges to bless themselves. They cut pieces from the dead animals. Some of them took bowls that were not broken and clothes that were not torn. Afterward we swept up the rice and sewed it back up into sacks. But the smells from the spilled

preserves lasted. Your aunt gave birth in the pigsty that night. The next morning when I went for the water, I found her and the baby plugging up the family well.

"Don't let your father know that I told you. He denies her. Now that you have started to menstruate, what happened to her could happen to you. Don't humiliate us. You wouldn't like to be forgotten as if you had never been born. The villagers are watchful."

Whenever she had to warn us about life, my mother 10 told stories that ran like this one, a story to grow up on. She tested our strength to establish realities. Those in the emigrant generations who could not reassert brute survival died young and far from home. Those of us in the first American generations have had to figure out how the invisible world the emigrants built around our childhoods fits in solid America.

The emigrants confused the gods by diverting their curses, misleading them with crooked streets and false names. They must try to confuse their offspring as well, who, I suppose, threaten them in similar ways—always trying to get things straight, always trying to name the unspeakable. The Chinese I know hide their names; sojourners take new names when their lives change and guard their real names with silence.

Chinese-Americans, when you try to understand what things in you are Chinese, how do you separate what is peculiar to childhood, to poverty, insanities, one family, your mother who marked your growing with stories, from what is Chinese? What is Chinese tradition and what is the movies?

If I want to learn what clothes my aunt wore, whether flashy or ordinary, I would have to begin, "Remember Father's drowned-in-the-well sister?" I cannot ask that. My mother has told me once and for all the useful parts. She will add nothing unless powered by Necessity, a riverbank that guides her life. She plants vegetable gardens rather than lawns; she carries the odd-shaped tomatoes home from the fields and eats food left for the gods.

Whenever we did frivolous things, we used up energy; we flew high kites. We children came up off the ground over the melting cones our parents brought home from work and the American movie on New Year's Day— *Oh, You Beautiful Doll* with Betty Grable[11] one year, and *She Wore a Yellow Ribbon* with John Wayne[12] another year. After the one carnival ride each, we paid in guilt; our tired father counted his change on the dark walk home.

Adultery is extravagance. Could people who hatch 15 their own chicks and eat the embryos and the heads for delicacies and boil the feet in vinegar for party food, leaving only the gravel, eating even the gizzard lining—could such people engender a prodigal aunt? To be a woman, to

---

[10] **bund** Embankment meant to control the flow of water.

[11] *Oh . . . Grable* Kingston's memory is confused, because *Oh, You Beautiful Doll* (1949) starred June Haver (1926–2005) and Gale Robbins (1924–1980). Perhaps she meant *The Dolly Sisters* (1946) with Betty Grable (1917–1973). Grable was a movie star in the 1940s, and her photograph became an icon during World War II, as a pin-up for U.S. servicemen.

[12] *She . . . Wayne* The movie appeared in 1949. Famous for action films, John Wayne (1907–1979) was a leading movie star from the late 1930s until the early 1970s.

have a daughter in starvation time was a waste enough. My aunt could not have been the lone romantic who gave up everything for sex. Women in the old China did not choose. Some man had commanded her to lie with him and be his secret evil. I wonder whether he masked himself when he joined the raid on her family.

Perhaps she had encountered him in the fields or on the mountain where the daughters-in-law collected fuel. Or perhaps he first noticed her in the marketplace. He was not a stranger because the village housed no strangers. She had to have dealings with him other than sex. Perhaps he worked an adjoining field, or he sold her the cloth for the dress she sewed and wore. His demand must have surprised, then terrified her. She obeyed him; she always did as she was told.

When the family found a young man in the next village to be her husband, she had stood tractably beside the best rooster, his proxy, and promised before they met that she would be his forever. She was lucky that he was her age and she would be the first wife,[13] an advantage secure now. The night she first saw him, he had sex with her. Then he left for America. She had almost forgotten what he looked like. When she tried to envision him, she only saw the black and white face in the group photograph the men had had taken before leaving.

The other man was not, after all, much different from her husband. They both gave orders: she followed. "If you tell your family, I'll beat you. I'll kill you. Be here again next week." No one talked sex, ever. And she might have separated the rapes from the rest of living if only she did not have to buy her oil from him or gather wood in the same forest. I want her fear to have lasted just as long as rape lasted so that the fear could have been contained. No drawn-out fear. But women at sex hazarded birth and hence lifetimes. The fear did not stop but permeated everywhere. She told the man, "I think I'm pregnant." He organized the raid against her.

On nights when my mother and father talked about their life back home, sometimes they mentioned an "outcast table" whose business they still seemed to be settling, their voices tight. In a commensal tradition, where food is precious, the powerful older people made wrongdoers eat alone. Instead of letting them start separate new lives like the Japanese, who could become samurais[14] and geishas,[15] the Chinese family, faces averted but eyes glowering sideways, hung on to the offenders and fed them leftovers. My aunt must have lived in the same house as my parents and eaten at an outcast table. My mother spoke about the raid as if she had seen it, when she and my aunt, a daughter-in-law to a different household, should not have been living together at all. Daughters-in-law lived with their husbands' parents, not their own; a synonym for marriage in Chinese is "taking a daughter-in-law." Her husband's parents could have sold her, mortgaged her, stoned her.

But they had sent her back to her own mother and father, a mysterious act hinting at disgraces not told me. Perhaps they had thrown her out to deflect the avengers.

She was the only daughter; her four brothers went with her father, husband, and uncles "out on the road" and for some years became western men. When the goods were divided among the family, three of the brothers took land, and the youngest, my father, chose an education. After my grandparents gave their daughter away to her husband's family, they had dispensed all the adventure and all the property. They expected her alone to keep the traditional ways, which her brothers, now among the barbarians, could fumble without detection. The heavy, deep-rooted women were to maintain the past against the flood, safe for returning. But the rare urge west had fixed upon our family, and so my aunt crossed boundaries not delineated in space.

The work of preservation demands that the feelings playing about in one's guts not be turned into action. Just watch their passing like cherry blossoms. But perhaps my aunt, my forerunner, caught in a slow life, let dreams grow and fade and after some months or years went toward what persisted. Fear at the enormities of the forbidden kept her desires delicate, wire and bone. She looked at a man because she liked the way the hair was tucked behind his ears, or she liked the question-mark line of a long torso curving at the shoulder and straight at the hip. For warm eyes or a soft voice or a slow walk—that's all—a few hairs, a line, a brightness, a sound, a pace, she gave up family. She offered us up for a charm that vanished with tiredness, a pigtail[16] that didn't toss when the wind died. Why, the wrong lighting could erase the dearest thing about him.

It could very well have been, however, that my aunt did not take subtle enjoyment of her friend, but, a wild woman, kept rollicking company. Imagining her free with sex doesn't fit, though. I don't know any women like that, or men either. Unless I see her life branching into mine, she gives me no ancestral help.

To sustain her being in love, she often worked at herself in the mirror, guessing at the colors and shapes that would interest him, changing them frequently in order to hit on the right combination. She wanted him to look back.

On a farm near the sea, a woman who tended her appearance reaped a reputation for eccentricity. All the married women blunt-cut their hair in flaps about their ears or pulled it back in tight buns. No nonsense. Neither style blew easily into heart-catching tangles. And at their weddings they displayed themselves in their long hair for the last time. "It brushed the backs of my knees," my mother tells me. "It was braided, and even so, it brushed the backs of my knees."

At the mirror my aunt combed individuality into her bob. A bun could have been contrived to escape into black streamers blowing in the wind or in quiet wisps about her face, but only the older women in our picture album wear buns. She brushed her hair back from her forehead,

---

[13] **first wife** Multiple wives, as well as concubines, were allowed in traditional Chinese society.
[14] **samurai** Japanese, "guard." In Japan, a military order, starting in feudal times and ending in the late 1800s. Samurai wore two swords, symbolic of their warrior status.
[15] **geisha** A Japanese courtesan, trained in music and dancing.

---

[16] **pigtail** Hairstyle worn by Chinese men, established under the Qing (Manchu) dynasty in the seventeenth century, as a mark of servitude to the emperor; the custom was abolished in 1912.

tucking the flaps behind her ears. She looped a piece of thread, knotted into a circle between her index fingers and thumbs, and ran the double strand across her forehead. When she closed her fingers as if she were making a pair of shadow geese bite, the string twisted together catching the little hairs. Then she pulled the thread away from her skin, ripping the hairs out neatly, her eyes watering from the needles of pain. Opening her fingers, she cleaned the thread, then rolled it along her hairline and the tops of her eyebrows. My mother did the same to me and my sisters and herself. I used to believe that the expression "caught by the short hairs" meant a captive held with a depilatory[17] string. It especially hurt at the temples, but my mother said we were lucky we didn't have to have our feet bound[18] when we were seven. Sisters used to sit on their beds and cry together, she said, as their mothers or their slaves removed the bandages for a few minutes each night and let the blood gush back into their veins. I hope that the man my aunt loved appreciated a smooth brow, that he wasn't just a tits-and-ass man.

Once my aunt found a freckle on her chin, at a spot that the almanac said predestined her for unhappiness. She dug it out with a hot needle and washed the wound with peroxide.

More attention to her looks than these pullings of hairs and pickings at spots would have caused gossip among the villagers. They owned work clothes and good clothes, and they wore good clothes for feasting the new seasons. But since a woman combing her hair hexes beginnings, my aunt rarely found an occasion to look her best. Women looked like great sea snails—the corded wood, babies, and laundry they carried were the whorls on their backs. The Chinese did not admire a bent back; goddesses and warriors stood straight. Still there must have been a marvelous freeing of beauty when a worker laid down her burden and stretched and arched.

Such commonplace loveliness, however, was not enough for my aunt. She dreamed of a lover for the fifteen days of New Year's,[19] the time for families to exchange visits, money, and food. She plied her secret comb. And sure enough she cursed the year, the family, the village, and herself.

Even as her hair lured her imminent lover, many other men looked at her. Uncles, cousins, nephews, brothers would have looked, too, had they been home between journeys. Perhaps they had already been restraining their curiosity, and they left, fearful that their glances, like a field of

nesting birds, might be startled and caught. Poverty hurt, and that was their first reason for leaving. But another, final reason for leaving the crowded house was the never-said.

She may have been unusually beloved, the precious [30] only daughter, spoiled and mirror gazing because of the affection the family lavished on her. When her husband left, they welcomed the chance to take her back from the in-laws; she could live like the little daughter for just a while longer. There are stories that my grandfather was different from other people, "crazy ever since the little Jap bayoneted him in the head." He used to put his naked penis on the dinner table, laughing. And one day he brought home a baby girl, wrapped up inside his brown western-style greatcoat. He had traded one of his sons, probably my father, the youngest, for her. My grandmother made him trade back. When he finally got a daughter of his own, he doted on her. They must have all loved her, except perhaps my father, the only brother who never went back to China, having once been traded for a girl.

Brothers and sisters, newly men and women, had to efface their sexual color and present plain miens. Disturbing hair and eyes, a smile like no other, threatened the ideal of five generations living under one roof. To focus blurs, people shouted face to face and yelled from room to room. The immigrants I know have loud voices, unmodulated to American tones even after years away from the village where they called their friendships out across the fields. I have not been able to stop my mother's screams in public libraries or over telephones. Walking erect (knees straight, toes pointed forward, not pigeon-toed, which is Chinese-feminine) and speaking in an inaudible voice, I have tried to turn myself American-feminine. Chinese communication was loud, public. Only sick people had to whisper. But at the dinner table, where the family members came nearest one another, no one could talk, not the outcasts nor any eaters. Every word that falls from the mouth is a coin lost. Silently they gave and accepted food with both hands. A preoccupied child who took his bowl with one hand got a sideways glare. A complete moment of total attention is due everyone alike. Children and lovers have no singularity here, but my aunt used a secret voice, a separate attentiveness.

She kept the man's name to herself throughout her labor and dying; she did not accuse him that he be punished with her. To save her inseminator's name she gave silent birth.

He may have been somebody in her own household, but intercourse with a man outside the family would have been no less abhorrent. All the village were kinsmen, and the titles shouted in loud country voices never let kinship be forgotten. Any man within visiting distance would have been neutralized as a lover—"brother," "younger brother," "older brother"—one hundred and fifteen relationship titles. Parents researched birth charts probably not so much to assure good fortune as to circumvent incest in a population that has but one hundred surnames. Everybody has eight million relatives. How useless then sexual mannerisms, how dangerous.

As if it came from an atavism deeper than fear, I used to add "brother" silently to boys' names. It hexed the boys,

---

[17] **depilatory** An agent for removing unwanted hair.
[18] **feet bound** In China, the custom of foot binding began when a girl reached the age of three. Her toes were first broken, and then the feet were bound tightly with cloth strips to keep the foot size to 10 centimeters (about 4 inches) or less. The goal was dainty feet that would resemble a "three-inch golden lotus"—a feudal ideal under the Sung dynasty, when the practice first began. In 1911, the new Chinese republic abolished the custom.
[19] **New Year's** A festival that falls on a different date each year. The changeable nature of the day reflects the Chinese calendar, which uses both lunar and solar schedules. The celebration begins with the new moon and ends with the full moon fifteen days later.

who would or would not ask me to dance, and made them less scary and as familiar and deserving of benevolence as girls.

But, of course, I hexed myself also—no dates. I should have stood up, both arms waving, and shouted out across libraries, "Hey, you! Love me back." I had no idea, though, how to make attraction selective, how to control its direction and magnitude. If I made myself American-pretty so that the five or six Chinese boys in the class fell in love with me, everyone else—the Caucasian, Negro, and Japanese boys—would too. Sisterliness, dignified and honorable, made much more sense.

Attraction eludes control so stubbornly that whole societies designed to organize relationships among people cannot keep order, not even when they bind people to one another from childhood and raise them together. Among the very poor and the wealthy, brothers married their adopted sisters, like doves. Our family allowed some romance, paying adult brides' prices and providing dowries so that their sons and daughters could marry strangers. Marriage promises to turn strangers into friendly relatives—a nation of siblings.

In the village structure, spirits shimmered among the live creatures, balanced and held in equilibrium by time and land. But one human being flaring up into violence could open up a black hole, a maelstrom that pulled in the sky. The frightened villagers, who depended on one another to maintain the real, went to my aunt to show her a personal, physical representation of the break she had made in the "roundness." Misallying couples snapped off the future, which was to be embodied in true offspring. The villagers punished her for acting as if she could have a private life, secret and apart from them.

If my aunt had betrayed the family at a time of large grain yields and peace, when many boys were born, and wings were being built on many houses, perhaps she might have escaped such severe punishment. But the men—hungry, greedy, tired of planting in dry soil—had been forced to leave the village in order to send food-money home. There were ghost plagues, bandit plagues, wars with the Japanese, floods. My Chinese brother and sister had died of an unknown sickness. Adultery, perhaps only a mistake during good times, became a crime when the village needed food.

The round moon cakes and round doorways, the round tables of graduated sizes that fit one roundness inside another, round windows and rice bowls—these talismans had lost their power to warn this family of the law: a family must be whole, faithfully keeping the descent line by having sons to feed the old and the dead, who in turn look after the family. The villagers came to show my aunt and her lover-in-hiding a broken house. The villagers were speeding up the circling of events because she was too shortsighted to see that her infidelity had already harmed the village, that waves of consequences would return unpredictably, sometimes in disguise, as now, to hurt her. This roundness had to be made coin-sized so that she would see its circumference: punish her at the birth of her baby. Awaken her to the inexorable. People who refused fatalism because they could invent small resources

insisted on culpability. Deny accidents and wrest fault from the stars.

After the villagers left, their lanterns now scattering in various directions toward home, the family broke their silence and cursed her. "Aiaa, we're going to die. Death is coming. Death is coming. Look what you've done. You've killed us. Ghost! Dead ghost! Ghost! You've never been born." She ran out into the fields, far enough from the house so that she could no longer hear their voices, and pressed herself against the earth, her own land no more. When she felt the birth coming, she thought that she had been hurt. Her body seized together. "They've hurt me too much," she thought. "This is gall,[20] and it will kill me." With forehead and knees against the earth, her body convulsed and then relaxed. She turned on her back, lay on the ground. The black well of sky and stars went out and out and out forever; her body and her complexity seemed to disappear. She was one of the stars, a bright dot in blackness, without home, without a companion, in eternal cold and silence. An agoraphobia[21] rose in her, speeding higher and higher, bigger and bigger; she would not be able to contain it; there would be no end to fear.

Flayed, unprotected against space, she felt pain return, focusing her body. This pain chilled her—a cold, steady kind of surface pain. Inside, spasmodically, the other pain, the pain of the child, heated her. For hours she lay on the ground, alternately body and space. Sometimes a vision of normal comfort obliterated reality: she saw the family in the evening gambling at the dinner table, the young people massaging their elders' backs. She saw them congratulating one another, high joy on the mornings the rice shoots came up. When these pictures burst, the stars drew yet further apart. Black space opened.

She got to her feet to fight better and remembered that old-fashioned women gave birth in their pigsties to fool the jealous, pain-dealing gods, who do not snatch piglets. Before the next spasms could stop her, she ran to the pigsty, each step a rushing out into emptiness. She climbed over the fence and knelt in the dirt. It was good to have a fence enclosing her, a tribal person alone.

Laboring, this woman who had carried her child as a foreign growth that sickened her every day, expelled it at last. She reached down to touch the hot, wet, moving mass, surely smaller than anything human, and could feel that it was human after all—fingers, toes, nails, nose. She pulled it up on to her belly, and it lay curled there, butt in the air, feet precisely tucked one under the other. She opened her loose shirt and buttoned the child inside. After resting, it squirmed and thrashed and she pushed it up to her breast. It turned its head this way and that until it found her nipple. There, it made little snuffling noises. She clenched her teeth at its preciousness, lovely as a young calf, a piglet, a little dog.

She may have gone to the pigsty as a last act of responsibility: she would protect this child as she had protected its father. It would look after her soul, leaving supplies on

---

[20] **gall** Bitterness.
[21] **agoraphobia** An abnormal fear of open space or public space.

her grave. But how would this tiny child without family find her grave when there would be no marker for her anywhere, neither in the earth nor the family hall? No one would give her a family hall name. She had taken the child with her into the wastes. At its birth the two of them had felt the same raw pain of separation, a wound that only the family pressing tight could close. A child with no descent line would not soften her life but only trail after her, ghost-like, begging her to give it purpose. At dawn the villagers on their way to the fields would stand around the fence and look.

Full of milk, the little ghost slept. When it awoke, she 45 hardened her breasts against the milk that crying loosens. Toward morning she picked up the baby and walked to the well.

Carrying the baby to the well shows loving. Otherwise abandon it. Turn its face into the mud. Mothers who love their children take them along. It was probably a girl; there is some hope of forgiveness for boys.

"Don't tell anyone you had an aunt. Your father does not want to hear her name. She has never been born." I have believed that sex was unspeakable and words so strong and fathers so frail that "aunt" would do my father mysterious harm. I have thought that my family, having settled among immigrants who had also been their neighbors in the ancestral land, needed to clean their name, and a wrong word would incite the kinspeople even here. But there is more to this silence: they want me to participate in her punishment. And I have.

In the twenty years since I heard this story I have not asked for details nor said my aunt's name; I do not know it. People who can comfort the dead can also chase after them to hurt them further—a reverse ancestor worship. The real punishment was not the raid swiftly inflicted by the villagers, but the family's deliberately forgetting her. Her betrayal so maddened them, they saw to it that she would suffer forever, even after death. Always hungry, always needing, she would have to beg food from other ghosts, snatch and steal it from those whose living descendants give them gifts. She would have to fight the ghosts massed at crossroads for the buns a few thoughtful citizens leave to decoy her away from village and home so that the ancestral spirits could feast unharassed. At peace, they could act like gods, not ghosts, their descent lines providing them with paper suits and dresses, spirit money, paper houses, paper automobiles, chicken, meat, and rice into eternity[22]—essences delivered up in smoke and flames, steam and incense rising from each rice bowl. In an attempt to make the Chinese care for people outside the family, Chairman Mao[23] encourages us now to give our paper replicas to the spirits of outstanding soldiers and workers, no matter whose ancestors they may be. My aunt remains forever hungry. Goods are not distributed evenly among the dead.

My aunt haunts me—her ghost drawn to me because now, after fifty years of neglect, I alone devote pages of paper to her, though not origamied into houses and clothes. I do not think she always means me well. I am telling on her, and she was a spite suicide, drowning herself in the drinking water. The Chinese are always very frightened of the drowned one, whose weeping ghost, wet hair hanging and skin bloated, waits silently by the water to pull down a substitute.

---

[22] **descent lines . . . eternity** Offerings to the dead, as part of ancestor worship.
[23] **Chairman Mao** Mao Zedong (1893–1973), Chinese leader of the Chinese Communist Party that defeated the Nationalist Party, in 1949, and established the People's Republic of China (PRC).

Questions for Critical Thinking

1. What does the story of No Name Woman reveal about the status of women in Chinese village culture in the early twentieth century?

2. Discuss Kingston's interweaving of American pop culture with traditional Chinese village culture. What is her artistic goal in this cultural blending?

ORHAN PAMUK
Selections from *My Name Is Red*

The writings—several novels and one memoir—of Orhan Pamuk (b. 1952) have placed Turkish literature on the global literary map. Before Pamuk, few Turkish writers found an audience outside their country. His works have been translated into over fifty languages and garnered many literary awards, including the 2006 Nobel Prize in Literature. At home, his books, while controversial because of their political themes, have been hugely popular, with some of them earning the largest sales of any other Turkish author to date.

In his works Pamuk mines Turkey's rich and varied past, ranging from its founding in the fifteenth century as an Islamic state, called the Ottoman Empire, to modern Turkey, a secular, parliamentary republic with a mainly Muslim population. The subjects of his books often explore aspects of contemporary or historic Turkish Islamic culture—a position that angers both nationalistic Turks, who object to his airing of their country's troubled heritage, and religious traditionalists, who are offended by his impartial treatment of Islam. Pamuk, a native of Istanbul, has traveled widely in the West, serving from 1985 to 1988 as a visiting scholar at Columbia University and the University of Iowa. In 2005 he ran afoul of Turkish authorities who charged him with "insulting Turkishness," because of an interview in which he criticized Turkey's historic treatment of Kurds and Armenian minorities. Although the government dropped the charges, Pamuk's arrest, widely reported in the world media, raises questions about Turkey's future admission to the European Union with its requirement of free speech for entry.

Of Pamuk's many works, *My Name Is Red* (2000) is probably the most memorable. Typical of his literary projects, the subject is the clash of civilizations, specifically of Islam with the West, as manifested in the introduction of the Western art technique of perspective to the sixteenth-century Ottoman court and its workshop of miniature artists. A murder mystery, the novel focuses on the death of one of the Ottoman court miniaturists, Master Elegant Effendi. Both victim and murderer are enmeshed in a web of intrigue, while vying for position at court and dealing with foreign influences in Ottoman art. Pamuk employs a postmodern narrative, assigning a single narrator to each chapter and with no two consecutive chapters in the same voice. The voices include living and dead humans, along with those of animals (a dog) and inanimate things (the color red). He is particularly adept in evoking the sights, sounds, and smells of the past. The result is a brilliant, kaleidoscopic window into sixteenth-century Turkish culture.

Reading the Selections

Chapter 20, "I Am Called Black," is narrated by Black, a miniaturist at the court of the Ottoman Sultan Murat III (r. 1574–1594). He describes the circumstances in which Western perspective came to be introduced into Turkish art. Black recounts a meeting between the sultan and Black's uncle Enishte, a workshop master who had been impressed with the uniqueness of Venetian portraiture. Murat III, fearing that Western perspective would lead to religious idolatry ("We'd begin to worship a picture we've hung on a wall"), nevertheless desired that his "portrait be made in the style of the Frankish masters." This chapter sets forth the clash of civilizations theme triggered by the importation of Western art methods into Islamic art.

The word "your" in the title of chapter 21, "I Am Your Beloved Uncle," establishes that the novel's hero is the miniaturist known as Black. Black's uncle is named Enishte, and Black usually refers to him as "my Enishte," an expression of endearment. In this chapter, Enishte elaborates on the difference between Islamic and Western art, pointing out, for instance, that Western painters depict shadows as a way of rendering the "unique and the exceptional"—a goal forbidden to painters in the Islamic tradition.

∞

Chapter 20
I Am Called Black[24]

I wondered whether Shekure's father[25] was aware of the letters we exchanged. If I were to consider her tone, which bespoke a timid maiden quite afraid of her father, I'd have to conclude that not a single word about me had passed between them. Yet, I sensed that this was not the case. The slyness in Esther's[26] looks, Shekure's enchanting appearance at the window, the decisiveness with which my Enishte[27] sent me to his illustrators and his despair when he ordered me to come this morning—all of it made me quite uneasy.

In the morning, as soon as my Enishte asked me to sit before him, he began to describe the portraits he saw in Venice.[28] As the ambassador of Our Sultan, Refuge of the World,[29] he'd visited quite a number of palazzos,[30] churches and the houses of prosperous men. Over a period of days, he stood before thousands of portraits. He saw thousands of framed faces depicted on stretched canvas or wood or painted directly onto walls. Each one was different from the next. "They were distinctive, unique human faces!" he said. He was intoxicated by their variety, their colors, the pleasantness—even severity—of the soft light that seemed to fall on them and the meaning emanating from their eyes.

"As if a virulent plague had struck, everyone was having his portrait made," he said. "In all of Venice, rich and influential men wanted their portraits painted as a symbol, a memento of their lives and a sign of their riches, power and influence—so they might always be there, standing before us, announcing their existence, nay, their individuality and distinction."

His words were belittling, as if he were speaking out of jealousy, ambition or greed. Though, at times, as he talked about the portraits he'd seen in Venice, his face would abruptly light up like a child's, invigorated.

Portraiture had become such a contagion among affluent men, princes and great families who were patrons of art that even when they commissioned frescoes of biblical scenes and religious legends for church walls, these infidels[31] would insist that their own images appear somewhere in the work. For instance, in a painting of the burial of St. Stephan[32] you'd suddenly see, ah yes, present among the tearful graveside mourners, the very prince who was giving you the tour—in a state of pure enthusiasm, exhilaration and conceit—of the paintings hanging on his palazzo walls. Next, in the corner of a fresco depicting St. Peter[33] curing the sick with his shadow, you'd realize with an odd sense of disillusionment that the unfortunate one writhing there in pain was, in fact, the strong-as-an-ox brother of your polite host. The following day, this time in a piece depicting the Resurrection of the Dead,[34] you'd discover the guest who'd stuffed himself beside you a lunch.

"Some have gone so far, just to be included in a painting," said my Enishte, fearfully as though he were talking about the temptations of Satan, "that they're willing to be portrayed as a servant filling goblets in the crowd, or a merciless man stoning an adulteress, or a murderer, his hands drenched in blood."

Pretending not to understand, I said, "Exactly the way we see Shah Ismail[35] ascending the throne in those illustrated books that recount ancient Persian legends. Or when we come across a depiction of Tamerlane,[36] who actually ruled long afterward, in the story of *Hüsrev and Shirin*."[37]

Was there a noise somewhere in the house?

"It's as if the Venetian paintings were made to frighten us," said my Enishte later, "And it isn't enough that we be in awe of the authority and money of these men who commission the works, they also want us to know that simply existing in this world is a very special, very mysterious event. They're attempting to terrify us with their unique faces, eyes, bearing and with their clothing whose every fold is defined by shadow. They're attempting to terrify us by being creatures of mystery."

He explained how once he'd gotten lost in the exquisite portrait gallery of a lunatic collector whose opulent

[24] **Black** Workshop name of one of the miniaturists at the Ottoman court. Boys in training in the workshop were given flowery nicknames by the head miniaturist, and the names followed them for the rest of their lives.
[25] **Shekure's father** Shekure is **Black's** love interest. Shekure's soldier-husband has disappeared, leaving her with two children. Shekure's father is **Enishte, Black's** uncle and a high-ranking official at the Ottoman court. **Enishte,** having served as a diplomat to Venice, has knowledge of Western Renaissance art.
[26] **Esther** Jewish matchmaker living in the Jewish quarter of Istanbul. She arranges secret letter exchanges between **Black** and **Shekure** (see footnotes 24 and 25).
[27] **Enishte** **Black's** beloved uncle and the father of **Shekure.**
[28] **Venice** As the leading maritime power in the Mediterranean in the 1500s (the time period of the novel), the Venetian Republic played a powerful role in mercantile, diplomatic, and cultural relations with the Ottoman Empire.
[29] **Sultan, Refuge of the World** Sultan Murat III (r. 1574–1595). His reign provides the time frame for the novel.
[30] **palazzo** Italian, palace.

[31] **infidel** Unbeliever. **Black,** the narrator, is a Muslim, and, as such, regards the Christian Venetians as infidels.
[32] **St. Stephan** The first Christian martyr (Acts 6, 7).
[33] **St. Peter** One of the original twelve disciples of Jesus Christ.
[34] **Resurrection of the Dead** A key belief of the Christian faith.
[35] **Shah Ismail** Perhaps Shah Ismail (r. 1501–1524), who founded the Safavid Empire, centered on Persia (modern Iran), and made Shi'a Islam its official religion.
[36] **Tamerlane** Also Timur, or Timur Lenk (Turkish, "Timur the Lame") (1336–1407), a Turkic warrior and Islamic believer who conquered the zone of land stretching from India and Russia to the Mediterranean Sea.
[37] *Hüsrev and Shirin* A Persian tale of the two legendary lovers.

estate was perched on the shores of Lake Como,[38] the proprietor had collected the portraits of all the great personages in Frankish[39] history from kings to cardinals, and from soldiers to poets: "When my hospitable host left me alone to roam as I wished throughout his palazzo, which he'd proudly given me a tour of, I saw that these supposedly important infidels—most of whom appeared to be real and some of whom looked me straight in the eye—had attained their importance in this world solely on account of having their portraits made. Their likenesses had imbued them with such magic, had so distinguished them, that for a moment among the paintings I felt flawed and impotent. Had I been depicted in this fashion, it seemed, I'd better understand why I existed in this world."

He was frightened because he suddenly understood—and perhaps desired—that Islamic artistry, perfected and securely established by the old masters of Herat,[40] would meet its end on account of the appeal of portraiture. "However, it was as if I too wanted to feel extraordinary, different and unique," he said. As if prodded by the Devil, he felt himself strongly drawn to what he feared. "How should I say it? It's as if this were a sin of desire, like growing arrogant before God, like considering oneself of utmost importance, like situating oneself at the center of the world."

Thereafter, this idea dawned on him: These methods which the Frankish artists made use of as if playing a prideful child's game, could be more than simply magic associated with Our Exalted Sultan—but could in fact become a force meant to serve our religion, bringing under its sway all who beheld it.

I learned that the idea of preparing an illuminated manuscript had arisen then: my Enishte, who'd returned to Istanbul from Venice, suggested it would be excellent indeed for Our Sultan to be the subject of a portrait in the Frankish style. But after His Excellency took exception, a book containing pictures of Our Sultan and the objects that represented Him was agreed upon.

"It is the story that's essential," our wisest and most Glorious Sultan had said. "A beautiful illustration elegantly completes the story. An illustration that does not complement a story, in the end, will become but a false idol. Since we cannot possibly believe in an absent story, we will naturally begin believing in the picture itself. This would be no different than the worship of idols in the Kaaba[41] that went on before Our Prophet,[42] peace and blessings be upon him, had destroyed them. If not as part

of a story, how would you propose to depict this red carnation, for example, or that insolent dwarf over there?"

"By exposing the carnation's beauty and uniqueness." 15

"In the arrangement of your scene, then, would you situate the flower at the precise center of the page?"

"I was afraid," my Enishte said." I panicked momentarily when I realized where Our Sultan's thoughts were taking me."

What filled my Enishte with fear was the notion of situating at the center of the page—and thereby, the world—something other than what God had intended.

"Thereafter," Our Sultan had said, "you'll want to exhibit a picture in whose center you've situated a dwarf." It was as I had assumed. "But this picture could never be displayed: after a while, we'd begin to worship a picture we've hung on a wall, regardless of the original intentions. If I believed, heaven forbid, the way these infidels do, that the Prophet Jesus[43] was also the Lord God himself, then I'd also hold that God could be observed in this world, and even, that He could manifest in human form; only then might I accept the depiction of mankind in full detail and exhibit such images. You do understand that, eventually, we would unthinkingly begin worshiping any picture that is hung on a wall, don't you?"

My Enishte said: "I understood it quite well, and be- 20 cause I did, I was afraid of what we both were thinking."

"For this reason," Our Sultan remarked, "I could never allow my portrait to be displayed."

"Though this is exactly what he wanted," whispered my Enishte, with a devilish titter.

It was my turn to be frightened now.

"Nonetheless, it is my desire that my portrait be made in the style of the Frankish masters," Our Sultan went on. "Such a portrait will, of course, have to be concealed within the pages of a book. Whatever that book might be, you shall be the one to tell me."

"In an instant of surprise and awe, I considered his 25 statement," said my Enishte, then grinning more devilishly than before, he seemed, suddenly, to become someone else.

"His Excellency Our Sultan ordered me to start working on His book posthaste. My head spun with joy. He added that it ought to be prepared as a present for the Venetian Doge,[44] whom I was to visit once again. Once the book was completed, it would become a symbol of the vanquishing power of the Islamic Caliph Our Exalted Sultan, in the thousandth year of the Hegira.[45] He requested that I prepare the illuminated manuscript in utmost secrecy, primarily to conceal its purpose as an olive branch extended to the Venetians, but also to avoid aggravating workshop jealousies. And in a state of great elation and sworn to secrecy, I embarked upon this venture."

---

[38] **Lake Como** Lake in northern Italy, surrounded by mountains.
[39] **Frank** Generic name for European, a relic of the Crusades. During the West's crusading era, roughly from 1095 to 1300, Anatolia, a major part of modern Turkey, was sometimes prey to European crusaders, including, most especially, the Franks, or the French.
[40] **Herat** City in northwest Afghanistan, famous for its miniature paintings (fifteenth century).
[41] **Kaaba** Arabic, "cube." Islam's most sacred shrine, located in Mecca, in modern Saudi Arabia; it was purged of its pagan elements by Muhammad.
[42] **Our Prophet** One of Muhammad's titles, reflecting his relationship to Allah.

[43] **Prophet Jesus** In Islam, Jesus is considered a prophet, but not the Messiah (Christ).
[44] **Doge** Venetian dialect, "duke" or "leader." The highest-ranking official in the Venetian Republic.
[45] **in the thousandth . . . Hegira** 1592 BCE. The Islamic calendar calculates time in lunar years, beginning with the Hegira, Muhammad's flight from Mecca to Medina (622, in the Western calendar).

❀

Chapter 21
I Am Your Beloved Uncle

And so it was on that Friday morning, I began to describe 1
the book that would contain Our Sultan's portrait painted
in the Venetian style. I broached the topic to Black by recounting how I'd brought it up with Our Sultan and how
I'd persuaded him to fund the book. My hidden purpose
was to have Black write the stories—which I hadn't even
begun—that were meant to accompany the illustrations.

I told him I'd completed most of the book's illustrations and that the last picture was nearly finished. "There's
a depiction of Death," I said, and I had the most clever of
miniaturists, Stork,[46] illustrate the tree representing the
peacefulness of Our Sultan's worldly realm. There's a picture of Satan and a horse meant to spirit us far far away.
There's a dog, always cunning and wily,[47] and also a gold
coin . . . I had the master miniaturists depict these things
with such beauty," I told Black, "that if you saw them but
once, you'd know straightaway what the corresponding
text ought to be. Poetry and painting, words and color,
these things are brothers to each other, as you well know."

For a while, I pondered whether I should tell him I
might marry off my daughter to him. Would he live together with us in this house? I told myself not to be taken
in by his rapt attention and his childlike expression. I
knew he was scheming to elope with my Shekure. Still, I
could rely on nobody else to finish my book.

Returning together from the Friday prayers, we discussed "shadow," the greatest of innovations manifest in
the paintings of the Venetian masters. "If," I said, "we intend to make our paintings from the perspective of pedes-
trians exchanging pleasantries and regarding their world;
that is, if we intend to illustrate from the street, we ought
to learn how to account for—as the Franks do—what is, in
fact, most prevalent there: shadows."[48]

"How does one depict shadow?" asked Black. 5

From time to time, as my nephew listened, I perceived impatience in him. He'd begin to fiddle with the
Mongol inkpot[49] he'd given me as a present. At times, he'd
take up the iron poker and stoke the fire in the stove. Now
and then I imagined that he wanted to lower that poker
onto my head and kill me because I dared to move the art
of illustrating away from Allah's[50] perspective; because I

would betray the dreams of the masters of Herat and their
entire tradition of painting; because I'd duped Our Sultan
into already doing so. Occasionally, Black would sit dead
still for long stretches and fix his eyes deeply into mine. I
could imagine what he was thinking: "I'll be your slave
until I can have your daughter." Once, as I would do when
he was a child, I took him out into the yard and tried to
explain to him, as a father might, about the trees, about
the light falling onto the leaves, about the melting snow
and why the houses seemed to shrink as we moved away
from them. But this was a mistake: It proved only that our
former filial relationship had long since collapsed. Now
patient sufferance of the rantings of a demented old man
had taken the place of Black's childhood curiosity and passion for knowledge. I was just an old man whose daughter
was the object of Black's love. The influence and experience of the countries and cities that my nephew had traveled through for a dozen years had been fully absorbed by
his soul. He was tired of me, and I pitied him. And he was
angry, I assumed, not only because I hadn't allowed him
to marry Shekure twelve years ago—after all, there was
no other choice then—but because I dreamed of paintings
whose style transgressed the precepts of the masters of
Herat. Furthermore, because I raved about this nonsense
with such conviction, I imagined my death at his hands.

I was not, however, afraid of him; on the contrary, I
tried to frighten him. For I believed that fear was appropriate to the writing I'd requested of him. "As in those pictures," I said, "one ought to be able to situate oneself at
the center of the world. One of my illustrators brilliantly
depicted Death for me. Behold."

Thus I began to show him the paintings I'd secretly
commissioned from the master miniaturists over the last
year. At first, he was a tad shy, even frightened. When he
understood that the depiction of Death was inspired by
familiar scenes that could be found in many *Book of Kings*
volumes—from the scene of Afrasiyab's decapitation of
Siyavush, for example, or Rüstem's murder of Suhrab without realizing this was his son—he quickly became interested in the subject.[51] Among the pictures that depicted the
funeral of the late Sultan Süleyman[52] was one I'd made with
bold but sad colors, combining a compositional sensibility
inspired by the Franks with my own attempt at shading—
which I'd added later. I pointed out the diabolic depth
evoked by the interplay of cloud and horizon. I reminded

---

[46] **Stork** The workshop name of one of **Master Osman's** disciples in the Ottoman miniature workshop (see footnote 54).
[47] **cunning and wily** Contrast this view of dogs as unclean with
the Western view that dogs are faithful and obedient.
[48] **shadow** Italian artists, wanting to represent nature in a
realistic fashion, first introduced shadows into their paintings
during the early Renaissance.
[49] **Mongol inkpot** An artifact from the Mongol period. The
Mongols captured Baghdad and abolished the Abbasid Caliph-
ate in 1258. Afterward, the Mongols established a short-lived
empire (until about 1335) based in Iran, which included most of
modern Iraq, northern Syria, and eastern and central Anatolia.
[50] **Allah** In Islam, God.

---

[51] ***Book of Kings . . . in the subject*** Typical subjects of Persian
miniature paintings, inspired by stories in the *Book of Kings*.
Known as the *Shah-nameh*, the *Book of Kings* is the Persian national epic, composed by the poet Ferdowsi in 1010.
[52] **Sultan Süleyman** Ottoman ruler, from 1520 to 1566, the
golden age of Ottoman culture. Under him, the arts flourished,
the first siege of Vienna (1529) was mounted, and Baghdad was
captured from the Safavids (1535).

him that Death was unique, just like the portraits of infidels I had seen hanging in Venetian palazzos; all of them desperately yearned to be rendered distinctly. "They want to be so distinct and different, and they want this with such passion that," I said, "look, look into the eyes of Death. See how men do not fear Death, but rather the violence implicit in the desire to be one-of-a kind, unique and exceptional. Look at this illustration and write an account of it. Give voice to Death. Here's paper and pen. I shall give what you write to the calligrapher straightaway."

He stared at the picture in silence. "Who painted this?" he asked later.

"Butterfly.[53] He's the most talented of the lot. Master Osman[54] had been in love with and awed by him for years."

"I've seen rougher versions of this depiction of a dog at the coffeehouse where the storyteller performs," Black said.

"My illustrators, most of whom are spiritually bound to Master Osman and the workshop, take a dim view of the labors performed for my book. When they leave here at night I imagine they have their vulgar fun over these illustrations which they draw for money and ridicule me at the coffeehouse. And who among them will ever forget the time Our Sultan had the young Venetian artist, whom He'd invited from the embassy at my behest, paint His portrait. Thereafter, He had Master Osman make a copy of that oil painting. Forced to imitate the Venetian painter, Master Osman held me responsible for this unseemly coercion and the shameful portrait that came of it. He was justified."

All day long, I showed him every picture—except the final illustration that I cannot, for whatever reason, finish. I prodded him to write. I discussed the temperaments of the miniaturists, and I enumerated the sums of money I meted out to them. We discussed "perspective" and whether the diminutive objects in the background of Venetian pictures were sacrilegious, and equally, we talked about the possibility that unfortunate Elegant Effendi[55] had been murdered for excessive ambition and out of jealousy over his wealth.

As Black returned home that night, I was confident he'd come again the next morning as promised and that he'd once again listen to me recount the stories that would constitute my book. I listened to his footsteps fading beyond the open gate; there was something to the cold night that seemed to make my sleepless and troubled murderer stronger and more devilish than me and my book.

I closed the courtyard gate tightly behind him. I placed the old ceramic water basin that I used as a basil planter behind the gate as I did each night. Before I reduced the stove to smoldering ashes and went to bed, I glanced up to see Shekure in a white gown looking like a ghost in the blackness.

"Are you absolutely certain that you want to marry him?" I asked.

"No, dear Father. I've long since forgotten about marriage. Besides, I am married."[56]

"If you still want to marry him, I'm willing to give you my blessing now."

"I wish not to be wed to him."

"Why?"

"Because it's against your will. In all sincerity, I desire nobody that you do not want."

I noticed, momentarily, the coals in the stove reflected in her eyes. Her eyes had aged, not out of unhappiness, but anger; yet there was no trace of offense in her voice.

"Black is in love with you," I said as if divulging a secret.

"I know."

"He listened to all I had to say today not out of his love of painting, but out of his love for you."

"He will complete your book, this is what matters."

"Your husband might return one day," I said.

"I'm not certain why, perhaps it's the silence, but tonight I've realized once and for all that my husband will never return. What I've dreamt seems to be the truth: They must've killed him. He's long since turned to dust." She whispered the last statement lest the sleeping children hear. And she said it with a peculiar tinge of anger.

"If they happen to kill me," I said, "I want you to finish this book to which I've dedicated everything. Swear that you will."

"I give my word. Who will be the one to complete your book?"

"Black! You can ensure that he does so."

"You are already ensuring that he does so, dear Father," she said. "You have no need for me."

"Agreed, but he's giving in to me because of you. If they kill me, he might be afraid to continue on."

"In that case, he won't be able to marry me," said my clever daughter, smiling.

Where did I come up with the detail about her smiling? During the entire conversation, I noticed nothing except an occasional glimmer in her eyes. We were standing tensely facing one another in the middle of the room.

"Do you communicate with each other, exchange signals?" I asked, unable to contain myself.

"How could you even think such a thing?"

A long agonizing silence passed. A dog barked in the distance. I was slightly cold and shuddered. The room was so black now that we could no longer see each other; we could each only sense the other's presence. We abruptly embraced with all our might. She began to cry, and said that she missed her mother. I kissed and stroked her head, which indeed smelled like her mother's hair. I walked her to her bedchamber and put her to bed next to the children who were sleeping side by side. And as I reflected back over the last two days, I was certain that Shekure had corresponded with Black.

---

[53] **Butterfly** The workshop name of one of **Master Osman's** disciples in the Ottoman miniature workshop (see footnote 54).
[54] **Master Osman** Nakkash Osman, the leader of the Ottoman miniaturists, during the reign of Murat III (see footnote 29).
[55] **Elegant Effendi** Elegant is the workshop name of one of **Master Osman's** disciples in the Ottoman miniature workshop (see footnote 54), while effendi is a Turkish term of respect. Elegant Effendi is the corpse, whose murder forms the main plot of *My Name Is Red*.

---

[56] **married** See footnote 25.

Questions for Critical Thinking

1. Discuss the narrative technique used by Pamuk in these two selections. What effect does this technique have upon you, the reader? Can the reader trust the narrative voice? Explain.

2. "Chapter 20 sets forth, among other things, a clash of civilizations between Islam and Western art." Explain. What is at issue with the Ottoman court painters who oppose the introduction of Western art techniques into their workshop?

DEREK WALCOTT
Selections from *Omeros*

The long epic poem *Omeros* (1990) is the masterpiece of Derek Walcott (b. 1930), the West Indian poet, playwright, and essayist. In his poem, Walcott transplants the *Iliad* and *Odyssey* to St. Lucia, where he was born, reinterpreting the Greek stories into the history, geography, and culture of his island homeland. In recognition of the perceived greatness of this poem, Walcott was awarded the Nobel Prize in Literature in 1992, thereby cementing his global reputation as a leading writer of his generation.

The literary form of *Omeros* draws on the West's long epic tradition, including the works of Homer, Virgil, and Dante. From Homer comes the work's title—*Omeros* is the Greek name for Homer—and many of the poem's main characters, including Achille, Hector, and Helen. From Virgil, Walcott adopts the idea of using the epic as a nation's founding narrative, thus the West Indies Federation, of which St. Lucia is a part, is presented as a new civilization whose future glory will rival that of ancient Rome. And from Dante, Walcott borrows the three-line stanza verse form—terza rima—freely adapting it, while ignoring the interconnected rhyming scheme Dante used.

Although indebted to the epic tradition, Walcott rejects most of its heroic features, preferring instead to make *Omeros* a populist work. Unlike the noble warriors of Homer and Virgil, who fought in battles and sought adventure, Walcott's characters are hardworking fishermen, struggling to make a living. Unlike the speech of traditional heroes, Walcott's men and women speak the creole French dialect of St. Lucia—a legacy of the island's years as a French colony. In the island setting, politics in Great Britain, France, the Netherlands, Africa, and the United States play the role that the Olympic gods and goddesses did in earlier epics, intervening fatefully in the lives of the characters.

Walcott's poetic mission is to give dignity to the ordinary people who have been marginalized by the periodic upheavals that sweep through Western culture. Without illusion, he describes the setting as "somewhere, with its sunlit islands, where what they called history could not happen." In this out-of-the-way corner, he chronicles not only the joys and the sorrows of daily life, but also offers the backstory of the characters, moving from past to present and ranging over St. Lucia's history from slavery and colonialism to its present status as a tourist destination under free market capitalism.

Reading the Selection

Chapters I to III of *Omeros* introduce five main characters, male and female, black and white, some with Homeric names. The Homeric-named characters are black residents of St. Lucia, including Philoctete (who, like his Greek counterpart, Philoctetes, has an open wound that refuses to heal and exudes a foul smell); Achille (the creole name for Achilles); and Hector. Walcott's giving of Homeric names to his characters is bitterly ironic, because, in St. Lucia's slavery days, slave owners often assigned classical names to some slaves. The non-Homeric characters introduced here include Ma Kilman, an Irish woman who operates the pub known as the No Pain Café, and Seven Seas, a blind retired sailor who is also Omeros, the title character.

Two major plot lines of Walcott's poem begin in these chapters. The first is the conflict between Achille and Hector, which echoes a key theme of the *Iliad.* Unlike Homer's *Iliad,* where the conflict is about honor, Walcott's Achille and Hector fight over a rusted tin cup and the beautiful Helen, a servant woman who is identified with the island of St. Lucia itself. The second is the curing of Philoctete's wound, a story derived from the *Iliad* and other Greek sources. In Greek versions of the tale, Philoctete is a victim of fate, but Walcott describes Philoctete's wound as caused by a rusted anchor, hence a symbol of St. Lucia's tortured history and its subsistence fishing culture.

❧

Book One
Chapter I

I

"This is how, one sunrise, we cut down them canoes."[57]   1
Philoctete[58] smiles for the tourists, who try taking
his soul with their cameras.[59] "Once wind bring the news

to the *laurier-cannelles,*[60] their leaves start shaking
the minute the axe of sunlight hit the cedars,
because they could see the axes in our own eyes.

Wind lift the ferns. They sound like the sea that feed us
fishermen all our life, and the ferns nodded 'Yes,
the trees have to die.' So, fists jam in our jacket,

cause the heights was cold and our breath making feathers   10
like the mist, we pass the rum.[61] When it came back, it
give us the spirit to turn into murderers.[62]

I lift up the axe and pray for strength in my hands
to wound the first cedar. Dew was filling my eyes,
but I fire one more white rum. Then we advance."

For some extra silver,[63] under a sea-almond,[64]
he shows them a scar made by a rusted anchor,[65]
rolling one trouser-leg up with the rising moan

of a conch. It has puckered like the corolla[66]
of a sea-urchin. He does not explain its cure.   20
"It have some things"—he smiles—"worth more than
   a dollar."

He has left it to a garrulous waterfall
to pour out his secret down La Sorcière,[67] since
the tall laurels fell, for the ground-dove's mating call

to pass on its note to the blue, tacit mountains
whose talkative brooks, carrying it to the sea,
turn into idle pools where the clear minnows shoot

and an egret stalks the reeds with one rusted cry
as it stabs and stabs the mud with one lifting foot.
Then silence is sawn in half by a dragonfly   30

---

[57] **"This is how . . . them canoes."** Philoctete (see footnote 58) is speaking. He speaks in creole English, one of the two languages used in St. Lucia and by the characters in this poem. The other language is creole French. The languages are legacies of St. Lucia's shifting fortunes, as the island changed hands fourteen times between France and England before becoming English, by the terms of an 1814 treaty.

[58] **Philoctete** The French version of Philoctetes. Walcott models this character on the Homeric warrior of the same name. Each has a wound that will not heal.

[59] **taking his soul . . . cameras** With the birth of the camera, a popular folk superstition claimed that "a photograph captured the soul" of a subject.

[60] *laurier-cannelle* Aromatic tree, indigenous to the Caribbean. Also, a type of laurel; hence, a classical allusion, because wreaths made of laurel leaves were worn by heroes in ancient Greece and Rome.

[61] **rum** The signature alcoholic liquor produced in the Caribbean, made from fermented sugar cane juice.

[62] **murderers Philoctete** (see footnote 58) is being metaphorical, as he describes himself and the other fishermen "murdering" the trees to make canoes.

[63] **silver** A tip. Philoctete is regaling tourists with stories of island life.

[64] **sea-almond** Indigenous almond tree in the Caribbean.

[65] **scar . . . anchor Philoctete,** like his Homeric namesake, has a wound that refuses to heal. Walcott's **Philoctete** was injured by an anchor, symbolic of the fishing culture of St. Lucia's colonial past and present-day life.

[66] **corolla** In botany, the whorl or whorls of petals that are the most conspicuous part of a flower; hence, flower-like display.

[67] **La Sorcière** French, "a female sorcerer" or "witch"; the name of a waterfall on St. Lucia.

as eels sign their names along the clear bottom-sand,
when the sunrise brightens the river's memory
and waves of huge ferns are nodding to the sea's sound.

Although smoke forgets the earth from which it ascends,
and nettles guard the holes where the laurels were killed,
an iguana hears the axes, clouding each lens

over its lost name, when the hunched island was called
"Iounalao,"[68] "Where the iguana is found."
But, taking its own time, the iguana will scale

the rigging of vines in a year, its dewlap[69] fanned,   40
its elbows akimbo, its deliberate tail
moving with the island. The slit pods of its eyes

ripened in a pause that lasted for centuries,
that rose with the Aruacs'[70] smoke till a new race
unknown to the lizard stood measuring the trees.

These were their pillars that fell, leaving a blue space
for a single God where the old gods stood before.
The first god was a gommier.[71] The generator

began with a whine, and a shark,[72] with sidewise jaw,
sent the chips flying like mackerel over water   50
into trembling weeds. Now they cut off the saw,

still hot and shaking, to examine the wound it
had made. They scraped off its gangrenous moss, then
        ripped
the wound clear of the net of vines that still bound it

to this earth, and nodded. The generator whipped
back to its work, and the chips flew much faster as
the shark's teeth gnawed evenly. They covered their eyes

from the splintering nest. Now, over the pastures
of bananas, the island lifted its horns. Sunrise
trickled down its valleys, blood splashed on the cedars,   60

and the grove flooded with the light of sacrifice.
A gommier was cracking. Its leaves an enormous
tarpaulin with the ridgepole gone. The creaking sound

made the fishermen leap back as the angling mast
leant slowly towards the troughs of ferns; then the ground
shuddered under the feet in waves, then the waves passed.

II

Achille[73] looked up at the hole the laurel had left.
He saw the hole silently healing with the foam
of a cloud like a breaker. Then he saw the swift

crossing the cloud-surf, a small thing, far from its home,   70
confused by the waves of blue hills. A thorn vine gripped
his heel. He tugged it free. Around him, other ships

were shaping from the saw. With his cutlass[74] he made
a swift sign of the cross, his thumb touching his lips
while the height rang with axes. He swayed back the
        blade,

and hacked the limbs from the dead god, knot after knot,
wrenching the severed veins from the trunk as he prayed:
"Tree! You can be a canoe! Or else you cannot!"

The bearded elders endured the decimation
of their tribe without uttering a syllable   80
of that language they had uttered as one nation,

the speech taught their saplings: from the towering babble
of the cedar to green vowels of *bois-campêche.*[75]
The *bois-flot*[76] held its tongue with the *laurier-cannelle,*

the red-skinned logwood endured the thorns in its flesh,
while the Aruacs' patois[77] crackled in the smell
of a resinous bonfire that turned the leaves brown

with curling tongues, then ash, and their language was
        lost.
Like barbarians striding columns they have brought down,
the fishermen shouted. The gods were down at last.   90

Like pygmies they hacked the trunks of wrinkled giants
for paddles and oars. They were working with the same
concentration as an army of fire-ants.

But vexed by the smoke for defaming their forest,
blow-darts of mosquitoes kept needling Achille's trunk.
He frotted white rum on both forearms that, at least,

those that he flattened to asterisks would die drunk.
They went for his eyes. They circled them with attacks
that made him weep blindly. Then the host retreated

---

[68] **Iounalao** St. Lucia, in the now-lost language of its former Amerindian inhabitants; the poem thus seeks to recover the "lost name."

[69] **dewlap** In iguanas, the loose fold of flesh hanging below the throat.

[70] **Aruac** Also spelled Arawak. The Spanish name for friendly Indians encountered in the Caribbean.

[71] **gommier** Candle tree, whose heartwood resembles mahogany.

[72] **shark** Saw; **Philoctete** is being metaphorical, when he describes the saw as biting like a "shark" through the tree trunk.

[73] **Achille** French version of Achilles; a main character. Modeled on Homer's hero.

[74] **cutlass** Knife; Walcott evokes the Homeric epic when he calls **Achille's** knife a "cutlass," the sword wielded by Homeric warriors.

[75] *bois-campêche* An ornamental tree, prized for its hard wood; its leaves and bark are valued for their medicinal properties and as sources for blue and black dyes.

[76] *bois-flot* A type of shrub or small tree in the Caribbean, in French; known as sea hibiscus or rope mangrove in English.

[77] **Aruacs' patois** The lost language spoken by the (now disappeared) Aruac (see footnote 70).

to high bamboo like the archers of Aruacs 100
running from the muskets of cracking logs, routed
by the fire's banner and the remorseless axe

hacking the branches. The men bound the big logs first
with new hemp and, like ants, trundled them to a cliff
to plunge through tall nettles. The logs gathered that
    thirst

for the sea which their own vined bodies were born with.
Now the trunks in eagerness to become canoes
ploughed into breakers of bushes, making raw holes

of boulders, feeling not death inside them, but use—
to roof the sea, to be hulls. Then, on the beach, coals 110
were set in their hollows that were chipped with an adze.

A flat-bed truck had carried their rope-bound bodies.
The charcoals, smouldering, cored the dugouts for days
till heat widened the wood enough for ribbed gunwales.

Under his tapping chisel Achille felt their hollows
exhaling to touch the sea, lunging towards the haze
of bird-printed islets, the beaks of their parted bows.

Then everything fit. The pirogues[78] crouched on the sand
like hounds with sprigs in their teeth. The priest
sprinkled them with a bell, then he made the swift's sign. 120

When he smiled at Achille's canoe, *In God We Troust*,
Achille said: "Leave it! Is God' spelling and mine."[79]
After Mass one sunrise the canoes entered the troughs

of the surpliced shallows, and their nodding prows
agreed with the waves to forget their lives as trees;
one would serve Hector[80] and another, Achilles.

---

[78] **pirogue** French, canoe of shallow draft, made from a hollowed-out tree trunk (see footnote 57). From Spanish, *piragua;* originally from an Indian word, *piraua.*
[79] **God' spelling and mine** Achille here defends his spelling of "trust," claiming God's authority for the mistake. Throughout *Omeros,* Walcott unapologetically presents the islanders in their natural exuberance and simplicity.
[80] **Hector** A main character; Hector's quarrel with **Achille** (see footnote 73) is modeled on the fight between Hector and Achilles in Homer's *Iliad.*

III

Achille peed in the dark, then bolted the half-door shut.
It was rusted from sea-blast. He hoisted the fishpot
with the crab of one hand; in the hole under the hut

he hid the cinder-block step. As he neared the depot, 130
the dawn breeze salted him coming up the grey street
past sleep-tight houses, under the sodium bars

of street-lamps, to the dry asphalt scraped by his feet;
he counted the small blue sparks of separate stars.
Banana fronds nodded to the undulating

anger of roosters, their cries screeching like red chalk
drawing hills on a board. Like his teacher, waiting,
the surf kept chafing at his deliberate walk.

By the time they met at the wall of the concrete shed
the morning star had stepped back, hating the odour 140
of nets and fish-guts; the light was hard overhead

and there was a horizon. He put the net by the door
of the depot, then washed his hands in its basin.
The surf did not raise its voice, even the ribbed hounds

around the canoes were quiet; a flask of l'absinthe[81]
was passed by the fishermen, who made smacking
    sounds
and shook at the bitter bark from which it was brewed.

This was the light that Achille was happiest in.
When, before their hands gripped the gunwales, they
    stood
for the sea-width to enter them, feeling their day begin. 150

---

[81] **l'absinthe** Absinthe, a French liqueur, made from wormwood and anise. Anise-flavored liqueurs are popular among all classes in Mediterranean cultures.

∞

Chapter II

I

Hector was there. Theophile also. In this light,   1
they have only Christian names. Placide, Pancreas,
Chrysostom, Maljo,[82] Philoctete with his head white

as the coiled surf. They shipped the lances of oars,
placed them parallel in the grave of the gunwales
like man and wife. They scooped the leaf-bilge from the
        planks,

loosened knots from the bodies of flour-sack sails,
while Hector, at the shallows' edge, gave a quick thanks,
with the sea for a font, before he waded, thigh-in.

The rest walked up the sand with identical stride   10
except for foam-haired Philoctete. The sore on his shin
still unhealed, like a radiant anemone. It had come

from a scraping, rusted anchor.[83] The pronged iron
peeled the skin in a backwash. He bent to the foam,
sprinkling it with a salt hiss. Soon he would run,

hobbling, to the useless shade of an almond,
with locked teeth, then wave them off from the shame
of his smell, and once more they would leave him alone

under its leoparding light. This sunrise the same
damned business was happening. He felt the sore twitch   20
its wires up to his groin. With his hop-and-drop

limp, hand clutching one knee, he left the printed beach
to crawl up the early street to Ma Kilman's shop.[84]
She would open and put the white rum within reach.

His shipmates watched him, then they hooked hands like
        anchors
under the hulls, rocking them; the keels sheared dry sand
till the wet sand resisted, rattling the oars

that lay parallel amidships; then, to the one sound
of curses and prayers at the logs jammed as a wedge,
one after one, as their tins began to rattle,   30

the pirogues slid to the shallows' nibbling edge,
towards the encouraging sea. The loose logs swirled
in surf, face down, like warriors from a battle

lost somewhere on the other shore of the world.
They were dragged to a place under the manchineels[85]
to lie there face upward, the sun moving over their brows

with the stare of myrmidons[86] hauled up by the heels
high up from the tide-mark where the pale crab burrows.
The fishermen brushed their palms. Now all the canoes

were riding the pink morning swell. They drew their   40
        bows
gently, the way grooms handle horses in the sunrise,
flicking the ropes like reins, pinned them by the nose—

Praise Him, Morning Star, St. Lucia, Light of My Eyes,[87]
threw bailing tins in them, and folded their bodies across
the tilting hulls, then sculled one oar in the slack

of the stern. Hector rattled out his bound canvas
to gain ground with the gulls, hoping to come back
before that conch-coloured dusk low pelicans cross.

II

Seven Seas[88] rose in the half-dark to make coffee.
Sunrise was heating the ring of the horizon   50
and clouds were rising like loaves. By the heat of the

glowing iron rose he slid the saucepan's base onto the ring and anchored it there. The saucepan shook
from the weight of water in it, then it settled.

His kettle leaked. He groped for the tin chair and took
his place near the saucepan to hear when it bubbled.
It would boil but not scream like a bosun's whistle

to let him know it was ready. He heard the dog's
morning whine under the boards of the house, its tail
thudding to be let in, but he envied the pirogues   60

already miles out at sea. Then he heard the first breeze
washing the sea-almond's wares; last night there had
        been
a full moon white as his plate. He saw with his ears.

---

[82] **Theophile . . . Placide, Pancreas, Chrysostom, Maljo** Non-Homeric names of fishermen. This list evokes Homer's "roll call of warriors" in the *Iliad*.
[83] **anchor** See footnote 65.
[84] **Ma Kilman's shop** The No Pain Café. Ma Kilman, of Irish origins, is also a medicine woman, who eventually heals **Philoctete's** wound.

---

[85] **manchineels** From French, *mancinelle*; Spanish, *manzinilla*. A tropical tree, bearing a poisonous fruit.
[86] **myrmidons** Faithful soldiers, prepared to die for their leader. Derived from Homer's *myrmidons,* the soldiers who fought with Achilles.
[87] ***Praise Him . . . Light of My Eyes*** Names of **pirogues,** oared by the various characters.
[88] **Seven Seas Omeros,** the blind, retired sailor on St. Lucia (see footnote 89).

He warmed with the roofs as the sun began to climb.
Since the disease had obliterated vision,
when the sunset shook the sea's hand for the last time—

and an inward darkness grew where the moon and sun
indistinctly altered—he moved by a sixth sense,
like the moon without an hour or second hand,

wiped clean as the plate that he now began to rinse   70
while the saucepan bubbled; blindness was not the end.
It was not a palm-tree's dial on the noon sand.

He could feel the sunlight creeping over his wrists.
The sunlight moved like a cat along the palings
of a sandy street; he felt it unclench the fists

of the breadfruit tree in his yard, run the railings
of the short iron bridge like a harp, its racing
stick rippling with the river; he saw the lagoon

behind the church, and in it, stuck like a basin,
the rusting enamel image of the full moon.   80
He lowered the ring to sunset under the pan.

The dog scratched at the kitchen door for him to open
but he made it wait. He drummed the kitchen table
with his fingers. Two blackbirds quarrelled at breakfast.

Except for one hand he sat as still as marble,
with his egg-white eyes, fingers recounting the past
of another sea, measured by the stroking oars.

O open this day with the conch's moan, Omeros,[89]
as you did in my boyhood, when I was a noun
gently exhaled from the palate of the sunrise.   90

A lizard on the sea-wall darted its question
at the waking sea, and a net of golden moss
brightened the reef, which the sails of their far canoes

avoided. Only in you, across centuries
of the sea's parchment atlas, can I catch the noise
of the surf lines wandering like the shambling fleece

of the lighthouse's flock, that Cyclops[90] whose blind eye
shut from the sunlight. Then the canoes were galleys
over which a frigate sawed its scythed wings slowly.

In you the seeds of grey almonds guessed a tree's shape,   100
and the grape leaves rusted like serrated islands,
and the blind lighthouse, sensing the edge of a cape,

paused like a giant, a marble cloud in its hands,
to hurl its boulder that splashed into phosphorous
stars; then a black fisherman, his stubbled chin coarse

---

[89] **Omeros** Greek name for Homer.
[90] **Cyclops** A lighthouse. With its single flashing light, a lighthouse evokes Homer's one-eyed Cyclops in the *Odyssey*.

as a dry sea-urchin's, hoisted his flour-sack
sail on its bamboo spar, and scanned the opening line
of our epic horizon; now I can look back

to rocks that see their own feet when light nets the waves,
as the dugouts set out with ebony captains,   110
since it was your light that startled our sunlit wharves

where schooners swayed idly, moored to their cold
     capstans.
A wind turns the harbour's pages back to the voice
that hummed in the vase of a girl's throat: "Omeros."

III

"O-meros," she laughed. "That's what we call him in
     Greek,"
stroking the small bust with its boxer's broken nose,
and I thought of Seven Seas sitting near the reek

of drying fishnets, listening to the shallows' noise.
I said: "Homer and Virg are New England farmers,[91]
and the winged horse guards their gas-station,[92] you're   120
     right."

I felt the foam head watching as I stroked an arm, as
cold as its marble, then the shoulders in winter light
in the studio attic. I said, "Omeros,"

and O was the conch-shell's invocation, *mer* was
both mother and sea in our Antillean patois,
os, a grey bone, and the white surf as it crashes

and spreads its sibilant collar on a lace shore.
Omeros was the crunch of dry leaves, and the washes
that echoed from a cave-mouth when the tide has ebbed.

The name stayed in my mouth. I saw how light was   130
     webbed
on her Asian cheeks, defined her eyes with a black
almond's outline, as Antigone[93] turned and said:

"I'm tired of America, it's time for me to go back
to Greece. I miss my islands." I write, it returns—
the way she turned and shook out the black gust of hair.

I saw how the surf printed its lace in patterns
on the shore of her neck, then the lowering shallows
of silk swirled at her ankles, like surf without noise,

---

[91] **Homer . . . Virg** Homer (eighth century BCE) and Virgil (70–19 BCE), the great epic poets. The assigning of these names to New England farmers signifies the appropriation of classical culture by white civilization.
[92] **winged horse . . . gas-station** The logo for Mobil gasoline, since 1911. Mobil's horse, named Pegasus after the Greek myth, is thus a classical marker for Walcott.
[93] **Antigone** Greek heroine of Sophocles' play of the same name. Here, the narrator recounts a sexual encounter with a Greek woman named Antigone.

and felt that another cold bust, not hers, but yours
saw this with stone almonds for eyes, its broken nose   140
turning away, as the rustling silk agrees.

But if it could read between the lines of her floor
like a white-hot deck uncaulked by Antillean heat,
to the shadows in its hold, its nostrils might flare

at the stench from manacled ankles, the coffled[94] feet
scraping like leaves, and perhaps the inculpable marble
would have turned its white seeds away, to widen

the bow of its mouth at the horror under her table,
from the lyre of her armchair draped with its white
    chiton,[95]
to do what the past always does: suffer, and stare.   150

She lay calm as a port, and a cloud covered her
with my shadow; then a prow with painted eyes
slowly emerged from the fragrant rain of black hair.

And I heard a hollow moan exhaled from a vase,
not for kings floundering in lances of rain; the prose
of abrupt fishermen cursing over canoes.

---

[94] **coffled** Bound at the ankles.

[95] **chiton** A long woolen tunic worn by the ancient Greeks.

∞

Chapter III

I

"Touchez-i, encore: N'ai fendre choux-ous-ou, salope!."   1
"Touch it again, and I'll split your arse, you bitch!"
"Moi t'a dire—'ous pas prêter un rien. 'Ous ni shallope,

'ous ni seine, 'ous croire 'ous ni choeur campêche?"
"I told you, borrow nothing of mine. You have a canoe,
and a net. Who you think you are? Logwood Heart?"

"'Ous croire 'ous c'est roi Gros Îlet? Voleur bomme!'
"You think you're king of Gros Îlet, you tin-stealer?"
Then in English: "I go show you who is king! Come!"[96]

Hector came out from the shade. And Achille, the   10
moment he saw him carrying the cutlass, *un homme
fou*,[97] a madman eaten with envy, replaced the tin

he had borrowed from Hector's canoe neatly back in the
    prow
of Hector's boat. Then Achille, who had had enough
of this madman, wiped and hefted his own blade.

And now the villagers emerged from the green shade
of the almonds and wax-leaved manchineels, for the
    face-off
that Hector wanted. Achille walked off and waited

at the warm shallows' edge. Hector strode towards him.
The villagers followed, as the surf abated   20
its sound, its fear cowering at the beach's rim.

Then, far out at sea, in a sparkling shower
arrows of rain arched from the emerald breakwater
of the reef, the shafts travelling with clear power

in the sun, and behind them, ranged for the slaughter,
stood villagers, shouting, with a sound like the shoal,
and hoisting arms to the light. Hector ran, splashing

in shallows mixed with the drizzle, towards Achille,
his cutlass lifted. The surf, in anger, gnashing
its tail like a foaming dogfight. Men can kill   30

their own brothers in rage, but the madman who tore
Achille's undershirt from one shoulder also tore
at his heart. The rage that he felt against Hector

was shame. To go crazy for an old bailing tin
crusted with rust! The duel of these fishermen
was over a shadow and its name was Helen.[98]

II

Ma Kilman had the oldest bar in the village.
Its gingerbread balcony had mustard gables
with green trim round the eaves, the paint wrinkled with
    age.

In the cabaret downstairs there were wooden tables   40
for the downslap of dominoes. A bead curtain
tinkled every time she came through it. A neon

---

[96] *Touchez-i . . . Come!* The exchange between **Achille** and **Hector,** which appears to be about the stealing of a "rusted tin cup" for bailing water from a pirogue.
[97] *un homme fou* French, "a madman."

[98] **Helen** The woman at the center of the love triangle between **Hector** and **Achille;** she also is the representation of St. Lucia itself. In interviews, Walcott described St. Lucia as "the Helen of the West," fought over by England and France.

sign endorsed Coca-Cola under the NO PAIN
CAFÉ ALL WELCOME. The NO PAIN was not her own
idea, but her dead husband's. "Is a prophecy,"

Ma Kilman would laugh. A hot street led to the beach
past the small shops and the clubs and a pharmacy
in whose angling shade, his khaki dog on a leash,

the blind man sat on his crate after the pirogues
set out, muttering the dark language of the blind,   50
gnarled hands on his stick, his ears as sharp as the dog's.

Sometimes he would sing and the scraps blew on the
        wind
when her beads rubbed their rosary. Old St. Omere.[99]
He claimed he'd sailed round the world. "Monsieur
        Seven Seas"

they christened him, from a cod-liver-oil label
with its wriggling swordfish. But his words were not
        clear.
They were Greek to her.[100] Or old African babble.

Across wires of hot asphalt the blind singer
seemed to be numbering things. Who knows if his eyes
saw through the shades, tapping his cane with one   60
        finger?

She helped him draw his veteran's compensation
every first of the month from the small Post Office.
He never complained about his situation

like the rest of them. The corner box, and the heat
on his hands would make him shift his box to the shade.
Ma Kilman saw Philoctete hobbling up the street,

so she rose from her corner window, and she laid
out the usual medicine for him, a flask of white
acajou,[101] and a jar of yellow Vaseline,

a small enamel basin of ice. He would wait   70
in the No Pain Café all day. There he would lean
down and anoint the mouth of the sore on his shin.

III

"Mais qui ça qui rivait-'ous, Philoctete?"

> *"Moin blessé."*

"But what is wrong wif you, Philoctete?"

"I am blest
wif this wound, Ma Kilman, *qui pas ka guérir pièce.*
Which will never heal."

"Well, you must take it easy.
Go home and lie down, give the foot a lickle rest."
Philoctete, his trouser-legs rolled, stares out to sea

from the worn rumshop window. The itch in the sore
tingles like the tendrils of the anemone,   80
and the puffed blister of Portuguese man-o'-war.

He believed the swelling came from the chained ankles[102]
of his grandfathers. Or else why was there no cure?
That the cross[103] he carried was not only the anchor's

but that of his race, for a village black and poor
as the pigs that rooted in its burning garbage,
then were hooked on the anchors of the abattoir.[104]

Ma Kilman was sewing. She looked up and saw his face
squinting from the white of the street. He was waiting
to pass out on the table. This went on for days.   90

The ice turned to warm water near the self-hating
gesture of clenching his head tight in both hands. She
heard the boys in blue uniforms, going to school,

screaming at his elbow: "Pheeloh! Pheelosophee!"
A mummy embalmed in Vaseline and alcohol.
In the Egyptian silence she muttered softly:

"It have a flower somewhere, a medicine, and ways
my grandmother would boil it. I used to watch ants
climbing her white flower-pot. But, God, in which place?"

Where was this root? What senna,[105] what tepid tisanes,[106]   100
could clean the branched river of his corrupted blood,
whose sap was a wounded cedar's? What did it mean,

this name that felt like a fever? Well, one good heft
of his garden-cutlass would slice the damned name clean
from its rotting yam. He said, *"Merci."* Then he left.

---

[99] **Old St. Omere** Seven Seas. St. Omere is a surname in the Caribbean, and Omere is a pun on Homer.
[100] **Greek to her** English slang, "Greek to me," meaning, "I don't understand."
[101] **white acajou** A type of mahogany.

---

[102] **chained ankles** A reference to St. Lucia's slavery days, when slaves were shackled at the ankles, to prevent their escape.
[103] **cross** Burden, a figure of speech; "cross" also suggests that Philoctete's grandfather was Christian, hence Walcott is reminding readers that white Christians enslaved black Christians.
[104] **abattoir** Slaughterhouse.
[105] **senna** A laxative made from a pod from the cassia tree.
[106] **tisane** An herbal infusion.

∞

Questions for Critical Thinking

1. Discuss the various elements of the epic genre that you can identify in Walcott's *Omeros*.

2. Characterize the islanders' world, set forth in *Omeros*. What effect on the reader is created by the use of epic language to describe this island world?

CREDITS

INDEX